D0981198

Scotland

Orkney & Shetland
p398

Northern Highlands & Islands
p349

Northeast Scotland
p209

Inverness & the Central Highlands
p293

Southern Highlands & Islands
p239

Central Scotland
p176

Edinburgh
p44

Glasgow
p103

Southern Scotland
p138

THIS EDITION WRITTEN AND RESEARCHED BY

Neil Wilson, Andy Symington

Contents

EDINBURGH P44

CAERLAVEROCK P165

GLEN CLOVA P321

Contents

Contents

ON THE ROAD

HOY P411

JUSTIN FOULKES / LONELY PLANET ©

Contents

UNDERSTAND

SURVIVAL GUIDE

SPECIAL FEATURES

Welcome to Scotland

Despite its small size, Scotland has many treasures crammed into its compact territory – big skies, lonely landscapes, spectacular wildlife, superb seafood and hospitable, down-to-earth people.

Outdoor Adventure

Scotland harbours some of the largest areas of wilderness left in Western Europe, a wildlife haven where you can see golden eagles soar above the lochs and mountains of the northern Highlands, spot otters tumbling in the kelp along the shores of the Outer Hebrides, and watch minke whales breach through shoals of mackerel off the coast of Mull. It's also an adventure playground where you can tramp the tundra plateaus of the Cairngorms, balance along tightrope ridges strung between the rocky peaks of the Cuillin, sea-kayak among the seal-haunted isles of the Outer Hebrides, and take a speed-boat ride into the surging white water of the Corryvreckan whirlpool.

Turbulent History

Scotland is a land with a rich, multilayered history, a place where every corner of the landscape is steeped in the past – a deserted croft on an island shore, a moor that was once a battlefield, a cave that sheltered Bonnie Prince Charlie. Hundreds of castles – from the plain but forbidding tower houses of Hermitage and Smailholm to the elaborate machicolated fortresses of Caerlaverock and Craigmillar – testify to the country's often turbulent past. And battles that played a pivotal part in the building of a nation are remembered and brought to life at sites such as Bannockburn and Culloden.

A Taste of Scotland

An increasing number of visitors have discovered that Scotland's restaurants have shaken off their old reputation for deep-fried food and unsmiling service and can now compete with the best in Europe. A new-found respect for top-quality local produce means that you can feast on fresh seafood mere hours after it was caught, beef and venison that was raised just a few miles away from your table, and vegetables that were grown in your hotel's own organic garden. Top it all off with a dram of single malt whisky – rich, evocative and complex, it's the true taste of Scotland.

The Culture

Be it the poetry of Robert Burns, the crime fiction of Ian Rankin or the songs of Emeli Sandé, Scotland's cultural exports are appreciated around the world every bit as much as whisky, tweed and tartan. But you can't beat reading Burns' poems in the village where he was born, enjoying an Inspector Rebus novel in Rankin's own Edinburgh, or catching the latest Scottish bands at the T in the Park festival. And museums such as Glasgow's Kelvingrove, Dundee's Discovery Point and Aberdeen's Maritime Museum recall the influence of Scottish artists, engineers, explorers, writers and inventors in shaping the modern world.

Why I Love Scotland

By Neil Wilson, Writer

It's the weather. Yes, seriously. We get four proper seasons here (sometimes all of them in one day) and that means that you get to enjoy the same landscapes over and over again in a range of different garbs – August hills clad in purple heather, native woodlands gilded with autumn colours, snowpatched winter mountains, and Hebridean machair sprinkled with a confetti of spring wildflowers. The unpredictability of the weather means that even the wettest day can be suddenly transformed by parting clouds and slanting shafts of golden light. Sheer magic.

For more about our writers, see p480

Above: Plockton (p373)

Scotland

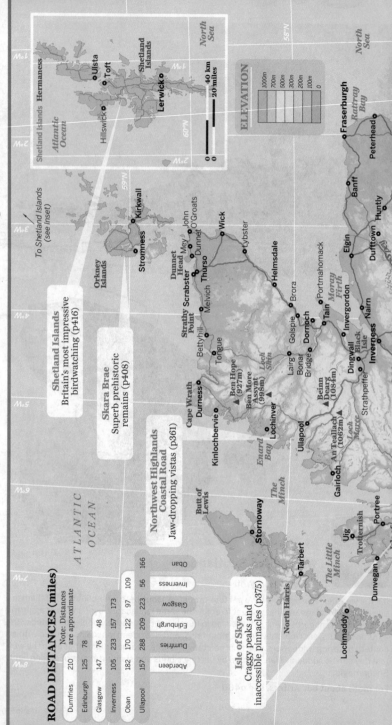

ROAD DISTANCES (miles)
Note: Distances are approximate

	Aberdeen	Dumfries	Edinburgh	Glasgow	Inverness	Oban
Dumfries	210					
Edinburgh	125	78				
Glasgow	147	76	48			
Inverness	105	233	157	173		
Oban	182	170	122	97	109	
Ullapool	157	288	209	223	56	166

Shetland Islands
Britain's most impressive birdwatching (p416)

Skara Brae
Superb prehistoric remains (p408)

Northwest Highlands
Coastal Road
Jaw-dropping vistas (p361)

Isle of Skye
Craggy peaks and inaccessible pinnacles (p375)

ELEVATION

| 1000m |
| 700m |
| 500m |
| 300m |
| 200m |
| 100m |
| 0 |

To Shetland Islands (see Inset)

Shetland Islands **Hermaness**

Ulsta
Toft
Hillswick
Shetland Islands
Lerwick

Atlantic Ocean

North Sea

Fraserburgh
Rattray Bay
Peterhead
Banff
Huntly
Dufftown
Elgin
Nairn
Inverness
Black Isle
Dingwall
Strathpeffer
Invergordon
Tain
Portmahomack
Moray Firth
Dornoch
Golspie
Brora
Helmsdale
Lybster
Wick
John O'Groats
Dunnet
Mey
Dunnet Head
Thurso
Scrabster
Melvich
Strathy Point
Bettyhill
Tongue
Ben Hope (927m)
Durness
Cape Wrath
Kinlochbervie
Lochinver
Ben More Assynt (998m)
Enard Bay
Ullapool
Beinn Dearg (1084m)
An Teallach (1062m)
Loch Maree
Gairloch
Lairg
Bonar Bridge
Loch Shin

Orkney Islands
Kirkwall
Stromness

Stornoway
Butt of Lewis
The Minch
North Harris
Tarbert
The Little Minch
Uig
Trotternish
Dunvegan
Portree
Lochmaddy
Lochmaddy

ATLANTIC OCEAN

North Sea

50 miles
100 km

40 km
20 miles

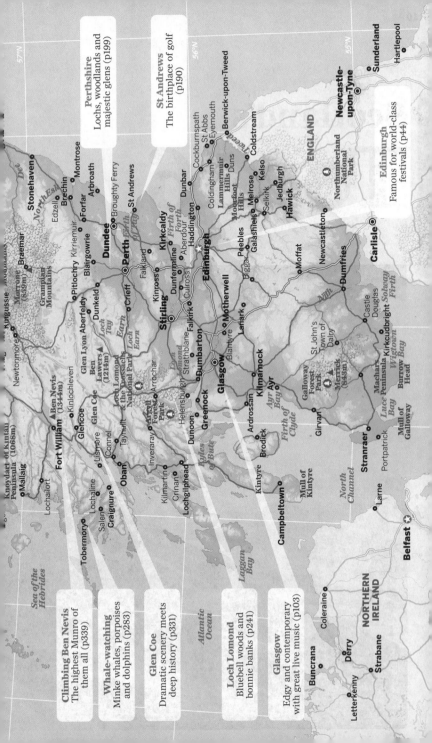

Perthshire
Lochs, woodlands and majestic glens (p199)

St Andrews
The birthplace of golf (p190)

Edinburgh
Famous for world-class festivals (p44)

Climbing Ben Nevis
The highest Munro of them all (p339)

Whale-watching
Minke whales, porpoises and dolphins (p283)

Glen Coe
Dramatic scenery meets deep history (p331)

Loch Lomond
Bluebell woods and bonnie banks (p241)

Glasgow
Edgy and contemporary with great live music (p103)

Scotland's
Top 16

Isle of Skye

1 In a country famous for stunning scenery, the Isle of Skye (p375) takes top prize. From the craggy peaks of the Cuillins and the bizarre pinnacles of the Old Man of Storr and the Quiraing to the spectacular sea cliffs of Neist Point, there's a photo opportunity at almost every turn. Walkers can share the landscape with red deer and golden eagles, and refuel at the end of the day in convivial pubs and top seafood restaurants. The Quiraing (p385), Trotternish

Edinburgh

2 Scotland's capital may be famous for its festivals, but there's much more to it than that. Edinburgh (p44) is a city of many moods: visit out of season to see the Old Town silhouetted against a blue spring sky and a yellow haze of daffodils; or on a chill December morning with the fog snagging the spires of the Royal Mile, rain on the cobblestones and a warm glow beckoning from the window of a pub.

CHRIS DAY / 500PX ©

TANGMAN PHOTOGRAPHY / GETTY IMAGES ©

Loch Lomond

3 Despite being less than an hour's drive from the bustle and sprawl of Glasgow, the bonnie banks and bonnie braes of Loch Lomond (p241) – immortalised in the words of one of Scotland's best-known songs – comprise one of the most scenic parts of the country. At the heart of Scotland's first national park, the loch begins as a broad, island-peppered lake in the south, its shores clothed in bluebell woods, narrowing in the north to a fjord-like trench ringed by 900m-high mountains.
Inchcailloch (p246)

Walking the West Highland Way

4 The best way to really get inside Scotland's landscapes is to walk them. Despite the wind, midges and drizzle, walking here is a pleasure, with numerous short- and long-distance trails, hills and mountains begging to be tramped. Top of the wish list for many hikers is the 96-mile West Highland Way (p34) from Milngavie (near Glasgow) to Fort William, challenging week-long walk through some of the country's finest scenery, finishing in the shadow of its highest peak, Ben Nevis.

TOM MARTIN / GETTY IMAGES ©

ANTON_IVANOV / SHUTTERSTOCK ©

Marine Wildlife Watching

5 Scotland is one of the best places in Europe for seeing marine wildlife. In the high season (July and August) many cruise operators on the west coast can almost guarantee sightings of minke whales and porpoises, and the Moray Firth is famous for its resident population of bottlenose dolphins. Basking sharks – at up to 12m, the biggest fish to be found in British waters – make another common sighting. Tobermory (p283) and Gairloch (near Oban) are top departure points.

Bottlenose dolphin

Climbing Ben Nevis

6 The allure of Britain's highest peak is strong – around 100,000 people a year set off up the summit trail, though not all make it to the top. Nevertheless, the highest Munro of them all is within reach of anyone who's reasonably fit. Treat Ben Nevis (p339) with respect and your reward (weather permitting) will be a truly magnificent view and a great sense of achievement. Real walking enthusiasts can warm up by hiking the 96-mile West Highland Way first.

Glasgow

7 Scotland's biggest city (p103) lacks Edinburgh's classical beauty, but more than makes up for it with a barrelful of things to do and a warmth and energy that leave every visitor impressed. Edgy and contemporary, it's a great spot to browse art galleries and museums, and to discover the works of local hero Charles Rennie Mackintosh. Add what is perhaps Britain's best pub culture and one of the world's best live-music scenes, and the only thing to do is live it.

Buchanan St shops

Golf

8 Scotland invented the game of golf and is still revered as its spiritual home by hackers and champions alike. Links courses are the classic experience here – bumpy coastal affairs where the rough is heather and machair (grass- and wildflower- covered dunes) and the main enemy is the wind, which can make a disaster of a promising round in an instant. St Andrews (p190), the historic Fife university town, is golf's headquarters, and an alluring destination for anyone who loves the sport. Old Course (p191)

Highlands

9 The Highlands abound in breathtaking views, but the far northwest is truly awe-inspiring. The coastal road between Durness and Kyle of Lochalsh offers jaw-dropping scenes at every turn: the rugged mountains of Assynt (p365), the desolate beauty of Torridon and the remote cliffs of Cape Wrath. These and the nooks of warm Highland hospitality found in classic rural pubs make this an unforgettable corner of the country. Cape Wrath (p364)

Perthshire – Big Tree Country

10 Blue-grey lochs shimmer, reflecting the changing moods of the weather; venerable trees centuries old, tower amid riverside forests; majestic glens scythe their way into remote wildernesses; and salmon leap upriver to the place of their birth. In Perthshire (p322), the heart of Scotland, picturesque towns bloom with flowers, distilleries emit tempting malty odours and sheep graze in impossibly green meadows. There's a feeling of the bounty of nature that no other place in Scotland can replicate.

Glen Coe

11 Scotland's most famous glen (p331) combines those two essential qualities of Highlands landscape: dramatic scenery and deep history. The peacefulness and beauty of this valley today belie the fact that it was the scene of a ruthless 17th-century massacre, when the local MacDonalds were murdered by soldiers of the Campbell clan. Some of the glen's finest walks – to the Lost Valley, for example – follow the routes used by the clanspeople fleeing to flee their attackers, and where many perished in the snow.

Whisky

12 Scotland's national drink – from the Gaelic *uisge bagh*, meaning 'water of life' – has been distilled here for more than 500 years. More than 100 distilleries are still in operation, producing hundreds of varieties of single malt, with new ones opening every year. Learning to distinguish the smoky, peaty whiskies of Islay (p262) from, say, the flowery, sherried malts of Speyside has become a hugely popular pastime. Many distilleries offer guided tours, rounded off with a tasting session. Trying local varieties is a great way to explore the whisky-making regions.

TTPHOTO / SHUTTERSTOCK ©

Castles

13 Desolate stone fortresses looming in the mist, majestic strongholds such as Stirling Castle (p177) towering over historic towns, or luxurious palaces built on expansive grounds by lairds more concerned with pampering than with defence: Scotland has a full range of castles that reflect its turbulent history and tense relations with its southern neighbour. Most castles have a story (or 10) to tell of plots, intrigues, imprisonments and treachery – as well as a ghost rumoured to stalk their halls.
Kinloch Castle (p346)

Island Hopping

14 Much of the unique character of western and northern Scotland is down to its expansive vistas of sea and islands – there are more than 700 islands off Scotland's coast, of which almost 100 are inhabited. A network of ferry services links these islands to the mainland and each other, providing a fascinating way to explore. It's possible to hop all the way from Arran or Bute to the Outer Hebrides (p386), touching the mainland only at Kintyre and Oban.
Lismore (p292)

Birdwatching in Shetland

15 Scotland is an important sanctuary for all sorts of wildlife. Amazing birdwatching is on offer throughout the country, but the seabird cities of the Shetland Islands take first prize for spectacle. From their first arrival in late spring to the raucous feeding frenzies of high summer, the vast colonies of gannets, guillemots, puffins and kittiwakes at Hermaness (p425), Noss and Sumburgh Head provide one of British birdwatching's most impressive experiences.
Puffin with a catch of sand eels

kara Brae

16 When visiting ancient sites it can be difficult to feel the gulf of ears or sense a connection with the people that uilt them, but Scotland's uperb prehistoric remains have an immediate mpact. Few places offer a etter glimpse of everyday tone Age life than Skara rae (p408) in Orkney, ith its carefully constructed fireplaces, beds, upboards and water sterns. Buried in coastal nd dunes for centuries, can feel as though the inabitants have just slipped ut to go fishing and could turn at any moment.

ABB PHOTO / SHUTTERSTOCK ©

Need to Know

For more information, see Survival Guide (p453)

Currency
Pounds sterling (£)

Language
English, Gaelic and Lallans

Money
ATMs widely available; credit cards widely accepted, though not in all restaurants or B&Bs.

Visas
Generally not needed for stays of up to six months. Not a member of the Schengen Zone.

Mobile Phones
Uses the GSM 900/1800 network. Local SIM cards can be used in unlocked phones.

Time
Scotland is on UTC/GMT +1 hour during summer daylight saving time (late March to late October), and UTC/GMT +0 the rest of the year.

Driving
In Scotland, drive on the left; the steering wheel is on the right-hand side of car.

When to Go

Cool to mild summers, cold winters

Lerwick
GO mid-May–mid July

Stornoway
• **GO** May–Sep

Inverness
• **GO** May–Sep

Fort William
• **GO** May–Sep

• Edinburgh
GO All year

High Season
(Jul & Aug)

➡ Accommodation prices 10%–20% higher (book in advance if possible).

➡ Warmest time of year, but often wet.

➡ Midges at their worst in Highlands and islands.

Shoulder Season (May, Jun & Sep)

➡ Wildflowers and rhododendrons bloom in May and June.

➡ Statistically, best chance of dry weather, minus midges.

➡ June evenings have daylight till 11pm.

Low Season
(Oct–Apr)

➡ Rural attractions and accommodation often closed.

➡ Snow on hills November to March.

➡ Gets dark at 4pm in December.

➡ Can be very cold and wet November to March.

Useful Websites

Lonely Planet (lonelyplanet. com/scotland) Destination information, forums, hotel bookings.

VisitScotland (www.visitscot land.com) Official tourism site; booking services.

Internet Guide to Scotland (www.scotland-info.co.uk) Best online tourist guide to Scotland.

Traveline (www.travelinescot land.com) Up-to-date public transport timetables.

ScotlandsPeople (www. scotlandspeople.gov.uk) Official genealogical website that lets you search the indexes to Old Parish Registers and Statutory Registers, as well as census returns, on a pay-per-view basis.

Important Numbers

Country code	+44
International access code	00
Emergencies	112 or 999
Police (non-emergencies)	101

Exchange Rates

Australia	A$1	£0.57
Canada	C$1	£0.59
Euro zone	€1	£0.84
Japan	¥100	£0.72
New Zealand	NZ$1	£0.55
USA	US$1	£0.75

For current exchange rates, see www.xe.com.

Daily Costs

Budget: Less than £40

➡ Dorm beds: £13–25

➡ Wild camping: free

➡ Takeaway fish and chips: £4–7

Midrange: £40–130

➡ Double room at midrange B&B: £50–100

➡ Bar lunch: £10; dinner at midrange restaurant: £25

➡ Car hire: £35 per day

➡ Petrol costs: around 15p per mile

Top End: More than £130

➡ Double room at high-end hotel: £130–250

➡ Dinner at high-end restaurant: £40–60

➡ Flights to islands: £65–130 each way

Opening Hours

Opening hours may vary throughout the year, especially in rural areas where many places have shorter hours, and a few close completely, from October or November to March or April.

Nightclubs 9pm or 10pm to 1am or later. Often only open Thursday to Saturday.

Pubs & Bars 11am to 11pm Monday to Thursday, 11am to 1am Friday and Saturday, 12.30pm to 11pm Sunday; lunch is served noon to 2.30pm, dinner 6pm to 9pm daily.

Shops 9am to 5.30pm (or 6pm in cities) Monday to Saturday, and often 11am to 5pm Sunday.

Restaurants Lunch noon to 2.30pm, dinner 6pm to 9pm or 10pm; in small towns and villages the chippy (fish-and-chip shop) is often the only place to buy cooked food after 8pm.

Arriving in Scotland

Edinburgh Airport (p463)
Trams to Edinburgh city centre depart every eight to 10 minutes from 6.15am to 10.45pm (£5.50); buses every 10 to 15 minutes from 4.30am to midnight (£4.50); and night buses every 30 minutes from 12.30am to 4am (£4). Taxis cost £18 to £28 and take about 20–30 minutes to the city centre.

Glasgow Airport (p463)
Buses to Glasgow city centre depart every 10 to 15 minutes from 6am to 11pm (£7); night buses depart hourly 11pm to 4am and half-hourly 4am to 6pm (£7). Taxis cost £24–£30 and take about 30 minutes to the city centre.

Getting Around

Transport in Scotland can be expensive compared to the rest of Europe; bus and rail services are sparse in the more remote parts of the country. For up-to-date timetables, visit Traveline Scotland (www. travelinescotland.com).

Car Useful for travelling at your own pace, or for visiting regions with minimal public transport. Cars can be hired in cities and major towns. Drive on the left.

Train Relatively expensive, with extensive coverage and frequent departures in central Scotland, but only a few lines in the northern Highlands and southern Scotland.

Bus Cheaper and slower than trains, but useful for more remote regions that aren't serviced by rail.

Boat A network of car ferries link the mainland to the islands of western and northern Scotland.

For much more on **getting around**, see p464

First Time Scotland

For more information, see Survival Guide (p453)

Checklist

☐ Make sure your passport is valid for at least six months past your arrival date.

☐ Make all necessary bookings (for accommodation, events and travel).

☐ Check the airline baggage restrictions.

☐ Inform your debit-/credit-card company of your travels.

☐ Arrange appropriate travel insurance.

☐ Check if you can use your mobile (cell) phone.

What to Pack

➡ Passport

➡ Driving licence

➡ Good walking shoes or boots

➡ Waterproof jacket

➡ Camera

➡ UK electrical adapter

➡ Insect repellent

➡ Binoculars

➡ Hangover cure (all that whisky, you know)

Top Tips for Your Trip

➡ Quality rather than quantity should be your goal: instead of a hair-raising race to see everything, pick a handful of destinations and give yourself time to linger. The most memorable experiences in Scotland are often the ones where you're doing very little at all.

➡ If you're driving, get off the main roads when you can. Some of the country's most stunning scenery is best enjoyed on secondary or tertiary roads that wind their narrow way through standout photo ops.

➡ Make the effort to greet the locals. The best experiences of Scotland are to be had courtesy of the Scots themselves, whose helpfulness, friendliness and fun has not been exaggerated.

➡ Be prepared for midges (p459) in summer in the Highlands. Bring along insect repellent, antihistamine cream and long-sleeved shirts and trousers.

What to Wear

Scotland is a fairly casual destination and you can wear pretty much whatever you like all the time. For fancy dinners, smart casual is all that's required. No restaurant will insist on jackets or ties, nor will any theatre or concert hall.

Summer days can be warm but rarely hot, so be prepared for when the inevitable cool sets in.

A light, waterproof jacket should always be close at hand, preferably one that can fold away easily.

Sleeping

Booking ahead is recommended, especially in summer, at weekends, and on islands (where options are often limited). Book at least two months ahead for July and August. If you're going to be in Edinburgh in August or at Hogmanay, book as much as a year ahead if possible.

B&Bs These small, family-run houses generally provide good value. More luxurious versions are more like a boutique hotel.

Hotels Scottish hotels range from half-a-dozen rooms above the pub to restored country houses and castles, with a commensurate range in rates.

Hostels There's a good choice of both institutional and independent hostels, many housed in rustic and/or historic buildings.

Money

➡ The British currency is the pound sterling (£), with 100 pence (p) to a pound. 'Quid' is the slang term for pound.

➡ Three Scottish banks issue their own banknotes, meaning there's quite a variety of different notes in circulation. They are legal currency in England too, but you'll sometimes run into problems changing them. They are also harder to exchange once you get outside the UK.

➡ Euros are accepted in Scotland only at some major tourist attractions and a few upmarket hotels – it's always better to use sterling.

Bargaining

A bit of mild haggling is acceptable at flea markets and antique shops, but everywhere else you're expected to pay the advertised price.

Tipping

Hotels One pound per bag is standard; gratuity for cleaning staff is completely at your discretion.

Pubs Not expected unless table service is provided, then £1 for a round of drinks.

Restaurants For decent service 10%, and up to 15% at more expensive places. Check to see if service has been added to the bill already (most likely for large groups).

Taxis Generally rounded up to nearest pound.

Compass atop Arthur's Seat (p58), Edinburgh

Etiquette

Although largely informal in their everyday dealings, the Scots do observe some rules of etiquette.

Greetings Shake hands with men, women and children when meeting for the first time and when saying goodbye. Scots expect a firm handshake with eye contact.

Conversation Generally friendly but often reserved, the Scots avoid conversations that might embarrass.

Language The Scots speak English with an accent that varies in strength – in places such as Glasgow and Aberdeen it can often be indecipherable. Oddly, native Gaelic speakers often have the most easily understood accent when speaking English.

Table service In general, cafes have table service but pubs do not. In some pubs, you should order food at the bar (after noting your table number); others will have food waiters to take your order.

Buying your round at the pub Like the English, Welsh and Irish, Scots generally take it in turns to buy a round of drinks for the whole group, and everyone is expected to take part. The next round should always be bought before the previous round is finished. In pubs, you are expected to pay for drinks when you order them.

Eating

You'll have plenty of choice for eating (p438) in Scotland. It's wise to book ahead for midrange restaurants in Scotland, especially at weekends. Top-end restaurants should be booked at least a couple of weeks in advance.

Cafes Open during daytime (rarely after 6pm), cafes are good for a casual breakfast or lunch, or simply a cup of coffee.

Pubs Most of Scotland's pubs serve reasonably priced meals, and many can compete with restaurants on quality.

Restaurants Scotland's restaurants range from cheap-and-cheerful to Michelin-starred, and cover every cuisine you can imagine.

What's New

V&A Museum of Design

Dundee's waterfront is graced by a stunning new building that is home to an outpost of London's Victoria & Albert Museum, a showcase for the best of Scottish art and design. (p212)

North Coast 500

This 500-mile circuit of northern Scotland's stunning coastline has proved an overnight hit, with thousands of people completing the route by car, campervan, motorbike or bicycle. (p360)

Borders Railway

The longest stretch of new railway line to be built in the UK for more than 100 years opened in September 2015, linking Edinburgh with Tweedbank, near Melrose (www.bordersrailway.co.uk).

Lews Castle

Stornoway's Lews Castle has been undergoing restoration and redevelopment for many years. It now provides an elegant new home for the Museum nan Eilean (Museum of the Isles), opened in late 2016. (p388)

Queensferry Crossing

The famous Forth Road Bridge (1964) has been joined by the impressive new Queensferry Crossing (opening May 2017), soaring across the Firth of Forth to the west of the city. (p98)

Loch Leven Heritage Trail

This 13-mile circuit of lovely Loch Leven, one of central Scotland's most scenic spots, was finally completed in 2014 and is now one of the best all-abilities walking and cycling trails in the country. (p203)

Craignure Bunkhouse

This brand new, purpose-built hostel provides much-needed backpacker accommodation just a short walk from Mull's main ferry terminal. It will prove very useful for travellers without cars. (p283)

Glasgow School of Art

Art-nouveau architect Charles Rennie Mackintosh's most famous creation was badly damaged by fire in 2014, but restoration is in full swing and the building should be open for tours again in 2018. (p106)

Doghouse Merchant City

Fraserburgh craft brewery Brewdog's plans for world domination continue apace with the opening of this cool, 25-tap beer bar and barbecue grill in Glasgow's trendiest district. (p127)

For more recommendations and reviews, see
lonelyplanet.com/scotland

If You Like...

Castles

The clash and conflict of Scotland's colourful history has left a legacy of military strongholds scattered across the country, from the border castles raised against English incursions to the island fortresses that controlled the seaways for the Lords of the Isles.

Edinburgh Castle The biggest, the most popular and the Scottish capital's reason for being. (p47)

Stirling Castle Perched on a volcanic crag at the top of the town, this historic royal fortress and palace has the lot. (p177)

Craigievar Castle The epitome of the Scottish Baronial style, all towers and turrets. (p235)

Culzean Castle Enormous, palatial 18th-century mansion in a romantic coastal setting. (p161)

Eilean Donan The perfect lochside location just by the main road to Skye makes this the Highlands' most photographed castle. (p375)

Hermitage Castle Bleak and desolate borderland fortress speaking of a turbulent relationship with England. (p149)

Wild Beaches

Nothing clears a whisky hangover like a walk along a wind-whipped shoreline, and Scotland is blessed with a profusion of wild beaches. The west coast in particular has many fine stretches of blinding white sands and turquoise waters that could pass for the Caribbean if not for the weather.

Kiloran Bay A perfect curve of deep golden sand – the ideal vantage point for stunning sunsets. (p269)

Sandwood Bay A sea stack, a ghost story and 2 miles of windblown sand – who could ask for more? (p366)

Bosta A beautiful and remote cove filled with white sand beside a reconstructed Iron Age house. (p390)

Durness A series of pristine sandy coves and duney headlands surrounds this northwestern village. (p363)

Scousburgh Sands Shetland's finest beach is a top spot for birdwatching as well as a bracing walk. (p422)

Orkney's Northern Islands Most of these islands, especially Sanday, Westray and North Ronaldsay, have spectacular stretches of white sand with seabirds galore and seals lazing on the rocks. (p412)

Good Food

Scotland's chefs have an enviable range of quality meat, game, seafood and vegetables at their disposal. The country has shaken off its once dismal culinary reputation as the land of deep-fried Mars Bars and now boasts countless regional specialities, farmers markets, artisan cheesemakers, smokeries and microbreweries.

Ondine Sustainably sourced seafood at one of Edinburgh's finest restaurants. (p82)

Café 1 International menu based on quality Scottish produce at this Inverness bistro. (p299)

Café Fish Perched on Tobermory waterfront, serving fresh seafood and shellfish straight off the boat. (p285)

Monachyle Mhor Utterly romantic location deep in the Trossachs and wonderful food with sound sustainable principles. (p252)

Peat Inn One of Scotland's most acclaimed restaurants sits in a hamlet amid the peaceful Fife countryside. (p195)

Albannach Fabulous gourmet retreat in the northwest – a real haven for relaxation. (p366)

Outdoor Adventures

Scotland is one of Europe's finest outdoor adventure playgrounds. The rugged mountain terrain and convoluted coastline of the Highlands and islands offer unlimited opportunities for hiking, mountain biking, surfing and snowboarding.

Fort William The self-styled Outdoor Capital of the UK, a centre for hiking, climbing, mountain biking, winter sports... (p335)

Shetland A top coastline for sea kayaking, with an abundance of bird and sea life to observe from close quarters. (p416)

7stanes Mountain-biking trails for all abilities in the forests of southern Scotland. (p171)

The Cairngorms Winter skiing and summer hill walking amid the epic beauty of this high, subarctic plateau. (p309)

Thurso An unlikely surfing mecca, but once you've got the wetsuit on the waves are pretty good. (p359)

River Tay Perhaps the finest salmon-fishing river in Europe, and famous for white-water rafting too. (p329)

Live Music & Festivals

Scotland's festival calendar has seen an explosion of events in the last decade, with music festivals especially springing up in the most unlikely corners. The ones that have stood the test of time are full of character, with superb settings and a smaller, more convivial scale than monster gigs like Glastonbury and Reading.

Groove Loch Ness Perhaps the most scenic festival site in the country, held in June with Loch Ness as a backdrop. (p307)

Top: The Horse Shoe (p128), Glasgow
Bottom: T in the Park (p196)

Arran Folk Festival June sees the fiddles pulled out all over this scenic island. (p272)

T in the Park The country's biggest rock festival kicks off in mid-July, at Strathallan Castle near Gleneagles. (p196)

King Tut's Wah Wah Hut Nightly live music at this legendary Glasgow venue. Perhaps the best thing about it is that it's one of many great places in the city. (p130)

Orkney Folk Festival Stromness vibrates to the wail of the fiddle and the stamping of feet in this good-natured, late-partying island festival. (p410)

Rural Museums

Every bit as interesting and worthy of study as the 'big picture' history – especially if you're investigating your Scottish ancestry – the history of rural communities is preserved in a wide range of fascinating museums, often in original farm buildings and historic houses.

Arnol Blackhouse Preserved in peat smoke since its last inhabitant left in the 1960s, this is a genuine slice of 'living history'. (p390)

Highland Folk Museum Fascinating outdoor museum populated with real historic buildings reassembled here on site. (p315)

Scottish Crannog Centre Head back to the Bronze Age in this excellent archaeological reconstruction of a fortified loch house. (p329)

Tain Through Time Really entertaining local museum with a comprehensive display on Scottish history and Tain's silversmithing tradition. (p353)

Stromness Museum Delightful small-town museum about the Orkney fishing industry, the world wars and marine wildlife. (p410)

Pubs

No visit to Scotland is complete without a night in a traditional Scottish hostelry, supping real ales, sipping whisky and tapping your toes to traditional music. The choice of pubs is huge, but in our opinion the old ones are the best.

Drover's Inn A classic Highland hostelry with kilted staff, candlelight and a stuffed bear. (p245)

Sandy Bell's A stalwart of the Edinburgh folk scene, with real ale and live trad music. (p91)

Glenelg Inn The beer garden here *is* actually a garden. What's more, it's got sensational views across the water to Skye. (p375)

Horse Shoe All real ales and polished brass, this is Glasgow's best traditional pub. (p128)

Stein Inn A lochside pub in Skye with fine ales, fresh seafood and a view to die for. (p385)

Shopping

Scotland offers countless opportunities for shoppers to indulge in retail therapy, from designer frocks and shoes in city malls, to local art, handmade pottery and traditional textiles in Highland and island workshops.

Glasgow The centre of Glasgow is a shopper's paradise, with everything from designer boutiques to secondhand records. (p131)

Edinburgh Competes with Glasgow as the country's shopping epicentre, with its Harvey Nicks, malls, cashmere, tartan and quirky little gift shops. (p93)

Wigtown An amazing array of secondhand and specialist bookshops cluster around the square in this small, out-of-the-way village. (p172)

Barras Glasgow's legendary flea market is a boisterous and intriguing place to browse for a taste of the city. (p132)

Classic Walks

Scotland's wild, dramatic scenery and varied landscape has made hiking a hugely popular pastime. There's something for all levels of fitness and enthusiasm, but the really keen will want to tick off some (or all) of the classic walks.

West Highland Way The granddaddy of Scottish long-distance walks, the one everyone wants to do. (p34)

Glen Affric to Shiel Bridge A classic two-day cross-country hike, with a night in a remote hostel. (p304)

Southern Upland Way Crosses Southern Scotland's hills from coast to coast; longer and harder than the WHW. (p150)

Ben Lawers One of central Scotland's classic hill walks, with super views over Loch Tay. (p252)

Fife Coastal Path Seascapes and clifftops galore on this picturesque route right around the 'Kingdom'. (p193)

Hidden Gems

For those who enjoy exploring off the beaten track, Scotland is littered with hidden corners, remote road-ends and quiet cul-de-sacs where you can feel as if you are discovering the place for the first time.

Benmore Botanic Garden Tucked away in a fold of the hills in the heart of the Cowal peninsula, this Victorian garden is a riot of colour in spring and early summer. (p254)

The Quiraing (p385), Trotternish, Isle of S

Glen Clova The loveliest of the Angus glens lies hidden away on the quiet side of the Cairngorms National Park. (p321)

Falls of Clyde Normally associated with shipbuilding, the River Clyde reveals its bucolic side further upstream. (p154)

Scotland's Secret Bunker It's back to the Cold War in this chilling but fascinating nuclear hideout hidden beneath a field in the middle of rural Fife. (p198)

Cape Wrath A curious boat-minibus combo grinds you through a missile range to this spectacular headland at Britain's northwest tip. (p364)

Natural Wonders

Scotland's stunning landscapes harbour many awe-inspiring natural features, including spectacular sea stacks and rock formations, thundering waterfalls, impressive gorges and swirling tidal whirlpools.

Old Man of Hoy While most of Orkney is fairly flat, Hoy is rugged and rocky; its spectacular west coast includes Britain's tallest sea stack. (p411)

Corryvreckan Whirlpool One of the world's three most powerful tidal whirlpools, squeezed between Jura and Scarba. (p268)

Falls of Measach A trembling suspension bridge provides a viewpoint for one of Scotland's most impressive waterfalls. (p370)

Quiraing This jumble of landslip blocks and pinnacles in northern Skye is one of the weirdest landscapes in the country. (p385)

Islands

Scotland has more than 700 islands scattered around its shore. While the vast majority of visitors stick to the larger, better-known ones such as Arran, Skye, Mull and Lewis, it's often the smaller, lesser-known islands that provide the real highlights.

Iona Beautiful, peaceful (once the day trippers have left) and of huge historic and cultural importance, Iona is the jewel of the Hebrides. (p288)

Eigg The most intriguing of the Small Isles, with its miniature mountain, massacre cave and singing sands. (p346)

Jura Wild and untamed, with more deer than people, and a dangerous whirlpool at its northern end. (p267)

Isle of May Just a mile long, this spot off the Fife coast erupts to the clamour of tens of thousands of puffins in spring and summer. (p197)

Month by Month

TOP EVENTS

Celtic Connections, January

West End Festival, June

T in the Park, July

Edinburgh Festival Fringe, August

Braemar Gathering, September

January

The nation shakes off its Hogmanay hangover and gets back to work, but only until Burns Night comes along. It's still cold and dark, but the skiing can be good.

🍴 Burns Night

Suppers all over the country (and the world for that matter) are held on 25 January to celebrate the anniversary of national poet Robert Burns, with much eating of haggis, drinking of whisky and reciting of poetry.

🎆 Celtic Connections

Glasgow hosts the world's largest winter music festival, a celebration of Celtic music, dance and culture, with participants arriving from all over the globe. Held mid- to late January. (p116)

🎆 Up Helly Aa

Half of Shetland dresses up with horned helmets and battleaxes in this spectacular re-enactment of a Viking fire festival, with a torchlit procession leading the burning of a full-size Viking longship. Held in Lerwick on the last Tuesday in January. (p417)

February

The coldest month of the year is usually the best for hill walking, ice-climbing and skiing. The days are getting longer now, and snowdrops begin to bloom.

☆ Six Nations Rugby Tournament

Scotland, England, Wales, Ireland, France and Italy battle it out in this prestigious tournament, held February to March. Home games are played at Murrayfield, Edinburgh. See www.rbs6nations.com.

🏃 Fort William Mountain Festival

The UK's Outdoor Capital celebrates the peak of the winter season with ski and snowboard learning workshops, talks by famous climbers, kids' events and a festival of mountaineering films. See www.mountain festival.co.uk.

April

The bluebell woods on the shores of Loch Lomond come into flower and ospreys arrive at their Loch Garten nests. Weather is improving, though heavy showers are still common.

☆ Rugby Sevens

A series of weekend, seven-a-side rugby tournaments held in various towns throughout the Borders region in April and May, kicking off with Melrose in early April. Fast and furious rugby (sevens was invented here), crowded pubs and great craic. (p142)

May

Wildflowers on the Hebridean machair, hawthorn hedges in bloom and cherry blossom in city parks – Scottish weather is often at its best in May.

✦ Burns an' a' That

Ayrshire towns are the venues for performances of poetry and music, children's events, art exhibitions and more in celebrations of the Scottish bard. (p158)

▾ Spirit of Speyside

Based in the Moray town of Dufftown, this festival of whisky, food and music involves five days of distillery tours, knocking back the 'water of life', cooking, art and outdoor activities. Held late April to early May in Moray and Speyside. (p237)

June

Argyllshire is ablaze with pink rhododendron blooms as the long summer evenings stretch on till 11pm. Border towns are strung with bunting to mark gala days and Common Ridings.

✦ Common Ridings

Following the age-old tradition that commemorates the ancient conflict with England, horsemen and -women ride the old boundaries of common lands, along with parades, marching bands and street parties. Held in various Border towns; Jedburgh (www.jethartcallantsfestival.com) is one of the biggest and best.

✦ Glasgow Festivals

June is Glasgow's equivalent of Edinburgh's August festival season, when the city hosts several major events, the most important of which is the West End Festival, the city's biggest music and arts event. (p118)

July

School holidays begin, as does the busiest time of year for resort towns. It's high season for Shetland birdwatchers.

☆ T in the Park

Held annually since 1994, and headlined by world-class acts such as the Who, REM, the Stone Roses and Calvin Harris, this major music festival is Scotland's answer to Glastonbury; held over a mid-July weekend at Strathallan Castle, near Gleneagles. See www.tinthepark.com. (p196)

August

Festival time in Edinburgh (www.edinburghfestivals.co.uk) and the city is crammed with visitors. On the west coast, this is the peak month for sighting minke whales and basking sharks.

☆ Edinburgh International Festival

The world's top musicians and performers congregate in Edinburgh for three weeks of diverse and inspirational music, opera, theatre and dance. Takes place over the three weeks ending on the first Saturday in September. The program is usually available from April. (p75)

☆ Edinburgh Festival Fringe

The biggest performing-arts festival anywhere in the world.

September

School holidays are over, midges are dying off, wild brambles are ripe for picking in the hedgerows, and the weather is often dry and mild – an excellent time of year for outdoor pursuits.

✦ Braemar Gathering

The biggest and most famous Highland Games in the Scottish calendar, traditionally attended by members of the royal family. Highland dancing, bagpipe-playing and caber-tossing. Held early September in Braemar, Royal Deeside. (p320)

December

Darkness falls mid-afternoon as the shortest day approaches. The often cold and wet weather is relieved by Christmas and New Year festivities.

✦ Hogmanay

Christmas celebrations in Edinburgh (www.edinburghschristmas.com) culminate in a huge street party on Hogmanay (31 December). The fishing town of Stonehaven echoes an ancient, pre-Christian tradition with its procession of fireball-swinging locals who parade to the harbour and fling their blazing orbs into the sea (www.stonehavenfireballs.co.uk). (p76)

Itineraries

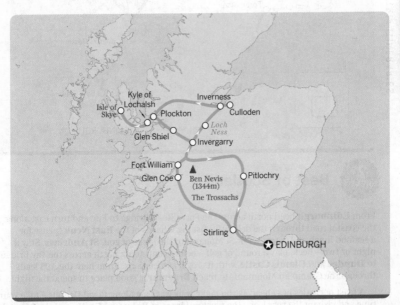

A Highland Fling

No trip to Scotland would be complete without a visit to **Edinburgh**, and even if your Scottish trip lasts only a week, the capital is worth two days of your time. On day three, head northwest to **Stirling** to see Scotland's other great castle, then on to the **Trossachs** for your first taste of Highland scenery (overnight in Callander).

Day four starts with a scenic drive north via **Glen Coe** and **Fort William**, then along the Great Glen to **Loch Ness** in time for an afternoon visiting Urquhart Castle and the Loch Ness Centre & Exhibition. An evening cruise on Loch Ness rounds off the day before spending the night in **Inverness**, on picturesque River Ness.

Spend the morning of day five visiting **Culloden Battlefield**, then drive west via Achnasheen and **Plockton** to **Kyle of Lochalsh** and cross the bridge to the **Isle of Skye**. Devote day six to exploring Skye – there will be time for a visit to Dunvegan Castle and a tour of the Trotternish peninsula.

Spend your last day taking the long drive back south – the scenic route goes via **Glen Shiel**, **Invergarry**, Spean Bridge (pause at the Commando Monument), Laggan and then south on the A9 to Edinburgh, with a stop in **Pitlochry**.

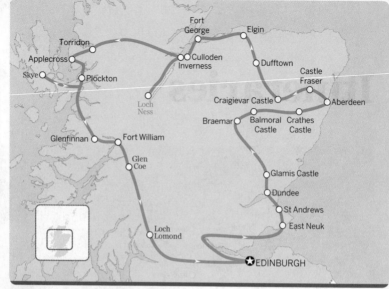

2 WEEKS Best of Scotland

From **Edinburgh** head north across the Forth Road Bridge to Fife and turn east along the coastal road through the delightful fishing villages of the **East Neuk** (pause for a seafood lunch at Anstruther or St Monans) to the home of golf, **St Andrews**. Stay a night or two – heck, play a round of golf – before continuing north across the Tay Bridge to **Dundee** and **Glamis Castle**, with its royal associations. From here the A93 leads through the Grampian Mountains to reach **Braemar**, a good place to spend the night.

A feast of castles lies ahead as you make your way east along Royal Deeside – take your time and visit (at the very least) the royal residence of **Balmoral Castle** and the fairy-tale **Crathes Castle** on your way to the granite city of **Aberdeen**. Plan to overnight here.

Now strike west again along the A944, making small detours to visit **Castle Fraser** and **Craigievar Castle** before heading north to **Dufftown** and Aberlour in the heart of Speyside. Base yourself here for at least a day while you explore the many whisky distilleries nearby – there are some good places to eat, plus the whisky bar at the Craigellachie Hotel.

Head northwest to **Elgin** and its magnificent ruined cathedral, then west on the A96 visiting **Fort George** and **Culloden** on the way to Inverness (you'll probably need a stopover in Nairn). **Inverness** itself is worth a night or two – there are some excellent hotels and restaurants, and the opportunity for a side trip to **Loch Ness** (Drumnadrochit for monster spotters; Dores Inn for foodies).

Now for a glorious drive from Inverness to **Torridon** via Kinlochewe through some of the country's finest mountain scenery; try to spend a night at the Torridon hotel. Then head south via **Applecross** and the pretty village of **Plockton** to Kyle of Lochalsh and the bridge to **Skye**.

Spend two days exploring Scotland's most famous island before taking the ferry from Armadale to Mallaig, and follow the Road to the Isles in reverse, stopping to visit **Glenfinnan**, where Bonnie Prince Charlie raised his Highland army in 1745. Overnight at **Fort William**, and drive back to Edinburgh via the scenic road through **Glen Coe** and along the bonnie banks of **Loch Lomond**.

Above: Plockton
(p373)

Right: Old Course
(p191), St Andrews

ADAMEDWARDS / SHUTTERSTOCK ©

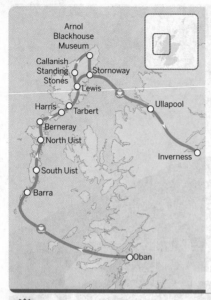

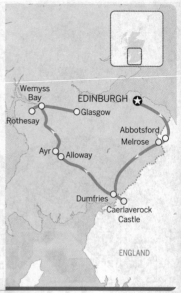

1 WEEK Island Hopscotch

This route is usually done by car, but it also makes a brilliant cycling tour (270 miles, including the 60 miles from Ullapool to Inverness train station, making both start and finish accessible by rail).

From **Oban** it's a five-hour ferry crossing to **Barra**; plan to spend the night here and book ahead. On day two, after a visit to Kisimul Castle and a tour around the island, take the ferry to **South Uist**. Walk the wild beaches of the west coast, sample the local seafood and perhaps go fishing on the island's trout lochs. Continue through Benbecula and **North Uist**, prime birdwatching country.

Overnight at Lochmaddy on North Uist (if you're camping or hostelling, a night at **Berneray** is a must) before taking the ferry to **Harris**, whose west coast has some of the most spectacular beaches in Scotland. The road continues north from **Tarbert**, where you'll find good hotels, through rugged hills to **Lewis**.

Loop west via the **Callanish Standing Stones** and **Arnol Blackhouse museum**. Spend your final night in **Stornoway** (eat at Digby Chick), then take the ferry to **Ullapool** for a scenic drive to **Inverness**.

5 DAYS Border Raid

From **Edinburgh** your first objective should be a visit to Sir Walter Scott's former home at **Abbotsford**, followed by a traipse around the beautiful Border abbeys of **Melrose** and nearby Dryburgh; Melrose is a charming place to stay the night, with a choice of good hotels and eating places.

Next morning head west along the A708 to Moffat, passing through glorious scenery around **St Mary's Loch**. Continue to **Dumfries** (and stop for the night), where you can visit the first of several sights related to Scotland's national poet Robert Burns, and make a short side trip to see spectacular **Caerlaverock Castle**.

Take the A76 northwest towards Ayr, and spend the rest of day three in **Alloway** visiting the birthplace of Robert Burns (and other Burns-related sites); nearby **Ayr** has plenty of accommodation options.

North now to **Wemyss Bay** and the ferry to **Rothesay** on the Isle of Bute, where you can visit stunning Mount Stuart, one of Scotland's most impressive stately homes. Spend the night on the island, then return to the mainland and head east to **Glasgow**.

Plan Your Trip
Walking in Scotland

Scotland's wild, dramatic scenery and varied landscape has made walking a hugely popular pastime for locals and tourists alike. There really is something for everyone, from after-breakfast strolls to the popular sport of Munro bagging.

Planning

For gentle walks along clearly defined tracks, the most planning you'll need to do is take a look at the weather forecast and decide how many layers you'll need to wear. Highland hikers should be properly equipped and cautious, as the weather can become vicious at any time of year. After rain, peaty soil can become boggy, so always wear stout shoes or boots and carry extra food and drink – many unsuspecting walkers have had to survive an unplanned night in the open. Don't depend on mobile phones (although carrying one with you is a good idea, and can be a lifesaver if you get a signal). If necessary leave a note with your route and expected time of return on the dashboard of your car.

When to Go

The best time of year for hill walking is usually May to September, although snow can fall on the highest summits even in midsummer. Winter walking on the higher hills of Scotland requires the use of an ice axe and crampons and is for experienced mountaineers only.

Access & Rights of Way

There is a tradition of relatively free access to open country in Scotland, a custom that was enshrined in law in the 2003 Land

Walking Essentials

Hillwalking Gear

☐ Good waterproofs

☐ Spare warm clothing

☐ Map and compass (know how to use them!)

☐ Mobile phone (but don't rely on it)

☐ First-aid kit

☐ Head torch

☐ Whistle (for emergencies)

☐ Spare food and drink

☐ Bivvy bag

Safety Checklist

☐ Check the weather forecast first

☐ Let someone know your plans

☐ Set your pace and objective to suit the slowest member of your party

☐ Don't be afraid to turn back if it's too difficult

Reform (Scotland) Bill, popularly known as 'the right to roam'. The Scottish Outdoor Access Code (www.outdooraccess-scotland.com) states that everyone has the right to be on most land and inland waters, providing they act responsibly.

You should avoid areas where you might disrupt or disturb wildlife, lambing (generally mid-April to the end of May), grouse shooting (from 12 August to the third week in October) or deer stalking (1 July to 15 February, but the peak period is August to October). You can get up-to-date information on deer stalking in various areas through the Heading for the Scottish Hills (www.www.outdooraccess-scotland.com/hftsh) service.

Local authorities aren't required to list and map rights of way, so they're not shown on Ordnance Survey (OS) maps of Scotland, as they are in England and Wales. However, the Scottish Rights of Way & Access Society (www.scotways.com) keeps records of these routes, provides and maintains signposting, and publicises them in its guidebook, *Scottish Hill Tracks*.

You are free to pitch a tent almost anywhere that doesn't cause inconvenience to others or damage to property, as long as you stay no longer than two or three nights in any one spot, take all litter away with you, and keep well away from houses and roads. (Note that this right does not extend to the use of motorised vehicles to reach camping spots.)

Best Walks

West Highland Way

This classic hike – the country's most popular long-distance trail – stretches for 96 miles through some of Scotland's most spectacular scenery, from Milngavie (mull-*guy*), on the northwestern fringes of Glasgow, to Fort William.

The route begins in the Lowlands but the greater part of the trail is among the mountains, lochs and fast-flowing rivers of the western Highlands. After following the eastern shore of Loch Lomond and passing Crianlarich and Tyndrum, the route crosses the vast wilderness of Rannoch Moor and reaches Fort William via Glen Nevis, in the shadow of Britain's highest peak, Ben Nevis.

The path is easy to follow, making use of old drove roads (along which Highland cattle were once driven to Lowland markets), an old military road (built by troops to help subdue the Highlands in the 18th century) and disused railway lines.

Best done from south to north, the walk takes about six or seven days. Many people round it off with an ascent of Ben Nevis. You need to be properly equipped with good boots, waterproofs, maps, a compass, and food and drink for the northern part of the walk. Midge repellent is also essential.

OFFICIAL LONG-DISTANCE FOOTPATHS

Scotland has no fewer than 26 official long-distance footpaths (ie waymarked trails), which are all described on the website www.scotlandsgreattrails.org.uk. Each trail also has its own dedicated website, and at least one print guidebook such as those published by Cicerone (www.cicerone.co.uk) and Rucksack Readers (www.rucsacs.com).

WALK	DISTANCE (MI)	FEATURES	DURATION (DAYS)	DIFFICULTY
Fife Coastal Path	78	Firth of Forth, undulating country	5-6	easy
Great Glen Way	73	Loch Ness, canal paths, forest tracks	4	easy
Pilgrims Way	25	Machars peninsula, standing stones, burial mounds	2-3	easy
Southern Upland Way	212	Remote hills & moorlands	9-14	medium-hard
Speyside Way	66	Follows river, whisky distilleries	3-4	easy-medium
St Cuthbert's Way	62	Follows the path of a famous saint	6-7	medium
West Highland Way	96	Spectacular scenery, mountains & lochs	6-8	medium

TOP 10 SHORT WALKS

Quiraing (p385; Isle of Skye) One to two hours; bizarre rock pinnacles.

Steall Meadows (p338; Glen Nevis) One to two hours; waterfall beneath Ben Nevis.

Lost Valley (p332; Glen Coe) Three hours; impressive mountain scenery.

Conic Hill (p245; Loch Lomond) Two hours; views over Loch Lomond.

Loch an Eilein (p309; Aviemore) One hour; lovely lochan amid Scots pines.

Linn of Quoich (p321; Braemar) One hour; rocky gorge and waterfall.

Plodda Falls (p304; Cannich) One hour; dizzying viewpoint above waterfall.

Duncansby Head (p359; John O'Groats) One hour; spectacular sea stacks.

Stac Pollaidh (p367; Coigach) Two to four hours; ascent of miniature mountain.

Old Man of Hoy (p411; Orkney) Three hours; Britain's tallest sea stack.

It's possible to do just a day's hike along part of the trail. For example, the Loch Lomond Water Bus allows you to walk the section from Rowardennan to Inversnaid, returning to your starting point by boat.

The West Highland Way Official Guide by Bob Aitken and Roger Smith is the most comprehensive guidebook, while the Harveys map *West Highland Way* covers the entire route in a single waterproof map sheet.

Accommodation shouldn't be too difficult to find, though between Bridge of Orchy and Kinlochleven it's limited. At peak times (May, July and August), book accommodation in advance. There are some youth hostels and bunkhouses on or near the path, and it's possible to camp in some parts. A list of accommodation is available from tourist offices.

For more information check out the website www.west-highland-way.co.uk.

Speyside Way

This long-distance footpath follows the course of the River Spey, one of Scotland's most famous salmon-fishing rivers. It starts at Buckie and first follows the coast to Spey Bay, east of Elgin, then runs inland along the river to Aviemore in the Cairngorms (with branches to Tomintoul and Dufftown). There are plans to extend the trail to Newtonmore in 2016–17.

The 66-mile route has been dubbed the 'Whisky Trail' as it passes near a number of distilleries, including Glenlivet and Glenfiddich (p237), which are open to the public. If you stop at them all, the walk may take considerably longer than the usual three or four days! The first 11 miles from Buckie to Fochabers makes a good day hike (allow four to five hours).

The Speyside Way, a guidebook by Jacquetta Megarry and Jim Strachan, describes the trail in detail. Check out the route at www.speysideway.org.

Isle of Skye

Skye is a walker's paradise, criss-crossed with trails both easy and strenuous that lead you through some of the country's most spectacular scenery.

Quiraing (3.5 miles; two to three hours) Start at the parking area at the highest point of the minor road between Staffin and Uig. A clear path leads northeast towards the obvious pinnacles, but after 200m or so strike north up the hill to reach another path that leads across the summit of Meall na Suiramach with fantastic views down into the Quiraing. The path continues to a saddle and break in the cliffs where you can descend and return to your starting point through the midst of the pinnacles.

Kilmarie to Coruisk (11 miles; at least six hours) One of the most spectacular and challenging of Skye's low-level walks begins at a parking area just south of Kilmarie, on the Broadford–Elgol road. A stony track leads over a hill pass to the gorgeous bay of Camasunary, and continues on the far side of the Camasunary River – at low tide you can cross on stepping stones, but if the tide is high you'll have to splash across further upstream. The notorious Bad Step is opposite the northern end of the little island in Loch na Cuilce; it's a rock slab that drops straight into the sea, where you scramble out onto a shelf and along a rising crack (the secret is to drop down leftward when you

MOUNTAIN WALKS IN THE CAIRNGORMS

The climb from the car park at the Coire Cas ski area to the summit of **Cairn Gorm** (1245m) is 2 miles and takes about two hours (one way). From there, you can continue south across the high-level plateau to Ben Macdui (1309m), Britain's second-highest peak. From the car park to the peak and then back is 12 miles and takes eight to 10 hours. It's a serious undertaking, and is for experienced and well-equipped walkers only.

The **Lairig Ghru trail**, which can take eight to 10 hours, is a demanding 24-mile walk from Aviemore through the Lairig Ghru pass (840m) to Braemar. An alternative to doing the full route is to make the six-hour return hike up to the summit of the pass and back to Aviemore. The path starts from Ski Rd, a mile east of Coylumbridge, and involves some very rough going.

Warning – the Cairngorm plateau is a sub-Arctic environment where navigation is difficult and weather conditions can be severe, even in midsummer. Hikers must have proper hill-walking equipment, and know how to use a map and compass. In winter it is a place for experienced mountaineers only. Trip durations are estimates only.

reach a niche in the crack). There are no further obstacles, and 15 minutes later you arrive at Loch Coruisk, one of the wildest and most remote spots in Scotland. Return by the same route, or arrange in advance to be picked up by one of the tour boats from Elgol.

Munro Bagging

At the end of the 19th century an eager hill walker, Sir Hugh Munro, published a list of Scottish mountains measuring over 3000ft (914m) in height – he couldn't have realised that in time his name would be used to describe all Scottish mountains over 3000ft, and that keen hill walkers would set themselves the target of reaching the summit of (or bagging) all of Scotland's 282 Munros.

To the uninitiated it may seem odd that Munro baggers see venturing into mist, cloud and driving rain as time well spent. However, for those who can add one or more ticks to their list, the vagaries of the weather are part of the enjoyment, at least in retrospect. Munro bagging is, of course, more than merely ticking off a list – it takes you to some of the wildest and most beautiful corners of Scotland.

Once you've bagged all the Munros you can move on to the Corbetts – hills over 2500ft (700m), with a drop of at least 500ft (150m) on all sides – and the Donalds, lowland hills over 2000ft (610m). And for connoisseurs of the diminutive, there are the McPhies: 'eminences in excess of 300ft (90m)' on the island of Colonsay.

Further Information

Every tourist office has leaflets (free or for a nominal charge) of suggested walks that take in local points of interest. Lonely Planet's *Walking in Scotland* is a comprehensive resource, covering short walks and long-distance paths; its *Walking in Britain* guide covers Scottish walks, too. For general advice, VisitScotland's **Walking in Scotland** (http://walking.visitscotland.com) website describes numerous routes in various parts of the country, and also offers safety tips and other useful information. **WalkHighlands** (www.walkhighlands.co.uk) is an online database of more than 1500 walks complete with maps and detailed descriptions.

Plan Your Trip
Golf

A round in the home of golf isn't about nostalgia: the sport is part of Scotland's fabric. Playing here is a unique experience; you're almost guaranteed heart-stopping scenery and a friendly atmosphere whatever the weather. Scotland's tradition of public courses means that outstanding golf is usually accompanied by sociable moments and warm hospitality.

History

The first known mention of golf is from 1457, when James II banned it to prevent archery, crucial for military reasons, being ignored as an activity.

The oldest course is at Musselburgh; the oldest club is the Honourable Company of Edinburgh Golfers (1744), based at Muirfield. In 1754 the Royal and Ancient of St Andrews, which became the game's governing body, was born.

Modern golf really evolved in the late 19th and early 20th centuries. Legendary figures such as James Braid and Old Tom Morris designed courses across Britain; the latter was a founding figure of the Open Championship and won it four times.

Scotland is also very much at the forefront of international professional golf, with high-profile events such as the 2014 Ryder Cup, 2015 Open and 2018 Open held at Gleneagles, St Andrews and Royal Troon respectively.

Where to Play

With more golf courses per capita than any other country, Scotland offers a bewildering choice. A selection of world golf's most iconic courses offers some of the sport's most famous holes, with deep, challenging bunkers where you might only get out

Golf Essentials

When to Play

Summer is most enjoyable – long daylight hours mean you can tee off at 6am or 7pm. Courses are busy in these months though; a good compromise is to play in May or September.

Resources

VisitScotland (www.visitscotland.com/golf) Useful information, including on discount golf passes. Publishes *Golf in Scotland*, a free annual brochure listing courses, costs and accommodation information.

Scotland Golf (www.scotlandgolf.com) Good for investigating courses to play.

Costs

A round at an unfashionable rural course may cost as little as £10. Showpiece courses charge green fees of £160 to £250 in high season. It's more economical in winter, it's often cheaper midweek, and 'twilight' rates (teeing off after 4pm or so) can save you up to 50% at some clubs.

backwards, if at all. But there's also great pleasure to be had on simpler, local fairways eked out by small Highland or island communities, where you'll have to improvise shots over the sheep or deer nibbling at the green.

Practical Tips

➡ Handicap certificates are often unnecessary, but bring one, along with an introduction letter from your home club, for more upmarket clubs. Some courses have a minimum handicap requirement.

➡ Dress regulations aren't generally too rigorous – think smart casual as a norm. Most

TEN OF THE BEST GOLF COURSES

St Andrews (p191) The public Old Course is the game's spiritual home and you can't help but be awed by the history and atmosphere here. The 17th – the Road Hole – is famous for its blind drive, nasty bunker and seriously sloping green. Several other courses for all abilities make this Scotland's premium golfing destination.

Turnberry (p161) Now owned by Donald Trump, Turnberry's Ailsa is one of Scotland's most prestigious links courses, with spectacular views. Pack a spare ball for the nasty 9th on the Ailsa course, where your ball will sleep with the fishes unless you manage the 200-yard carry off the tee. Luckily there's the renowned Halfway Hut to drown your sorrows before taking on the 10th.

Carnoustie (☑01241-802270; www.carnoustiegolflinks.co.uk; 20 Links Parade, Carnoustie, Angus) Widely known as Scotland's toughest challenge, it's nicknamed Car-nasty, as much for near-constant winds as for the course itself. It ain't over till it's over here: the Barry Burn on the 18th has undone many a leader in social games and Open Championships alike. Hosts the Open in 2018.

Loch Lomond (p241) On the shores of the famous loch, this course – not a links – has a picturesque, romantic location, including an impressive clubhouse and a ruined castle by the 18th green. Nevertheless, it's a real test, with plenty of water hazards and cunningly placed sand traps. You have to be a member or be invited by one.

Royal Troon (p157) Making its way along the dunes, this classic seaside venue could define a links course. The short 8th is known as the Postage Stamp for its tiny, well-protected green. It was the Open venue in 2016.

Royal Dornoch (p355) Up north, the sumptuous championship course rewards the journey with picture-perfect links scenery and a quieter pace to things. If this was nearer the southern population centres, many would rate it Scotland's best.

Machrihanish Dunes (p261) On the Kintyre peninsula, this Old Tom Morris–designed course is one of Scotland's most scenic. There's no easing into your round here; strike long and clean on the 1st or you'll be on the beach – literally.

Gleneagles (☑01764-662231; www.gleneagles.com/golf; near Auchterarder, Perthshire) Three brilliant courses and a five-star hotel with truly excellent service make this legendary Perthshire destination a great choice for golfing breaks. Plenty on offer for golf widowers, widows and/or kids.

Muirfield (☑01620-842123; www.muirfield.org.uk; Duncur Rd, Muirfield, Gullane) Handy for Edinburgh, this private course on land reclaimed from the sea allocates some public tee times. It's one of Scotland's more traditional – and many would say outrageously sexist – institutions, and hit the headlines again in 2016 for its members' failure to pass a motion to allow females to join their ranks.

Trump International (☑01358-743300; www.trumpgolfscotland.com; Balmedie, Aberdeenshire) Environmentally controversial course near Aberdeen featuring spectacular high-dune scenery.

places prohibit jeans, trainers and T-shirts, and several don't look kindly upon shorts. Mobile-phone use on course is frowned upon. Stricter dress regulations may apply for the clubhouse.

➡ Club hire is usually available, but it's not cheap (up to £70 on elite courses), so if you'll play a few rounds, it's worth bringing your own bag.

➡ Motorised carts are widely available, but are less used than in the US or Australia. They tend to be hired mostly by people with mobility difficulties and are prohibited on some courses.

➡ Book rounds at desirable courses well ahead – many months in the case of prestigious links like the Old Course at St Andrews.

➡ Caddies can help greatly. They know the layout, and will advise when to attack the pin and when caution is the better part of valour. Their local lore and fund of anecdotes also often makes for a special Scottish experience. Caddies should be booked, though you may be able to hire one on the day. Think around £50 plus tip for the round.

➡ Some courses have starters, whose job is to get your group out on time. It's worth chatting to these savvy folk for tips on not embarrassing yourself off the 1st tee with everyone watching.

➡ Solo players may be put into existing groups. Some busier courses won't allow single players to book, allocating places in twosomes or threesomes on a first-come, first-served basis.

Links Courses

Links, the seaside courses where modern golf was born, present unique challenges with their undulating fairways, unforgiving rough, vertical bunkers and enormous greens that can resemble the Scottish Highlands in miniature. They're usually wholly treeless, with gorse, heather and machair making up the vegetation. But that's not to say that they're easy. Far from it.

On sandy uncultivable ground between the fields and the sea and largely un-planned, they follow the contours of the land. Exposed and unprotected, they are at the mercy of wind and weather: on a sunny day you can post flattering scores, but a healthy sea breeze means that approaches into scarily angled greens need meticulous execution. It pays to listen to locals.

Regions at a Glance

Which regions of Scotland you choose to visit will naturally depend on how much time you have, and whether you've been here before. First-time visitors will want to squeeze in as many highlights as possible, so could try following the well-trodden route through Edinburgh, the Trossachs, Pitlochry, Inverness, Loch Ness and the Isle of Skye.

It takes considerably more time to explore the further-flung corners of the country, but the ruined abbeys and castles of the Borders, the jaw-dropping scenery of the northwest Highlands and the gorgeous white-sand beaches of the Outer Hebrides are less crowded and ultimately more rewarding. The long journey to Orkney or Shetland means that you'll want to devote more than just a day or two to these regions.

Edinburgh

Culture
History
Food

Festival City

The Scottish capital is a city of high culture where, each summer, the world's biggest arts festival gets rave reviews.

Capital History

Perched on a brooding black crag overlooking the city centre, Edinburgh Castle has played a pivotal role in Scottish history. The growth of the city from its medieval origins and the parallel development of Scottish nationhood is documented in its excellent museums.

Eating Out

Edinburgh has more restaurants per head of population than any city in the UK. Eating out is commonplace, not just for special occasions, and the eateries range from stylish but inexpensive bistros and cafes to gourmet restaurants with Michelin stars.

p44

Glasgow

Museums
Music
Design

Kelvingrove Art Gallery & Museum

Glasgow's mercantile, industrial and academic history has left the city with a wonderful legacy of museums and art galleries, dominated by the grand Kelvingrove, boasting a bewildering variety of exhibits.

King Tut's Wah Wah Hut

Glasgow is the star of Scotland's live-music scene, with legendary venues like King Tut's Wah Wah Hut staging gigs ranging from local start-ups to top international acts.

Charles Rennie Mackintosh

With Charles Rennie Mackintosh's iconic buildings, the centre's grand Victorian architecture, the fashion boutiques of the Italian Centre and design exhibitions at the Lighthouse, Glasgow is Scotland's most stylish city.

p103

Southern Scotland

Historic Buildings
Architecture
Activities

Great Abbeys

Ruined abbeys dot Scotland's southern border. The Gothic ruins of Melrose, Jedburgh, Dryburgh and Sweetheart and the martial towers of Hermitage Castle, Caerlaverock Castle and Smailholm are testimony to a turbulent past.

Dumfries House

This region is rich in Adam-designed mansions such as Culzean Castle, Paxton House, Floors Castle and Mellerstain House, but Dumfries House takes top place.

Mountain Biking

The hills of the Southern Uplands can't compete with the Highlands for scenery, but Galloway and Arran are prime hill-walking country, and the 7stanes trails offer some of the UK's best and most challenging mountain biking.

p138

Central Scotland

Golf
Coastal Scenery
Castles

St Andrews

Scotland is the home of golf, and the Old Course at St Andrews is on every golfer's wish list. The game has been played here for more than 600 years; the Royal & Ancient Golf Club, the game's governing body, was founded in 1754.

East Neuk of Fife

The scenic coastline of the East Neuk of Fife is dotted with picturesque harbours and quaint fishing villages, their history recounted in the excellent Scottish Fisheries Museum in Anstruther.

Stirling Castle

Some say that Stirling has the finest castle in the country, but the region has plenty of others worth visiting, including St Andrews Castle, Castle Campbell, Kellie Castle and Doune Castle.

p176

Northeast Scotland

Whisky
Castles
History

Speyside Distilleries

Don't leave Scotland without visiting a whisky distillery; the Speyside region, around Dufftown in Moray, is the epicentre of the industry. More than 50 distilleries open during the Spirit of Speyside festival; many open year-round.

Scottish Baronial Style

Aberdeenshire and Moray have the greatest concentration of Scottish Baronial castles in the country, from the turreted splendour of Craigievar and Fyvie to the elegance of Crathes and Balmoral.

Pictish Stones

The Picts carved mysterious stones (dating from the 7th and 8th centuries) can be seen in places such as Aberlemno and St Vigeans Museum (near Arbroath).

p209

Southern Highlands & Islands

Wildlife
Islands
Food

Whales & Eagles

See some of Scotland's most spectacular wildlife, from magnificent white-tailed sea eagles in Mull to majestic minke whales and basking sharks cruising the west coast. Beavers have also been reintroduced into the wild here.

Island-Hopping

Island-hopping is one of the best ways to explore the western seaboard, and the cluster of islands here – Islay Jura, Mull, Iona, and the beaches of Colonsay, Coll and Tiree – provide a brilliant introduction.

Seafood

Whether you dine at a top restaurant in Oban or Tobermory, or eat with your fingers on the harbourside, the rich harvest of the sea is one of the region's biggest drawcards.

p239

Inverness & the Central Highlands

Activities
Royalty
Legends

Hiking & Skiing

The Highland towns of Aviemore and Fort William offer outdoor adventure galore. Be it climbing, walking, biking or skiing, there's something for everyone.

Royal Deeside

The valley of the River Dee between Ballater and Braemar has been associated with the royal family since Queen Victoria acquired her holiday home, Balmoral Castle.

The Loch Ness Monster

Scotland's most iconic legend, the Loch Ness monster, lurks in here. You might not spot Nessie, but the magnificent scenery of the Great Glen makes a visit worthwhile, as does Culloden battlefield, the undoing of another Scottish legend, Bonnie Prince Charlie.

p293

Northern Highlands & Islands

Scenery
Activities
History

Mountains & Lochs

From the peaks of Assynt and Torridon to the pinnacles of the Cuillin Hills and the beaches of the Outer Hebrides, the big skies and lonely landscapes of the northern Highlands and islands are the very essence of Scotland.

Adventure Sports

The northwest's vast spaces make one huge adventure playground for hikers, mountain bikers, climbers and kayakers, and provide the chance to see some of the UK's most spectacular wildlife.

The Clearances

The abandoned rural communities of the north teach much about the Clearances, especially Arnol Blackhouse. Prehistoric remains include the famous standing stones of Callanish.

p349

Orkney & Shetland

History
Wildlife
Music

Skara Brae

These islands have a fascinating Viking heritage and unique prehistoric villages, tombs and stone circles. Skara Brae is northern Europe's best-preserved prehistoric village; Maeshowe is one of Britain's finest Neolithic tombs.

Birdwatching

Shetland is a birdwatcher's paradise, its cliffs teeming in summer with gannets, fulmars, kittiwakes, razorbills and puffins, and Europe's largest colony of Arctic terns. Hermaness on Unst is Scotland's northernmost inhabited island.

Folk Tradition

The pubs of Kirkwall, Stromness and Lerwick are fertile ground for exploring the traditional-music scene. Both Orkney and Shetland host annual folk music festivals.

p398

On the Road

Edinburgh

POP 498,810

Best Places to Eat

➡ Castle Terrace (p86)
➡ Gardener's Cottage (p83)
➡ The Dogs (p83)
➡ Ondine (p82)
➡ Fishers Bistro (p87)
➡ Timberyard (p86)

Best Places to Sleep

➡ Witchery by the Castle (p76)
➡ Knight Residence (p78)
➡ Sheridan Guest House (p79)
➡ Southside Guest House (p78)
➡ Millers 64 (p79)

Why Go?

Edinburgh is a city that begs to be explored. From the vaults and wynds (narrow lanes) that riddle the Old Town to the urban villages of Stockbridge and Cramond, it's filled with quirky, come-hither nooks that tempt you to walk just a little bit further. And every corner turned reveals sudden views and unexpected vistas – green sunlit hills, a glimpse of rust-red crags, a blue flash of distant sea.

But there's more to Edinburgh than sightseeing – there are top shops, world-class restaurants and a bacchanalia of bars to enjoy. This is a city of pub crawls and impromptu music sessions, late-night drinking, all-night parties and wandering home through cobbled streets at dawn.

All these superlatives come together at festival time in August, when it seems as if half the world descends on Edinburgh for one enormous party. If you can possibly manage it, join them.

When to Go
Edinburgh

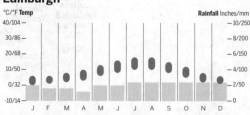

May Good weather (usually), flowers and cherry blossom everywhere and (gasp!) no crowds.

Aug Festival time! Crowded and mad but irresistible.

Dec Christmas decorations, cosy pubs with open fires, ice skating in Princes Street Gardens.

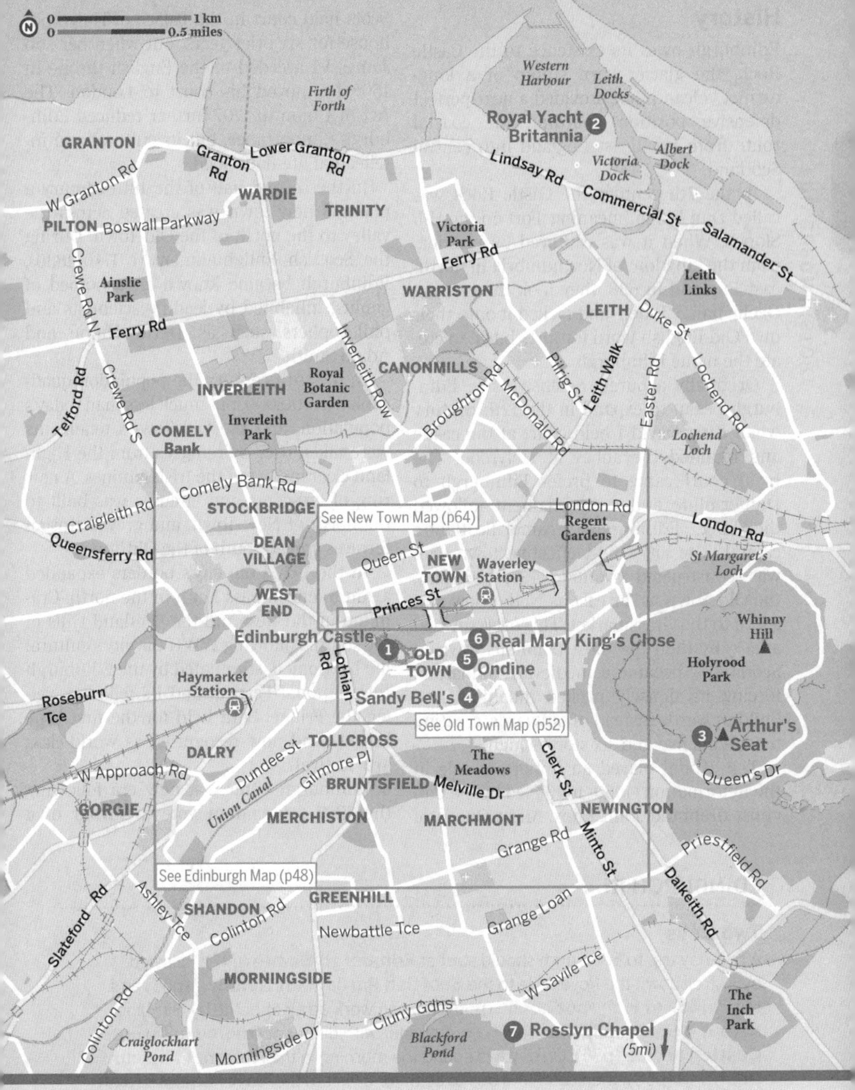

Map legend and labels:

- Firth of Forth
- Western Harbour
- Leith Docks
- Albert Dock
- **Royal Yacht Britannia** ②
- Victoria Dock
- GRANTON
- Lower Granton Rd
- Granton Rd
- W Granton Rd
- Lindsay Rd
- Commercial St
- Salamander St
- WARDIE
- TRINITY
- PILTON
- Boswall Parkway
- Victoria Park Rd
- Ferry Rd
- Leith Links
- LEITH
- Ainslie Park
- Crewe Rd N
- Ferry Rd
- WARRISTON
- Duke St
- Easter Rd
- Lochend Rd
- Telford Rd
- Crewe Rd S
- INVERLEITH
- Royal Botanic Garden
- CANONMILLS
- Broughton Rd
- McDonald Rd
- Pilrig St
- Leith Walk
- Lochend Loch
- COMELY Bank
- Inverleith Park
- Inverleith Row
- Craigleith Rd
- Comely Bank Rd
- STOCKBRIDGE
- See New Town Map (p64)
- London Rd
- Regent Gardens
- London Rd
- St Margaret's Loch
- Queensferry Rd
- DEAN VILLAGE
- Queen St
- **NEW TOWN**
- Waverley Station
- Whinny Hill
- WEST END
- Princes St
- Holyrood Park
- Roseburn Tce
- Haymarket Station
- **Edinburgh Castle** ①
- Lothian Rd
- **OLD TOWN**
- ⑤ **Ondine**
- ⑥ **Real Mary King's Close**
- **Sandy Bell's** ④
- See Old Town Map (p52)
- ③ ▲ **Arthur's Seat**
- DALRY
- TOLLCROSS
- W Approach Rd
- Dundee St
- Gilmore Pl
- The Meadows
- Melville Dr
- Clerk St
- Queen's Dr
- GORGIE
- Union Canal
- BRUNTSFIELD
- MARCHMONT
- NEWINGTON
- See Edinburgh Map (p48)
- MERCHISTON
- Grange Rd
- Minto St
- Priestfield Rd
- Slateford Rd
- Ashley Tce
- Colinton Rd
- GREENHILL
- SHANDON
- Newbattle Tce
- Grange Loan
- Dalkeith Rd
- MORNINGSIDE
- W Savile Tce
- The Inch Park
- Colinton Rd
- Morningside Dr
- Cluny Gdns
- Craiglockhart Pond
- Blackford Pond
- ⑦ **Rosslyn Chapel** (5mi)

Edinburgh Highlights

① **Edinburgh Castle** (p47) Taking in the views from the battlements.

② **Royal Yacht Britannia** (p68) Nosing around the Queen's private quarters.

③ **Arthur's Seat** (p58) Climbing to the summit of the city's miniature mountain.

④ **Sandy Bell's** (p91) Listening to live folk music.

⑤ **Ondine** (p82) Enjoying the finest of Scottish seafood.

⑥ **Real Mary King's Close** (p53) Exploring Edinburgh's subterranean history in these haunted vaults.

⑦ **Rosslyn Chapel** (p99) Trying to decipher the Da Vinci Code at this mysterious chapel.

History

Edinburgh owes its existence to the Castle Rock, the glacier-worn stump of a long-extinct volcano that provided a near-perfect defensive position guarding the coastal route from northeast England into central Scotland.

In the 7th century the Castle Rock was called Dun Eiden (meaning 'Fort on the Hill Slope'). When it was captured by invaders from the kingdom of Northumbria in north-east England in 638, they took the existing Gaelic name 'Eiden' and tacked it onto their own Old English word for fort, 'burh', to create the name Edinburgh.

Originally a purely defensive site, Edinburgh began to expand in the 12th century when King David I held court at the castle and founded the abbey at Holyrood. The royal court came to prefer Edinburgh to Dunfermline and, as parliament followed the king, Edinburgh became Scotland's capital. The city's first effective town wall was constructed around 1450, enclosing the Old Town as far east as Netherbow and south to the Grassmarket. This overcrowded area – by then the most populous town in Scotland – became a medieval Manhattan, forcing its densely packed inhabitants to build upwards instead of outwards, creating tenements five and six storeys high.

The capital played an important role in the Reformation (1560–1690), led by the Calvinist firebrand John Knox. Mary, Queen of Scots held court in the Palace of Holyroodhouse for six brief years, but when her son James VI acceded to the English throne in 1603 he moved his court to London. The Act of Union in 1707 further reduced Edinburgh's importance, but its cultural and intellectual life flourished.

In the second half of the 18th century a planned new town was created across the valley to the north of the Old Town. During the Scottish Enlightenment (c 1740–1830), Edinburgh became known as 'a hotbed of genius', inhabited by leading scientists and philosophers such as David Hume and Adam Smith.

In the 19th century the population quadrupled to 400,000, not much less than today's population, and the Old Town's tenements were taken over by refugees from the Highland clearances and the Irish famines. A new ring of crescents and circuses was built to the north of New Town, and grey Victorian terraces spread south of the Old Town.

In the 1920s the city's borders expanded again to encompass Leith in the north, Cramond in the west and the Pentland Hills in the south. Following WWII the city's cultural life blossomed, stimulated by the Edinburgh International Festival and its fellow traveller, the Fringe, both held for the first time in 1947 and now recognised as world-class arts festivals.

Edinburgh entered a new era following the 1997 referendum vote in favour of a

EDINBURGH IN...

Two Days

A two-day trip to Edinburgh should start at Edinburgh Castle (p47), followed by a stroll down the Royal Mile to the Scottish Parliament Building (p55) and the Palace of Holyroodhouse (p55). You can work up an appetite by climbing Arthur's Seat (p58), then satisfy your hunger with dinner at Ondine (p82) or Castle Terrace (p86). On day two spend the morning in the National Museum of Scotland (p58), then catch the bus to Leith for a visit to the Royal Yacht Britannia (p68). In the evening, have dinner at one of Leith's many excellent restaurants, or scare yourself silly on a guided ghost tour.

Four Days

Two more days will give you time for a morning stroll around the Royal Botanic Garden (p68), followed by a trip to the enigmatic and beautiful Rosslyn Chapel (p99), or a relaxing afternoon visit to the seaside village of Cramond (p69) – bring binoculars (for birdwatching and yacht-spotting) and a book (to read in the sun). Dinner at Gardener's Cottage (p83) could be before or after your sunset walk to the summit of Calton Hill (p66). On day four head out to the pretty harbour village of Queensferry (p98), nestled beneath the Forth Bridges, and take a cruise to Inchcolm (p98) island.

devolved Scottish parliament, which first convened in 1999 in a controversial modern building at the foot of the Royal Mile. The 2014 independence referendum saw Scots vote to remain part of the United Kingdom.

◉ Sights

Edinburgh's main attractions are concentrated in the city centre – on and around the Old Town's Royal Mile between the castle and Holyrood, and in the New Town. A major exception is the Royal Yacht *Britannia*, which is in the redeveloped docklands district of Leith, two miles northeast of the centre.

If you tire of sightseeing, good areas for aimless wandering include the posh suburbs of Stockbridge and Morningside, the pretty riverside village of Cramond and the winding footpaths of Calton Hill and Arthur's Seat.

◉ Old Town

Edinburgh's Old Town stretches along a ridge to the east of the castle, and tumbles down Victoria St to the broad expanse of the Grassmarket. It's a jagged and jumbled maze of masonry riddled with closes (alleys) and wynds, stairs and vaults, and cleft along its spine by the cobbled ravine of the Royal Mile.

Until the founding of the New Town in the 18th century, old Edinburgh was an overcrowded and insanitary hive of humanity squeezed between the boggy ground of the Nor' Loch (North Loch, now drained and occupied by Princes Street Gardens) to the north and the city walls to the south and east. The only way for the town to expand was upwards, and the five- and six-storey tenements that were raised along the Royal Mile in the 16th and 17th centuries were the skyscrapers of their day, remarked upon with wonder by visiting writers such as Daniel Defoe. All classes of society, from beggars to magistrates, lived cheek by jowl in these urban ant nests, the wealthy occupying the middle floors – high enough to be above the noise and stink of the streets, but not so high that climbing the stairs would be too tiring – while the poor squeezed into attics, basements, cellars and vaults amid rats, rubbish and raw sewage.

The renovated Old Town tenements still support a thriving city-centre community, and today the street level is crammed with cafes, restaurants, bars, backpacker hostels and tacky souvenir shops. Few visitors wander beyond the main drag of the Royal Mile, but it's worth taking time to explore the countless closes that lead into quiet courtyards, often with unexpected views of city, sea and hills.

◉ Royal Mile

This mile-long street earned its regal nickname in the 16th century when it was used by the king to travel between the castle and the Palace of Holyroodhouse. There are five sections (the Castle Esplanade, Castlehill, Lawnmarket, High St and Canongate), the names of which reflect their historical origins.

★**Edinburgh Castle** CASTLE
(Map p52; www.edinburghcastle.gov.uk; Castle Esplanade; adult/child £16.50/9.90, audioguide additional £3.50; ⊘9.30am-6pm Apr-Sep, to 5pm Oct-Mar, last admission 1hr before closing; ▣23, 27, 41, 42) Edinburgh Castle has played a pivotal role in Scottish history, both as a royal residence – King Malcolm Canmore (r 1058–93) and Queen Margaret first made their home here in the 11th century – and as a military stronghold. The castle last saw military action in 1745; from then until the 1920s it served as the British army's main base in Scotland. Today it is one of Scotland's most atmospheric and popular tourist attractions.

The brooding, black crags of Castle Rock, rising above the western end of Princes St, are the very reason for Edinburgh's existence. This rocky hill was the most easily defended hilltop on the invasion route between England and central Scotland, a route followed by countless armies from the Roman legions of the 1st and 2nd centuries AD to the Jacobite troops of Bonnie Prince Charlie in 1745.

The **Entrance Gateway**, flanked by statues of Robert the Bruce and William Wallace, opens to a cobbled lane that leads up beneath the 16th-century **Portcullis Gate** to the cannons ranged along the Argyle and Mills Mount Batteries. The battlements here have great views over the New Town to the Firth of Forth.

At the far end of Mills Mount Battery is the famous **One O'Clock Gun**, where crowds gather to watch a gleaming WWII 25-pounder fire an ear-splitting time signal at exactly 1pm (every day except Sundays, Christmas Day and Good Friday).

Edinburgh

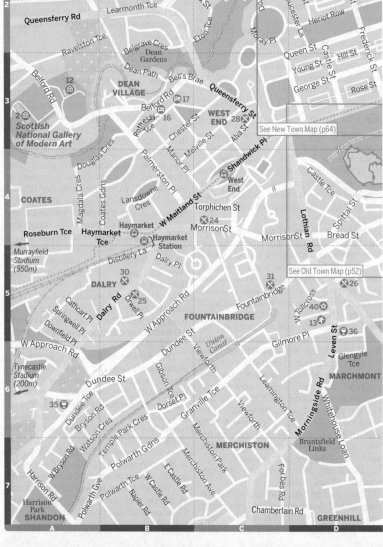

Royal Botanic
Garden (400m)

Water of
Leith

Brandon Tce
43
Henderson Row

COMELY
BANK

STOCKBRIDGE

Raeburn Pl
45
33

Fettes Ave

Clarence St

Fettes
Row

Comely Bank Rd

Dean St

Cumberland St

Orchard Brae

Comely Bank Ave

Comely Bank St

Dean Park Mews

Raeburn St

Leslie Pl

Circus Pl

Great
King St

India St

Howe St

S Learmonth Gdns

Danube St

Doune Tce

Gloucester La

Heriot Row

Queensferry Rd

Learmonth Tce

Ann St

Queen St

Castle St

Hill St

Frederick St

Ravelston Tce

Eton Tce

Moray Pl

Young St

George St

Rose St

Belgrave Cres

Dean Gardens

12

Belford Rd

Dean Path

Bell's Brae

Queensferry St

See New Town Map (p64)

2
Scottish
National Gallery
of Modern Art

DEAN
VILLAGE

Belford Rd

17

16

WEST
END

28

Rothesay
Tce

Chester St

Ala St

Douglas Cres

Melville Pl

Manor Pl

Palmerston Pl

Shandwick Pl

Castle Tce

COATES

Magdala Cres

Coates Gdns

Lansdowne
Cres

West
End

Torphichen St

Lothian Rd

Spittal St

Bread St

Roseburn Tce

Haymarket
Tce

W Maitland St

24
Morrison St

Morrison St

Murrayfield
Stadium
(950m)

Haymarket

Haymarket
Station

Distillery La

Dalry Pl

See Old Town Map (p52)

DALRY

30

Dalry Rd

Orwell Pl

25

W Approach Rd

FOUNTAINBRIDGE

31

Fountainbridge

26

Tollcross

40

13

36

Leven St

Cathcart Pl

Springwell Pl

Downfield Pl

W Approach Rd

Dundee St

Union Canal

Viewforth

Gilmore Pl

Glengyle
Tce

MARCHMONT

Tynecastle
Stadium
(200m)

Dundee St

35

Dundee Tce

Bryson Rd

Watson Cres

Gibson Tce

Dorset Pl

Granville Tce

Viewforth

Leamington Tce

Morningside Rd

Whitehouse Loan

Harrison Rd

W Bryson Rd

Temple Park Cres

Polwarth Gve

Polwarth Tce

W Castle Rd

Napier Rd

Polwarth Gdns

Merchiston Park

MERCHISTON

Merchiston Ave

E Castle Rd

Forbes Rd

Bruntsfield
Links

Harrison
Park

SHANDON

Chamberlain Rd

GREENHILL

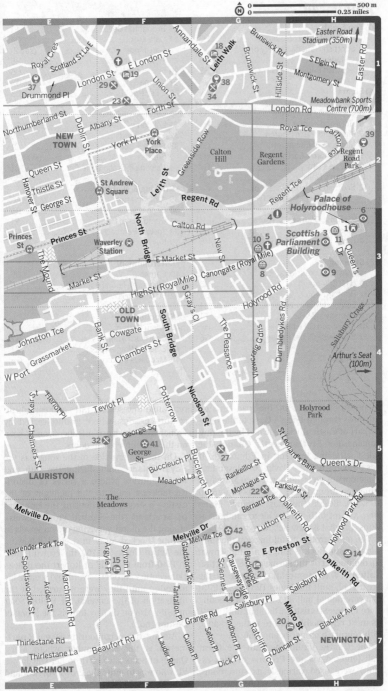

Edinburgh

South of Mills Mount, the road curls up leftwards through **Foog's Gate** to the highest part of Castle Rock, crowned by the tiny, Romanesque **St Margaret's Chapel**, the oldest surviving building in Edinburgh. It was probably built by David I or Alexander I in memory of their mother, Queen Margaret, sometime around 1130 (she was canonised in 1250). Beside the chapel stands **Mons Meg**, a giant 15th-century siege gun built at Mons (in what is now Belgium) in 1449.

The main group of buildings on the summit of Castle Rock is ranged around Crown Sq, dominated by the shrine of the **Scottish National War Memorial**. Opposite is the Great Hall, built for James IV (r 1488–1513) as a ceremonial hall and used as a meeting place for the Scottish parliament until 1639. Its most remarkable feature is the original, 16th-century hammer-beam roof.

The **Castle Vaults** beneath the Great Hall (entered via the **Prisons of War** exhibit) were used variously as storerooms, bakeries and a prison. The vaults have been renovated to resemble 18th- and early 19th-century prisons, where graffiti carved by French and American prisoners can be seen on the ancient wooden doors.

On the eastern side of the square is the **Royal Palace**, built during the 15th and 16th centuries, where a series of historical tableaux leads to the highlight of the castle – a strongroom housing the **Honours of Scotland** (the Scottish crown jewels), among the oldest surviving crown jewels in Europe. Locked away in a chest following the Act of Union in 1707, the crown (made in 1540 from the gold of Robert the Bruce's 14th-century coronet), sword and sceptre lay forgotten until they were unearthed at the instigation of the novelist Sir Walter Scott in 1818. Also on display here is the Stone of Destiny (p62).

Among the neighbouring **Royal Apartments** is the bedchamber where Mary, Queen of Scots gave birth to her son James VI, who was to unite the crowns of Scotland and England in 1603.

→ **National War Museum of Scotland**
(Map p52; www.nms.ac.uk; admission incl in Edinburgh Castle ticket; ⊘9.45am-5.45pm Apr-Oct, to 4.45pm Nov-Mar; 🚌23, 27, 41, 42) At the western end of Edinburgh Castle (p47), to the left of the castle tearooms, a road leads down to the National War Museum of Scotland, which brings Scotland's military history vividly to life. The exhibits have been personalised by telling the stories of the original owners of the objects on display, making it easier to empathise with the experiences of war than any dry display of dusty weaponry ever could.

Scotch Whisky Experience   MUSEUM
(Map p52; www.scotchwhiskyexperience.co.uk; 354 Castlehill; adult/child incl tour & tasting £14.50/7.25; ⊘10am-6pm Apr-Aug, to 5pm Sep-Mar; 🚌23, 27, 41, 42) A former school houses this multimedia centre explaining the making of whisky from barley to bottle in a series of exhibits, demonstrations and talks that combine sight, sound and smell, including the world's largest collection of malt whiskies (3384 bottles!). More expensive tours include more extensive whisky tastings and samples of Scottish cuisine. There's also a restaurant (p82) that serves traditional Scottish dishes with, where possible, a dash of whisky thrown in.

Camera Obscura   MUSEUM
(Map p52; www.camera-obscura.co.uk; Castlehill; adult/child £14.50/10.50; ⊘9am-9pm Jul & Aug, 9.30am-7pm Apr-Jun & Sep-Oct, 10am-6pm Nov-Mar; 🚌23, 27, 41, 42) Edinburgh's camera obscura is a curious 19th-century device – in constant use since 1853 – that uses lenses and mirrors to throw a live image of the city onto a large horizontal screen. The accompanying commentary is entertaining and the whole experience has a quirky charm, complemented by an intriguing exhibition dedicated to illusions of all kinds. Stairs lead up through various displays to the **Outlook Tower**, which offers great views over the city.

Gladstone's Land   HISTORIC BUILDING
(NTS; Map p52; www.nts.org.uk/Property/Gladstones-Land; 477 Lawnmarket; adult/child £6.50/5; ⊘10am-6.30pm Jul & Aug, to 5pm Apr-Jun & Sep-Oct; 🚌23, 27, 41, 42) One of Edinburgh's most prominent 17th-century merchants was Thomas Gledstanes, who in 1617 purchased the tenement later known as Gladstone's Land. It contains fine painted ceilings, walls and beams, and some splendid furniture from the 17th and 18th centuries. The volunteer guides provide a wealth of anecdotes and a detailed history.

St Giles Cathedral   CHURCH
(Map p52; www.stgilescathedral.org.uk; High St; suggested donation £3; ⊘9am-7pm Mon-Fri, to 5pm Sat, 1-5pm Sun May-Sep, 9am-5pm Mon-Sat, 1-5pm Sun Oct-Apr; 🚌23, 27, 41, 42) The great grey bulk of St Giles Cathedral dates largely from the 15th century, but much of it was restored in the 19th century. One of the most interesting corners of the kirk is the **Thistle Chapel**, built in 1911 for the Knights of the Most Ancient & Most Noble Order of the Thistle. The elaborately carved Gothic-style stalls have canopies topped with the helms and arms of the 16 knights – look out for the bagpipe-playing angel amid the vaulting.

CASTLE TO CANONGATE

Castle Esplanade Open area outside the castle gates; originally a parade ground, it forms the stage for the Military Tattoo (p75) during festival time.

Castlehill The short slope connecting the Castle Esplanade to the Lawnmarket.

Lawnmarket A corruption of 'Landmarket', a market selling goods from land outside the city; takes its name from the large cloth market that flourished here until the 18th century. This was the poshest part of the Old Town, where many of its most distinguished citizens made their homes.

High St Stretches from George IV Bridge down to the Netherbow at St Mary's St. It's the heart and soul of the Old Town, home to the city's main church, the law courts, the city council and – until 1707 – the Scottish parliament.

Canongate The stretch of the Royal Mile from Netherbow to Holyrood takes its name from the Augustinian canons (monks) of Holyrood Abbey. From the 16th century it was home to aristocrats attracted to the Palace of Holyroodhouse. Originally governed by the monks, Canongate was an independent burgh separate from Edinburgh until 1856.

Old Town

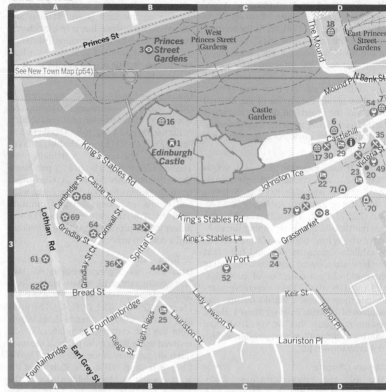

Properly called the High Kirk of Edinburgh (it was only a true cathedral – the seat of a bishop – from 1633 to 1638 and from 1661 to 1689), the church was named after the patron saint of cripples and beggars. The interior lacks grandeur but is rich in history: a Norman-style church was built here in 1126 but was destroyed by English invaders in 1385 (the only substantial remains are the central piers that support the tower). St Giles was at the heart of the Scottish Reformation, and John Knox served as minister here from 1559 to 1572.

There are several ornate monuments in the church, including the tombs of **James Graham, Marquis of Montrose**, who led Charles I's forces in Scotland and was hanged in 1650 at the Mercat Cross; and his Covenanter opponent **Archibald Campbell, Marquis of Argyll**, who was decapitated in 1661 after the Restoration of Charles II. There's also a bronze memorial to author

Robert Louis Stevenson, and a copy of the National Covenant of 1638.

By the side of the street, outside the western door of St Giles, is the **Heart of Midlothian** (Map p52; High St; ☐ 23, 27, 41, 42), set into the cobblestone paving. This marks the site of the Tolbooth. Built in the 15th century and demolished in the early 19th century, the Tolbooth served variously as a meeting place for parliament, the town council and the General Assembly of the Reformed Kirk, before becoming law courts and, finally, a notorious prison and place of execution. Passers-by traditionally spit on the heart for luck (don't stand downwind!).

At the other end of St Giles is the **Mercat Cross** (Map p52; ☐ 35), a 19th-century copy of the 1365 original, where merchants and traders met to transact business and royal proclamations were read.

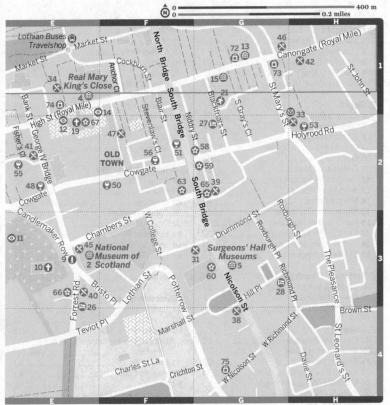

(Map p52;

★ **Real Mary King's Close** HISTORIC BUILDING
(Map p52; ☑0845 070 6244; www.realmary
kingsclose.com; 2 Warriston's Close, High St; adult/
child £14.50/8.75; ⏱10am-9pm daily Apr-Oct,
10am-5pm Sun-Thu, 10am-9pm Fri & Sat Nov-Mar;
☐23, 27, 41, 42) Edinburgh's 18th-century City
Chambers were built over the sealed-off
remains of Mary King's Close, and the lower
levels of this medieval Old Town alley have
survived almost unchanged amid the foundations for 250 years. Now open to the public, this spooky, subterranean labyrinth gives
a fascinating insight into the everyday life of
17th-century Edinburgh. Costumed characters lead tours through a 16th-century town
house and the plague-stricken home of a
17th-century gravedigger. Advance booking
recommended.

The scripted tour, complete with ghostly
tales and gruesome tableaux, can seem a
little naff, milking the scary and scatological
aspects of the close's history for all they're
worth. But there are many things of genuine
interest to see; there's something about the
crumbling 17th-century **tenement room**
that makes the hairs rise on the back of your
neck, with tufts of horsehair poking from
the collapsing lath-and-plaster, the ghost of
a pattern on the walls, and the ancient smell
of stone and dust thick in your nostrils.

In one of the former bedrooms off the
close, a psychic once claimed to have been
approached by the ghost of a little girl
called Annie. It's hard to tell what's more
frightening – the story of the ghostly child,
or the bizarre heap of tiny dolls and teddies
left in a corner by sympathetic visitors.

Museum of Childhood MUSEUM
(Map p52; ☑0131-529 4142; www.edinburgh
museums.org.uk; 42 High St; ⏱10am-5pm Mon-
Sat, noon-5pm Sun; ☐35) FREE Halfway down
the Royal Mile is 'the noisiest museum in
the world'. Often filled with the chatter of
excited children, it covers serious issues

Old Town

related to childhood – health, education, upbringing etc – but also has an enormous collection of toys, dolls, games and books, recordings of school lessons from the 1930s, and film of kids playing street games in 1950s Edinburgh.

John Knox House　　　　　HISTORIC BUILDING
(Map p52; www.scottishstorytellingcentre.co.uk; 43-45 High St; adult/child £5/1; ⊙10am-6pm Mon-Sat year-round, noon-6pm Sun Jul & Aug; 🚌35) The Royal Mile narrows at the foot of High St beside the jutting facade of John Knox House. This is the oldest surviving tenement in Edinburgh, dating from around 1490. John Knox, an influential church reformer and leader of the Protestant Reformation in Scotland, is thought to have lived here from 1561 to 1572. The labyrinthine interior has some beautiful painted-timber ceilings and an interesting display on Knox's life and work.

People's Story MUSEUM
(Map p48; www.edinburghmuseums.org.uk; 163 Canongate; ⊙10am-5pm Mon-Sat year-round, noon-5pm Sun Aug; ☐35) **FREE** One of the surviving symbols of the Canongate district's former independence is the Canongate Tolbooth. Built in 1591 it served successively as a collection point for tolls (taxes), a council house, a courtroom and a jail. With picturesque turrets and a projecting clock, it's an interesting example of 16th-century architecture. It now houses a fascinating museum called the People's Story, which covers the life, work and pastimes of ordinary Edinburgh folk from the 18th century to today.

Museum of Edinburgh MUSEUM
(Map p48; ☑0131-529 4143; www.edinburghmuseums.org.uk; 142 Canongate; ⊙10am-5pm Mon-Sat year-round, noon-5pm Sun Aug; ☐35) **FREE** You can't miss the colourful facade of Huntly House, brightly renovated in red and yellow ochre, opposite the Tolbooth clock on the Royal Mile. Built in 1570, it houses a museum covering Edinburgh from its prehistory to the present. Exhibits of national importance include an original copy of the National Covenant of 1638, but the big crowd-pleaser is the dog collar and feeding bowl that once belonged to Greyfriars Bobby (p59), the city's most famous canine citizen.

Canongate Kirkyard CHURCH
(Map p48; canongatekirk.org.uk; Canongate; ⊙24hr; ☐35) The attractive curved gable of the Canongate Kirk, built in 1688, overlooks a kirkyard that contains the graves of several famous people, including the economist Adam Smith, author of The Wealth of Nations; Agnes MacLehose (the 'Clarinda' of Robert Burns' love poems); and poet Robert Fergusson (1750–74; there's a statue of him on the street outside the church). An information board just inside the gate lists famous graves and their locations.

Fergusson was much admired by Robert Burns, who paid for his gravestone and penned the epitaph – take a look at the inscription on the back.

◉ Holyrood & Arthur's Seat

★Scottish
Parliament Building NOTABLE BUILDING
(Map p48; ☑0131-348 5200; www.scottish.parliament.uk; Horse Wynd; ⊙9am-6.30pm Tue-Thu & 10am-5pm Mon, Fri & Sat in session, 10am-5pm Mon-Sat in recess; ☐6, 35) **FREE** The Scottish parliament building, on the site of a former brewery, was officially opened by HM the Queen in October 2005. Designed by Catalan architect Enric Miralles (1955–2000), the ground plan of the parliament complex represents a 'flower of democracy rooted in Scottish soil' (best seen looking down from Salisbury Crags). Free, one-hour guided tours (advance booking recommended) include a visit to the Debating Chamber, a committee room, the Garden Lobby and an MSP's (Member of the Scottish Parliament) office.

Miralles believed that a building could be a work of art. However, this weird concrete confection at the foot of Salisbury Crags has left the good people of Edinburgh staring and scratching their heads in confusion. What does it all mean? The strange forms of the exterior are all symbolic in some way, from the oddly shaped windows on the west wall (inspired by the silhouette of the *Reverend Robert Walker Skating on Duddingston Loch,* one of Scotland's most famous paintings), to the asymmetric panels on the main facade (representing a curtain being drawn aside, a symbol of open government).

The Main Hall, inside the public entrance, has a low, triple-arched ceiling of polished concrete, like a cave, or cellar, or castle vault. It is a dimly lit space, the starting point for a metaphorical journey from this relative darkness up to the Debating Chamber (sitting directly above the Main Hall), which is, in contrast, a palace of light – the light of democracy. This magnificent chamber is the centrepiece of the parliament, designed not to glorify but to humble the politicians who sit within it. The windows face Calton Hill, allowing MSPs to look up to its monuments (reminders of the Scottish Enlightenment), while the massive, pointed oak beams of the roof are suspended by steel threads above the MSPs' heads like so many Damoclean swords.

The public areas of the parliament building – the Main Hall, where there is an exhibition, a shop and cafe, and the public gallery in the Debating Chamber – are open to visitors (free tickets needed for public gallery – see website for details). If you want to see the parliament in session, check the website to see when it will be sitting – business days are normally Tuesday to Thursday year-round.

★ **Palace of Holyroodhouse** PALACE
(Map p48; www.royalcollection.org.uk; Horse Wynd; adult/child incl audioguide £12/7.20; ⊙9.30am-6pm Apr-Oct, to 4.30pm Nov-Mar; ☐6, 35) This palace is the royal family's official residence

Royal Mile

A GRAND DAY OUT

Planning your own procession along the Royal Mile involves some tough decisions – it would be impossible to see everything in a single day, so it's wise to decide in advance what you don't want to miss and shape your visit around that. Remember to leave time for lunch, for exploring some of the Mile's countless side alleys and, during festival time, for enjoying the street theatre that is bound to be happening in High St.

The most pleasant way to reach the Castle Esplanade at the start of the Royal Mile is to hike up the zigzag path from the footbridge behind the Ross Bandstand in Princes Street Gardens (in springtime you'll be knee-deep in daffodils). Starting at **Edinburgh Castle** ❶ means that the rest of your walk is downhill. Fo a superb view up and down the length of the Mile, climb the **Camera Obscura's Outlook Tower** ❷ before visiting **Gladstone's Land** ❸ and **St Giles Cathedral** ❹.

ROYAL VISITS TO THE ROYAL MILE

1561: Mary, Queen of Scots arrives from France and holds an audience with John Knox.
1745: Bonnie Prince Charlie fails to capture Edinburgh Castle, and instead sets up court in Holyroodhouse.
2004: Queen Elizabeth II officially opens the Scottish Parliament building.

Edinburgh Castle

If you're pushed for time, visit the Great Hall, the Honours of Scotland and the Prisons of War exhibit. Head for the Half Moon Battery for a photo looking down the length of the Royal Mile.

Royal Scottish Academy

Scott Monument

Heart of Midlothian

City Chambers

NORTH BR

Scottish National Gallery

Princes Street Gardens

THE MOUND

❺

HIGH

❷

❸

❹

CASTLEHILL

GEORGE IV BRIDGE

❶

Scotch Whisky Experience

Gladstone's Land

The 1st floor houses a faithful recreation of how a wealthy Edinburgh merchant lived in the 17th century. Check out the beautiful Painted Bedchamber, with its ornately decorated walls and wooden ceilings.

LUNCH BREAK

Burger and a beer at **Holyrood 9A**; steak and chips at **Maxie's Bistro**; slap-up seafood at **Ondine**.

history's your thing, you'll want to add
Real Mary King's Close ⑤, **John Knox House** ⑥ and the **Museum of Edinburgh** ⑦ to your must-see list.

At the foot of the mile, choose between modern and ancient seats of power – the **Scottish Parliament** ⑧ or the **Palace of Holyroodhouse** ⑨. Round off the day with an evening ascent of Arthur's Seat or, slightly less strenuously, Calton Hill. Both make great sunset viewpoints.

TAKING YOUR TIME

Minimum time needed for each attraction:

- » **Edinburgh Castle:** two hours
- » **Gladstone's Land:** 45 minutes
- » **St Giles Cathedral:** 30 minutes
- » **Real Mary King's Close:** one hour (tour)
- » **Scottish Parliament:** one hour (tour)
- » **Palace of Holyroodhouse:** one hour

Real Mary King's Close
The guided tour is heavy on ghost stories, but a highlight is standing in an original 17th-century room with tufts of horsehair poking from the crumbling plaster, and breathing in the ancient scent of stone, dust and history.

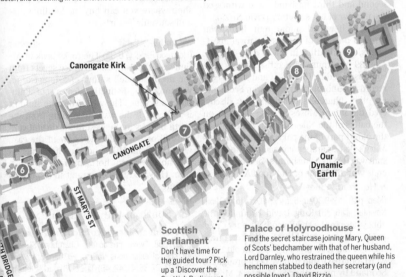

Canongate Kirk

CANONGATE

ST MARY'S ST

TH BRIDGE

Our Dynamic Earth

Scottish Parliament
Don't have time for the guided tour? Pick up a 'Discover the Scottish Parliament Building' leaflet from reception and take a self-guided tour of the exterior, then hike up to Salisbury Crags for a great view of the complex.

Palace of Holyroodhouse
Find the secret staircase joining Mary, Queen of Scots' bedchamber with that of her husband, Lord Darnley, who restrained the queen while his henchmen stabbed to death her secretary (and possible lover), David Rizzio.

St Giles Cathedral
Look out for the Burne-Jones stained-glass window (1873) at the west end, showing the crossing of the River Jordan, and the bronze memorial to Robert Louis Stevenson in the Moray Aisle.

in Scotland, but is more famous as the 16th-century home of the ill-fated Mary, Queen of Scots. The highlight of the tour is **Mary's Bed Chamber**, home to the unfortunate queen from 1561 to 1567. It was here that her jealous second husband, Lord Darnley, restrained the pregnant queen while his henchmen murdered her secretary – and favourite – Rizzio. A plaque in the neighbouring room marks the spot where he bled to death.

The palace developed from a guesthouse, attached to Holyrood Abbey, which was extended by King James IV in 1501. The oldest surviving part of the building, the northwestern tower, was built in 1529 as a royal apartment for James V and his wife, Mary of Guise. Mary, Queen of Scots spent six turbulent years here, during which time she debated with John Knox, married both her second and third husbands, and witnessed the murder of her secretary David Rizzio.

The self-guided audio tour leads you through a series of impressive royal apartments, culminating in the **Great Gallery**. The 89 portraits of Scottish kings were commissioned by Charles II and supposedly record his unbroken lineage from Scota, the Egyptian pharaoh's daughter who discovered the infant Moses in a reed basket on the banks of the Nile. The tour continues to the oldest part of the palace, which contains Mary's Bed Chamber, connected by a secret stairway to her husband's bedroom, and ends with the ruins of Holyrood Abbey.

➡ **Holyrood Abbey**

(Map p48; ⊙9.30am-6pm Apr-Oct, to 4.30pm Nov-Mar; ▨6, 35) King David I founded the abbey here in the shadow of Salisbury Crags in 1128. It was probably named after a fragment of the True Cross (*rood* is an old Scots word for cross), said to have been brought to Scotland by his mother, St Margaret. Most of the surviving ruins date from the 12th and 13th centuries, although a doorway in the far southeastern corner has survived from the original Norman church.

Admission to the abbey is included in the cost of the Palace of Holyroodhouse (p55) ticket.

➡ **Queen's Gallery**

(Map p48; www.royalcollection.org.uk; Horse Wynd; adult/child £6.70/3.40, combined admission to gallery & Holyroodhouse £16.90/9.50; ⊙9.30am-6pm Apr-Oct, to 4.30pm Nov-Mar; ▨6, 35) This stunning modern gallery, which occupies the shell of a former church and

school, is a showcase for exhibitions of art from the Royal Collections. The exhibitions change every six months or so; for details of the latest, check the website.

Our Dynamic Earth   EXHIBITION

(Map p48; www.dynamicearth.co.uk; Holyrood Rd; adult/child £13.50/9; ⊙10am-5.30pm Easter-Oct, to 6pm Jul-Aug, 10am-5.30pm Wed-Sun Nov-Easter, last admission 90min before closing; ▨; ▨6, 35) Housed in a modernistic white marquee, Our Dynamic Earth is billed as an interactive, multimedia journey of discovery through Earth's history from the Big Bang to the present day. Hugely popular with kids of all ages, it's a slick extravaganza of whiz-bang special effects and 3D movies cleverly designed to fire up young minds with curiosity about all things geological and environmental. Its true purpose, of course, is to disgorge you into a gift shop where you can buy model dinosaurs and souvenir T-shirts.

⭐ **Arthur's Seat**   VIEWPOINT

(Holyrood Park; ▨6, 35) The rocky peak of Arthur's Seat (251m), carved by ice sheets from the deeply eroded stump of a long-extinct volcano, is a distinctive feature of Edinburgh's skyline. The view from the summit is well worth the walk, extending from the Forth Bridges in the west to the distant conical hill of North Berwick Law in the east, with the Ochil Hills and the Highlands on the northwestern horizon. You can hike from Holyrood to the summit in around 45 minutes

⊙ South of the Royal Mile

⭐ **National Museum of Scotland**   MUSEUM

(Map p52; www.nms.ac.uk; Chambers St; fee for special exhibitions varies; ⊙10am-5pm; ▨; ▨2, 23, 27, 35, 41, 42, 45) **FREE** Broad, elegant Chambers St is dominated by the long facade of the National Museum of Scotland. Its extensive collections are spread between two buildings, one modern, one Victorian – the golden stone and striking modern architecture of the new building, opened in 1998, is one of the city's most distinctive landmarks. The five floors of the museum trace the history of Scotland from its geological beginnings to the 1990s, with many imaginative and stimulating exhibits. Audioguides are available in several languages.

The new building connects with the original Victorian museum, dating from 1861, the stolid, grey exterior of which gives way to a beautifully bright and airy, glass-roofed exhibition hall. The old building houses an eclectic collection covering natural history, archaeology, scientific and industrial technology, and the decorative arts of ancient Egypt, Islam, China, Japan, Korea and the West.

Greyfriars Kirkyard   CEMETERY
(Map p52; www.greyfriarskirk.com; Candlemaker Row; ⊙ 8am-dusk; ▣ 2, 23, 27, 35, 41, 42, 45) Greyfriars Kirkyard is one of Edinburgh's most evocative cemeteries, a peaceful green oasis dotted with elaborate monuments. Many famous Edinburgh names are buried here, including the poet Allan Ramsay (1686–1758), architect William Adam (1689–1748) and William Smellie (1740–95), the editor of the first edition of the *Encyclopedia Britannica*. If you want to experience the graveyard at its scariest – inside a burial vault, in the

dark, at night – go on one of the City of the Dead (p70) guided tours.

Greyfriars Bobby Statue   MONUMENT
(Map p52; cnr George IV Bridge & Candlemaker Row; ▣ 2, 23, 27, 35, 41, 42, 45) Probably the most popular photo opportunity in Edinburgh, the life-size statue of Greyfriars Bobby, a Skye terrier who captured the hearts of the British public in the late 19th century, stands outside Greyfriars Kirkyard. From 1858 to 1872, the wee dog maintained a vigil over the grave of his master, an Edinburgh police officer. The story was immortalised in a novel by Eleanor Atkinson in 1912, and in 1963 was made into a movie by – who else? – Walt Disney.

The statue is always surrounded by crowds of visitors taking photos of themselves posing beside the little dog. Bobby's own grave, marked by a small, pink granite

THE RESURRECTION MEN

In 1505 Edinburgh's newly founded Royal College of Surgeons was officially allocated the corpse of one executed criminal per year for the purposes of dissection. But this was not nearly enough to satisfy the curiosity of the city's anatomists, and in the following centuries an illegal trade in dead bodies emerged, which reached its culmination in the early 19th century when the anatomy classes of famous surgeons such as Professor Robert Knox drew audiences of up to 500.

The readiest supply of corpses was to be found in the city's graveyards, especially Greyfriars. Grave robbers – who came to be known as 'resurrection men' – plundered newly buried coffins and sold the cadavers to the anatomists, who turned a blind eye to the source of their research material.

This gruesome trade led to a series of countermeasures, including the mort-safe – a metal cage that was placed over a coffin until the corpse had begun to decompose; you can see examples in **Greyfriars Kirk** (Map p52; www.greyfriarskirk.com; Candlemaker Row; ⊙ 10.30am-4.30pm Mon-Fri, 11am-2pm Sat Apr-Oct, closed Nov-Mar; ▣ 2, 23, 27, 35, 41, 42, 45) FREE and on Level 5 of the National Museum of Scotland (p58). Watchtowers, where a sexton, or relatives of the deceased, would keep watch over new graves, survive in St Cuthbert's and Duddingston kirkyards.

The notorious William Burke and William Hare, who kept a lodging house in Tanner's Close at the west end of the Grassmarket, took the body-snatching business a step further. When an elderly lodger died without paying his rent, Burke and Hare stole his body from the coffin and sold it to the famous Professor Knox. Seeing a lucrative business opportunity, they figured that rather than waiting for someone else to die, they could create their own supply of fresh cadavers by resorting to murder.

Burke and Hare preyed on the poor and weak of Edinburgh's Grassmarket, luring them back to Hare's lodging house, plying them with drink and then suffocating their victims. Between December 1827 and October 1828, they murdered at least 16 people, selling their bodies to Professor Knox. When the law finally caught up with them, Hare turned King's evidence and testified against Burke.

Burke was hanged outside St Giles Cathedral in January 1829 and, in an ironic twist, his body was given to the anatomy school for public dissection. His skeleton, and a wallet made from his flayed skin, are still on display in the Surgeons' Hall Museums (p69).

It was as a result of the Burke and Hare case that the Anatomy Act of 1832 – regulating the supply of cadavers for dissection, and still in force today – was passed.

ROB CRANDALL / SHUTTERSTOCK ©

1. Highland Folk Museum (p315), Newtonmore 2. People's Story
(p55), Edinburgh 3. Riverside Museum (p111), Glasgow
4. Kelvingrove Art Gallery & Museum (p112), Glasgow

CHRISDORNEY / SHUTTERSTOCK ©

THE PEOPLE'S STORY

Scotland's Museums

Scotland's rich culture and history are celebrated in countless museums, from internationally important collections to specialist exhibits such as the Grampian Transport Museum in Alford, and tiny museums such as Groam House Museum in Rosemarkie, with its carved Pictish stones.

National Museums

The National Museum of Scotland is complemented by several other nationally important collections, including Glasgow's Kelvingrove Museum and the Riverside Museum, a modern masterpiece celebrating transport, with a tall ship moored alongside. There are more things nautical at Dundee's Discovery Point, a shrine to polar exploration, and Aberdeen's superb Maritime Museum.

Folk Museums

The culture and traditions of Scottish rural life come to the fore in places such as the Highland Folk Museum, where a farming township is re-created with historic buildings and demonstrations of traditional crafts. Other, smaller folk museums include the Glencoe Folk Museum and the Kildonan Museum (South Uist).

Island Museums

Each Scottish island has its own culture and identity. The hardy lifestyle of Hebridean crofters is told in the Arnol Blackhouse Museum in Lewis, and in the Skye Museum of Island Life in Trotternish, while the Norse influences of the Northern Isles is explored in the Stromness Museum and the Shetland Museum.

Offbeat Museums

The Museum of Lead Mining in Wanlockhead is one of the country's more unusual museums, offering fascinating insights into a little-known subject. Similar places include the Surgeons' Hall Museum in Edinburgh (pathology), the British Golf Museum in St Andrews and the Scottish Lighthouse Museum in Fraserburgh.

stone, is just inside the entrance to Greyfriars Kirkyard, behind the monument, and you can see his original collar and bowl in the Museum of Edinburgh (p55).

Grassmarket STREET
(Map p52; 🚇2) The site of a cattle market from the 15th century until the start of the 20th century, the Grassmarket has always been a focal point of the Old Town. It was once the city's main place of execution, and over 100 martyred Covenanters are commemorated by a monument at the eastern end, where the gallows used to stand. The notorious murderers Burke and Hare operated from a now-vanished close off the western end.

Nowadays the broad, open square, lined by tall tenements and dominated by the looming castle, has many lively pubs and restaurants, including the White Hart Inn (p88), which was once patronised by Robert Burns. Claiming to be the city's oldest pub in continuous use (since 1516), it also hosted William Wordsworth in 1803. **Cowgate** – the long, dark ravine leading eastwards from the Grassmarket – was once the road along which cattle were driven from the pastures around Arthur's Seat to the safety of the city walls. Today it is the heart of Edinburgh's nightlife, with around two dozen clubs and bars within five minutes' walk of each other.

New Town

Edinburgh's New Town lies north of the Old, on a ridge running parallel to the Royal Mile and separated from it by the valley of Princes Street Gardens. Its regular grid of elegant, Georgian terraces is a complete contrast to the chaotic tangle of tenements and wynds that characterises the Old Town, and is the world's most complete and unspoilt example of Georgian architecture and town planning.

Apart from the streetscape, the main sights are the art galleries and gardens on Princes St, and the Scottish National Portrait Gallery near St Andrew Sq, all within walking distance of each other.

Princes Street

Princes St is one of the world's most spectacular shopping streets. Built up on the north side only, it catches the sun in summer and allows expansive views across Princes Street

---

THE STONE OF DESTINY

On St Andrew's Day 1996 a block of sandstone – 26.5 inches by 16.5 inches by 11 inches in size, with rusted iron hoops at either end – was installed with much pomp and ceremony in Edinburgh Castle. For the previous 700 years it had lain in London, beneath the Coronation Chair in Westminster Abbey. Almost all English, and later British, monarchs from Edward II in 1307 to Elizabeth II in 1953 have parked their backsides firmly over this stone during their coronation ceremony.

The legendary Stone of Destiny – said to have originated in the Holy Land, and on which Scottish kings placed their feet during their coronation (not their bums; the English got that bit wrong) – was stolen from Scone Abbey near Perth by King Edward I of England in 1296. It was taken to London and there it remained for seven centuries – except for a brief removal to Gloucester during WWII air raids, and a three-month sojourn in Scotland after it was stolen by Scottish Nationalist students on Christmas in 1950 – as an enduring symbol of Scotland's subjugation by England.

The Stone of Destiny returned to the political limelight in 1996, when the then Scottish Secretary and Conservative Party MP Michael Forsyth arranged for the return of the sandstone block to Scotland. A blatant attempt to boost the flagging popularity of the Conservative Party in Scotland prior to a general election, Forsyth's publicity stunt failed miserably. The Scots said thanks very much for the stone and then, in May 1997, voted every Conservative MP in Scotland into oblivion.

Many people, however, believe Edward I was fobbed off with a shoddy imitation in 1296 and that the true Stone of Destiny remains safely hidden somewhere in Scotland. This is not impossible – some descriptions of the original stone state that it was made of black marble and decorated with elaborate carvings. Interested parties should read *Scotland's Stone of Destiny* by Nick Aitchinson, which details the history and cultural significance of Scotland's most famous lump of rock.

Gardens to the castle and the crowded skyline of the Old Town.

Princes Street Gardens (Map p52; Princes St; ☉dawn-dusk; ▣all Princes St buses) **FREE** lie in a valley that was once occupied by the Nor' Loch, a boggy depression that was drained in the early 19th century. The gardens are split in the middle by **The Mound**, which was created from around two million cartloads of earth excavated from the foundations of the New Town and dumped here to provide a road link across the valley to the Old Town. It was completed in 1830.

Scott Monument
MONUMENT

(Map p64; www.edinburghmuseums.org.uk; East Princes Street Gardens; admission £5; ☉10am-7pm Apr-Sep, 10am-4pm Oct-Mar; ▣Princes St) The eastern half of Princes Street Gardens is dominated by the massive Gothic spire of the Scott Monument, built by public subscription in memory of the novelist Sir Walter Scott after his death in 1832. The exterior is decorated with 64 carvings of characters from his novels; inside you can see an exhibition on Scott's life, and climb the 287 steps to the top for a superb view of the city.

Scottish National Gallery
GALLERY

(Map p52; www.nationalgalleries.org; The Mound; fee for special exhibitions varies; ☉10am-5pm Fri-Wed, to 7pm Thu; ▣Princes St) **FREE** Designed by William Playfair, this imposing classical building with its Ionic porticoes dates from the 1850s. Its octagonal rooms, lit by skylights, have been restored to their original Victorian decor of deep-green carpets and dark-red walls. The gallery houses an important collection of European art from the Renaissance to post-Impressionism, with works by Verrocchio (Leonardo da Vinci's teacher), Tintoretto, Titian, Holbein, Rubens, Van Dyck, Vermeer, El Greco, Poussin, Rembrandt, Gainsborough, Turner, Constable, Monet, Pissarro, Gauguin and Cézanne.

The upstairs galleries house portraits by Sir Joshua Reynolds and Sir Henry Raeburn, and a clutch of **Impressionist paintings**, including Monet's luminous *Haystacks,* Van Gogh's demonic *Olive Trees* and Gauguin's hallucinatory *Vision After the Sermon.* But the painting that really catches your eye is the gorgeous portrait of *Lady Agnew of Lochnaw* by John Singer Sargent.

The basement galleries dedicated to **Scottish art** include glowing portraits by Allan Ramsay and Sir Henry Raeburn,

rural scenes by Sir David Wilkie and Impressionistic landscapes by William MacTaggart. Look out for Sir George Harvey's hugely entertaining *A Schule Skailin* (A School Emptying) – a stern dominie (teacher) looks on as the boys stampede for the classroom door, one reaching for a confiscated spinning top. Kids will love the fantasy paintings of Sir Joseph Noel Paton in room B5; the incredibly detailed canvases are crammed with hundreds of tiny fairies, goblins and elves.

Recent research has suggested that the iconic 1790s painting of *Reverend Robert Walker Skating on Duddingston Loch,* historically attributed to Sir Henry Raeburn, may in fact be the work of French artist Henri-Pierre Danloux.

Each January the gallery exhibits its **collection of Turner watercolours**, bequeathed by Henry Vaughan in 1900. Room X is graced by Antonio Canova's white marble sculpture, *The Three Graces;* it is owned jointly with London's Victoria & Albert Museum.

Royal Scottish Academy
GALLERY

(Map p64; ☎0131-225 6671; www.royalscottish academy.org; The Mound; fee for special exhibitions varies; ☉10am-5pm Mon-Sat, noon-5pm Sun; ▣Princes St) **FREE** This Greek Doric temple, with its northern pediment crowned by a seated figure of Queen Victoria, is the home of the Royal Scottish Academy. Designed by William Playfair and built between 1823 and 1836, it was originally called the Royal Institution; the RSA took over the building in 1910. The galleries display a collection of paintings, sculptures and architectural drawings by academy members dating from 1831, and they also host temporary exhibitions throughout the year.

The RSA and the Scottish National Gallery are linked via an underground mall – the Weston Link – which gives them twice the temporary exhibition space of the Prado in Madrid and three times that of the Royal Academy in London, as well as housing cloakrooms, a lecture theatre and a restaurant.

◉ George Street & Charlotte Square

Until the 1990s George St – the major axis of the New Town – was the centre of Edinburgh's financial industry and Scotland's equivalent of Wall St. Today the big

New Town

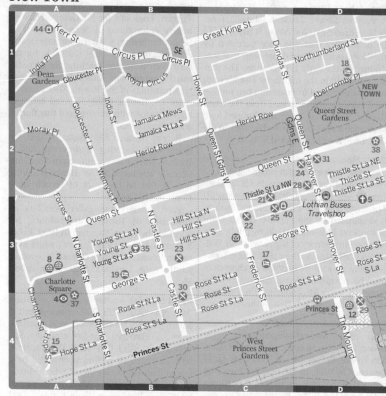

financial firms have moved to premises in the new Exchange office district west of Lothian Rd, and George St's former banks and offices house upmarket shops, pubs and restaurants.

At the western end of George St is **Charlotte Sq** (Map p64; ⬚ 19, 36, 37, 41, 47), the architectural jewel of the New Town, designed by Robert Adam shortly before his death in 1791. The northern side of the square is Adam's masterpiece and one of the finest examples of Georgian architecture anywhere. **Bute House** (Map p64; 6 Charlotte Sq; ⬚ 19, 36, 37, 41, 47), in the centre at No 6, is the official residence of Scotland's first minister, the equivalent of London's 10 Downing St.

Georgian House   HISTORIC BUILDING
(NTS; Map p64; www.nts.org.uk; 7 Charlotte Sq; adult/child £7/5.50; ☉10am-6pm Jul & Aug, 10am-5pm Apr-Jun & Sep-Oct, 11am-4pm Mar & Nov; ⬚36, 47) The National Trust for Scotland's Georgian House has been beautifully restored and furnished to show how Edinburgh's wealthy elite lived at the end of the 18th century. The walls are decorated with paintings by Allan Ramsay, Sir Henry Raeburn and Sir Joshua Reynolds, and there's a fully equipped 18th-century kitchen complete with china closet and wine cellar.

◉ St Andrew Square

Not as architecturally distinguished as its sister Charlotte Sq (p63) at the opposite end of George St, St Andrew Sq is dominated by the fluted column of the **Melville Monument** (Map p64; St Andrew Sq; ⬚St Andrew Sq), commemorating Henry Dundas, 1st Viscount Melville (1742–1811). Dundas was the most powerful Scottish politician of his time, often referred to when alive as 'Harry IX, the Uncrowned King of Scotland'. The impressive Palladian mansion of **Dundas House** (Map p64; St Andrew Sq; ⬚St Andrew Sq), built between 1772 and 1774, on

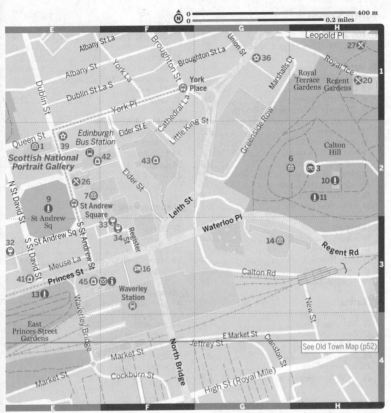

the eastern side of the square, was built for Sir Laurence Dundas (1712–81; no relation to Viscount Melville). It has been the head office of the Royal Bank of Scotland since 1825 and has a spectacular domed banking hall dating from 1857 (you can nip inside for a look).

A short distance along George St is the **Church of St Andrew & St George** (Map p64; www.stagw.org.uk; 13-17 George St; ⊙10am-3pm Mon-Fri, 11am-1pm Sat, 9am-1pm Sun; 🚌10,11,12,16) **FREE**, built in 1784 with an unusual oval nave. It was the scene of the Disruption of 1843, when 451 dissenting ministers left the Church of Scotland to form the Free Church.

★Scottish National Portrait Gallery

GALLERY

(Map p64; www.nationalgalleries.org; 1 Queen St; ⊙10am-5pm; ♿; 🚇St Andrew Sq) **FREE** The Venetian Gothic palace of the Scottish National Portrait Gallery reopened its doors in 2011 after a two-year renovation, emerging as one of the city's top attractions. Its galleries illustrate Scottish history through paintings, photographs and sculptures, putting faces to famous names from Scotland's past and present, from Robert Burns, Mary, Queen of Scots and Bonnie Prince Charlie to Sean Connery, Billy Connolly and poet Jackie Kay.

The gallery's interior is decorated in Arts and Crafts style, and nowhere more splendidly than in the **Great Hall**. Above the Gothic colonnade a processional frieze painted by William Hole in 1898 serves as a 'visual encyclopedia' of famous Scots, shown in chronological order from Calgacus (the chieftain who led the Caledonian tribes into battle against the Romans) to writer and philosopher Thomas Carlyle (1795–1881). The murals on the 1st-floor balcony depict scenes from Scottish history, while the ceiling is painted with the constellations of the night sky.

New Town

The gallery's selection of 'trails' leaflets adds a bit of background information while leading you around the various exhibits; the Hidden Histories trail is particularly interesting.

◉ Calton Hill

Rising dramatically above the eastern end of Princes St, **Calton Hill** (Map p64; ▣all Leith St buses) (100m) is Edinburgh's acropolis, its summit scattered with grandiose memorials dating mostly from the first half of the 19th century. It is also one of the best viewpoints in the city, with a panorama that takes in the castle, Holyrood, Arthur's Seat, the Firth of Forth, New Town and the full length of Princes St.

On the southern side of the hill, on Regent Rd, is the modernist facade of **St Andrew's House** (Map p64; ▣15, 26, 44), built between 1936 and 1939 and housing the civil servants of the Westminster government's Scottish Office until they were moved to the

new Scottish Executive building in Leith in 1996.

Just beyond St Andrew's House, and on the opposite side of the road, is the imposing **Royal High School** building, dating from 1829 and modelled on the Temple of Theseus in Athens. Former pupils include Robert Adam, Alexander Graham Bell and Sir Walter Scott. It now stands empty. To its east, on the other side of Regent Rd, is the 1830 **Burns Monument** (Map p48; ▣104, 113), a Greek-style memorial to Robert Burns.

You can reach the summit of Calton Hill via the road beside the Royal High School or by the stairs at the eastern end of Waterloo Pl. The largest structure on the summit is the **National Monument** (Map p64; ▣all Leith St buses), an over-ambitious attempt to replicate the Parthenon in Athens and intended to honour Scotland's dead in the Napoleonic Wars. Construction – paid for by public subscription – began in 1822, but funds ran dry when only 12 columns had been completed.

Looking a bit like an upturned telescope – the similarity is intentional – and offering superb views, the **Nelson Monument** (Map p64; www.edinburghmuseums.org.uk; Calton Hill; admission £5; ⊙10am-7pm Mon-Sat, noon-5pm Sun Apr-Sep, 10am-3pm Mon-Sat Oct-Mar; 🚌 all Leith St buses) was built to commemorate Admiral Lord Nelson's victory at Trafalgar in 1805.

The design of the **City Observatory** (Map p64; ✆ 0131-556 1264; www.collectivegallery. net; Calton Hill; ⊙10am-5pm Tue-Sun Apr-Jul & Sep, to 4pm Oct-Mar, to 6pm daily Aug; 🚌 all Leith St buses) FREE, built in 1818, was based on the ancient Greek Temple of the Winds in Athens. Its original function was to provide a precise, astronomical time-keeping service for marine navigators, but smoke from Waverley train station forced the astronomers to move to Blackford Hill in the south of Edinburgh in 1895. It has been redeveloped as a stunning space for contemporary visual art, and opened to the public for the first time in its history.

⊙ Dean Village

★ **Scottish National Gallery of Modern Art** GALLERY
(Map p48; www.nationalgalleries.org; 75 Belford Rd; fee for special exhibitions varies; ⊙10am-5pm; 🚌13) FREE Edinburgh's gallery of modern art is split between two impressive neo-classical buildings surrounded by land-scaped grounds some 500m west of Dean Village. As well as showcasing a stunning collection of paintings by the popular, post-Impressionist Scottish Colourists – in *Reflections, Balloch,* Leslie Hunter pulls off the improbable trick of making Scotland look like the south of France – the gallery is the starting point for a walk along the Water of Leith, following a trail of sculptures by Antony Gormley.

The main collection, known as **Modern One**, concentrates on 20th-century art, with various European movements represented by the likes of Matisse, Picasso, Kirchner, Magritte, Miró, Mondrian and Giacometti. American and English artists are also represented, but most space is given to Scottish painters – from the Scottish Colourists of the early 20th century to contemporary artists such as Peter Howson and Ken Currie.

There's an excellent **cafe** (Map p48; mains £4-8; ⊙9am-4.30pm Mon-Fri, 10am-4.30pm Sat & Sun; 🥗♿) downstairs, and the surrounding park features sculptures by Henry Moore, Rachel Whiteread and Bar-bara Hepworth, among others, as well as a 'landform artwork' by Charles Jencks, and the **Pig Rock Bothy**, a rustic timber perfor-mance and exhibition space created in 2014 as part of the Bothy Project (www.thebothy project.org).

A footpath and stairs at the rear of the gallery lead down to the **Water of Leith Walkway**, which you can follow along the river for 4 miles to Leith. This takes you past **6 Times**, a sculptural project by Antony Gormley consisting of six human figures standing at various points along the river. (The statues are designed to fall over in flood conditions, so some of them may not be visible after heavy rain.)

➡ **Scottish National Gallery of Modern Art - Modern Two**
(Map p48; www.nationalgalleries.org; Belford Rd; ⊙10am-5pm; 🚌13) FREE Directly across Belford Rd from Modern One, another neo-classical mansion (formerly an orphanage) houses its annexe, Modern Two, which is home to a large collection of sculpture and graphic art created by the Edinburgh-born artist Sir Eduardo Paolozzi. One of the 1st-floor rooms houses a re-creation of Paoloz-zi's studio, while the rest of the building stages temporary exhibitions of modern art.

⊙ Leith

Two miles northeast of the city centre, Leith has been Edinburgh's seaport since the 14th century and remained an independent burgh with its own town council until it was incor-porated by the city in the 1920s. Like many of Britain's dockland areas, it fell into decay in the decades following WWII but has been undergoing a revival since the late 1980s.

Old warehouses have been turned into luxury flats, and a lush crop of trendy bars and restaurants has sprouted along the wa-terfront. The area was given an additional boost in the late 1990s when the Scottish Ex-ecutive (a government department) moved to a new building on Leith docks.

The city council has formulated a major redevelopment plan for the entire Edin-burgh waterfront from Leith to Granton, the first phase of which is **Ocean Termi-nal** (✆0131-555 8888; www.oceanterminal.com; Ocean Dr; ⊙10am-8pm Mon-Fri, to 7pm Sat, 11am-6pm Sun; 📞; 🚌11, 22, 34, 35, 36), a shopping and leisure complex that includes the for-mer Royal Yacht *Britannia* (p68) and a berth for visiting cruise liners.

★ **Royal Yacht Britannia**   SHIP
(www.royalyachtbritannia.co.uk; Ocean Terminal; adult/child £15/8.50; ⏱ 9.30am-6pm Jul-Sep, to 5.30pm Apr-Jun & Oct, 10am-5pm Nov-Mar, last admission 90min before closing; 🚌 11, 22, 34, 35, 36) Built on Clydeside, the former Royal Yacht *Britannia* was the British royal family's floating holiday home during their foreign travels from the time of her launch in 1953 until her decommissioning in 1997, and is now moored permanently in front of Ocean Terminal (p67). The tour, which you take at your own pace with an audioguide (included in the admission fee and available in 20 languages), lifts the curtain on the everyday lives of the royals, and gives an intriguing insight into the Queen's private tastes.

Britannia is a monument to 1950s decor, and the accommodation reveals Her Majesty's preference for simple, unfussy surroundings. There was nothing simple or unfussy, however, about the running of the ship. When the Queen travelled, with her went 45 members of the royal household, five tons of luggage and a Rolls-Royce that was carefully squeezed into a specially built garage on the deck. The ship's company consisted of an admiral, 20 officers and 220 yachtsmen.

The decks (of Burmese teak) were scrubbed daily, but all work near the royal accommodation was carried out in complete silence and had to be finished by 8am. A thermometer was kept in the Queen's bathroom to make sure the water was the correct temperature, and when in harbour one yachtsman was charged with ensuring that the angle of the gangway never exceeded 12 degrees. Note the mahogany windbreak that was added to the balcony deck in front of the bridge. It was put there to stop wayward breezes from blowing up skirts and inadvertently revealing the royal undies.

Britannia was joined in 2010 by the 1930s racing yacht *Bloodhound,* which was owned by the Queen in the 1960s. She is moored alongside *Britannia* (except in July and August, when she is away cruising).

The Majestic Tour bus (p72) runs from Waverley Bridge to *Britannia* during opening times.

◉ Greater Edinburgh

★ **Royal Botanic Garden**   GARDENS
(☑ 0131-248 2909; www.rbge.org.uk; Arboretum Pl; ⏱ 10am-6pm Mar-Sep, to 5pm Feb & Oct, to 4pm Nov-Jan; 🚌 8, 23, 27) **FREE** Edinburgh's Royal

---

EDINBURGH FOR CHILDREN

Edinburgh has a multitude of attractions for children, and most things to see and do are child-friendly. During the Edinburgh and Fringe Festivals there's lots of street theatre for kids, especially on High St and at the foot of The Mound; in December there's a Ferris wheel, an open-air ice rink and fairground rides in Princes Street Gardens.

There are good, safe playgrounds in most Edinburgh parks, including Princes Street Gardens West, Inverleith Park (opposite the Royal Botanic Garden), George V Park (New Town), the Meadows and Bruntsfield Links.

Some more ideas for outdoor activities include exploring the Royal Botanic Garden, going to see the animals at Edinburgh Zoo, visiting the statue of Greyfriars Bobby, and feeding the swans and playing on the beach at Cramond.

If it's raining, you can visit the Discovery Centre, a hands-on activity zone on level 3 of the National Museum of Scotland, play on the flumes at the Royal Commonwealth Pool, try out the earthquake simulator at Our Dynamic Earth, or take a tour of the haunted Real Mary King's Close.

Need to Know

Resources Edinburgh for Under Fives (www.efuf.co.uk) has a useful website and guidebook. *The List* (www.list.co.uk) magazine has a special kids' section with activities and events in and around Edinburgh.

Public Transport Up to two children under five may travel free when accompanied by a fare-paying adult. Children between 5 and 15 inclusive pay half the adult fare.

Babysitting You can hire a babysitter from agencies including **Super Mums** (☑ 0131-225 1744; www.supermums.co.uk) and **Panda's Nanny Agency** (☑ 0131-663 3967; www.pandasnannyagency.co.uk), and get further information from **Edinburgh Childcare Information Service** (☑ 0131-529 2103; www.scottishfamilies.gov.uk).

QUIRKY EDINBURGH

Edinburgh is full of unusual attractions and out-of-the-way corners that most visitors never see – even though they may be standing just a few metres away. Here are a few of the city's less-mainstream attractions.

Surgeons' Hall Museums

(Map p52; www.museum.rcsed.ac.uk; Nicolson St; adult/child £6/3.50; ⊙10am-5pm daily Apr-Oct, noon-4pm Mon-Fri Nov-Mar; 🚌 all South Bridge buses) Housed in a grand Ionic temple designed by William Playfair in 1832, these three fascinating museums were originally established as teaching collections. The **History of Surgery Museum** provides a look at surgery in Scotland from the 15th century – when barbers supplemented their income with bloodletting, amputations and other surgical procedures – to the present day. The highlight is the exhibit on Burke and Hare (p59), which includes Burke's death mask and a pocketbook made from his skin. The adjacent **Dental Collection**, with its wince-inducing collections of extraction tools, covers the history of dentistry, while the **Pathology Museum** houses a gruesome but compelling 19th-century collection of diseased organs and massive tumours pickled in formaldehyde.

Gilmerton Cove

(www.gilmertoncove.org.uk; 16 Drum St; adult/child £7.50/4; ⊙10am-4pm) While ghost tours of Edinburgh's underground vaults and haunted graveyards have become a mainstream attraction, Gilmerton Cove remains an off-the-beaten-track gem. Hidden in the southern suburbs, the mysterious 'cove' is a series of subterranean caverns hacked out of the rock, their origin and function unknown. Advance booking essential through **Rosslyn Tours** (☎07914-829177; www.rosslyntours.co.uk).

Mansfield Place Church

(Map p48; www.mansfieldtraquair.org.uk; Mansfield Pl; ⊙1-4pm 2nd Sun of the month Jan-Nov, 11am-1pm most days during Aug; 🚌8) **FREE** In complete contrast to the austerity of most of Edinburgh's religious buildings, this 19th-century, neo-Romanesque church at the foot of Broughton St contains a remarkable series of Renaissance-style frescos painted in the 1890s by Irish-born artist Phoebe Anna Traquair (1852–1936). The murals have been restored and are on view to the public (check the website for any changes to viewing times).

Botanic Garden is the second oldest institution of its kind in Britain (after Oxford), and one of the most respected in the world. Founded near Holyrood in 1670 and moved to its present location in 1823, its 70 beautifully landscaped acres include splendid Victorian glasshouses (admission £5.50), colourful swaths of rhododendron and azalea, and a world-famous rock garden.

The John Hope Gateway visitor centre is housed in a striking, environmentally friendly building overlooking the main entrance on Arboretum Pl, and has exhibitions on biodiversity, climate change and sustainable development, as well as displays of rare plants from the institution's collection and a specially created biodiversity garden.

Edinburgh Zoo   ZOO

(www.edinburghzoo.org.uk; 134 Corstorphine Rd; adult/child £19/14.55; ⊙9am-6pm Apr-Sep, to 5pm Oct & Mar, to 4.30pm Nov-Feb; 👶) Opened in 1913, Edinburgh Zoo is one of the world's leading conservation zoos. Edinburgh's captive breeding program has helped save many endangered species, including Siberian tigers, pygmy hippos and red pandas. The main attractions are the two giant pandas, Tian Tian and Yang Guang, who arrived in December 2011, and the penguin parade (the zoo's penguins go for a walk every day at 2.15pm).

The zoo is 2.5 miles west of the city centre; take Lothian Bus 12, 26 or 31, First Bus 16, 18, 80 or 86, or the Airlink Bus 100 westbound from Princes St.

Cramond   AREA

With its moored yachts, stately swans and whitewashed houses spilling down the hillside at the mouth of the River Almond, Cramond is the most picturesque corner of Edinburgh. It is also rich in history. The Romans built a fort here in the 2nd century AD, but recent archaeological excavations have revealed evidence of a Bronze Age settlement dating from 8500 BC, the oldest-known site in Scotland. It's 5 miles northwest of the city centre; take bus 41 from George St (westbound) or Queensferry St.

Activities

Edinburgh has plenty of places to perk up your sagging muscles with a spot of healthy exercise.

Walking

Edinburgh is lucky to have several good walking areas within the city boundary, including Arthur's Seat (p58), Calton Hill (p66), **Blackford Hill** (Charterhall Rd; 24, 38, 41), **Hermitage of Braid** (www.fohb.org; 5, 11, 15, 16), **Corstorphine Hill** and the coast and river at Cramond (p69). The **Pentland Hills** (www.pentlandhills.org) FREE, which rise to over 500m, stretch southwest from the city for over 15 miles, offering excellent high- and low-level walking.

You can follow the Water of Leith Walkway (p67) from the city centre to Balerno (8 miles), and continue across the Pentlands to Silverburn (6.5 miles) or Carlops (8 miles), and return to Edinburgh by bus. Another good walk is along the **Union Canal towpath**, which begins in Fountainbridge and runs all the way to Falkirk (31 miles). You can return to Edinburgh by bus at Ratho (8.5 miles) or Broxburn (12 miles), and by bus or train from Linlithgow (21 miles).

Scottish Rights of Way & Access Society (0131-558 1222; www.scotways.com; 24 Annandale St) provides information and advice on walking trails and rights of way in Scotland.

Cycling

Edinburgh and its surroundings offer many excellent opportunities for cycling (see www.cyclingedinburgh.info and www.cycling-edinburgh.org.uk). The main off-road routes from the city centre out to the countryside follow the **Union Canal towpath** then the **Water of Leith Walkway** from Tollcross southwest to Balerno (7.5 miles) on the edge of the Pentland Hills, and the **Innocent Railway Cycle Path** from the southern side of Arthur's Seat eastwards to Musselburgh (5 miles) and on to Ormiston and Pencaitland.

There are several routes through the **Pentland Hills** that are suitable for mountain bikes. For details ask at any bike shop or check out the Pentland Hills Regional Park website (www.pentlandhills.org). The

Spokes Edinburgh Cycle Map (www.spokes.org.uk; available from cycle shops) shows all the city's cycle routes.

Cycle Scotland   CYCLING
(Map p52; 0131-556 5560; www.cyclescotland.co.uk; 29 Blackfriars St; per day £20-25; 10am-6pm Mon-Sat) The friendly and helpful folk here rent out top-quality bikes; rates include helmet, lock and repair kit. You can hire tents and touring equipment too. The company also organises cycle tours in Edinburgh and all over Scotland – check the website for details.

Golf

There are no fewer than 19 golf courses in Edinburgh – the following are two of the best city courses.

Braid Hills Public Golf Course   GOLF
(0131-447 6666; www.edinburghleisure.co.uk/venues; Braid Hills Approach; green fees weekday/weekend £24.80/26.50) A scenic but challenging course to the south of the city centre.

Duddingston Golf Course   GOLF
(www.duddingstongolfclub.co.uk; Duddingston Rd West; green fees weekday/weekend £45/55) Enjoys a picturesque setting at the foot of Arthur's Seat.

Swimming

The Firth of Forth is a bit on the chilly side for enjoyable swimming, but there are indoor alternatives.

Edinburgh's main facility, the **Royal Commonwealth Pool** (Map p48; 0131-667 7211; www.edinburghleisure.co.uk/venues; 21 Dalkeith Rd; adult/family £6/15; 5.30am-10pm Mon-Fri, to 8pm Sat, 7.30am-8pm Sun; 2, 14, 30, 33) – built for the 1970 Commonwealth Games, and serving again as a venue for the 2014 Glasgow games – is affectionately known as the 'Commie Pool'. Recently refurbished, it has a 50m eight-lane pool, diving pool, teaching/children's pool, fitness centre and kids' soft play area.

Tours

Walking Tours

There are plenty of organised walks around Edinburgh, many of them related to ghosts, murders and witches.

City of the Dead Tours   WALKING
(www.cityofthedeadtours.com; adult/concession £10/8) This tour of Greyfriars Kirkyard is probably the scariest of Edinburgh's 'ghost' tours. Many people have reported encoun-

UNDERGROUND EDINBURGH

As Edinburgh expanded in the late 18th and early 19th centuries, many old tenements were demolished and new bridges were built to link the Old Town to the newly built areas to its north and south. South Bridge (built between 1785 and 1788) and George IV Bridge (built between 1829 and 1834) lead south from the Royal Mile over the deep valley of Cowgate, but so many buildings have been constructed around them you can hardly tell they are bridges – George IV Bridge has a total of nine arches but only two are visible; South Bridge has no fewer than 18 hidden arches.

These **subterranean vaults** were originally used as storerooms, workshops and drinking dens. But as Edinburgh's population swelled in the early 19th century with an influx of penniless Highlanders cleared from their lands, and Irish refugees from the potato famine, the dark, dripping chambers were given over to slum accommodation and abandoned to poverty, filth and crime.

The vaults were eventually cleared in the late 19th century, then lay forgotten until 1994 when the **South Bridge vaults** were opened to guided tours. Certain chambers are said to be haunted and one particular vault was investigated by paranormal researchers in 2001.

Nevertheless, the most ghoulish aspect of Edinburgh's hidden history dates from much earlier – from the plague that struck the city in 1645. Legend has it that the disease-ridden inhabitants of **Mary King's Close** (a lane on the northern side of the Royal Mile, on the site of the City Chambers – you can still see its blocked-off northern end from Cockburn St) were walled up in their houses and left to perish. When the lifeless bodies were eventually cleared from the houses, they were so stiff that workmen had to hack off limbs to get them through the small doorways and narrow, twisting stairs.

From that day on, the close was said to be haunted by the spirits of the plague victims. The few people who were prepared to live there reported seeing apparitions of severed heads and limbs, and the largely abandoned close fell into ruin. When the Royal Exchange (now the City Chambers) was constructed between 1753 and 1761, it was built over the lower levels of Mary King's Close, which were left intact and sealed off beneath the building.

Interest in the close revived in the 20th century when Edinburgh's city council began to allow occasional guided tours to enter. Visitors have reported many supernatural experiences – the most famous ghost is 'Annie', a little girl whose sad tale has prompted people to leave gifts of dolls in a corner of one of the rooms. In 2003 the close was opened to the public as the **Real Mary King's Close** (p53).

ters with the 'Mackenzie Poltergeist', the ghost of a 17th-century judge who persecuted the Covenanters, and now haunts their former prison in a corner of the kirkyard. Not suitable for young children.

Cadies & Witchery Tours WALKING
(Map p52; ☎ 0131-225 6745; www.witcherytours. com; adult/child £10/7.50; ☒ 2) The becloaked and pasty-faced Adam Lyal (deceased) leads a 'Murder & Mystery' tour of the Old Town's darker corners. These tours are famous for their 'jumper-ooters' – costumed actors who 'jump oot' when you least expect it.

Edinburgh Literary Pub Tour WALKING
(www.edinburghliterarypubtour.co.uk; adult/student £14/10; ⊙ 7.30pm daily May-Sep, limited days Oct-Apr) An enlightening two-hour trawl through Edinburgh's literary history – and its asso-

ciated howffs (pubs) – in the entertaining company of Messrs Clart and McBrain. One of the city's best walking tours.

Mercat Tours WALKING
(Map p52; ☎ 0131-225 5445; www.mercattours. com; Mercat Cross; adult/child £12/7) Mercat offers a wide range of fascinating history walks and 'Ghosts & Ghouls' tours, but its most famous is a visit to the hidden, haunted, underground vaults beneath South Bridge.

Invisible (Edinburgh) WALKING
(☎ 07500-773709; www.invisible-cities.org; per person £8) A new venture that trains homeless people as tour guides to explore a different side of the city. Tour themes include Crime & Punishment (includes Burke and Hare) and Powerful Women (from Maggie

Dickson to JK Rowling). Must be booked in advance; check website for times.

Trainspotting Tours
WALKING

(www.leithwalks.co.uk; per person £6, min charge £24) A tour of locations from Irvine Welsh's notorious 1993 novel *Trainspotting*, and the 1996 film of the book, delivered with wit and enthusiasm. Not suitable for kids.

Rebus Tours
WALKING

(☑ 0131-553 7473; www.rebustours.com; per person £10; ☉ noon Sat) A two-hour guided tour of the 'hidden Edinburgh' frequented by novelist Ian Rankin's fictional detective, John Rebus. Not recommended for children under 10.

Bus Tours

Open-topped buses leave from Waverley Bridge, outside the main train station, and offer hop-on, hop-off tours of the main sights, taking in New Town, the Grassmarket and the Royal Mile. They're a good way to get your bearings, although with a bus map and a Day Saver bus ticket (£4) you could do much the same thing (but without the commentary).

Majestic Tour
BUS

(www.edinburghtour.com; adult/child £15/7.50; ☉ daily year-round except 25 Dec) Hop-on, hop-off tour departing every 15 to 20 minutes from Waverley Bridge to the Royal Yacht *Britannia* at Ocean Terminal via the New Town, Royal Botanic Garden and Newhaven, returning via Leith Walk, Holyrood and the Royal Mile.

MacTours
BUS

(www.edinburghtour.com; adult/child £15/7.50; ☉ every 30 min Apr-Oct) A quick tour around the highlights of the Old and New Towns, from the castle to Calton Hill, aboard an open-topped vintage bus.

City Sightseeing
BUS

(www.edinburghtour.com; adult/child £15/7.50; ☉ daily year-round except 25 Dec) Bright-red, open-top buses depart every 20 minutes from Waverley Bridge.

🎊 Festivals & Events

Edinburgh hosts an amazing number of festivals throughout the year, notably the Edinburgh International Festival, the Edinburgh Festival Fringe and the Military Tattoo. Hogmanay, Scotland's New Year's celebrations, is also a peak party time.

🚶 City Walk
Old Town Alleys

START CASTLE ESPLANADE
END COCKBURN ST
LENGTH 1 MILE; ONE TO TWO HOURS

This walk explores the alleys and side streets around the the Royal Mile, and involves a bit of climbing up and down steep stairs.

Begin on the ❶ **Castle Esplanade**, which provides a grandstand view south over Grassmarket; the prominent quadrangular building with all the turrets is George Heriot's School, which you'll be passing later on. Head towards Castlehill and the start of the Royal Mile.

The 17th-century house on the right is known as ❷ **Cannonball House** because of the iron ball lodged in the wall (look between, and slightly below, the two largest windows on the wall facing the castle). It was not fired in anger, but marks the gravitation height to which water would flow naturally from the city's first piped water supply.

The low, rectangular building across the street (now a touristy tartan-weaving mill) was originally the reservoir that held the Old Town's water supply. On its west wall is the ❸ **Witches Well**, where a bronze fountain commemorates around 4000 people (mostly women) who were executed between 1479 and 1722 on suspicion of witchcraft.

Go past the reservoir and turn left down Ramsay Lane. Take a look at ❹ **Ramsay Garden** – one of Edinburgh's most desirable addresses – where late-19th-century apartments were built around the octagonal Ramsay Lodge, once home to poet Allan Ramsay. The cobbled street continues around to the right below student residences to the towers of the ❺ **New College**, home to Edinburgh University's Faculty of Divinity. Nip into the courtyard to see the statue of John Knox (a firebrand preacher who led the Protestant Reformation in Scotland, and was instrumental in the creation of the Church of Scotland in 1560).

Just past New College turn right and climb the stairs into Milne's Court, a student residence belonging to Edinburgh University. Exit into Lawnmarket, cross

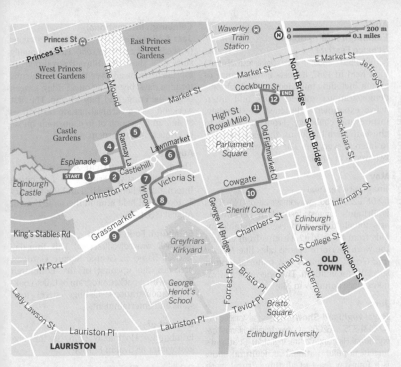

the street (bearing slightly left) and duck into **6 Riddell's Court**, a typical Old Town close at No 322–8. You'll find yourself in a small courtyard, but the house in front of you (built in 1590) was originally the edge of the street (the building you just walked under was added in 1726 – look for the inscription in the doorway on the right). The arch with the inscription *Vivendo discimus* (We live and learn) leads into the original 16th-century courtyard.

Go back into the street, turn right and right again down Fisher's Close, which leads to the delightful Victoria Terrace, strung above the cobbled curve of shop-lined Victoria St. Wander right, enjoying the view – **7 Maxie's Bistro** (p82), at the far end of the terrace, is a great place to stop for a drink – then descend the stairs at the foot of Upper Bow and continue downhill to the Grassmarket. At the east end, outside Maggie Dickson's pub, is the **8 Covenanters Monument**, which marks the site of the gallows where more than 100 Covenanters were martyred in the 17th century.

If you're feeling peckish, the Grassmarket has several good places to eat and a couple of good pubs – Robert Burns once stayed at the **9 White Hart Inn** (p88). Head east

along the gloomy defile of the Cowgate, passing under the arch of George IV Bridge – the buildings to your right are the new law courts, while high up to the left you can see the complex of buildings behind Parliament Sq. Past the courts, on the right, is **10 Tailors Hall** (built 1621, extended 1757), now a hotel and bar but formerly the meeting place of the Companie of Tailzeours (Tailors' Guild).

Turn left and climb steeply up Old Fishmarket Close, a typical cobbled Old Town wynd, and emerge once more onto the Royal Mile. Across the street and slightly downhill is **11 Anchor Close**, named for a tavern that once stood there. It hosted the Crochallan Fencibles, an 18th-century drinking club that provided its patrons with an agreeable blend of intellectual debate and intoxicating liquor. The club was founded by William Smellie, editor of the first edition of the *Encyclopedia Brittanica*; its best-known member was the poet Robert Burns.

Go down Anchor Close, to finish the walk on **12 Cockburn St**, one of the city's coolest shopping streets, lined with record shops and clothing boutiques. The street was cut through Old Town tenements in the 1850s to provide an easy route between Waverley Station and the Royal Mile.

April

Edinburgh International Science Festival FESTIVAL

(☎0844-557 2686; www.sciencefestival.co.uk) First held in 1987, it hosts a wide range of events, including talks, lectures, exhibitions, demonstrations, guided tours and interactive experiments designed to stimulate, inspire and challenge. From dinosaurs to ghosts to alien life forms, there's something to interest everyone. The festival runs over two weeks in April.

May

Imaginate Festival ART

(☎0131-225 8050; www.imaginate.org.uk) This is Britain's biggest festival of performing arts for children, with events suitable for kids from three to 12. Groups from around the world perform classic tales like *Hansel and Gretel*, as well as new material written specially for children. The one-week festival takes place annually in May.

June

Royal Highland Show AGRICULTURE

(☎0131-335 6200; www.royalhighlandshow.org; Royal Highland Centre, Ingliston) Scotland's hugely popular national agricultural show is a four-day feast of all things rural, with everything from show jumping and tractor driving to sheep shearing and falconry. Countless pens are filled with coiffed show cattle and pedicured prize ewes. The show is held over a long weekend (Thursday to Sunday) in late June.

Edinburgh International Film Festival FILM

(Map p52; www.edfilmfest.org.uk) One of the original Edinburgh Festival trinity, having first been staged in 1947 along with the International Festival and the Fringe, the two-week June film festival is a major international event, serving as a showcase for new British and European films, and staging the European premieres of one or two Hollywood blockbusters.

July

Scottish Real Ale Festival BEER

(www.sraf.camra.org.uk; Corn Exchange, Chesser Ave) A celebration of all things fermented and yeasty, Scotland's biggest beer-fest gives you the opportunity to sample a wide range of traditionally brewed beers from Scotland and around the world. Froth-topped bliss. The festival is held over a long weekend in June or July.

Edinburgh International Jazz & Blues Festival MUSIC

(www.edinburghjazzfestival.com) Held annually since 1978, the Jazz & Blues Festival pulls in top talent from all over the world. It runs for nine days, beginning on a Friday, a week before the Fringe and Tattoo begin. The first weekend sees a carnival parade on Princes St and an afternoon of free, open-air music in Princes Street Gardens.

August

The Edinburgh International Festival, the Edinburgh Festival Fringe, the Edinburgh International Book Festival and the Military Tattoo are all held around the same time in August (see p75).

Edinburgh Food Festival FOOD & DRINK

(Map p48; www.edfoodfest.com) This four-day festival, based in George Square Gardens, precedes the opening of the Edinburgh Fringe with a packed program of talks, cookery demonstrations, tastings, street food stalls and entertainment.

December

Edinburgh's Hogmanay (p76) is the biggest winter festival in Europe.

Edinburgh's Christmas CHRISTMAS

(☎0844 545 8252; www.edinburghschristmas.com) First held in 2000, the Christmas bash runs from late November to early January and includes a big street parade, a Christmas market, a fairground and Ferris wheel, and an open-air ice rink in Princes Street Gardens.

Sleeping

Edinburgh offers a wide range of accommodation options, from moderately priced guesthouses set in lovely Victorian villas and Georgian town houses to expensive and stylish boutique hotels. There are also plenty of international chain hotels, and a few truly exceptional hotels housed in magnificent historic buildings. At the budget end of the range, there is no shortage of youth hostels and independent backpacker hostels, which often have inexpensive double and twin rooms available.

Old Town

★**Malone's Old Town Hostel** HOSTEL £

(Map p52; ☎0131-226 7648; www.maloneshostel.com; 14 Forrest Rd; dm £12-20; @ 📶; 🚌2, 23, 27, 41, 42, 45) No fancy decor or style

FESTIVAL CITY

August in Edinburgh sees a frenzy of festivals, with several world-class events running at the same time.

Edinburgh Festival Fringe

When the first Edinburgh Festival was held in 1947, there were eight theatre companies who didn't make it onto the main program. Undeterred, they grouped together and held their own mini-festival – on the fringe – and an Edinburgh institution was born. Today the **Edinburgh Festival Fringe** (☏0131-226 0026; www.edfringe.com) is the biggest festival of the performing arts anywhere in the world.

Since 1990 the Fringe has been dominated by stand-up comedy, but the sheer variety of shows on offer is staggering – everything from chainsaw juggling and performance poetry to Tibetan yak-milk gargling. So how do you decide what to see? There are daily reviews in the *Scotsman* newspaper – one good *Scotsman* review and a show sells out in hours – but the best recommendation is word of mouth. If you have the time, go to at least one unknown show – it may be crap, but at least you'll have your obligatory 'worst show I ever saw' story.

The big names play at megavenues organised by big agencies such as Assembly (www.assemblyfestival.com) and the Gilded Balloon (www.gildedballoon.co.uk), and charge megaprices (£15 to £20 a ticket and up, with some famous comedians notoriously charging more than £30), but there are plenty of good shows in the £5 to £15 range and, best of all, lots of free stuff. **Fringe Sunday** – usually the second Sunday – is a smorgasbord of free performances, staged in the Meadows park to the south of the city centre.

The Fringe takes place over 3½ weeks, the last two weeks overlapping with the first two of the Edinburgh International Festival.

For bookings and information, head to the **Edinburgh Festival Fringe Office** (☏0131-226 0026; www.edfringe.com; 180 High St; ☉noon-3pm Mon-Sat mid-Jun–mid-Jul, 10am-6pm daily mid-Jul–1 Aug, 9am-9pm daily Aug; ◪all South Bridge buses).

Edinburgh International Festival

First held in 1947 to mark a return to peace after the ordeal of WWII, the **Edinburgh International Festival** (☏0131-473 2000; www.eif.co.uk) is festooned with superlatives – the oldest, the biggest, the most famous, the best in the world. The original was a modest affair, but today hundreds of the world's top musicians and performers congregate in Edinburgh for three weeks of diverse and inspirational music, opera, theatre and dance.

The festival takes place over the three weeks ending on the first Saturday in September; the program is usually available from April. Tickets for popular events – especially music and opera – sell out quickly, so it's best to book as far in advance as possible. You can buy tickets in person at the **Hub** (Map p52; ☏0131-473 2015; www.thehub-edinburgh.com; Castlehill; ☉ticket centre 10am-5pm Mon-Fri), or by phone or internet.

Edinburgh Military Tattoo

August in Edinburgh kicks off with the **Edinburgh Military Tattoo** (☏0131-225 1188; www.edintattoo.co.uk), a spectacular display of military marching bands, massed pipes and drums, acrobats, cheerleaders and motorcycle display teams, all played out in front of the magnificent backdrop of the floodlit castle. Each show traditionally finishes with a lone piper, dramatically lit, playing a lament on the battlements. The Tattoo takes place over the first three weeks of August (from a Friday to a Saturday); there's one show at 9pm Monday to Friday and two (at 7.30pm and 10.30pm) on Saturday, but no performance on Sunday.

Edinburgh International Book Festival

Held in a little village of marquees in the middle of Charlotte Sq, the **Edinburgh International Book Festival** (Map p64; ☏0845 373 5888; www.edbookfest.co.uk) is a fun fortnight of talks, readings, debates, lectures, book signings and meet-the-author events, with a cafe-bar and tented bookshop thrown in. The festival lasts for two weeks (usually the first two weeks of the Edinburgh International Festival).

EDINBURGH'S HOGMANAY

The biggest winter festival in Europe, **Edinburgh's Hogmanay** (☎ 0844 573 8455; www.
edinburghshogmanay.com; tickets £20), has events running from 27 December to 1 January,
including a torchlight procession, huge street party and the famous 'Loony Dook', a chilly
sea-swimming event on New Year's Day. To get into the main party area in the city centre
after 8pm on 31 December you'll need a ticket – book well in advance.

Traditionally, the New Year has always been a more important celebration for Scots
than Christmas. In towns, cities and villages all over the country, people fill the streets at
midnight on 31 December to wish each other a Guid New Year and, yes, to knock back a
dram or six to keep the cold at bay.

In 1993 Edinburgh's city council had the excellent idea of spicing up Hogmanay by
organising some events, laying on some live music in Princes St and issuing an open
invitation to the rest of the world. Most of them turned up, or so it seemed, and had such
a good time that they told all their pals and came back again the next year.

credentials here, but they've got the basics right: it's clean, comfortable and friendly, and set upstairs from an Irish pub where guests get discounts on food and drink. The cherry on the cake is its superbly central location, an easy walk from the Royal Mile, the castle, the Grassmarket and Princes St.

Kickass Hostel HOSTEL £

(Map p52; ☎ 0131-226 6351; https://kickasshostels.co.uk; 2 West Port; dm/tw £27/57; @ 🤶; 🖵 2) Great value and great location (the castle is just five minutes away) are the main attractions here, but the colourful decor, cheap cafe-bar and helpful staff are added bonuses. Bunks have free lockers, bedside lights and phone-charging stations too.

Castle Rock Hostel HOSTEL £

(Map p52; ☎ 0131-225 9666; www.scotlands-top-hostels.com; 15 Johnston Tce; dm £14-17, d £55; @ 🤶; 🖵 2) With its bright, spacious, mixed or female-only dorms, superb views and friendly staff, the 200-bed Castle Rock has lots to like. It has a great location – the only way to get closer to the castle would be to pitch a tent on the esplanade – a games room, reading lounge and big-screen video nights. No under-18s.

Safestay Edinburgh HOSTEL £

(Map p52; ☎ 0131-524 1989; www.smartcityhostels.com; 50 Blackfriars St; dm £13-20; @ 🤶) A big, modern hostel, with a convivial cafe where you can buy breakfast, and mod cons such as keycard access and charging stations for mobile phones, MP3 players and laptops. Lockers in every room, a huge bar and a central location just off the Royal Mile make this a favourite among the young, party-mad crowd – don't expect a quiet night!

⭐ **Witchery by the Castle** B&B £££

(Map p52; ☎ 0131-225 5613; www.thewitchery.com; Castlehill; ste £325-395; 🖵 23, 27, 41, 42) Set in a 16th-century Old Town house in the shadow of Edinburgh Castle, the Witchery's nine lavish Gothic suites are extravagantly furnished with antiques, oak panelling, tapestries, open fires, four-poster beds and roll-top baths, and supplied with flowers, chocolates and complimentary champagne. Overwhelmingly popular – you'll have to book several months in advance to be sure of getting a room.

Grassmarket Hotel HOTEL £££

(Map p52; ☎ 0131-220 2299; www.grassmarkethotel.co.uk; 94-96 Grassmarket; s/d from £120/140; 🤶; 🖵 2) An endearingly quirky hotel set in a historic Grassmarket tenement in the heart of the Old Town, this place has bedroom walls plastered with front pages from the *Dandy* (a DC Thomson comic published in Dundee) and coffee stations supplied with iconically Scottish Tunnock's teacakes and Irn Bru. Some bargain rates available direct through the website.

🛏 Holyrood & Arthur's Seat

⭐ **Prestonfield** BOUTIQUE HOTEL £££

(☎ 0131-668 3346; www.prestonfield.com; Priestfield Rd; r/ste from £285/361; 🅿 🤶) If the blonde wood and brushed steel of modern boutique hotels leaves you cold, then this is the place for you. A 17th-century mansion set in 8 hectares of parkland (complete with peacocks and Highland cattle), Prestonfield is draped in damask and packed with antiques – look out for original tapestries, 17th-century embossed-leather panels, and £500-a-roll hand-painted wallpaper.

⊨ New Town

Code Hostel
HOSTEL **£**

(Map p64; ☑ 0131-659 9883; www.codehostel. com; 50 Rose St N Lane; dm from £25, d £99; ☎; 🚇 Princes St) This upmarket hostel, bang in the middle of the New Town, combines cute designer decor with innovative sleeping cubicles that offer more privacy than bunks (four to six people per dorm, each with en suite shower room). There's also a luxurious double apartment called the Penthouse, complete with kitchenette and roof terrace.

Gerald's Place
B&B **££**

(Map p64; ☑ 0131-558 7017; www.geraldsplace. com; 21b Abercromby Pl; d £89-149; @ ☎; 🚇 23, 27) Gerald is an unfailingly charming and helpful host, and his lovely Georgian garden flat (just two guest bedrooms, each with a private bathroom) has a great location across from a peaceful park, an easy stroll from the city centre. There may be a minimum three-night stay in peak season.

Ramsay's B&B
B&B **££**

(Map p48; ☑ 0131-557 5917; www.ramsaysbed andbreakfastedinburgh.com; 25 East London St; d £115; ☎; 🚇 8) The four bright and fresh bedrooms in this tastefully decorated Georgian town house make a great base for exploring the New Town, with the vibrant bar and restaurant scene of Broughton's gay village just around the corner. Breakfasts are freshly prepared, with kippers on the menu as well the usual suspects.

Angels Share Hotel
HOTEL **££**

(Map p64; ☑ 0131-247 7000; http://angelsshare hotel.com/; 9-11 Hope St; r from £115; ☎; 🚇 all Princes St buses) You'll be right in the middle of the New Town action at this small but buzzing hotel, with Princes St shops and George St cocktail bars just a short stagger away. Rooms are understated but stylish, each decorated with a huge image of a Scottish celeb – fine if you don't mind Lulu or Rod Stewart looming over your bed!

Balmoral Hotel
HOTEL **£££**

(Map p64; ☑ 0131-556 2414; www.thebalmoral hotel.com; 1 Princes St; s/d from £277/299; P ☎ ☀; 🚇 all Princes St buses) The sumptuous Balmoral – a prominent landmark at the eastern end of Princes St – offers some of the best accommodation in Edinburgh, including suites with 18th-century decor, marble bathrooms and stunning sunset views of Princes St and the Scott Monument. There's

also a spa and gym with 20m pool in the basement.

Tigerlily
BOUTIQUE HOTEL **£££**

(Map p64; ☑ 0131-225 5005; www.tigerlilyedin burgh.co.uk; 125 George St; r from £175; ☎; 🚇 all Princes St buses) Georgian meets gorgeous at this glamorous, glittering boutique hotel (complete with its own nightclub) decked out in mirror mosaics, beaded curtains, swirling Timorous Beasties textiles and wall coverings, and atmospheric pink uplighting. Book the Georgian Suite (from £400) for a truly special romantic getaway.

⊨ West End & Dean Village

★ B+B Edinburgh
HOTEL **£££**

(Map p48; ☑ 0131-225 5084; www.bb-edinburgh. com; 3 Rothesay Tce; d/ste from £138/190; ☎; 🚇 West End) Built in 1883 as a grand home for the proprietor of the *Scotsman* newspaper, this Victorian extravaganza of carved oak, parquet floors, stained glass and elaborate fireplaces was given a designer makeover to create a striking contemporary hotel. Rooms on the 2nd floor are the most spacious, but the smaller top-floor rooms enjoy the finest views.

Bonham Hotel
BOUTIQUE HOTEL **£££**

(Map p48; ☑ 0131-226 6050; www.townhouse company.com/thebonham; 35 Drumsheugh Gardens; r from £160; P ☎; 🚇 19, 36, 37, 41) The Bonham manages a successful fusion of Victorian interiors with bold modern colours

---

ACCOMMODATION AGENCIES

If you arrive in Edinburgh without a room, the Edinburgh Information Centre (p95) booking service will try to find a room to suit you (and will charge a £5 fee if successful). If you have the time, pick up the tourist office's accommodation brochure and ring around yourself.

VisitScotland (www.edinburgh.org) Wide range of options from the official website.

Lonely Planet (lonelyplanet.com/ hotels) Recommendations and bookings.

Edinburgh & the Lothians (www. edinburgh.org) Official tourist website, with wide range of accommodation and weekend break offers.

and contemporary design. Cool, crisp bed linen, luxury bathrooms and friendly but unobtrusive service make for a memorable stay. Though set in a quiet, West End backstreet, the Bonham is only five minutes' walk from Princes St.

🛏 South Edinburgh

Argyle Backpackers   HOSTEL $
(Map p48; ☑0131-667 9991; www.argyle-back packers.co.uk; 14 Argyle Pl; dm £16-18, s/tw from £54/60; @🕾; 🖵41) The Argyle, spread across three adjacent terrace houses, is a quiet and relaxed hostel offering single, double and twin rooms as well as four- to six-bed dorms (mixed or female-only). There is a comfortable TV lounge, an attractive little conservatory and a pleasant walled garden at the back where you can sit outside in summer.

⭐ Southside Guest House   B&B $$
(Map p48; ☑0131-668 4422; www.southside guesthouse.co.uk; 8 Newington Rd; s/d from £80/105; 🕾; 🖵all Newington buses) Though set in a typical Victorian terrace, the Southside transcends the traditional guesthouse category and feels more like a modern boutique hotel. Its eight stylish rooms ooze interior design, standing out from other Newington B&Bs through the clever use of bold colours and modern furniture. Breakfast is an event, with Bucks Fizz (cava mixed with orange juice) on offer to ease the hangover!

Sherwood Guest House   B&B $$
(Map p48; ☑0131-667 1200; www.sherwood-edin burgh.com; 42 Minto St; s/d from £70/85; P🕾; 🖵all Newington buses) One of the most attractive guesthouses on Minto St's B&B strip, the Sherwood is a refurbished Georgian terrace house decked out with hanging baskets and shrubs. Inside are six en suite rooms that combine period features with modern fabrics and pine furniture.

No 45   B&B $$
(☑0131-667 3536; www.edinburghbedbreakfast. com; 45 Gilmour Rd; s/d £70/120; 🕾; 🖵all Newington buses) A peaceful setting, large garden and friendly owners contribute to the appeal of this Victorian terrace house, which overlooks the local bowling green. The decor is a blend of 19th and 20th century, with bold Victorian reds, pine floors and a period fireplace in the lounge, and a 1930s vibe in the three spacious bedrooms.

Aonach Mor Guest House   B&B $$
(☑0131-667 8694; www.aonachmor.com; 14 Kilmaurs Tce; r per person £33-65; @🕾; 🖵2, 14, 30, 33) This elegant Victorian terrace house is located on a quiet backstreet and has seven bedrooms, beautifully decorated, with many original period features. Our favourite is the four-poster bedroom with polished mahogany furniture and period fireplace. Located 1 mile southeast of the city centre.

Knight Residence   APARTMENT $$$
(Map p52; ☑0131-622 8120; www.theknightresi dence.co.uk; 12 Lauriston St; 1-/2-bedroom apt from £180/270; P🕾; 🖵2) Works by contemporary artists adorn these modern studio, one- and two-bedroom apartments (available by the night; the latter sleep up to four adults and one child), each with fully equipped kitchen and comfortable lounge with cable TV, video and stereo. It has a good central location in a quiet street only a few minutes' walk from the Grassmarket.

Ten Hill Place   HOTEL $$$
(Map p52; ☑0131-662 2080; www.tenhillplace. com; 10 Hill Pl; r from £185; P🕾; 🖵all South Bridge buses) 🅿 This attractive modern hotel offers good-value accommodation close to the city centre. The standard bedrooms are comfortable and stylish with a sober but sophisticated colour scheme in rich browns, purples and tweedy greens, and appealing modern bathrooms. For a special weekend, ask for one of the four 'skyline' rooms on the top floor, with panoramic views of Salisbury Crags.

🛏 Leith

Edinburgh Central SYHA   HOSTEL $
(SYHA; Map p48; ☑0131-524 2090; www. syha.org.uk; 9 Haddington Pl, Leith Walk; dm/s/ tw £22/46/74; @🕾; 🖵all Leith Walk buses) This modern, purpose-built hostel, about a half-mile north of Waverley train station, is a big (300 beds), flashy, five-star establishment with its own cafe-bistro as well as self-catering kitchen, smart and comfortable eight-bed dorms and private rooms, and mod cons including keycard entry and plasma-screen TVs.

⭐ Wallace's Arthouse   B&B $$
(☑07941 343714; www.wallacesarthousescotland. com; 41/4 Constitution St; s/d £99/120; 🕾; 🖵12, 16) This Georgian apartment, housed in the neoclassical Leith Assembly Rooms (a Grade A listed building), offers two beautifully nos-

talgic bedrooms styled by former fashion designer Wallace, who comes as part of the package – your charming host and breakfast chef is an unfailing source of colourful anecdotes and local knowledge.

★**Sheridan Guest House** B&B ££
(☑0131-554 4107; www.sheridanedinburgh.com; 1 Bonnington Tce, Newhaven Rd; r from £95; P☎; ▣7, 11, 14) Flowerpots filled with colourful blooms line the steps of this little haven hidden away to the north of the New Town. The eight bedrooms (all en suite) blend crisp colours with contemporary furniture, stylish lighting and colourful paintings, which complement the house's clean-cut Georgian lines, while the breakfast menu adds omelettes, pancakes with maple syrup, and scrambled eggs with smoked salmon to the usual offerings.

Millers 64 B&B ££
(☑0131-454 3666; www.millers64.com; 64 Pilrig St; s from £80, d £90-150; ☎; ▣11) Luxury textiles, colourful cushions, stylish bathrooms and fresh flowers added to a warm Edinburgh welcome make this Victorian town house a highly desirable address. There are just two bedrooms (and a minimum three-night stay during festival periods), so book well in advance.

Sandaig Guest House B&B ££
(☑0131-554 7357; www.sandaigguesthouse.co.uk; 5 East Hermitage Pl, Leith Links; s/d from £90/105; ☎; ▣21, 25) From the welcoming tot of whisky liqueur to the cheerful goodbye wave, the owners of the Sandaig know a thing or two about hospitality. There are plenty of things that make staying here a pleasure, from the boldly coloured decor to the crisp cotton sheets, big fluffy towels and refreshing power showers, and a breakfast menu that includes porridge with cream and maple syrup.

✗ **Eating**

Eating out in Edinburgh has changed beyond all recognition in the last 20 years. Two decades ago, sophisticated dining meant a visit to the Aberdeen Angus Steak House for a prawn cocktail, steak (well done) and chips, and Black Forest gateau. Today, eating out has become a commonplace event and the city has more restaurants per head of population than any other city in the UK, including a handful with Michelin stars.

✗ **Old Town**

★**Mums** CAFE £
(Map p52; ☑0131-260 9806; www.monstermashcafe.co.uk; 4a Forrest Rd; mains £8-11; ⊙9am-10pm Mon-Sat, 10am-10pm Sun; ☎♿; ▣23, 27, 41, 42) ✔ This nostalgia-fuelled cafe serves up classic British comfort food that wouldn't look out of place on a 1950s menu – bacon and eggs, bangers and mash, shepherd's pie, fish and chips. But there's a twist – the food is all top-quality nosh freshly prepared from local produce. There's also a good selection of bottled craft beers and Scottish-brewed cider.

Wings FAST FOOD £
(Map p52; ☑0131-629 1234; http://wingsedinburgh.com; 5/7 Old Fishmarket Close; per portion £3.50; ⊙4-11pm Mon, noon-11pm Tue-Sun; ▣23, 27, 41, 42) Eateries don't come much simpler. Order some bowls of barbecued chicken wings (six wings per portion) with the sauce of your choice (a couple of dozen to choose from, whether soused in tequila and lime juice or slathered with hot chilli) and a drink. If you're still hungry, order more. Genius. Great sci-fi/comic-book decor too.

Pancho Villa's MEXICAN £
(Map p52; ☑0131-557 4416; www.panchovillas.co.uk; 240 Canongate; mains £9-12; ⊙noon-10pm Mon-Sat, 5-10pm Sun; ♿♿) With a Mexican-born owner and lots of Latin American and Spanish staff, it's not surprising that this colourful and lively restaurant is one of the most authentic-feeling Mexican places in town. The dinner menu includes delicious steak fajitas and great vegetarian spinach enchiladas. It's often busy, so book ahead.

★**Cannonball Restaurant** SCOTTISH ££
(Map p52; ☑0131-225 1550; www.contini.com/contini-cannonball; 356 Castlehill, Royal Mile; mains £15-25; ⊙noon-5pm & 5.30-10pm Tue-Sat; ☎♿; ▣23, 27, 41, 42) The historic Cannonball House next to Edinburgh Castle's esplanade has been transformed into a sophisticated restaurant (and whisky bar) where the Contini family work their Italian magic on Scottish classics to produce dishes such as haggis balls with spiced pickled turnip and whisky marmalade, and lobster with wild garlic and lemon butter.

Mother India's Cafe INDIAN ££
(Map p52; ☑0131-524 9801; www.motherindia.co.uk; 3-5 Infirmary St; dishes £4-6; ⊙noon-2pm & 5-10.30pm Mon-Wed, noon-11pm Thu-Sun; ☎♿;

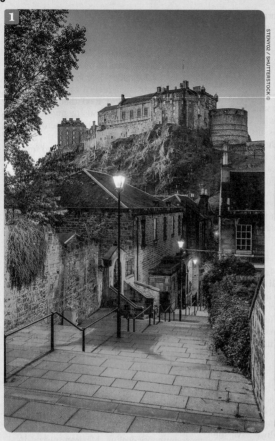

STENY02 / SHUTTERSTOCK ©

ANTON_IVANOV / SHUTTERSTOCK ©

STUDIOSJ / SHUTTERSTOCK ©

3

Edinburgh Castle (p47)
ce used as a royal residence, a prison and an
ny base, the castle now houses the Scottish
wn jewels and the Stone of Destiny.

**National Museum of Scotland,
Edinburgh (p58)**
hibits tracing the history of Scotland are divided
ween a striking modern museum building and a
e example of Victorian architecture.

**View of Edinburgh from Calton
Hill (p66)**
ted with historic monuments, Calton Hill offers
noramic views of Edinburgh's highlights.

Balmoral Hotel & Princes St (p77)
e clock on the Balmoral Hotel is traditionally
ee minutes fast so that you don't miss your
n.

🚌 all South Bridge buses) A simple concept pioneered in Glasgow has captured hearts and minds – and stomachs – here in Edinburgh: Indian food served in tapas-size portions, so that you can sample a greater variety of deliciously different dishes without busting a gut. Hugely popular, so book a table to avoid disappointment.

Devil's Advocate
PUB FOOD ££

(Map p52; 📞0131-225 4465; http://devilsadvocate edinburgh.co.uk; 9 Advocates Close; mains £14-24; ⏰food served noon-4pm & 5-10pm; 🔊; 🚌6, 23, 27, 41, 42) No trip to Edinburgh is complete without exploring the narrow closes (alleys) that lead off the Royal Mile. Lucky you if your explorations lead to this cosy split-level pub-restaurant set in a converted Victorian pump house, with a menu of top-quality pub grub – the burgers are among the best in town. It gets rammed on weekends, so book a table.

Maison Bleue
FRENCH ££

(Map p52; 📞0131-226 1900; http://maisonbleu erestaurant.com; 36-38 Victoria St; mains £10-27; ⏰noon-10pm Sun-Thu, to 11pm Fri & Sat; 🔊; 🚌2, 23, 27, 41, 42) Eating here is a comfortably laid-back affair – the candlelit ground-floor dining room has chunky wooden tables and modern art on bare stone walls; upstairs is brighter and more cafe-like. The menu lists *bouchées* (French for 'mouthfuls') – starter-size helpings of which you can have as many or as few as you wish – and the food is an eclectic mix of French and North African influences.

Amber
SCOTTISH ££

(Map p52; 📞0131-477 8477; www.amber-restau rant.co.uk; 354 Castlehill; mains £13-22; ⏰noon-8.30pm Sun-Thu, to 9pm Fri & Sat; 🔊🍴; 🚌23, 27, 41, 42) You've got to love a place where the waiter greets you with the words, 'I'll be your whisky adviser for this evening'. Located in the Scotch Whisky Experience (p51), this whisky-themed restaurant manages to avoid the tourist clichés and creates genuinely interesting and flavoursome dishes using top Scottish produce, with a suggested whisky pairing for each dish.

Petit Paris
FRENCH ££

(Map p52; 📞0131-226 2442; www.petitparis -restaurant.co.uk; 38-40 Grassmarket; mains £14-19; ⏰noon-3pm & 5.30-10pm; 🚌2) Like the name says, this is a little piece of Paris, complete with chequered tablecloths, friendly waiters and good-value grub – the *moules-*

frites (mussels and chips) are excellent. There's a lunch/pre-theatre deal (noon to 3pm and 5.30pm to 7pm) offering two courses for £12.90.

Maxie's Bistro
BISTRO ££

(Map p52; 📞0131-226 7770; www.maxiesbistro. com; 5b Johnston Tce; mains £9-22; ⏰11am-11pm; 🔊🍴; 🚌23, 27, 41, 42) This candlelit bistro, with its cushion-lined nooks set amid stone walls and wooden beams, is a pleasant setting for a cosy dinner, but at summer lunchtimes people queue for the outdoor tables on the terrace overlooking Victoria St. The food is dependable, ranging from pasta, steaks and stir-fries to seafood platters and daily specials. Best to book, especially in summer.

⭐ Grain Store
SCOTTISH ££££

(Map p52; 📞0131-225 7635; www.grainstore -restaurant.co.uk; 30 Victoria St; mains £20-32; ⏰noon-2.30pm & 6-9.45pm Mon-Sat, 6pm-9.30pm Sun; 🚌2, 23, 27, 41, 42) An atmospheric upstairs dining room on picturesque Victoria St, the Grain Store has a well-earned reputation for serving the finest Scottish produce, perfectly prepared – from wood pigeon with leek and hickory risotto to seared monkfish with scallop ravioli and mustard beurre blanc. The three-course lunch for £16 is good value.

⭐ Ondine
SEAFOOD £££

(Map p52; 📞0131-226 1888; www.ondinerestau rant.co.uk; 2 George IV Bridge; mains £17-40, 2-/3-course lunch £25/30; ⏰noon-3pm & 5.30-10pm Mon-Sat; 🔊; 🚌23, 27, 41, 42) Ondine is one of Edinburgh's finest seafood restaurants, with a menu based on sustainably sourced fish. Take a seat at the curved Oyster Bar and tuck into oysters Kilpatrick, smoked haddock chowder, lobster thermidor, a roast shellfish platter or just good old haddock and chips (with minted pea purée, just to keep things posh).

Wedgwood
SCOTTISH £££

(Map p52; 📞0131-558 8737; www.wedgwoodthe restaurant.co.uk; 267 Canongate; mains £17-23, 2-/3-course lunch £15/19; ⏰noon-3pm & 6-10pm; 🚌35) 🌿 Fine food without the fuss is the motto at this friendly, unpretentious restaurant. Scottish produce is served with an inventive flair in dishes such as venison mince pie with black pudding mash and onion puree, or sesame and soy-glazed sea trout with crisped scallop roe, while the menu includes foraged wild salad leaves collected by the chef himself.

Witchery by the Castle   SCOTTISH, FRENCH £££
(Map p52; ☑ 0131-225 5613; www.thewitchery.
com; Castlehill; mains £23-45, 2-course lunch £20;
⊙ noon-11.30pm; ☑ 23, 27, 41, 42) Set in a merchant's town house dating from 1595, the
Witchery is a candlelit corner of antique
splendour with oak-panelled walls, low ceilings, opulent wall hangings and red leather
upholstery; stairs lead down to a second,
even more romantic, dining room called the
Secret Garden. The menu ranges from oysters to Aberdeen Angus steak and the wine
list runs to almost 1000 bins.

Tower   SCOTTISH £££
(Map p52; ☑ 0131-225 3003; www.tower-restau
rant.com; National Museum of Scotland, Chambers
St; mains £19-40, 2-course lunch & pre-theatre
menu £19; ⊙ 10am-11pm; ☑ 2, 23, 27, 41, 42, 45)
Chic and sleek, with a great view of the
castle, Tower is perched in a turret atop
the National Museum of Scotland building.
A star-studded guest list of celebrities has
enjoyed its menu of quality Scottish food,
simply prepared – try half a dozen oysters
followed by roast loin of venison. Afternoon
tea (£20) is served from 2.30pm to 5.30pm.

✖ Holyrood & Arthur's Seat

★Rhubarb   SCOTTISH £££
(☑ 0131-225 1333; Prestonfield, Priestfield Rd;
mains £18-35; ⊙ noon-2pm Mon-Sat, 12.30-3pm
Sun, 6-10pm daily; **P**) Set in the splendid
17th-century Prestonfield hotel (p76),
Rhubarb is a feast for the eyes as well as the
taste buds. The over-the-top decor of rich
reds set off with black and gold and the sen-
suous surfaces – damask, brocade, marble,
gilded leather – that make you want to touch
everything are matched by the intense flavours and rich textures of the modern Scottish cuisine.

Take your postprandial coffee and bran-
dy upstairs to the sumptuous fireside sofas
in the Tapestry and Leather rooms. A two-
course lunch menu is available for £20.

✖ New Town

Broughton Deli   CAFE £
(Map p48; ☑ 0131-558 7111; www.broughton-deli.
co.uk; 7 Barony St; mains £6-10; ⊙ 8am-7pm
Mon-Fri, 9am-6pm Sat, 10am-5pm Sun; 🐾🖊👶;
☑ 8) Mismatched cafe tables and chairs in
a bright back room behind the deli counter
provide an attractive setting for brunch just
off the main drag of the New Town's bohemian Broughton St. Brunch is served till

2pm weekdays or 3pm on weekends; choose
from American-style pancakes, veggie fry-
ups, and poached eggs on toast with organic
smoked salmon.

★Gardener's Cottage   SCOTTISH ££
(Map p64; ☑ 0131-558 1221; www.thegardeners
cottage.co; 1 Royal Terrace Gardens, London Rd;
lunch mains £16-17, dinner set menu £40; ⊙ noon-
2pm & 5-10pm Mon & Wed-Fri, 10am-2pm & 5-10pm
Sat & Sun; 🔊 all London Rd buses) ⏩ This country cottage in the heart of the city, bedecked
with flowers and fairy lights, offers one of
Edinburgh's most interesting dining experiences – two tiny rooms with communal
tables made of salvaged timber, and a menu
based on fresh local produce (most of the
vegetables and fruit are grown in a local
organic garden). Bookings essential; brunch
served at weekends.

★Dogs   BRITISH ££
(Map p64; ☑ 0131-220 1208; www.thedogsonline.
co.uk; 110 Hanover St; mains lunch £6, dinner £9-
22; ⊙ noon-2.30pm & 6-10pm Mon-Fri, noon-4pm
& 6-10pm Sat & Sun; 🖊; ☑ 23, 27) ⏩ One of
the coolest tables in town, this bistro-style
place uses cheaper cuts of meat and less
well-known, more sustainable species of
fish to create hearty, no-nonsense dishes
such as devilled kidneys on toast; shredded
lamb with skirlie (fried oatmeal and onion),
pomegranate seeds and almonds; and beetroot and horseradish spelt risotto.

★Contini   ITALIAN ££
(Map p64; ☑ 0131-225 1550; www.contini.com/
contini-ristorante; 103 George St; mains £11-30;
⊙ 7.30am-11pm Mon-Fri, 9am-midnight Sat, 9am-
11pm Sun; 🐾🖊👶; 🔊 all Princes St buses) A palatial Georgian banking hall enlivened by
fuchsia-pink banners and lampshades is
home to this lively, child-friendly Italian bar
and restaurant, where the emphasis is on
fresh, authentic ingredients (produce import-
ed weekly from Milan; homemade bread and
pasta) and uncomplicated enjoyment of food.

★Urban Angel   CAFE ££
(Map p64; ☑ 0131-225 6215; www.urban-angel.
co.uk; 121 Hanover St; mains £6-13; ⊙ 8am-5pm
Mon-Fri, 9am-5pm Sat & Sun; 🖊👶; ☑ 23, 27) ⏩
A wholesome deli that puts the emphasis on
fair-trade, organic and locally sourced produce, Urban Angel is also a delightfully informal cafe-bistro that serves all-day brunch
(porridge with honey, French toast, eggs
Benedict), tapas and a wide range of light,
snacky meals.

Hadrian's Brasserie SCOTTISH, FRENCH ££
(Map p64; ☎0131-557 5000; www.roccofortehotels.com; Balmoral Hotel, 1 Princes St; mains £15-22; ⏲7-10.30am, noon-2.30pm & 5.30-10pm Mon-Fri, 7.30-11am & 12.30-10.30pm Sat & Sun; 👪; 🚌all Princes St buses) The brasserie at the Balmoral Hotel (p77) has a 1930s art-deco feel, with pale-green walls, dark-wood furniture, and waiters dressed in white aprons and black waistcoats. The menu includes posh versions of popular dishes such as fish and chips, haggis with whisky sauce, and rump steak with Café de Paris sauce.

Seasons SCANDINAVIAN ££
(Map p48; ☎0131-466 9851; www.seasonstasting.co.uk; 36 Broughton St; 5-course dinner £35; ⏲noon-2.30pm & 5-9.30pm Wed-Sun; 📶; 🚌8) The Swedish chef at Seasons creates a dynamic fusion of Scottish and Scandinavian influences, trading in the traditional á la carte menu for a set list of seasonal produce from which your meal will be created (you can point out any you don't fancy), then beautifully garnished with foraged ingredients and edible flowers.

Bon Vivant BISTRO ££
(Map p64; ☎0131-225 3275; http://bonvivantedinburgh.co.uk; 55 Thistle St; mains £9-15; ⏲noon-1pm; 📶; 🚌23, 27) Candlelight reflected in the warm glow of polished wood makes for an intimate atmosphere in this New Town favourite. The food is superb value for this part of town, offering a range of tapas-style 'bites' as well as normal main courses, with a changing menu of seasonal, locally sourced dishes such as tempura of cod with chorizo, puy lentils and garlic cream.

Scottish Cafe & Restaurant SCOTTISH ££
(Map p64; ☎0131-226 6524; www.thescottishcafeandrestaurant.com; The Mound; mains £13-15; ⏲9am-5.30pm Fri-Wed, to 7pm Thu; 📶👪; 🚌Princes St) 🍃 This appealing modern restaurant (part of the Scottish National Gallery complex) has picture windows providing a view along Princes Street Gardens. Try traditional Scottish dishes such as Cullen skink (smoked haddock soup) and leek and potato soup, or seasonal, sustainably sourced produce including smoked salmon and trout, free-range chicken and pork.

Café Marlayne FRENCH ££
(Map p64; ☎0131-226 2230; www.cafemarlayne.com; 76 Thistle St; mains lunch £8-10, dinner £15-18; ⏲noon-10pm; 🚌24, 29, 42) All weathered wood and candlelit tables, Café Marlayne is a cosy nook offering French and Mediterranean cooking – think sea bream with ratatouille and pea shoots salad, stuffed rabbit wrapped in Parma ham, *boudin noir* (black pudding) with bacon and mustard dressing – at very reasonable prices. Bookings recommended.

L'Escargot Bleu FRENCH ££
(Map p48; ☎0131-557 1600; www.lescargotbleu.co.uk; 56 Broughton St; mains £13-19; ⏲noon-2.30pm & 5.30-10pm Mon-Thu, noon-3pm & 5.30-10.30pm Fri & Sat; 👪; 🚌8) As with its sister restaurant, **L'Escargot Blanc** (Map p48; ☎0131-226 1890; www.lescargotblanc.co.uk; 17 Queensferry St; 3-course lunch/dinner £13.90/25; ⏲noon-2.30pm & 5.30-10pm Mon-Thu, noon-3pm & 5.30-10.30pm Fri & Sat; 👪; 🚌19, 36, 37, 41, 47) 🍃 on Queensferry St, this cute little bistro is as Gallic as garlic but makes fine use of quality Scottish produce – the French-speaking staff will lead you knowledgeably through a menu that includes authentic Savoyard *tartiflette, quenelle* of pike with lobster sauce, and pigs' cheeks braised in red wine. Two-course lunch/early-bird menu £12.90.

Fishers in the City SEAFOOD ££
(Map p64; ☎0131-225 5109; www.fishersbistros.co.uk; 58 Thistle St; mains £17-23; ⏲noon-10.30pm Mon-Sat, 12.30-10.30pm Sun; 📶👪; 🚌13, 19, 37, 41) 🍃 This more sophisticated version of the famous Fishers Bistro (p87) in Leith, with granite-topped tables, split-level dining area and nautical theme, specialises in superior Scottish seafood – the knowledgeable staff serve up plump and succulent oysters, meltingly sweet scallops, and sea bass that's been grilled to perfection.

21212 FRENCH £££
(Map p64; ☎0131-523 1030; www.21212restaurant.co.uk; 3 Royal Tce; 3-course lunch/dinner £32/55; ⏲noon-1.45pm & 7-9pm Tue-Sat; 📶; 🚌all London Rd buses) A grand Georgian town house on the side of Calton Hill is the elegant setting for one of Edinburgh's Michelin stars. Divine decor by Timorous Beasties and Ralph Lauren provide the backdrop to an exquisitely prepared five-course dinner (£70 a head) that changes weekly and features fresh, seasonal delights such as baby turbot poached in olive oil with saffron pancake, and lamb and merguez kebab with banana and cucumber confit.

Number One SCOTTISH £££
(Map p64; ☎0131-557 6727; www.restaurantnumberone.com; Balmoral Hotel, 1 Princes St; 3-course dinner £75; ⏲6.30-10pm Mon-Thu,

6-10pm Fri-Sun; 🕿; 🚌all Princes St buses) This is the stylish and sophisticated chatelaine of Edinburgh's city-centre restaurants, all gold-and-velvet elegance with a Michelin star sparkling on her tiara. The food is top-notch modern Scottish (a seven-/10-course tasting menu costs £85/110 per person) and the service is just on the right side of fawning.

Forth Floor Restaurant & Brasserie
SCOTTISH £££

(Map p64; 🕿0131-524 8350; www.harveynichols.com; 30-34 St Andrew Sq; mains £18-25; ⊗noon-3pm Mon-Fri, to 3.30pm Sat & Sun, 6-10pm Tue-Sat; 🚇St Andrew Sq) The in-store restaurant at Harvey Nichols (p94) has floor-to-ceiling windows overlooking St Andrew Sq, making it a great place to enjoy sunset views across the New Town rooftops. The food has as much

designer chic as the surroundings, while the less formal brasserie offers simpler dishes and also serves Sunday brunch (11am to 5pm).

✖ West End & Dean Village

Cafe Milk
CAFE £

(Map p48; 🕿0131-629 6022; www.cafemilk.co.uk; 232 Morrison St; mains £4-7; ⊗7.30am-4pm Mon-Fri, 8am-4pm Sat, 8am-3pm Sun; 🕿🖉; 🚇Haymarket) 🖉 This is fast food with a conscience – natural, nutritious, locally sourced and freshly prepared, from organic porridge to courgette, lemon and feta fritters, to North Indian dhal with rice or flatbread. Take away, or sit in and soak up the retro vibe with old Formica tables, battered school benches, enamel plates and junk-shop cutlery stacked in golden syrup tins.

TOP FIVE VEGETARIAN RESTAURANTS

Many Edinburgh restaurants offer vegetarian options on the menu – some good, some bad, some indifferent. The places listed here are all 100% veggie and fall into the 'good' category.

David Bann (Map p52; 🕿0131-556 5888; www.davidbann.com; 56-58 St Mary's St; mains £11-13; ⊗noon-10pm Mon-Fri, 11am-10pm Sat & Sun; 🖉; 🚌35) If you want to convince a carnivorous friend that cuisine à la veg can be as tasty and inventive as a meat-muncher's menu, take them to David Bann's stylish restaurant – dishes such as Thai fritter of broccoli and smoked tofu, and aubergine, chickpea and cashew kofta are guaranteed to win converts.

Henderson's (Map p64; 🕿0131-225 2131; www.hendersonsofedinburgh.co.uk; 94 Hanover St; mains £6-12; ⊗8am-9pm Mon-Sat, 10.30am-4pm Sun; 🕿🖉🚹; 🚌23, 27) Established in 1962, Henderson's is the grandmother of Edinburgh's vegetarian restaurants. The food is mostly organic and guaranteed GM-free, and special dietary requirements can be catered for. The place still has something of a 1970s canteen feel to it (in a good, nostalgic way), and the daily salads and hot dishes are as popular as ever.

Right around the corner on Thistle St is **Henderson's Vegan**, a new and 100% vegan branch.

Kalpna (Map p48; 🕿0131-667 9890; www.kalpnarestaurant.com; 2-3 St Patrick Sq; mains £6-11; ⊗noon-2pm & 5.30-9.30pm Mon-Sat year-round, 6pm-10.30pm Sun May-Sep; 🖉; 🚌all Newington buses) A long-standing Edinburgh favourite, Kalpna is one of the best Indian restaurants in the country, vegetarian or otherwise. The cuisine is mostly Gujarati, with a smattering of dishes from other parts of India. The all-you-can-eat lunch buffet (£8) is superb value.

Forest Café (Map p48; 🕿0131-229 4922; http://blog.theforest.org.uk/cafe; 141 Lauriston Pl; mains £3-6; ⊗10am-11pm; 🕿🖉🚹; 🚌all Tollcross buses) A chilled-out, colourful and comfortably scuffed-around-the-edges antidote to squeaky-clean espresso bars, this volunteer-run, not-for-profit art space and cafe serves up humongous helpings of hearty vegetarian and vegan fodder, ranging from nachos to falafel wraps.

Mosque Kitchen (Map p52; www.mosquekitchen.com; 31 Nicolson Sq; mains £4-7; ⊗11.30am-10pm, closed 12.50-1.50pm Fri; 🖉🚹; 🚌all South Bridge buses) Expect shared tables and disposable plates, but this is the place to go for cheap, authentic and delicious homemade curries, kebabs, pakoras and naan bread, all washed down with lassi or mango juice. Caters to Edinburgh's Central Mosque, but welcomes all – local students have taken to it big time. No alcohol.

Kanpai Sushi JAPANESE ££
(Map p52; ☑ 0131-228 1602; www.kanpaisushi.
co.uk; 8-10 Grindlay St; mains £9-15, sushi per piece
£4-10; ⏱ noon-2.30pm & 5-10.30pm Tue-Sun; 🔲 all
Lothian Rd buses) What is probably Edinburgh's
best sushi restaurant impresses with its minimalist interior, fresh, top-quality fish and
elegantly presented dishes – the squid tempura comes in a delicate woven basket, while
the sashimi combo is presented as a flower
arrangement in an ice-filled stoneware bowl.

★**Timberyard** SCOTTISH £££
(Map p52; ☑ 0131-221 1222; www.timberyard.co;
10 Lady Lawson St; 4-course lunch or dinner £55;
⏱ noon-2pm & 5.30-9.30pm Tue-Sat; 🛜🍴; 🔲 2,
35) 🌿 Ancient worn floorboards, cast-iron

pillars, exposed joists, and tables made from
slabs of old mahogany create a rustic, retro
atmosphere in this slow-food restaurant
where the accent is on locally sourced produce from artisan growers and foragers.
Typical dishes include seared scallop with
apple, Jerusalem artichoke and sorrel; and
juniper-smoked pigeon with wild garlic
flowers and beetroot.

★**Castle Terrace** SCOTTISH £££
(Map p52; ☑ 0131-229 1222; www.castleterrace
restaurant.com; 33-35 Castle Tce; 3-course lunch/
dinner £29.50/65; ⏱ noon-2.15pm & 6.30-10pm
Tue-Sat; 🔲2) 🌿 It was little more than a year
after opening in 2010 that Castle Terrace was
awarded a Michelin star under chef-patron

TOP FIVE EDINBURGH CAFES

Cafe culture is firmly ensconced in Edinburgh, and it is as easy to get your daily caffeine
fix here as it is in New York or Paris. Most cafes offer some kind of food, from cakes and
sandwiches to full-on meals.

Loudon's Café & Bakery (Map p48; www.loudons-cafe.co.uk; 94b Fountainbridge; mains
£5-10; ⏱8am-5pm; 🛜🍴; 🔲1, 34, 35) A cafe that bakes its own organic bread and cakes
on the premises, ethically sourced coffee, daily and weekend newspapers scattered
about, even some outdoor tables – what's not to like? All-day brunch (8am to 3pm)
served at weekends includes eggs Benedict, warm spiced quinoa with dried fruit, and
specials such as blueberry pancakes with fruit salad.

Brew Lab (Map p52; ☑ 0131-662 8963; www.brewlabcoffee.co.uk; 6-8 South College St;
mains £4-5; ⏱8am-6pm Mon-Fri, 9am-6pm Sat & Sun; 🛜; 🔲all South Bridge buses) Students
with iPads lolling in armchairs, sipping carefully crafted espressos amid artfully distressed brick and plaster, recycled school gym flooring, old workshop benches and lab
stools...this is coffee nerd heaven. There's good food too, with hearty soups and crusty
baguette sandwiches. In summer, try their refreshing cold brew coffee.

Peter's Yard (Map p48; ☑ 0131-228 5876; www.petersyard.com; 27 Simpson Loan;
mains £5-9; ⏱7.30am-6pm Mon-Fri, 9am-6pm Sat & Sun; 🍴; 🔲23, 27, 35, 45, 47) This
Swedish-style coffee house produces its own home-baked breads, from sourdough to
focaccia, which form the basis of lunchtime sandwiches with fillings such as roast beef
with beetroot and caper salad, and roast butternut squash with sunblush tomato pesto.
Breakfast (served till noon) can be a basket of breads with conserves and cheeses, or
yoghurt with granola and fruit.

Social Bite (Map p64; ☑ 0131-220 8206; http://social-bite.co.uk; 131 Rose St; mains £4-8;
⏱7am-3pm Mon-Fri; 🛜; 🔲all Princes St buses) Describing its mission as 'good food for a
good cause', this cafe is a social enterprise set up to support the homeless (25% of em-
ployees are from a homeless background). The food – from freshly prepared sandwiches
to hot lunches including Jamaican chicken, and haggis, neeps and tatties – is delicious,
and you can donate a 'suspended item' to be claimed by a homeless person.

Valvona & Crolla Caffé Bar (Map p48; ☑ 0131-556 6066; www.valvonacrolla.co.uk; 19
Elm Row, Leith Walk; mains £10-15; ⏱8.30am-5.30pm Mon-Thu, 8am-6pm Fri & Sat, 10.30am-
4.30pm Sun; 🛜🍴; 🔲all Leith Walk buses) Try breakfast (served till 11.30am) with an Italian
flavour – full *paesano* (meat) or *verdure* (veggie) fry-ups, or deliciously light and crisp
panettone in *carrozza* (sweet brioche dipped in egg and fried) – or choose from almond
croissants, muesli, yoghurt and fruit, freshly squeezed orange juice and perfect Italian
coffee. There's also a tasty lunch menu (noon to 3pm) of classic Italian dishes.

Dominic Jack. The menu is seasonal and applies sharply whetted Parisian skills to the finest of local produce, be it Ayrshire pork, Aberdeenshire lamb or Newhaven crab – even the cheese in the sauces is Scottish.

✗ Stockbridge

Scran & Scallie   GASTROPUB ££
(Map p48; ☑0131-332 6281; https://scranand scallie.com; 1 Comely Bank Rd; mains £10-22; ⊙noon-3pm & 6-10pm Mon-Fri, 8.30-11am & noon-10pm Sat & Sun; ��⌑⌗; ⌑24, 29, 42) Established by the Michelin-starred team responsible for the Kitchin and Castle Terrace (p86), this laid-back gastropub adds a modern chef's touch to old-time dishes such as chicken liver parfait, ham hock terrine, and steak pie. There's also quality versions of classic pub grub such as burgers, seafood pie, and fish and chips, and veggie options that include a spelt and lentil burger.

✗ South Edinburgh

★First Coast   SCOTTISH ££
(Map p48; ☑0131-313 4404; www.first-coast. co.uk; 97-101 Dalry Rd; mains £12-20; ⊙noon-2pm & 5-11pm Mon-Sat; ⓖ⌑⌗; ⌑2, 3, 4, 25, 33, 44) This popular neighbourhood bistro has a striking main dining area with sea-blue wood panelling and stripped stonework, and a short and simple menu offering hearty comfort food such as fish with creamy mash, brown shrimp and garlic butter, or leek and bread pudding, creamed leeks and braised fennel. Lunchtime and early evening there's an excellent two-course meal for £12.50.

★Locanda de Gusti   ITALIAN ££
(Map p48; ☑0131-346 8800; www.locandade gusti.com; 102 Dalry Rd; mains £9-26; ⊙5.30-10pm Mon-Sat, 12.30-2.15pm Thu-Sat; ⌗; ⌑2, 3, 4, 25, 33, 44) This bustling family bistro, loud with the buzz of conversation and the clink of glasses and cutlery, is no ordinary Italian but a little corner of Naples complete with hearty Neapolitan home cooking by friendly head chef Rosario. The food ranges from light and tasty ravioli tossed with butter and sage to delicious platters of grilled seafood.

★Aizle   SCOTTISH ££
(Map p48; ☑0131-662 9349; http://aizle.co.uk; 107-109 St Leonard's St; 5-course dinner £45; ⊙6-9.30pm Wed, Thu & Sun, 5-9.30pm Fri & Sat; ⓖ; ⌑14) If you're the sort who has trouble deciding what to eat, Aizle will do it for you (the name is an old Scots word for 'spark' or

'ember'). There's no menu, just a five-course dinner conjured from a monthly 'harvest' of the finest and freshest of local produce (listed on a blackboard), and presented beautifully – art on a plate.

✗ Leith

★Fishers Bistro   SEAFOOD ££
(☑0131-554 5666; www.fishersbistros.co.uk; 1 The Shore; mains £12-25; ⊙noon-10.30pm Mon-Sat, 12.30-10.30pm Sun; ⓖ⌑⌗; ⌑16, 22, 35, 36) This cosy little restaurant, tucked beneath a 17th-century signal tower, is one of the city's best seafood places. The menu ranges widely in price, from cheaper dishes such as classic fish cakes with lemon and chive mayonnaise to more expensive delights such as North Berwick lobster thermidor.

Leith Chop House   STEAK ££
(☑0131-629 1919; www.chophousesteak.co.uk; 102 Constitution St; mains £10-26; ⊙noon-3pm & 5-10pm Mon-Fri, 10am-11pm Sat & Sun; ⓖ; ⌑12, 16) A modern take on the old-fashioned steakhouse, this 'bar and butchery' combines slick designer decor (the ceramic brick tiles are a nod to traditional butcher shops) with a meaty menu of the best Scottish beef, dry-aged for at least 35 days and char-grilled to perfection. Sauces include bone marrow gravy, and Argentinian *chimmichurri*. Cool cocktails too.

Shore   SEAFOOD ££
(☑0131-553 5080; www.fishersrestaurants.co.uk; 3-4 The Shore; mains £12-26; ⊙noon-10.30pm Mon-Sat, 12.30-10.30pm Sun; ⓖ⌗; ⌑16, 22, 35, 36) The atmospheric dining room in the popular Shore pub is a haven of wood-panelled peace, with old photographs, nautical knick-knacks, fresh flowers and an open fire adding to the romantic theme. The menu changes regularly and specialises in fresh Scottish seafood, beef, pork and game.

★The Kitchin   SCOTTISH £££
(☑0131-555 1755; http://thekitchin.com/; 78 Commercial Quay; 3-course lunch/dinner £30/70; ⊙12.15-2.30pm & 6.30-10pm Tue-Thu, to 10.30pm Fri & Sat; ⌗; ⌑16, 22, 35, 36) Fresh, seasonal, locally sourced Scottish produce is the philosophy that has won a Michelin star for this elegant but unpretentious restaurant. The menu moves with the seasons, of course, so expect fresh salads in summer and game in winter, and shellfish dishes such as baked scallops with white wine, vermouth and herb sauce when there's an 'r' in the month.

Drinking & Nightlife

Edinburgh has always been a drinker's city. It has more than 700 pubs – more per square mile than any other UK city – and they are as varied and full of character as the people who drink in them, from Victorian palaces to stylish pre-club bars, and from real-ale howffs to trendy cocktail lounges.

 ## Old Town

The pubs in the Grassmarket have outdoor tables on sunny summer afternoons, but in the evenings are favoured by boozed-up lads on the pull, so steer clear if that's not your thing. The Cowgate – the Grassmarket's extension to the east – is Edinburgh's clubland.

 ★Bow Bar PUB

(Map p52; www.thebowbar.co.uk; 80 West Bow; ⊘noon-midnight Mon-Sat, to 11.30pm Sun; 🐾; 🚍2, 23, 27, 41, 42) One of the city's best traditional-style pubs (it's not as old as it looks), serving a range of excellent real ales, Scottish craft gins and a vast selection of malt whiskies, the Bow Bar often has standing-room only on Friday and Saturday evenings.

★Cabaret Voltaire CLUB

(Map p52; www.thecabaretvoltaire.com; 36-38 Blair St; ⊘5pm-3am Mon-Thu, noon-3am Fri-Sun; 🐾; 🚍all South Bridge buses) An atmospheric warren of stone-lined vaults houses this self-consciously 'alternative' club, which eschews huge dance floors and egotistical DJ worship in favour of a 'creative crucible' hosting an eclectic mix of DJs, live acts, comedy, theatre, visual arts and the spoken word. Well worth a look.

Bongo Club CLUB

(Map p52; www.thebongoclub.co.uk; 66 Cowgate; admission free-£6; ⊘11pm-3am Tue & Thu, 7pm-3am Fri-Sun; 🐾; 🚍2) Owned by a local arts charity, the weird and wonderful Bongo Club boasts a long history of hosting everything from wild club nights and local bands to performance art and kids' comedy shows, and is open as a cafe and exhibition space during the day.

OX 184 BAR

(Map p52; ☑0131-226 1645; www.ox184.co.uk; 184-186 Cowgate; ⊘11am-3am; 🐾; 🚍35, 45) A big, booming industrial-chic bar with more than 100 whiskies on offer (Scotch, Irish, American and Japanese), as well as a fine selection of real ales and craft beers, the OX's standout feature is a huge wood-fired grill on

which burgers, ribs and steaks are constantly sizzling. DJs and live bands every night .

Jolly Judge PUB

(Map p52; www.jollyjudge.co.uk; 7a James Ct; ⊘noon-11pm Mon-Thu, to midnight Fri & Sat, 12.30-11pm Sun; 🐾; 🚍23, 27, 41, 42) A snug little howff tucked away down a close, the Judge exudes a cosy 17th-century atmosphere (low, timber-beamed painted ceilings) and has the added attraction of a cheering open fire in cold weather. No music or gaming machines, just the buzz of conversation.

White Hart Inn PUB

(Map p52; ☑0131-226 2806; www.whitehart-edinburgh.co.uk; 34 Grassmarket; ⊘11am-11pm Mon-Fri, to 12.30am Sat & Sun; 🚍2) A brass plaque outside this pub proclaims: 'In the White Hart Inn Robert Burns stayed during his last visit to Edinburgh, 1791.' Claiming to be the city's oldest pub in continuous use (since 1516), it also hosted William Wordsworth in 1803. Not surprisingly, it's a traditional, cosy, low-raftered place. It has folk/acoustic music sessions seven nights a week.

Holyrood 9A PUB

(Map p52; www.theholyrood.co.uk; 9a Holyrood Rd; ⊘9am-midnight Sun-Thu, to 1am Fri & Sat; 🐾; 🚍36) Candlelight flickering off hectares of polished wood creates an atmospheric setting for this superb real-ale bar, with more than 20 taps pouring craft beers from all corners of the country and, indeed, the globe. If you're peckish, it serves excellent gourmet burgers too.

BrewDog BAR

(Map p52; www.brewdog.com; 143 Cowgate; ⊘noon-1am Mon-Sat, 12.30pm-1am Sun; 🐾; 🚍35, 45) The Edinburgh outpost of Scotland's self-styled 'punk brewery', BrewDog stands out among the sticky-floored dives that line the Cowgate, with its polished concrete bar and cool, industrial-chic decor. As well as its own highly rated beers, there's a choice of guest real ales, and – a sign of a great trad pub – coat hooks under the edge of the bar.

Liquid Room CLUB

(Map p52; www.liquidroom.com; 9c Victoria St; admission free-£20; ⊘live music from 7pm, club 10.30pm-3am Wed, Fri & Sat; 🚍23, 27, 41, 42) Set in a subterranean vault deep beneath Victoria St, the Liquid Room is a superb club venue with a thundering sound system. There are regular club nights on Wednesday, Friday and Saturday, as well as live bands.

TOP FIVE TRADITONAL PUBS

Bennet's Bar (Map p48; ☑ 0131-229 5143; www.bennetsbaredinburgh.co.uk; 8 Leven St; ⊙ 11am-1am; ᰥ all Tollcross buses) Situated beside the King's Theatre, Bennet's has managed to hang on to almost all of its beautiful Victorian fittings, from the leaded stained-glass windows and ornate mirrors to the wooden gantry and the brass water taps on the bar (for your whisky – there are over 100 malts from which to choose).

Café Royal Circle Bar (Map p64; www.caferoyaledinburgh.co.uk; 17 West Register St; ⊙ 11am-11pm Mon-Wed, to midnight Thu, to 1am Fri & Sat, 12.30-11pm Sun; ☎; ᰥ Princes St) Perhaps *the* classic Edinburgh pub, the Café Royal's main claims to fame are its magnificent oval bar and its Doulton tile portraits of famous Victorian inventors. Sit at the bar or claim one of the cosy leather booths beneath the stained-glass windows, and choose from the seven real ales on tap.

Athletic Arms (Diggers; Map p48; ☑ 0131-337 3822; 1-3 Angle Park Tce; ⊙ 11am-1am Mon-Sat, 12.30pm-1am Sun; ᰥ 1, 34, 35) Nicknamed for the cemetery across the street – gravediggers used to nip in and slake their thirst here – the Diggers dates from the 1890s. It's still staunchly traditional – the decor has barely changed in 100 years – and is a real-ale drinker's mecca, serving locally brewed 80-shilling ale. Packed to the gills with football and rugby fans on match days.

Abbotsford (Map p64; ☑ 0131-225 5276; www.theabbotsford.com; 3 Rose St; ⊙ 11am-11pm Mon-Thu, to midnight Fri & Sat, 12.30-11pm Sun; ☎; ᰥ all Princes St buses) One of the few pubs in Rose St that has retained its Edwardian splendour, the Abbotsford has long been a hang-out for writers, actors, journalists and media people, and has many loyal regulars. Dating from 1902, and named after Sir Walter Scott's country house, the pub's centrepiece is a splendid mahogany island bar. Good selection of real ales.

Sheep Heid Inn (www.thesheepheidedinburgh.co.uk; 43-45 The Causeway; ⊙ 11am-11pm Mon-Thu, to midnight Fri & Sat, noon-11pm Sun; ᰥ; ᰥ 42) Possibly the oldest inn in Edinburgh (with a licence dating back to 1360) the Sheep Heid feels more like a country pub than an Edinburgh bar. Set in the semirural shadow of Arthur's Seat, it's famous for its 19th-century skittles alley and the lovely little beer garden.

Dragonfly　　　　　　COCKTAIL BAR

(Map p52; ☑ 0131-228 4543; www.dragonfly cocktailbar.com; 52 West Port; ⊙ 4pm-1am; ☎; ᰥ 2) A super-stylish lounge bar with a Raffles of Singapore vibe – it's all crystal chandeliers, polished wood and oriental art – Dragonfly has won rave reviews both for its innovative cocktails and its designer decor. Grab a seat in the neat little mezzanine, from where you can look down on the bar as the Singapore Slings are being slung.

🍺 New Town

Oxford Bar　　　　　　　　　PUB

(Map p64; ☑ 0131-539 7119; www.oxfordbar.co.uk; 8 Young St; ⊙ 11am-midnight Mon-Sat, 12.30-11pm Sun; ☎; ᰥ 19, 36, 37, 41, 47) The Oxford is that rarest of things: a real pub for real people, with no 'theme', no music, no frills and no pretensions. 'The Ox' has been immortalised by Ian Rankin, author of the Inspector Rebus novels, whose fictional detective is a regular here. Occasional live folk music.

Joseph Pearce's　　　　　　　PUB

(Map p48; ☑ 0131-556 4140; www.bodabar.com/joseph-pearces; 23 Elm Row; ⊙ 11am-midnight Sun-Thu, to 1am Fri & Sat; ☎ ᰥ; ᰥ all Leith Walk buses) This traditional Victorian pub has been remodelled and given a new lease of life by the Swedish owners. It's a real hub of the local community with good food (very family friendly before 5pm), a relaxed atmosphere, and events like Monday night Scrabble games and August crayfish parties.

Cumberland Bar　　　　　　　PUB

(Map p48; ☑ 0131-558 3134; www.cumberlandbar. co.uk; 1-3 Cumberland St; ⊙ noon-midnight Mon-Wed, to 1am Thu-Sat, 11am-midnight Sun; ☎; ᰥ 23, 27) Immortalised as the stereotypical New Town pub in Alexander McCall Smith's *44 Scotland Street,* the Cumberland has an authentic, traditional wood-brass-and-mirrors look (despite being relatively new) and serves cask-conditioned ales and a wide range of malt whiskies. There's also a pleasant little beer garden outside.

Tigerlily
COCKTAIL BAR

(Map p64; ☎0131-225 5005; www.tigerlilyedin burgh.co.uk; 125 George St; ◷11am-1am; ☎; ☐all Princes St buses) Swirling wallpapers, glittering chain-mail curtains, crystal chandeliers, and plush pink and gold sofas have won a cluster of design awards for this boutique hotel bar, where sharp suits and stiletto heels line the banquettes. There's expertly mixed cocktails, as well as Czech Staropramen beer on draught and Innis & Gunn Scottish ale in bottles.

Bramble
COCKTAIL BAR

(Map p64; ☎0131-226 6343; www.bramblebar. co.uk; 16a Queen St; ◷4pm-1am; ☐23, 27) One of those places that easily earns the sobriquet 'best-kept secret', Bramble is an unmarked cellar bar where a maze of stone and brick hideaways conceals what is arguably the city's best cocktail venue. No beer taps, no fuss, just expertly mixed drinks.

Guildford Arms
PUB

(Map p64; ☎0131-556 4312; www.guildfordarms. com; 1 West Register St; ☎; ☐Princes St) Located in a side alley off the east end of Princes St, the Guildford is a classic Victorian pub full of polished mahogany, brass and ornate cornices. The range of real ales is excellent – try to get a table in the unusual upstairs gallery, with a view over the sea of drinkers below.

Leith

★Roseleaf
BAR

(☎0131-476 5268; www.roseleaf.co.uk; 23-24 Sandport Pl; ◷10am-1am; ☎☐; ☐16, 22, 35, 36) Cute, quaint and verging on chintzy, the Roseleaf could hardly be further from the average Leith bar. Decked out in flowered wallpaper, old furniture and rose-patterned china (cocktails are served in teapots), the real ales and bottled beers are complemented by a range of speciality teas, coffees and fruit drinks (including rose lemonade), and well-above-average pub grub (served from 10am to 10pm).

Lioness of Leith
BAR

(☎0131-629 0580; www.facebook.com/Thelioness ofleith; 21-25 Duke St; ◷noon-midnight Mon-Thu, 11am-1am Fri & Sat, 12.30pm-midnight Sun; ☎; ☐21, 25, 34, 35, 49) Duke St was always one of the rougher corners of Leith, but the emergence of pubs like the Lioness is a sure sign of creeping gentrification. Distressed timber and battered leather benches are surrounded by vintage *objets trouvés* from chandeliers and glitterballs to mounted animal heads, a pinball machine and a pop-art print of Allen Ginsberg. Good beers and cocktails.

GAY & LESBIAN EDINBURGH

Edinburgh has a small – but perfectly formed – gay and lesbian scene, centred on the area around Broughton St (known affectionately as the 'Pink Triangle') at the eastern end of New Town.

Scotsgay (www.scotsgay.co.uk) is the local monthly magazine covering gay and lesbian issues, with listings of gay-friendly pubs and clubs. See also www.edinburghgayscene. com for online listings.

Useful contacts:

Edinburgh LGBT Centre (☎0131-523 1100; www.lgbthealth.org.uk; 9 Howe St)

Lothian LGBT Helpline (☎0300 123 2523; www.lgbt-helpline-scotland.org.uk; ◷noon-9pm Tue & Wed)

Pubs & Clubs

CC Blooms (Map p64; ☎0131-556 9331; http://ccbloomsedinburgh.com; 23 Greenside Pl; ◷11am-3am Mon-Sat, 12.30pm-3am Sun; ☎; ☐all Leith Walk buses) New owners have given the raddled old queen of Edinburgh's gay scene a shot in the arm, with two floors of deafening dance and disco every night. It can get overcrowded after 11pm and the drinks are a bit overpriced, but it's worth a visit – go early, or sample the wild Church of High Kicks talent contest on Sunday nights.

Regent (Map p48; www.theregentbar.co.uk; 2 Montrose Tce; ◷noon-1am Mon-Sat, 12.30pm-1am Sun; ☐35, 104, 113) This is a pleasant gay local with a relaxed atmosphere (no loud music), serving coffee and croissants as well as excellent real ales, including Deuchars IPA and Caledonian 80/-. Meeting place for the Lesbian and Gay Real Ale Drinkers club (first Monday of the month at 9pm).

Sofi's
BAR

(📞0131-555 7019; www.bodabar.com/sofis; 65 Henderson St; ⏱2pm-1am Mon-Fri, noon-1am Sat, 1pm-1am Sun; 🛜♿; 🚌22, 35, 36) Sofi's brings a little bit of Swedish sophistication to this former Leith pub, feeling more like a bohemian cafe with its mismatched furniture, candlelit tables, fresh flowers and colourful art. It's a real community place too, hosting film screenings, book clubs, open-mic music nights, and even a knitting club!

Teuchters Landing
PUB

(📞0131-554 7427; www.aroomin.co.uk; 1 Dock Pl; ⏱10.30am-1am; 🛜; 🚌16, 22, 35, 36) A cosy warren of timber-lined nooks and crannies housed in a single-storey red-brick building (once a waiting room for ferries across the Firth of Forth), this real-ale and malt-whisky bar also has outdoor tables on a floating terrace in the dock.

☆ Entertainment

Edinburgh has a number of fine theatres and concert halls, and there are independent art-house cinemas as well as mainstream movie theatres. Many pubs offer entertainment ranging from live Scottish folk music to pop, rock and jazz, as well as karaoke and quiz nights, while a range of stylish bars purvey house, dance and hip-hop to the pre-clubbing crowd.

The comprehensive source for what's-on info is the *List* (www.list.co.uk), an excellent listings magazine covering Edinburgh and Glasgow. It's available from most newsagents, and is published fortnightly on a Thursday.

Live Music

Edinburgh is a great place to hear traditional Scottish (and Irish) folk music, with a mix of regular spots and impromptu sessions. The Gig Guide (www.gigguide.co.uk) is a free email newsletter and listing website covering live music in Edinburgh and Scotland.

★ Sandy Bell's
TRADITIONAL MUSIC

(Map p52; www.sandybellsedinburgh.co.uk; 25 Forrest Rd; ⏱noon-1am Mon-Sat, 12.30pm-midnight Sun; 🚌2, 23, 27, 41, 42, 45) This unassuming pub is a stalwart of the traditional music scene (the founder's wife sang with The Corries). There's music almost every evening at 9pm, and from 3pm Saturday and Sunday, plus lots of impromptu sessions.

Jam House
LIVE MUSIC

(Map p64; 📞0131-220 2321; www.thejamhouse.com; 5 Queen St; admission from £4; ⏱6pm-3am Fri & Sat; 🚌10, 11, 12, 16, 26, 44) The brainchild of rhythm-and-blues pianist and TV personality Jools Holland, the Jam House is set in a former BBC TV studio and offers a combination of fine dining and live jazz and blues performances. Admission is for over-21s only, and there's a smart-casual dress code.

Caves
LIVE MUSIC

(Map p52; 📞0131-557 8989; www.thecavesedinburgh.com; 8-12 Niddry St South; 🚌35) A spectacular subterranean club venue set in the ancient stone vaults beneath the South Bridge, the Caves stages a series of one-off club nights and live-music gigs, as well as *ceilidh* nights during the festival – check the What's On link on the website for upcoming events.

Bannerman's
LIVE MUSIC

(Map p52; www.bannermanslive.co.uk; 212 Cowgate; ⏱noon-1am Mon-Sat, 12.30pm-1am Sun; 🛜; 🚌35, 45) A long-established music venue – it seems like every Edinburgh student for the last four decades spent half their youth here – Bannerman's straggles through a warren of old vaults beneath South Bridge. It pulls in crowds of students, locals and backpackers alike with live rock, punk and indie bands six nights a week.

Royal Oak
TRADITIONAL MUSIC

(Map p52; www.royal-oak-folk.com; 1 Infirmary St; ⏱11.30am-2am Mon-Sat, 12.30pm-2am Sun; 🚌all South Bridge buses) This popular folk music pub is tiny, so get there early (9pm start weekdays, 2.30pm Saturdays) if you want to be sure of a place. Sundays from 4pm to 7pm is open session – bring your own instruments (or a good singing voice).

Henry's Cellar Bar
LIVE MUSIC

(Map p52; 📞0131-629 2992; www.henryscellarbar.co.uk; 16 Morrison St; admission free-£6; ⏱5pm-1am Sun-Thu, to 3am Fri & Sat; 🚌all Lothian Rd buses) One of Edinburgh's most eclectic live-music venues, Henry's has something going on most nights of the week, from rock and indie to 'Balkan-inspired folk' and from funk to hip-hop to hardcore, staging both local bands and acts from around the world.

Jazz Bar
JAZZ, BLUES

(Map p52; www.thejazzbar.co.uk; 1a Chambers St; admission £3-7; ⏱5pm-3am Mon-Fri, 2.30pm-3am Sat & Sun; 🛜; 🚌35, 45) This atmospheric cellar bar, with its bare stone walls, candlelit tables and stylish steel-framed chairs, is owned and operated by jazz musicians. There's live music every night from 9pm to 3am, and on Saturday from 3pm; as well as jazz, expect bands playing blues, funk, soul and fusion.

Voodoo Rooms
LIVE MUSIC

(Map p64; ☑0131-556 7060; www.thevoodoo rooms.com; 19a West Register St; admission free-£10; ☺noon-1am Fri-Sun, 4pm-1am Mon-Thu; ☑St Andrew Sq) Decadent decor of black leather, ornate plasterwork and gilt detailing create a funky setting for this complex of bars and performance spaces above the Café Royal that host everything from classic soul and Motown to Vegas lounge club nights (www. vegasscotland.co.uk) and live local bands.

Cinemas

Film buffs will find plenty to keep them happy in Edinburgh's art-house cinemas, while popcorn munchers can choose from a range of multiplexes.

Cameo
CINEMA

(Map p48; ☑0871 902 5723; www.picturehouses. co.uk; 38 Home St; ☎; ☑all Tollcross buses) The three-screen, independently owned Cameo is a good, old-fashioned cinema showing an imaginative mix of mainstream and art-house movies. There is a good program of late-night films and Sunday matinees, and the seats in screen 1 are big enough to get lost in.

Filmhouse
CINEMA

(Map p52; ☑0131-228 2688; www.filmhouse cinema.com; 88 Lothian Rd; ☎; ☑all Lothian Rd buses) The Filmhouse is the main venue for the annual Edinburgh International Film Festival (p74) and screens a full program of art-house, classic, foreign and second-run films, with lots of themes, retrospectives and 70mm screenings. It has wheelchair access to all three screens.

Classical Music, Opera & Ballet

Edinburgh is home to the Scottish Chamber Orchestra (SCO; www.sco.org.uk), one of Europe's finest orchestras and well worth hearing. Their performances are usually held at the Queen's Hall or the Usher Hall.

Edinburgh Festival Theatre
THEATRE

(Map p52; ☑0131-529 6000; www.edtheatres. com/festival; 13-29 Nicolson St; ☺box office 10am-6pm Mon-Sat, to 8pm show nights, 4pm-showtime Sun; ☑all South Bridge buses) A beautifully restored art-deco theatre with a modern frontage, the Festival is the city's main venue for opera, dance and ballet, but also stages musicals, concerts, drama and children's shows.

Usher Hall
CLASSICAL MUSIC

(Map p52; ☑0131-228 1155; www.usherhall.co.uk; Lothian Rd; ☺box office 10.30am-5.30pm, to 8pm show nights; ☑all Lothian Rd buses) The architec-turally impressive Usher Hall hosts concerts by the Royal Scottish National Orchestra (RSNO) and performances of popular music.

St Giles Cathedral
CLASSICAL MUSIC

(Map p52; www.stgilescathedral.org.uk; High St; ☑23, 27, 41, 42) The big kirk on the Royal Mile plays host to a regular and varied program of classical music, including popular lunchtime and evening concerts and organ recitals. The cathedral choir sings at the 10am and 11.30am Sunday services.

Theatre, Musicals & Comedy

★Summerhall
THEATRE

(Map p48; ☑0131-560 1580; www.summerhall. co.uk; 1 Summerhall; ☑41, 42, 67) Formerly Edinburgh University's veterinary school, the Summerhall complex is a major cultural centre and entertainment venue, with old halls and lecture theatres (including an original anatomy lecture theatre) now serving as venues for drama, dance, cinema and comedy performances. It's also one of the main venues for Edinburgh Festival events.

Royal Lyceum Theatre
THEATRE

(Map p52; ☑0131-248 4848; www.lyceum.org. uk; 30b Grindlay St; ☺box office 10am-6pm Mon-Sat, to 8pm show nights; ☑; ☑all Lothian Rd buses) A grand Victorian theatre located beside the Usher Hall, the Lyceum stages drama, concerts, musicals and ballet.

Traverse Theatre
THEATRE

(Map p52; ☑0131-228 1404; www.traverse.co.uk; 10 Cambridge St; ☺box office 10am-6pm Mon-Sat, to 8pm show nights; ☎; ☑all Lothian Rd buses) The Traverse is the main focus for new Scottish writing and stages an adventurous program of contemporary drama and dance. The box office is only open on Sunday (from 4pm) when there's a show on.

Stand Comedy Club
COMEDY

(Map p64; ☑0131-558 7272; www.thestand. co.uk; 5 York Pl; tickets £2-15; ☺from 7.30pm Mon-Sat, from 12.30pm Sun; ☑St Andrew Sq) The Stand, founded in 1995, is Edinburgh's main independent comedy venue. It's an intimate cabaret bar with performances every night and a free Sunday lunchtime show.

Sport

Edinburgh has two rival football (soccer) teams playing in the Scottish Premier League – Heart of Midlothian (aka Hearts, nicknamed the Jam Tarts or Jambos), founded in 1874, and Hibernian (aka Hibs, Hibbies or Hi-bees), founded in 1875.

Hearts has its home ground at Tynecastle Stadium (www.heartsfc.co.uk; Gorgie Rd; 📮2, 3, 4, 25, 33, 44), southwest of the city centre in Gorgie. Hibernian's home ground is northeast of the city centre at Easter Road Stadium (www.hibernianfc.co.uk; 12 Albion Pl).

Each year, from January to March, Scotland's national rugby team takes part in the Six Nations Rugby Union Championship (www.rbs6nations.com). The most important fixture is the clash against England for the Calcutta Cup, which takes place in Edinburgh in even-numbered years (and at Twickenham in London in odd-numbered years). At club level, the season runs from September to May. Murrayfield Stadium (www.scottishrugby .org; 112 Roseburn St; 📮Murrayfield Stadium), about 1.5 miles west of the city centre, is the venue for international matches.

Other sporting events, including athletics and cycling, are held at Meadowbank Sports Centre (📞0131-661 5351; www.edin burghleisure.co.uk/venues; 139 London Rd), Scotland's main sports arena.

Horse-racing fans head 6 miles east to Musselburgh Racecourse (www.mussel burgh-racecourse.co.uk; Linkfield Rd; tickets from £20), Scotland's oldest racecourse (founded 1816), where meetings are held throughout the year.

🔒 Shopping

Princes St is Edinburgh's principal shopping street, lined with all the big high-street stores, with many smaller shops along pedestrianised Rose St, and more expensive designer boutiques on George St and Thistle St.

For more off-beat shopping – including fashion, music, crafts, gifts and jewellery – head for the cobbled lanes of Cockburn, Victoria and St Mary's Sts, all near the Royal Mile in the Old Town; William St in the western part of the New Town; and the Stockbridge district, immediately north of the New Town.

There are two big shopping centres in the New Town – Waverley Mall (Map p64; 📞0131-557 3759; www.waverleymall.com; Waverley Bridge; ⏰9am-6pm Mon-Wed & Fri-Sat, to 7pm Thu 11am-5pm Sun; 📮all Princes St buses), at the eastern end of Princes St, and the nearby St James Centre (Map p64; 📞0131-558 1200; www.stjamesshopping.com; 1 Leith St; ⏰9am-6pm Mon-Wed & Fri-Sat, to 8pm Thu, 10am-6pm Sun; 📮York Pl) at the top of Leith St, plus Multrees Walk (Map p64; www.multreeswalk.co.uk; 📮St Andrew Sq), a designer shopping complex with a flagship Harvey Nichols store on the eastern side of St Andrew Sq.

The huge Ocean Terminal (p67) in Leith is the biggest shopping centre in the city.

Woollen textiles and knitwear are some of Scotland's classic exports. Scottish cashmere – a fine, soft wool from young goats and lambs – provides the most luxurious and expensive knitwear and has been seen gracing the torsos of pop star Robbie Williams and England footballer David Beckham. There are dozens of shops along the Royal Mile and Princes St where you can buy kilts and tartan goods.

🔒 Old Town

Armstrong's
VINTAGE
(Map p52; 📞0131-220 5557; www.armstrongs vintage.co.uk; 83 Grassmarket; ⏰10am-5.30pm Mon-Thu, to 6pm Fri & Sat, noon-6pm Sun; 📮2) Armstrong's is an Edinburgh fashion institution (established in 1840, no less), a quality vintage clothes emporium offering everything from elegant 1940s dresses to funky 1970s flares. As well as having retro fashion, it's a great place to hunt for 'previously owned' kilts and Harris tweed, or to seek inspiration for that fancy-dress party.

Ragamuffin
FASHION & ACCESSORIES
(Map p52; 📞0131-557 6007; 278 Canongate; ⏰10am-5pm Mon-Sat, noon-5pm Sun; 📮35) Quality Scottish knitwear and fabrics including cashmere from Johnstons of Elgin, Fair Isle sweaters and Harris tweed.

Bill Baber
FASHION & ACCESSORIES
(Map p52; 📞0131-225 3249; www.billbaber. com; 66 Grassmarket; ⏰9am-5.30pm Mon-Sat; 📮2) This family-run designer knitwear studio has been in the business for more than 30 years, producing stylish and colourful creations using linen, merino wool, silk and cotton.

Geoffrey (Tailor) Inc
FASHION & ACCESSORIES
(Map p52; 📞0131-557 0256; www.geoffreykilts. co.uk; 57-59 High St; ⏰9.30am-6pm Mon-Sat, 10.30am-5.30pm Sun; 📮35) Geoffrey can fit you out in traditional Highland dress, or run up a kilt in your own clan tartan. Its offshoot, 21st Century Kilts (p94), offers modern fashion kilts in a variety of fabrics.

Royal Mile Whiskies
DRINKS
(Map p52; 📞0131-225 3383; www.royalmile whiskies.co.uk; 379 High St; ⏰10am-6pm Mon-Sat, 12.30-6pm Sun mid-Sep–Jun, 12.30-8pm daily Jul–mid-Sep; 📮23, 27, 41, 42) If it's a drap of the cratur ye're after, this place has a selection of single malts in miniature and full-size

bottles. There's also a range of blended whiskies, Irish whiskey and bourbon, and you can buy online too.

New Town

21st Century Kilts
FASHION & ACCESSORIES

(Map p64; http://21stcenturykilts.com; 48 Thistle St; ⊘10am-6pm Tue-Sat; 🚊23, 27) 21st Century Kilts offers modern fashion kilts in a variety of fabrics; celebrity customers include Robbie Williams and Vin Diesel.

Jenners
DEPARTMENT STORE

(Map p64; 🖉0344 800 3725; www.houseoffraser. co.uk; 48 Princes St; ⊘9.30am-6.30pm Mon-Wed, 8am-9pm Thu, 8am-8pm Fri, 8am-7pm Sat, 11am-6pm Sun; 🚇Princes St) Founded in 1838, and acquired by House of Fraser in 2005, Jenners is the *grande dame* of Scottish department stores. It stocks a wide range of quality goods, both classic and contemporary.

Harvey Nichols
DEPARTMENT STORE

(Map p64; 🖉0131-524 8388; www.harveynichols. com; 30-34 St Andrew Sq; ⊘10am-6pm Mon-Wed, 10am-8pm Thu, 10am-7pm Fri & Sat, 11am-6pm Sun; 🚇St Andrew Sq) The jewel in the crown of Edinburgh's shopping scene has four floors of designer labels and eye-popping price tags.

South Edinburgh

Meadows Pottery
CERAMICS

(Map p48; 🖉0131-662 4064; www.themeadows pottery.com; 11a Summerhall Pl; ⊘10.30am-7.30pm Mon & Tue, to 6pm Wed-Sat; 🚊2, 41, 42, 67) This little shop sells a range of colourful, high-fired oxidised stoneware, both domestic and decorative, all hand-thrown on the premises. If you can't find what you want, you can commission custom-made pieces.

Courtyard Antiques
ANTIQUES

(Map p48; 🖉0131-662 9008; www.edinburgh courtyardantiques.co.uk; 108a Causewayside; ⊘9.30am-5.30pm; 🚊42) Hidden down a lane, the Courtyard has two crowded floors of wooden furniture (19th century to the 1970s), toys and militaria, including some fascinating bric-a-brac that ranges from 78rpm records to model trains, boats and aircraft.

Word Power
BOOKS

(Map p52; 🖉0131-662 9112; www.word-power. co.uk; 43 West Nicolson St; ⊘10am-6pm Mon-Sat, noon-5pm Sun; 🚊41, 42) Word Power is a radical, independent bookshop that supports both small publishers and local writers. It stocks a wide range of political, gay and feminist literature, as well as non-mainstream fiction and nonfiction.

Leith

Kinloch Anderson
FASHION & ACCESSORIES

(🖉0131-555 1390; www.kinlochanderson.com; 4 Dock St; ⊘9am-5.30pm Mon-Sat; 🚊16, 22, 35, 36) One of the best tartan shops in Edinburgh, Kinloch Anderson was founded in 1868 and is still family run. It is a supplier of kilts and Highland dress to the royal family.

Stockbridge

Stockbridge Market
MARKET

(Map p64; www.stockbridgemarket.com; cnr Kerr St & Saunders St; ⊘10am-5pm Sun; 🚊24, 29, 36, 42) On Sundays, Stockbridge Market is the focus of the community, set in a leafy square next to the bridge that gives the district its name. Stalls range from fresh Scottish produce to handmade ceramics, jewellery, soaps and cosmetics. Grab an espresso from Steampunk Coffee, which operates out of a 1970s VW campervan.

Galerie Mirages
JEWELLERY

(Map p48; 🖉0131-315 2603; www.galeriemirages. com; 46a Raeburn Pl; ⊘10am-5.30pm Mon-Sat, 12-4.30pm Sun; 🚊24, 29, 42) An Aladdin's cave packed with jewellery, textiles and handicrafts from all over the world, it's best known for its silver, amber and gemstone jewellery in both ethnic and contemporary designs.

Adam Pottery
CERAMICS

(Map p48; 🖉0131-557 3978; www.adampottery. co.uk; 76 Henderson Row; ⊘11am-6pm Wed-Sat, to 5pm Jan-Mar; 🚊36) This small, independent pottery produces its own colourfully glazed ceramics, both decorative and functional, in a wide range of styles, with objects ranging from coffee cups to garden planters. Visitors are welcome to visit the studio to watch potters at work.

ℹ Information

EMERGENCY

In an emergency, dial 🖉999 or 112 (free from public payphones) and ask for police, ambulance, fire brigade or coastguard.

Police Scotland New Town (🖉non-emergency 101; www.scotland.police.uk; Gayfield Sq; ⊘24hr; 🚇all Leith Walk buses)

Police Scotland West End (🖉non-emergency 101; www.scotland.police.uk; 3-5 Torphichen Pl; ⊘9am-5pm Mon-Fri)

INTERNET ACCESS

There are internet-enabled telephone boxes scattered around the city centre, and countless wi-fi hot spots. Internet cafes, such as **Coffee Home** (☑ 0131-477 8336; www.coffeehome. co.uk; 28 Crighton Pl, Leith Walk; per 20min 60p; ⊙ 10am-9pm Mon-Fri, 10am-8pm Sat, noon-8pm Sun; 🛜 🖥 ; 🚌 all Leith Walk buses) in Leith, are spread around the city and most cafes and bars offer free wi-fi for customers.

MEDIA

The Scotsman (www.scotsman.com) Quality daily covering Scottish, UK and international news, sport and current affairs; *Scotland on Sunday* is the weekend newspaper from the same publisher.

Edinburgh Evening News (www.edinburgh news.com) Covers news and entertainment in the city and its environs.

BBC Radio Scotland (www.bbc.co.uk/radio scotland) *Good Morning Scotland* from 6am weekdays covers Scottish current affairs.

MEDICAL SERVICES

For urgent medical advice you can call the **NHS 24 Helpline** (☑ 111; www.nhs24.com). Chemists (pharmacists) can advise you on minor ailments. At least one local chemist remains open round the clock – its location will be displayed in the windows of other chemists.

For urgent dental treatment, you can visit the walk-in **Chalmers Street Dental Clinic** (☑ 0131-536 4800; 3 Chalmers St; ⊙ 9am-4.45pm Mon-Thu, to 4.15pm Fri; 🚌 23, 27, 35, 45, 47). In the case of a dental emergency in the evenings or at weekends, call **Lothian Dental Advice Line** (☑ 0131-536 4800; ⊙ 5-10pm Mon-Fri, 9am-10pm Sat & Sun).

Boots (☑ 0131-225 6757; 48 Shandwick Pl; ⊙ 7.30am-8pm Mon-Fri, 9am-6pm Sat, 10.30am-5pm Sun; 🚌 West End) Chemist open longer hours than most.

Edinburgh Royal Infirmary (☑ 0131-536 1000; www.nhslothian.scot.nhs.uk; 51 Little France Cres, Old Dalkeith Rd; ⊙ 24hr) Edinburgh's main general hospital; has 24-hour accident and emergency department.

Western General Hospital (☑ 0131-537 1000; www.nhslothian.scot.nhs.uk; Crewe Rd South; ⊙ 8am-9pm) For non-life-threatening injuries and ailments, you can attend the Minor Injuries Clinic here without having to make an appointment.

Royal Hospital for Sick Children (☑ 0131-536 0000; www.nhslothian.scot.nhs.uk; 9 Sciennes Rd; ⊙ 24hr) Casualty department for children aged under 13 years; located in Marchmont (moving to a new location near the Edinburgh Royal Infirmary in autumn or winter of 2017).

Edinburgh Rape Crisis Centre (☑ 08088-01 03 02; www.rapecrisisscotland.org.uk)

POST

The UK postal system is generally reliable. You can find up-to-date rates at www.royalmail.com.

Frederick St Post Office (Map p64; 40 Frederick St; ⊙ 9am-5.30pm Mon & Wed-Fri, 9.30am-5.30pm Tue, 9.30am-12.30pm Sat)

Waverley Mall Post Office (Map p64; Waverley Mall; ⊙ 9am-5.30pm Mon & Wed-Sat, 9.30am-5.30pm Tue)

St Mary's St Post Office (Map p52; 46 St Mary's St; ⊙ 9am-5.30pm Mon-Fri, to 12.30pm Sat)

TOURIST INFORMATION

Edinburgh Information Centre (Map p64; ☑ 0131-473 3868; www.edinburgh.org; Waverley Mall, 3 Princes St; ⊙ 9am-7pm Mon-Sat, 10am-7pm Sun Jul & Aug, to 6pm Jun, to 5pm Sep-May; 🛜 ; 🚌 St Andrew Sq) Has an accommodation booking service, currency exchange, gift and bookshop, internet access and counters selling tickets for Edinburgh city tours and Scottish Citylink bus services.

Edinburgh Airport Information Centre (☑ 0131-473 3690; www.edinburghairport. com; Edinburgh Airport; ⊙ 7.30am-7.30pm Mon-Fri, to 8pm Sat & Sun) VisitScotland Information Centre in the airport's terminal extension..

USEFUL WEBSITES

Edinburgh Festival Guide (www.edinburghfes-tivals.co.uk) Everything you need to know about Edinburgh's many festivals.

CITY MAPS

For coverage of the whole city in detail, the best maps are Nicolson's *Edinburgh Citymap* and the Ordnance Survey's (OS) *Edinburgh Street Atlas*. You can buy these at the Edinburgh Information Centre (p95), bookshops and newsagents. Note that long streets may be known by different names along their length. For example, the southern end of Leith Walk is variously called Union Pl and Antigua St on one side, and Elm Row and Greenside Pl on the other.

The OS's 1:50,000 Landranger map *Edinburgh, Penicuik & North Berwick* (sheet No 66) covers the city and the surrounding region to the south and east at a scale of 1.25 inches to 1 mile; it's useful for walking in the Pentland Hills and exploring Edinburgh's fringes and East Lothian.

Lonely Planet (www.lonelyplanet.com/edin burgh) Destination information, hotel bookings, great for planning.

VisitScotland Edinburgh (www.edinburgh.org) Official Scottish tourist board site.

The List (www.list.co.uk) Local listings and reviews for restaurants, bars, clubs and theatres.

ⓘ Getting There & Away

AIR

Edinburgh Airport (p463), 8 miles west of the city, has numerous flights to other parts of Scotland and the UK, Ireland and mainland Europe. There's a VisitScotland Information Centre (p95) in the airport's terminal extension.

FlyBe/Loganair (☑ 0371 700 2000; www. loganair.co.uk) operates daily flights to Inverness, Wick, Orkney, Shetland and Stornoway.

BUS

Edinburgh Bus Station (Map p64; entrances on Elder St & St Andrew Sq; left luggage lockers per 12hr £5-8; ⏱ 4.30am-midnight Sun-Thu, 4.30am-12.30am Fri & Sat) is at the northeast corner of St Andrew Sq, with pedestrian entrances from the square and from Elder St. For timetable information, contact **Traveline** (☑ 0871 200 22 33; www.traveline scotland.com).

Scottish Citylink (☑ 0871 266 3333; www. citylink.co.uk) buses connect Edinburgh with all of Scotland's cities and major towns. The following are sample one-way fares departing from Edinburgh.

DESTINATION	FARE (£)
Aberdeen	31
Dundee	16.60
Fort William	35
Glasgow	7.50
Inverness	31
Portree	56
Stirling	8.20

It's also worth checking with **Megabus** (☑ 0141-352 4444; www.megabus.com) for cheap intercity bus fares (from as little as £5) from Edinburgh to Aberdeen, Dundee, Glasgow, Inverness and Perth.

There are various buses to Edinburgh from London and the rest of the UK.

CAR & MOTORCYCLE

Arriving in or leaving Edinburgh by car during the morning and evening rush hours (7.30am to 9.30am and 4.30pm to 6.30pm Monday to Friday) is an experience you can live without. Try to time your journey to avoid these periods.

Major roads leading in and out of Edinburgh:
- M90 north to Perth
- M9 northwest to Stirling
- M8 west to Glasgow
- A7 south to Galashiels
- A68 south to Melrose and Jedburgh
- A1 southeast to Berwick-upon-Tweed

TRAIN

The main train terminus in Edinburgh is **Waverley train station**, located in the heart of the city. Trains arriving from, and departing for, the west also stop at Haymarket station, which is more convenient for the West End.

You can buy tickets, make reservations and get travel information at the **Edinburgh Rail Travel Centre** (⏱ 5am-midnight Mon-Sat, 7am-midnight Sun) in Waverley station. For fare and timetable information, phone the **National Rail Enquiry Service** (☑ 08457-48 49 50; www. nationalrail.co.uk) or use the journey planner on the website.

If you're travelling as a pair, consider purchasing a **Two Together Railcard** (p467), which offers you up to 30% off your combined fares on train rides taken throughout Great Britain.

ScotRail (☑ 0344-811 0141; www.scotrail. co.uk) operates regular train services to the following:

Glasgow (£12.50, 50 minutes, every 15 minutes)
Aberdeen (£35, 2½ hours)
Dundee (£17.90, 1¼ hours)
Inverness (£42, 3½ hours)

ⓘ Getting Around

TO/FROM THE AIRPORT

Bus Lothian Buses' **Airlink** (www.flybybus.com) service 100 runs from Waverley Bridge, outside the train station, to the airport (one way/return £4.50/7.50, 30 minutes, every 10 minutes from 4am to midnight) via the West End and Haymarket.

Tram Edinburgh Trams (www.edinburghtrams. com) run from the airport to the city centre (one way/return £5.50/8.50, 33 minutes, every six to eight minutes from 6am to midnight).

Taxi An airport taxi to the city centre costs around £20 and takes about 20 to 30 minutes. Trams, buses and taxis all depart from outside the arrivals hall; go out through the main doors and turn left.

BICYCLE

Thanks to the efforts of local cycling campaign group Spokes and a bike-friendly city council, Edinburgh is well equipped with bike lanes and dedicated cycle tracks. You can buy a map of the city's cycle routes from most bike shops.

Biketrax (Map p48; ☑ 0131-228 6633; www.biketrax.co.uk; 11-13 Lochrin Pl; per day from £17; ⊘ 9.30am-6pm Mon-Fri, to 5.30pm Sat, noon-5pm Sun; 🚊 all Tollcross buses) rents out hybrid bikes, road bikes and Brompton folding bikes (no mountain bikes, though). You'll need a £100 cash or credit-card deposit and photographic ID.

BUS

Bus timetables, route maps and fare guides are posted at all main bus and tram stops, and you can pick up a copy of the free *Lothian Buses Route Map* from Lothian Buses Travelshops on **Waverley Bridge** (Map p52; 31 Waverley Bridge; ⊘ 9am-6pm Mon-Wed & Fri, to 7pm Thu, to 5.30pm Sat, 10am-5.30pm Sun) and **Hanover St** (Map p64; 27 Hanover St; ⊘ 9am-6pm Mon-Fri, 9am-5.30pm Sat).

Adult fares within the city are £1.60; purchase from the bus driver. Children aged under five travel free and those aged five to 15 pay a flat fare of 80p.

On Lothian Buses you must pay the driver the exact fare, but First buses will give change. Lothian Bus drivers also sell a day ticket (£4) that gives unlimited travel on Lothian buses and trams for a day; a family day ticket (up to two adults and three children) costs £8.50.

Night-service buses, which run hourly between midnight and 5am, charge a flat fare of £3.50.

You can also buy a Ridacard (from Travelshops; not available from bus drivers) that gives unlimited travel for one week for £18.

The Lothian Buses lost-property office is in the Hanover St Travelshop.

CAR & MOTORCYCLE

Though useful for day trips beyond the city, a car in central Edinburgh is more of a liability than a convenience. There is restricted access on Princes St, George St and Charlotte Sq; many streets are one-way, and finding a parking place in the city centre is like striking gold. Queen's Dr around Holyrood Park is closed to motorised traffic on Sunday.

Car Rental

All the big, international car-rental agencies have offices in Edinburgh, including **Avis** (☑ 0844 544 6059; www.avis.co.uk; 24 East London St; ⊘ 8am-6pm Mon-Fri, 8am-2pm Sat, 10am-2pm Sun) and **Europcar** (☑ 0871 384 3453; www. europcar.co.uk; Platform 2, Waverley Train Station, Waverley Bridge; ⊘ 7am-8pm Mon-Fri, 7am-5pm Sat & Sun).

There are many smaller, local agencies that offer better rates. **Arnold Clark** (☑ 0141-237 4374; www.arnoldclarkrental.co.uk) charges from £32 a day, or £185 a week for a small car, including VAT and insurance.

BUS INFO ON YOUR PHONE

Lothian Buses has created free smart-phone apps that provide route maps, timetables and live waiting times for city buses. Search for EdinBus (iPhone), My Bus Edinburgh (Android) or BusTracker Edinburgh (Windows Phone).

Parking

There's no parking on main roads into the city from 7.30am to 6.30pm Monday to Saturday. Also, parking in the city centre can be a nightmare.

On-street parking is controlled by self-service ticket machines from 8.30am to 6.30pm Monday to Saturday, and costs £1.80 to £3.60 per hour, with a 30-minute to four-hour maximum.

If you break the rules, you'll get a fine, often within minutes of your ticket expiring – Edinburgh's parking wardens are both numerous and notorious. The fine is £60, reduced to £30 if you pay up within 14 days. Cars parked illegally will be towed away. There are large, long-stay car parks at the St James Centre, Greenside Pl, New St, Castle Tce and Morrison St. Motorcycles can be parked free at designated areas in the city centre.

TAXI

Edinburgh's black taxis can be hailed in the street, ordered by phone (extra 80p charge) or picked up at one of the many central ranks. The minimum charge is £2.10 (£3.10 at night) for the first 450m, then 25p for every subsequent 188m – a typical 2-mile trip across the city centre will cost around £6 to £7. Tipping is up to you – because of the high fares local people rarely tip on short journeys, but occasionally round up to the nearest 50p on longer ones.

Central Taxis (☑ 0131-229 2468; www.taxis -edinburgh.co.uk)

City Cabs (☑ 0131-228 1211; www.citycabs. co.uk)

ComCab (☑ 0131-272 8001; www.comcab -edinburgh.co.uk)

TRAM

Edinburgh's tram system (www.edinburghtrams. com) began service in 2014. The line runs from Edinburgh Airport to York Pl, at the top of Leith Walk, via Haymarket, the West End and Princes St.

Tickets are integrated with the city's Lothian Buses, costing £1.60 for a single journey within the city boundary, or £5.50 to the airport. Trams run every eight to 10 minutes Monday to Saturday and every 12 to 15 minutes on a Sunday, from 5.30am to 11pm.

AROUND EDINBURGH

Edinburgh is small enough that, when you need a break from the city, the beautiful surrounding countryside isn't far away and is easily accessible by public transport, or even by bike. The old counties around Edinburgh are called Midlothian, West Lothian and East Lothian, often referred to collectively as 'the Lothians'.

Queensferry

POP 9000

Queensferry is at the narrowest part of the Firth of Forth, where ferries have crossed to Fife from the earliest times. The village takes its name from Queen Margaret (1046–93), who gave pilgrims free passage across the firth on their way to St Andrews. Ferries continued to operate until 1964 when the graceful **Forth Road Bridge** was opened; this was followed by a second road bridge, the **Queensferry Crossing** (2017).

Predating the first road bridge by 74 years, the magnificent **Forth Bridge** – only outsiders ever call it the Forth Rail Bridge – is one of the finest engineering achievements of the 19th century. Completed in 1890 after seven years' work, its three huge cantilevers span 1447m and took 59,000 tonnes of steel, eight million rivets and the lives of 58 men to build.

◉ Sights

Hopetoun House   HISTORIC BUILDING
(www.hopetoun.co.uk; house & grounds adult/child £9.85/5.45, grounds only £4.55/2.80; ⊙10.30am-5pm Easter-Sep, last admission 4pm; P) One of Scotland's finest stately homes, Hopetoun House has a superb location in lovely grounds beside the Firth of Forth. There are two parts – the older built to Sir William Bruce's plans between 1699 and 1702 and dominated by a splendid stairwell with (modern) trompe l'oeil paintings; and the newer designed between 1720 and 1750 by three members of the Adam family, William and sons Robert and John.

The highlights are the red and yellow Adam drawing rooms, lined in silk damask, and the view from the roof terrace. Britain's most elegant equine accommodation – where the marquis once housed his pampered racehorses – is now the stylish **Stables Tearoom** (☑0131-331 3661; mains £5-10, afternoon tea £20; ⊙11am-4.30pm Easter-Sep), a delightful spot for lunch or afternoon tea.

Hopetoun House is 2 miles west of Queensferry along the coast road. Driving from Edinburgh, turn off the A90 onto the A904 just before the Forth Bridge and follow the signs.

Queensferry Museum   MUSEUM
(www.edinburghmuseums.org.uk; 53 High St; ⊙10am-1pm & 2.15-5pm Mon & Thu-Sat, noon-5pm Sun) FREE In the pretty, terraced High St in Queensferry is the small Queensferry Museum. It contains some interesting background information on the Forth bridges, and a fascinating exhibit on the 'Burry Man', part of the village's summer gala festivities.

🛏 Sleeping & Eating

Orocco Pier   BOUTIQUE HOTEL ££
(☑0870-118 1664; www.oroccopier.co.uk; 17 High St; r from £115; 🖎) This stylish hotel has an enviable situation overlooking the Firth of Forth, with views of the Forth bridges.

Hawes Inn   PUB FOOD ££
(☑0131-331 1990; www.vintageinn.co.uk; Newhalls Rd; mains £9-19; ⊙food served noon-10pm; P🖎📶; 🚍First Edinburgh 43) The atmospheric Hawes Inn, famously mentioned in Robert Louis Stevenson's novel *Kidnapped*, serves excellent pub grub; it's opposite the Inchcolm ferry, right beside the Forth railway bridge.

ⓘ Getting There & Away

Queensferry lies on the southern bank of the Firth of Forth, 8 miles west of Edinburgh city centre. To get there, take Stagecoach bus 40 (£3.30, 30 to 40 minutes, three or four hourly) from Edinburgh Bus Station. It's a 10-minute walk from the bus stop to the Hawes Inn and the Inchcolm ferry.

Trains go from Edinburgh's Waverley and Haymarket stations to Dalmeny station (£4.50, 15 minutes, two to four hourly). From the station exit, the Hawes Inn is five minutes' walk along a footpath (across the road, behind the bus stop) that leads north beside the railway and then downhill under the Forth Bridge.

Inchcolm

Known as the 'Iona of the East', the island of Inchcolm (meaning 'St Columba's Island') lies east of the Forth bridges, less than a mile off the coast of Fife. Only 800m long, it is home to the ruins of **Inchcolm Abbey** (HS; adult/child £5.50/3.30; ⊙9.30am-5.30pm Apr-Oct), one of Scotland's best-preserved medieval abbeys, founded by Augustinian priors in 1123.

WORTH A TRIP

ROSSLYN CHAPEL

The success of Dan Brown's novel *The Da Vinci Code* and the subsequent Hollywood film has seen a flood of visitors descend on Scotland's most beautiful and enigmatic church – **Rosslyn Chapel** (Collegiate Church of St Matthew; www.rosslynchapel.org.uk; Chapel Loan, Roslin; adult/child £9/free; ⊙9.30am-6pm Mon-Sat Apr-Sep, to 5.30pm Oct-Mar, noon-4.45pm Sun year-round; P). The chapel was built in the mid-15th century for William St Clair, third earl of Orkney, and the ornately carved interior – at odds with the architectural fashion of its time – is a monument to the mason's art, rich in symbolic imagery. Hourly talks by qualified guides are included in the admission price.

As well as flowers, vines, angels and biblical figures, the carved stones include many examples of the pagan 'Green Man'; other figures are associated with Freemasonry and the Knights Templar. Intriguingly, there are also carvings of plants from the Americas that predate Columbus' voyage of discovery. The symbolism of these images has led some researchers to conclude that Rosslyn is some kind of secret Templar repository, and it has been claimed that hidden vaults beneath the chapel could conceal anything from the Holy Grail or the head of John the Baptist to the body of Christ himself. The chapel is owned by the Episcopal Church of Scotland and services are still held here on Sunday mornings.

The chapel is on the eastern edge of the village of Roslin, 7 miles south of Edinburgh's centre. Lothian Bus 15 (not 15A) runs from the west end of Princes St in Edinburgh to Roslin (£1.60, 30 minutes, every 30 minutes).

It's a half-hour sail to Inchcolm and you get 1½ hours ashore. As well as the abbey, the trip gives you the chance to see the island's grey seals, puffins and other seabirds.

The ferry boat **Maid of the Forth** (www.maidoftheforth.co.uk; adult/child £18.50/9.30) sails to Inchcolm from Hawes Pier in Queensferry. There are one to four sailings most days from April to October. The return fare includes admission to the abbey.

North Berwick & Around

POP 6600

North Berwick is an attractive Victorian seaside resort with long sandy beaches, three golf courses and a small harbour.

⊙ Sights & Activities

North Berwick is a popular golfing destination, with four courses in and around the town and a dozen more within easy reach, including the world-famous Open Championship course at **Muirfield** (www.muirfield.org.uk).

Off High St, a short steep path climbs **North Berwick Law** (184m), a conical hill that dominates the town. When the weather's fine there are great views to spectacular Bass Rock, iced white in spring and summer with guano from thousands of nesting gannets. **Sula II** (☑01620-880770; www.sulaboat trips.co.uk; adult/child £15/10; ⊙daily Apr-Sep) runs boat trips around Bass Rock, departing from North Berwick's harbour.

Scottish Seabird Centre　　WILDLIFE CENTRE
(www.seabird.org; The Harbour; adult/child £8.95/4.95; ⊙10am-6pm Apr-Aug, to 5pm Feb, Mar, Sep & Oct, to 4pm Nov-Jan; P☒) Top marks to the bright spark who came up with the idea for this centre, an ornithologist's paradise that uses remote-control video cameras sited on Bass Rock and other islands to relay live images of nesting gannets and other seabirds – you can control the cameras yourself, and zoom in on scenes of cosy gannet domesticity.

Tantallon Castle　　CASTLE
(HS; adult/child £5.50/3.30; ⊙9.30am-5.30pm Apr-Sep, 10am-4pm Oct-Mar; P) Perched on a cliff 3 miles east of North Berwick is the spectacular ruin of Tantallon Castle. Built around 1350, it was the fortress residence of the Douglas earls of Angus (the Red Douglases), defended on one side by a series of ditches and on the other by an almost sheer drop into the sea.

Dirleton Castle　　CASTLE
(HS; adult/child £5.50/3.30; ⊙9.30am-5.30pm Apr-Sep, 10am-4pm Oct-Mar; P) Two miles west of North Berwick is this impressive medieval fortress with massive round towers, a drawbridge and a horrific pit dungeon, surrounded rather incongruously by beautiful, manicured gardens.

Rosslyn Chapel

DECIPHERING ROSSLYN

Rosslyn Chapel is a small building, but the density of decoration inside can be overwhelming. It's well worth buying the official guidebook by the Earl of Rosslyn first; find a bench in the gardens and have a skim through before going into the chapel – the background information will make your visit all the more interesting. The book also offers a useful self-guided tour of the chapel, and explains the legend of the Master Mason and the Apprentice.

Entrance is through the **north door** ①. Take a pew and sit for a while to allow your eyes to adjust to the dim interior; then look up at the ceiling vault, decorated with engraved roses, lilies and stars, (Can you spot the sun and the moon?). Walk left along the north aisle to reach the Lady Chapel, separated from the rest of the church by the **Mason's Pillar** ② and the **Apprentice Pillar** ③. Here you'll find carvings of **Lucifer** ④, the Fallen Angel, and the **Green Man** ⑤. Nearby are **carvings** ⑥ that appear to resemble Indian corn (maize). Finally, go to the western end and look up at the wall – in the left corner is the head of the **Apprentice** ⑦; to the right is the (rather worn) head of the **Master Mason** ⑧.

EXPLORE SOME MORE

After visiting the chapel, head downhill to see the spectacularly sited ruins of Roslin Castle, then take a walk along leafy Roslin Glen.

Lucifer, the Fallen Angel
At head height, to the left of the second window from the left, is an upside-down angel bound with rope, a symbol often associated with Freemasonry. The arch above is decorated with the Dance of Death.

The Apprentice
High in the corner, beneath an empty statue niche, is the head of the murdered Apprentice, with a deep wound in his forehead above the right eye. Legend says the Apprentice was murdered in a jealous rage by the Master Mason. The worn head on the side wall to the left of the Apprentice is that of his mother.

The Master Mason ⑧

Baptistery

ROSSLYN CHAPEL & THE DA VINCI CODE

Dan Brown was referencing Rosslyn Chapel's alleged links to the Knights Templar and the Freemasons – unusual symbols found among the carvings, and the fact that a descendant of its founder, William St Clair, was a Grand Master Mason – when he chose it as the setting for his novel's denouement. Rosslyn is indeed a coded work, written in stone, but its meaning depends on your point of view. See The Rosslyn Hoax? by Robert LD Cooper for an alternative interpretation of the chapel's symbolism.

PRACTICAL TIPS

Local guides give hourly talks throughout the day, which are included in the admission price. No photography is allowed inside the chapel.

Green Man

On a boss at the base of the arch between the second and third windows from the left is the finest example of more than a hundred 'green man' carvings in the chapel, pagan symbols of spring, fertility and rebirth.

2

4

5

Mason's Pillar

Lady Chapel

3

Sacristy

Aisle

Altar

Choir

South Aisle

6

The Apprentice Pillar

This is perhaps the chapel's most beautiful carving. Four vines spiral up the pillar, issuing from the mouths of eight dragons at its base. At the top is Isaac, son of Abraham, lying bound upon the altar.

Indian Corn

The frieze around the second window on the south wall is said to represent Indian corn (maize), but it predates Columbus' discovery of the New World in 1492. Other carvings seem to resemble aloe vera.

🛏 Sleeping & Eating

Glebe House B&B **££**
(☑ 01620-892608; www.glebehouse-nb.co.uk; Law Rd; r per person £65; P 🤶) Glebe House is a beautiful Georgian country house with three spacious bedrooms.

Buttercup Cafe CAFE **£**
(☑ 01620-894985; 92 High St; mains £4-6; ⊙ 9am-4pm Mon-Sat, 10am-4pm Sun; 🖼) The delightful Buttercup Cafe is an ideal place to break for coffee and cake, or a lunchtime baked potato, salad or sandwich.

Grange STEAK **££**
(☑ 01620-893344; www.grangenorthberwick.co.uk; 35 High St; mains £11-25; ⊙ noon-2pm & 5-9pm Mon-Thu, from 10am Fri-Sun; 🖼) The Grange, one of North Berwick's top eating places, is a grill restaurant that serves burgers, steaks and hot dogs, plus deli spreads and breakfasts Friday to Sunday (till 12.30pm). Two-/three-course lunches cost £13/15 and are served from 11am to 2pm.

ℹ Getting There & Away

North Berwick is 24 miles east of Edinburgh. First bus 124 runs between Edinburgh and North Berwick (£4.20, 1¼ hours, every 30 minutes).

There are frequent trains between North Berwick and Edinburgh (£6.40, 35 minutes, hourly).

Linlithgow

POP 13,500

This ancient royal burgh is one of Scotland's oldest towns, though much of it 'only' dates from the 15th to 17th centuries. Its centre retains a certain charm, despite some ugly modern buildings and occasional traffic congestion, and the town makes an excellent day trip from Edinburgh.

There's a self-service **tourist information point** (☑ 01506-282720; Burgh Halls, The Cross; ⊙ 9am-5pm Mon-Sat, 11am-5pm Sun) in the Burgh Halls, near the Linlithgow Palace entrance.

👁 Sights & Activities

Linlithgow Palace PALACE
(HS; Church Peel; adult/child £5.50/3.30; ⊙ 9.30am-5.30pm Apr-Sep, 10am-4pm Oct-Mar) The building of this magnificent palace, begun by James I in 1425, continued for over a century and it became a favourite royal residence – James V was born here in 1512, as was his daughter Mary (later Queen of Scots) in 1542, and Bonnie Prince Charlie visited briefly in 1745. The elaborately carved **King's Fountain**, the centrepiece of the palace courtyard, flowed with wine during Charlie's stay; commissioned by James V in 1537, it is the oldest in Britain.

Linlithgow Canal Centre MUSEUM
(www.lucs.org.uk; Manse Rd; ⊙ 1.30-5pm Sat & Sun Easter-Sep, 1.30-5pm Mon-Fri Jul–mid-Aug) FREE Just 150m south of the town centre lies the Union Canal and this pretty little museum that records the history of the canal. The centre runs 2½-hour canal boat trips (adult/child £8/5) west to the Avon Aqueduct, departing at 2pm Saturday and Sunday, Easter to September, and occasionally to the Falkirk Wheel (£22). Shorter 20-minute cruises (adult/child £4/3) leave every half hour during the centre's opening times.

🍴 Eating & Drinking

Four Marys PUB FOOD **££**
(www.fourmarys-linlithgow.co.uk; 65-76 High St; mains £8-13; ⊙ food served noon-2.30pm & 6-9pm Mon-Fri, noon-9pm Sat, 12.30-8.30pm Sun) The Four Marys is an attractive traditional pub (opposite the entrance to Linlithgow Palace) that serves real ales and good-value pub grub, including haggis, neeps and tatties (haggis, mashed turnip and mashed potato).

Champany Inn STEAK **£££**
(☑ 01506-834532; www.champany.com; mains £33-45; ⊙ 12.30-2pm Mon-Fri, 7-10pm Mon-Sat; P) This rustic inn is a trencherman's delight, famous for its excellent Aberdeen Angus steaks and Scottish lobsters (booking essential). The neighbouring **Chop & Ale House** (mains £12-25; ⊙ noon-2.30pm & 6.30-10pm Mon-Thu, noon-10pm Fri & Sat, 12.30-10pm Sun; P) is a less-expensive alternative to the main dining room. The inn is 2 miles northeast of Linlithgow, on the A803/A904 road towards Bo'ness and Queensferry.

ℹ Getting There & Away

Linlithgow is 15 miles west of Edinburgh, and is served by frequent trains from the capital (£5.20, 20 minutes, four every hour); the train station is 250m east of the town centre.

You can also cycle from Edinburgh to Linlithgow along the Union Canal towpath (21 miles); allow two hours.

Glasgow

POP 596,500

Best Places to Eat

➡ Ubiquitous Chip (p126)

➡ Stravaigin (p125)

➡ Mother India (p125)

➡ Ox & Finch (p124)

➡ Saramago Café Bar (p123)

➡ Topolabamba (p123)

Best Places to Sleep

➡ Alamo Guest House (p122)

➡ Grasshoppers (p118)

➡ 15Glasgow (p122)

➡ Hotel du Vin (p122)

➡ Malmaison (p119)

Why Go?

Disarmingly blending sophistication and earthiness, Scotland's biggest city has evolved over the last couple of decades to become one of Britain's most intriguing metropolises.

The soberly handsome Victorian buildings, legacies of wealth generated from manufacturing and trade, suggest a staid sort of place. Very wrong. They are packed with stylish bars, top-notch restaurants and one of Britain's best live-music scenes. The place's sheer vitality is gloriously infectious: the combination of edgy urbanity and the residents' legendary friendliness is captivating.

Glasgow also offers plenty by day. Its shopping – whether you're looking for Italian fashion or pre-loved denim – is famous and there are top-drawer museums and galleries. Charles Rennie Mackintosh's sublime designs dot the city, which – always proud of its working-class background – also innovatively displays its industrial heritage.

When to Go
Glasgow

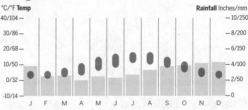

Feb The drizzle won't lift? Maroon yourself in one of Glasgow's fabulous pubs or clubs.

Jun The West End Festival and the Glasgow Jazz Festival make the city music heaven.

Aug Glasgow is super-friendly at any time, but when the sun is shining it's the happiest city in Britain.

Glasgow Highlights

1 Art Exploring the city's fabulous wealth of paintings, beginning at the Kelvingrove Art Gallery & Museum (p112).

2 Architecture Discovering the work of Charles Rennie Mackintosh, starting with his masterpiece, the Glasgow School of Art (p106).

3 Ubiquitous Chip (p126) Dining in the restaurant that set the scene for the West End's culinary excellence.

4 Live Music Seeing a band at King Tut's Wah Wah Hut (p130) or at any other venue in the city's legendary, diverse live-music scene.

5 Vintage Shops Browsing the city's excellent selection of

vintage shops – Mr Ben (p132) being among the favourites.

6 **Football** Catching a match at either of the local teams' massive cauldrons of football – Celtic Park (p131) or Ibrox Stadium (p131)'.

7 **Sub Club** (p127) Showing your latest dance moves at this iconic club.

8 **Clyde Walkway** (p116) Grabbing a bike for a leisurely exploration of Glasgow's industrial heritage and green

surroundings on this great cycle route.

9 **Pink Triangle** Immersing yourself in Glasgow's friendly LGBT culture in one of the bars of the Pink Triangle such as Speakeasy (p128).

History

Glasgow grew around the cathedral founded by St Kertigan, later to become St Mungo, in the 6th century. Unfortunately, with the exception of the cathedral, virtually nothing of the medieval city remains. It was swept away by the energies of a new age – the age of capitalism, the Industrial Revolution and the British Empire.

In the 18th century, much of the tobacco trade between Europe and the USA was routed through Glasgow, providing a great source of wealth. Even after the tobacco trade declined in the 19th century, the city continued to prosper as a centre of textile manufacturing, shipbuilding and the coal and steel industries. The outward appearance of prosperity, however, was tempered by the dire working conditions in the factories.

In the first half of the 20th century Glasgow was the centre of Britain's munitions industry, supplying arms and ships for the two world wars, in the second of which the city was carpet-bombed. Post-war, however, the port and heavy industries began to dwindle, and by the early 1970s, the city looked doomed. Glasgow became synonymous with unemployment, economic depression and urban violence, centred around high-rise housing schemes such as the infamous Gorbals. More recently, urban development and a booming cultural sector have injected style and confidence into the city; though the standard of living remains low for Britain and life continues to be tough for many, the ongoing regeneration process gives grounds for optimism. The successful hosting of the 2014 Commonwealth Games highlighted this regeneration to a wide global audience.

◉ Sights

Glasgow's major sights are fairly evenly dispersed, with many found along the Clyde. Many museums are free.

◉ City Centre

The grid layout and pedestrian streets of the city centre make it easy to get around, and there are numerous cafes and pubs that make good pit stops between attractions.

★ **Glasgow School of Art**   HISTORIC BUILDING
(Map p108; ☑ 0141-353 4526; www.gsa.ac.uk/ tours; 167 Renfrew St; tours adult/child £9.75/4.75; ☺ 10am-4.30pm) Charles Rennie Mackintosh's greatest building – extensively damaged by fire in 2014, and due to re-open in 2018 – still fulfils its original function, so just follow the steady stream of eclectically dressed students up the hill to find it. It's one of Glasgow's architectural showpieces and has now been joined by Steven Holl's spectacular glacial, green School of Design right opposite. A risqué combination, but it works. Tours leave from the new building, which also holds a free design exhibition.

Visits to the Mackintosh building are by excellent hour-long guided tours (11am and 3pm, plus 1pm May to September, multi-

---

GLASGOW IN...

Two Days

On your first day, hit the East End for **Glasgow Cathedral** (p108), **St Mungo's Museum** (p110) and a wander through the hillside **necropolis** (p110). Later, take in one of the city's top museums: either the **Burrell Collection** (p113) or the **Kelvingrove** (p112). As evening falls, head to trendy Merchant City for a stroll and dinner; try **Café Gandolfi** (p124). Check out **Artà** (p127) for a pre- or post-meal drink. The next day, visit whichever museum you missed yesterday, and then it's Mackintosh time. **Glasgow School of Art** (p106) is his finest work: if you like his style, head to the West End for **Mackintosh House** (p112). Hungry? Thirsty? Some of the city's best restaurants and bars are up this end of town, so you could make a night of it. Make sure to check out one of the numerous excellent **music venues** around the city.

Four Days

A four-day stay gives better scope to get to grips with Glasgow. Spend a day along the Clyde – the **Riverside Museum** (p111) and the **Glasgow Science Centre** (p111). Plan your weekend around a night out at the **Cathouse** (p129) or the legendary **Sub Club** (p127), and a day strolling the stylish city-centre clothing emporia or attending a football game. Don't miss trying at least one of the city's classic curry houses.

lingual translations available) run by architecture students. While reconstruction is ongoing, they visit the building's exterior only. Book online or by phone at busy times. Once the building is reopened, tour frequency will likely increase.

Particularly impressive is the thoroughness of the design; the architect's pencil seems to have shaped everything down to the smallest detail. The interior is strikingly austere, with simple colour combinations (often just black and cream) and the uncomfortable-looking high-backed chairs for which Mackintosh is famous. The library, designed as an addition in 1907, is a masterpiece.

There's a Mackintosh shop at the end of the tour. If you liked the visit, the same folk run recommended architecturally minded **walking tours** of central Glasgow; see the website for details.

Willow Tearooms HISTORIC BUILDING

(Map p108; 217 Sauchiehall St) FREE The location of the original tearoom that Mackintosh designed and furnished in the early 20th century for restaurateur Kate Cranston was undergoing extensive work at the time of research and will reopen as an authentic reconstruction in 2018 or 2019. You'll be able to relive the original splendour while admiring the architect's distinctive touch in just about every element; he had a free rein and even the teaspoons were given his attention. Other reconstructions operate as tearooms further down Sauchiehall St and on Buchanan St.

There's a Mackintosh gift shop here too.

★**City Chambers** HISTORIC BUILDING

(Map p108; www.glasgow.gov.uk; George Sq; ⊙9am-5pm Mon-Fri) FREE The grand seat of local government was built in the 1880s at the high point of Glasgow's wealth. The interior is even more extravagant than the exterior, and the chambers have sometimes been used as a movie location to represent the Kremlin or the Vatican. You can have a look at the opulent ground floor during opening hours. To see more, free guided tours are held at 10.30am and 2.30pm Monday to Friday; it's worth popping in earlier that day to prebook.

Gallery of Modern Art GALLERY

(GoMA; Map p108; ☑ 0141-287 3050; www.glasgow museums.com; Royal Exchange Sq; ⊙10am-5pm Mon-Thu & Sat, until 8pm Thu, 11am-5pm Fri & Sun)

FREE Scotland's most popular contemporary-art gallery features modern works from international artists, housed in a graceful neoclassical building. The original interior is an ornate contrast to the daring, inventive art often on display. There's also a big effort made to keep the kids entertained. Usually the horseback statue of the Duke of Wellington outside is cheekily crowned with a traffic cone; the authorities grumble, but it keeps happening and is now an icon.

The Lighthouse HISTORIC BUILDING

(Map p108; ☑ 0141-276 5365; www.thelighthouse. co.uk; 11 Mitchell Lane; ⊙10.30am-5pm Mon-Sat, noon-5pm Sun) FREE Mackintosh's first building, designed in 1893, was a striking new headquarters for the *Glasgow Herald*. Tucked up a narrow lane off Buchanan St, it now serves as Scotland's Centre for Architecture & Design, with fairly technical temporary exhibitions (sometimes admission is payable for these), as well as the Mackintosh Interpretation Centre, a detailed (if slightly dry) overview of his life and work. On the top floor of the 'lighthouse', drink in great views over the rooftops and spires of the city centre.

★**Sharmanka Kinetic Theatre** EXHIBITION

(Map p108; ☑ 0141-552 7080; www.sharmanka. com; 103 Trongate; adult/child short show £6/5, long show £8/6; ⊙45min shows 3pm Wed-Sun plus 4.15pm Sat, 70min shows 7pm Thu & Sun) This extraordinary mechanical theatre is located at the Trongate 103 arts centre. The amazing creativity of Eduard Bersudsky, a Russian sculptor and mechanic, now resident in Scotland, has created a series of large, wondrous figures sculpted from bits of scrap and elaborate carvings. Set to haunting music, these perform humorous and tragic stories of the human spirit. It's great for kids and very moving for adults: inspirational one moment and macabre the next, but always colourful, clever and thought-provoking.

The gallery is open just before performances Wednesday to Sunday – the sculptures and their stories are fascinating even when not in motion.

⊙ **East End**

The oldest part of the city is concentrated around Glasgow Cathedral, to the east of the modern centre. It's a 15-minute walk from George Sq, but numerous buses pass nearby, including buses 11, 12, 36, 37, 38 and 42.

Central Glasgow

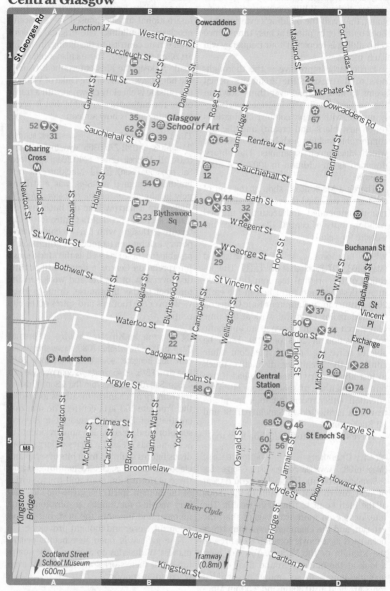

★ **Glasgow Cathedral** CATHEDRAL
(HES; Map p108; ☎ 0141-552 8198; www.historic environment.scot; Cathedral Sq; ⓧ 9.30am-5.30pm Mon-Sat & 1-5pm Sun Apr-Sep, 10am-4pm Mon-Sat & 1-4pm Sun Oct-Mar) **FREE** Glasgow Cathedral has a rare timelessness. The dark, imposing interior conjures up medieval might and can send a shiver down the spine. It's a shining example of Gothic architecture, and unlike nearly all of Scotland's cathedrals, survived the turmoil of the Reformation mobs almost intact. Most

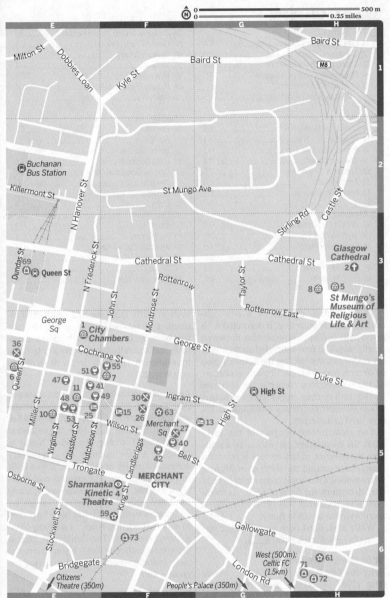

0 — 500 m
0 — 0.25 miles

Baird St

Baird St

M8

Milton St

Dobbies Loan

Kyle St

Buchanan Bus Station

St Mungo Ave

Killermont St

N Hanover St

Dundas St

Queen St

Cathedral St

Rottenrow

Stirling Rd

Castle St

Cathedral St

Glasgow Cathedral
2

8 5
St Mungo's Museum of Religious Life & Art

N Frederick St

John St

Montrose St

Taylor St

Rottenrow East

George Sq

1 **City Chambers**

George St

Duke St

36

Queen St

Cochrane St

51 55
47 7
11 41
48 49
10
53 25

30

Ingram St

15
26

Merchant Sq

63
27

40

High St

13

High St

Miller St

Virginia St

Glassford St

Hutcheson St

Wilson St

Candleriggs

42

Bell St

King St

Trongate

MERCHANT CITY

Osborne St

Sharmanka Kinetic Theatre
4

59

Stockwell St

73

Gallowgate

Bridgegate

London Rd

West (500m); Celtic FC (1.5km)

61
71
72

Citizens' Theatre (350m)

People's Palace (350m)

of the current building dates from the 15th century.

Entry is through a side door into the nave, hung with regimental colours. The wooden roof has been restored many times since its original construction, but some of the tim-

ber dates from the 14th century; note the impressive shields. Many of the cathedral's stunning, narrow stained-glass windows are modern; to your left is Francis Spear's 1958 work *The Creation*, which fills the west window.

Central Glasgow

The cathedral, divided by a late-15th-century stone choir screen, is decorated with seven pairs of figures representing the seven deadly sins. The four stained-glass panels of the east window, depicting the Apostles (also by Francis Spear) are particularly evocative. At the northeastern corner is the entrance to the 15th-century upper chapter house, where Glasgow University was founded. It's now used as a sacristy.

The most interesting part of the cathedral, the lower church, is reached by a stairway. Its forest of pillars creates a powerful atmosphere around the tomb of St Mungo, who founded a monastic community here in the 5th century, the focus of a famous medieval pilgrimage that was believed to be as meritorious as a visit to Rome.

While here, don't miss a stroll in the **necropolis** (◷8.30am-4.30pm) FREE.

★**St Mungo's Museum of
Religious Life & Art** MUSEUM
(Map p108; ☑0141-276 1625; www.glasgow museums.com; 2 Castle St; ◷10am-5pm Tue-Thu & Sat, 11am-5pm Fri & Sun) FREE Set in a reconstruction of the bishop's palace that once stood in the cathedral forecourt, this museum audaciously attempts to capture the world's major religions in an artistic nutshell. A startling achievement, it presents the similarities and differences of how various religions approach common themes such as birth, marriage and death. The attraction is twofold: firstly, impressive art that blurs the lines between religion and culture; and secondly, the opportunity to delve into different faiths, as deeply or shallowly as you wish.

Provand's Lordship HISTORIC BUILDING
(Map p108; ☑0141-276 1625; www.glasgowmuse ums.com; 3 Castle St; ◷10am-5pm Tue-Thu & Sat, 11am-5pm Fri & Sun) FREE Near the cathedral is Provand's Lordship, the oldest house in Glasgow. A rare example of 15th-century domestic Scottish architecture, it was built in 1471 as a manse. The ceilings and doorways are low, and the rooms are sparsely furnished with period artefacts, except for an upstairs room, which has been furnished to reflect the living space of an early-16th-century chaplain. The building's biggest draw is its authentic feel – if you ignore the tacky imitation-stone linoleum covering the ground floor.

People's Palace MUSEUM
(☑0141-276 0788; www.glasgowmuseums.com; Glasgow Green; ◷10am-5pm Tue-Thu & Sat, 11am-5pm Fri & Sun) FREE Set in the city's oldest park, Glasgow Green, is the solid orange stone People's Palace. It is an impressive museum of social history, telling the story of Glasgow from 1750 to the present through creative, inventive family-friendly displays.

The palace was built in the late 19th century as a cultural centre for Glasgow's East End. The attached greenhouse, the **Winter Gardens** (10am to 5pm daily), has tropical plants and is a nice spot for a coffee.

⊙ The Clyde

Once a thriving shipbuilding area, the Clyde sank into dereliction during the post-war era but has been subject to extensive rejuvenation.

There are several good attractions along the Clyde, but the walk along its banks still isn't all that it could be; it can feel bleak and impersonal, with oversized buildings dwarfing the humble pedestrian.

★ **Riverside Museum**　　　MUSEUM
(☑0141-287 2720; www.glasgowmuseums.com; 100 Pointhouse Pl; ⊙10am-5pm Mon-Thu & Sat, 11am-5pm Fri & Sun; ⊕) **FREE** This visually impressive modern museum at Glasgow Harbour owes its striking curved forms to late British-Iraqi architect Zaha Hadid. A transport museum forms the main part of the collection, featuring a fascinating series of cars made in Scotland, plus assorted railway locos, trams, bikes (including the world's first pedal-powered bicycle from 1847) and model Clyde-built ships. An atmospheric recreation of a Glasgow shopping street from the early 20th century puts the vintage vehicles into a social context. There's also a cafe.

It's west of the centre. Get bus 100 from the north side of George Sq or walk the signposted path from the Kelvingrove Museum – about 0.6 miles.

The magnificent three-masted *Glenlee,* launched in 1896, is the **Tall Ship** (www.thetallship.com; Riverside Museum; ⊙10am-5pm; ⊕) **FREE**, which is berthed alongside the museum. On board are family-friendly displays about the ship's history, restoration and shipboard life during its heyday. Upkeep costs are high, so do donate something or have a coffee below decks.

★ **Glasgow Science Centre**　　　MUSEUM
(Map p114; ☑0141-420 5000; www.glasgowsciencecentre.org; 50 Pacific Quay; adult/child £11/9, IMAX, tower or planetarium extra £2.50-3.50; ⊙10am-5pm Wed-Sun Nov-Mar, 10am-5pm daily Apr-Oct; ⊕) This ultramodern science museum will keep the kids entertained for hours (that's middle-aged kids, too!). It brings science and technology alive through hundreds of interactive exhibits on four floors: a bounty of discovery for inquisitive minds. There's also an **IMAX theatre** (see www.cineworld.com for current screenings), a rotating 127m-high **observation tower**; a **planetarium**, and a **Science Theatre**, with live science demonstrations. To get here, take bus 89 or 90 from Union St.

◉ West End

With its appealing studenty buzz, trendy bars and cafes and nonchalant swagger, the West End is probably the most engaging area of Glasgow – it's great for people-watching, and is as close as Glasgow gets to bohemian. From the centre, buses 9, 16 and 23 run towards Kelvingrove; buses 8, 11, and 16 to the university; and buses 20, 44 and 66 to Byres Rd (among others).

★ **Kelvingrove Art Gallery & Museum** GALLERY, MUSEUM
(Map p114; www.glasgowmuseums.com; Argyle St; ☉ 10am-5pm Mon-Thu & Sat, 11am-5pm Fri & Sun) **FREE** A magnificent stone building, this grand Victorian cathedral of culture is a fascinating and unusual museum, with a bewildering variety of exhibits. You'll find fine art alongside stuffed animals, and Micronesian shark-tooth swords alongside a Spitfire plane, but it's not mix 'n' match: rooms are carefully and thoughtfully themed, and the collection is a manageable size. It has an excellent room of Scottish art, a room of fine French Impressionist works, and quality Renaissance paintings from Italy and Flanders.

Salvador Dalí's superb *Christ of St John of the Cross* is also here. Best of all, nearly everything, including the paintings, has an easy-reading paragraph of interpretation. You can learn a lot about art here, and it's excellent for children, with plenty to do and displays aimed at a variety of ages. Free hour-long guided tours begin at 11am and 2.30pm. Bus 17, among many others, runs here from Renfield St.

Hunterian Museum MUSEUM
(Map p114; www.hunterian.gla.ac.uk; University Ave; ☉ 10am-5pm Tue-Sat, 11am-4pm Sun) **FREE** Housed in the glorious sandstone university building, which is in itself reason enough to pay a visit, this quirky museum contains the collection of renowned one-time student of the university, William Hunter (1718–83). Hunter was primarily an anatomist and physician, but as one of those wonderfully well-rounded Enlightenment figures, he interested himself in everything the world had to offer. This collection is scheduled to become part of the new museum at Kelvin Hall but probably not until 2020.

Pickled organs in glass jars take their place alongside geological phenomena, potsherds gleaned from ancient brochs, dinosaur skeletons and a creepy case of deformed animals. The main halls of the exhibition, with their high vaulted roofs, are magnificent in themselves. A highlight is the 1674 Chinese *Map of the Whole World* in the World Culture section.

Hunterian Art Gallery GALLERY
(Map p114; www.hunterian.gla.ac.uk; 82 Hillhead St; ☉ 10am-5pm Tue-Sat, 11am-4pm Sun) **FREE** Across the road from the Hunterian Museum, and part of the same bequest, the bold tones of the Scottish Colourists (Samuel Peploe, Francis Cadell, JD Fergusson and Leslie Hunter) are well represented in this gallery. There are William MacTaggart's Impressionistic Scottish landscapes and a gem by Thomas Millie Dow. There's also a special collection of James McNeill Whistler's limpid prints, drawings and paintings. Upstairs, in a section devoted to late-19th-century Scottish art, you can see works by several of the Glasgow Boys.

This collection is scheduled to become part of the new museum at Kelvin Hall but likely not until 2020.

★ **Mackintosh House** HISTORIC BUILDING
(Map p114; www.hunterian.gla.ac.uk; 82 Hillhead St; adult/child £5/3; ☉ 10am-5pm Tue-Sat, 11am-4pm Sun) Attached to the Hunterian Art Gallery, this is a reconstruction of the first home that Charles Rennie Mackintosh bought with his wife, noted designer/artist Margaret Macdonald. It's fair to say that interior decoration was one of their strong points; Mackintosh House is startling even today. The house is scheduled to become part of the new museum at Kelvin Hall (Map p114; www.glasgowlife.org.uk; 1445 Argyle St), but probably not until 2020.

The quiet elegance of the hall and dining room on the ground floor give way to a stunning drawing room. There's something otherworldly about the very mannered style of the beaten silver panels, the long-backed chairs and the surface decorations echoing Celtic manuscript illuminations. You wouldn't have wanted to be the guest that spilled a glass of red on this carpet. Visits are by guided tour on the half hour.

Botanic Gardens PARK
(Map p114; ☑ 0141-276 1614; www.glasgowbotanicgardens.com; 730 Great Western Rd; ☉ 7am-dusk, glasshouse 10am-6pm summer, to 4.15pm winter) A marvellous thing about walking in here is the way the noise of Great Western Rd suddenly recedes into the background. The

wooded gardens follow the riverbank of the River Kelvin and there are plenty of tropical species to discover. **Kibble Palace**, an impressive Victorian iron and glass structure dating from 1873, is one of the largest glasshouses in Britain; check out the herb garden, too, with its medicinal species.

The gorgeous hilly grounds make the perfect place for a picnic lunch. There are also organised walks and concerts in summer – have a look at the noticeboard near the entrance to see what's on.

◉ South Side

The south side is a tangled web of busy roads with a few oases giving relief from the urban congestion. It does, however, contain some excellent attractions.

Burrell Collection GALLERY
(☑ 0141-287 2550; www.glasgowmuseums.com; Pollok Country Park; ⊘ Closed) **FREE** One of Glasgow's top attractions, this outstanding museum 3 miles out of town houses everything from Chinese porcelain and medieval furniture to paintings by Cézanne. It's closed for refurbishment, and is due to reopen in 2020.

Scotland Street School Museum NOTABLE BUILDING
(☑ 0141-287 0504; www.glasgowmuseums.com; 225 Scotland St; ⊘ 10am-5pm Tue-Thu & Sat, 11am-5pm Fri & Sun) **FREE** Mackintosh's Scotland Street School seems a bit forlorn these days, on a windswept industrial street with no babble of young voices filling its corridors. Nevertheless it's worth a visit for its stunning facade and the interesting museum of education that occupies the interior. Reconstructions of classrooms from various points in the school's lifetime, combined with grumbling headmaster and cleaner, will have older visitors recalling their own schooldays. It's right opposite Shields Rd subway station and there's also an OK cafe.

House for an Art Lover NOTABLE BUILDING
(☑ 0141-353 4770; www.houseforanartlover.co.uk; Bellahouston Park, Dumbreck Rd; adult/child £4.50/3; ⊘ 10am-4pm Mon-Wed, to 12.30pm Thu-Sun) Although designed in 1901 as an entry in a competition run by a German magazine, the House for an Art Lover was not built until the 1990s. Mackintosh worked closely with his wife on the design and her influence is evident, especially in the rose motif.

THE GENIUS OF CHARLES RENNIE MACKINTOSH

Great cities have great artists, designers and architects contributing to their urban environment while expressing their soul and individuality. Charles Rennie Mackintosh was all of these and his quirky, linear and geometric designs have had an enormous influence on Glasgow. Many of the buildings Mackintosh designed are open to the public, and you'll see his tall, thin, art-nouveau typeface repeatedly reproduced.

Born in 1868, Mackintosh studied at the Glasgow School of Art. It was there that he met the influential artist and designer Margaret Macdonald, whom he married; they collaborated on many projects and were major influences on each other's work. In 1896, aged only 27, he won a competition for his design of the School of Art's new building, Mackintosh's supreme architectural achievement. The first section was opened in 1899 and is considered to be the earliest example of art nouveau in Britain. This building demonstrates his skill in combining function and style.

Although Mackintosh's genius was quickly recognised on the Continent, he did not receive the same encouragement in Scotland. His architectural career here lasted only until 1914, when he moved to England to concentrate on furniture design. He died in 1928, and it is only since the last decades of the 20th century that Mackintosh's genius has been widely recognised. For more about the man and his work, contact the **Charles Rennie Mackintosh Society** (Map p114; ☑ 0141-946 6600; www.crmsociety.com; Mackintosh Church, 870 Garscube Rd). Check its website for special events.

Another of Mackintosh's finest works is **Hill House** (p247), in Helensburgh. If you're planning to visit some of the farther-flung attractions, the **Mackintosh Trail ticket** (£10), available at the **tourist office** (p133) or any Mackintosh building, gives you a day's admission to Hill House, the **Mackintosh Church** (p115) and **House for an Art Lover** (p113) as well as unlimited bus and subway travel.

West End

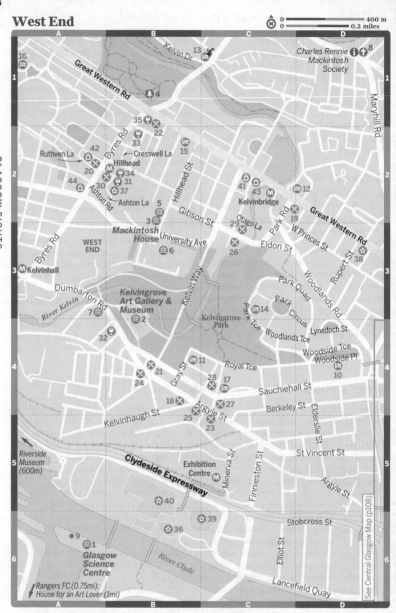

The overall effect of this brilliant architect's design is one of space and light. Buses 3, 9, 54, 55 and 56 all run here from downtown; check the website beforehand, as it's regularly booked for events.

Holmwood House HISTORIC BUILDING

(NTS; ☑ 0141-571 0184; www.nts.org.uk; 61-63 Netherlee Rd, Cathcart; adult/child £6.50/5; ⊙ noon-5pm Thu-Mon Apr-Oct, from 11am Jul & Aug) An interesting building designed by Alexander 'Greek' Thomson, Holmwood House dates

West End

from 1857. Despite ongoing renovations, it's well worth a visit. Look for sun symbols downstairs and stars upstairs in this attractive house with its adaptation of classical Greek architecture. Cathcart is 4 miles south of the centre; get a train via Queen's Park or Neilston. Otherwise, take bus 44, 44A, 44D or 66 from the city centre. Follow Rhannan Rd for about 800m to find the house.

Scottish Football Museum   MUSEUM
(The Hampden Experience; ☑0141-616 6139; www.
scottishfootballmuseum.org.uk; Hampden Park;
adult/child £8/3; ⊙10am-5pm Mon-Sat, 11am-
5pm Sun) At Hampden Park, the national
stadium, this museum covers the history of
the game in Scotland and the considerable
influence of Scots on the world game. It's
crammed full of impressive memorabilia, including a cap and match ticket from the very
first international football game ever played,
held in Glasgow in 1872. You can also take
a tour of the stadium (adult/child £8/3.50;
combined ticket with museum £12/5),
home ground to both Scotland and lower
league outfit Queens Park. The museum is
at Hampden Park, off Aikenhead Rd. Take a
train to Mount Florida station or take bus 5,
31, 37 or 75 from Stockwell St.

⊙ North Side

Mackintosh Church   CHURCH
(Queen's Cross Church; Map p114; ☑0141-946
6600; www.mackintoshchurch.com; 870 Garscube
Rd; adult/child £4/free; ⊙10am-5pm Mon-Fri
Apr-Oct, 10am-4pm Mon, Wed & Fri Nov-Dec &
Feb-Mar, closed Jan) Now headquarters of the
Charles Rennie Mackintosh Society, this is
the only one of Mackintosh's church designs
to be built. It has an excellent stained-glass
window and exquisite relief carvings, and
the wonderful simplicity and grace of the
barrel-shaped design is particularly inspiring. The luminous church hall is arguably
even finer. It has a good gift shop and a detailed Mackintosh DVD playing. Garscube
Rd is the northern extension of Rose St in
the city centre.

🏃 Activities

There are numerous green spaces within the
city. **Pollok Country Park** surrounds the
Burrell Collection and has several woodland

trails. Nearer the centre of the city, the **Kelvin Walkway** follows the River Kelvin through Kelvingrove Park, the Botanic Gardens and on to Dawsholm Park.

Walking & Cycling

The **Clyde Walkway** stretches from Glasgow upriver to the Falls of Clyde near New Lanark, about 40 miles away. The tourist office (p133) has information outlining different sections of this walk. The 10-mile section through Glasgow has interesting parts, though most of the old shipyards are no longer there.

The well-trodden, long-distance footpath the **West Highland Way** begins in Milngavie, 8 miles north of Glasgow (you can walk to Milngavie from Glasgow along the River Kelvin), and runs for 95 spectacular miles to Fort William.

There are several long-distance pedestrian/cycle routes that begin in Glasgow and follow off-road routes for most of the way. Check www.sustrans.org.uk for more details. The **Clyde–Loch Lomond route** traverses residential and industrial areas in a 20-mile ride from Bell's Bridge to Loch Lomond. This route continues to Inverness, part of the **Lochs and Glens National Cycle Route**.

The **Clyde to Forth cycle route** runs through Glasgow. One way takes you to Edinburgh via Bathgate, the other takes you via Paisley to Greenock and Gourock, the first section partly on roads. Another branch heads down to Irvine and Ardrossan, for the ferry to Arran. An extension via Ayr, Maybole and Glentrool leads to the Solway coast and Carlisle.

☞ Tours

Waverley   BOATING
(Map p114; ☑ 0845 130 4647; www.waverley excursions.co.uk; ☺ mid-May–mid-Aug plus some Oct departures) The world's last ocean-going paddle steamer (built in 1947) cruises Scotland's west coast in summer, with many different routes; the website details days of departure. It serves several towns and the islands of Bute, Great Cumbrae, Arran and more. Its Glasgow departures are from the Glasgow Science Centre, while it also has frequent departures from Largs and Ayr among others.

Seaforce   BOATING
(☑ 0141-221 1070; www.seaforce.co.uk; Riverside Museum) Departing from the Riverside Museum, Seaforce offers speedy all-weather powerboat jaunts along the Clyde. There's a variety of trips, including a 20-minute 'Clyde Ride' around central Glasgow (adult/child £10/5), an hour-long trip to the Erskine Bridge (£15/10) or four-hour rides to local wildlife hot spots (£45/35).

Rabbies   BUS
(☑ 0141-291 5005; www.rabbies.com) This popular outfit runs a range of minibus tours around the city and up to the Highlands, including popular long day-trips that take in Glencoe and Loch Ness, or West Highland castles.

Hidden Heritage Tours   CYCLING
(☑ 07857 974178; www.hiddenheritagetours.co.uk) These tours explore Glasgow's industrial and mercantile heritage. They offer a two-hour walking tour of Merchant City (£10), a half-day bike tour of major attractions (£20/30 with own/hire bike), or a full-day exploration of the Clyde's shipbuilding past (£30/40 with own/hire bike).

Glasgow Taxis City Tour   DRIVING
(☑ 0141-429 7070; www.glasgowtaxis.co.uk) If you're confident you can understand the driver's accent, a taxi tour is a good way to get a feel of the city and its sights. The 60-minute tour takes you around all the centre's important landmarks, with commentary. The standard tour costs £35 for up to five people, or £65 for a two-hour affair.

☆ Festivals & Events

Celtic Connections   MUSIC
(☑ 0141-353 8000; www.celticconnections.com; ☺ Jan) This two-week music festival focuses on roots music and folk from Scotland and around the world.

Glasgow Film Festival   FILM
(www.glasgowfilm.org; ☺ Feb) Ten-day film festival with screenings in various locations across the city.

Glasgow International Festival of Visual Art   ART
(☑ 0141-276 8384; www.glasgowinternational.org; ☺ late Apr) Held in even years, this festival features a range of innovative installations, performances and exhibitions around town.

Glasgow Jazz Festival   MUSIC
(www.jazzfest.co.uk; ☺ Jun) Excellent festival sees big-name international acts come to town, with stages set up in George Sq and Merchant City.

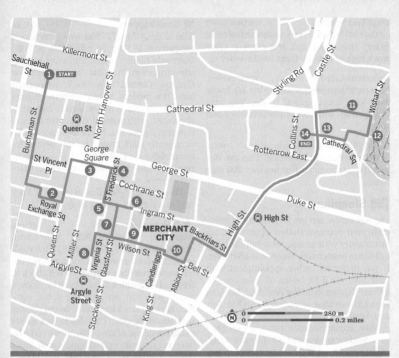

City Walk
Glasgow

START BUCHANAN ST
END PROVAND'S LORDSHIP
LENGTH 1¾ MILES; 1½ HOURS

This stroll takes you to Glasgow Cathedral through trendy Merchant City, once headquarters for Glasgow industrialists.

Start at the junction of two major shopping thoroughfares, Sauchiehall and Buchanan Sts, overseen by a bronze **1 statue of Donald Dewar**, Scotland's inaugural First Minister. Stroll down pedestrian Buchanan St, then left through one of the handsome gateways into Merchant City. Here, the strikingly colonnaded **2 Gallery of Modern Art** (p107) was once the Royal Exchange and now hosts some of the country's best contemporary art displays. Turn left up Queen St to **3 George Square**, surrounded by imposing Victorian architecture, including the grandiose **4 City Chambers** (p107). Statues include Robert Burns, James Watt and, atop a Doric column, Sir Walter Scott.

Walk down South Frederick St. Ahead of you, the former Court House cells now house the **5 Corinthian Club** (p127); drop

into the bar for a glimpse of the extravagant interior, then continue to **6 Hutcheson's Hall**. This was built in 1805 as a hospital and school for the poor with a bequest from the brothers whose statues stand in the facade. Retrace your steps one block and continue south down Glassford St past **7 Trades Hall**, designed by Robert Adam in 1791 to house the trades guild. Turn right into Wilson St and left along Virginia St, lined with the old warehouses of the Tobacco Lords; many of these have been converted into posh flats. The **8 Tobacco Exchange** is flanked by pretty Virginia Court. Sugar and tobacco were traded here in the 18th and 19th centuries.

Back on Wilson St, the **9 Old Sheriff Court** fills a whole block and has been both Glasgow's town hall and main law court. Continue east on Wilson St past Ingram Sq to **10 Merchant Square**, a covered courtyard that was once the city's fruit market but now bustles with cafes and bars.

Head up Albion St, then right into Blackfriars St. Emerging onto High St, turn left and follow it up to **11 Glasgow Cathedral** (p108). Behind the cathedral wind your way up through the **12 necropolis** (p110), which offers great city views. Lastly, check out **13 St Mungo's Museum of Religious Life & Art** (p110) and **14 Provand's Lordship** (p110).

West End Festival

PERFORMING ARTS

(☏ 0141-341 0844; www.westendfestival.co.uk; ☉ Jun) This music and arts event is Glasgow's biggest festival. Runs for three weeks.

Merchant City Festival

STREET CARNIVAL

(www.merchantcityfestival.com; ☉ late Jul) Lively week-long street festival in the Merchant City quarter, with lots of performances and stalls.

World Pipe Band Championships

MUSIC

(www.theworlds.co.uk; ☉ mid-Aug) This two-day bagpipe extravaganza features over 200 pipe bands.

🛏 Sleeping

The city centre can get very rowdy at weekends, and accommodation options fill up fast, mostly with groups who will probably roll home boisterously some time after 3am. If you prefer an earlier appointment with your bed, you'll be better off in a smaller, quieter lodging, or in the West End. Booking ahead is essential at weekends and in July and August.

Most accommodation providers set prices according to demand, so if there's a big-name concert on a Saturday, expect to pay a hefty premium, even for mediocre places.

🛏 City Centre

Glasgow Metro Youth Hostel

HOSTEL £

(SYHA; Map p108; ☏ 0345-293 7373; www.syha. org.uk; 89 Buccleuch St; s £34, without bathroom £27; ☉ late Jun-Aug; 🛜) Student accommodation belonging to the nearby Glasgow School of Art provides the venue for this summer hostel. All rooms are comfortable singles, many with en suite, there are kitchen facilities and it's a very good deal for solo travellers or groups. It's slightly cheaper midweek.

Euro Hostel

HOSTEL £

(Map p108; ☏ 08455 399956; www.euro-hostels. co.uk; 318 Clyde St; dm £16-26, d £50-80; 🛜) With hundreds of beds, this mammoth hostel is handily central. While it can feel over-businesslike, and is often booked out by rowdy groups, it has lots of facilities, including en suite dorms (some recently modernised) with lockers, a compact kitchen, breakfast, bar, games room and laundry. Aimed at groups, the 'suites' section is attractively modern, with its own little garden and lounge area.

★ Grasshoppers

HOTEL ££

(Map p108; ☏ 0141-222 2666; www.grasshoppers glasgow.com; 87 Union St; r £100-120; ❋ 🛜 🐾) Discreetly hidden atop a timeworn railway administration building right alongside Glasgow Central, this small, well-priced hotel is a modern, upbeat surprise. Rooms are compact (a few are larger) but well-appointed, with unusual views over the station roof's glass sea. Numerous nice touches: friendly staff, interesting art, proper in-room coffee, free cupcakes, and weeknight suppers make this among the centre's homiest choices.

There's a very good deal available (£6 per day) at a car park a block away.

★ Citizen M

HOTEL ££

(Map p108; ☏ 0141-404 9485; www.citizenm. com; 60 Renfrew St; r £72-130; @ 🛜) This modern chain does away with some normal hotel accoutrements in favour of self-check-in terminals and minimalist, plasticky modern rooms with just two features: a big, comfortable king-sized bed and a decent shower with mood lighting. The idea is that guests make liberal use of the public areas, and why wouldn't you, with upbeat, super-comfortable designer furniture, 24-hour cafe, and iMacs.

Indigo

HOTEL ££

(Map p108; ☏ 0141-226 7700; www.hotelindigo glasgow.com; 75 Waterloo St; r £110-190; ❋ @ 🛜) Once the power station for early trams, this boutique-chain conversion of an elegant building has resulted in a satisfying, surprisingly quiet option in the heart of things. Rooms have mural-style artwork, great beds and free minibar (the contents improve as you go up the room grades). Space is good, and bathrooms have rainfall showers. Prices vary; there are usually good online deals.

Rab Ha's

INN ££

(Map p108; ☏ 0141-572 0400; www.rabhas.com; 83 Hutcheson St; r £69-89; 🛜) This Merchant City favourite is an atmospheric pub-restaurant with four stylish rooms upstairs. They are all quite distinct and colourful. Room 1 is the best and largest, but all are comfortable, and the location is great. The personal touches like fresh flowers, iPod docks, a big welcome and any-time breakfast make you feel special.

Pipers Tryst Hotel

HOTEL ££

(Map p108; ☏ 0141-353 5551; www.thepiping centre.co.uk; 30-34 McPhater St; s/d £89/99; 🛜) The name is no tartan tourist trap; rather this intimate, cosy hotel in a noble building is actually run by the adjacent bagpiping centre, and profits go towards maintaining it. Cheery staff, great value and a prime city-centre location make this a wise choice. You won't have far to migrate after a night of Celtic music and fine single malts in the snug bar-restaurant downstairs.

Grand Central Hotel   HOTEL ££
(Map p108; ☏ 0141-240 3700; www.thegrandcentralhotel.co.uk; 99 Gordon St; r £100-180; @ 🛜) This handsome Victorian hotel is part of the central railway station: some rooms overlook the platforms. High ceilings, vast corridors stretching into the distance and a fabulous ballroom are highlights of this throwback to rail's golden age. Modern bathrooms and spacious rooms – superior categories are worth the upgrade – make this a far more comfortable trainspotting base than a footbridge in the drizzle.

Brunswick Hotel   HOTEL ££
(Map p108; ☏ 0141-552 0001; www.brunswickhotel.co.uk; 106 Brunswick St; d £50-95; 🛜🛁) Especially suiting people wanting a nightlife base, this is a pleasing Merchant City option. The rooms are all stylish with a mixture of minimalism and rich, sexy colours. Compact and standard doubles are small but will do if you're here for a night out, but king-sized rooms are well worth the upgrade. It has a good restaurant downstairs and hosts events in the basement space.

Babbity Bowster   INN ££
(Map p108; ☏ 0141-552 5055; www.babbitybowster.com; 16-18 Blackfriars St; s/d £55/75; P🛜) Smack bang in the heart of the trendy Merchant City, this lively, pleasant pub has simple rooms with sleek furnishings and a minimalist design (No 3 is a good one). Staying here is an excellent Glaswegian experience – the building's design is attributed to Robert Adam. Unusually, room rates do not include breakfast – but that helps keep prices down.

Malmaison   HOTEL £££
(Map p108; ☏ 0141-572 1000; www.malmaison.com; 278 West George St; r £135-215; 🛜) This former church is a longtime favourite for its decadent decor and plush lines. Stylish rooms with mood lighting have a dark, brooding tone and opulent furnishings. It's a hedonistic sort of place and can be cheerfully boisterous at weekends. It's best to book online, as it's cheaper, and various suite offers can be mighty tempting.

Blythswood Square   HOTEL £££
(Map p108; ☏ 0141-248 8888; www.blythswoodsquare.com; 11 Blythswood Sq; r £195-265; @🛜🛁🛁) In a gorgeous Georgian terrace, this elegant five-star offers inner-city luxury, with grey and cerise tweeds providing casual soft-toned style throughout. Room grades go from standard to penthouse with corresponding increases in comfort; it's hard to resist the traditional 'classic' ones with windows onto the delightful square, but at weekends you'll have a quieter sleep in the new wing at the back.

It has an excellent bar and a superb restaurant, as well as a very handsome floor-boarded and colonnaded salon space on the 1st floor that functions as an evening spot for cocktails. Other facilities include valet parking and a seductive spa complex.

Dakota Deluxe   HOTEL £££
(Map p108; ☏ 0141-404 3680; www.dakotahotels.co.uk; 179 West Regent St; r £150-200; 🛁🛜🛁) This newcomer is suave and seductive in dark wood and grey tones and carries a strong design concept right the way from low-lit basement restaurant to light-filled suites. Rooms are very spacious and feature appealing sitting areas as well as inviting beds. Service is excellent, and the bar area – see how many Jacks you can name – a delight.

🛏 West End

Glasgow SYHA   HOSTEL £
(SYHA; Map p114; ☏ 0141-332 3004; www.syha.org.uk; 8 Park Tce; dm/tw £26/62; @🛜) Perched on a hill overlooking Kelvingrove Park in a charming town house, this place is one of Scotland's best official hostels. Dorms are mostly four to six beds with padlock lockers, and all have their own en suite. The common rooms are spacious, plush and good for lounging about. There's no curfew, it has a good kitchen, and meals are available.

The prices listed reflect maximums and are usually cheaper. Non-members pay £3 extra, but it's cheap to join. There's a good self-catering two-bedroom apartment that sleeps six and will appeal to families.

Heritage Hotel   HOTEL £
(Map p114; ☏ 0141-339 6955; www.theheritagehotel.net; 4 Alfred Tce, Great Western Rd; s/d £40/60; P🛜🛁) A stone's throw from all the action of the West End, this friendly hotel has an open, airy feel despite the rather dilapidated raised terrace it's located on.

Glasgow Cathedral (p108)
...e example of Gothic architecture
...some roof timbers dating from the
... century.

**Gallery of Modern Art
...07), Glasgow**
...ornate features of its neoclassical
...ding contrast with the modern
...orks displayed in this gallery.

**Kibble Palace (p113),
...asgow**
...ated within the Botanic Gardens,
...le Palace is one of Britain's largest
...shouses.

Generally, rooms on the 1st and 2nd floors are a bit more spacious (No 21 is best of the doubles) and have a better outlook. The location, parking option and very fair prices mark it out.

Red Deer Village Holiday Park
CAMPSITE £

(Craigendmuir Camping & Caravan Park; ☑ 0141-779 4159; www.craigendmuir.co.uk; 1 Village Dr, Stepps; sites for 1/2 people £15/18; P 🛜) The nearest campsite to town is about 800m from Stepps station. It has sites for caravans and tents, and there are a few well-equipped chalets and holiday homes for weekly rental.

★15Glasgow
B&B ££

(Map p114; ☑ 0141-332 1263; www.15glasgow.com; 15 Woodside Pl; d/ste £125/155; P 🛜) Glasgow's 19th-century merchants certainly knew how to build a beautiful house, and this 1840s terrace is a sumptuous example. Huge rooms with lofty ceilings have exquisite period detail complemented by attractive modern greys, striking bathrooms and well-chosen quality furniture. Your welcoming host makes everything easy for you: an in-room breakfast, overlooking the park, is a real treat. The host prefers no under-5s.

★Alamo Guest House
B&B ££

(Map p114; ☑ 0141-339 2395; www.alamoguesthouse.com; 46 Gray St; basic/superior d £99/149, d without bathroom £69-79; @🛜) The Alamo may not sound a peaceful spot, but that's exactly what this great place is. Opposite Kelvingrove Park, it feels miles from the city's hustle, but several of the best museums and restaurants in town are close by. The decor is an enchanting mixture of antique furnishings and modern design, with excellent bathrooms, and the owners will make you very welcome.

The superior rooms are a sumptuous sight to behold and may be a cheap upgrade at quiet times. Breakfast is abundant and events such as whisky tastings are regularly offered.

Amadeus Guest House
B&B ££

(Map p114; ☑ 0141-339 8257; www.amadeusguesthouse.co.uk; 411 North Woodside Rd; s £50-55, s without bathroom £35-38, d £80-90; 🛜) Just off the bustle of Great Western Rd, a minute's walk from the subway but on a quiet street by the riverside pathway, this B&B has compact bright rooms with a cheerful, breezy feel. There's a variety of room types, but prices are very good for all of them and come down substantially midweek. It's a friendly spot; breakfast is continental.

Embassy Apartments
APARTMENT ££

(Map p114; ☑ 0141-946 1018; www.embassy-apartments.co.uk; 8 Kelvin Dr; 1-/2-/4-person apt £70/80/110; P 🛜) This elegant self-catering place offers both facilities and location. Situated on a quiet, exclusive street right on the edge of the Botanical Gardens, the studio-style apartments sleep one to seven, have fully-equipped kitchens and are sparklingly clean. They're a particularly good option for couples and families with older kids. Available by the day, but prices drop for longer rentals and vary by demand.

Kirklee Hotel
B&B ££

(Map p114; ☑ 0141-334 5555; www.kirkleehotel.co.uk; 11 Kensington Gate; s/d £68/85; 🛜) In a leafy West End neighbourhood, Kirklee is a quiet little gem that offers a warm welcome in an elegant Edwardian terrace house. This could be the city's most beautiful street. The rooms are furnished in comfortable classical style and mostly look onto lush gardens; bathrooms are appropriately veteran. Breakfast is served in the room. You can park free on the street.

For families, there is an excellent downstairs room with enormous en suite.

Sandyford Lodge
HOTEL ££

(Map p114; ☑ 0141-332 9009; www.sandyfordlodge.com; 21 Royal Cres; s £59-79, d £109-129; 🛜) Recently refurbished, this elegant Victorian building is handy for the West End's museums and the Finnieston restaurant strip. Rooms offer decent value – except on busy weekends – with good facilities and comfort, while staff go out of their way to be helpful. Don't confuse with the nearby Sandyford Hotel.

Hotel du Vin
HOTEL £££

(One Devonshire Gardens; ☑ 0141-378 0385; www.hotelduvin.com; 1 Devonshire Gardens; r £169-279; P @ 🛜 🐾) This is traditionally Glasgow's favoured hotel of the rich and famous, and the patriarch of sophistication and comfort. A study in elegance, it's sumptuously decorated and occupies three classical sandstone terrace houses. There's a bewildering array of room types, all different in style and size. The hospitality is old-school courteous, and there's an excellent restaurant on site with a vast wine selection.

✗ Eating

Glasgow is the best place to eat in Scotland, with an excellent range of eateries. The West End is the culinary centre, with Merchant City also boasting a high concentration of quality restaurants and cafes. Many Glasgow restaurants post offers on the internet (changing daily) at 5pm.co.uk. Pubs and bars are often good mealtime options too.

✗ City Centre

★ Saramago Café Bar   CAFE £

(Map p108; ☑0141-352 4920; www.facebook. com/saramagocafebar; 350 Sauchiehall St; light meals £3-9; ☺food noon-10pm Sun-Wed, noon-11.30pm Thu-Sat; ☎🖉) In the airy atrium of the Centre for Contemporary Arts, this place does a great line in eclectic vegan fusion food, with a range of top flavour combinations from around the globe. The upstairs bar has a great deck on steep Scott St and packs out inside with a friendly hipstery crowd enjoying the DJ sets and quality tap beers.

★ Riverhill Coffee Bar   CAFE £

(Map p108; ☑0141-204 4762; www.riverhillcafe. com; 24 Gordon St; rolls £4-5; ☺7am-5pm Mon-Fri, 8am-5pm Sat, 10am-5pm Sun; ☎) 🖋 Chain cafes plaster Glasgow's centre, so it's a joy to come across this tiny place, which offers great coffee and hot chocolate as well as delicious filled rolls and tempting pastries. Ingredients are sustainably sourced and seriously tasty. It's extremely friendly; you'd come every day if you lived nearby.

Brutti Ma Buoni   MEDITERRANEAN £

(Map p108; ☑0141-552 0001; www.brunswickho tel.co.uk; 106 Brunswick St; mains £7-11; ☺11am-10pm Sun-Thu, to 11pm Fri & Sat; ☎🍴) If you like dining in a place that has a sense of fun, Brutti delivers – it's the antithesis of some of the pretentious places around the Merchant City and offers decent food at happily low prices. Italian and Spanish influences give rise to tapas-like servings or full-blown meals, which are imaginative, fresh and frankly delicious. The £5 mini-dishes make a more-than-decent lunch.

Wee Curry Shop   INDIAN £

(Map p108; ☑0141-353 0777; www.weecurryshop. co.uk; 7 Buccleuch St; 2-course lunch £5.50, dinner mains £6-8; ☺noon-2pm & 5.30-10.30pm Mon-Thu, noon-11pm Fri, noon-2pm & 5.30-11pm Sat, 5-10pm Sun; ☎🖉) This tiny place has great home-cooked curries. It's wise to book – it's a snug place with a big reputation, a limited menu and a sensational-value two-course lunch.

Lily's   CAFE, CHINESE £

(Map p108; ☑0141-552 8788; 103 Ingram St; mains £3-6; ☺9.30am-4pm Mon-Sat; ☎🖉) Don't be put off by the slightly sterile feel: Lily's is a top lunch spot fusing a creative blend of East and West with made-to-order Chinese food (such as dumpling buns and mandarin-duck wraps) and standards like tarted-up burgers and baked potatoes. The Chinese food is particularly outstanding – fresh, lively and served with fruits and salad.

Chippy Doon the Lane   FISH & CHIPS £

(Map p108; ☑0141-225 6650; www.thechippy glasgow.com; McCormick Lane, 84 Buchanan St; meals £6-12; ☺noon-9.30pm; ☎) 🖋 Don't be put off by its location in a down-at-heel alleyway off the shopping precinct: this is a cut above your average chip shop. Sustainable seafood is served in a chic space: all old-time brick, metal archways and jazz. Otherwise, chow down on your takeaway at the wooden tables in the lane or out on Buchanan St itself.

Bar 91   PUB FOOD £

(Map p108; ☑0141-552 5211; www.bar91.co.uk; 91 Candleriggs; mains £6-10; ☺meals noon-9pm Mon-Sat, 1-7pm Sun; ☎) This happy, buzzy bar serves excellent meals, far better than your average pub food. Salads, pasta and burgers are among the many tasty offerings, and in summer tables spill out onto the sidewalk – ideal for people-watching.

Willow Tearooms   CAFE £

(Map p108; ☑0141-332 0521; www.willowtea rooms.co.uk; 3rd fl, 119 Sauchiehall St; light meals £4-8; ☺9am-5pm Mon-Sat, 10.30am-5pm Sun; ☎) One of two separate locations for these famous tearooms, which are re-creations of the tearooms designed by Charles Rennie Mackintosh in 1904. On the 3rd floor of the Watt Brothers department store, this backs up its wonderful design elements with good teas and reasonable bagels, pastries or, more splendidly, afternoon teas. At busy times the queues for a table can be long.

★ Topolabamba   MEXICAN ££

(Map p108; ☑0141-248 9359; www.topolabamba. com; 89 St Vincent St; portions £5-10; ☺food noon-10pm Sun-Thu, noon-10.30pm Fri & Sat; ☎🖉) Lots of fun and attractively kitted-out in hipster Mexican decor – all skulls, figurines and tequila crates – this brings a real slice of authentic cuisine to Glasgow, with zingy tacos, tasty tostadas and not a plate of nachos in sight. The stuffed calamari are especially good, but it's all refreshingly flavoursome. Portions are tapa-sized, so order a few and share.

An interesting list of mescal, *raicilla* and other distillates make out-of-the-ordinary accompaniments.

★ Ox & Finch   FUSION £

(Map p114; ☑ 0141-339 8627; www.oxandfinch. com; 920 Sauchiehall St; portions £4-8; ⊙ noon-10pm; 🕱) This fashionable place could almost sum up the thriving modern Glasgow eating scene, with a faux-pub name, sleek but comfortable contemporary decor, tapas-sized dishes and an open kitchen. Grab a cosy booth and be prepared to have your tastebuds wowed with innovative, delicious creations aimed at sharing, drawing on French and Mediterreanean influences but focusing on quality Scottish produce.

★ Loon Fung   CHINESE ££

(Map p108; ☑ 0141-332 1240; 417 Sauchiehall St; mains £9-15; ⊙ noon-11pm; 🕱🍴) This elegant Cantonese oasis is one of Scotland's most authentic Chinese restaurants; indeed, it's quite a surprise after a traditional dining experience here to emerge to boisterous Sauchiehall rather than Hong Kong. The dim-sum choices are toothsome, and the seafood – try the sea bass – really excellent.

Café Gandolfi   CAFE, BISTRO ££

(Map p108; ☑ 0141-552 6813; www.cafegandolfi. com; 64 Albion St; mains £10-16; ⊙ 8am-11.30pm Mon-Sat, 9am-11.30pm Sun; 🕱) In Merchant City, this cafe was once part of the old cheese market. It's been pulling in the punters for years and attracts an interesting mix of die-hard Gandolfers, the upwardly mobile and tourists. It covers all the bases with excellent breakfasts and coffee, an enticing upstairs bar, and top-notch bistro food, including Scottish and Continental options, in an atmospheric medieval-like setting.

There's an expansion, specialising in fish, a couple of doors up, with a takeaway outlet.

Red Onion   BISTRO ££

(Map p108; ☑ 0141-221 6000; www.red-onion. co.uk; 257 West Campbell St; mains £11-18; ⊙ noon-11pm; 🕱🖶) This comfortable split-level bistro buzzes with contented chatter.

French, Mediterranean and Asian touches add intrigue to the predominantly British menu, and a good-value fixed-price deal is available at weekday lunchtimes.

Smoak   AMERICAN ££

(Map p108; ☑ 0141-228 4721; www.smoakbbq. co.uk; 6 Royal Exchange Sq; dishes £6-16; ⊙ 10am-9.30pm; 🕱) This simple, cosy wood-lined eatery is among the best of the many barbecue-type restaurants that have popped up in Glasgow in recent years. The menu is short and focuses on burgers, ribs and pulled pork. The slow-cooking works wonders with the melt-in-your-mouth meat, and the rich sauces make even a simple burger into a sinful, sticky experience. No alcohol: bring your own.

Dakhin   INDIAN ££

(Map p108; ☑ 0141-553 2585; www.dakhin. com; 89 Candleriggs; mains £9-16; ⊙ noon-2pm & 5-11pm Mon-Fri, 1-11pm Sat & Sun; 🕱🍴) This South Indian restaurant is a pleasing change of air from the majority of the city's excellent curry scene. Dishes are from all over the South, and include *dosas* (thin rice-based crêpes) and a yummy variety of fragrant coconut-based curries. If you're really hungry, try a *thali*: an assortment of Indian 'tapas'.

Bar Soba   ASIAN ££

(Map p108; ☑ 0141-204 2404; www.barsoba. co.uk; 11 Mitchell Lane; mains £10-13; ⊙ noon-10pm; 🕱) With candles flickering in windows there's a certain sense of intimacy in stylish Bar Soba where industrial meets plush. A great stop in the heart of the shopping zone for lunch; both the bar and downstairs restaurant do quality Asian fusion. Background beats are also perfect for chilling with a cocktail. A couple of other branches have sprung up.

Meat Bar   AMERICAN ££

(Map p108; ☑ 0141-204 3605; www.themeatbar. co.uk; 142 West Regent St; mains £9-20; ⊙ food noon-10pm; 🕱) Like a mafia film speakeasy where some minor henchman gets whacked, this has underworld ambience carried off with style. As the name suggests, it's all about meat here: it even makes its way into some of the cocktails. Daily cuts of prime Scottish beef (£25 to £35) accompany a range of American-style slow-smoked meats. Tasty and atmospheric, with interesting beers.

Gamba

SEAFOOD £££

(Map p108; ☑0141-572 0899; www.gamba.
co.uk; 225a West George St; mains £20-28;
◷noon-2.30pm & 5-10pm Mon-Thu, noon-2.15pm
& 5-10.30pm Fri & Sat, 5-9.30pm Sun; ☎) This
business-district basement is easily missed
but is actually one of the city's premier seafood restaurants. Presentation is elegant,
with carefully selected flavours allowing the
fish, sustainably sourced from Scotland and
beyond, to shine. There's a good lunch deal,
costing £19/25 for two/three courses.

✕ West End

There are numerous excellent restaurants
in the West End. They cluster along Byres
Rd and just off it, on Ashton Lane and Ruthven Lane. Gibson St and Great Western Rd
also have plenty to offer, while the Argyle
Rd strip in Finnieston has lots of interesting
new options.

Bay Tree Café

CAFE £

(Map p114; ☑0141-334 5898; www.thebaytree
westend.co.uk; 403 Great Western Rd; mains £7-
11; ◷9am-10.30pm Mon-Sat, 9am-9.30pm Sun;
☎🖉) There are many good cafes in the two
or three blocks around here, but the Bay
Tree is still a solid choice. It has lots of vegan and vegetarian options, smiling staff,
filling mains (mostly Middle Eastern and
Greek), generous salads and a good range of
hot drinks. The cafe is famous for its all-day
breakfasts.

78 Cafe Bar

CAFE, VEGETARIAN £

(Map p114; ☑0141-576 5018; www.the78cafebar.
com; 10 Kelvinhaugh St; mains £5-8; ◷noon-9pm;
☎🖉) More a comfortable lounge than your

typical veggie restaurant, this offers cosy
couch seating and reassuringly solid wood-
en tables, as well as an inviting range of ales.
The low-priced vegan food includes hearty
stews and curries, and there's regular live
music in a very welcoming atmosphere.

Hanoi Bike Shop

VIETNAMESE £

(Map p114; ☑0141-334 7165; www.thehanoibike
shop.co.uk; 8 Ruthven Lane; mains £6-11; ◷noon-
11pm Mon-Thu, noon-12.30am Fri, 11am-12.30am
Sat, 11am-11pm Sun; ☎) 🖉 Tucked away just
off Byres Rd, this upbeat spot offers creative
takes on Vietnamese food, using fresh ingredients and homemade tofu. The various *pho*
dishes are delicious.

★ Stravaigin

SCOTTISH, FUSION ££

(Map p114; ☑0141-334 2665; www.stravaigin.
co.uk; 28 Gibson St; bar dishes £6-12, restaurant
mains £15-19; ◷food 9am-11pm Mon-Fri, 11am-
11pm Sat & Sun; ☎) Stravaigin is a serious
foodie's delight, with a menu constantly
pushing the boundaries of originality and offering creative culinary excellence. The cool
contemporary dining space in the basement
has booth seating and helpful, laid-back
waitstaff. Entry level has a buzzing two-level
bar with a different menu. Scottish classics
like haggis take their place alongside a range
of Asian-influenced dishes. It's all delicious.

★ Mother India

INDIAN ££

(Map p114; ☑0141-221 1663; www.motherindia.
co.uk; 28 Westminster Tce, Sauchiehall St; mains
£8-16; ◷5.30-10.30pm Mon-Thu, noon-11pm Fri,
1-11pm Sat, 1-10pm Sun; ☎🖉🖢) Glasgow curry
buffs forever debate the merits of the city's
numerous excellent South Asian restaurants, and this features in every discussion.

GLASGOW FOR CHILDREN

Glasgow is easy with children due to its extensive public transport system and friendly
locals. The city boasts excellent family attractions:

➡ **Glasgow Science Centre** (p111)

➡ **Sharmanka Kinetic Theatre** (p107)

➡ **Riverside Museum** (p111)

➡ **People's Palace** (p110)

For suggestions for short-term child-care agencies, get in touch with the council-run
Glasgow Family Information Service (☑0141-287 4702; www.gfis.org.uk).

KidsGlasgow (www.kidsglasgow.com) lists upcoming events for children, as well as
soft play areas and other recommendations.

Most parks in Glasgow have playgrounds for children. In the centre of town, the major
shopping complexes are handy stops, with baby-changing facilities, soft play areas and
shops and activities designed to keep the kids occupied for an hour or two.

It may lack the trendiness of some of the up-and-comers, but it's been a stalwart for years, and the quality and innovation on show are superb. The three dining areas are all attractive and it makes an effort for kids, with a separate menu.

There are various other innovative, distinct sister restaurants around town.

Left Bank
BISTRO ££

(Map p114; ☏ 0141-339 5969; www.theleftbank. co.uk; 33 Gibson St; mains £8-16; ⏰ 9am-10pm Mon-Fri, 10am-10pm Sat & Sun; 🛜 🖉 👪) 🖉 Huge windows fronting the street reveal this outstanding eatery specialising in gastronomic delights and lazy afternoons. Lots of little spaces filled with couches and chunky tables make for intimacy. The large starter-menu is good for devising a shared meal. Lots of delightful creations use seasonal and local produce, with an eclectic variety of influences. Breakfasts and brunches are also highlights.

Finnieston
SEAFOOD ££

(Map p114; ☏ 0141-222 2884; www.thefinnieston bar.com; 1125 Argyle St; mains £13-19; ⏰ food noon-10pm Mon-Sat, noon-9pm Sun; 🛜) 🖉 A flagship of this increasingly vibrant strip, this gastropub recalls the area's sailing heritage with a cosily romantic below-decks atmosphere and artfully placed nautical motifs. It's been well thought through, with excellent mixed drinks and cocktails accompanying a short menu of high-quality upmarket pub fare focusing on sustainable Scottish seafood.

Gannet
SCOTTISH ££

(Map p114; ☏ 0141-204 2081; www.thegannetgla. com; 1155 Argyle St; mains £16-22; ⏰ noon-2.30pm & 5-9.30pm Tue-Sat, 1-7.30pm Sun; 🛜) 🖉 Trendy but comfortably so, this jewel of the Finnieston strip offers a cosy wood-panelled ambience and gourmet food that excels on presentation and taste without venturing towards cutting edge. The short, polished daily menu features quality produce sourced mostly from southern Scotland and the interesting wine list backs it up very well indeed. Solicitous, professional service is another plus point.

Firebird
BISTRO ££

(Map p114; ☏ 0141-339 0594; www.firebirdglas gow.com; 1321 Argyle St; mains £10-14; ⏰ food noon-10pm; 🛜 👪) A combined bar and bistro with a cheery feel, Firebird has zany artwork on its bright walls and, more importantly, quality nosh whisked under the noses of its patrons. Local flavours and Mediterran-

an highlights (mainly North African, Italian and Spanish) are evident and organic produce is used wherever possible. Taste sensations range from wood-fired pizzas to Moroccan-influenced salads.

Bothy
SCOTTISH ££

(Map p114; ☏ 0845 166 6032; www.bothyglas gow.co.uk; 11 Ruthven Lane; mains £12-20; ⏰ food noon-10pm Mon-Fri, 10am-10pm Sat & Sun; 🛜) This West End player, boasting a combo of modern design and comfy retro furnishings, blows apart the myth that Scottish food is stodgy and uninteresting. The Bothy dishes out traditional home-style fare with a modern twist. It's filling, but leave room for dessert. Smaller lunch plates are a good deal, and there's an attractive outdoor area.

★ Ubiquitous Chip
SCOTTISH £££

(Map p114; ☏ 0141-334 5007; www.ubiquitous chip.co.uk; 12 Ashton Lane; 2-/3-course lunch £17/21, mains £22-35, brasserie mains £10-15; ⏰ noon-2.30pm & 5-11pm Mon-Sat, 12.30-3pm & 5-11pm Sun; 🛜) 🖉 The original champion of Scottish produce, this is legendary for its unparalleled Scottish cuisine and lengthy wine list. Named to poke fun at Scotland's culinary reputation, it offers a French touch but resolutely Scottish ingredients, carefully selected and following sustainable principles. The elegant courtyard space offers some of Glasgow's best dining, while, above, the cheaper brasserie offers exceptional value for money.

Two bars, including the cute 'Wee Pub' down the side alley, offer plenty of drinking pleasure. There's always something going on at the Chip – check the website for upcoming events.

Butchershop Bar & Grill
STEAK £££

(Map p114; ☏ 0141-339 2999; www.butchershop glasgow.com; 1055 Sauchiehall St; steaks £18-33; ⏰ noon-10pm; 🛜) Offering several different cuts of traceably sourced, properly aged beef, this is just about the best spot in Glasgow for a tasty, served-as-you-want-it steak. It's a perfect lunch venue after the Kelvingrove museum. There are seats out the front if the weather happens to be fine. It also has a little seafood on the menu and decently mixed cocktails.

Cail Bruich
SCOTTISH £££

(Map p114; ☏ 0141-334 6265; www.cailbruich. co.uk; 725 Great Western Rd; mains £16-24; ⏰ 5.30-9pm Mon & Tue, noon-2.30pm & 5.30-9pm Wed-Sat, 1-7pm Sun; 🛜) In an elegant if rather nondescript dining room, the kitchen here turns out some memorable modern Scottish fare. The forage ethos brings surprising, tangy, herbal flavours to plates that are always interesting but never pretentious. Everything from the amuse-bouche to the homemade bread is top-notch; the degustation menu (£55) with optional wine flight (£35) combines the best on offer.

🍷 Drinking & Nightlife

Some of Britain's best nightlife is found in the din and sometimes roar of Glasgow's pubs and bars. There are as many different styles of bar as there are punters to guzzle in them. Some pubs and, especially, clubs have begun to enforce a 21-year-old minimum age.

Glasgow's clubbing scene has been hit by recent closures, but it's still lively. Glaswegians usually hit clubs after the pubs have closed, so many clubs offer discounted admission and cheaper drinks if you go early. Entry costs £5 to £10 (up to £25 for big events), although bars often hand out free passes. Clubs shut comparatively early, so keep your ear to the ground to find out where the after parties are at.

📍 City Centre

★ DogHouse Merchant City   BAR
(Map p108; 📞0141-552 6363; www.brewdog. com; 99 Hutcheson St; ⊙11am-midnight Mon-Fri, 10am-midnight Sat & Sun; 🛜) Brewdog's zingy beers are matched by its upbeat attitude, so this recent opening in Merchant City was always going to be a fun place. An open kitchen doles out slidery, burgery smoked-meat fare while 25 taps run quality craft beer from morning till night.

Sub Club   CLUB
(Map p108; www.subclub.co.uk; 22 Jamaica St; ⊙typically 10pm-4am Tue-Sun) Saturdays at the Sub Club are one of Glasgow's legendary nights, offering serious clubbing with a sound system that aficionados usually rate as the city's best. The claustrophobic, last-one-in vibe is not for those faint of heart. Check the website for other nights. Closes one of Sunday or Monday.

Babbity Bowster   PUB
(Map p108; 📞0141-552 5055; www.babbitybow ster.com; 16-18 Blackfriars St; ⊙11am-midnight Mon-Sat, 12.30pm-midnight Sun; 🛜) In a quiet corner of Merchant City, this handsome spot

is perfect for a tranquil daytime drink, particularly in the adjoining beer garden. Service is attentive, and the smell of sausages may tempt you to lunch; it also offers accommodation. This is one of the city centre's most charming pubs, in one of its noblest buildings. There's a regular folk-music scene here.

Corinthian Club   BAR
(Map p108; 📞0141-552 1101; www.thecorinthian club.co.uk; 191 Ingram St; ⊙10am-2am Sun-Thu, 10am-3am Fri & Sat; 🛜) A breathtaking domed ceiling and majestic chandeliers make this casino a special space. Originally a bank and later Glasgow's High Court, this regal building's main bar, Teller's, has to be seen to be believed. Cosy wraparound seating and space to spare are complemented by a snug wine bar and a plush club downstairs in old court cells.

Butterfly & the Pig   PUB
(Map p108; 📞0141-221 7711; www.thebutterfly andthepig.com; 153 Bath St; ⊙11am-1am Mon-Thu, 11am-3am Fri & Sat, 12.30pm-midnight Sun; 🛜) A breath of fresh air, this offbeat spot makes you feel comfortable as soon as you plunge into its basement depths. The decor is eclectic with a cosy retro feel. There's regular live jazz or similar and a sizeable menu – if you can decipher it – of pub grub, plus a rather wonderful tearoom upstairs, great for breakfast before the pub opens.

Artà   BAR, CLUB
(Map p108; www.arta.co.uk; 62 Albion St; ⊙5pm-1am Thu, 5pm-3am Sat; 🛜) This place is so baroque that when you hear a Mozart concerto over the sound system, it wouldn't surprise you to see the man himself at the other end of the bar. Set in a former cheese market, it really does have to be seen to be believed. Despite the luxury, it's got a relaxed, chilled vibe and does a decent cocktail.

It also does Spanish-influenced food but is better as a bar in our opinion.

West   BREWERY
(📞0141-550 0135; www.westbeer.com; Binnie Pl; ⊙11am-11pm Sun-Thu, 11am-midnight Fri & Sat; 🛜) Something a bit different, this welcoming, spacious brewpub on the edge of Glasgow Green churns out beers brewed to the traditional German purity laws (which basically means they're bloody good) in a bizarrely ornate former carpet factory opposite the People's Palace. German dishes such as sausages and pork knuckle (mains £9 to £13)

can accompany the amber fluid. There's a great grassy beer garden outside.

Horse Shoe
PUB

(Map p108; www.horseshoebar.co.uk; 17 Drury St; ⊙10am-midnight Sun-Fri, 9am-midnight Sat) This legendary city pub and popular meeting place dates from the late 19th century and is largely unchanged. It's a picturesque spot, with the longest continuous bar in the UK, but its main attraction is what's served over it – real ale and good cheer. Upstairs in the lounge is some of the best-value pub food (three-course lunch £4.50) in town.

Blackfriars
PUB

(Map p108; www.blackfriarsglasgow.com; 36 Bell St; ⊙11am-midnight Mon-Sat, 12.30pm-midnight Sun; 🐾) One of Merchant City's most relaxed and atmospheric pubs, and far less posh than the rest on this square, Blackfriars' friendly staff and regular live music make it special. It takes its cask ales seriously, and there's a seating area with large windows, which are great for people-watching. Buzzy and inclusive.

Slouch Bar
BAR

(Map p108; www.slouch-bar.co.uk; 203 Bath St; ⊙11am-2am or 3am; 🐾) There's a basement bar for all types on Bath St, with subver-

---

GAY & LESBIAN GLASGOW

Glasgow has a vibrant LGBTIQ scene, with the gay quarter found in and around the Merchant City (particularly Virginia, Wilson and Glassford Sts). The city's gay community has a reputation for being very friendly.

To tap into the scene, check out *The List* (www.list.co.uk) and the free *Scots Gay* (www.scotsgay.co.uk) magazine and website.

Many straight clubs and bars have gay and lesbian nights.

AXM (Map p108; ☑0141-552 5761; www.axmgroup.co.uk; 80 Glassford St; ⊙11pm-4.30am Sun-Thu, 10am-5.30am Fri & Sat) This popular Manchester club's Glasgow branch is a cheery spot, not too scene-y, with all welcome. It makes for a fun place to finish off a night out.

Delmonica's (Map p108; ☑0141-552 4803; www.delmonicas.co.uk; 68 Virginia St; ⊙noon-1am) In the heart of the Pink Triangle, this is a popular bar with a good mix of ages and orientations. It's packed on weekday evenings, but is a pleasant spot for a quiet drink during the day. Drop in here before heading to the adjacent Polo Lounge, as it often gives out free or cheaper passes.

Underground (Map p108; ☑0141-553 2456; www.underground-glasgow.com; 6a John St; ⊙noon-midnight; 🐾) Downstairs on cosmopolitan John St, Underground sports a relaxed crowd and, crucially, a free jukebox. You'll be listening to indie rather than Abba here.

Speakeasy (Map p108; www.speakeasyglasgow.co.uk; 10 John St; ⊙5pm-3am Wed-Sat) Relaxed and friendly bar that starts out pub-like and gets louder with gay anthem DJs as the night progresses. Serves food too, so it's a good all-rounder.

Katie's Bar (Map p108; ☑0141-237 3030; www.katiesbar.co.uk; 17 John St; ⊙noon-midnight; 🐾) With an easily missed entrance between a Spanish and an Italian restaurant, this basement space is a friendly LGBT pub with a pool table and regular gigs at weekends. It's a pleasant, low-key space to start off the night and especially popular with women.

Waterloo Bar (Map p108; www.facebook.com/waterloobar1; 306 Argyle St; ⊙noon-midnight Fri & Sat, noon-11pm Sun-Thu) This traditional pub is Scotland's oldest gay bar. It attracts punters of all ages. It's very friendly and, with a large group of regulars, a good place to meet people away from the scene.

Polo Lounge (Map p108; www.pologlasgow.co.uk; 84 Wilson St; ⊙11pm-3am Sun-Thu, 10pm-3am Fri, 9pm-3am Sat) This doesn't have the friendliest staff, but it still attracts talent. It's an attractive spot, with opulent furnishings. The downstairs Polo Club and Club X areas still pack out on weekends; just the main bars open on other nights. One of them, the Riding Room, has cabaret shows.

sive hideaways under brokers' offices and a range of vibes. This is low-lit and casual but handsomely designed, with an American South feel to the decor, drinks and rock soundtrack. It's got an intriguing spirits selection, more-than-acceptable comfort food and regular live music.

Nice 'n' Sleazy   BAR, CLUB

(Map p108; ☑0141-333 0900; www.nicensleazy.com; 421 Sauchiehall St; ☺noon-3am Mon-Sat, 1pm-3am Sun; ☎) On the rowdy Sauchiehall strip, students from the nearby School of Art make the buzz here reliably friendly. If you're over 35, you'll feel like a professor not a punter, but retro decor, a big selection of tap and bottled beers, 3am closing, and nightly alternative live music downstairs followed by a club at weekends make this a winner.

A couple of similar options alongside mean that you can pick and choose. There's also popular, cheap Tex-Mex food here (dishes £6 to £9).

Tiki Bar & Kitsch Inn   BAR

(Map p108; ☑0141-332 1341; www.tikibarglasgow.com; 214 Bath St; ☺10am-midnight; ☎) Hawaiian shirts, palms and leis provide an appropriate backdrop to colourful cocktails in this hedonistic and amiable basement bar. Upstairs, Kitsch plays the relative straight man, though *MAD* magazine covers mean it's not all poker-faces. It also does a good line in Thai food. Order top-shelf spirits to watch the bar staff negotiate the ladder.

Classic Grand   CLUB

(Map p108; ☑0141-847 0820; www.classicgrand.com; 18 Jamaica St; ☺variable; ☎) Rock, industrial, electronic and powerpop grace the stage and the turntables at this unpretentious central venue. It doesn't take itself too seriously, drinks are cheap and the locals are welcoming. Hours vary according to events, but core opening is 11pm to 3am Thursday to Saturday.

Cathouse   CLUB

(Map p108; www.cathouse.co.uk; 15 Union St; ☺10.30pm-3am Wed-Sun; ☎) It's mostly rock, alternative and metal with a touch of goth and post-punk at this long-standing indie venue. There are two dance floors: upstairs is pretty intense with lots of metal and hard rock; downstairs is a little more tranquil.

ABC   CLUB

(O₂ABC; Map p108; ☑0141-332 2232; www.o2abcglasgow.co.uk; 300 Sauchiehall St; ☺club 11pm-3am Thu-Sat; ☎) Both nightclub and venue, this reference point on Sauchiehall has two large concert spaces with big-name gigs, plus several attractive bars. It's a good all-rounder, with a variety of DJs playing every Thursday to Saturday.

Buff Club   CLUB

(Map p108; ☑0141-248 1777; www.thebuffclub.com; 142 Bath Lane; ☺11pm-3am Mon, Tue & Thu-Sat; ☎) Tucked away in a laneway behind the Bath St bar strip, this club presents eclectic, honest music without dress pretensions. The sounds vary substantially depending on the night, and can range from hip-hop to disco via electronica. It's more down-to-earth than many Glasgow venues, and has seriously cheap drinks midweek.

🍷 West End

Brewdog Glasgow   PUB

(Map p114; ☑0141-334 7175; www.brewdog.com; 1397 Argyle St; ☺noon-midnight; ☎) Perfect for a pint after the Kelvingrove Museum, this great little spot offers the delicious range of artisanal beers from the brewery of the same name. Punk IPA is refreshingly hoppy, more so than formidable WattDickie, which comes in at a whisky-like 35%. Tasting flights mean you can try several, while burgers and dogs are on hand to soak it up.

Hillhead Bookclub   BAR

(Map p114; ☑0141-576 1700; www.hillheadbookclub.co.uk; 17 Vinicombe St; ☺11am-midnight Mon-Fri, 10am-midnight Sat & Sun; ☎) Atmosphere in spades is the call sign of this easygoing West End bar. An ornate wooden ceiling overlooks two levels of well-mixed cocktails, seriously cheap drinks, comfort food and numerous intriguing decorative touches. There's even a ping-pong table in a cage.

Òran Mór   BAR, CLUB

(Map p114; ☑0141-357 6200; www.oran-mor.co.uk; cnr Byres & Great Western Rds; ☺9am-2am Mon-Wed, 9am-3am Thu-Sat, 10am-3am Sun; ☎) Now some may be a little uncomfortable with the thought of drinking in a church. But we say: the Lord giveth. This sizeable converted church is now a bar, restaurant, club and theatre venue. Look out for the 'A Play, a Pie and a Pint' deals. There's an excellent array of whiskies. The only thing missing is holy water on your way in.

Brel BAR
(Map p114; ☑0141-342 4966; www.brelbar.
com; 39 Ashton Lane; ⏲11am-midnight Mon-Sat,
noon-midnight Sun; ☏) Perhaps the best bar on
Ashton Lane, this can seem tightly packed,
but there's a conservatory for eating out
the back so you can pretend you're sitting
outside when it's raining, and when the sun
does peek through, there's a beer garden. Its
got a huge range of Belgian beers, and also
does mussels and langoustines among other
tasty fare.

Jinty McGuinty's PUB
(Map p114; ☑0141-339 0747; 23 Ashton Lane;
⏲11am-midnight Mon-Sat, 12.30pm-midnight Sun;
☏) Unlike many, there's actually something
rather authentically Irish about this place,
which has an aged wooden floor, unusual
booth seating, a literary hall of fame and a
beer garden alongside. There's live music
most nights.

☆ Entertainment

Glasgow is Scotland's entertainment city,
from classical music, fine theatres and ballet
to an amazing range of live-music venues.
To tap into the scene, check out *The List*
(www.list.co.uk), an invaluable events guide
released every four weeks and available at
newsagents and bookshops.

For theatre tickets, book directly with the
venue. For concerts, a useful booking centre
is **Tickets Scotland** (Map p108; ☑0141-204
5151; www.tickets-scotland.com; 237 Argyle St;
⏲9am-6pm Mon-Wed & Fri- Sat, 9am-7pm Thu,
11.30am-5.30pm Sun).

Live Music

Glasgow is the king of Scotland's live-music
scene. Year after year, touring musicians and
travellers alike name Glasgow one of their
favourite cities in the world to enjoy live
music. Much of Glasgow's character is encapsulated in the soul and humour of its inhabitants, and the main reason for the city's
musical success lies within its audience and
the musical community it has bred and nur-
tured for years.

There are so many venues it's impossible to keep track of them all. For the latest
listings, pick up a copy of the *Gig Guide* or
check its website (www.gigguide.co.uk). It's
available free in most pubs and venues.

One of the city's premier live-music pub
venues, the excellent King Tut's Wah Wah
Hut hosts bands every night of the week;
Oasis were signed after playing here. Classic

Grand (p129) and Nice 'n' Sleazy (p129)
are also great for live music, and the ABC
(p129) is a popular venue.

★ King Tut's Wah Wah Hut LIVE MUSIC
(Map p108; ☑0141-221 5279; www.kingtuts.
co.uk; 272a St Vincent St; ⏲noon-midnight) One
of the city's premier live-music pub venues,
hosting bands every night of the week. A
staple of the local scene, and a real Glasgow
highlight.

Hydro LIVE PERFORMANCE
(Map p114; ☑0141-248 3000; www.thessehydro.
com; Finnieston Quay; ☏) Another spectacular
modern building to keep the adjacent 'Armadillo' company, the Hydro amphitheatre is a
phenomenally popular venue for big-name
concerts and shows.

13th Note Café LIVE MUSIC
(Map p108; www.13thnote.co.uk; 50-60 King St;
⏲noon-midnight; ☏) Cosy basement venue
with small independent bands as well as
weekend DJs and regular comedy and theatre performances. At street level the cafe
does decent vegetarian and vegan food (£6
to £8)

Hug and Pint LIVE MUSIC
(Map p114; ☑0141-331 1901; www.thehugand
pint.com; 171 Great Western Rd; ⏲noon-midnight;
☏) With bands almost daily in the downstairs space, this comfortable local is a great
destination. It would be anyway for its excellent atmosphere, highly original Asian-influenced vegan food and colourful interior.

Barrowland Ballroom CONCERT VENUE
(The Barrowlands; Map p108; www.glasgow-bar
rowland.com; 244 Gallowgate) A down-at-heel
but exceptional old dancehall catering for
some of the larger acts that visit the city. It's
one of Scotland's most atmospheric venues.

Clyde Auditorium LIVE PERFORMANCE
(Map p114; ☑0844 395 4000; www.secc.co.uk;
Finnieston Quay) Also known as the Armadillo
because of its bizarre shape, the Clyde adjoins the SECC auditorium, and caters for
big national and international acts.

SECC LIVE PERFORMANCE
(Map p114; ☑0844 395 4000; www.secc.co.uk;
Finnieston Quay) The headquarters of the com-
plex that includes the Clyde Auditorium and
Hydro and hosts major national and inter-
national acts.

Audio CONCERT VENUE
(Map p108; www.facebook.com/audioglasgow; 14
Midland St) In the bowels of Central Station,
this is an atmospheric venue for regular concerts by touring acts, particularly of the rock
and metal varieties.

Cinemas

★ **Glasgow Film Theatre** CINEMA
(Map p108; ☑0141-332 6535; www.glasgowfilm.
org; 12 Rose St; adult/child £8.80/5) This much-
loved three-screener off Sauchiehall St
shows art-house cinema and classics.

Grosvenor Cinema CINEMA
(Map p114; ☑0845 166 6002; www.grosvenor
westend.co.uk; Ashton Lane) This sweet cinema
puts you in the heart of West End eating and
nightlife for post-show debriefings.

Theatres & Concert Halls

Theatre Royal CONCERT VENUE
(Map p108; ☑0844 871 7647; www.glasgowthe
atreroyal.org.uk; 282 Hope St) Proudly sporting
an eyecatching modern facelift, Glasgow's
oldest theatre is the home of Scottish Opera
and Scottish Ballet.

**City Halls &
Old Fruitmarket** CONCERT VENUE
(Map p108; ☑0141-353 8000; www.glasgowcon
certhalls.com; Candleriggs) In the heart of Merchant City, there are regular performances
here by the Scottish Chamber Orchestra and
the Scottish Symphony Orchestra. The adjacent Old Fruitmarket venue, a spectacular
vaulted space, also has concerts, both classical and rock.

Glasgow Royal Concert Hall CONCERT VENUE
(Map p108; ☑0141-353 8000; www.glasgow
concerthalls.com; 2 Sauchiehall St; ☎) A feast of
classical music is showcased at this concert
hall, the modern home of the Royal Scottish
National Orchestra. There are also regular
pop, folk and jazz performances, typically by
big-name solo artists.

Citizens' Theatre THEATRE
(☑0141-429 0022; www.citz.co.uk; 119 Gorbals
St) South of the Clyde, this is one of the top
theatres in Scotland. It's well worth trying to
catch a performance here.

Centre for Contemporary Arts ARTS CENTRE
(Map p108; ☑0141-352 4900; www.cca-glasgow.
com; 350 Sauchiehall St; ☺10am-midnight Mon-
Thu, 10am-1am Fri & Sat, noon-midnight Sun) This
is a chic venue making terrific use of space
and light. It showcases the visual and per-

forming arts, including movies, talks and
galleries. There's a good cafe-bar here too.

Tramway PERFORMING ARTS
(☑0141-276 0950; www.tramway.org; 25 Albert
Dr) Attracts cutting-edge theatrical groups,
the visual and performing arts, and a varied
range of artistic exhibitions. It's very close to
Pollokshields East train station.

Sport
Two football clubs – Rangers and Celtic –
dominate the sporting scene in Scotland,
having vastly more resources than other
clubs and a long history (and rivalry). This
runs along partisan lines, with Rangers
representing Protestant supporters, and
Celtic, Catholic. It's worth going to a game;
both play in magnificent arenas with great
atmosphere. Games between the two (normally four a year) are fiercely contested,
but tickets aren't sold to the general public;
you'll need to know a season-ticket holder.
In recent years, Rangers have had to work
their way back up the divisions after a financial meltdown, arriving back in the top flight
in 2016.

Celtic FC FOOTBALL
(☑0871 226 1888; www.celticfc.net; Celtic Park,
Parkhead) Playing in green and white hoops,
Celtic are one of Glasgow's big two football
clubs and traditionally represent the Catholic side of the divide. There are daily stadium
tours (adult/child £10/6). Catch bus 61 or 62
from outside St Enoch centre.

Rangers FC FOOTBALL
(☑0871 702 1972; www.rangers.co.uk; Ibrox Stadium, 150 Edmiston Dr) One of Glasgow's big
two football clubs, Rangers play in blue
and traditionally represent the Protestant,
pro-Union side of the divide. They recently
returned to the top division after a financial
meltdown. Tours of the stadium and trophy room run Friday to Sunday (£10/5.50
per adult/child). Take the subway to Ibrox
station.

🅰 Shopping

Boasting the UK's largest retail phalanx
outside London, Glasgow is a shopaholic's
paradise. The 'Style Mile' around Buchanan
St, Argyle St and Merchant City (particularly
upmarket Ingram St) is a fashion hub, while
the West End has quirkier, more bohemian
shopping options: Byres Rd is great for vintage clothing.

DON'T MISS

VINTAGE CLOTHING – GLASGOW'S BEST

Snag a bargain and bring out the hipster in you with Glasgow's fabulous range of retro rag stores.

Mr Ben (Map p108; ✆ 0141-553 1936; www.mrbenretroclothing.com; 101 King St; ⊙ 10.30am-5.30pm Mon-Sat, 1-5pm Sun) This cute place is one of Glasgow's best destinations for vintage clothing, with a great selection of brands like Fred Perry, as well as more glam choices, on offer.

Vintage Guru (Map p114; ✆ 0141-339 4750; www.vintageguru.co.uk; 195 Byres Rd; ⊙ 10am-6pm Mon-Sat, 11am-6pm Sun) You might have to elbow your way into this tightly packed West End favourite, but it's worth it for the always-intriguing and frequently updated selection and fair prices.

Circa Vintage (Map p114; ✆ 0141-334 6660; www.circavintage.co.uk; 37 Ruthven Lane; ⊙ roughly 11.30am-5.30pm Mon-Sat, 1-5pm Sun) Tucked away off Byres Rd in a little market of secondhand and quirky shops, this offers online shopping as well as a fab range of in-store jewellery and well-kept clothes.

Glasgow Vintage Company (Map p114; ✆ 0141-339 6633; www.glasgowvintage.co.uk; 453 Great Western Rd; ⊙ 11am-6pm Mon-Sat, 11am-5pm Sun) With a little more breathing room than some of Glasgow's vintage shops, this offers relaxed browsing.

Barras MARKET

(Map p108; www.glasgow-barrowland.com; btwn Gallowgate & London Rd; ⊙ 10am-5pm Sat & Sun) At Glasgow's legendary weekend flea market, the Barras on Gallowgate, cheap tat rules the roost these days. But it's still an intriguing stroll, as much for the assortment of local characters as what's on offer. People come here just for a wander, and it's got a real feel of a nearly vanished Britain of whelk stalls and rag-and-bone merchants. Watch your wallet.

Barras Art & Design ARTS & CRAFTS

(BAaD; Map p108; www.baadglasgow.com; 54 Calton Entry; ⊙ 9am-4pm Sat & Sun) This workshop space for artists and designers in the heart of the Barras market area has pepped up the area. It opens as a market at weekends, when you can browse the creatives' wares and enjoy the family-friendly enclosed space.

Princes Square SHOPPING CENTRE

(Map p108; www.princessquare.co.uk; 48 Buchanan St; ⊙ 10am-7pm Mon-Fri, 9am-6pm Sat, 11am-5pm Sun) Set in a magnificent 1841 renovated square with elaborate ironwork and an exuberant metal leaf-and-peacock facade, this place has lots of beauty and fashion outlets, including Vivienne Westwood. There's a good selection of restaurants and cafes, as well as a bar with roof terrace.

Argyll Arcade JEWELLERY

(Map p108; www.argyll-arcade.com; Buchanan St; ⊙ 10am-5.30pm Mon-Sat, noon-5pm Sun) This splendid historic arcade doglegs between Buchanan and Argyle Sts. It's quite a sight with its end-to-end jewellery and watch shops. Top-hatted doorpeople greet nervously excited couples shopping for diamond rings.

Caledonia Books BOOKS

(Map p114; ✆ 0141-334 9663; www.caledonia books.co.uk; 483 Great Western Rd; ⊙ 10.30am-6pm Mon-Sat) This characterful spot is just what a secondhand bookshop should be, with a smell of dust and venerability and a wide range of intriguing volumes on the slightly chaotic shelves.

Slanj Kilts CLOTHING

(Map p108; ✆ 0141-248 5632; www.slanjkilts. com; 80 St Vincent St; ⊙ 9.30am-5.30pm Mon-Wed, Fri & Sat, 9.30am-6.30pm Thu, 11am-4pm Sun) This upbeat shop is a top spot to hire or buy kilts both traditional and modern, as well as other tartan wear and a range of T-shirts and other accessories. Always worth a look.

Adventure 1 OUTDOOR

(Map p108; ✆ 0141-353 3788; www.adventure1. co.uk; 38 Dundas St; ⊙ 9am-5.30pm Mon-Sat) This friendly, no-frills outdoor shop up the side of Queen Street station is an excellent place to buy hiking boots, backpacks and military surplus gear.

ℹ️ Information

Available from newsagents *The List* (www.list.
co.uk) is Glasgow and Edinburgh's invaluable
guide to films, theatre, cabaret, music and
clubs, released every four weeks. The excellent
Eating & Drinking Guide, published by the *List*
every second April, covers both Glasgow and
Edinburgh.

INTERNET ACCESS

There's a free wi-fi zone across the city centre
(network: GlasgowCC Wifi). You can get a local
SIM card for about a pound and data packages
are cheap.

Gallery of Modern Art (☏ 0141-229 1996;
Royal Exchange Sq; ⊙10am-5pm Mon-Thu &
Sat, 11am-5pm Fri & Sun; 🕾) Basement library;
free internet access. Bookings recommended.

Hillhead Library (☏ 0141-276 1617; www.
glasgowlife.org.uk; 348 Byres Rd; ⊙10am-8pm
Mon-Thu, 10am-5pm Fri & Sat, noon-5pm Sun;
🕾) Free internet terminals.

iCafe (www.icafe.uk.com; 250 Woodlands Rd;
per hr £2.50; ⊙8.30am-9.30pm; 🕾) Sip a
coffee and munch on a pastry while you check
your emails on super-fast connections. Wi-fi
too. It's actually a very good cafe in its own
right. There are other branches, including one
on Sauchiehall St (315 Sauchiehall St; ⊙7am-
10pm Mon-Fri, 8am-10pm Sat & Sun; 🕾).

Mitchell Library (☏ 0141-287 2999; www.
glasgowlife.org.uk; North St; ⊙9am-8pm Mon-
Thu, 9am-5pm Fri & Sat) Free internet access;
bookings recommended.

Yeeha Internet Cafe (www.yeeha-internet
-cafe.co.uk; 48 West George St; per hr £2.50;
⊙9.30am-6pm Mon-Fri, 10am-6pm Sat)
Upstairs location in the heart of the city.

MEDICAL SERVICES

Glasgow Dental Hospital (☏ 0141-211 9600;
www.nhsggc.org.uk; 378 Sauchiehall St)

Glasgow Royal Infirmary (☏ 0141-211 4000;
www.nhsggc.org.uk; 84 Castle St) Medical
emergencies and outpatient facilities.

Queen Elizabeth University Hospital (☏ 0141-
201 1100; www.nhsggc.org.uk; 1345 Govan Rd)
Modern; south of the river.

POST

Many shops across the centre offer postal service, including some supermarkets that are open
Sundays.

Post Office (Map p108; www.postoffice.
co.uk; 136 West Nile St; ⊙9am-5.30pm Mon-
Sat) The most central full-service post office.

TOURIST INFORMATION

Glasgow Information Centre (Map p108;
www.visitscotland.com; Gallery of Modern
Art, Royal Exchange Sq; ⊙10am-4.45pm, till

7.45pm Thu, from 11am Fri & Sun; 🕾) In the
Gallery of Modern Art.

Glasgow Airport Information Centre (☏ 0141-
566 4089; www.visitscotland.com; Glasgow
International Airport; ⊙7.30am-5pm Mon-Sat,
8am-3.30pm Sun)

ℹ️ Getting There & Away

AIR

Glasgow International Airport (GLA; ☏ 0844
481 5555; www.glasgowairport.com; 🕾) Ten
miles west of the city. Handles international
and domestic flights.

Glasgow Prestwick Airport (PIK; ☏ 0871 223
0700; www.glasgowprestwick.com) Thirty
miles southwest of Glasgow. Used by Ryanair
and some other budget airlines, with connections mostly to southern Europe.

BUS

All long-distance buses arrive at and depart
from **Buchanan bus station** (Map p108;
☏ 0141-333 3708; www.spt.co.uk; Killermont
St; 🕾), which has pricey lockers, ATMs and
wi-fi.

Megabus (☏ 0141-352 4444; www.megabus.
com) Your first port of call if you're looking for
the cheapest fare. Megabus offers very cheap
demand-dependent prices on many major bus
routes, including to Edinburgh and London.

National Express (p464) Also runs daily to
several English cities.

Scottish Citylink (☏ 0871 266 3333; www.
citylink.co.uk) Has buses to Edinburgh (£7.50,
1¼ hours, every 15 minutes) and most major
towns in Scotland.

TRAIN

As a general rule, Glasgow Central station
serves southern Scotland, England and Wales,
and Queen Street station serves the north and
east. Buses run between the two stations every
10 minutes. There are direct trains to London's
Euston station; they're much quicker (advance
purchase single £62, full fare off-peak/peak
£134/183, 4½ hours, more than hourly) and
more comfortable than the bus.

Scotrail (☏ 0344-811 0141; www.scotrail.
co.uk) runs Scottish trains. Destinations include
the following:

Aberdeen £39.60, 2½ to 3½ hours, hourly

Dundee £22, 1½ hours, hourly

Edinburgh £13.60, 50 minutes, every 15
minutes

Fort William £29.20, 3¾ hours, four to five
daily

Inverness £87.70, 3½ to four hours, 10 daily
(four on Sunday)

Oban £23.90, three hours, three to six daily

ℹ️ Getting Around

TO/FROM THE AIRPORT

There are buses every 10 or 15 minutes from Glasgow International Airport to Buchanan bus station via Central and Queen Street train stations (single/return £7/9.50, 25 minutes). This is a 24-hour service. You can include a day ticket on the bus network for £9 total.

Another bus, the 747, covers the same route via Finnieston and Kelvingrove, taking longer (£5).

A taxi costs around £25.

There are also buses from Buchanan bus station direct to/from Edinburgh Airport (£11.40, one hour, half-hourly).

BICYCLE

The **Nextbike** (www.nextbike.co.uk; per 30min £1) citybike scheme is easy; download the app for the most convenient use.

There are several places to hire a bike; the **tourist office** (p133) has a full list.

Gear Bikes (📞 0141-339 1179; www.gearbikes. com; 19 Gibson St; half-day/1 day/3 days/wk £15/20/40/70; ⊙10am-6pm Mon-Sat, noon-5pm Sun)

Bike Station (📞 0141-248 5409; www.thebike station.org.uk; 65 Haugh Rd; half-day/day/wk £15/20/70; ⊙9am-5pm Mon-Sat, to 8pm Wed)

CAR & MOTORCYCLE

The most difficult thing about driving in Glasgow is the sometimes-confusing one-way system. For short-term parking (up to two hours), you've got a decent chance of finding something on the street, paying at the meters, which cost up to £4 per hour. Otherwise, multistorey car parks are probably your best bet and are not so expensive. Ask your hotel in advance if they offer parking discounts.

There are numerous car-rental companies; both big names and discount operators have airport offices.

Arnold Clark (📞 0141-423 9559; www.arnold clarkrental.com; 43 Allison St; ⊙8am-5.30pm Mon-Fri, 8am-4pm Sat, 11am-4pm Sun)

Avis (📞 0844 544 6064; www.avis.co.uk; 70 Lancefield St; ⊙8am-6pm Mon-Fri, 8am-1pm Sat, 10am-2pm Sun)

Europcar (📞 0141-204 1280; www.europcar. co.uk; 76 Lancefield Quay; ⊙8am-6pm Mon-Fri, 8am-4pm Sat)

Enterprise (📞 0141-221 2124; www.enterprise. co.uk; 40 Oswald St; ⊙7am-9pm Mon-Fri, 8am-4pm Sat, 10am-3pm Sun)

Hertz (📞 0849 309 3032; www.hertz.co.uk; 138 Hydepark St; ⊙8am-6pm Mon-Fri, 8am-1pm Sat)

PUBLIC TRANSPORT

Public transport in and around Glasgow is coordinated by SPT (www.spt.co.uk).

Bus

City bus services, mostly run by **First Glasgow** (📞 0141-420 7600; www.firstglasgow.com), are frequent. You can buy tickets when you board buses, but on most you must have the exact change. Short journeys in town cost £1.40 or £2.15; a day ticket (£4.50) is good value and is valid until 1am, when a night network starts. A weekly ticket is £15.50. Check route maps online at www.spt.co.uk.

Train & Underground

There's an extensive suburban network of trains in and around Glasgow; tickets should be bought before travel if the station is staffed, or from the conductor if it isn't. There's also an underground line, the Subway, that serves 15 stations in the centre, west and south of the city (single £1.60). The train network connects with the Subway at Buchanan St underground station, next to Queen St overground station, and St Enoch underground station, near Central railway station. The All Day Ticket (£4) gives unlimited travel on the Subway for a day, while the Roundabout ticket gives a day's unlimited train and Subway travel for £6.60. The subway annoyingly shuts down at around 6pm on a Sunday.

Combined Ticket

The Daytripper ticket gives you a day's unlimited travel on buses, the Subway, rail and some ferries in the Glasgow region, including Loch Lomond, Ayrshire and Lanarkshire. It costs £11.60 for one adult or £20.50 for two. Two kids per adult are included free.

TAXI

There's no shortage of taxis, and if you want to know anything about Glasgow, striking up a conversation with a cabbie is a good place to start. Fares are very reasonable – you can get across the centre for around £6, and there's no surcharge for calling a taxi. You can pay by credit card with **Glasgow Taxis** (📞 0141-429 7070; www.glasgowtaxis.co.uk) if you order by phone; most of its taxis are wheelchair accessible. Download its app to make booking easy.

AROUND GLASGOW

Good transport connections mean it's easy to plan day trips out of Glasgow. There are some excellent sights along the southern shore of the Clyde, where the ghosts of shipbuilding haunt places like Greenock, and Paisley's magnificent abbey tells a tale of nobler architectural times.

Greenock & Gourock

POP 53,700

Fused together these days, the towns of Gourock and Greenock were always warming sights to a Glasgow mariner's heart as their ships rounded the point from the Firth of Clyde into the river proper and thence to home. Gourock's firthside views are spectacular, and Greenock's historical buildings – despite the scrappy shopping complexes in its centre – invite a stop. Before the Clyde was dredged, larger ships couldn't progress further than Greenock, which consequently raked in considerable customs dues. In summer and on fine days, these become little resort towns for Glasgow families looking for a day out.

◉ Sights

McLean Museum & Art Gallery   MUSEUM, GALLERY

(☑ 01475-715624; www.inverclyde.gov.uk; 15 Kelly St; ⊙10am-5pm Mon-Sat) FREE In the historic centre of Greenock and well worth checking out. There's quite an extensive collection, with displays charting the history of steam power and Clyde shipping. The art gallery has some fine pieces, and several canvases give you an idea of just how busy Greenock's harbour once was. There's also a pictorial history of Greenock through the ages, while upstairs are small displays from China, Japan and Egypt. The natural history section highlights species extinction in the modern world. There are free internet terminals here.

🛏 Sleeping & Eating

Tontine Hotel   HOTEL ££

(☑ 01475-723316; www.tontinehotel.co.uk; 6 Ardgowan Sq; s/d £68/78, superior s/d £88/98; P 🛜) This noble hotel in the nicest part of Greenock has appealing recently refurbished rooms that provide comfort without taking away from the building's older features. Superior rooms in the old part of the building are more spacious. An old fashioned lounge bar and decent restaurant are here, and staff are very welcoming. Book ahead in summer.

One Cove Road   CAFE £

(☑ 01475-637336; www.onecoveroad.co.uk; 1 Cove Rd; light meals £3-9; ⊙9am-6pm; 🛜) The area's best cafe by some distance occupies a sweet corner with views over the water as you enter Gourock from Greenock on the right.

All-day breakfast is tasty, sourced from local producers, and lunch specials appeal, but it's the cakes piled on the counter that stand out. It's difficult to stop for a coffee and not succumb to temptation.

ℹ Getting There & Away

Greenock is 27 miles west of Glasgow, and Gourock is 3 miles further west. The Glasgow–Greenock–Gourock leg of the Clyde to Forth pedestrian and cycle route follows an old train track for 10 miles.

There are trains from Glasgow Central station (£6.90, 35 to 50 minutes, two to three per hour) and hourly buses stopping in both towns.

Gourock's train station is next to the ferry terminal. Gourock is an important ferry hub:

Argyll Ferries (☑ 01475-650338; www.argyllferries.co.uk) A passenger service to Dunoon (£4.50, 25 minutes, half-hourly Monday to Saturday, hourly Sunday) on Argyll's Cowal Peninsula.

Kilcreggan Ferry (☑ 0871 705 0888; www.kilcregganferry.com) A passenger-only ferry service to Kilcreggan (adult/child £2.60/1.30, 15 minutes, 12 to 13 daily Monday to Saturday); buy tickets on board.

Western Ferries (☑ 01369-704452; www.western-ferries.co.uk) Also has a service (adult/child/car £4.40/2.10/12.40, 20 minutes, two to three hourly) to Dunoon from McInroy's Point, 2 miles south from Gourock train station on the Irvine road; Scottish Citylink buses run to here.

Paisley

POP 76,600

Once a proud weaving town, but these days effectively a southwestern suburb of Glasgow, Paisley gave its name to the funky patterned fabric. Though flanked by green countryside, it's not an engaging place, but it has an ace up its sleeve in the shape of the magnificent **Paisley Abbey** (☑ 0141-889 7654; www.paisleyabbey.org.uk; Abbey Close; ⊙10am-3.30pm Mon-Sat) FREE, which is well worth the short trip from Glasgow to see.

This majestic Gothic building was founded in 1163 by Walter Fitzalan, first high steward of Scotland and ancestor of the Stuart dynasty. Apart from the magnificent perspective down the nave, points of interest include royal tombs, some excellent 19th- and 20th-century stained glass, including three windows by Edward Burne-Jones, and the 10th-century Celtic Barochan Cross.

A monastery for Cluny monks, it was damaged by fire during the Wars of Independence in 1306 but rebuilt soon after. Most of the nave is 14th or 15th century. The building was mostly a ruin from the 16th century until the 19th-century restoration, completed in 1928. A window commemorates the fact that William Wallace was educated by monks from this monastery.

At the western end of High St, worthwhile **Paisley Museum** (☑ 0141-889 3151; www.renfrewshire.gov.uk; High St; ⊙ 11am-4pm Tue-Sat, 2-5pm Sun) FREE is housed in an elegant Victorian Grecian edifice and has a decent collection of 19th-century Scottish art as well as a bit of everything else, from dinosaur footprints to a stuffed terrier, and plenty of information on the town's textile history and the famous Paisley pattern's origins in ancient Mesopotamia. Plans are under way to convert it to a national museum of textiles by 2021, so you may find it closed.

Trains run from Glasgow's Central station to Paisley (10 minutes, eight per hour).

Blantyre

POP 17,000

Though technically part of Lanarkshire, Blantyre, birthplace of David Livingstone, is an outlying suburb of Glasgow these days. It was founded as a cotton mill in the late 18th century. Livingstone, a zealous and pious doctor, missionary and explorer, was raised in a one-room tenement and worked in the mill by day from the age of 10, going to the local school at night. Amazingly for a time in which most mill-workers were barely able to write their names, he managed to get himself into university to study medicine.

The **David Livingstone Centre** (NTS; www.nts.org.uk; 165 Station Rd, Blantyre; adult/child £6.50/5; ⊙ 11am-4pm Sat-Tue Apr-Sep; ⊕) This tells the story of David Livingstone's life from his early days in Blantyre to the 30 years he spent in Africa, where he named the Victoria Falls on one of his numerous journeys. It's a good display and brings to life the incredible hardships of his missionary existence, his battles against slavery, and his famous meeting with Stanley. There's a child-friendly African wildlife feature, and the grassy park the museum is set in makes a perfect picnic spot.

Head straight down the hill from the station to reach the museum.

It's a 30-minute walk from Blantyre along the river to **Bothwell Castle** (HES; www.historicenvironment.scot; Castle Ave, Uddingston; adult/child £4.50/2.70; ⊙ 9.30am-5.30pm Apr-Sep, 10am-4pm Sat-Wed Oct-Mar), regarded as the finest 13th-century castle in Scotland. The stark, roofless, red-sandstone ruins are substantial and, largely due to their beautiful green setting, romantic.

Trains run from Glasgow Central station to Blantyre (20 minutes, three hourly).

The Campsies & Strathblane

The beautiful Campsies reach an altitude of nearly 600m and lie just 10 miles north of Glasgow. The plain of the River Forth lies to the north; Strathblane and Loch Lomond are to the west.

One of several villages around the Campsies, attractive **Killearn** is known for its 31m-high obelisk, raised in honour of George Buchanan, James VI's tutor. Eight miles to the east, **Fintry** has carved itself a gorgeous spot deep in the Campsies on the banks of Endrick Water, which has an impressive 28m waterfall, the Loup of Fintry.

One of the best walks in the area is the ascent of spectacular **Dumgoyne hill** (427m) from Glengoyne distillery near Killearn: allow at least one hour for the 1.5-mile climb. It's another 1.5 miles (one hour) to Earl's Seat, and 3 miles (1½ hours) to return from there to the distillery. From Drymen, the **Rob Roy Way** (www.robroyway.com) is a great week's walk through Central Scotland's most beautiful lochlands.

⊙ Sights

Glengoyne Distillery   DISTILLERY
(☑ 01360-550254; www.glengoyne.com; A81; tours from £9; ⊙ 10am-6pm Mar-Nov, 10am-5pm Dec-Feb, last tour 1hr before closing) Glengoyne distillery, about 2 miles south of Killearn, is a traditional place run by genuine people in lovely surrounds. There are various tours: the basic ones run on the hour and are reliably excellent.

Culcreuch Castle   HOTEL **££**
(☑ 01360-860555; www.culcreuch.com; Kippen Rd, Fintry; s/d from £83/116; P ⊛ ❄) Fancy a night in a 700-year-old castle? Parts of Culcreuch date to 1296 and the whole is a remarkably well-preserved historic building. The rooms vary substantially in size, price and comfort,

and most look out onto the collage of greenery engulfing the surrounding estate. A little dowdy perhaps and popular with groups, but this place, with its period furnishings, has real character.

There are also self-catering lodges, a little removed from the castle itself, which are great for families; one is pet-friendly.

🛏 Sleeping & Eating

★ **Inn at Kippen** INN ££
(☎ 01786-870500; www.theinnatkippen.co.uk; Fore Rd, Kippen; mains £12-21; ⊗ breakfast 9-11am, lunch noon-6pm, dinner 6-8pm or 9pm; P 🛜 🐾) Though it doesn't promise a great deal from outside, this atmospheric and historic pub is one of the best places in the region at which to eat, and offers exceptional value for this quality of food. Elaborate, imaginative dishes are solidly grounded in British tradition with the odd exotic influence; everything is reliably delicious. There are also four gorgeous rooms (doubles £65 to £95) available.

Kippen is just off the A811 between Balfron and Stirling.

❶ Getting There & Away
First bus 10 runs from Glasgow to Killearn (£5.20, 50 minutes) regularly. Change at Balfron for Fintry and Kippen.

Southern Scotland

Best Places to Eat

➡ Cobbles (p150)

➡ Auld Alliance (p170)

➡ Coltman's (p142)

➡ Campbell's (p175)

➡ MacCallum's (p157)

Best Places to Sleep

➡ Corsewall Lighthouse Hotel (p175)

➡ Knockinaam Lodge (p175)

➡ Old Bank House (p143)

➡ Old Priory (p150)

➡ Edenbank House (p150)

Why Go?

Though wise folk are well aware of its charms, for many people southern Scotland is just something to drive through on the way to northern Scotland. Big mistake. But it does mean you'll find breathing room here in summer, and peaceful corners.

Proximity to England brought raiding and strife; grim borderland fortifications saw skirmishes aplenty. There was loot to be had in the Borders, where large prosperous abbeys ruled over agricultural communities. Regularly ransacked before their destruction in the Reformation, the ruins of these churches, linked by cycling and walking paths, are among Scotland's most atmospheric historic sites.

The rolling west enjoys extensive forest cover between bustling market towns. The hills cascade down to sandy stretches of coastline blessed with Scotland's sunniest weather. It's the land of Robert Burns, whose verse reflected his earthy attitudes and active social life.

When to Go

Ayr

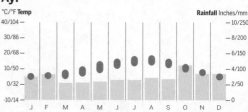

May Take a fortnight to cross the whole region, hiking the gorgeous Southern Upland Way.

Jun The perfect time to visit the region's numerous stately homes, with spectacular gardens in bloom.

Oct Hit Galloway's forests to see red deer battling it out in the rutting season.

BORDERS REGION

The Borders has had a rough history: centuries of war and plunder have left a battle-scarred landscape, encapsulated by the magnificent ruins of the Border abbeys. Their wealth was an irresistible magnet during cross-frontier wars, and they were destroyed and rebuilt numerous times. Today these massive stone shells are the region's finest attraction. And don't miss Hermitage Castle: nothing encapsulates the region's turbulent history like this spooky stronghold.

But the Borders is also genteel. Welcoming villages with ancient traditions pepper the countryside and grandiose mansions await exploration. It's fine walking and cycling country too, the hills lush with shades of green. Offshore is some of Europe's best cold-water diving.

Peebles

POP 8600

With a picturesque main street set on a ridge between the River Tweed and the Eddleston Water, Peebles is one of the most handsome of the Border towns. Though it lacks a major sight, the agreeable atmosphere and good walking options in the rolling, wooded hills thereabouts will entice you to linger for a couple of days.

◉ Sights & Activities

A mile west of the town centre, Neidpath Castle is a tower house perched on a bluff above the river; it's closed but worth a look from the riverbank.

The riverside walk along the River Tweed has plenty of grassed areas ideal for a picnic, and there's a children's playground (near the main road bridge).

Nearby in Glentress forest is the busiest of the **7stanes mountain-biking hubs** (p171), as well as osprey viewing and marked walking trails. There are also swing and zipline forest routes, not to mention camping huts (see www.glentressforestlodges.co.uk). In town, you can hire bikes to explore the region from **Bspoke Cycles** (☎01721-723423; www.bspokepeebles.co.uk; Old Tweeddale Garage, Innerleithen Rd; bikes per day from £25; ⊙9am-5.30pm Mon-Sat).

There are further mountain-biking trails at Innerleithen, 7 miles east of Peebles.

Go Ape   ADVENTURE SPORTS
(www.goape.co.uk; Glentress Forest; adult/child £33/25; ⊙Feb-Nov) This forest-top adventure course features rope bridges, swings and a glorious long zip line over trees and a reservoir. Opening times and days vary widely through the season, so check the website and book ahead online.

🛏 Sleeping

Rosetta Holiday Park   CAMPSITE £
(☎01721-720770; www.rosettaholidaypark.com; Rosetta Rd; tent site for 1/2 £12/20; ⊙Apr-Oct; P 🛜🐾) This campsite, about 800m north of the town centre, has an appealing green setting with lots of trees and grass. There are plenty of amusements for the kids, such as a bowling green and a games room. It also has static caravans of various grades for week-long stays.

Tontine Hotel   HOTEL ££
(☎01721-720892; www.tontinehotel.com; High St; s £60, d £110-120; P🛜🐾) Right in the heart of things, this is a bastion of Borders hospitality. Refurbished rooms have high comfort levels, modish colours and top-notch bathrooms, while service couldn't be more helpful. There's a small supplement for rooms with four-poster beds and/or river views. There are also a good restaurant and bar here. It's in the heart of town.

Rowanbrae   B&B ££
(☎01721-721630; www.aboutscotland.co.uk/peebles/rowanbrae.html; 103 Northgate; s/d £45/68; 🛜) In a quiet cul-de-sac but not far from

---

THE RIDING OF THE MARCHES

The Riding of the Marches, also known as the Common Riding, takes place in early summer in the major Borders towns. Like many Scottish festivals, it has ancient origins, dating back to the Middle Ages when riders would be sent to the town boundary to check on the common lands. The colourful event normally involves extravagant convoys of horse riders following the town standard as it is paraded along a well-worn route. Festivities vary between towns but usually involve lots of singing, sport, pageants and concerts, and plenty of whisky. If you want to zero in on the largest of the Ridings, head to Jedburgh for the **Jethart Callant's Festival** (p148).

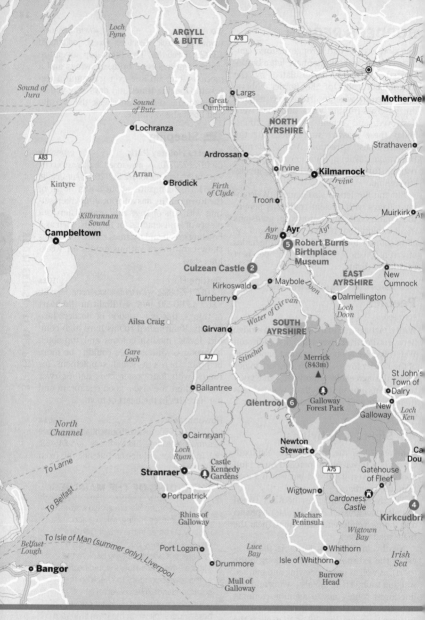

Southern Scotland Highlights

1 Border Abbeys Exploring the noble, evocative ruins of these abbeys – **Dryburgh** (p144) is our favourite – and the area's several other excellent historic sights

2 Culzean Castle (p161) Admiring the 18th-century architectural genius of a castle perched on wild sea cliffs.

3 Hermitage Castle (p149) Pondering the tough old life on the England–

Scotland frontier at this desolate castle.

4 Kirkcudbright (p168) Exploring this charming, dignified town, marvelling at the creative flair of its inhabitants.

5 **Robert Burns Birthplace Museum** (p159) Learning Lallans words from the Scottish Bard's verses.

6 **Glentrool** (p170) Whooshing down forest trails at Glentrool and other 7stanes mountain-biking hubs in the region.

7 **New Lanark** (p153) Admiring the radical social reform instituted in this handsome mill community.

8 **Hiking & Cycling** (p150) Completing one of the region's grand long-distance routes.

9 **Scuba Diving** Plunging the deeps off picturesque **St Abbs** (p153) for top-notch diving.

the main street, this hospitable spot treats its guests like family friends. The traditional old building has modern comforts but retains a pleasant, comfortably old-fashioned feel; there are three upstairs bedrooms, two of them en suite, and a commodious guest lounge for relaxation.

Eating

Cocoa Black
CAFE £

(☏ 01721-721662; www.cocoablack.com; 1 Cuddy Bridge; sweets £1.50-3; ⏱ 9.30am-5pm Mon-Fri, 9am-5pm Sat, 10.30am-4pm Sun; 🛜🚻) Chocaholics should make a beeline for this friendly cafe, where exquisite cakes and other patisserie offerings will satisfy any cacao-focused cravings. It also runs a school where you can learn to make them yourself.

★ Coltman's
BISTRO, DELI ££

(☏ 01721-720405; www.coltmans.co.uk; 71 High St; mains £11-19; ⏱ 10am-5pm Sun-Wed, 10am-10pm Thu-Sat; 🛜) 🍴 This main street deli has numerous temptations, such as excellent cheeses and Italian smallgoods, as well as perhaps Scotland's tastiest sausage roll – buy two to avoid the walk back for another one. Behind the shop, the good-looking dining area serves up confident bistro fare and light snacks with a variety of culinary influences, using top-notch local ingredients.

Tontine Hotel
SCOTTISH ££

(☏ 01721-720892; www.tontinehotel.com; High St; mains £11-19; ⏱ noon-2.30pm & 6-8.45pm; 🛜) Glorious is the only word to describe the Georgian dining room here, complete with musicians' gallery, fireplace and fabulous windows. It'd be worth it even for cat food on mouldy bread, but luckily the meals – ranging from pub classics like steak-and-ale pie to more ambitious fare – are tasty and backed up by very welcoming service. Afternoon tea is served between meal times.

ⓘ Information

Peebles Tourist Office (☏ 01721-728095; www.visitscottishborders.com; 23 High St; ⏱ 9am-5pm Mon-Sat, 11am-4pm Sun) is closed Sundays from January to March. Open until 5.30pm mid-June to August.

ⓘ Getting There & Away

The bus stop is beside the post office on Eastgate. Bus 62A/X62 runs half-hourly (hourly on Sundays) to Edinburgh (£5.20, 1¼ hours). In the other direction it heads for Galashiels, where you can change for Melrose (£6, some through services).

Melrose

POP 2500

Tiny, charming Melrose is a polished village running on the well-greased wheels of tourism. Sitting at the feet of the three heather-covered Eildon Hills, Melrose has a classic market square and one of the great abbey ruins. Just outside town is Abbotsford (p144), the home of Sir Walter Scott, which makes another superb visit.

⊙ Sights

★ Melrose Abbey
RUINS

(HES; ☏ 01896-822562; www.historicenvironment. scot; adult/child £5.50/3.30; ⏱ 9.30am-5.30pm Apr-Sep, 10am-4pm Oct-Mar) Perhaps the most interesting of the Border abbeys, redsandstone Melrose was repeatedly destroyed by the English in the 14th century. The remaining broken shell is pure Gothic and the ruins are famous for their decorative stonework – look out for the pig gargoyle playing the bagpipes. Though Melrose had a monastery way back in the 7th century, this abbey was founded by David I in 1136 for Cistercian monks, and later rebuilt by Robert the Bruce, whose heart is buried here.

The ruins date from the 14th and 15th centuries, and were repaired by Sir Walter Scott in the 19th century. The museum has many fine examples of 12th- to 15th-century stonework and pottery found in the area. Note the impressive remains of the 'great drain' outside – a medieval sewerage system.

🏃 Activities

There are many attractive walks in the **Eildon Hills**, accessible via a footpath off Dingleton Rd (the B6359) south of Melrose, or via the trail along the River Tweed. The tourist office has details of local walks.

The St Cuthbert's Way (p150) long-distance walking path starts in Melrose, while the coast-to-coast Southern Upland Way (p150) passes through town. You can do a day's walk along St Cuthbert's Way as far as Harestanes (16 miles), on the A68 near Jedburgh, and return to Melrose on the hourly Jedburgh–Galashiels bus. The Tweed Cycle Route (p150) also passes through Melrose.

🎊 Festivals & Events

Melrose Rugby Sevens
SPORTS

(www.melrose7s.com; ⏱ mid-Apr) Rugby followers fill the town to see this famous one-day sevens competition.

TRAQUAIR HOUSE

One of Scotland's great country houses, **Traquair House** (☎ 01896-830323; www.traquair.co.uk; adult/child/family £8.70/4.40/24; ⊙ 11am-5pm Easter-Sep, 11am-4pm Oct, 11am-3pm Sat & Sun Nov) has a powerful, ethereal beauty, and exploring it is like time travel. Odd, sloping floors and a musty odour bestow a genuine feel, and parts of the building are believed to have been constructed long before the first official record of its existence in 1107. The massive tower house was gradually expanded but has remained virtually unchanged since the 17th century.

Since the 15th century, the house has belonged to various branches of the Stuart family, and the family's unwavering Catholicism and loyalty to the Stuart cause led to famous visitors like Mary, Queen of Scots and Bonnie Prince Charlie, but also to numerous problems after the deposal of James II of England in 1688. The family's estate, wealth and influence were gradually whittled away, as life as a Jacobite became a furtive, clandestine affair.

One of Traquair's most interesting places is the concealed room where priests secretly lived and performed Mass – up until 1829 when the Catholic Emancipation Act was finally passed. Other beautiful, time-worn rooms hold fascinating relics, including the cradle used by Mary for her son, James VI of Scotland (who also became James I of England), and fascinating letters from the Jacobite Earls of Traquair and their families, including one particularly moving one written from death row in the Tower of London.

The main gates to the house were locked by one earl in the 18th century until the day a Stuart king reclaimed the throne in London, so meanwhile you'll have to enter by a side gate.

In addition to the house, there's a garden **maze**, a small **brewery** producing the tasty Bear Ale, and a series of **craft workshops**.

Traquair is 1.5 miles south of Innerleithen, about 6 miles southeast of Peebles. Bus 62 runs from Edinburgh via Peebles to Innerleithen and on to Galashiels and Melrose.

Borders Book Festival LITERATURE
(www.bordersbookfestival.org) This book festival is run in Melrose over four days in late June.

🛏 Sleeping

Braidwood B&B **£**
(☎ 01896-822488; www.braidwoodmelrose.co.uk; Buccleuch St; s £40-45, d £60-65; 🛜🐾) This popular option near the abbey is solid and comfortable. The bright rooms have a well-cared-for feel, and the twin room has great views. Breakfast features fresh fruit salad. The owners are courteous and generally leave you to your own devices. No singles are available in summer.

⭐**Old Bank House** B&B **££**
(☎ 01896-823712; www.oldbankhousemelrose.co.uk; 27 Buccleuch St; s/d £50/75; 🛜🐾) Right in the centre, this is a superb B&B in a charming old building. The owner's artistic touch is evident throughout, from walls covered with paintings, some his own, to a house full of curios and tasteful art nouveau features, and a sumptuous breakfast room. Rooms are spacious with comfortable furniture and top modern bathrooms; they are complemented by a generous can-do attitude.

It goes the extra mile, and that makes it a great Borders base.

⭐**The Townhouse** HOTEL **£££**
(☎ 01896-822645; www.thetownhousemelrose.co.uk; Market Sq; s/d/superior d £95/132/149; 🅿🛜) The classy Townhouse exudes warmth and professionalism, and has some of the best rooms in town, tastefully furnished with attention to detail. The superior rooms are enormous in size with lavish furnishings and excellent en suites, some with Jacuzzi. Standard rooms are a fair bit smaller but recently refurbished and very comfortable. It's well worth the price.

Burts Hotel HOTEL **£££**
(☎ 01896-822285; www.burtshotel.co.uk; Market Sq; s/d/superior d £75/140/150; 🅿🛜🐾) Set in an early-18th-century house, Burts is a famously reliable central hotel that retains much of its period charm. Rooms vary – the renovated ones with modern plaid fabrics

are very smart, and the superiors are extra spacious. It's got an air of friendly formality that makes it a favourite with older visitors. Appealing food is served too.

Eating

Russell's CAFE £
(28 Market Sq; light meals £6-10; ⊙9.30am-5pm Tue-Sat) Solid wooden furniture and big windows looking out over the centre of Melrose make this stylish little tearoom a popular option. It has a large range of snacks and some more substantial lunch offerings, with daily specials. It's famous throughout the Borders for its excellent scones. New owners were refurbishing at time of last research, so things may change.

The Townhouse SCOTTISH ££
(☑ 01896-822645; www.thetownhousemelrose.co.uk; Market Sq; mains £13-19; ⊙noon-2pm & 6-9pm Sun-Thu, noon-2pm & 6-9.30pm Fri & Sat; 🛜) The brasserie and restaurant here turn out just about the best gourmet cuisine in town and offer decent value. There's some rich, elaborate, beautifully presented fare here, with plenty of venison and other game choices, but for a lighter feed you can always opt for the range of creative lunchtime sandwiches.

ℹ Information

The **Melrose Tourist Office** (☑ 01896-820178; www.visitscottishborders.com; Abbey St; ⊙10am-5pm Mon-Sat, 1-5pm Sun Apr-Oct) is located by the abbey.

ℹ Getting There & Away

The reopened Borders Railway runs from Edinburgh to Tweedbank (£10.10, one hour, half-hourly), which is 1½ miles from Melrose. Some buses run from here to Melrose, but check with Traveline Scotland (www.travelinescotland.com) first, as there may be a faster connection if you get off the train in nearby Galashiels. Otherwise a taxi into Melrose is inexpensive.

Buses run to/from Galashiels, which has bus connections to Edinburgh (£7.20, 1½ to two hours, hourly) and other Borders destinations.

Around Melrose

In the vicinity of Melrose are a couple of excellent attractions intimately connected with Sir Walter Scott.

Abbotsford

Just outside Melrose, **Abbotsford** (☑01896-752043; www.scottsabbotsford.com; visitor centre free, house adult/child £8.95/4.50; ⊙10am-5pm Apr-Oct, 10am-4pm Nov-Mar, house closed Dec-Feb) is where to discover the life and works of Sir Walter Scott, to whom we arguably owe both the modern novel and our mind's-eye view of Scotland. This whimsical, fabulous house where he lived – and which ruined him when his publishers went bust – really brings this 19th-century writer to life. The grounds on the banks of the Tweed are lovely, and Scott drew much inspiration from rambles in the surrounding countryside.

A modern visitor centre displays memorabilia and gives an intriguing overview of the man, before a swish audioguide system – with one designed for kids – shows you round the house. In the house are some gloriously over-the-top features, with elaborate carvings, enough swords and dirks to equip a small army, a Chinese drawing room and a lovely study and library.

A wing of the house offers luxurious self-catering accommodation designed for large groups.

Abbotsford is 2 miles west of Melrose; buses between Galashiels and Melrose will drop you at the nearby Tweedbank roundabout. It's an easy walk from Tweedbank station, reachable in under an hour from Edinburgh. You can also walk from Melrose along the southern bank of the Tweed. There's a cafe-restaurant atop the visitor centre.

Dryburgh Abbey

Partly because the neighbouring town of Dryburgh no longer exists (another victim of the wars) and partly because of its lovely site by the Tweed in a sheltered birdsong-filled valley, **Dryburgh Abbey** (HES; ☑ 01835-822381; www.historicenvironment.scot; adult/child £5.50/3.30; ⊙9.30am-5.30pm Apr-Sep, 10am-4pm Oct-Mar) is the most beautiful and complete of the Border abbeys. Dating from about 1150, the abbey belonged to the Premonstratensians, a religious order founded in France, and evokes 12th-century monastic life more successfully than its nearby counterparts. The pink-hued stone ruins are the burial place of Sir Walter Scott.

The abbey is 5 miles southeast of Melrose on the B6404, which passes the famous Scott's View outlook. Hike there along the southern bank of the River Tweed, or take a bus to the nearby village of Newtown St Boswells.

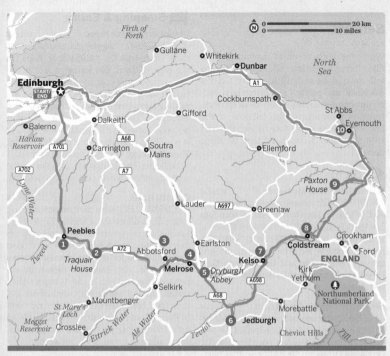

Driving Tour
Historic Sights of the Borders

START EDINBURGH
END EDINBURGH
LENGTH 155 MILES; ONE TO THREE DAYS

You could do this drive in a long day, but to give yourself time to explore better take two or three. All the towns mentioned have good overnighting options.

Starting in Edinburgh, head south on the A701 to **1 Peebles** (p139); Rosslyn Chapel is an easy detour along the way. Stroll around Peebles, a typically pretty Borders town, then head east along the A72, deviating at Innerleithen to historic **2 Traquair House** (p143), offering 10 centuries of history and great insights into the Jacobite cause and rebellions. Continue eastwards on the A72, pausing at excellent **3 Abbotsford** (p144), Sir Walter Scott's one-time home. The attractive bijou village of **4 Melrose** (p142), with its fabulous abbey, is a must-see and a good meal or overnight stop. Head east again, then south down the A68 to **5 Dryburgh Abbey** (p144), perhaps the most evocative of the great Borders ruins.

Continue along the A68 to attractive **6 Jedburgh** (p147), dominated by the skeleton of the third of the abbeys. The turbulent history of these once-powerful communities tells of the constant strife in these frontier lands.

From Jedburgh, take the A698 northeast to **7 Kelso** (p149), a historic market town and the location of grandiose Floors Castle, the last and least intact of the abbey ruins. Several other historic buildings are close by, so this makes an appealing stop for a night or two to explore them: Mellerstain House and the Smailholm Tower are particularly worthwhile.

Beyond Kelso, the A698 takes you to **8 Coldstream**, which gives its name to the famous regiment once based here. Here the road crosses the Tweed into England and leads to the coast near Berwick-upon-Tweed. Head north and take the left turn to the magnificent 18th-century **9 Paxton House** (p152), just back over the border in Scotland. Continue north to **Eyemouth** (p151), with its fascinating maritime history. Here, Gunsgreen House is an elegant mansion with an intriguing smuggling past. From here, drive up the A1 through East Lothian and back to Edinburgh.

Selkirk

POP 5600

While the noisy throb of machinery once filled the valleys below Selkirk, a prosperous mill town in the early 19th century, today it sits placid and pretty – apart from busy traffic through the centre – atop its steep ridge. Naughty millworkers who fell foul of the law would have come face to face in court with Sir Walter Scott, sheriff here for three decades.

◎ Sights

Halliwell's House Museum   MUSEUM
(☑ 01750-726456; www.scotborders.gov.uk; Halliwell's Close; ⊙ 11am-4pm Mon-Sat & noon-3pm Sun Apr-Oct) FREE Halliwell's House Museum is the oldest building (1712) in Selkirk. The museum charts local history with an engrossing exhibition, and the **Robson Gallery** has changing exhibitions. It is inside the tourist office.

Sir Walter Scott's Courtroom   MUSEUM
(☑ 01750-726456; www.scotborders.gov.uk; Market Sq; ⊙ 10am-4pm Mon-Fri & 11am-3pm Sat Mar-Sep, plus 11am-3pm Sun May-Aug, noon-3pm Mon-Sat Oct) FREE Drop into Sir Walter Scott's Courtroom, where there's an exhibition on the man's life and writings, plus a fascinating account of the courageous explorer Mungo Park (born near Selkirk) and his search for the River Niger.

🛏 Sleeping & Eating

Philipburn House Hotel   HOTEL **££**
(☑ 01750-720747; www.bw-philipburnhousehotel.co.uk; Linglie Rd/A708; r £105-145; P🐾🛜🐕) On the edge of town, this former dower house has a jazzy 21st-century look that hasn't ruined its historic features, as well as appealing renovated rooms and a snug bar and restaurant. The luxury rooms are particularly good – some have a Jacuzzi, while another is a split-level affair with a double balcony. There's a range of online booking options.

Self-catering facilities are on offer in the separate lodges, where pets are also welcome.

County Hotel   INN **££**
(☑ 01750-721233; www.countyhotelselkirk.co.uk; 1 High St; s/d/executive d £50/67/73; P🛜🐕) Located in the centre of town, this is a former coaching inn. It has the odd Norwegian touch and comfortable, modernised rooms that vary in size. Executive rooms are super-spacious and handsome. It has a stylish restaurant and lounge with original art and upmarket bar meals (£10 to £16; food noon to 9pm). Room-only rates are also available for £7.50 less per person. You can get a discount advance booking via the website.

Buon Gusto   ITALIAN **££**
(☑ 01750-778174; www.buongustoristorante.co.uk; 73 High St; mains £8-14; ⊙ noon-2.30pm & 5.30-9.30pm Wed-Fri, noon-9.30pm Sat, 5.30-9.30pm Sun) On the main street, this does rather tasty pizza, elaborate pasta creations and other Italian plates and adaptations.

SIR WALTER SCOTT

Sir Walter Scott (1771–1832) is one of Scotland's greatest literary figures. Born in Edinburgh, he spent time on his grandparents' farm at Sandyknowe in the Borders as a child. It was here, rambling around the countryside, that he developed a passion for historical ballads and Scottish heroes. After studying in Edinburgh he bought Abbotsford (p144), a country house in the Borders.

The Lay of the Last Minstrel (1805) was an early critical success. Further works earning him an international reputation included *The Lady of the Lake* (1810), set around Loch Katrine and the Trossachs. He later turned his hand to novels and was instrumental in their development. His first novel, *Waverley* (1814), which dealt with the 1745 Jacobite rebellion, set the classical pattern of the historical novel. Other works included *Guy Mannering* (1815) and *Rob Roy* (1817). He became something of an international superstar, and heavily influenced writers and artists such as Austen, Dickens and Turner. His writings virtually single-handedly revived interest in Scottish history and legend, and much of our Scottish cliches of today – misty glens, fierce warriors, tartan – are largely down to him. His organisation of the visit of George IV to Edinburgh reintegrated Highland dress into society.

Later in life Scott wrote obsessively to stave off bankruptcy. Tourist offices stock a *Sir Walter Scott Trail* booklet, which details many places associated with him in the Borders.

ℹ️ Information

Selkirk Tourist Office (📞 01750-20054; www.visitscottishborders.com; Halliwell's Close; 🕐 11am-4pm Mon-Sat, noon-3pm Sun Apr-Oct) The helpful tourist office is tucked away off Market Square. Inside is Halliwell's House Museum (p146).

ℹ️ Getting There & Away

First buses 95 and X95 run at least hourly between Carlisle and Edinburgh (£7.20, two hours) via Hawick, Selkirk and Galashiels. It's usually faster to hop off a bus at Galashiels and catch the train into Edinburgh.

Hawick

POP 13,900

Straddling the River Teviot, Hawick (pronounced 'hoik') is one of the largest towns in the Borders and has long been a major production centre for knitwear. There are several large outlets to buy jumpers and other woollens around town. Hawick is also famous for rugby; the local club has produced dozens of Scotland internationals.

◉ Sights

Heart of Hawick VISITOR CENTRE
(www.heartofhawick.co.uk; Kirkstile) Three buildings form the 'heart' of Hawick. A former mill holds the tourist office and a cinema. Opposite, historic **Drumlanrig's Tower**, once a major seat of the Douglas clan, now houses the **Borders Textile Towerhouse** (📞 01450-377615; www.heartofhawick.co.uk; 1 Tower Knowe; 🕐 10am-4.30pm Mon-Sat & noon-3pm Sun Apr-Oct, 10am-4pm Mon-Sat Nov-Mar). This tells the story of the town's knitwear-producing history. Behind the tourist office, the **Heritage Hub** (📞 01450-360699; www.heartofhawick.co.uk; Kirkstile; 🕐 9.30am-12.45pm & 1.15-4.45pm Mon-Fri, to 7pm by appointment Tue & Thu, 10am-2pm Sat) **FREE** is a state-of-the-art facility open to anyone wishing to trace their Scottish heritage or explore other local archives.

Hawick Museum & Art Gallery MUSEUM, GALLERY
(📞 01450-364747; Wilton Lodge Park; 🕐 10am-noon & 1-5pm Mon-Fri, 2-5pm Sat & Sun Apr-Sep, noon-3pm Mon-Fri, 1-3pm Sun Oct-Mar) **FREE** This museum has an interesting collection of mostly 19th-century manufacturing and domestic memorabilia as well as details on a tragic pair of local motorcycling legends. There are usually a couple of temporary exhibitions on as well.

🛏️ Sleeping & Eating

Bank Guest House B&B ££
(📞 01450-363760; www.thebankno12highst.com; 12 High St; s £50-65, d £75-85; 🅿️ 🛜) This posh boutique B&B in the centre of Hawick brings out the best in this solid 19th-century building with modish wallpapers and designer furniture and fabrics. Modern comforts as well as numerous thoughtful extras make this a great place to stay.

Damascus Drum CAFE £
(📞 07707-856123; www.damascusdrum.co.uk; 2 Silver St; light meals £5-10; 🕐 10am-5pm Mon-Sat; 🛜 ✍️) The Middle East meets the Borders in this enticing cafe behind the tourist office. Patterned rugs and a secondhand bookshop make for a relaxing environment to enjoy breakfasts, bagels, burgers and tasty Turkish-style meze options.

Night Safe Bistro BISTRO ££
(📞 01450-377045; www.hawicknightsafebistro.co.uk; 12 High St; dinner mains £15-19; 🕐 10am-4pm & 6.30-9pm Tue-Sat; 🛜) Lively and attractive, this high street coffee stop and restaurant occupies the ground level of a handsome bank building. Morning coffees and light lunches give way to sturdier dinner mains based around well-sourced duck, fish and meat. Service is very welcoming.

ℹ️ Information

Hawick Tourist Office (📞 01450-360688; www.visitscottishborders.com; Kirkstile; 🕐 10am-5.30pm Mon & Wed, 10am-6.15pm Tue & Thu, 10am-7.15pm Fri & Sat, noon-2.45pm Sun; 🛜) Located in Tower Mill, part of the Heart of Hawick complex.

ℹ️ Getting There & Away

Half-hourly First buses 95 and X95 connect Hawick with Galashiels, Selkirk and Edinburgh (£7.20, two hours). Buses leave from Mart St at the northern end of the town centre.

Jedburgh

POP 4000

Attractive Jedburgh, where many old buildings and wynds (narrow alleys) have been intelligently restored, invites exploration by foot.

◉ Sights

⭐ **Jedburgh Abbey** RUINS
(HES; www.historicenvironment.scot; Abbey Rd; adult/child £5.50/3.30; 🕐 9.30am-5.30pm Apr-Sep, 10am-4pm Oct-Mar) Dominating the town

skyline, this was the first of the great Border abbeys to be passed into state care, and it shows – audio and visual presentations telling the abbey's story are scattered throughout the carefully preserved ruins (good for the kids). The red-sandstone ruins are roofless but relatively intact, and the ingenuity of the master mason can be seen in some of the rich (if somewhat faded) stone carvings in the nave.

The abbey was founded in 1138 by David I as a priory for Augustinian canons.

Mary, Queen of Scots' Visitor Centre
HISTORIC BUILDING

(Queen St; ⊙9.30am-4.30pm Mon-Sat, 10.30am-4pm Sun Mar-Nov) FREE Mary stayed at this beautiful 16th-century tower house in 1566 after her famous ride to visit the injured earl of Bothwell, her future husband, at Hermitage Castle. The interesting exhibition evokes the sad saga of Mary's life and death. Various objects associated with her – including a lock of her hair – are on display.

Activities

The tourist office has handy booklets for walks around the town, including sections of the Southern Upland Way (p150) or Borders Abbeys Way (p150). Jedburgh is also a popular stop for walkers on St Cuthbert's Way (p150), which passes nearby.

Festivals & Events

Jethart Callant's Festival
CULTURAL

(www.jethartcallantsfestival.com; ⊙from late Jun) This two-week cavalcade recalls the perilous time when people rode out on horseback checking for English incursions. It's perhaps the most notable of the Common Riding festivals of the Borders (p139). There are various rides and processions over the fortnight, involving hundreds of costumed horseriders.

Sleeping

Maplebank
B&B £

(☑01835-862051; maplebank3@btinternet.com; 3 Smiths Wynd; s/d £30/50; ℗🐕🐾) It's very pleasing to come across places like this, where it really feels like you're staying in someone's home. Here, that someone is like your favourite aunt: friendly, chaotic and generous. There's lots of clutter and it's very informal. Rooms are comfortable and large, sharing a good bathroom. Breakfast (including fruit, yoghurts and homemade jams) is brilliant – much better than at most posher places.

Willow Court
B&B ££

(☑01835-863702; www.willowcourtjedburgh.co.uk; the Friars; s/d £75/86; ℗🐾) It seems inadequate to call this impressive option a B&B; it's more like a boutique hotel. Impeccable rooms with elegant wallpaper, showroom bathrooms and great beds are complemented by a courteous, professional welcome. Every time we visit it's been improved in some way: the sign of a standout establishment. The conservatory lounge is great for admiring the views over garden and town.

Glenbank House Hotel
HOTEL ££

(☑01835-862258; www.jedburgh-hotel.com; Castlegate; s/d/superior d £55/75/90; ℗🐾) This lovely old building has modern, comfortable rooms – some of which are rather compact – shiny contemporary bathrooms, and nice views over the town and hills. It's a likeable place, with a bar and decent food, as well as a very friendly owner who is great value for a breakfast-time chat.

Eating

Capon Tree
SCOTTISH ££

(☑01835-869596; www.thecapontree.com; 61 High St; mains £13-19; ⊙noon-2.30pm & 6-9pm Tue-Sat year-round, daily Jun-Aug; 🐾) Attractively combining smart and casual, this welcoming bistro and bar does modern Scottish cuisine. Plates are beautifully, though not fussily, presented and ingredients are of high quality. A couple of flavour combinations don't work so well, but the overall package is appealing, the service good and the ambience romantic. There are handsome rooms available too.

Carters Rest
PUB FOOD ££

(☑01835-864745; Abbey Pl; mains £10-13; ⊙food noon-8pm Sun-Fri, noon-9pm Sun; 🐾) Right opposite the abbey, here you'll find upmarket pub grub in an attractive lounge bar. The standard fare is fleshed out with an evening dinner menu featuring local lamb and other goodies. Portions are generous and served with a smile.

ℹ Information

There's a free wi-fi zone around the centre, which is strongest around the tourist office.

Jedburgh Library (☑01835-863592; www.scotborders.gov.uk; Castlegate; ⊙10am-1pm & 2-5pm Mon & Thu, 2-7pm Tue, 2-7pm Tue, 9.30am-12.30pm Sat) has free internet.

The very helpful **Jedburgh Tourist Office** (☑01835-863170; www.visitscotland.com; Mur-

HERMITAGE CASTLE

The 'guardhouse of the bloodiest valley in Britain', Hermitage Castle (HES; www.historic environment.scot; adult/child £4.50/2.70; ⊗ 9.30am-5.30pm Apr-Sep) embodies the brutal history of the Scottish Borders. Desolate but proud with its massive squared stone walls, it looks more like a lair for orc raiding parties than a home for Scottish nobility, and is one of the bleakest and most stirring of Scottish ruins. The castle is about 12 miles south of Hawick on the B6357.

Strategically crucial, the castle was the scene of many a dark deed and dirty deal with the English invaders, all of which rebounded heavily on the perfidious Scottish lord in question. Here, in 1338, Sir William Douglas imprisoned his enemy Sir Alexander Ramsay and deliberately starved him to death. Ramsay survived for 17 days by eating grain that trickled into his pit (which can still be seen) from the granary above. In 1566 Mary, Queen of Scots famously visited the wounded tenant of the castle, Lord Bothwell, here. Fortified, he recovered to (probably) murder her husband, marry her himself, then abandon her months later and flee into exile.

ray's Green; ⊗ 9am-5.30pm Mon-Sat, 10am-5pm Sun Apr-Oct, 10am-4pm Mon-Sat Nov-Mar; 🖝) is the head tourist office for the Borders region.

❶ Getting There & Away

Jedburgh has good bus connections to Hawick, Melrose and Kelso (all around 25 minutes, roughly hourly, two-hourly on Sunday). Buses also run to Edinburgh (£7.30, two hours, three to six daily).

Kelso

POP 5600

Kelso, a prosperous market town with a broad, cobbled square flanked by Georgian buildings, has a cheery feel and historic appeal. During the day it's a busy little place, but after 8pm you'll have the streets to yourself. The town has a lovely site at the junction of the Tweed and Teviot, and is one of the most enjoyable places in the Borders.

◉ Sights

Floors Castle   HISTORIC BUILDING
(✆ 01573-223333; www.floorscastle.com; adult/child castle & grounds £8.50/4.50, incl gardens £12.50/6.50; ⊗ 10.30am-5pm mid-Apr–mid-Oct) Grandiose Floors Castle is Scotland's largest inhabited mansion, home to the Duke of Roxburghe, and overlooks the Tweed about a mile west of Kelso. Built by William Adam in the 1720s, the original Georgian simplicity was 'improved' in the 1840s with the addition of rather ridiculous battlements and turrets. Inside, view the vivid colours of the 17th-century Brussels tapestries in the drawing room and the intricate oak carv-

ings in the ornate ballroom. The impressive walled garden is entered by a separate ticket.

Kelso Abbey   RUINS
(HES; www.historicenvironment.scot; Bridge St; ⊗ 9.30am-5.30pm Apr-Sep, 9.30am-4.30pm Sat-Wed Oct-Mar) **FREE** Once one of the richest abbeys in southern Scotland, Kelso Abbey was built by the Tironensians, an order founded in Picardy and brought to the Borders around 1113 by David I. English raids in the 16th century reduced it to ruins, though what little remains today is some of the finest surviving Romanesque architecture in Scotland.

🏃 Activities

The Kelso–Jedburgh section (12 miles) of the Borders Abbeys Way (p150) is a fairly easy walk, largely following the River Teviot. The tourist office has a free leaflet with map and route description.

For a shorter ramble, leave the Square by Roxburgh St and take the signposted alley to Cobby Riverside Walk, a pleasant stroll along the river to Floors Castle (rejoin Roxburgh St to gain admission to the castle).

🛏 Sleeping

Central Guest House   GUESTHOUSE **£**
(✆ 01890-883664; www.thecentralguesthousekelso. co.uk; 51 The Square; s/d/f £45/60/120; 🖝) A reasonable cheaper option in sometimes pricey Kelso and just on the central square. The owners live off-site, so call ahead first. The rooms are dated but fine: spacious, with firm beds, carpets and good bathrooms. Rates are

room-only, but you get a fridge, toaster and microwave, so you can create your own breakfast. There's some street noise.

★ **Edenbank House**   B&B **££**
(☎ 01573-226734; www.edenbank.co.uk; Stichill Rd; s/d £50/80; P 🖳) Half-a-mile down the Stichill road, this grand Victorian house sits in spacious grounds where only bleating lambs in the green fields and birds in the garden break the silence. It's a fabulous place, with huge opulent rooms, lovely views over the fields, and incredibly warm, generous hospitality. Breakfast features homemade produce, and a laissez-faire attitude makes for an utterly relaxing stay. Don't just show up: call ahead.

★ **Old Priory**   B&B **££**
(☎ 01573-223030; www.theoldpriorykelso.com; 33 Woodmarket; s/d £55/85; P 🖳) Fantastic rooms here are allied with numerous personal details – the operators turn down the beds at night and make you feel very welcome. Doubles are top-notch and the family room really excellent. The good news extends to the garden – perfect for a coffee in the morning – and a comfortable conservatory lounge. The huge windows flood the rooms with natural light. Top-class B&B.

Inglestone House   B&B **££**
(☎ 01573-225800; www.inglestonehouse.co.uk; Abbey Row; s/d/f £55/80/120; 🖳) The Northumbrian owners here are welcoming and very cordial but also leave you space for yourself, giving this spot behind the main street an appealing blend of hotel and guesthouse. Rooms are a good size with firm mattresses and – unusually for the Borders – the wi-fi is fast.

✖ Eating & Drinking

★ **Cobbles**   BISTRO **££**
(☎ 01573-223548; www.thecobbleskelso.co.uk; 7 Bowmont St; mains £10-17; ⊙ food noon-2.30pm & 5.45-9pm Mon-Fri, noon-9pm Sat, noon-8pm Sun; 🖳) This inn off the main square is so popular you will need to book a table at weekends. It's cheery, very welcoming and warm, and serves excellent upmarket pub food in generous portions. Pick and mix from bar menu, steaks and gourmet options. Leave room for cheese and/or dessert. The bar's own microbrewed ales are excellent. A cracking place.

WALKING & CYCLING IN SOUTHERN SCOTLAND

Walking

The region's most famous walk is the challenging 212-mile **Southern Upland Way** (www.southernuplandway.gov.uk). If you want a sample, one of the best bits is the three- to four-day section from Dalry to Beattock.

Another long-distance walk is 62-mile **St Cuthbert's Way** (http://stcuthbertsway.info), inspired by the travels of St Cuthbert, a 7th-century saint who lived at the first Melrose monastery. It crosses some superb scenery between Melrose and Lindisfarne (in England).

In Galloway, the **Pilgrims Way** follows a 25-mile trail from Glenluce Abbey to the Isle of Whithorn.

The **Borders Abbeys Way** (www.bordersabbeysway.com) links all the great Border abbeys in a 65-mile circuit. For shorter walks and especially circular loops in the hills, the towns of Melrose, Jedburgh and Kelso all make ideal bases.

For baggage transfer on these walks, contact **Walking Support** (☎ 01896-822079; www.walkingsupport.co.uk). In early September, look out for the **Scottish Borders Walking Festival** (www.borderswalking.com; ⊙ early Sep), with a week of walks for all abilities and an instant social scene.

Cycling

With the exception of the main A-roads, traffic is sparse, which, along with the beauty of the countryside, makes this ideal cycling country.

The **Tweed Cycle Route** is 95 waymarked miles along the beautiful Tweed Valley, following minor roads from Biggar to Peebles (22 miles), Melrose (25 miles), Coldstream (28 miles) and Berwick-upon-Tweed (19 miles). The **4 Abbeys Cycle Route** is a 55-mile circuit of the Border abbeys. Local tourist offices have route maps; these and other routes are also detailed at www.cyclescottishborders.com.

Oscar's
BISTRO ££

(☑ 01573-224008; www.oscars-kelso.com; 35 Horse-market; mains £11-19; ⊙ 6-9.30pm Thu-Sat, opens extra days in summer; ☎ ☑) Posh comfort food and the work of local artists sit side by side in this likeable bar-restaurant-gallery in the centre of town. A list of excellent daily specials complements the more standard permanent selection. A wide choice of wines is available, and you can browse the exhibition space downstairs while you wait for your meal.

★ Rutherfords
PUB

(☑ 07803-208460; www.rutherfordsmicropub.co.uk; 38 The Square; ⊙ 4-9pm Mon, noon-9pm Tue-Thu & Sun, noon-10pm Fri & Sat) This enchanting small bar prioritises conversation and has no TV or music. It's a charming place with gin on tap poured through a microscope, carefully selected craft beers and spirits, and a warm, convivial atmosphere. Unusual and excellent.

❶ Information

Kelso Library (☑ 01573-223171; www.scot border.gov.uk; Bowmont St; ⊙ 10am-5pm Mon & Thu, 1-7pm Tue, 10am-2pm Wed, 10am-4pm Fri, 9.30am-12.30pm Sat; ☎ ❸) has free internet access and wi-fi.

Kelso Tourist Office (☑ 01573-221119; www.visitscottishborders.com; The Square; ⊙ 10am-3.30pm Mon-Sat Apr-Oct, to 5pm plus 10am-2pm Sun mid-Jun–Aug) is in the town hall building.

❶ Getting There & Away

There are six daily direct bus services to Edinburgh (£7.30, two hours, one to two on Sunday) and regular routes to other Borders towns and Berwick-upon-Tweed.

Around Kelso

The area around Kelso has two starkly contrasting historic buildings to visit, and the twin walkers' villages of Town Yetholm and Kirk Yetholm.

◉ Sights

Mellerstain House HISTORIC BUILDING

(☑ 01573-410225; www.mellerstain.com; adult/child £8.50/4; ⊙ 12.30-5pm Fri-Mon Easter & May-Sep) Finished in 1778, this is considered to be Scotland's finest Robert Adam–designed mansion. It is famous for its classic elegance, ornate interiors and plaster ceilings; the library in particular is outstanding. The upstairs bedrooms are less attractive, but have a peek at the bizarre puppet-and-doll

collection in the gallery. It's about 6 miles northwest of Kelso, near Gordon.

Smailholm Tower
TOWER

(HES; www.historicenvironment.scot; adult/child £4.50/2.70; ⊙ 9.30am-5.30pm Sat & Sun Apr-Sep) Perched on a rocky knoll above a small lake, this narrow stone tower provides one of the most evocative sights in the Borders and keeps its bloody history alive. Although displays inside are sparse, the panoramic view from the top is worth the climb. The tower is 6 miles west of Kelso, a mile south of Smailholm village on the B6397.

The nearby privately owned farm, **Sandy-knowe**, was owned by Sir Walter Scott's grandfather. As Scott himself recognised, his imagination was fired by the ballads and stories he heard as a child at Sandyknowe, and by the ruined tower a stone's throw away.

Eyemouth
POP 3500

Eyemouth is a busy fishing port and popular domestic holiday destination. The harbour itself is very atmospheric – you may even spot seals frolicking in the water, as well as tourists frolicking around the boats, snapping pics of old fishing nets accompanied by the cry of seagulls.

The community here suffered its greatest catastrophe in October 1881, when a terrible storm destroyed the coastal fishing fleet, killing 189 fishermen, 129 of whom were locals. Peter Aitchison's *Black Friday* is a good book about the disaster.

◉ Sights & Activities

Eyemouth Maritime Centre MUSEUM

(☑ 01890-751020; www.worldofboats.org/emc; Harbour Rd; adult/child £3/2; ⊙ 10am-5pm Mon-Sat, 10am-4pm Sun Apr-Oct) Situated right on Eyemouth's working fishing harbour, what was once the fish market has been decked out to resemble an 18th-century man o' war. A changing yearly exhibition occupies most of the interior, drawing on the museum's large collection of well-loved wooden coastal craft. The friendly museum guides are happy to provide extra information

Gunsgreen House MUSEUM

(☑ 01890-752062; www.gunsgreenhouse.org; Gunsgreen Quay; adult/child £6.50/4; ⊙ 11am-5pm Apr-Oct) Standing proud and four-square across the harbour, this elegant 18th-century John Adam mansion was built on the profits of

WORTH A TRIP

PAXTON HOUSE

Six miles west of Berwick-upon-Tweed, **Paxton House** (☑ 01289-386291; www.paxton house.co.uk; B6461; adult/child £8.50/free; ☉ 10am-5pm Easter-Oct, grounds 10am-sunset) is beside the River Tweed and surrounded by parkland and gardens. It was built in 1758 by Patrick Home for his intended wife, the daughter of Prussia's Frederick the Great. Unfortunately she stood him up, but it was her loss; designed by the Adam family – brothers John, James and Robert – it's acknowledged as one of the finest 18th-century Palladian houses in Britain.

It contains a large collection of Chippendale and Regency furniture, and its picture gallery houses paintings from the national galleries of Scotland. The nursery is designed to provide insight into a child's 18th-century life. In the grounds are walking trails and a riverside museum on salmon fishing. There's plenty to keep the kids entertained here.

Bus 32 runs past here every couple of hours from Berwick.

smuggling: Eyemouth was an important landing point for illegal cargoes from northern Europe and the Baltic. The house has been beautifully restored to reflect this and other aspects of its varied past. Both the house and the adjacent tower-like dovecote can be hired out as self-catering accommodation.

Eyemouth Museum   MUSEUM
(www.eyemouthmuseum.org; Manse Rd; adult/child £3.50/free; ☉ 10am-4pm Tue-Sat, noon-4pm Sun Apr-Oct) Has intriguing local history displays, particularly relating to the town's fishing heritage. Its centrepiece is the tapestry commemorating the 1881 fishing disaster.

Eyemouth RIB Trips   BOATING
(☑ 07941-441995; www.eyemouthribtrips.co.uk) Offers a range of fun boat trips, some focused on coastal scenery and wildlife spotting, others on giving you a thrill and a soaking from the spray.

🛏 Sleeping & Eating

Bantry   B&B ££
(Mackays; ☑ 01890-751900; www.mackaysofeye mouth.co.uk; 20 High St; s/d/f £50/75/80; [P] 🛜) Above a restaurant on the main drag, this B&B has redecorated and refurbished rooms (some with shared bathroom) with muted tones and a luxurious, modern feel and is positioned right on the waterfront. Try to get room No 3 for sea views. There's a fabulous deck, with loungers and a summer hot tub, overlooking the lapping waves. No-breakfast rates available too.

Oblò   BISTRO ££
(☑ 01890-752527; www.oblobar.com; 20 Harbour Rd; mains £11-17; ☉ food 10am-9pm Sun-Thu, to 9.30pm Fri & Sat; 🛜 ☑) For a meal any time, find your way upstairs to this modern Mediterranean-fusion bar-bistro with comfy seating and a modish interior. It's just down from the tourist office, and it's got a great deck to lap up the sunshine. Service is attentive and the food is delicious. Try the local seafood, then duck around the back of the building for authentic Italian gelato.

ℹ Information

The very helpful **Eyemouth Tourist Office** (☑ 01890-750678; www.visiteyemouth.com; ☉ 10am-4pm Tue-Sat, noon-4pm Sun Apr-Oct) is inside Eyemouth Museum near the harbour.

ℹ Getting There & Away

Eyemouth is 5 miles north of the Scotland–England border. Buses go to Berwick-upon-Tweed (£2.80, 15 minutes, frequent), which has a train station, and to Edinburgh (£10.40, 1¾ hours, six to eight daily Monday to Saturday, three Sunday).

Coldingham & St Abbs

This picturesque area is fantastic for those who love the great outdoors. There's some of the UK's best diving here, as well as great cycling, walking, angling and birdwatching. From the village of Coldingham, with its twisting streets, take the B6438 downhill to the small fishing village of St Abbs, a gorgeous, peaceful little community with a picture-perfect harbour nestled below the cliffs.

◉ Sights & Activities

St Abbs Visitor Centre   MUSEUM
(☑ 01890-771672; www.stabbsvisitorcentre.co.uk; Coldingham Rd, St Abbs; ☉ 10am-5pm Apr-Oct) **FREE** This modern exhibition in St Abbs

has interesting interactive displays on the often stormy history of this harbour village. Spoken reminiscences from locals like a fisherman and lighthouse keeper are the highlight.

St Abbs & Eyemouth Voluntary Marine Reserve
NATURE RESERVE
(☏01890-771443; www.marine-reserve.co.uk) 🏊
The clear, clean waters around St Abbs form part of St Abbs & Eyemouth Voluntary Marine Reserve, one of the best cold-water diving sites in Europe. The reserve is home to a variety of marine life, including grey seals and porpoises. Visibility is about 7m to 8m but has been recorded at up to 24m. Beds of brown kelp form a hypnotically undulating forest on the seabed.

Coldingham Bay
BEACH, SURFING
In Coldingham, a signposted turn-off to the east leads just under a mile down to away-from-it-all Coldingham Bay, which has a sandy beach and a clifftop walking trail to Eyemouth (3 miles). At **St Vedas Surf Shop** (☏01890-771679; www.stvedas.co.uk; surfboard hire per hr £6, kayaks per hr/half-day/day £14/32/49; ☺9am-dusk) you can hire surfboards, sea kayaks and snorkelling gear; there's a hotel here that serves cheap food. Surfing lessons (£35) are also available.

Diving
The sea around St Abbs forms part of the St Abbs & Eyemouth Voluntary Marine Reserve. Three dive boats operate out of St Abbs, run by **Paul Crowe** (☏07710-961050, 01890-771945; http://divestabbs.com; Rock House, St Abbs; 2 dives £40), **Paul O'Callaghan** (☏01890-771525, 07780-980179; www.stabbsdiving.com; Priory View, Eyemouth Rd, Coldingham) and **Peter Gibson** (☏07702-687606; st.abbsboatcharter@gmail.com; 2 dives £40). You can charter them whole, or phone to book a spot on a boat; these spots cost around £40 per person for two dives.

The St Abbs Visitor Centre (p152) can provide some diving advice. A guide to local dive sites costs £7.50.

🛌 Sleeping

Rock House
HOSTEL £
(☏01890-771945; www.divestabbs.com; Harbour, St Abbs; dm £23; 🛜) Right by the harbour in St Abbs, this is run by a friendly dive skipper; you can almost roll out of bed onto the boat. The bunkhouse, which is normally booked up by groups at the weekend, has three rooms and sleeps a total of 10.

Glenlea
B&B ££
(☏01890-771368; www.glenlea-bb.co.uk; the Bow, Coldingham; s/d £60/70; 🅿🛜) In the centre of Coldingham, this cute blue-trimmed whitewashed cottage offers upright B&B and courteous hospitality. Two sweet rooms offer plenty of comfort, and the owners are used to dealing with surfboards, scuba tanks and the like. This little road gets tight beyond here, so back out if you've got a big vehicle.

ℹ Getting There & Away
Perryman's Buses No 253 (six to eight daily Monday to Saturday, three Sunday) between Edinburgh (£9.20) and Berwick-upon-Tweed (£3.60) stops in Coldingham (some go to St Abbs on request). Bus 235 runs hourly from Berwick via Eyemouth to Coldingham and St Abbs.

SOUTH LANARKSHIRE

South Lanarkshire combines a highly urbanised area south of Glasgow with scenically gorgeous country around the Falls of Clyde and the World Heritage–listed area of New Lanark, by far the biggest drawcard of the region. The handsome town of Biggar is also worth a visit.

Lanark & New Lanark
POP 8900

Below the market town of Lanark, in an attractive gorge by the River Clyde, is the World Heritage Site of New Lanark – an intriguing collection of restored mill buildings and warehouses.

Once Britain's largest cotton-spinning complex, it is better known for the pioneering social experiments of Robert Owen, who managed the mill from 1800. New Lanark is really a memorial to this enlightened capitalist. He provided his workers with housing, a cooperative store, the world's first nursery school, adult-education classes, a sick-pay fund for workers and a social centre he called the New Institute for the Formation of Character. Devote half a day to exploring this site as there's plenty to see and do, including appealing walks along the riverside. What must once have been a thriving, noisy, industrial village is now a peaceful oasis with only the swishing of trees and the rushing of the River Clyde to be heard.

◉ Sights & Activities

★ New Lanark Visitor Centre
MUSEUM

(☑ 01555-661345; www.newlanark.org; adult/child/family £9.50/7/30; ⊙ 10am-5pm Apr-Oct, 10am-4pm Nov-Mar) The main attractions of this World Heritage mill town are accessed via a single ticket. These include a huge working spinning mule, producing woollen yarn, and the **Historic Schoolhouse**, which contains an innovative, high-tech journey to New Lanark's past via a 3D hologram of the spirit of Annie McLeod, a 10-year-old mill girl who describes life here in 1820. The kids will love it as it's very realistic, although the 'do good for all mankind' theme is a little overbearing.

Included in your admission is entrance to a millworker's house, Robert Owen's home and exhibitions on 'saving New Lanark'. There's also a 1920s-style village store.

★ Falls of Clyde
WALKING

From New Lanark, you can walk through the beautiful nature reserve up to **Corra Linn** (0.75 miles) and **Bonnington Linn** (1½ miles), two of the Falls of Clyde that inspired Turner and Wordsworth. You could return via the muddier path on the opposite bank, pass New Lanark and cross the river further downstream to make a circular walk of it (3 miles).

🛏 Sleeping & Eating

Wee Row Hostel
HOSTEL £

(☑ 01555-666710; www.newlanarkhostel.co.uk; Rosedale St, New Lanark; s/tw £49/59; P @ 🛜) This hostel has a great location in an old mill building in the heart of the New Lanark complex. It has comfortable en suite rooms with both beds and bunks and a really good downstairs common area. Prices come down substantially outside high season. Dorm rates (£16 to £18) may be offered subject to availability. Closed between 11am and 3pm.

New Lanark Mill Hotel
HOTEL ££

(☑ 01555-667200; www.newlanarkmillhotel.co.uk; New Lanark; r £107-125; P @ 🛜 ♨ ✿) Cleverly converted from an 18th-century mill, this hotel is full of character and is a stone's throw from the major attractions. It has luxury rooms (only a little extra for a spacious superior room), with contemporary art on the walls and views of the churning Clyde below. It also has self-catering accommodation in charming cottages.

There are good facilities for people with disability here. The hotel also serves good meals (bar meals £5 to £11; restaurant mains £14 to £16).

La Vigna
ITALIAN £££

(☑ 01555-664320; www.lavigna.co.uk; 40 Wellgate; mains £17-24; ⊙ noon-2.30pm & 5-10pm Mon-Sat, noon-3pm & 5-9.30pm Sun; 🛜) This well established local favourite is a great spot, seemingly plucked from some bygone age with its quietly efficient service and a separate menu for 'ladies' – without prices. The food is distinctly Italian, albeit using Scottish venison, beef and fish, and there are also vegetarian options. The set-price meals are great value.

ℹ Information

Lanark Tourist Office (☑ 01555-668249; www.visitscotland.com; 18 Ladyacre Rd; ⊙ 10am-5pm Mon-Fri year-round, plus 10am-5pm Sat & Sun Apr-Oct) Close to the bus and train stations.

ℹ Getting There & Away

Lanark is 25 miles southeast of Glasgow. Express bus 240X runs hourly Monday to Saturday (£6.20, one hour); trains from Glasgow Central also run (£6.90, 55 minutes, every 30 minutes, hourly on Sundays).

It's a pleasant walk to New Lanark, but there's also a half-hourly bus service from the train station (daily). If you need a taxi, call **Clydewide** (☑ 0800-050 9264; www.clydewidetaxis.co.uk).

Biggar
POP 2300

Biggar is a pleasant town in a rural setting dominated by Tinto Hill (712m). The town has a worthwhile museum and a famous puppet theatre. It's also known for the nationalist, leftist poet Hugh MacDiarmid, who lived near here for nearly 30 years until his death in 1978.

◉ Sights & Activities

Biggar & Upper Clydesdale Museum
MUSEUM

(☑ 01899-221050; www.biggarmuseumtrust.co.uk; 156 High St; adult/child £5/2; ⊙ 10am-5pm Tue-Sat & 1-5pm Sun Apr-Oct, 10am-5pm Sat & 1-5pm Sun Nov-Mar) This museum has been a major community project pursued by dedicated volunteers, and finally opened with heartwarming enthusiasm in 2015. The pièce de résistance is Gladstone Court, a reconstructed street with historic Victorian-era nook-and-cranny shops that you can pop into to steal a glimpse of the past. A working telephone exchange is an impressive highlight. Other displays cover archaeology, geography and history of the area, with features both on the Covenanters and the Polish soldiers billeted in Biggar in WWII.

Biggar Puppet Theatre   THEATRE
(☏ 01899-220631; www.purvespuppets.com; Broughton Rd; seats £8; ☻ Easter-Sep) A well-loved local institution that runs matinee shows every couple of days throughout the summer using miniature Victorian puppets and bizarre glow-in-the-dark modern ones over 1m high. Different shows are suitable for varying age groups, so inquire before you take along the kids. Check the website for performance times.

Tinto Hill   WALKING
The hill dominates the town from a distance. It is a straightforward ascent by the northern ridge from the car park, just off the A73 by Thankerton Crossroads. Look out for the Stone Age **fort** on your way up. Allow two hours for the return trip (4½ miles).

🛏 Sleeping & Eating

★ **Cornhill Castle**   HOTEL **££**
(☏ 01899-220001; www.cornhillcastle.co.uk; r £114-165; P🛜) Two miles west of Biggar, just off the A72, is this fabulous country hotel on the Clyde. It's a striking château-style building that offers artistic, opulent decor with not a hint of tartan. There are nine rooms and they are huge, with loads of character and appealing furniture such as leather sofas or four-poster beds. It books out at weekends for weddings.

There's a good on-site restaurant.

Barony   BRITISH **££**
(☏ 01899-221159; www.barony-biggar.co.uk; 55 High St; mains £13; ☻ noon-2.30pm & 5-9pm Wed-Sat, noon-3pm & 5-8pm Sun; 🛜) A classier option than Biggar's decent pubs, this well-run restaurant features a handsome dining area with exposed stone, candlelight, posh glassware and inviting chairs. The short menu covers upmarket comfort food and a few more ambitious creations. There are good lunch specials. Book at weekends.

ⓘ Getting There & Away

Biggar is 33 miles southeast of Glasgow. There are hourly buses (four on Sunday) to/from Edinburgh (£4.80, 1¼ hours). For Glasgow, change at Lanark (30 minutes). Other buses run to Peebles.

AYRSHIRE

Ayrshire is synonymous with golf and Robert Burns – and there's plenty on offer here to satisfy both of these pursuits. Troon and Turnberry have world-famous courses, and there's enough Burns memorabilia in the region to satisfy even his most fanatical admirers.

The best way to appreciate the Ayrshire coastline is on foot: the **Ayrshire Coastal Path** (www.ayrshirecoastalpath.org; 🚶) offers 100 miles of spectacular waterside walking.

Largs
POP 11,300

On a sunny day, there are few places in southern Scotland more beautiful than Largs, where green grass meets the sparkling water of the Firth of Clyde. It's a resort-style waterfront town that harks back to seaside days in times of gentler pleasures, and the minigolf, amusements, old-fashioned eateries and bouncy castle mean you should get into the spirit, buy an ice cream and stroll around this slice of retro Scotland.

◎ Sights

Víkingar!   MUSEUM
(☏ 01475-689777; www.kaleisure.com; Greenock Rd; adult/child £4.50/3.50; ☻ 11.30am-2.30pm Sat & Sun Feb & Nov, 11.30am-1.30pm Mar, 10am-2.30pm Apr-Jun & Sep-Oct, 10.30am-3.30pm Mon-Fri & 11.30am-3.30pm Sat & Sun Jul-Aug; 🚶) The town's main attraction is a multimedia exhibition describing Viking influence in Scotland until its demise at the Battle of Largs in 1263. It's got a slightly downbeat municipal feel these days, but tours with staff in Viking outfits run every hour; ring ahead to check, though. It also has a swimming pool, soft play area and leisure centre. It's on the waterfront road; you can't miss it, as it's the only place with a longship outside.

👉 Tours

In summer, the *Waverley* (p116), the last ocean-going paddle steamer ever built, runs spectacular coastal voyages. There are several departures a week from Largs; book online or at the information office.

🎆 Festivals & Events

Largs Viking Festival   HISTORIC
(www.largsvikingfestival.com; ☻ 1st week Sep) This festival celebrates the Battle of Largs and the end of Viking political domination

WORTH A TRIP

IRVINE

Boat lovers should check out the **Scottish Maritime Museum** (☑ 01294-278283; www.scottishmaritimemuseum.org; Harbour Rd; adult/child £7.50/free; ⊙ 10am-5pm) by the train station in Irvine, which long ago was west Scotland's busiest port. In the massive **Linthouse Engine Shop** – an old hangar with a cast-iron framework – is an absorbing collection of boats and machinery. Displays cover ropeworking, the age of steam and the Clyde's shipbuilding industry. Every boat here has a story – some tragic. Free guided tours take you down to the dock where you can clamber over various ships, and visitors can also see a shipyard worker's restored flat.

Further along the harbour road, be sure to drop into the **Ship Inn** (☑ 01294-279722; www.theshipinnirvine.co.uk; 120 Harbour St; mains £9-13; ⊙ food 10am-9pm Sun-Thu, 10am-9.30pm Fri, 10am-10pm Sat; ☎). It's the oldest pub in Irvine (1597), serves tasty bar meals and has bucket-loads of character.

Irvine is 26 miles from Glasgow. There are frequent buses from Ayr (30 minutes) and Largs (45 minutes). Trains run to/from Glasgow Central station; the other way they go to Ayr.

in Scotland. The highlights are the authentic Viking village peopled by costumed locals and the re-enactment of the battle, complete with longship aflame.

🍴 Sleeping & Eating

St Leonards Guest House
B&B ££

(☑ 01475-673318; www.stleonardsguesthouse.com; 9 Irvine Rd; s £40-65, d £65-80; ᴘ☎) On the main road through town, but excellently soundproofed, this spot offers a cordial welcome and spotless, well-decorated rooms, some of which share a top-notch modern bathroom. Breakfast is a pleasure.

Glendarroch
B&B ££

(☑ 01475-676305; www.glendarrochlargs.com; 24 Irvine Rd; d £65-70; ᴘ☎) This B&B on the main road through town has warm and friendly owners who keep their prices fair and their four lovely rooms very shipshape. All are en suite and the kingsized double is particularly desirable.

Lounge
BISTRO ££

(☑ 01475-689968; www.loungeatlargs.com; 33 Main St; mains £11-16; ⊙ noon-3.30pm & 5-9.30pm Mon-Fri, noon-4pm & 5-9.30pm Sat & Sun; ☎) Tucked away above the Royal Bank of Scotland on the main road, this stunningly attractive bar and bistro comes as quite a surprise. Eating is done in an elegant tea-room space, with hardwood floor, ceramic fireplace and leather seats. Service is willing, and there's a nice range of classic Scottish pub fare alongside tasty seafood and a few fusion dishes.

Nardini's
CAFE, BISTRO ££

(☑ 01475-689300; www.nardinis.co.uk; 2 Greenock Rd; mains £8-16; ⊙ 9am-10pm; ☎⛱) Nothing typifies the old-time feel of Largs more than this giant art deco gelateria. The ice creams are decadently delicious, with rich flavours that'll have parents licking more than their fair share from their kids' cones. It also has a cafe with outdoor seating, and a franchise restaurant that does decent pizza and pasta, and some more elaborate mains and tapas portions.

❶ Getting There & Away

Largs is 32 miles west of Glasgow by road. There are trains from Glasgow Central (£8, one hour, hourly). Buses run the route more slowly via Greenock and Gourock. Buses also run once or twice hourly to Ayr (£6.60, 1½ hours) via Ardrossan and Irvine. You can also reach these by rail, some with a change at Kilwinning.

Great Cumbrae

POP 1400

Walking or cycling is the best way to explore this accessible, hilly island (it's only 4 miles long), ideal for a day trip from Largs. **Millport** is the only town, strung out around the bay overlooking neighbouring Little Cumbrae. The town boasts Britain's smallest **cathedral** (☑ 01475-530353; www.cumbraecathedralfriends.com; College St; ⊙ daylight hours) FREE.

The island's minor roads have well-marked walking and cycling routes. Take the Inner Circle route up to the island's highest point, **Glaid Stone**, where you get good views of Arran and Largs, and even as far as the Paps of Jura on a clear day. You can walk between the ferry and the town via here in about an hour. There are several bike-hire places in Millport.

If you're staying overnight on the island, modernised **College Guesthouse** (☑ 01475-530353; www.cumbraeguesthouse.co.uk; College St; d £86, s/d without bathroom £43/76; P ☎) is run by a religious college and is part of the cathedral complex. It's a quiet, comfortable place to stay; it has a refectory-style dining room (half- and full-board rates available) and a library.

The **Dancing Midge** (24 Glasgow St; light meals £3-8; ☉ 10am-4pm Thu-Sun, extended hours summer; ☎) is a cheerful cafe on the seafront providing tasty alternatives to the chippies in town, as well as an ideal spot to read the newspaper.

A frequent CalMac ferry links Largs with Great Cumbrae (passenger/car return £3.20/12.20, 10 minutes). Buses meet the ferries for the 3.5-mile journey to Millport.

Troon
POP 14,640

Troon, a major sailing centre on the coast 7 miles north of Ayr, has excellent sandy beaches and six golf courses, including one of the world's finest. Nearby Dundonald Castle is also well worth a visit.

The demanding championship course **Royal Troon** (☑ 01292-311555; www.royaltroon.com; Craigend Rd; ☉ mid-Apr–mid-Oct), host of the 2016 Open Championship and considered one of golf's classic links challenges, has offers on its website; the standard green fee is £220, which includes a complimentary round at the Portland course.

Dundonald Castle (HES; ☑ 01563-851489; www.dundonaldcastle.org.uk; Winehouse Yett, Dundonald; adult/child £4.50/2.70; ☉ 10am-5pm Apr-Oct) commands impressive views and, in its main hall, has one of the finest barrel-vaulted ceilings preserved in Scotland. It was the first home of the Stuart kings, built by Robert II in 1371, and reckoned to be the third most important castle in Scotland in its time, after Edinburgh and Stirling. The visitor centre has good information on prior settlements, and scale models of the castle and its predecessors. Buses running between Troon and Kilmarnock stop in Dundonald.

Right at the end of the harbour road, where yachts have given way to fishing boats, **MacCallum's** (☑ 01292-319339; www.

maccallumsoftroon.co.uk; Harbour Rd; seafood mains £14-20, fried fish £3.50-6.50; ☉ restaurant noon-2.30pm & 6.30-9.30pm Tue-Sat, noon-2.30pm Sun, chip shop noon-8pm Sun & Tue-Thu, noon-9pm Fri & Sat) set-up has two parts, both worthwhile. The Oyster Bar offers excellent fresh seafood in a smart, uncluttered setting. Next door, the Wee Hurrie does fish 'n' chips, with excellent fish choices like sea bass. Order the fritto misto to try different varieties.

❶ Getting There & Away

There are half-hourly trains to Ayr (£3.30, 15 minutes) and Glasgow (£7.70, 50 minutes). The ferry service to Northern Ireland is no longer running.

Ayr
POP 46,710

Ayr's long sandy beach has made it a popular family seaside resort since Victorian times, but it has struggled in the recent economic climate. Parts of the centre have a neglected air, though there are many fine Georgian and Victorian buildings, and it makes a convenient base for exploring this section of coast. The huge drawcard is Alloway (p159), 3 miles south, with its Robert Burns heritage. Most things to see in Ayr are also Robert Burns–related.

◉ Sights

St John's Tower TOWER
(Eglinton Tce) This is the only remnant of a church where a parliament was held in 1315, the year after the celebrated victory at the battle of Bannockburn. John Knox's son-in-law was the minister here, and Mary, Queen of Scots stayed overnight in 1563. You can only admire it from the street, but it's very photogenic.

Auld Brig BRIDGE
(Old Bridge) Several of Burns' poems are set here in Ayr; in *Twa Brigs,* Ayr's old and new bridges argue with one another. The Auld Brig was built in 1491 and spans the river just north of the church.

---

❶ ARDROSSAN

An otherwise unremarkable coastal town, Ardrossan is the main ferry port for Arran. From May to September there are also services to Campbeltown on the Kintyre peninsula.

Ayr

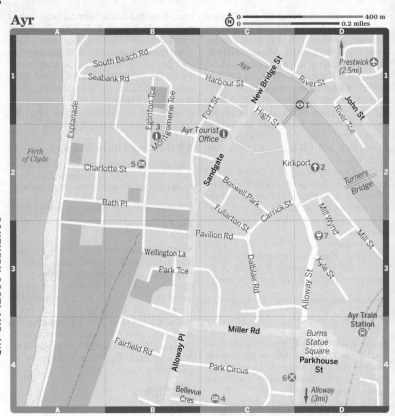

Ayr

⊙ Sights
1 Auld Brig	D1
2 Auld Kirk	D2
3 St John's Tower	B2

🛏 Sleeping
4 26 The Crescent	C4
5 Arrandale Hotel	B2

⊗ Eating
6 XXII	C4

🍸 Drinking & Nightlife
7 Tam O'Shanter	D3

Auld Kirk   CHURCH
(Old Church; www.auldkirk.org; Blackfriars Walk; ⊗1-2pm Tue Mar-Jun & Sep-Nov, 10.30am-12.30pm Sat Jul & Aug) FREE Robert Burns was baptised in the Auld Kirk (Old Church). The at-mospheric cemetery here overlooks the river and is good for a stroll, offering an escape from the bustle of High St.

✨ Festivals & Events

Burns an' a' That   CULTURAL
(www.burnsfestival.com; ⊗ late May) This festival has a bit of everything, from wine-tasting and horseracing to concerts, some of it Burns-related.

🛏 Sleeping

**Heads of Ayr
Caravan Park**   CAMPSITE £
(☑ 01292-442269; www.headsofayr.com; Dunure Rd; sites £18-25; ⊗ Mar-Oct; P 🛜) This caravan park is in a lovely, quiet location close to the beach. There are various caravans and chalets available to rent by the week or for a few days. From Ayr take the A719 south for about 5 miles.

26 The Crescent
B&B **££**

(☏ 01292-287329; www.26crescent.co.uk; 26 Bellevue Cres; d £70-97; ☏) When the blossoms are out, this is Ayr's prettiest street, and it boasts an excellent place to stay. The rooms are impeccable – an upgrade to the spacious four-poster room is a sound investment. Bathrooms are excellent. Though there's more space on the 1st floor, we like the top-floor chambers with sloping roof. The welcome is genuinely friendly.

Arrandale Hotel
GUESTHOUSE **££**

(☏ 01292-289959; www.arrandalehotel.co.uk; 2 Cassillis St; s £38, d £60-95; ☏) In a quiet and pleasant part of town, the mixture of new and old here doesn't always work, but it's a relaxed, friendly place offering comfort at a reasonable price. Sparklingly clean bathrooms are a highlight, and the spacious lounge is an appealing space. Room-only rates are the norm, with breakfast £7 per person.

✖ Eating & Drinking

XXII
BISTRO **££**

(No 22 Bar & Grill; ☏ 01292-280820; www.22ayr.com; 22 Beresford Tce; mains £9-16; ⊙ food 9am-9.30pm; ☏) Buzzy and attractive, this serves a wide-ranging fusion menu as well as cocktails, breakfasts and more. Mediterranean and, particularly, Italian influences take pride of place, backed up by things like tempura and steaks. It's very hit-and-miss but outranks the local competition: not a tough task. There's a wide choice of wines by the glass.

Tam O'Shanter
PUB

(☏ 01292-611684; 230 High St; ⊙ 11am-11pm Mon-Sat, 12.30-11pm Sun; ☏) In Robert Burns' poem 'Tam o' Shanter', Tam spends a boozy evening in this pub, which now bears his name. Opened in the mid-18th century, it's an atmospheric old place with a good atmosphere as well as mediocre pub grub (served noon to 9pm).

ℹ Information

Ayr Tourist Office (☏ 01292-290300; www.ayrshire-arran.com; 22 Sandgate; ⊙ 9am-5pm Mon-Sat year-round, plus 10am-5pm Sun Apr-Sep; 🖳) is in the centre.

Carnegie Library (☏ 01292-286385; www.south-ayrshire.gov.uk; 12 Main St; ⊙ 9am-7.30pm Mon & Tue, 9am-5pm Wed & Fri-Sat, 10am-7.30pm Thu; ☏) has free internet access.

ℹ Getting There & Away

Ayr is 33 miles from Glasgow and is Ayrshire's major transport hub. There are frequent express services to Glasgow (£6.20, 50 minutes to one hour) via Prestwick Airport, as well as services to Stranraer (£8.60, two hours, four to eight per day) and several Ayrshire towns. The bus station sits at the corner of Fullarton St and Sandgate.

There are at least two trains an hour that run between Ayr and Glasgow Central station (£8.30, 55 minutes), and some trains continue south from Ayr to Stranraer (£10.90, 1½ hours).

Alloway
POP 6100

The pretty, lush village of Alloway (3 miles south of Ayr) should be on the itinerary of every Robert Burns fan – he was born here on 25 January 1759. Even if you haven't been seduced by Burnsmania, it's still well worth a visit, as the Burns-related exhibitions give a good impression of life in Ayrshire in the late 18th century.

◉ Sights

★ Robert Burns Birthplace Museum
MUSEUM

(NTS; ☏ 0844-493 2601; www.burnsmuseum.org.uk; Murdoch's Lone; adult/child £9/7; ⊙ 10am-5pm Oct-Mar, to 5.30pm Apr-Sep, closed Christmas-early Jan) This impressive museum has collected a solid range of Burns memorabilia, including manuscripts and possessions of the poet, like the pistols he packed for his daily work as a taxman. There's good biographical information, and a series of displays that bring to life individual poems via background snippets, translations and recitations. Appropriately, the museum doesn't take itself too seriously: there's plenty of humour that the poet surely would have approved of, and entertaining audio and visual performances will keep the kids amused.

The admission ticket also covers the atmospheric **Burns Cottage**, connected via a walkway to the Birthplace Museum. Born in the little box-bed in this cramped thatched dwelling, the poet spent the first seven years of his life here. It's an attractive display that gives you a context for reading plenty of his verse. Much-needed translation of some of the more obscure Scots farming terms he loved to use decorate the walls.

Alloway Auld Kirk
RUIN, CHURCH

(Monument Rd; ⊙24hr) FREE Near the Robert Burns Birthplace Museum (p159) are the ruins of the kirk, the setting for part of Burns' verse tale 'Tam o' Shanter'. Burns' father, William, is buried in the kirkyard; read the poem on the back of the gravestone.

Burns Monument & Memorial Gardens
GARDENS

(⊙24hr) FREE Within these gardens near the Robert Burns Birthplace Museum (p159) is a striking neo-Grecian monument to the poet, completed in 1823. It affords a view of the nearby 13th-century Brig o' Doon, another Burns landmark.

🛌 Sleeping

Brig O'Doon House
HOTEL ££

(📞01292-442466; www.brigodoonhouse.com; High Maybole Rd; s/d £85/120; 🅿) On the main road right by the monument and bridge, a charming ivy-covered facade conceals this romantic, rather luxurious hotel, which will appeal greatly to Burns fans. The heavyish decor of plaid carpets is relieved by slate-floored bathrooms; rooms are spacious and very comfortable, and there's a decent restaurant (mains £10 to £13). Often booked up by wedding parties at weekends.

Across the road, there are more bedrooms in Doonbrae, blessed with a lovely garden, and a couple of cottages – Rose, traditionally decorated, and Gables, more contemporary.

THE SCOTTISH BARD

> I see her in the dewy flowers,
> I see her sweet and fair:
> I hear her in the tunefu' birds,
> I hear her charm the air:
> There's not a bonnie flower that springs
> By fountain, shaw, or green;
> There's not a bonnie bird that sings,
> But minds me o' my Jean.
>
> *Robert Burns, 'Of a' the Airts', 1788*

Best remembered for penning the words of 'Auld Lang Syne', Robert Burns (1759–96) is Scotland's most famous poet and a popular hero; his birthday (25 January) is celebrated as Burns Night by Scots around the world.

Burns was born in Alloway to a poor family, who scraped a living gardening and farming. At school he soon showed an aptitude for literature and a fondness for the folk song. He later began writing his own songs and satires. When the problems of his arduous farming life were compounded by the threat of prosecution from the father of Jean Armour, with whom he'd had an affair, he decided to emigrate to Jamaica. He gave up his share of the family farm and published his poems to raise money for the journey.

The poems were so well reviewed in Edinburgh that Burns decided to remain in Scotland and devote himself to writing. He went to Edinburgh in 1787 to publish a 2nd edition, but the financial rewards were not enough to live on and he had to take a job as an excise man in Dumfriesshire. Though he worked well, he wasn't a taxman by nature, and described his job as 'the execrable office of whip-person to the blood-hounds of justice'. He contributed many songs to collections, and a 3rd edition of his poems was published in 1793. A prodigious writer, Burns composed more than 28,000 lines of verse over 22 years. He died (probably of heart disease) in Dumfries in 1796, aged 37, having fathered more than a dozen children to several different women. Generous-spirited Jean bore nine of them and took in another, remarking 'Oor Robbie should hae had twa wives'.

Many of the local landmarks mentioned in the verse tale 'Tam o' Shanter' can still be visited. Farmer Tam, riding home after a hard night's drinking in a pub in Ayr, sees witches dancing in Alloway churchyard. He calls out to the one pretty witch, but is pursued by them, and has to reach the other side of the River Doon to be safe. He just manages to cross the Brig o' Doon, but his mare loses her tail to the witches.

The Burns connection in southern Scotland is milked for all it's worth and tourist offices have a *Burns Heritage Trail* leaflet leading you to every place that can claim some link with the bard. Burns fans should have a look at www.robertburns.org.

ⓘ Getting There & Away

Bus 361 runs hourly between Alloway and Ayr (£1.85, six minutes). The X77 runs direct here from Glasgow via Prestwick airport and Ayr. Otherwise walk or cycle here from Ayr.

Culzean Castle

The Scottish National Trust's flagship property, magnificent **Culzean Castle & Country Park** (kull-*ane*; NTS; ☑ 01655-884400; www.culzeanexperience.org; castle adult/child/family £15.50/11.50/38; ⊗ castle 10.30am-5pm Apr-Oct, last entry 4pm, park 9.30am-sunset year-round; 🐾) is one of the most impressive of Scotland's great stately homes. On approach the castle floats into view like a mirage. Designed by Robert Adam, who was encouraged to exercise his romantic genius, this 18th-century mansion is perched dramatically on a clifftop.

There's a great play area for kids, which re-creates the castle on a smaller scale, as well as a re-creation of a Victorian vinery, an orangery, a deer park and an aviary.

Robert Adam was the most influential architect of his time, renowned for his meticulous attention to detail and the elegant classical embellishments with which he decorated his ceilings and fireplaces.

The beautiful oval staircase here is regarded as one of his finest achievements. On the 1st floor, the opulence of the circular saloon contrasts violently with the views of the wild sea below. Lord Cassillis' bedroom is said to be haunted by a lady in green, mourning for a lost baby. Even the bathrooms are palatial: the dressing room beside the state bedroom is equipped with a Victorian state-of-the-art shower.

If you really want to experience the magic of this place, it's possible to stay in the **castle** (☑ 01655-884455; www.culzean-eisenhower.com s/d from £150/225, Eisenhower ste s/d £250/375; ⊗ Apr-Oct; 🅿 🛇) from April to October. There's also a **campsite** (☑ 01655-760627; www.campingandcaravanningclub.co.uk; sites per adult/child from £10.50/5.25, plus per site for non-members £7.50; ⊗ Apr-Oct; 🅿 🛇 🐾) at the entrance to the park, offering grassy pitches with great views.

Wildlife in the area includes otters.

Stagecoach buses running between Ayr and Girvan stop outside the gates, from where it's a 1-mile walk to the castle itself.

WORTH A TRIP

DUMFRIES HOUSE

A Palladian mansion designed in the 1750s by the Adam brothers, **Dumfries House** (☑ 01290-425959; www.dumfries-house.org.uk; adult/child £9/4, HS members £6.75; ⊗ tours 10.45am-3.30pm Sun-Fri, 10.45am & noon Sat Mar-Oct, 12.15pm & 1.45pm Sat & Sun Nov-Feb, closed mid-Dec–early Jan) is an architectural jewel: such is its preservation that Prince Charles personally intervened to ensure its protection. It contains an extraordinarily well-preserved collection of Chippendale furniture and numerous objets d'art. Visits are by guided tour; book ahead by phone or internet. There's a discount for Historic Scotland members. The daily Grand Tour (adult/child £13/4) also takes you to the bedrooms upstairs and the grounds. There's a cafe here.

The house is located 13 miles east of Ayr, near Cumnock. Bus it from Ayr or Dumfries to Cumnock and walk or cab it the 2 miles to the house; you can also get a train from Glasgow to Auchinleck.

Kirkoswald

Between the towns of Maybole and Kirkoswald, by the A77, **Crossraguel Abbey** (HES; ☑ 01655-883113; www.historicenvironment.scot; A77; adult/child £4.50/2.70; ⊗ 9.30am-5.30pm Apr-Sep) is a substantial ruin dating back to the 13th century that's good fun to explore. The renovated 16th-century gatehouse is the best part – you'll find decorative stonework and superb views from the top. Inside, if you have the place to yourself, you'll hear only the whistling wind – an apt reflection of the abbey's long-deceased monastic tradition. Don't miss the echo in the chilly sacristy.

Turnberry

Turnberry basically consists of one of Scotland's great golf links and a massive, super-luxurious resort and self-catering complex opposite it. The whole thing was bought by Donald Trump in 2015 and has had a recent facelift.

Turnberry's **Ailsa** (☑ 01655-331991; www.turnberry.co.uk; Maidens Rd, Turnberry) is one of Scotland's most prestigious links courses, with spectacular views of Ailsa Craig offshore. You don't need a handicap certificate to play, just plenty of pounds – the summer weekend green fee is £275. In summer though, take advantage of the after-3pm 'sunset' rate and you can go round for less than half that.

The super-luxurious, recently renovated **Trump Turnberry** (☎01655-331000; www.turnberryresort.co.uk; r without/with view £345/395; P ❄ @ ☎ ≋ 🐾) resort opposite the famous golf course offers everything you can think of, including kilted staff, an airstrip and a helipad. As well as the luxurious rooms and excellent restaurant, there's a series of self-contained lodges. Rooms with sea views cost somewhat more. Some cheaper rooms above the spa complex have views and cost £130 for a double.

Ailsa Craig

The curiously shaped island of Ailsa Craig can be seen from much of southern Ayrshire. While its unusual blue-tinted granite – famous for making the best curling stones – has been used by geologists to trace the movements of the great Ice Age ice sheet, birdwatchers know Ailsa Craig as the world's second-largest gannet colony – around 10,000 pairs breed annually on the island's sheer cliffs.

To see the island close up, take a cruise from Girvan on the **MV Glorious** (☎01465-713219, 07773-794358; www.ailsacraig.org.uk; 7 Harbour St). It's possible to land if the sea is reasonably calm; a four-hour trip costs £20/15 per adult/child (£25 per person if you want three hours ashore). Mull of Kintyre Seatours (p262) also runs sightseeing trips here from Campbeltown.

Trains going to Girvan run approximately hourly (less frequently on Sundays) from Ayr (£5.40, 30 minutes).

> **DUMFRIES & GALLOWAY BUS PASS**
>
> Buses are the main mode of local transport with **Stagecoach** (☎01387-253496; www.stagecoachbus.com) the primary operator. Its Megarider ticket costs £23 and gives you unlimited travel on Stagecoach buses within Dumfries and Galloway for a week – not a bad deal.

DUMFRIES & GALLOWAY

Some of Southern Scotland's finest attractions lie in the gentle hills and lush valleys of Dumfries and Galloway. It's an ideal destination for families, as there's plenty on offer for the kids. Galloway Forest – with its sublime views, mountain-biking and walking trails, red deer, kites and other wildlife – is a highlight, as are the dream-like ruins of Caerlaverock Castle. Adding to the appeal of this enticing region is a string of southern Scotland's most idyllic towns, which are charming when the sun shines. And shine it does. Warmed by the Gulf Stream, this is the mildest region in Scotland, a phenomenon that has allowed the development of some famous gardens.

Dumfries

POP 32,900

Lovely, red-hued sandstone bridges crisscross the wide, grassy-banked River Nith, which runs through the centre of pleasant Dumfries. Historically the town held a strategic position in the path of vengeful English armies; consequently, although it has existed since Roman times, the oldest standing building dates from the 17th century. Plenty of famous names have passed through: Robert Burns lived here and worked as a tax collector, Peter Pan creator JM Barrie was schooled here and DJ Calvin Harris hails from the town.

Sights

★Burns House MUSEUM
(☎01387-255297; www.dumgal.gov.uk/museums; Burns St; ⏲10am-5pm Mon-Sat & 2-5pm Sun Apr-Sep, 10am-1pm & 2-5pm Tue-Sat Oct-Mar) FREE
This is a place of pilgrimage for Burns enthusiasts. It's here that the poet spent the last years of his life, and there are various possessions of his in glass cases, as well as manuscripts and, entertainingly, letters: make sure you have a read.

Devorgilla Bridge BRIDGE
The red sandstone bridges arching over the River Nith are the most attractive feature of the town. Devorgilla Bridge (1431) is one of the oldest bridges in Scotland. Built into its southwestern end is the city's oldest extant house.

Dumfries

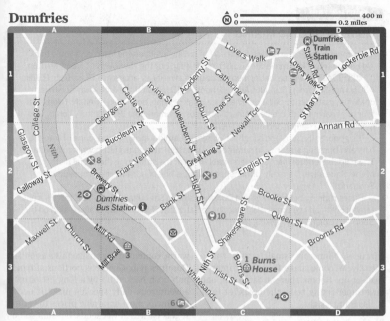

Robert Burns Centre   MUSEUM

(📞 01387-253374; www.dumgal.gov.uk/museums; Mill Rd; audiovisual presentation £2.30; ⊙10am-5pm Mon-Sat & 2-5pm Sun Apr-Sep, 10am-1pm & 2-5pm Tue-Sat Oct-Mar) **FREE** A worthwhile Burns exhibition in an old mill on the banks of the River Nith; it tells the story of the poet and Dumfries in the 1790s. The optional audiovisual presentations give more background on Dumfries, and explain the exhibition's contents. The centre functions as a cinema in the evenings.

Ellisland Farm   MUSEUM

(📞 01387-740426; www.ellislandfarm.co.uk; Holywood Rd, Auldgirth; adult/child £4/free; ⊙10am-1pm & 2-5pm Mon-Sat, 2-5pm Sun Apr-Sep, 10am-1pm & 2-5pm Tue-Sat Oct-Mar) If you're not Burnsed out, you can head 6 miles northwest of Dumfries and visit the farm he leased. It still preserves some original features from when he and his family lived here, and there's a small exhibition. It's signposted off the A76 to Kilmarnock.

Robert Burns Mausoleum   TOMB

(St Michael's Kirk) **FREE** Burns' mausoleum is in the graveyard at St Michael's Kirk. It's in the far corner from the entrance. There's a grisly account of his reburial on the information panel.

Dumfries

🛏 Sleeping

★ Merlin   B&B £

(📞 01387-261002; www.themerlin.webeden.co.uk; 2 Kenmure Tce; s/d without bathroom £35/56; 📶) Beautifully located on the riverbank across a pedestrian bridge from the centre, this is a top place to hole up. So much work goes on behind the scenes here that it seems

WORTH A TRIP

MUSEUM OF LEAD MINING

'Lead mining': even the phrase has a sort of dulling effect on the brain, and you'd think it'd be a tough ask to make the subject interesting. But the **Museum of Lead Mining** (☑ 01659-74387; www.leadminingmuseum.co.uk; Wanlockhead; adult/child £8.25/6.25; ⊙ 11am-4.30pm Apr-Sep, from 10am Jul & Aug), signposted 10 miles off the motorway northwest of Moffat, manages to pull it off. The place is fascinating, and family-friendly, taking in a tour of a real mine, re-created miners' cottages, a remarkable 18th-century library, and a display on lead mining and other minerals.

It's apparently Scotland's highest village, set amid a striking landscape of treeless hills and burbling streams. In summer the museum also runs gold-panning activities. The palpable enthusiasm and personableness of the staff bring the social history of the place alive. It's really rather special, and is one of our favourite museums in Scotland.

Buses running between Ayr and Dumfries stop in Sanquhar, from where there's a bus to Wanlockhead five times daily Monday to Saturday. Wanlockhead is also a stop on the Southern Upland Way walking route.

effortless. Numerous small details and a friendly welcome make this a very impressive set-up. Rooms share a bathroom, and have super-comfy beds; the breakfast table is also quite a sight.

Ferintosh Guest House
B&B **££**

(☑ 01387-252262; www.ferintosh.net; 30 Lovers Walk; s £35-40, d £64-68; ☎ 🐾) A Victorian villa opposite the train station, Ferintosh is a good-humoured place with excellent rooms and a warm welcome. These people have the right attitude towards hospitality, with comfortable plush beds, a free dram on arrival, and plenty of good chat on distilleries. The showers sound like aircraft taking off but deliver impressive results. The owner's original artwork complements the decor.

Cyclists are welcomed with a shed and bike-washing facilities.

Torbay Lodge
B&B **££**

(☑ 01387-253922; www.torbaylodge.co.uk; 31 Lovers Walk; s £36-48, d/f £68/77; 🅿 ☎) This high-quality guesthouse has beautifully presented bedrooms with big windows, elegant bedsteads and generously sized en suites (and a single without); the good vibe is topped off by an excellent breakfast. It's handy for the station and there's a laundry service.

🍴 Eating & Drinking

Cavens Arms
PUB FOOD **£**

(☑ 01387-252896; 20 Buccleuch St; mains £8-12; ⊙ food 11.30am-9pm Tue-Sat, noon-8.30pm Sun; ☎) Engaging staff, 10 real ales on tap and a

warm, contented buzz make this a legendary Dumfries pub. Generous portions of typical pub nosh backed up by a long list of more adventurous daily specials make it one of the town's most enjoyable places to eat too. It gets packed at weekends, but staff still try to find a table for all.

If you were going to move to Dumfries, you'd make sure you were within a block or two of this place. There's no food on Monday, but the pub's still open.

Kings
CAFE **£**

(☑ 01387-254444; www.kings-online.co.uk; 12 Queensberry St; snacks £2-6; ⊙ 8am-5.30pm Mon-Sat, noon-4pm Sun; ☎) This buzzy cafe in the centre of town doubles as a bookshop. It does tasty fair-trade coffee, has big windows for observing Dumfries life passing by and serves toothsome sweet things, breakfasts and filled rolls.

Hullabaloo
CAFE, BISTRO **££**

(☑ 01387-259679; www.hullabaloorestaurant.co. uk; Mill Rd; mains £9-20; ⊙ noon-3pm Mon, noon-3pm & 5.30-8.30pm Tue-Sat year-round, plus 12.30-3pm Sun Easter-Sep; 🍴) The best eating option in Dumfries is this cosy space upstairs at the Robert Burns Centre. For lunch there's wraps, melts and ciabattas, but come dinner time it's inventive angles and interesting cuts and combinations. There's a distinct Mediterranean flavour to the regularly changing specials, including expertly prepared fish dishes and appetising vegetarian choices. It has vegan and gluten-free menus.

Globe Inn PUB
(📞 01387-252335; www.globeinndumfries.co.uk; 56 High St; ⏱ 10am-11pm Mon-Wed, to midnight Thu, to 1am Fri & Sat, 11.30am-midnight Sun) A traditional, rickety old nook-and-cranny pub down a narrow wynd off the main pedestrian drag, this was reputedly Burns' favourite watering hole, and scene of one of his numerous seductions. It's not an upmarket place, but can have good atmosphere created more by its welcoming locals and staff than the numerous pictures of the 'ploughman poet' himself.

ℹ Information

By the river, **Dumfries Tourist Office** (📞 01387-253862; www.visitdumfriesandgalloway.co.uk; 64 Whitesands; ⏱ 9.30am-4.30pm Mon-Sat Nov-Mar, 9.30am-5pm or 5.30pm Mon-Sat, 11am-4pm Sun Apr-Oct) offers plenty of information on the region.

Ewart Library (📞 01387-253820; www.dumgal.gov.uk; Catherine St; ⏱ 9am-6.30pm Mon & Wed, 9am-5pm Tue & Fri, 9am-6pm Thu, 10am-3pm Sat; 📶) Free internet access.

Post Office (www.postoffice.co.uk; 73-74 Whitesands; ⏱ 8am-9pm Mon-Sat, 11.30am-5.30pm Sun)

ℹ Getting There & Away

Buses run via towns along the A75 to Stranraer (£7.40, 2¼ hours, seven daily Monday to Saturday, three on Sunday) as well as to Castle Douglas and Kirkcudbright. Bus 102 runs to/from Edinburgh (£9.20, 2¾ to three hours, four to seven daily), via Moffat and Biggar.

There are **trains** between Carlisle and Dumfries (£10.80, 40 minutes, every hour or two), and direct trains between Dumfries and Glasgow (£16.20, 1¾ hours, nine daily Monday to Saturday. Services are reduced on Sundays.

Ruthwell

Seven miles east of Caerlaverock Castle, in tiny Ruthwell, the church holds one of Europe's most important early Christian monuments. The 6m-high 7th-century **Ruthwell Cross** (HES; www.historicenvironment.scot; B724; ⏱ daylight hour) FREE is carved top to bottom in New Testament scenes and is inscribed with a poem called 'The Dream of the Rood'; written in a Saxon runic alphabet, it's considered one of the earliest examples of English-language literature.

Bus 79 running between Dumfries and Carlisle stops in Ruthwell on request.

Caerlaverock

The ruins of **Caerlaverock Castle** (HES; 📞 01387-770244; www.historicenvironment.scot; Glencaple; adult/child £5.50/3.30; ⏱ 9.30am-5.30pm Apr-Sep, 10am-4pm Oct-Mar), by Glencaple on a beautiful stretch of the Solway coast, are among the loveliest in Britain. Surrounded by a moat, lawns and stands of trees, the unusual pink-stoned triangular castle looks impregnable. In fact, it fell several times, most famously when it was attacked in 1300 by Edward I: the siege became the subject of an epic poem, 'The Siege of Caerlaverock'.

The current castle dates from the late 13th century but, once defensive purposes were no longer a design necessity, it was refitted as a luxurious Scottish Renaissance mansion house in 1634. Ironically, the rampaging Covenanter militia sacked it a few years later. With nooks and crannies to explore, passageways and remnants of fireplaces, this castle is great for the whole family.

Nearby the **Caerlaverock Wetland Centre** (📞 01387-770200; www.wwt.org.uk/caerlaverock; Eastpark Farm; adult/child £7.45/3.64, free for WWT members; ⏱ 10am-5pm) protects 546 hectares of salt marsh and mud flats, the habitat for numerous birds, including barnacle geese. There are various activities, including badger-watching, dawn goose flights, and child-focused events. It also has a good nature-watching bookshop and a coffee shop that serves organic food. Accommodation in private rooms with a shared kitchen (double £60 to £84) is also available.

From Dumfries, bus 6A runs several times a day (twice on Sunday) to Caerlaverock Castle (£2.70, 30 minutes). If you're travelling by car, take the B725 south.

New Abbey

The small, picturesque whitewashed village of New Abbey lies 7 miles south of Dumfries and has several worthwhile things to see and do in and around it.

◎ Sights & Activities

Sweetheart Abbey RUINS
(HES; www.historicenvironment.scot; adult/child £4.50/2.70; ⏱ 9.30am-5.30pm Apr-Sep, 10am-4pm Sat-Wed Oct-Mar) The shattered red-sandstone remnants of this 13th-century Cistercian abbey stand in stark contrast to the manicured lawns surrounding them. The abbey, last of Scotland's major monasteries to be

established, was founded by Devorgilla of Galloway in 1273 in honour of her dead husband John Balliol (the couple founded Balliol College, Oxford). On his death, she had his heart embalmed and carried it with her until she died 22 years later. She and the heart were buried by the altar: hence the name.

7stanes Mabie MOUNTAIN BIKING
(www.7stanesmountainbiking.com; A710) `FREE`
Mabie Forest Park is one of southern Scotland's 7stanes mountain-biking hubs, set among forested hills a couple of miles north of New Abbey. There are nearly 40 miles of trails for all levels; the closest bike hire is in Dumfries. It's very close to the **Mabie Farm Park** (☑ 01387-259666; www.mabiefarmpark. co.uk; Burnside Farm, Mabie; adult/child/family £8/7.50/30; ☺ 10am-5pm Apr-Oct, plus weekends Mar; ♿), which is handy if you've got kids of different ages.

🛏 Sleeping

Mabie House Hotel HOTEL **££**
(☑ 01387-263188; www.mabiehousehotel.co.uk; d £90-120, ste £170; 🅿 🛜 🐾) Four miles north of New Abbey, this welcoming country-house hotel is a great base, especially for families, as the farm park and mountain-biking trails are on the doorstep. Rooms are stylish and luxurious, offering excellent comfort at fair prices. In the garden are cosy mini-huts sleeping four (£40), which are a good budget option for bikers or youngsters seeking some independence.

❶ Getting There & Away

To get to New Abbey, take Bus 372 from Dumfries (15 minutes).

Annandale & Eskdale

These valleys, in Dumfries and Galloway's east, form part of two major routes that cut across Scotland's south. Away from the highways, the roads are quiet and there are some interesting places to visit, especially if you're looking to break up a road trip.

Gretna & Gretna Green
POP 3100

Firmly on the coach-tour circuit for its romantic associations, Gretna Green is on the outskirts of the town of Gretna, just across the river from Cumbria in England. Historically famous as a destination at which eloping couples get married, it's still one of Britain's most popular wedding venues.

A mile away from Gretna Green in Gretna's shopping centre, the very helpful **tourist office** (☑ 01461-335208; www.visitscotland. com; Gretna Gateway, Gretna; ☺ 10am-6pm Apr-Oct, 10am-4.30pm Mon-Sat & 10am-4pm Sun Nov-Mar) is a good first stop for information on Scotland if you're arriving from England

Trains run from Gretna Green to Dumfries (£8.60, 25 minutes) and Carlisle (£4.70, 11 minutes).

Bus 79 between Dumfries (£8 discovery ticket, one hour) and Carlisle (£3.50, 35 minutes) stops in Gretna (hourly Monday to Saturday, every two hours Sunday).

Famous Blacksmith's Shop MUSEUM
(☑ 01461-338441; www.gretnagreen.com; Gretna Green; exhibition adult/child £3.50/free; ☺ 9am-5pm Oct-Mar, to 5.30pm Apr-May, to 6pm Jun-Sep) At the centre of the village of Gretna Green, the touristy Famous Blacksmith's Shop com-

---

TYING THE KNOT IN GRETNA GREEN

The Marriage Act that passed in England in 1754 suddenly required couples that did not have their parents' consent to be 21 years of age before they could marry. But cunning teenage sweethearts soon realised that the law didn't apply in Scotland, where a simple declaration in front of a pair of witnesses would suffice. As the first village in Scotland, Gretna Green's border location made it the most popular venue for eloping couples to get hitched.

Locals competed for the incoming trade, and marriages were performed by just about anyone who could round up a couple of witnesses from the nearest pub. One legendary Gretna vow-taker was the local blacksmith, who became known as the 'Anvil Priest'. In 1856 eloping was made more difficult when a law was passed obliging couples to have spent at least three weeks in Scotland prior to tying the knot, but Gretna Green remained popular. And it still is: some 5000 couples annually take or reaffirm their marriage vows in the village. If you want to get married over the famous anvil in the Old Blacksmith's Shop at Gretna Green, check out www.gretnagreen.com or www.gretnaweddings.co.uk.

plex has a number of mediocre shops and eateries, a maze, and a quite entertaining multilingual exhibition on Gretna Green's history, with tales of intrigues, elopements, scoundrels and angry parents arriving minutes too late. There's a re-creation of a blacksmith's forge, a collection of handsome carriages and a few marriage rooms: you may well run into a modern-day wedding as you walk through.

Smith's at Gretna Green HOTEL ££

(☎ 01461-337007; www.smithsgretnagreen.com; s/d from £92/102; P ☎) A large contemporary hotel close to the Gretna Green complex. Though the blocky exterior won't delight everybody, the interior is much more stylish; rooms are decorated in a chic, restrained style with king-sized beds. Various grades are available; the rates here represent typical online booking offers. The restaurant (restaurant mains £17-23, bar mains £11-14; ☺ noon-9pm; ☎ ☻) is the best around. There's a little noise from the adjacent motorway.

Langholm

POP 2200

The waters of three rivers – the Esk, Ewes and Wauchope – meet at Langholm, nicknamed the 'Muckle Toon', a gracious old town at the centre of Scotland's tweed industry. Most people come for fishing and walking in the surrounding moors and woodlands; check out the Langholm Walks website (www.langholmwalks.co.uk) for details.

Hugh MacDiarmid – poet, communist and seminal figure in 20th-century Scottish nationalism – was born Christopher Grieve here in Langholm in 1892. Thomas Telford was also born nearby. Another famous visitor was Neil Armstrong, who accepted an honorary Freemanship of Langholm, which is the traditional seat of Clan Armstrong.

Buses between Edinburgh and Carlisle pass through Langholm. There are frequent services to Lockerbie, where you can change to other routes.

Eskdale Hotel HOTEL ££

(☎ 01387-380357; www.eskdalehotel.co.uk; Market Pl; s/d £48/85; P ☎) Pleasantly genteel, this main-street Victorian hotel has light, modernised rooms and bathrooms as well as a decent restaurant and a small bar. A courteous owner and staff make this a reliable choice.

Border House B&B ££

(☎ 01387-380376; www.border-house.co.uk; 28 High St; s £40-50, d £70-75; P ☎ ☻) On the main road, this central accommodation option has large rooms, a friendly owner and big sink-in-and-smile beds. There's a good room if you're travelling with a child, and you won't pay extra for the fold-out. If you're lucky, you may be treated to afternoon scones. The garden runs right down to the river.

Castle Douglas & Around

POP 4100

Castle Douglas attracts a lot of day trippers but hasn't been 'spruced up' for tourism. It's an open, attractive, well-cared-for town, with some remarkably beautiful areas close to the centre, such as the small Carlingwark Loch. The town was laid out in the 18th century by Sir William Douglas, who had made a fortune in the Americas.

☉ Sights & Activities

Threave Castle CASTLE

(HES; www.historicenvironment.scot; adult/child incl ferry £4.50/2.70; ☺ 10am-5pm Apr-Sep, to 4pm Oct) Two miles west of Castle Douglas, this impressive tower sits on a small river island. Built in the late 14th century, it became a principal stronghold of the Black Douglases, including the excellently named Archibald the Grim. It's now basically a shell, having been badly damaged by the Covenanters in the 1640s, but it's a romantic ruin nonetheless. It's a 15-minute walk from the car park to the ferry landing, where you ring a bell for the custodian to take you across.

Also from the car park, where there's a small nature exhibition, a 1.5-mile circular nature path gives you the chance to spot deer and ospreys, as well as waterbirds from hides. At dusk it's good for batwatching.

Loch Ken LAKE

Stretching for 9 miles northwest of Castle Douglas between the A713 and A762, Loch Ken is a popular outdoor recreational area. The range of water sports includes windsurfing, sailing, canoeing, power-boating and kayaking. There are also walking trails and rich bird life. The Royal Society for the Protection of Birds (RSPB) has a nature reserve (p168) on the western bank, north of Glenlochar.

★Galloway
Activity Centre WATERSPORTS, MOUNTAIN BIKING
(☑01556-502011; www.lochken.co.uk; ☉10am-
5pm, plus an evening session Jun-Aug; 👍) On the
eastern bank of Loch Ken north of Parton,
this excellent set-up runs a wide range of
activities, and also provides equipment and
a variety of camping and hostel accommodation. Activities run in sessions of 1½ hours;
one session costs £20.50 each for two, and
the price reduces substantially for further
sessions. Best to book in advance.

Ken-Dee Marshes
Nature Reserve BIRDWATCHING
(☑01556-670464; www.rspb.org.uk) **FREE** This
birdwatching reserve is on the western bank
of Loch Ken, 3½ miles north of Glenlochar.
It's a scenic spot where the River Dee meets
the loch, and a nature trail and hides allow
you to view a range of species, including
pied flycatchers, redstarts and wintering
geese.

🛏 Sleeping & Eating

Lochside Caravan &
Camping Site CAMPSITE £
(☑01556-504682; www.dumgal.gov.uk/caravan
andcamping; Lochside Park; tent sites without/with
power £11.50/15, plus car £4; ☉Apr-Oct; P🐾)
Very central campsite attractively situated
beside Carlingwark Loch; there's plenty of
grass and fine trees provide shade.

★**Douglas House** B&B ££
(☑01556-503262; www.douglas-house.com; 63
Queen St; s £40-41, d £77-85; 🛜🐾) Set in a
beautiful 200-year-old stone house, this has
big beautiful bathrooms that complement
the light, stylish chambers, which include
flatscreen digital TVs with inbuilt DVD players. The two upstairs doubles are the best,
although the downstairs double is huge and
has a superking-sized bed – you could sleep
four in it! Breakfast is recommended, with
locally sourced produce.

★**Designs** CAFE £
(☑01556-504552; www.designsgallery.co.uk; 179
King St; lunches £6.50; ☉9.30am-4.45pm; 🛜)
This excellent cafe under a gallery and shop
is the best spot in town for a coffee, with
cosy wood fittings offset by a garden space
out the back. There's a nice line in ciabatta
and bruschetta options complemented by
chalkboard lunch specials. The carrot cake
also comes warmly recommended.

Nikos Greek Restaurant GREEK ££
(☑01556-504345; www.blackwaterproduce.co.uk;
139 King St; mains £12-17; ☉11am-3pm & 6-9pm
Mon-Sat; 🐾) On the main street, it's quite a
surprise to find authentic Greek food here in
provincial Castle Douglas. The charismatic,
welcoming host prepares delicious, authentic meze (£14.95 per person) and mains, has
a special night-time fish and seafood menu
(£17.50 for two courses) and a variety of
cheaper lunchtime specials (£5 to £7).

🛈 Information

Castle Douglas Library (☑01556-505260;
www.dumgal.gov.uk; King St; ☉9am-5pm Mon,
Thu & Fri, 1-7pm Tue, 9am-noon Wed, 10am-
1pm Sat; 🐾) Free internet access.
Castle Douglas Tourist Office (☑01556-
502611; www.visitscotland.com; King St;
☉10am-5pm Mon-Sat Apr–mid-Jun & Sep-Oct,
10am-6pm Mon-Sat, 11am-3pm Sun mid-Jun–
Aug) Located in a small park behind the library.

🛈 Getting There & Away

Buses run roughly hourly from Castle Douglas
to Dumfries (£7.20, 50 minutes); there are also
services to Kirkcudbright (20 minutes), Stranraer, New Galloway and Ayr.

Kirkcudbright
POP 3400

Kirkcudbright (kirk-*coo*-bree), with its dignified streets of 17th- and 18th-century
merchants' houses and appealing harbour,
is the ideal base from which to explore the
south coast. Look out for the nook-and-
cranny closes and wynds in the elbow of
beautifully restored High St. With its architecture and setting, it's easy to see why Kirkcudbright has been an artists' colony since
the late 19th century.

🔘 Sights

Broughton House GALLERY
(NTS; ☑01557-330437; www.nts.org.uk; 12 High St;
adult/child £6.50/5; ☉noon-5pm Apr-Oct, 11am-
4pm Thu-Sat Nov–mid-Dec) The 18th-century
Broughton House displays paintings by EA
Hornel (he lived and worked here), one of
the Glasgow Boys. The library, with its wood
panelling and stone carvings, is probably the
most impressive room. Behind the house is
a lovely Japanese-style garden (also open
11am to 4pm Monday to Friday in February
and March).

MacLellan's Castle
CASTLE

(☑01557-331856; www.historicenvironment.scot; Castle St; adult/child £4.50/2.70; ⊘9.30am-1pm & 2-5.30pm Apr-Sep) Near the harbour, this is a large, atmospheric ruin built in 1577 by Thomas MacLellan, then provost of Kirkcudbright, as his town residence. Inside look for the 'lairds' lug', a 16th-century hidey-hole designed for the laird to eavesdrop on his guests.

Tolbooth Art Centre
GALLERY

(☑01557-331556; www.dumgal.gov.uk; High St; ⊘10am-4pm Mon-Sat, 1-4pm Sun mid-Apr–Sep, 11am-4pm Mon-Sat Oct–mid-Apr) FREE As well as catering for today's local artists, this centre has an exhibition on the history of the town's artistic development. The place is as interesting for the building itself as for the artistic works on display; it's one of the oldest and best-preserved tollbooths in Scotland, and there are interpretative signboards to explain its past.

Festivals & Events

Thursdays in high summer are Scottish theme nights, with music, dancing and more in the centre of town.

Art & Crafts Trail
ART

(www.artandcraftstrail.com; ⊘late Jul) Each year the town revels in a four-day community artistic extravaganza with a theme that changes annually. There's something quirky – sculpture, music, handcraft workshops – going on all over the place in numerous venues: people's homes, improvised outdoor spaces, the castle. Infectious fun is guaranteed.

Wickerman Festival
MUSIC

(www.thewickermanfestival.co.uk; ⊘Jul) A diverse two-day music festival held on farmland a few miles southeast of town. From punk to reggae via indie rock, there's something for everyone. The festival climaxes with the burning of an enormous wickerman; much of the 1973 cult movie of the same name was filmed around this area.

Kirkcudbright Jazz Festival
MUSIC

(www.kirkcudbrightjazzfestival.co.uk; ⊘Jun) Four days of swing, trad and dixie.

Sleeping

Silvercraigs Caravan & Camping Site
CAMPSITE £

(☑07824-528482; www.dumgal.gov.uk/caravanand camping; Silvercraigs Rd; tent site without/with power £11.50/15, plus car £4; ⊘Apr-Oct; P 🐾) There are brilliant views from this campsite; you feel like you're sleeping on top of the town. It's great for stargazing on clear nights, and there are good facilities, including a laundry.

★ Greengate
B&B ££

(☑01557-331895; www.thegreengate.co.uk; 46 High St; s/d £60/80; 🐾) The artistically inclined should snap up the one double room in this lovely place, which has both historic and current painterly connections. The chamber is a comfortable front room with large bathroom and your own lounge alongside. The artistic, good-humoured hosts are a delight.

While staying, make sure you head down the side laneway – with cottages that were used by students of artist Jessie M King and her husband EA Taylor – to the huge, extraordinary and offbeat garden, complete with houseboat and piano, down the back.

★ Selkirk Arms Hotel
HOTEL ££

(☑01557-330402; www.selkirkarmshotel.co.uk; High St; s/d £84/110, budget d £96; P @ 🐾) What a haven of hospitality this is. All the rooms have been recently refurbished, and are looking good with a stylish purply finish and slate-floored bathrooms. Wood furnishings and views over the back garden give some of them an extra rustic appeal. Staff are happy to be there, and you will be too.

Baytree House
B&B ££

(☑01557-330824; www.baytreekirkcudbright.co.uk; 110 High St; s £65, d £78-84; @ 🐾) This is a very high-standard B&B, but always directed towards the guest's comfort: it never feels too posh. Rooms are spacious and feature plush, comfortable beds and lots of little extras like a sherry decanter, earplugs (not that you need them) and fresh milk. A great lounge space has DVDs and reading material. Room-only rates are available.

There's a self-catering flat out the back too.

Kirkcudbright Bay Hotel
PUB ££

(☑01557-339544; www.kirkcudbrightbay.com; 25 St Cuthbert St; s/d £60/75; 🐾) This well-run central pub is a very pleasant place to lay your head, with comfortable modernised en suite rooms – the large room 1 is especially appealing – and an attractive downstairs bar and restaurant. Room-only rates are available but breakfast is generous and includes haggis.

Anchorlee
B&B ££

(✆ 01557-330197; www.anchorlee.co.uk; 95 St Mary St; s/d £66/78; 🅿 🛜 🐾) This elegant residence on the main road is a comfortable, classic B&B. Welcoming hosts, cheerfully flowery rooms and a solid breakfast make staying here a pleasure. Up for sale at time of research, so change is possible.

✘ Eating

★ Auld Alliance
SCOTTISH, FRENCH ££

(✆ 01557-330888; www.auldalliancekirkcudbright. co.uk; 29 St Cuthbert St; mains £14-21; ⊗ 6-9pm Thu-Sat, plus Wed Jul-Sep; 🛜) Overlooking the heart of town, this restaurant's cuisine is true to its name, which refers to the historic bond between Scotland and France. Local produce is given a Gallic and Mediterranean twist, with dishes like Galloway lamb tagine or local haddock encrusted with oatmeal and black olive tapenade.

Selkirk Arms Hotel
BISTRO ££

(www.selkirkarmshotel.co.uk; High St; mains £12-16; ⊗ noon-2pm & 6-9pm; 🅿 🛜 🍴) Cheery servers and a wide-ranging menu of well-presented dishes give you plenty of options here, where you can sit in the more formal restaurant area (dinner only) or the more casual bar zone. Local scallops are a highlight, and some fairly elaborate mains can round out the meal, but you can also chow down on upmarket fish and chips. All positive.

ⓘ Information

Check out www.kirkcudbright.co.uk and www. artiststown.org.uk for heaps of information on the town.

Kirkcudbright Tourist Office (✆ 01557-330494; www.visitdumfriesandgalloway.co.uk; Harbour Sq; ⊗ 11am-3pm Mon-Sat, 11am-5pm Sun Apr–mid-Jun, 9.30am-6pm Mon-Sat & 10am-5pm Sun mid-Jun–Aug, 10am-5pm Mon-Sat & 11am-3pm Sun Sep-Oct, 11am-4pm Mon-Sat Nov-Mar) is a handy office with useful brochures detailing walks and road tours in the surrounding district.

ⓘ Getting There & Away

Kirkcudbright is 28 miles southwest of Dumfries. Buses run to Dumfries (£4.40, 1¼ hours) via/changing in Castle Douglas (£1.35, 15 minutes). Change at Ringford or Gatehouse of Fleet for Stranraer.

Galloway Forest Park

South and northwest of the small town of New Galloway is 300-sq-mile Galloway Forest Park, with numerous lochs and great whale-backed mountains covered in heather and pine. The highest point is **Merrick** (843m). The park is criss-crossed by off-road bike routes (p171) and some superb signposted walking trails, from gentle strolls to long-distance paths, including the Southern Upland Way (p150).

Walkers and cyclists should head for **Glentrool** in the park's west, accessed by the forest road east from Bargrennan off the A714, north of Newton Stewart. Located just over a mile from Bargrennan is the Glentrool Visitor Centre (p171). The road then winds and climbs up to Loch Trool, where there are magnificent views.

The park is very family focused; look out for the booklet of annual events in tourist offices. It's also great for **stargazing**; it has been named a Dark Sky Park by the International Dark-Sky Association (www.darksky. org).

🏃 Activities

Red Kite Feeding Station
BIRDWATCHING

(✆ 01644-450202; www.gallowaykitetrail.com; Bellymack Hill Farm, Laurieston; adult/child £5/free) Just off the B795, this farm has daily feedings of red kites at 2pm. There's a visitor centre (with cafe) here, from which you can observe these beautiful raptors, which congregate from about 1pm. There are often RSPB volunteers present who can inform you about the birds' lifestyles.

Galloway Red Deer Range
WILDLIFE WATCHING

(www.gallowayforestpark.com) FREE At the Galloway Red Deer Range you can observe Britain's largest land-based beast from a hide and viewing area. During rutting season in autumn, it's a bit like watching a bullfight as snorting, charging stags compete for the harem. From April to September there are guided ranger-led visits (adult/child £5/3) to see these impressive beasts.

Raiders Road
DRIVING TOUR

(http://scotland.forestry.gov.uk; per vehicle £2; ⊗ vehicles Apr-Oct) About a mile west of Clatteringshaws Visitor Centre (p171), Raiders Rd is a 10-mile drive through the forest with various picnic spots, child-friendly activities, and short walks marked along the way. Drive slowly as there's plenty of wildlife about. One of the nicest spots is a cascade where you might spot otters. Walkers and cyclists can access the road year-round.

❶ Information

Clatteringshaws Visitor Centre (✆ 01644-420285; www.gallowayforestpark.com; A712; ⏰ 10am-4.30pm mid-Mar–Oct, to 5.30pm Jul & Aug) On the shore of Clatteringshaws Loch, 6 miles west of New Galloway, this is basically a cafe but has the odd display panel. From the visitor centre you can walk to a replica of a Romano-British **homestead** (0.5 miles), and to **Bruce's Stone** (1 mile), where Robert the Bruce is said to have rested after defeating the English at the Battle of Rapploch Moss in 1307. Pick up a copy of the *Galloway Red Kite Trail* leaflet here, which details a circular route through impressive scenery that offers a good chance to spot one of these majestic reintroduced birds.

Glentrool Visitor Centre (✆ 01671-840302; www.gallowayforestpark.com; ⏰ 10am-4.30pm mid-Mar–Oct, to 5.30pm Jul & Aug) Located just over a mile from Bargrennan, this place stocks information on activities, including mountain biking, in the area. There is a coffee shop with snacks.

Kirroughtree Visitor Centre (✆ 01671-402165; www.gallowayforestpark.com; Palnure, off A75; ⏰ 10am-5pm) This park tourist office 3 miles southeast of Newton Stewart has a cafe and a nature-watching hide. This is also one of the **7Stanes mountain-biking hubs** (www.7stanesmountainbiking.com; Kirroughtree Tourist Office), and there's a good bike shop here that does hires and repairs.

❶ Getting There & Away

The scenic 19-mile A712 (Queen's Way) between New Galloway and Newton Stewart slices through the southern section of the park. It's the only road through the park, but no buses run along it. The nearest public transport point for the western part of this road is Newton Stewart, for the east New Galloway. There's bike hire available in Newton Stewart.

Newton Stewart

POP 4000

On the banks of the sparkling River Cree, Newton Stewart is at the heart of some beautiful countryside, and is popular with hikers and anglers. On the eastern bank, across the bridge, is the older and smaller settlement of Minnigaff. Both towns makes a convenient base for exploring the Galloway Forest Park.

This is great angling country. Drop into **Galloway Angling Centre** (✆ 01671-401333; www.gallowayangling.co.uk; 1 Queen St; ⏰ 9am-1pm & 2-5pm Mon-Sat) and check out the very useful website www.fishgalloway.co.uk.

🛏 Sleeping & Eating

Creebridge House Hotel   HOTEL ££

(✆ 01671-402121; www.creebridge.co.uk; Minnigaff; s/d/superior d £65/116/130; 🅿 🛜 🐾) This is a magnificent refurbished 18th-century mansion built for the Earl of Galloway. A maze inside, it has tastefully decorated refurbished rooms with a classical style and plenty of character. Bathrooms are OK, but don't have the same wow factor. Try to get a room overlooking the garden (No 7 is good).

There's also tasty food here (mains £11 to £18, noon to 2pm, and 6pm to 9pm).

Flowerbank Guest House   B&B ££

(✆ 01671-402629; www.flowerbankgh.com; Millcroft Rd; s £44, d £66-74; ⏰ Apr-Oct; 🅿 🛜 🐾)

MOUNTAIN-BIKING HEAVEN

A brilliant way to experience southern Scotland's forests is by pedal power. The **7stanes** (stones) are seven mountain-biking centres around southern Scotland, featuring trails through some of the finest forest scenery you'll find in the country.

Glentrool (www.7stanesmountainbiking.com; Glentrool Tourist Office) FREE is one of these centres; the **Blue Route** here is 5.6 miles in length and is a lovely ride climbing up to Green Torr Ridge overlooking Loch Trool. If you've more serious intentions, the **Big Country Route** is 36 miles of challenging ascents and descents that afford magnificent views of the Galloway Forest. It takes a full day and is not for wimps.

Another of the trailheads is at **Kirroughtree Visitor Centre** (p171), 3 miles southeast of Newton Stewart. This centre offers plenty of singletrack at four different skill levels. You can hire also bikes here (www.thebreakpad.com). For more information on routes see www.7stanesmountainbiking.com.

This dignified 18th-century house is set in a magnificent landscaped garden in Minnigaff on the banks of the River Cree. The two elegantly furnished rooms at the front of the house are slightly more expensive but are spacious and have lovely garden and river views. It's a quiet, peaceful stop.

Galloway Arms Hotel
HOTEL ££

(☑ 01671-402653; www.gallowayarmshotel.com; 54 Victoria St; s/d £43/79; P 🛜 🐾) There are attractive renovated rooms at this historic main-street pub; the best ones are upstairs, with plenty of space. The hotel is walker- and cyclist-friendly, with bike storage and a drying room, while the bar and restaurant dole out good local fare.

Galloway Arms Hotel
PUB FOOD ££

(☑ 01671-402653; www.gallowayarmshotel.com; 54 Victoria St; mains £7-16; ⊙ noon-2pm & 5-9pm; P 🛜 🐾) This historic high street pub is distinctive and cosy, and has a fireplace. It does a wide range of uncomplicated good grub, with a nice line in burgers – try the pork and apple one. Sandwiches are good value, and there's a range of fuller meals. Up for lease, so things may change.

ℹ Information

Named after the striped local breed of cow, the **Belted Galloway Tourist Office** (☑ 01671-403458; www.thebeltedgalloway.co.uk; Riverside View; ⊙ 10am-5pm Mon-Sat Sep-May, 10am-5pm Jun, 10am-7pm Jul & Aug; 🛜) is just off the main street. It offers a good licensed cafe, a giftshop selling books and maps, and displays on local history and attractions. It's the best spot for information on the many walks to be done in the Newton Stewart area. Good disabled access.

ℹ Getting There & Around

Buses stop in Newton Stewart (Dashwood Sq) on their way to Stranraer (£3.90, 40 minutes) and Dumfries (£7.40, 1½ hours); both run several times daily. There are also connections to Ayr and Glasgow via Girvan. Frequent buses run south to the Machars.

Kirkcowan Cycle Hire (☑ 01671-401529; www.kirkcowancycles.co.uk; Victoria Lane; half-/full-day £10/18; ⊙ 9am-5pm Mon-Sat) is a good bike shop with hybrids for hire that are handy for exploring the Galloway Forest Park.

The Machars

South of Newton Stewart, the Galloway Hills give way to the softly rolling pastures of the triangular peninsula known as the Machars. The south has many early Christian sites and the 25-mile Pilgrims Way walk.

Bus 415 runs every hour or so (only twice on Sundays) between Newton Stewart and Isle of Whithorn (£3, one hour) via Wigtown (15 minutes) and Whithorn. There are some intermediate services also.

Wigtown
POP 900

Little Wigtown, officially Scotland's National Book Town, has more than a dozen bookshops offering an astonishingly wide selection of volumes, giving book enthusiasts the opportunity to get lost here for days. A major **book festival** (www.wigtownbookfestival.com; ⊙ late Sep) is also held here.

⊙ Sights

Bladnoch Distillery
DISTILLERY

(www.bladnoch.com; Bladnoch) Browsing books can be thirsty work, so it's fortunate that Bladnoch Distillery is just a couple of miles away from Wigtown, in the village of Bladnoch. Recently bought and now Australian-owned, it wasn't open for tours at time of last research, though these may resume.

Torhouse Stone Circle
RUINS

Four miles west of Wigtown, off the B733, this well-preserved ruin dates from the 2nd millennium BC.

🛌 Sleeping & Eating

Hillcrest House
B&B ££

(☑ 01988-402018; www.hillcrest-wigtown.co.uk; Station Rd; s/d £50/75; P 🛜 🐾) A noble stone building in a quiet part of town, this offers a genuine welcome and a lovely interior featuring high ceilings and huge windows. Spend the extra for one of the superior rooms, which have stupendous views overlooking rolling green hills and the sea beyond. This is all complemented by a ripper breakfast involving fresh local produce. Dinners also often available.

ReadingLasses Bookshop Café
CAFE £

(☑ 01988-403266; www.facebook.com/reading-lasses; 17 South Main St; mains £7-8; ⊙ 10am-4pm Mon-Wed & 10am-4.30pm Thu-Sat year-round, plus

10.30am-4pm Sun May-Oct; 🛜📶) 🏃 This bookshop is set around a brilliantly welcoming cafe serving decent coffee to prolong your reading time. It also offers a toothsome range of home cooking prepared with care, including several vegetarian/vegan options. It specialises in books on the social sciences and women's studies.

Craft   BURGERS
(📞01988-403326; www.craftrestaurant.co.uk; 30 South Main St; burgers £7-9; ⊙food noon-2.30pm & 5-9pm Wed-Sun; 🛜📶) Innovative, scrumptious burgers washed down by Brewdog and other craft beers is the template at this central restaurant and bar. It regularly hosts acoustic sessions on weekends.

🛍 Shopping

The Bookshop   BOOKS
(📞01988-402499; www.the-bookshop.com; 17 North Main St; ⊙9am-5pm Mon-Sat) This claims to be Scotland's largest secondhand bookshop, and has a great collection of Scottish and regional titles.

ℹ️ Getting There & Away

Bus 415 runs every hour or so (thrice on Sundays) between Newton Stewart and Isle of Whithorn (£1.95, 15 minutes). Buses continue to Whithorn and Isle of Whithorn.

Whithorn

POP 800

Whithorn has a broad, attractive High St that is virtually closed at both ends (it was designed to enclose a medieval market). There are few facilities in town, but it's worth visiting because of its fascinating history.

In 397, while the Romans were still in Britain, St Ninian established the first Christian mission beyond Hadrian's Wall in Whithorn (pre-dating St Columba on Iona by 166 years). After his death, **Whithorn Priory**, the earliest recorded church in Scotland, was built to house his remains, and Whithorn became the focus of an important medieval pilgrimage.

Today the ruined priory is part of the excellent **Whithorn Trust Discovery Centre** (📞01988-500508; www.whithorn.com; 45 George St; adult/child £4.50/2.25; ⊙10.30am-5pm Apr-Oct).

Bus 415 runs every hour or so (only twice on Sundays) between Newton Stewart and Whithorn (£3, 50 minutes) via Wigtown. Buses run on to Isle of Whithorn.

Isle of Whithorn

POP 300

The Isle of Whithorn, once an island but now linked to the mainland by a causeway, is a curious place with an attractive natural harbour and colourful houses. The roofless 13th-century **St Ninian's Chapel**, probably built for pilgrims who landed nearby, sits evocatively on the windswept rocky headland. Around Burrow Head, to the southwest but accessed off the A747 before you enter the Isle of Whithorn, is **St Ninian's Cave**, where the saint went to pray.

Bus 415 runs every hour or so (only twice on Sundays) between Newton Stewart and Isle of Whithorn (£3, one hour) via Wigtown and Whithorn. There are some Whithorn–Isle of Whithorn services also.

Steam Packet Inn   PUB ££
(📞01988-500334; www.thesteampacketinn.biz; Harbour Row; r per person £40-45; ⊙food noon-2pm & 6.30-9pm; 🛜🐾) The quayside Steam Packet Inn is a popular pub with real ales, scrumptious bar meals (mains £7 to £11) and comfy lodgings with no single supplement. Try to get a room to the front of the building as they have lovely views over the little harbour (No 2 is a good one).

Stranraer

POP 10,400

The friendly but somewhat ramshackle port of Stranraer has seen its tourist mainstay, the ferry traffic to Northern Ireland, move up the road to Cairnryan. The town's still wondering what to do with itself, but there's lots to explore in the surrounding area.

◉ Sights

Castle Kennedy Gardens   GARDENS, CASTLE
(📞01776-702024; www.castlekennedygardens.com; Sheuchan; adult/child £5.50/2; ⊙10am-5pm daily Apr-Oct, Sat & Sun only Feb-Mar) Three miles east of Stranraer, these magnificent gardens are among Scotland's most renowned. They cover 30 hectares and are set on an isthmus between two lochs and two castles. The landscaping was undertaken in 1730 by the Earl of Stair, who used unoccupied soldiers to do the work. Buses heading east from Stranraer stop at the gate on the main road; it's a pleasant 20-minute stroll from here to the gardens' entrance.

Stranraer Museum
MUSEUM

(☑ 01776-705088; www.dumgal.gov.uk; 55 George St; ☉ 10am-5pm Mon-Fri, 10am-1pm & 1.30-4.30pm Sat) FREE This museum houses exhibits on local history and you can learn about Stranraer's polar explorers. The highlight is the carved stone pipe from Madagascar.

🛏 Sleeping & Eating

Purgatory must look something like Stranraer at dinnertime. Several pubs and cafes do mediocre standards in big portions, so you won't go hungry at least.

Ivy House
B&B £

(☑ 01776-704176; www.ivyhouse-ferrylink.co.uk; 3 Ivy Pl; s/d £35/55, s without bathroom £30; 🕸) This is a great guesthouse that does Scottish hospitality proud, with excellent facilities, tidy en suite rooms and a smashing breakfast. Nothing is too much trouble for the genial host, who always has a smile for her guests. The room at the back overlooking the churchyard is particularly light and quiet. Room-only rates available.

Cairnryan B&B
B&B ££

(☑ 07759-498130; www.cairnryan-bb.co.uk; Cairnryan Rd; s/d £55/70; P🕸) Overlooking the water in the centre of little Cairnryan, this is a modern bungalow with comfortable en suite rooms, but it's the genuinely welcoming hosts – old hands at excellent B&B – who make this a special experience. Breakfast features the odd homegrown treat.

North West Castle Hotel
HOTEL ££

(☑ 01776-704413; www.mcmillanhotels.com; s £54 d £79-89; P🕸🌊🏊) Showing its age but still an enjoyable time-warp experience, this was formerly the home of Arctic explorer Sir John Ross. Rooms are quaint but comfortable enough – try for sea views. Service is excellent. It was the first hotel in the world to have an indoor curling rink.

The bar is a great place to sit and watch those unusual ice antics when there's a match on.

ℹ Information

Stranraer Library (☑ 01776-707400; www.dumgal.gov.uk; North Strand St; ☉ 9am-5pm Mon-Thu, 9am-4pm Fri, 10am-1pm Sat; 🕸) Free internet access.

Stranraer Tourist Office (☑ 01776-702595; www.visitscotland.com; 28 Harbour St; ☉ 10am-3pm Mon-Sat, plus 11am-3pm Sun mid-Jun–early Sep) Efficient and friendly.

ℹ Getting There & Away

Stranraer is 6 miles south of Cairnryan, which is on the eastern side of Loch Ryan. A service coinciding with Stena Line ferries runs between Stranraer and Cairnryan. Buses running frequently between Stranraer and Ayr also stop in Cairnryan. For a taxi, call **McLean's Taxis** (☑ 01776-703343; www.mcleanstaxis.com; 21 North Strand St; ☉ 24hr): about £8.

BOAT

P&O (☑ 0800 130 0030; www.poferries.com) Runs six to eight fast ferries a day from Cairnryan to Larne (Northern Ireland). The crossing takes two hours.

Stena Line (☑ 0844 770 7070; www.stenaline.co.uk) runs five to six daily fast ferries from Cairnryan to Belfast (2¼ hours).

Prices for crossings vary but in high season are around £30/99 per person/car.

BUS

Scottish Citylink (www.citylink.co.uk) buses run to Glasgow (£18.50, 2½ hours, three daily) and Edinburgh (£21.50, four hours, three daily).

There are also several daily local buses to Kirkcudbright and the towns along the A75, such as Newton Stewart (£3.90, 40 minutes, at least hourly) and Dumfries (£7.40, 2¼ hours, seven daily Monday to Saturday, three on Sunday).

TRAIN

First Scotrail runs to/from Glasgow (£12.80, 2¼ hours). There are four direct services Monday to Saturday and none on Sunday; with more frequent daily connections changing in Ayr.

The Rhinns of Galloway

The Rhinns (or Rhins) of Galloway is a hammerhead-shaped peninsula west of Stranraer that runs 25 miles from north to south. Its coastal scenery includes rugged cliffs, tiny harbours and sandy beaches. Dairy cattle graze on the greenest grass you've ever seen, and the warm waters of the Gulf Stream give the peninsula the mildest climate in Scotland.

Pretty Portpatrick, set around a harbour, is a big drawcard. Further south, sleepy **Port Logan** has an excellent sandy beach and a famous botanical garden. From **Drummore**, a fishing village on the east coast, it's another 5 miles to the spectacular Mull of Galloway, Scotland's most southerly point.

Scotland's southernmost point, **Mull of Galloway** (www.mull-of-galloway.co.uk) is a spectacular spot, with windswept green grass and views of Scotland, England, the Isle of Man and Northern Ireland. The lighthouse here was built by Robert Stevenson, grandfather of the writer, in 1826. The Mull of Galloway RSPB nature reserve, home to thousands of seabirds, is also important for its wildflowers. At the entrance to the reserve is a spectacular clifftop cafe. The former homes of the lightkeepers are available as accommodation; check out www.lighthouseholidaycottages.co.uk.

The mild climate in this southwestern part of Scotland is demonstrated at **Logan Botanic Garden** (☑01776-860231; www.rbge.org.uk/logan; Port Logan; adult/child £6.50/free; ☺10am-4pm Sun Feb, 10am-5pm daily mid-Mar–Oct), a mile north of Port Logan, where an array of subtropical flora includes tree ferns and cabbage palms. The garden is an outpost of the Royal Botanic Garden in Edinburgh. There's a good cafe here.

It's just you and the cruel sea out here at **Corsewall Lighthouse Hotel** (☑01776-853220; www.lighthousehotel.co.uk; Kirkcolm; d £140-250; P☎), the the fabulously romantic 200-year-old lighthouse. On a sunny day, the water shimmers with light, and you can see Ireland, Kintyre, Arran and Ailsa Craig. But when wind and rain beat in, it's just great to be cosily holed up in the bar-restaurant or snuggling under the covers in your room.

It's right at the northwest tip of the peninsula, 13 miles northwest of Stranraer. Rooms in the lighthouse building itself are attractive if necessarily compact; chalets are also available. Dinner, bed and breakfast rates are available for an extra £20 per person.

Invisible from above, thanks to its turf roof, clifftop **Gallie Craig** (☑01776-840558; www.galliecraig.co.uk; Mull of Galloway; light meals £3-8; ☺11am-4pm Sun-Wed Feb-Mar, 10am-5.30pm daily Apr-Oct, 11am-4pm Sat & Sun Nov) cafe offers spectacular vistas, great cakes and tasty savouries.

Buses from Stranraer cover the peninsula.

Portpatrick

POP 500

Portpatrick is a charming harbour village on the rugged west coast of the Rhinns of Galloway peninsula. It is a good base from which to explore the area, and it's the starting or finishing point for the Southern Upland Way (p150). You can follow part of the Way to Stranraer (9 miles). It's a clifftop walk, with sections of farmland and heather moor.

Bus 367 runs to Stranraer (20 minutes, hourly Monday to Saturday, three Sunday).

🛏 Sleeping & Eating

Harbour House Hotel INN ££
(☑01776-810456; www.theharbourhousehotel.co.uk; 53 Main St; s £65-85, d £98-120; ☎☺) Formerly the customs house, this is now a popular, solid old pub. Some of the tastefully furnished rooms have brilliant views over the harbour. The hotel is also a warm nook for a traditional bar meal (mains £8 to £10).

★**Knockinaam Lodge** HOTEL £££
(☑01776-810471; www.knockinaamlodge.com; dinner & B&B s £210-325, d £350-450; P☎☺) For a real dose of luxury, head 3 miles southeast to this former hunting lodge in a dramatic, secluded location with grassy lawns rolling down to a sandy cove. It's where Churchill plotted the endgame of WWII – you can stay in his suite – and it's a very romantic place to get away from it all.

Excellent French-influenced cuisine (lunch/dinner £40/68) is backed up by a great range of wines and single malts, and breakfast features homemade jams.

★**Campbell's** SEAFOOD ££
(☑01776-810314; www.campbellsrestaurant.co.uk; 1 South Crescent; mains £13-29; ☺noon-2.30pm & 6-9pm Tue-Sat, noon-2.30pm & 6.30-9pm Sun; ☎) Fresh local seafood is the stock-in-trade of this unprepossessing local favourite, and it does it very well. Ask for whatever is good that day or choose one of the sharing platters and enjoy the flavour burst of locally caught fish or shellfish.

Central Scotland

Best Places to Eat

➡ Cellar Restaurant (p198)

➡ The Peat Inn (p195)

➡ Sangster's

➡ Loch Leven's Larder (p203)

➡ Adamson (p194)

Best Places to Sleep

➡ Old Fishergate House (p194)

➡ Spindrift (p197)

➡ Merlindale (p206)

➡ Pitcullen Guest House (p202)

➡ Victoria Square Guesthouse (p182)

Why Go?

The country's historic roots are deeply embedded in central Scotland. Key battles around Stirling shaped the nation's fortunes; significant castles from the region's history pepper the landscape; and Perth, the former capital, is where kings were crowned on the Stone of Destiny.

Arriving from Glasgow and Edinburgh, visitors begin to get a sense of the country further north as the Lowland scenery ramps up towards Highland splendour. It is here that the majesty of Scotland's landscape begins to unfold among woodlands and waterfalls, craggy hills and rushing rivers, with the silhouettes of soaring, sentinel-like peaks on the northern horizon.

Whether in the softly wooded country of lowland Perthshire or the green Fife coastline dotted with fishing villages, opportunities to enjoy the outdoors abound: walking, cycling and angling are all easy possibilities. The region also has some of the country's best pubs and restaurants, which greet weary visitors at day's end.

When to Go
Stirling

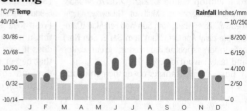

May A magical time before summer crowds arrive, and for the Perth Arts Festival.

Jul–Aug Summer is best for seafood feasts in Fife, and fresh raspberries in Blairgowrie.

Oct–Nov Autumn colours enliven walks in the woods around Crieff, Comrie and Blairgowrie.

STIRLING REGION

Covering Scotland's wasplike waist, this region has always been a crucial strategic point dividing the Lowlands from the Highlands. Scotland's two most important independence battles were fought here, within sight of Stirling's hilltop stronghold. William Wallace's victory over the English at Stirling Bridge in 1297, followed by Robert Bruce's triumph at Bannockburn in 1314, established Scottish nationhood. The region remains a focus of much national pride.

Stirling

POP 36,150

With an impregnable position atop a mighty wooded crag (the plug of an extinct volcano), Stirling's beautifully preserved Old Town is a treasure trove of historic buildings and cobbled streets winding up to the ramparts of its impressive castle, which offer views for miles around. Clearly visible is the brooding Wallace Monument, a strange Victorian Gothic creation honouring the legendary freedom fighter of *Braveheart* fame. Nearby is Bannockburn, scene of Robert the Bruce's pivotal triumph over the English in 1314.

The castle makes a fascinating visit, but make sure you also spend time exploring the Old Town and the picturesque Back Walk footpath that encircles it. Below the Old Town, retail-oriented modern Stirling doesn't offer the same appeal; stick to the high ground as much as possible and you'll love the place.

⊙ Sights

★**Stirling Castle**   CASTLE
(HS; www.stirlingcastle.gov.uk; Castle Wynd; adult/child £14.50/8.70; ⊙ 9.30am-6pm Apr-Sep, to 5pm Oct-Mar; P) Hold Stirling and you control Scotland. This maxim has ensured that a fortress of some kind has existed here since prehistoric times. You cannot help drawing parallels with Edinburgh Castle, but many find Stirling's fortress more atmospheric – the location, architecture, historical significance

CENTRAL SCOTLAND STIRLING

Central Scotland Highlights

❶ **Stirling Castle** (p177) Admiring the views across ancient independence battlefields from this magnificent castle.

❷ **St Andrews** (p190) Pacing through the historic

birthplace of golf to play the famous Old Course.

❸ **Scone Palace** (p200) Strutting with the peacocks at this noble palace where Scottish kings were once crowned.

❹ **Falkirk Wheel** (p185) Taking a canal-boat trip through an engineering marvel.

❺ **East Neuk of Fife** (p196) Feasting on local seafood in picturesque fishing villages.

and commanding views combine to make it a grand and memorable sight. It's best to visit in the afternoon; many tourists come on day trips, so you may have the castle almost to yourself by about 4pm.

The current castle dates from the late 14th to the 16th century, when it was a residence of the Stuart monarchs. The undisputed highlight of a visit is the fabulous **Royal Palace**, which underwent a major restoration in 2011. The idea was that it should look brand new, just as when it was constructed by French masons under the orders of James V in the mid-16th century with the aim of impressing his new (also French) bride and other crowned heads of Europe.

The suite of six rooms – three for the king, three for the queen – is a sumptuous riot of colour. Particularly notable are the **Stirling Heads** – reproductions of painted oak roundels in the ceiling of the king's audience chamber (originals are in the Stirling Heads Gallery). The **Stirling tapestries** are modern reproductions, painstakingly woven by expert hands and based on 16th-century originals in New York's Metropolitan Museum. They depict the hunting of a unicorn – an event ripe with Christian metaphor – and are breathtakingly beautiful. Don't miss the palace exterior, studded with beautiful sculptures.

The **Stirling Heads Gallery**, above the royal chambers, displays some of the original carved oak roundels that decorated the king's audience chamber – a real rogue's gallery of royals, courtiers, and biblical and classical figures. In the vaults beneath the palace is a child-friendly **exhibition** on various aspects of castle life.

The other buildings surrounding the main castle courtyard are the vast **Great Hall**, built by James IV; the **Royal Chapel**, remodelled in the early 17th century by James VI and with the colourful original mural painting intact; and the King's Old Building. The latter is now home to the **Argyll & Sutherland Highlanders Regimental Museum** (www.argylls.co.uk; admission included in Stirling Castle entry; ◷ 9.30am-5pm Apr-Sep, 10am-4.35pm Oct-Mar).

The **Great Kitchens**, bring to life the bustle and scale of the enterprise of cooking for the king while, near the entrance, the **Castle Exhibition** gives good background information on the Stuart kings and updates on current archaeological investigations. There are magnificent vistas from the ramparts towards the Highlands.

Admission includes an audioguide, and free guided tours leave regularly from near the entrance. Your ticket also includes admission to nearby Argyll's Lodging.

Argyll's Lodging HISTORIC BUILDING
(www.stirlingcastle.gov.uk; Castle Wynd; admission included in Stirling Castle entry; ◷ 12.45-4pm) This elegant building is Scotland's most impressive 17th-century town house, built for a wealthy local merchant and later acquired by the Earl of Argyll when he thought that King Charles II might use Stirling Castle as a royal residence. It has been tastefully restored and gives an insight into the lavish lifestyle of 17th-century aristocrats. You can join a 20-minute guided tour (included in the Stirling Castle admission fee) or wander through the house at your leisure.

National Wallace Monument MONUMENT
(☑ 01786-472140; www.nationalwallacemonument. com; Abbey Craig; adult/child £9.99/6.25; ◷ 9.30am-5pm Apr-Jun, Sep & Oct, to 6pm Jul & Aug, 10.30am-4pm Nov-Feb, 10am-5pm Mar; P ♿) Perched high on a crag above the floodplain of the River Forth, this Victorian monument is so Gothic it deserves circling bats and croaking ravens. In the shape of a medieval

---

STIRLING'S OLD TOWN

Sloping steeply down from Stirling Castle, the Old Town has a remarkably different feel to modern Stirling, its cobblestone streets packed with 15th- to 17th-century architectural gems, and surrounded by Scotland's best-surviving town wall. Its growth began when Stirling became a royal burgh (about 1124), and reached a peak in the 15th and 16th centuries when rich merchants built their houses here.

Stirling's **town wall** was built around 1547 when Henry VIII of England began the 'Rough Wooing' – attacking Scottish towns in order to force Mary, Queen of Scots to marry his son so the two kingdoms could be united. The wall can be explored on the **Back Walk**, which follows the line of the wall from Dumbarton Rd to the castle. You pass the town cemeteries (check out the **Star Pyramid**, an outsized affirmation of Reformation values dating from 1863), then continue around the back of the castle to Mote Hill and the **Beheading Stone**.

Stirling

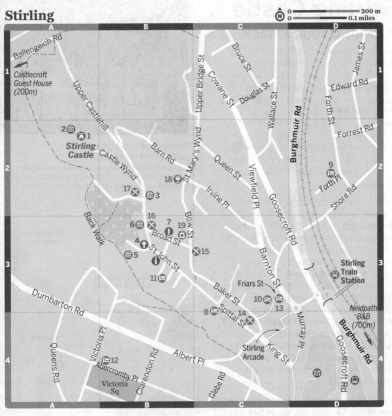

Stirling

◎ Top Sights
1	Stirling Castle	A2

◎ Sights
2	Argyll & Sutherland Highlanders Regimental Museum	A2
3	Argyll's Lodging	B2
4	Church of the Holy Rude	B3
5	Cowane's Hospital	B3
6	Mar's Wark	B3
7	Mercat Cross	B3

⊟ Sleeping
8	Colessio Hotel	C3
9	Forth Guest House	D2
10	Friars Wynd	C3
11	Stirling SYHA	B3
12	Victoria Square Guesthouse	B4
13	Willy Wallace Backpackers Hostel	C3

⊗ Eating
14	Breá	C4
15	Darnley Coffee House	C3
16	Hermann's	B3
17	Portcullis	B2

◗ Drinking & Nightlife
	Brewdog	(see 14)
18	Settle Inn	B2

⊡ Shopping
19	Stirling Bagpipes	B3

tower, it commemorates William Wallace, the hero of the bid for Scottish independence depicted in the film *Braveheart*. The view from the top over the flat, green gorgeousness of the Forth Valley, including the site of Wal-lace's 1297 victory over the English at Stirling Bridge, almost justifies the steep entry fee.

The climb up the narrow staircase inside leads through a series of galleries including the Hall of Heroes, a marble pantheon of

Stirling Castle

PLANNING YOUR ATTACK

Stirling's a sizeable fortress, but not so huge that you'll have to decide what to leave out – there's time to see it all. Unless you've got a working knowledge of Scottish monarchs, head to the **Castle Exhibition ❶** first: it'll help you sort one James from another. That done, take on the sights at leisure. First, stop and look around you from the **ramparts ❷**; the views high over this flat valley, a key strategic point in Scotland's history, are magnificent.

Track back towards the citadel's heart, stopping for a quick tour through the **Great Kitchens ❸**; looking at all that fake food might make you seriously hungry, though. Then enter the main courtyard. Around you are the principal castle buildings, including the **Royal Chapel ❹**. During summer there are events (such as Renaissance dancing) in the **Great Hall ❺** – get details at the entrance. The **Museum of the Argyll & Sutherland Highlanders ❻** is a treasure trove if you're interested in regimental history, but missable if you're not. Leave the best for last – crowds thin in the afternoon – and enter the sumptuous **Royal Palace ❼**.

Take time to admire the beautiful **Stirling Tapestries ❽**, skillfully woven by hand on-site between 2001-2014.

THE WAY UP & DOWN

If you have time, take the atmospheric Back Walk, a peaceful, shady stroll around the Old Town's fortifications and up to the castle's imposing crag-top position. Afterwards, wander down through the Old Town to admire its facades.

TOP TIPS

» **Admission** Entrance is free for Historic Scotland members. If you'll be visiting several Historic Scotland sites a membership will save you plenty.

» **Vital Statistics** First constructed: before 1110; number of sieges: at least nine; last besieger: Bonnie Prince Charlie (unsuccessful); money spent refurbishing the Royal Palace: £12 million.

Museum of the Argyll & Sutherland Highlanders
The history of one of Scotland's legendary regiments – now subsumed into the Royal Regiment of Scotland – is on display here, featuring memorabilia, weapons and uniforms.

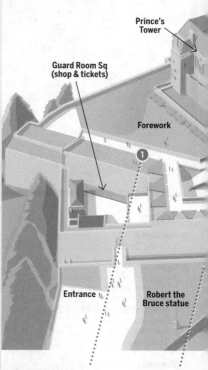

Prince's Tower

Guard Room Sq (shop & tickets)

Forework

❶

Entrance

Robert the Bruce statue

Castle Exhibition
A great overview of the Stewart dynasty here will get your facts straight, and also offers the latest archaeological titbits from the ongoing excavations under the citadel. Analysis of skeletons has revealed surprising amounts of biographical data.

Royal Palace
The impressive highlight of a visit to the castle is this recreation of the royal lodgings originally built by James V. The finely worked ceiling, ornate furniture and sumptuous unicorn tapestries dazzle.

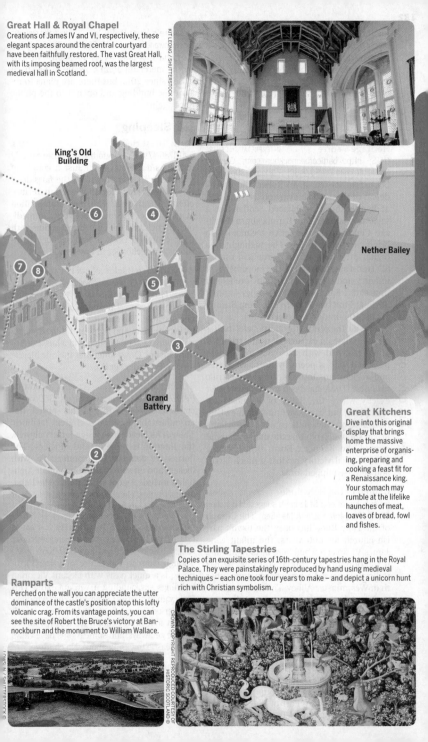

Great Hall & Royal Chapel

Creations of James IV and VI, respectively, these elegant spaces around the central courtyard have been faithfully restored. The vast Great Hall, with its imposing beamed roof, was the largest medieval hall in Scotland.

KIT LEONG / SHUTTERSTOCK ©

King's Old Building

Nether Bailey

⑥ ④

⑦ ⑧

⑤

③

Grand Battery

Great Kitchens

Dive into this original display that brings home the massive enterprise of organising, preparing and cooking a feast fit for a Renaissance king. Your stomach may rumble at the lifelike haunches of meat, loaves of bread, fowl and fishes.

The Stirling Tapestries

Copies of an exquisite series of 16th-century tapestries hang in the Royal Palace. They were painstakingly reproduced by hand using medieval techniques – each one took four years to make – and depict a unicorn hunt rich with Christian symbolism.

Ramparts

Perched on the wall you can appreciate the utter dominance of the castle's position atop this lofty volcanic crag. From its vantage points, you can see the site of Robert the Bruce's victory at Bannockburn and the monument to William Wallace.

LOVEISN / SHUTTERSTOCK ©

CROWN COPYRIGHT REPRODUCED COURTESY OF HISTORIC SCOTLAND ©

lugubrious Scottish luminaries. Admire Wallace's broadsword and see the man himself re-created in a 3D audiovisual display.

Buses 62 and 63 run from Murray Pl in Stirling to the visitor centre (£2.30, 10 minutes, every 30 minutes). From the visitor centre, walk or shuttle-bus up the hill to the monument itself.

Bannockburn
Heritage Centre
INTERPRETATION CENTRE

(NTS; http://battleofbannockburn.com; Glasgow Rd; adult/child £11.50/8.50; ⊙10am-5.30pm Mar-Oct, to 5pm Nov-Feb; P ⏾) Robert the Bruce's defeat of the English army on 24 June 1314 at Bannockburn established Scotland as a separate nation. The Bannockburn Heritage Centre uses interactive technology to bring the battle to life. The highlight is a digital projection of the battlefield onto a 3D landscape that shows the movements of infantry and cavalry (entry is by prebooked time slots). Bannockburn is 2 miles south of Stirling; First bus 24 or 54 run from Stirling (£1.80, 10 minutes, three per hour).

Outside the centre, the 'battlefield' itself is no more than an expanse of neatly trimmed grass, crowned with a circular monument inscribed with a poem by Kathleen Jamie, and a Victorian statue of the victor astride his horse. There has been much debate over exactly where the Battle of Bannockburn took place, but it was definitely somewhere near here on the southern edge of Stirling's urban sprawl. Exploiting the marshy ground around the Bannock Burn, Bruce won a great tactical victory against a much larger and better-equipped force.

Church of the Holy Rude
CHURCH

(www.holyrude.org; St John St; suggested donation £2; ⊙11am-4pm Easter & May-Sep) The Church of the Holy Rude has been the town's parish church for 600 years; the infant King James VI was crowned here in 1567, making it the only British church still in daily use to have witnessed a royal coronation, other than Westminster Abbey. The nave and tower date from 1456, and the church has one of the few surviving medieval open-timber roofs. Stunning stained-glass windows and huge stone pillars create a powerful effect.

Mar's Wark
HISTORIC BUILDING

(Castle Wynd) Mar's Wark (*wark* is an old Scots word for 'building') is the ornate facade of a Renaissance town house commissioned in 1569 by the wealthy Earl of Mar, regent of Scotland during James VI's minority.

Cowane's Hospital
HISTORIC BUILDING

(www.cowanes.org.uk; 49 St John St) Cowane's Hospital was built as an almshouse in 1637 by the merchant John Cowane. It has been closed since 2015, but there are plans to restore the building and open it to the public once again.

🛏 Sleeping

Forth Guest House
B&B £

(✆01786-471020; www.forthguesthouse.co.uk; 23 Forth Pl; s/d £55/60; P ⏾) Just a couple of minutes' walk from town, on the far side of the railway, this elegant Georgian terrace offers attractive and stylish accommodation at a fair price. The rooms are very commodious, particularly the cute garret rooms with their coombed ceilings and modern bathrooms. Even cheaper in low season.

Willy Wallace Backpackers Hostel
HOSTEL £

(✆01786-446773; www.willywallacehostel.com; 77 Murray Pl; dm/tw from £15/46; @ ⏾) This highly convenient central hostel is friendly, roomy and sociable. The colourful, spacious dormitories are clean and light, and it has free tea and coffee, a good kitchen and a laissez-faire atmosphere. Other amenities include bicycle hire and laundry service.

Stirling SYHA
HOSTEL £

(✆01786-473442; www.syha.org.uk; St John St; dm/tw £17.50/44; P @ ⏾) This hostel has an unbeatable location and great facilities. Though its facade is that of a former church, the interior is modern and efficient. The dorms are compact but comfortable, with lockers and en suite bathrooms; other highlights include a pool table, a bike shed and, at busy times, cheap meals on offer. Lack of atmosphere can be the only downside.

★ Victoria Square Guesthouse
B&B ££

(✆01786-473920; www.victoriasquareguesthouse. com; 12 Victoria Sq; s/d from £70/105; P ⏾) Though close to the centre of town, Victoria Sq is a quiet oasis with elegant Victorian buildings surrounding a verdant park. This luxury guesthouse's huge rooms, bay windows and period features make it a winner – there's a great four-poster room (from £110) for romantic getaways, and some rooms have views to the castle towering above. No children.

Castlecroft Guest House
B&B ££

(✆01786-474933; www.castlecroft-uk.com; Ballengeich Rd; s/d £75/85; P ⏾) Nestling into the hillside under the back of the castle, this great hideaway feels like a rural retreat but is a short, spectacular walk from the heart of Stirling. The lounge and deck area enjoy views over green fields to the nearby hills, the rooms have excellent modern bathrooms and the welcome couldn't be more hospitable. Breakfast features homemade bread, among other delights.

Neidpath B&B
B&B ££

(☑ 01786-469017; www.accommodationinstirling. co.uk; 24 Linden Ave; s/d/f £55/70/95; P ଵ) Offering excellent value and a genuine welcome, this fine choice is easily accessed by car. A particularly appealing front room is one of three excellent modernised bedrooms with fridges and good bathrooms. The owners also run various self-catering apartments around town; details via the website. Two-night minimum stay most nights in July and August.

★ Friars Wynd
HOTEL £££

(☑ 01786-473390; www.friarswynd.co.uk; 17 Friars St; r from £129; ଵ) Set in a lovingly restored 19th-century town house just a short walk from the train station, Friars Wynd offers eight bedrooms of varying sizes, many with period features such as Victorian cast-iron fire surrounds or exposed patches of original red-brick walls. Be aware that the 1st-floor rooms are directly above the bar and restaurant, so can be a little noisy at weekends.

Colessio Hotel
BOUTIQUE HOTEL £££

(☑ 01786-448880; www.hotelcolessio.com; 33 Spittal St; r from £129; ଵ) This new luxury hotel and spa occupies a landmark neoclassical building (a former hospital) in the heart of the Old Town. The luxury conversion includes sumptuous rooms and suites with a touch of designer decadence, and a sophisticated cocktail bar and restaurant.

✕ Eating & Drinking

Darnley Coffee House
CAFE £

(☑ 01786-474468; www.facebook.com/Darnley CoffeeHouse; 18 Bow St; mains £3-5; ⊙ 11am-4pm Mon-Sat, noon-4pm Sun; ଵ) Just down the hill from Stirling Castle, this is a good pit stop for home baking, soup and speciality coffees during a walk around the Old Town. The cafe is in the vaulted cellars of a 16th-century house where Darnley, the lover and later husband of Mary, Queen of Scots, once stayed while visiting her.

Birds & Bees
PUB FOOD ££

(☑ 01786-473663; www.thebirdsandthebees-stirling. com; Easter Cornton Rd, Causewayhead; mains £9-14; ⊙ food served noon-2.30pm & 5-10pm; P ଵ ⊕) A bit of a local secret this – a country pub in a converted barn, hidden away on a back road on the northern fringes of the city. There's faux-rustic decor and a crowd-pleasing pub-grub menu that runs from nachos and tempura king prawns to steaks, burgers, ribs and fish and chips. Outdoor seating and plenty of space for kids to run around.

Breá
BISTRO ££

(www.brea-stirling.co.uk; 5 Baker St; mains £9-17; ⊙ noon-9pm Sun-Thu, to 10pm Fri-Sat; ⊘ ⊕) 🌱 Bringing a bohemian touch to central Stirling, this busy bistro has pared-back contemporary decor and a short menu showcasing carefully sourced Scottish produce, including beef, venison, seafood, haggis and Brewdog beers, as well as gourmet burgers, pizza and a handful of vegetarian dishes.

CENTRAL SCOTLAND STIRLING

WILLIAM WALLACE, SCOTTISH PATRIOT

William Wallace is one of Scotland's best-known historical figures, a patriot whose exploits set the scene for Scotland's wars of independence. Born in 1270, he was catapulted into fame and a place in history as a highly successful guerrilla commander who harassed the English invaders for many years.

In the wake of his victory over the English at Stirling Bridge in 1297, Wallace was knighted by Robert the Bruce and proclaimed Guardian of Scotland. However, it was only a short time before English military superiority and the fickle loyalties of the Scots nobility turned against the defender of Scottish independence.

Disaster struck in July 1298 when King Edward's forces defeated the Scots at the Battle of Falkirk. Wallace went into hiding and travelled throughout Europe to drum up support for the Scottish cause. But many Scottish nobles were prepared to side with Edward, and Wallace was betrayed after his return to Scotland in 1305; he was found guilty of treason at Westminster and hanged, beheaded and disembowelled at Smithfield, London.

Hermann's
AUSTRIAN, SCOTTISH ££

(☑ 01786-450632; www.hermanns.co.uk; 58 Broad St; mains £11-20, 2-/3-course lunch £12/15; ⊙noon-3pm & 6-10pm; 🅿🖷) This elegant Scottish-Austrian restaurant is a reliable and popular choice, with conservative decor oddly offset by magazine-spread skiing photos, but the food doesn't miss a beat and ranges from Scottish favourites such as Cullen skink to Austrian schnitzel and *spätzle* noodles. Vegetarian options are good, and quality Austrian wines provide an out-of-the-ordinary accompaniment.

Portcullis
PUB FOOD ££

(☑ 01786-472290; www.theportcullishotel.com; Castle Wynd; mains £9-18; ⊙food served noon-3.30pm & 5.30-9pm; 🖀) Built in stone as solid as the castle that it stands below, this former school is just the spot for a pint and a pub lunch after your castle visit. With bar meals that would have had even William Wallace loosening his belt a couple of notches, a little beer garden and a cosy buzz indoors, it's well worth a visit.

Brewdog
BAR

(☑ 01786-440043; www.brewdog.com/bars/uk/stirling; 7 Baker St; ⊙noon-midnight Sun-Thu, to 1am Fri-Sat; 🖀) The burgeoning Brewdog empire has come to Stirling, with a cool bar done out in designer-distressed timber offering no fewer than 16 taps dispensing craft beers from all over the world, including several from their own famously crowdfunded brewery near Fraserburgh in Aberdeenshire.

Settle Inn
PUB

(☑ 01786-474609; 91 St Mary's Wynd; ⊙11am-11pm Mon-Sat, 12.30-11pm Sun; 🖀) A warm welcome is guaranteed at Stirling's oldest pub (1733), a spot redolent with atmosphere, with its log fire, vaulted back room, low-slung ceilings and Friday night folk-music sessions. Guest ales, atmospheric nooks where you can settle in for the night, and a blend of local characters make it a classic of its kind.

🛍 Shopping

Stirling Bagpipes
MUSIC

(☑ 01786-448886; www.stirlingbagpipes.com; 8 Broad St; ⊙10am-6pm Mon, Tue & Thu-Sat) Bagpipes are handmade and repaired in this combined shop and workshop, which also houses a collection of antique bagpipes and piping paraphernalia. The place is a focus for local pipers, and sells books and CDs of bagpipe music.

ℹ Information

There's free internet access at **Stirling Library** (Corn Exchange Rd; ⊙9.30am-5.30pm Mon, Wed, Fri, to 7pm Tue & Thu, to 5pm Sat).

Stirling Community Hospital (☑ 01786-434000; www.nhsforthvalley.com; Livilands Rd) is south of the town centre. The nearest emergency department is Forth Valley Royal Hospital in Larbert, 9 miles southeast of Stirling.

You'll find a **post office** (44 Thistles Centre, Goosecroft Rd; ⊙9am-5.30pm Mon-Sat, 11am-3pm Sun) in the WH Smith newspaper shop.

Information can be found and accommodation booked at **Stirling Tourist Office** (☑ 01786-475019; www.destinationstirling.com; Old Town Jail, St John St; ⊙10am-5pm).

ℹ Getting There & Away

BUS

The bus station is on Goosecroft Rd. **Citylink** (☑ 0871-266-3333; www.citylink.co.uk) offers a number of services to/from Stirling including the following:

Dundee £14.40, 1¾ hours, hourly

Edinburgh £8.20, 1¼ hours, hourly

Glasgow £7.70, 45 minutes, hourly

Perth £9.20, 50 minutes, at least hourly

Some buses continue to Aberdeen, Inverness and Fort William; more frequently a change will be required.

TRAIN

ScotRail (www.scotrail.co.uk) has services to/from a number of destinations, including the following:

Aberdeen £30, 2¼ hours, hourly weekdays, every two hours Sunday

Dundee £12, one hour, hourly weekdays, every two hours Sunday

Edinburgh £8.60, one hour, twice hourly Monday to Saturday, hourly Sunday

Glasgow £8.90, 50 minutes, twice hourly Monday to Saturday, hourly Sunday

Perth £13, 30 minutes, hourly weekdays, every two hours Sunday

Dunblane
POP 8800

Dunblane, 5 miles northwest of Stirling, is a pretty town with a notable cathedral. It's difficult not to remember the horrific massacre that took place in the primary school in 1996, but happier headlines have come the town's way in recent years with the success of Dunblane-born tennis star Andy Murray – a gold-painted letterbox at the north end of

THE FALKIRK WHEEL & THE KELPIES

Scotland's canals were once vital avenues for goods transport, but the railway age left them to fall into dereliction. A millennium project restored two of Scotland's major canals, the Union and the Forth & Clyde, which were once linked by an arduous series of 11 locks covering the difference in level of 115ft. The construction of the unique Falkirk Wheel changed all that. Its rotating arms literally scoop boats up and lift them to the higher waterway.

Falkirk is a large town about 10 miles southeast of Stirling. Regular buses and trains link the two, and also connect Falkirk with Glasgow and Edinburgh.

Completed in 2002, the **Falkirk Wheel** (www.thefalkirkwheel.co.uk; Lime Rd, Falkirk; visitor centre free, boat trips adult/child £12.50/7.50; ⊘10am-5.30pm daily Mar-Oct, 11am-4pm Wed-Sun Nov-Feb; P) is a modern engineering marvel, a rotating boat lift that raises vessels 115ft from the Forth & Clyde Canal to the Union Canal. Boat trips depart from the lower basin every 40 minutes (hourly in winter) and travel into the wheel, which delivers you to the Union Canal high above. Boats then go through Roughcastle Tunnel before the return descent on the wheel. Anyone with an interest in engineering should not miss this boat ride – it's great for kids, too.

There's also water playpark, a cafe and a newly revamped visitor centre that explains the workings of the mighty wheel – it only takes the power of about eight toasters for a full rotation!

A pair of stunning equine statues gracing the eastern entrance to the Forth & Clyde Canal, **the Kelpies** (☑01324-506850; www.thehelix.co.uk; The Helix, Falkirk; guided tours adult/child £7/4; ⊘visitor centre 10am-5pm, tours 11am-4pm; P) are named after mythical Scottish water-horses. The two 30m-tall horse's heads are fashioned out of stainless steel, and are a tribute to the working horses that once hauled barges along the canal. You can view them for free (indeed, they are clearly visible from the M9 motorway between Edinburgh and Stirling), but the 45-minute guided tour takes you inside the sculptures.

the High St commemorates his 2012 Olympic gold medal.

There are frequent trains from Stirling to Dunblane (£3.50, 12 minutes, every 30 minutes). Bus services are slower and less convenient.

Dunblane Cathedral (HS; www.dunblanecathedral.org.uk; Cathedral Sq; ⊘9.30am-12.30pm & 1.30-5pm Mon-Sat, 2-5pm Sun Apr-Sep, 9.30am-4pm Mon-Sat, 2-4pm Sun Oct-Mar) **FREE** is a superbly elegant example of Gothic architecture – the lower parts of the bell tower date from the 11th century, the rest mainly from the 13th century, though it was all restored in late Victorian times. There are fine 15th-century carved-wood misericord stalls in the chancel, and a 9th-century carved Celtic cross stands in the north aisle; a modern standing stone commemorates the town's slain children.

The musty old **Leighton Library** (www.leightonlibrary.org.uk; 61 High St; ⊘11am-1pm Mon-Sat May-Sep) **FREE**, dating from 1684, is the oldest purpose-built library in Scotland. There are 4500 books in 90 languages.

Riverside PUB FOOD ££
(☑01786-823318; www.theriversidedunblane.co.uk; Stirling Rd; mains £9-20; ⊘food 10am-2.30pm & 5-9pm Mon-Fri, 10am-9pm Sat-Sun;) The name describes the location of this pub-cafe-restaurant that champions local produce and serves everything from free-range eggs Benedict for breakfast and pulled-pork sandwiches for lunch, to seafood risotto for dinner or just a glass of local beer on the terrace overlooking the Allan Water.

Doune

POP 1630

Doune is best known for its castle, which was famously used as a film set for *Monty Python and the Holy Grail* (1975), and more recently for the TV series *Outlander*. But it's a picturesque village in its own right, with a cluster of craft shops and some lovely walks along the River Teith.

Doune is 8 miles northwest of Stirling. Buses run from Stirling to Doune every hour or two (£4.10, 25 minutes), less frequently on Sunday.

Magnificent **Doune Castle** (HS; www. historicenvironment.scot; adult/child £5.50/3.30; ⏱9.30am-5.30pm Apr-Sep, 10am-4pm Oct-Mar; 🅿) is one of the best-preserved medieval fortresses in Scotland, having remained largely unchanged since it was built for the Duke of Albany in the 14th century. It has been used as a film set for the movie *Monty Python and the Holy Grail* (1975) – the audioguide is narrated by Python member Terry Jones – and the TV series *Outlander* and *Game of Thrones*. Highlights include the cathedral-like Great Hall, and a kitchen fireplace big enough to roast a whole ox.

The castle was a favourite royal hunting lodge, but was also of great strategic importance because it controlled the route between the Lowlands and Highlands. Mary, Queen of Scots once stayed here, as did Bonnie Prince Charlie. There are great views from the castle walls, and the lofty gatehouse is very impressive, rising nearly 30m.

Right in the middle of the village, cute **Buttercup Cafe** (📞01786-842511; www.butter cupcafe.co.uk; 7 Main St; mains £4-10; ⏱9am-5pm Mon-Fri, 9am-4pm Sat, 10am-4pm Sun; 🛜🧒) serves good breakfasts (including eggs Benedict, pancakes, omelettes and gluten-free options, until 11.30am) and hot lunches, and is licensed so you can enjoy a glass of Prosecco with your smoked salmon sandwiches.

Dollar

One of central Scotland's most dramatically situated castles, **Castle Campbell** (HS; www. historicenvironment.scot; adult/child £5.50/3.30; ⏱9.30am-5.30pm Apr-Sep, to 4.30pm Oct, to 4.30pm Sat-Wed Nov-Mar; 🅿) sits on a spur between two deep, wooded ravines known as the Burn of Sorrow and the Burn of Care. A former stronghold of the Dukes of Argyll, it was originally known as 'Castle Gloom'. There are interesting rooms in the 15th-century tower house, but the main attraction is the spectacular view from the top. The castle lies a mile north of charming Dollar village, about 11 miles east of Stirling.

There's a superb circular walk (30 minutes) from the lower car park, up the track to the castle and then back down via a walkway through the ravine.

FIFE

The Kingdom of Fife (www.visitfife.com) as it calls itself – it was home to Scottish kings for 500 years – is a tongue of land protruding between the Firths of Forth and Tay that has managed to maintain an individual Lowland identity quite separate from the rest of the country. Though southern Fife is part of Edinburgh's commuter-belt territory, eastern Fife's rolling green farmland and quaint fishing villages are prime turf for exploration, and the fresh sea air feels like it's doing you a power of good. Fife's biggest attraction, St Andrews, has Scotland's most venerable university and a wealth of historic buildings. It's also, of course, the headquarters of golf and draws professionals and keen slashers alike to take on the Old Course – the classic links experience.

The **Fife Coastal Path** (www.fifecoastal path.co.uk) runs more than 80 miles, following the entire Fife coastline from the Forth Road Bridge to the Tay Bridge and beyond. It's well waymarked, picturesque and not too rigorous, though winds can buffet. It's easily accessed for shorter sections or day walks, and long stretches of it can also be tackled on a mountain bike.

❶ Getting Around

The main bus operator here is **Stagecoach East Scotland** (www.stagecoachbus.com). You can buy a Fife Dayrider ticket (£8.40), which gives one day's unlimited travel around Fife on Stagecoach buses.

Fife Council produces a useful transport map, *Getting Around Fife*, available from tourist offices. Good public transport information can be found at www.fifedirect.org.uk.

If you are driving from the Forth bridges to St Andrews, a slower but much more scenic route than the M90/A91 is along the signposted Fife Coastal Tourist Route.

Culross

POP 400

Instantly familiar to fans of the TV series *Outlander,* in which it appears as the fictional village of Cranesmuir, Culross (*koo-ross*) is Scotland's best-preserved example of a 17th-century town. Limewashed white and yellow-ochre houses with red-tiled roofs stand amid a maze of cobbled streets, and the winding Back Causeway to the abbey is lined with whimsical cottages. The National Trust for Scotland (NTS) owns no fewer than 20 of the town's buildings.

As the birthplace of St Mungo, Glasgow's patron saint, Culross was an important religious centre from the 6th century. The burgh developed under Sir George Bruce by extracting coal through ingenious tunnels extending under the seabed. When mining was ended by flooding of the tunnels, the town switched to making linen and shoes.

More large house than palace, **Culross Palace** (NTS; www.nts.org.uk; Low Causewayside; adult/child £10.50/7.50; noon-5pm daily Jun-Aug, Wed-Sun only Apr-May & Sep, noon-4pm Wed-Sun Oct), the 17th-century residence of local laird Sir George Bruce features an interior largely unchanged since his time. The decorative wood panelling and painted timber ceilings are of national importance, particularly the allegorical scenes in the Painted Chamber, which survive from the early 1600s. Don't miss the re-creation of a 17th-century garden at the back, with gorgeous views from the top terrace.

The Town House (with ticket and information desk downstairs) and the Study, both dating from the early 17th century, can be visited on a 45-minute guided tour of the town (£2 per person, available between 1pm and 3pm).

Ruined **Culross Abbey** (HS; www.historicenvironment.scot; Back Causeway; dawn-dusk), **FREE**, founded by the Cistercians in 1217, sits atop a hill in a lovely peaceful spot with vistas of the firth. The choir was converted into the parish church in the 16th century; it's worth a peek inside for the stained glass and the Gothic Argyll tomb.

Above a pottery workshop behind the Town House, **Biscuit Café** (www.culrosspottery.com; Sandhaven; mains £3-6; 10am-5pm) has a tranquil little garden and sells coffee, tempting organic cakes and scones, and tasty light meals.

Culross is 16 miles east of Stirling, and 12 miles west of the Forth bridges. Buses run from Dunfermline (£2.90, 30 minutes, hourly) via Culross to Stirling (£4.80, 50 minutes, hourly Monday to Saturday).

Dunfermline

POP 49,700

Dunfermline is a large and unlovely town, but rich in history, boasting the evocative Dunfermline Abbey, its neighbouring palace and the attractive grounds of Pittencrieff Park, the latter gifted to the city by local boy

WORTH A TRIP

DEEP SEA WORLD

If the kids are tiring of historic buildings, a trip to **Deep Sea World** (www.deepseaworld.com; North Queensferry; adult/child £14/9.75; 10am-5pm; P) might make them feel more kindly towards Fife. Situated at North Queensferry, beneath the Forth Bridge, this is a blockbuster aquarium with all those 'respect' species like sharks and piranhas, as well as seals and touch pools with rays and other sea creatures. You can even arrange guided dives with sharks. It's a little cheaper if you pre-purchase tickets online.

made good, Andrew Carnegie (1835–1919), of US steel industry fame.

Dunfermline Abbey & Palace (HES; www.historicenvironment.scot; St Margaret St; adult/child £4.50/2.70; 9.30am-5.30pm Apr-Sep, 9.30am-4.30pm Sat-Wed Oct-Mar) was founded by David I in the 12th century as a Benedictine monastery. The abbey and its neighbouring palace was already favoured by religious royals: Malcolm III married the exiled Saxon princess Margaret here in the 11th century, and both chose to be interred here. More royal burials followed, none more notable than Robert the Bruce, whose remains were interred here in 1329.

What remains of the abbey are the ruins of the impressive three-tiered refectory building, and the atmosphere-laden nave of the old church, endowed with geometrically patterned columns and fine Romanesque and Gothic windows. It adjoins the 19th-century abbey church where Robert the Bruce lies entombed beneath the ornate pulpit.

Next to the refectory (and included in your abbey admission) is **Dunfermline Palace**. Once the abbey guesthouse, it was converted for James VI, whose son, the ill-fated Charles I, was born here in 1600. Below stretches the leafy, strollable **Pittencrieff Park**.

Dunfermline Abbey Church (10am-4.30pm Mon-Sat, 2-4.30pm Sun Apr-Oct) is a 19th-century construction, adjoining the medieval nave of the old church to the east. It contains the tomb of Robert the Bruce, which lies beneath the ornate pulpit.

Set in a Georgian town house a block east of Dunfermline Abbey, **De Brus** (☑ 01383-747757; http://debrusbrewery.com; 25 Canmore St; ⊙ noon-11pm Mon-Thu, to midnight Fri-Sat, to 10pm Sun) is a stylish and intimate bar and brewery that serves its own distinctive range of beers and ciders, as well as tempting sharing platters of Scottish artisan cheeses and charcuterie.

There are frequent buses between Dunfermline and Edinburgh (£6, 50 minutes), Stirling (£4.80, 1¼ hours) and St Andrews (£11.10, 1¼ hours), plus trains to/from Edinburgh (£5.30, 40 minutes).

Aberdour

POP 1630

Aberdour is a popular seaside town with an impressive castle and a lovely family beach, known as the Silver Sands.

Long a residence of the Douglases of Morton, **Aberdour Castle** (HS; www.historicenvironment.scot; adult/child £5.50/3.30; ⊙ 9.30am-5.30pm Apr-Sep, 10am-4pm Sat-Wed Oct-Mar; ℗) is a stately structure that exhibits several architectural phases. It's worth purchasing the guidebook to better comprehend what you see. Most charming of all is the elaborate *doocot* (dovecote) at the bottom of the garden. Be sure to pop into the beautiful Romanesque **church of St Fillan's**, next door to the castle.

Aberdour Hotel (☑ 01383-860325; www.aberdourhotel.co.uk; 38 High St; s/d £80/99; 🛜🐾) is a family-run hotel on the main road is not only a good place to stay, but also does bar meals with an emphasis on hearty, home-cooked food. There are real ales and good vegetarian choices on the menu.

It's difficult to imagine a more enchanting setting than that enjoyed by friendly **B&B Forth View Hotel** (☑ 01383-860402; www.forthviewhotel.co.uk; Hawkcraig Point; s £45-85, d £65-110; ⊙ Apr-Oct; ℗🛜) in a secluded seafront location. The front rooms offer fabulous views across the firth to Edinburgh and the hospitality is most welcoming. It's tough to find – follow signs for Silver Sands beach, through the car park and down a narrow lane on the other side.

There's also an excellent little seafood restaurant, **Room with a View** (☑ 01383-860402; www.roomwithaviewrestaurant.co.uk; Forth View Hotel, Hawkcraig Point; mains lunch £11-17, dinner £14-24; ⊙ noon-2pm Wed-Sun, 6-10pm Wed-

Sat) 🍴, in the B&B's front room that is open year-round.

There are hourly trains to Edinburgh (£6, 30 minutes) and Dundee (£14, 1¼ hours) from Aberdour, as well as buses to nearby Dunfermline (£4.20, 45 minutes, twice hourly).

Kirkcaldy

POP 49,700

Kirkcaldy (kir-*caw*-day) wins no prizes for prettiness; its slightly shabby promenade sprawls along the edge of the sea for several miles, with spectacular pounding surf on windy days. The town is famous as the birthplace of 18th-century Enlightenment philosopher and economist **Adam Smith** (who features on English £20 notes issued between 2007 and 2016), but is only worth a stop for its excellent museum.

Kirkcaldy Galleries (☑ 01592-583206; www.onfife.com/venues/kirkcaldy-galleries; War Memorial Gardens, Abbotshall Rd; ⊙ noon-7pm Mon, 9.30am-7pm Tue & Thu, 9.30am-5pm Wed & Fri, 9.30am-4pm Sat, noon-4pm Sun; ℗) FREE is a museum and art gallery showcasing Kirkcaldy's history as a trading port and producer of linen, canvas and linoleum (floor covering). The kids will have a ball as there are plenty of hands-on attractions. There's also an impressive collection of Scottish paintings from the 18th to the 20th century, including works by the Scottish Colourists, William McTaggart and Jack Vettriano. The museum is a short walk east from the train and bus stations, and also houses a **tourist information point**.

There are hourly buses to St Andrews (£8.20, 1¼ hour) and Anstruther (£7.50, 1¼ hours). Two to four trains an hour run to Edinburgh (£7.90, 45 minutes) and Dundee (£11.70, 45 minutes).

Falkland

POP 1100

Below the soft ridges of the Lomond Hills in the centre of Fife lies the charming village of Falkland, a cluster of whitewashed cottages with red pantile roofs and crowstep gables. A handful of tea rooms and antique shops dot the narrow street, and rising majestically over the village square is Falkland Palace, a 16th-century country residence of the Stuart monarchs.

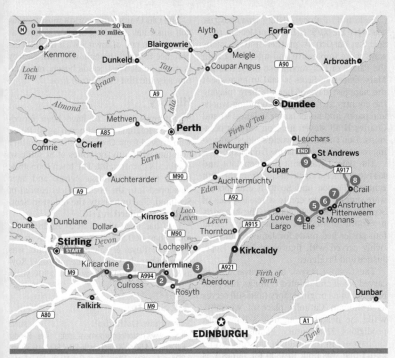

Driving Tour
The Fife Coast

START STIRLING
END ST ANDREWS
LENGTH 76 MILES; ONE DAY

This tour links two of the most popular tourist towns in Central Scotland via the scenic delights of the Fife coast.

Head south from  **1 Stirling** (p177) on the M9 and at Junction 7 turn east towards Kincardine Bridge. As you approach the bridge, follow signs for Kincardine and Kirkcaldy; then once across the Firth of Forth, follow the Fife Coastal Tourist Route signposts to the historic village of **2 Culross** (p186). Spend an hour or so exploring the medieval buildings of Culross before continuing via the A994 to **3 Dunfermline** (p187), for a look at its fine abbey and palace ruins.

From Dunfermline take the M90 towards the Forth Road Bridge, but leave at Junction 1 (signposted A921 Dalgety Bay) and continue to the attractive seaside village of **4 Aberdour** (p188) for lunch at the Aberdour Hotel or the Room with a View restaurant. Stay on the A921 as far as Kirkcaldy, then take the faster A915 (signposted St Andrews) as far as Upper Largo where you follow the A917 towards Elie; from here on, you will be following the brown Fife Coastal Tourist Route signs.

5 Elie (p199), with its sandy beaches and coastal footpaths, is a great place to stretch your legs and take in some bracing sea air before driving just a couple of miles further on to explore the neighbouring fishing villages of **6 St Monans** (p198) and **7 Pittenweem** (p198). Just 1 mile beyond Pittenweem, **8 Anstruther** (p197) deserves a slightly longer stop for a visit to the Scottish Fisheries Museum, a stroll by the harbour and an ice cream. If time allows, you may want to detour inland a couple of miles to visit Kellie Castle or Scotland's Secret Bunker.

The final stop before St Andrews is the pretty fishing village of **9 Crail** (p196), where the late afternoon or early evening light will provide ideal conditions for capturing one of Scotland's most photographed harbours. A brisk hike along the coastal path towards Fife Ness, keeping an eye out for seals and seabirds, will round off the day before driving the last 10 miles into **St Andrews** (p190).

Falkland Palace (NTS; www.nts.org.uk; adult/child £12.50/9; ⊙ 11am-5pm Mon-Sat, noon-5pm Sun Mar-Oct) is prettier and in many ways more impressive and interesting than the Palace of Holyroodhouse in Edinburgh. Mary, Queen of Scots is said to have spent the happiest days of her life here 'playing the country girl' in the surrounding woods and parks, and kings James V, James VI and Charles II all stayed here on various occasions. Don't miss the world's oldest surviving real tennis court, dating from 1539.

The palace was built between 1501 and 1541 to replace a castle dating from the 12th century; French and Scottish craftspeople were employed to create a masterpiece of Scottish Gothic architecture. The keeper's bedroom houses an extraordinary royal four-poster bed made for James VI in 1618, richly carved with figures of Faith, Hope, Justice and Prudence.

The Chapel Royal, an extravaganza of carved wood and painted ceiliings, has been restored to its original glory (and still serves as a Roman Catholic place of worship), while the neighbouring hall is hung with prodigious 17th-century Flemish hunting tapestries. In the grounds, the real tennis court that was built in 1539 for James V is the oldest still in use anywhere in the world (the one at London's Hampton Court Palace was originally built in 1528, but was renovated for Charles II in the 17th century).

Falkland village is 11 miles north of Kirkcaldy. Stagecoach bus 64 links St Andrews to Falkland direct (£6.20, 1¾ hours, hourly Monday to Saturday, five on Sunday). If travelling from Edinburgh (£13, hourly Monday to Saturday, five on Sunday), change buses at Glenrothes.

St Andrews

POP 16,900

For a small town, St Andrews has made a big name for itself: firstly as a religious centre and place of pilgrimage, then as Scotland's oldest (and Britain's third-oldest) university town. But it is its status as the home of golf that has propelled it to even greater fame, and today's pilgrims mostly arrive with a set of clubs in hand. Nevertheless, it's a lovely place to visit even if you've no interest in the game, with impressive medieval ruins, stately university buildings, idyllic white sands and excellent guesthouses and restaurants.

The Old Course, the world's most famous golf links, has a striking seaside location at the western end of town – it's a thrilling experience to stroll the hallowed turf. Nearby is magnificent West Sands beach, made famous by the film *Chariots of Fire*.

History

St Andrews is said to have been founded by St Regulus (also known as St Rule), who arrived from Greece in the 4th century bringing with him the bones of St Andrew, Scotland's patron saint. The town soon grew into a major pilgrimage centre and later developed into the ecclesiastical capital of Scotland. The university, the oldest in Scotland, was founded in 1410.

Golf has been played at St Andrews for more than 600 years; the game's governing body, the Royal & Ancient Golf Club, was founded here in 1754 and the imposing Royal & Ancient Clubhouse was built 100 years later.

◉ Sights

St Andrews Cathedral　　RUINS
(HES; www.historicenvironment.scot; The Pends; adult/child £4.50/2.70, incl castle £8/4.80; ⊙ 9.30am-5.30pm Apr-Sep, 10am-4pm Oct-Mar) All that's left of one of Britain's most magnificent medieval buildings are ruined fragments of wall and arch, and a single towering gable, but you can still appreciate the scale and majesty of the edifice from these scant remains. There's also a museum with a collection of superb 17th- and 18th-century grave slabs, 9th- and 10th-century Celtic crosses, and the late 8th-century St Andrews Sarcophagus, Europe's finest example of early medieval stone carving.

Founded in 1160 and consecrated in 1318, the cathedral stood as the focus of this important pilgrimage centre until 1559, when it was pillaged during the Reformation. The bones of St Andrew himself lie beneath the altar; until the cathedral was built, they had been enshrined in the nearby Church of St Regulus (or Rule). All that remains of this church is St Rule's Tower, worth the claustrophobic climb for the view across St Andrews. The admission fee only applies for the museum and tower; you can wander freely around the atmospheric ruins.

St Andrews Castle　　CASTLE
(HS; www.historicenvironment.scot; The Scores; adult/child £5.50/3.30, incl cathedral £8/4.80; ⊙ 9.30am-5.30pm Apr-Sep, 10am-4pm Oct-Mar)

The castle is mainly in ruins, but the site itself is evocative and has dramatic coastline views. It was founded around 1200 as a fortified home for the bishop of St Andrews. After the execution of Protestant reformers in 1545, other reformers retaliated by murdering Cardinal Beaton and taking over the castle. They spent almost a year holed up, during which they and their attackers dug a complex of **siege tunnels**; you can walk (or stoop) along their damp mossy lengths.

The visitor centre gives a good audiovisual introduction and has a small collection of Pictish stones.

British Golf Museum MUSEUM
(www.britishgolfmuseum.co.uk; Bruce Embankment; adult/child £7/3; ⊘9.30am-5pm Mon-Sat, 10am-5pm Sun Apr-Oct, 10am-4pm daily Nov-Mar) This museum provides a comprehensive overview of the history and development of the game and the role of St Andrews in it. Favourite fact: bad players were formerly known as 'foozlers'. The huge collection ranges from the world's oldest set of clubs (late 17th century, used with feather-stuffed golf balls) to modern equipment, clothing and trophies, and there's a large collection of memorabilia from Open winners both male and female.

St Andrews Aquarium AQUARIUM
(⊘01334-474786; www.standrewsaquarium.co.uk; The Scores; adult/child £10.50/8; ⊘10am-5pm Mon-Fri, to 6pm Sat & Sun; ⊛) As well as a seal sanctuary, rays and sharks from Scottish waters and exotic tropical favourites, St Andrews Aquarium has penguins, alligators and a cute family of meerkats.

St Andrews Museum MUSEUM
(www.onfife.com/venues/st-andrews-museum; Doubledykes Rd; ⊘10.30am-4pm daily Apr-Sep, Wed-Sun Oct-Mar) FREE St Andrews Museum has interesting displays that chart the history of the town from its founding by St Regulus to its growth as an ecclesiastical, academic and sporting centre.

Museum of the University of St Andrews MUSEUM
(MUSA; www.st-andrews.ac.uk/musa; 7a The Scores; ⊘10am-5pm Mon-Sat, noon-4pm Sun Apr-Oct, noon-4pm Thu-Sun Nov-Mar) FREE MUSA celebrates the history of Scotland's oldest university, and showcases treasures such as

---

PLAYING THE OLD COURSE

The **Old Course** (⊘Reservations Department ⊘01334-466718; www.standrews.com; Golf Pl) at St Andrews is the oldest and most famous golf course in the world. Golf has been played at St Andrews since the 15th century, and by 1457 it was apparently so popular that James II had to ban it because it was interfering with his troops' archery practice. Although it lies beside the exclusive Royal & Ancient Golf Club, the Old Course is a public course and is not owned by the club.

To play the Old Course, you'll need to book in advance via the website, or by contacting the Reservations Department. Reservations open on the last Wednesday in August the year before you wish to play. No bookings are taken for weekends or the month of September (check the latest guidelines on the website).

Unless you've booked months in advance, getting a tee-off time is literally a lottery; enter the ballot at the **caddie office** (⊘01334-466666; West Sands Rd) or by phone before 2pm two days before you wish to play (there's no Sunday play). Be warned that applications by ballot are normally heavily oversubscribed, and green fees are £175 in summer.

Singles are not accepted in the ballot and should start queuing as early as possible on the day – 5am is good – in the hope of joining a group. You'll need a handicap certificate (24/36 for men/women). If your number doesn't come up, there are six other public courses in the area (book up to seven days in advance on 01334-466718, no handicap required), including the prestigious Castle Course (£120). Other summer green fees: New £75, Jubilee £75, Eden £45, Strathtyrum £30 and Balgove (nine-holer for beginners and kids) £15. There are various multiple-day tickets available. A caddie for your round costs £50 plus tip. If you play on a windy day, expect those scores to balloon: Nick Faldo famously stated, 'When it blows here, even the seagulls walk'.

There are **guided walks** (www.standrews.com; per person £10; ⊘11am & 2pm daily Apr-Sep) of the Old Course, and you are free to walk over the course on Sunday, or follow the footpaths around the edge at any time.

St Andrews

Map labels:

St Andrews Bay

North Sea

The Scores

North St

Murray Park

Murray Pl

Greyfriars Gdn

Bell St

St Mary's Pl

Hope St

Golf Pl

The Links

Old Course

Old Pavilion

West Sands Rd

West Sands (200m)

Old Course Hotel (350m); Leuchars Train Station (5mi); Dundee (13mi)

David Russell Hall (700m)

Kinburn Park

Doubledykes Rd

Station Rd

City Rd

Bus Station

Alexandra Pl

Argyle St

Queen's Gdns

Church Sq

Holy Trinity Church

Church St

College St

Butts Wynd

Market St

Bell St

South St

West Burn La

Abbey St

North Castle St

South Castle St

Museum

The Pends

Crail (10mi); Anstruther (10mi)

200 m

0.1 miles

St Andrews

medieval silver maces, rare books and manuscripts, and 16th-century astronomical instruments.

Activities

Apart from the obvious activity – **golf** – the tourist office has a list of local **walks** and also sells OS maps. **Fergus Cook** (www.guidedtoursofstandrews.co.uk; per person £10) offers guided walking tours of the town. The section of the **Fife Coastal Path** (www.fifecoastalpath.co.uk) between St Andrews and the East Neuk is fun, either on foot or mountain bike. Parts of the track can be covered by the tide, so check tide times before you go. The tourist office has a detailed map.

One-hour guided tours of **Eden Mill Distillery** (p195) depart at noon and 4pm, beginning with a G&T and ending with a tasting session.

All the main East Neuk attractions are within reasonable **cycling** distance.

Festivals & Events

Open Championship SPORTS
(www.theopen.com; ☉ Jul) One of international golf's four major championships. The tournament venue changes from year to year, and comes to St Andrews every five years (next in 2020) – check the website for future venues.

St Andrews Highland Games CULTURAL
(www.standrewshighlandgames.co.uk) Held on the North Haugh on the last Sunday in July.

Sleeping

St Andrews' accommodation is expensive and often heavily booked, especially in summer, at weekends and during university events such as graduation, so reserve well in advance. Almost every house on super-central Murray Park and Murray Pl is a guesthouse.

During summer (June to August), three student residences open up as visitor accommodation (see www.discoverstandrews.com) – **Agnes Blackadder Hall** (☎ 01334-463000; www.discoverstandrews.com; North Haugh; s/d £59/79; ☉ Jun-Aug; P@⊛) ⌀, **David Russell Hall** (☎ 01334-463000; www.discoverstandrews.com; Buchanan Gdns; s/d from £59/79; ☉ Jun-Aug; P@⊛) ⌀ and **McIntosh Hall** (☎ 01334-467035; www.discoverstandrews.com; Abbotsford Cres; s/tw £45/65; ☉ Jun-Aug; P@⊛) ⌀. Prices are good value for the standard of accommodation on offer.

St Andrews Tourist Hostel HOSTEL **£**
(☎ 01334-479911; St Marys Pl; dm £13-15; ⊛) Laid-back and central, this hostel is the only backpacker accommodation in town. Occupying a stately old building, it has high corniced ceilings, especially in the huge lounge. There's a laissez-faire approach, which can verge on chaotic at times, but the staff and location can't be beaten. Reception closed between 2pm and 5pm.

Cairnsmill Caravan Park CAMPSITE **£**
(☎ 01334-473604; www.cairnsmill.co.uk; Largo Rd; tent without/with car £10/18, bunkhouse per person

£20; ☺ Apr-Oct; P 🤖 ⛱ 🐾) About a mile west of St Andrews on the A915, this campsite has brilliant views over the town. Facilities are good, though it's very caravan-heavy. There's also a simple bunkhouse.

★ Fairways of St Andrews
B&B ££

(☎ 01334-479513; www.fairwaysofstandrews.co.uk; 8a Golf Pl; d £98-130; 🛜) Just a few paces from golf's most famous 18th green, this is more like a boutique hotel than a B&B, despite its small size. There are just three super-stylish rooms; the best on the top floor is huge and has its own balcony with views over the Old Course.

★ Old Fishergate House
B&B ££

(☎ 01334-470874; www.oldfishergatehouse.co.uk; North Castle St; s/d £85/115; 🛜) This historic 17th-century town house, furnished with period pieces, is in a great location – the oldest part of town, close to the cathedral and castle. The two twin rooms are very spacious and even have their own sitting room. On a scale of one to 10 for quaintness, we'd rate it about a 9½. Cracking breakfast menu features fresh fish and pancakes.

34 Argyle St
B&B ££

(☎ 07712 863139; www.34argylestreet.com; 34 Argyle St; r from £120; 🛜) A new guesthouse set in a fine old terrace just west of the town centre, the Argyle has spacious, hotel-quality bedrooms with huge modern bathrooms of dark tile, chrome and glass (two of the four have free-standing bath tubs). Little touches like drinks offered on arrival, fresh flowers and sweets add to the atmosphere of hospitality.

Five Pilmour Place
B&B ££

(☎ 01334-478665; www.5pilmourplace.com; 5 Pilmour Pl; s/d from £75/110; 🛜) Just around the corner from the Old Course, this luxurious and intimate spot offers stylish, compact rooms with plenty of designer touches. The king-size beds are especially comfortable, and the lounge area is an Edwardian-style retreat of leather armchairs, polished wood and swagged curtains.

Cameron House
B&B ££

(☎ 01334-472306; www.cameronhouse-sta.co.uk; 11 Murray Park; s/d £50/90; 🛜) Beautifully decorated rooms and warm, cheerful hosts make this a real home away from home on this guesthouse-filled street. The two single rooms share a bathroom. Prices drop £10 per person outside peak season.

Old Course Hotel
HOTEL £££

(☎ 01334-474371; www.oldcoursehotel.co.uk; Old Station Rd; r from £275; P 🤖 ⛱) A byword for golfing luxury, this hotel is right alongside the famous 17th green (Road Hold) on the Old Course and has huge rooms, excellent service and a raft of facilities, including a spa complex. Fork out the extra £50 or so for a view over the Old Course. You can usually find good deals online.

Hazelbank Hotel
HOTEL £££

(☎ 01334-472466; www.hazelbank.com; 28 The Scores; d £129-189; 🛜) Offering a genuine welcome, the family-run Hazelbank is the most likeable of the pleasingly old-fashioned hotels along The Scores. The more expensive front rooms have marvellous views along the beach and out to sea; prices drop significantly outside the height of summer. There's good karma if you are playing golf – Bobby Locke won the Open in 1957 while a guest here.

✖ Eating

Tailend
FISH & CHIPS £

(www.thetailend.co.uk; 130 Market St; takeaway £4-9; ☺ 11.30am-10pm) 🍴 Delicious fresh fish sourced from Arbroath, just up the coast, puts this a class above most chippies. It fries to order and it's worth the wait. The array of exquisite smoked delicacies at the counter will have you planning a picnic or fighting for a table in the licensed cafe out the back.

Northpoint Cafe
CAFE £

(☎ 01334-473997; northpoint@dr.com; 24 North St; mains £3-7; ☺ 8.30am-5pm Mon-Fri, 9am-5pm Sat, 10am-4pm Sun; 🛜) The cafe where Prince William famously met his future wife Kate Middleton while they were both students at St Andrews serves good coffee and a broad range of breakfast fare, from porridge topped with banana to toasted bagels, pancake stacks and classic fry-ups. It's bit too busy for its own good these days, so get in early for lunch.

★ Adamson
BRASSERIE ££

(☎ 01334-479191; http://theadamson.com; 127 South St; mains £13-27; ☺ noon-3pm & 5-10pm Mon-Fri, noon-10pm Sat-Sun; 🛜♿) Housed in the former post-office building, this loud and bustling brasserie panders to a youngish clientele of local families, well-heeled students and tourists with a crowd-pleasing menu of steaks and seafood, including local lobster with chips. Service can be over-eager or occasionally chaotic, but it all adds to the hectic buzz.

Mitchell's Deli
DELI, SCOTTISH ££

(☑ 01334-441396; www.mitchellsdeli.co.uk; 110-112 Market St; ⊙ 8am-11pm Mon-Thu, 8am-midnight Fri-Sat, 9am-11pm Sun; 🛜🧒) 🍽 Railway sleeper floors, cut-down workbench tables and seats upholstered with old tweed jackets lend a utilitarian air to this excellent deli-cafe-restaurant where local produce is king. Breakfast (served till noon) includes free-range eggs Benedict, organic porridge and Arbroath smokies, while the evening menu runs to mussels and chips, steak and ale pie, and pork chop with black pudding.

★ Vine Leaf
SCOTTISH £££

(☑ 01334-477497; www.vineleafstandrews.co.uk; 131 South St; 2-/3-course dinner £28/30; ⊙ 6-10pm Tue-Sat; 🧒) 🍽 Classy, comfortable and well established, the friendly Vine Leaf offers a changing menu of sumptuous Scottish seafood, game and vegetarian dishes. There's a huge selection within the set-price menu, all well presented, and an interesting, mostly old-world wine list. It's down a close off South St. Reservations recommended.

Seafood Restaurant
SEAFOOD £££

(☑ 01334-479475; www.theseafoodrestaurant.com; The Scores; lunch mains £15-17, 3-course dinner £50; ⊙ 10am-10pm) 🍽 The Seafood Restaurant occupies a stylish glass-walled room, built out over the sea, with polished wooden floors, crisp white linen, an open kitchen and panoramic views of St Andrews Bay. It offers top-notch seafood and an excellent wine list; look out for its special winter deals.

Drinking & Nightlife

St Andrews Brewing Co
MICROBREWERY1

(www.standrewsbrewingcompany.com; 177 South St; ⊙ noon-midnight; 🛜🧒🍸) Good beer, good food and good company are the order of the day in this friendly modern brewpub, with 16 beers on tap (inlcuding several of their own brews), more than 170 varieties in bottles, and around 30 craft gins.

Eden Mill Distillery
DISTILLERY

(☑ 01334-834038; www.edenmill.com; Main St, Guardbridge; tours per person £10; ⊙ 10am-6pm) This combined brewery and distillery produces both beer and whisky, but is especially known for its range of craft gins made using locally grown botanicals. Eden Mill is 4 miles northwest of town, on the road to Leuchars.

THE PEAT INN

This superb Michelin-starred restaurant, backed by a commodious suite of bedrooms, makes an ideal gourmet break. The chef makes a great effort to source premium-quality Scottish produce and presents it in innovative ways that never feel pretentious or over-modern. The **Peat Inn** (☑ 01334-840206; www.thepeatinn.co.uk; Peat Inn; 3-course lunch/dinner £22/50; ⊙ 12.30-2pm & 6.30-9pm Tue-Sat; 🅿) is 6 miles from St Andrews; head southwest on the A915 then turn right on the B940.

The split-level **bedrooms** (s/d £205/225; 🅿🛜) look over the garden and fields beyond. There are various all-inclusive offers available.

West Port
PUB

(www.thewestport.co.uk; 170 South St; ⊙ 9am-11.30pm Sun-Thu, to 12.30am Fri & Sat; 🛜🧒) Just by the town gate of the same name, this sleek, modernised pub has several levels and a great beer garden out the back. Cheap cocktails rock the uni crowd, mixed drinks are above average and there's some OK bar food.

Vic
BAR

(www.vicstandrews.co.uk; 1 St Mary's Pl; ⊙ 10am-2am; 🛜) Warehouse chic meets medieval conviviality in this strikingly restored student favourite. Walls plastered with black-and-white pop culture give way to a handsome, high-ceilinged bar with sociable long tables down the middle and an eclectic assortment of seating. Other spaces include a more romantic bar, a dance floor and a smokers' deck. There are regular events.

☆ Entertainment

Byre Theatre
THEATRE

(☑ 01334-475000; www.byretheatre.com; Abbey St; 🛜) This theatre company started life in a converted cow byre in the 1930s, but now occupies a flashy modern premises making clever use of light and space.

ⓘ Information

Free internet access is offered at the **library** (Church Sq; ⊙ 9.30am-5pm Mon, Fri & Sat, to 7pm Tue-Thu).

Services are available at **St Andrews Community Hospital** (☑ 01334-465656; www.nhsfife. org; Largo Rd).

St Andrews has a central **post office** (90-92 South St; ⊘ 9am-5.30pm Mon-Sat, noon-4pm Sun).

The helpful staff at **St Andrews Tourist Office** (☑ 01334-472021; www.visitstandrews.com; 70 Market St; ⊘ 9.15am-6pm Mon-Sat, 10am-5pm Sun Jul & Aug, shorter hrs rest of yr) have a good knowledge of the city and Fife.

❶ Getting There & Away

BUS

All buses leave from the **bus station** (Station Rd).

Anstruther £4.20, 25 minutes, hourly

Crail £4.20, 25 minutes, hourly

Dundee £4.80, 30 minutes, at least half-hourly

Edinburgh £11.70, two hours, hourly

Glasgow £11.70, 2½ hours, hourly

Stirling £8.20, two hours, every two hours Monday to Saturday

TRAIN

There is no train station in St Andrews itself, but you can take a train from Edinburgh (grab a seat on the right-hand side of the carriage for great sea views) to Leuchars (£13.90, one hour, half-hourly), 5 miles to the northwest. From here, buses leave regularly for St Andrews (£2.90, 10 minutes, every 10 minutes) or a taxi costs around £13.

❶ Getting Around

To order a cab, call **Golf City Taxis** (☑ 01334-477788; www.golfcitytaxis.co.uk).

Spokes (☑ 01334-477835; www.spokes cycles.com; 37 South St; per day/week £20/95; ⊘ 8.45am-5.30pm Mon-Sat) hires out mountain bikes.

T IN THE PARK

Scotland's biggest music festival, **T in the Park** (www.tinthepark.com), rocks this corner of the country over the second weekend in July. A major event, with six stages and top-name acts, it takes places in the grounds of Strathallan Castle near Auchterarder. It's a three-day affair, with camping available from the night before the kick-off. The site is 2.5 miles north of the A9, about halfway between Perth and Stirling.

East Neuk

This charming stretch of coast runs south from St Andrews to the headland at Fife Ness, then as far west as Earlsferry. Neuk is an old Scots word for 'corner', and it's certainly an appealing nook of the country to investigate, with picturesque fishing villages whose distinctive red pantiled roofs and crowstep gables are a legacy of centuries-old trading links with the Low Countries.

The Fife Coastal Path's most scenic stretches are in this area. It's easily visited from St Andrews, or even as a day trip from Edinburgh, but also offers many pleasant places to stay.

Crail

POP 1640

Pretty and peaceful, little Crail has a much-photographed stone-built harbour surrounded by quaint cottages with red-tiled roofs. The village's history is outlined in the Crail Museum (www.crailmuseum.org.uk; 62 Marketgate; ⊘ 11am-4pm Mon-Sat, 1-4pm Jun-Sep, Sat & Sun only May & Oct) FREE, but the main attraction is just wandering the winding streets and hanging out by the harbour. There are views across to the Isle of May.

Cambo Estate, 2.5 miles north of Crail, is the country seat of the Erskine family. Its walled garden (www.camboestate.com; Cambo Estate; admission £5.50; ⊘ 10am-5pm; ℗) at, with an ornamental stream running through the middle, is famously beautiful in spring and summer, but also in January and February when its spectacular displays of snowdrops are in flower. There are woodland walks which lead to the Fife coastal path, and the kids can feed potatoes to the estate's pigs.

Kingsbarns Distillery (☑ 01333-451300; www.kingsbarnsdistillery.com; East Newhall Farm, Kingsbarns; guided tour £10; ⊘ 10am-6pm Apr-Sep, to 5pm Mar & Oct, shorter hours Nov-Feb; ℗) ois a brand new distillery pened in 2015. It uses Fife-grown barley to create a distinctive lowland whisky – it takes a minimum of three years maturation to create a single malt, so the first bottles will go on sale in 2018. Meanwhile, one-hour tours explain the process and offer tasting sessions, while the on-site cafe serves excellent tea and scones.

Hazelton Guest House (☑ 01333-450250; www.thehazelton.co.uk; 29 Marketgate North; r £55-85; ☎) is a welcoming, walker-friendly B&B

in the centre of the village. The Victorian house is filled with period features, and the two top-floor rooms have great views across the rooftops to the Firth of Forth and the Isle of May.

Lobster Store (☑ 01333-450476; 34 Shoregate; mains £4-11; ◷ noon-4pm Tue-Sun Jun-Sep, Sat-Sun only Oct-Apr), a quaint little shack overlooking Crail harbour, serves dressed crab and freshly boiled lobster that has been caught locally. You can have a whole lobster (split) or lobster rolls. This is no-fuss takeaway – there's a single table out front, but you can find a place to sit and eat your catch anywhere around the harbour.

Crail is 10 miles southeast of St Andrews. Stagecoach (www.stagecoachbus.com) bus 95 between Leven, Anstruther, Crail and St Andrews passes through Crail hourly every day (£4.20, 25 minutes to St Andrews).

Anstruther

POP 3450

Once among Scotland's busiest fishing ports, cheery Anstruther (pronounced *enster* by locals) has ridden the tribulations of the declining fishing industry better than some, and now offers a pleasant mixture of bobbing boats, historic streets and visitors ambling around the harbour grazing on fish and chips, or contemplating a boat trip to the Isle of May.

◉ Sights & Activities

Scottish Fisheries Museum MUSEUM
(www.scotfishmuseum.org; East Shore; adult/child £8/free; ◷ 10am-5.30pm Mon-Sat, 11am-5pm Sun Apr-Sep, 10am-4.30pm Mon-Sat, noon-4.30pm Sun Oct-Mar) This excellent museum covers the history of the Scottish fishing industry in fascinating detail, including plenty of hands-on exhibits for kids. Displays include the **Zulu Gallery**, which houses the huge, partly restored hull of a traditional 19th-century Zulu-class fishing boat, redolent with the scents of tar and timber; and afloat in the harbour outside the museum lies the **Reaper**, a fully restored Fifie-class fishing boat built in 1902.

Isle of May NATURE RESERVE
The mile-long Isle of May, 6 miles southeast of Anstruther, is a spectacular nature reserve. Between April and July the island's cliffs are packed with breeding kittiwakes, razorbills, guillemots, shags and around 40,000 puffins. Inland are the remains of

the 12th-century St Adrian's Chapel, dedicated to a monk who was murdered on the island by the Danes in 875. Several boats operating out of Anstruther harbour offer trips to the island.

May Princess BOATING
(☑ 07957 585200; www.isleofmayferry.com; adult/child £25/11; ◷ Apr-Sep) A five-hour boat trip to the Isle of May, including two to three hours ashore, sails from three to seven times weekly (weather permitting) from April to September (daily July to September). You can make reservations and buy tickets at the harbour kiosk at least an hour before departure. Departure times vary depending on the tide – check times for the coming week or so by calling, or check the website.

🛏 Sleeping & Eating

★**Murray Library Hostel** HOSTEL £
(☑ 01333-311123; http://murraylibraryhostel.com; 7 Shore St; dm/d £20/56; ☏) Set in a handsome, red-sandstone, waterfront building that once housed the local library, this brand-new hostel is beautifully furnished and equipped. There are four- to six-bed dorms, many with sea views, plus private twins and doubles, a gorgeous modern kitchen and a comfortable lounge.

★**Spindrift** B&B ££
(☑ 01333-310573; www.thespindrift.co.uk; Pittenweem Rd; d/f £92/120; 🅿 ☏ 🐾) Arriving from the west, there's no need to go further than Anstruther's first house on the left, a redoubt of Scottish cheer and warm hospitality. The rooms are elegant, classy and extremely comfortable – some have views across to Edinburgh and one is a wood-panelled re-creation of a ship's cabin, courtesy of the sea captain who once owned the house.

There are DVD players and teddies for company, an honesty bar with characterful ales and malts, and fine company from your hosts. Breakfast includes porridge once voted the best in the kingdom. Dinner (£25 per person) is also available, but must be booked in advance.

Lahloo B&B ££
(☑ 01333-312202; www.lahloobandb.co.uk; 15 East Green; r £80; ☏ 🐾) The unusual name comes from the clipper ship whose captain once lived in this lovely Georgian house, but there's nothing spartan or sailor-like about the accommodation here – there are spotless, super-comfy rooms decorated in

soothing shades of cream and taupe, waterfall showers in the en suite bathrooms, and tea and scones on arrival.

Anstruther Fish Bar
FISH & CHIPS **£**

(☑ 01333-310518; www.anstrutherfishbar.co.uk; 42-44 Shore St; mains £5-8; ⊙ 11.30am-10pm) An award-winning chippie famous for its deep-fried haddock and chips, this place also offers classy takes on traditional takeaway dishes, including dressed crab and battered prawns (both locally caught).

★ Cellar Restaurant
SCOTTISH **£££**

(☑ 01333-310378; www.thecellaranstruther.co.uk; 24 East Green; 3-course lunch/dinner £28/48; ⊙ 12.30-1.45pm Thu-Sun, 6.30-9pm Wed-Sun, no lunch Thu Oct-Mar) 🍽 Tucked away in an alley behind the Scottish Fisheries Museum, the elegant and upmarket Cellar has been famous for its superb food and fine wines since 1982; under new management from 2014, and the recipient of a Michelin star in 2015, it is better than ever, offering a creative menu built around Scottish seafood, lamb, pork and beef. Advance booking essential.

❶ Getting There & Away

Stagecoach (www.stagecoachbus.com) bus X60 runs hourly from Edinburgh to Anstruther (£11.70, 2¼ hours) and on to St Andrews (£4.20, 25 minutes). Bus 95 links Anstruther to all the other East Neuk villages, including Crail (£2.15, 15 minutes, hourly).

Troywood

Three miles north of Anstruther, off the b9131 to St Andrews, is Scotland's Secret Bunker (www.secretbunker.co.uk; Troywood; adult/child/family £12/8/33; ⊙ 10am-6pm Mar-Oct, last admission 5pm; Ⓟ). This fascinating – and chilling – monument to Cold War paranoia was built in the 1950s to serve as one of Britain's regional command centres in the event of a nuclear war. Hidden 30m underground and encased in nearly 5m of reinforced concrete, it houses two levels of austere operation rooms, communication centres, broadcasting studios, weapons stores and dormitories, filled with period artefacts and museum displays. The bunker is 3 miles north of Anstruther, off the B9131 to St Andrews.

You can book a Go-Flexi (☑ 01334-840340; www.go-flexi.org) 'taxibus' from Anstruther, or take a standard taxi (around £20) from St Andrews.

An authentic example of Lowland Scottish domestic architecture, Kellie Castle (NTS; www.nts.org.uk; adult/child £10.50/7.50; ⊙ castle 10.30am-5pm daily Jun-Aug, Sat-Thu Apr-May & Sep, 10.30am-4pm Sat-Thu Oct; Ⓟ) has creaky floors, crooked little doorways, superb decorative plasterwork and some marvellous works of art. The original part of the building dates from 1360; it was enlarged to its present dimensions around 1606. It's set amid beautiful gardens (open year-round from 9.30am to 6pm or dusk), 3 miles northwest of Pittenweem on the B9171.

Pittenweem
POP 1490

Pittenweem is the main fishing port on the East Neuk coast, and there are lively morning fish sales at the harbour. The village is a great place to wander, with boats bobbing along the harbour front, and art galleries, cafes and craft shops on the High St a block above – the two linked by steep, narrow alleys.

The village name means 'place of the cave', referring to St Fillan's Cave (Cove Wynd; adult/child £1/free; ⊙ 10am-6pm). The cave was used as a chapel by a 7th-century missionary who reputedly possessed miraculous powers – apparently, when he wrote his sermons in the dark cave, his arm would throw light on his work by emitting a luminous glow. The cave is protected by a locked gate, but a key and information leaflet are available from the nearby Cocoa Tree Cafe at 9 High St.

Bus details for Pittenweem are the same as for Anstruther.

St Monans
POP 450

This ancient fishing village is named after a cave-dwelling saint who was probably killed by pirates. Apart from a historic windmill overlooking the sea, its main sight is the picturesque parish church, built in 1362 on the orders of a grateful King David II, who was rescued by villagers from a shipwreck in the Firth of Forth. It was burned by the English in 1544 but restored. The church commands sweeping views of the firth, and the past echoes inside its cold, whitewashed walls.

The range of fish on offer at Craig Millar @ 16 West End (☑ 01333-730327; www.16westend.com; 16 West End; lunch mains £15-25, 3-course dinner £45; ⊙ 12.30-2pm Wed-Sun, 6.30-9pm Wed-Sat) 🍽 changes daily at this comfortable but classy seafood restaurant on the harbour – oysters, scallops, cod, turbot, monkfish (the menu details the provenance of these sustainable catches) – so just swim with the tide.

Stagecoach bus X60 runs daily from St Monans to St Andrews (£4.20, 35 minutes, hourly), via Anstruther.

Elie & Earlsferry

POP 680

These two attractive villages mark the south-western end of the East Neuk. There are great sandy beaches, two golf courses and good walks along the coast – seek out the **Chain Walk**, an adventurous scramble along the rocky shoreline at Kincraig Point, west of Earlsferry, using chains and steel rungs cemented into the rock (allow two hours, and ask local advice about tides before setting off). On a more relaxing note, there's nothing better than a lazy summer Sunday in Elie, watching the local team play cricket on the beach.

The **Ship Inn** (☑ 01333-330246; www.ship inn.scot; The Toft; mains £10-22; ⊘ food served noon-3pm & 5-9pm; 🐾), down by Elie harbour, is a pleasant and popular place for a bar lunch of local seafood. The best bit is the outside tables overlooking the wide sweep of the bay.

The hourly Stagecoach (www.stagecoach bus.com) X60 bus service from St Andrews stops at Elie (£4.20, 40 minutes), and continues to Edinburgh (£11.70, two hours). Bus 95 links Elie to the other East Neuk villages, including Anstruther (£3.10, 17 minutes, hourly) and Crail (£4.20, 35 minutes, hourly).

LOWLAND PERTHSHIRE & KINROSS

For sheer scenic variety, Perthshire is the pick of Scotland's counties and a place where everyone will find a special, personal spot. The county straddles the Highland border with Highland Perthshire (p322), stretching north from Dunkeld, while Lowland Perthshire ranges from the sedate streets of Perth itself, a fair city with a fabulous attraction in lavish Scone Palace, to the rural market towns of Crieff and Blairgowrie. Kinross, once one of Scotland's smallest counties, is famous for lovely Loch Leven with its historic island castle, scenic walks and good trout fishing.

Perth

POP 46,970

Elegantly arranged along the banks of the Tay, Perth is a pleasantly liveable city with large tracts of enticing parkland surrounding an easily managed centre. The Scottish parliament once sat here and, save for the murder of King James I at Blackfriars monastery in 1437, Perth might have been the capital of Scotland. Instead it built its fortune on the weaving, dyeing, fishing and brewing industries, and gave the country some of its most famous brand names, including Pullars (dry cleaning), Dewars and Bells (both whisky). To learn more about the city's history, pick up a copy of the *Walks Around Historic Perth* booklet at the museum.

On the outskirts of Perth lies Scone Palace, a country house of staggering luxury built alongside the ancient crowning place

---

GLENEAGLES

Deep in rural Perthshire near the town of Auchterarder lies **Gleneagles Hotel** (☑ 01764-662231; www.gleneagles.com; Gleneagles, near Auchterarder; r from £535; 🅿 @ 🛜 🏊), one of Scotland's most famous resorts. Not your typical bed-and-breakfast, this is a no-holds-barred luxury spot with three championship golf courses, Michelin-starred Andrew Fairlie – often referred to as Scotland's best restaurant (open for dinner Tuesday to Saturday) – and a variety of extravagantly elegant rooms and suites.

Despite the imposing building and kilted staff snapping to attention, it's welcoming to non-VIPs, and family-friendly to boot, with lots of activities available. There's Gleneagles train station if you wish to arrive sustainably; if not, limousine transfers are available. Check the website for deals.

The **Phoenix Falconry** (☑ 01764-682823; www.scottishfalconry.co.uk; Easterton Farm, by Gleneagles; per person £30-180), just along the road from Gleneagles Hotel, near Auchterarder, offers experiences that range from bird-handling sessions to all-day hunts with a harris hawk, hunting rabbits that have been flushed from their burrows using a ferret.

of Scotland's kings. The palace is a must-see, and the town itself – known as the Fair City – is endowed with fine galleries and good restaurants, and is within easy striking distance of both Edinburgh and Glasgow.

◉ Sights

★ Scone Palace
PALACE

(☑01738-552300; www.scone-palace.co.uk; Scone Estate; adult/child £11/8; ⊙9.30am-6pm May-Sep, 10am-5pm Easter-Apr & Oct, last admission 1hr before closing; P) 'So thanks to all at once and to each one, whom we invite to see us crowned at Scone.' This line from *Macbeth* indicates the importance of Scone (pronounced 'skoon') as the coronation place of Scottish monarchs. The original palace of 1580, laying claim to this historic site, was rebuilt in the early 19th century as a Georgian mansion of extreme elegance and luxury. The self-guided tour takes you through a succession of sumptuous rooms filled with fine French furniture and noble portraits.

Scone has belonged for centuries to the Murray family, Earls of Mansfield, and many of the objects have a fascinating history attached to them (friendly guides are on hand to explain). Each room has comprehensive multilingual information; there are also panels relating histories of some of the Scottish kings crowned at Scone over the centuries. Outside, peacocks – each named after a monarch – shriek and strut around the magnificent grounds, which incorporate woods, a butterfly garden and a maze.

Ancient kings were crowned on **Moot Hill**, now topped by a chapel next to the palace. It's said that the hill was created by bootfuls of earth, brought by nobles attending the coronations as an acknowledgement of the king's rights over their lands, although it's more likely the site of an ancient motte-and-bailey castle. Here in 838, Kenneth MacAlpin became the first king of a united Scotland and brought to Scone the **Stone of Destiny**, on which Scottish kings were ceremonially invested. In 1296 Edward I of England carted this talisman off to Westminster Abbey, where it remained for 700 years before being returned to Scotland in 1997 (it now sits in Edinburgh Castle, but there are plans afoot to return it to Perth).

Scone Palace is 2 miles north of Perth; from the town centre, cross the bridge, turn left, and keep bearing left until you reach the gates of the estate. From here, it's a another half-mile to the palace (about 45 minutes' walk). Various buses from town stop here; the tourist office can advise.

Fergusson Gallery
GALLERY

(www.pkc.gov.uk/article/6471/The-Fergusson-Gallery; cnr Marshall Pl & Tay St; ⊙10am-5pm Tue-Sat year-round, noon-4.30pm Sun Apr-Oct) FREE Beautifully set in a circular cast-iron building that was once a waterworks, this gallery exhibits an extensive collection of paintings by the Scottish Colourist JD Fergusson in a most impressive display. Fergusson spent time in Paris, and the influence of artists such as Matisse on his work is evident; his voluptuous female portraits against a tropical-looking Riviera background are memorable, as is the story of his lifelong relationship with noted Scottish dancer Margaret Morris.

Perth Museum & Art Gallery
MUSEUM

(www.pkc.gov.uk/perthmuseumandartgallery; cnr George & Charlotte Sts; ⊙10am-5pm Tue-Sat year-round, 10am-5pm Sun Apr-Oct) FREE This elegant neoclassical building, based on the Pantheon in Rome, houses one of the oldest purpose-built museums in Britain. There's a varied range of exhibits covering the city's history and natural environment, from portraits of dour lairds to carved Pictish stones and a plaster cast of Britain's record rod-caught salmon (29kg, hooked on the River Tay in 1922) along with an account of its capture by the angler, Georgina Ballantine.

Black Watch Museum
MUSEUM

(☑01738-638152; www.theblackwatch.co.uk; Hay St; adult/child £7.50/3.50; ⊙9.30am-4.30pm Apr-Oct, 10am-4pm Nov-Mar; P) Housed in Balhousie Castle on the edge of North Inch park, this museum honours what was once Scotland's foremost regiment (it was subsumed into the new Royal Regiment of Scotland in 2006). Formed in 1725 to control rebellious Highlanders following the Jacobite uprising of 1715, the Black Watch fought in numerous famous campaigns, re-created here with paintings, memorabilia and anecdotes.

St John's Kirk
CHURCH

(www.st-johns-kirk.co.uk; St John's St; ⊙10am-4pm Mon-Sat May-Sep) FREE Imposing St John's Kirk was founded in 1126 and is still the centrepiece of the town. In 1559 John Knox preached a powerful sermon here that helped begin the Reformation, inciting a frenzied destruction of Scone abbey and other religious sites. Perth used to be known as St John's Town after this church,

Perth

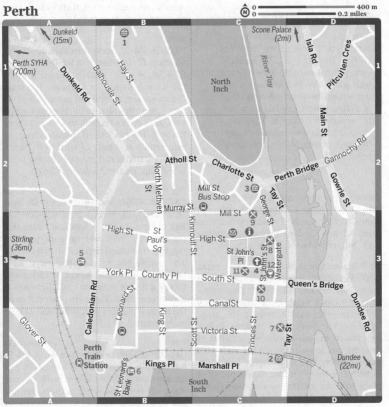

Perth

and the local football team is still called St Johnstone.

🛏 Sleeping

Heidl Guest House　　　　　　　　B&B **£**

(☎ 01738-635031; http://heidlguesthouse.co.uk; 43 York Pl; s/d/f £34/50/100; P 🛜) It may lack a little character from outside, but the Heidl is an excellent guesthouse and enthusiastic owners have mad a good job of renovation,

leaving the seven bedrooms very spruce indeed. Most are en suite; the two that aren't have separate but private bathrooms. Writer John Buchan (of *The Thirty-Nine Steps* fame) was born in the house opposite.

Perth SYHA　　　　　　　　　　HOSTEL **£**

(☎ 01738-877800; www.syha.org.uk; Crieff Rd; dm/tw £26/58; ☺ late Jun–late Aug) A 20-minute stroll from the centre, this summer-only hostel is set in a student residence at Perth

FAIR CITY FESTIVAL

If you're in Perth in the last two weeks of May, you'll come across **Perth Festival of the Arts** (☎01738-621031; www.perthfestival.co.uk), a low-profile but high-quality arts festival. Various venues around town host a diverse range of cultural events; don't be surprised to see some big-name bands (Jools Holland is a regular) or quality ballet troupe appearing at very reasonable prices.

College. The rooms are all en-suite twins, with good share kitchens and common rooms. Turn into the Brahan entrance on Crieff Rd, and the hostel is by the large car park. Numerous buses stop outside.

★**Pitcullen Guest House** B&B ££
(☎01738-626506; www.pitcullen.co.uk; 17 Pitcullen Cres; d/f £78/140; P🖘) This excellent B&B has a much more contemporary look than other guesthouses on this strip. Great-looking fabrics and modern styling give the rooms an upbeat feel, and lots of thought has gone into making your stay more comfortable, with things like fridges with free drinks in the rooms, plenty of plugs to make recharging easy and handy maps on the walls.

Parklands HOTEL ££
(☎01738-622451; www.theparklandshotel.com; 2 St Leonard's Bank; s/d £114/129; P🖘) This relaxing hotel occupies a luxurious villa set amid lush hillside gardens overlooking the parklands of the South Inch. While the rooms preserve the character of this beautiful building, formerly the residence of the town's mayors, they also offer modern conveniences and plenty of style. There's a great terrace and garden area to lap up the Perthshire sun.

✕ Eating & Drinking

Santé INTERNATIONAL ££
(☎01738-449710; www.sante-winebar.co.uk; 10 St John's Pl; tapas £4-8, 3-course dinner £19; ⏱9.30am-10pm Sun-Thu, to 11pm Fri-Sat; 🖘) This laid-back wine bar and restaurant mixes up Spanish, French and Scottish cuisine with an informal approach to dining out – you can order a selection of tapas or a chargrilled steak, or choose from a seafood menu (in

season). As you'd expect, there's also a good selection of wines by the glass.

Breizh BISTRO, FRENCH ££
(☎01738-444427; www.cafebreizh.co.uk; 28 High St; mains £7-17; ⏱9am-9pm Sun-Thu, to 9.30pm Fri & Sat; 🖈) This funkily French bistro – the name is Breton for Brittany – is a treat. Dishes are served with real panache, and the salads, featuring all sorts of delicious ingredients, are a feast of colour, texture and subtle flavours. The blackboard specials offer great value and a real taste of northwest France, including traditional *galettes* (Breton buckwheat pancakes with savoury fillings).

Pig'Halle FRENCH ££
(☎01738-248784; www.pighalle.co.uk; 38 South St; mains £10-19; ⏱noon-3pm & 5.30-9pm Sun-Wed, to 10pm Thu-Sat) A spacious bistro that presents the very best of pork products through traditional regional French cuisine. The sample platter of charcuterie is fabulous value, there are succulent mains and there's a decent selection of Gallic wines to accompany them. There are other dishes on the menu if pig ain't your thing, and a cheap early dinner deal.

Paco's INTERNATIONAL ££
(☎01738-622290; www.pacos.co.uk; 3 Mill St; mains £9-20; ⏱noon-11pm; 🖈) Something of an institution, Paco's keeps Perthers coming back over and over, perhaps because it would take dozens of visits to even try half the menu. There's something for everyone: steak, seafood, pizza, pasta and Mexican, all served in generous portions. The fountain-tinkled terrace is the place for a sunny day.

★**63 Tay Street** SCOTTISH £££
(☎01738-441451; www.63taystreet.com; 63 Tay St; mains lunch £13, dinner £23; ⏱noon-2pm Thu-Sat, 6.30-9pm Tue-Sat; 🖈) 🍴 Classy and warmly welcoming, this understated restaurant is Perth's best, featuring a lightly decorated dining area, excellent service and quality food. In a culinary Auld Alliance, French influence is applied to the best of Scottish produce to produce memorable game, seafood, beef and vegetarian plates.

Greyfriars Bar PUB
(www.perth-bars.co.uk; 15 South St; ⏱11am-11pm Mon-Sat, 12.30-11pm Sun) The smallest and friendliest pub in Perth serves up live music (usually Thursday and Saturday), great fish and chips, and fine ales from the local In-

veralmond Brewery – try a pint of Ossian, a golden ale with a fresh, zesty, hoppy flavour.

ℹ Information

Internet access is available at **AK Bell Library** (www.pkc.gov.uk/AKBell; York Pl; ⊘ 9.30am-5pm Wed & Fri, to 8pm Tue & Thu, to 1pm Sat).

Perth Royal Infirmary (☏ 01738-623311; www.nhstayside.scot.nhs.uk; Taymount Tce) is west of the town centre.

The usual services are available at the **post office** (WH Smith, High St; ⊘ 9am-5.30pm Mon-Sat, noon-4pm Sun).

Perth Tourist Office (☏ 01738-450600; www.perthshire.co.uk; 45 High St; ⊘ 9.30am-5pm Mon-Sat & 11am-4pm, longer hours Jul-Aug) is efficiently run.

ℹ Getting There & Away

BUS

Citylink (www.citylink.co.uk) coaches operate from the **bus station** (Leonard St), with services to/from the following:

Dundee £7.70, 40 minutes, hourly
Edinburgh £12.30, 1¾ hours, hourly
Glasgow £12.40, 1¾ hours, hourly
Inverness £22.10, three hours, at least five daily
Stirling £9.20, 55 minutes, hourly

Further buses run from the Broxden Park & Ride on Glasgow Rd; this is connected regularly with the bus station by shuttle bus. These include **Megabus** (www.megabus.com) discount services to Aberdeen, Edinburgh, Glasgow, Dundee and Inverness.

Stagecoach (www.stagecoach.com) buses serving local Perthshire destinations depart from Mill St. A Tayside Megarider ticket gives you seven days travel in Perth & Kinross and Dundee & Angus for £27.

TRAIN

Trains run between Perth and various destinations, including the following:

Dundee £7.90, 20 to 30 minutes, twice hourly, fewer on Sunday
Edinburgh £16.20, 1½ hours, at least hourly Monday to Saturday, every two hours Sunday
Glasgow £16.20, 1½, at least hourly Monday to Saturday, every two hours Sunday
Pitlochry £13.60, 30 minutes, two hourly, fewer on Sunday
Stirling £8, 30 minutes, one or two per hour

Kinross & Loch Leven

The town of Kinross sits on the banks of pretty Loch Leven, a haven for walkers, cyclists and anglers. Just east of the town sits the recently restored **Kinross House** (http://kinrosshouse.com), the finest Palladian mansion in Scotland, built by Sir William Bruce in 1693. Sadly it's not open to the public (it can be rented by the super-rich), but you can get a glimpse of it from the lochside trail.

Evocative **Lochleven Castle** (HS; www.historicenvironment.scot; Kinross Pier; adult/child incl boat ride £5.50/3.30; ⊘10am-5.15pm Apr-Sep, to 4.15pm Oct, last sailing 1hr before closing; P) served as an island fortress and prison from the late 14th century; its most famous captive was Mary, Queen of Scots, who was incarcerated here in 1567. Her famous charms bewitched Willie Douglas, who managed to get hold of the cell keys to release her, then rowed her across to the shore. The castle is now roofless but basically intact and makes for an atmospheric visit, crossing to the island by boat (included in admission fee).

One of the best all-abilities hiking and biking routes in Scotland, **Loch Leven Heritage Trail** (www.lochlevenheritagetrail.co.uk) is this scenic 14-mile circuit of Loch Leven, linking Kinross Pier, the RSPB Loch Leven nature reserve, and Loch Leven's Larder. Allow two hours to cycle the trail or five hours to walk it; you can hire bikes and mobility scooters at Kinross Pier.

The circuit offers great views of the Lomond Hills and even a sandy beach northeast of Kinross.

Three miles east of Kinross, **Loch Leven's Larder** (☏ 01592-841000; http://lochlevenslarder.com; Channel Farm; mains £7-10; ⊘ 9.30am-5.30pm; P🔊♿🐕) 🅿 is a family-run farm shop and restaurant overlooking Loch Leven. It is the ideal place to enjoy fresh local food, much of it from the family's own farm, whether it's a breakfast of soft-boiled free-range eggs with hot buttered toast, a platter of Scottish cheeses, or a lunch of Arbroath smoked haddock quiche with potato salad.

There's an outdoor terrace with a panorama over the loch, a children's playground, and a footpath that connects to the Loch Leven Heritage Trail, making it an ideal break on a walking or cycling circuit of the loch.

Stagecoach bus X55 runs between Kinross and Perth (£6, 35 minutes, hourly). In the other direction it goes to Edinburgh (£8.70, 1½ hours, hourly).

1. Doune Castle (p186) 2. Dunstaffnage Castle (p291)
3. Glamis Castle (p218) 4. Caerlaverock Castle (p165)

BILL MCKELVIE / SHUTTERSTOCK ©

Scottish Castles

Scotland is home to more than 1000 castles, ranging from meagre 12th-century ruins to magnificent Victorian mansions. They all began with one purpose: to serve as fortified homes for the landowning aristocracy. But as society became more settled and peaceful, defensive features gave way to ostentatious displays of wealth and status.

Curtain Wall Castles

Norman castles of the 12th century were mainly of the 'motte-and-bailey' type, consisting of earthwork mounds and timber palisades. The first wave of stonebuilt castles emerged in the 13th century, characterised by massive curtain walls up to 3m thick and 30m tall to withstand sieges, well seen at Dunstaffnage Castle and Caerlaverock Castle.

Tower Houses

The appearance of the tower house in the 14th century marks the beginning of the development of the castle as a residence. Clan feuds, cattle raiders and wars between Scotland and England meant that local lords built fortified stone towers in which to live, from diminutive Smailholm Tower in the Borders to impressive Doune Castle near Stirling.

Artillery Castles

The arrival of gunpowder and cannon in the 15th century transformed castle design, with features such as gun loops, round towers, bulwarks and bastions making an appearance. Forbidding Hermitage Castle is a prime example of a castle adapted for artillery defence.

Status Symbols

The Scottish Baronial style of castle architecture, characterised by a profusion of pointy turrets, crenellations and stepped gables, had its origins in 16th- and 17th-century castles such as Craigievar and Castle Fraser, and reached its apotheosis in the royal residences of Glamis and Balmoral.

Upper Strathearn

The Highland villages of Comrie and St Fillans in upper Strathearn are surrounded by forests and bare, craggy hilltops where deer and mountain hares live in abundance.

Comrie is a cute litte village that played its part in the history of science – on its western edge stands the **Earthquake House**, a tiny stone building that was the world's first seismic observatory. It was built in 1874 to monitor earth tremors in the vicinity of the Highland Boundary Fault, which runs nearby. There are many excellent local walks, a favourite being to the spectacular gorge and waterfall known as the **Deil's Cauldron**, 1 mile north of the village.

St Fillans enjoys an excellent location at the eastern end of scenic **Loch Earn**, which reflects the silhouettes of distant peaks. The loch has good **fishing** for brown trout and pike – you can buy permits (£11 for one day) from the village shop in St Fillans.

The **Four Seasons** (☑ 01765-685333; www.thefourseasonshotel.co.uk; St Fillans; d from £114; ☺ Mar-Dec; P 🗻 🐾) is a historic hotel – the Beatles stayed here while on tour in 1964 – that has been given a classy modern makeover. Two beautifully appointed lounges and an atmospheric wee bar enjoy great views over the loch. The superior rooms – worth the upgrade – have the best vistas, and there are also six chalets nestled in the slopes behind the hotel. There are many activities to choose from, including waterskiing, quad biking and pony trekking, and a noted fine-dining restaurant.

The foodie epicentre of Upper Strathearn, **Hansen's Kitchen** (☑ 01764-670253; www.hansenskitchen.com; Drummond St, Comrie; mains £4-6; ☺ 8am-5pm Mon-Sat, 10am-4pm Sun; 🍴) 🌱 is a hugely popular delicatessen and cafe (there's barely a dozen seats crammed into the crowded interior) serving superb coffee, cheese and charcuterie platters, and lunch dishes such as home-baked panini stuffed with salami, mozzarella and pesto. If you can't get a table, grab some takeaway and head for the riverside benches beneath the church.

Comrie is 24 miles west of Perth, and St Fillans is about 5 miles further west. Buses run from Perth via Crieff to Comrie (£3.70, one hour, roughly hourly Monday to Saturday, every two hours Sunday) and St Fillans (£5.40, 1½ hours, five daily Monday to Saturday).

Crieff

POP 7370

Elegant Crieff is an old resort-style town, as popular with tourists today as it was in Victorian times. It sits in a valley amid some glorious Perthshire countryside and, with excellent eating and accommodation options, it's a fine base for exploring this part of the country.

◉ Sights

Famous Grouse Experience DISTILLERY
(http://experience.thefamousgrouse.com; Hosh; standard tour adult/concession £10/9; ☺ 10am-6pm Apr-Oct, 10am-5pm Nov-Mar; P) At the old Glenturret Distillery, the highly rated Famous Grouse Experience has a better-than-average one-hour distillery tour that details the making of malt whisky and the blending process to create Famous Grouse whisky. There's also a dizzying audiovisual that takes you on a grouse's flight around Scotland. Two tiny drams are included in the standard tour; more expensive tours offer more detailed tasting sessions. The distillery is 1 mile north of Crieff.

🛏 Sleeping & Eating

Comrie Croft HOSTEL, CAMPSITE £
(☑ 01764-670140; www.comriecroft.com; Braincroft; campsites per person £10, dm/s/d £20/32/64; P @ 🗻 🐾) 🌱 A rustic, hospitable place, Comrie Croft has a bit of everything: camping; a pleasant, airy hostel; and Sami-style tepees (£85 per night) with wood stove that sleep up to four. Activities include mountain biking (purpose-built trails, bike hire available), fishing, walking, lots of games for the kids and plenty of places to just laze about. It's 4 miles west of Crieff on the A85.

★ **Merlindale** B&B ££
(☑ 01764-655205; www.merlindale.co.uk; Perth Rd; s/d £70/95; ☺ Mar-Nov; P 🗻) Georgian architecture meets generous hospitality at this excellent guesthouse at the eastern end of town. The four fabulous rooms all have individual character, and two have sumptuous bathrooms with free-standing tubs. There's a comfy lounge/library, the owner is a Cordon Bleu–trained chef, and thoughtful touches abound.

Comely Bank Guest House B&B ££
(☑ 01764-653409; www.comelybankguesthouse.co.uk; 32 Burrell St; s/d £52/77; 🗻 🐾) Just down-

THE LIBRARY OF INNERPEFFRAY

Scotland's oldest lending library (founded in 1680), **Innerpeffray Library** (☑ 01764-652819; www.innerpeffraylibrary.co.uk; Innerpeffray; adult/child £7.50/free; ⊙ 10am-12.45pm & 2-4.45pm Wed-Sat, 2-4pm Sun Mar-Oct, by appointment only Nov-Feb; P) houses a huge collection of rare, interesting and ancient books, some of them 500 years old. If you have any interest in books you could easily spend half a day here in the company of voluntary guides who will point out interesting volumes, or find ancient books on subjects that interest you. The library is signposted along a farm road, about 5 miles southeast of Crieff off the B8062.

Next to the library is **Innerpeffray Chapel**, built in 1507 as a private Catholic chapel for the Drummond family (who also founded the library). It contains some fragments of painted plaster, and the remarkable **Faichney monument** (1707), an ornately carved gravestone that reveals the mason's pride in his family.

hill from Crieff's main street, Comely Bank is homely and neat as a pin. The downstairs double is huge and could accommodate four at a pinch, while upstairs rooms are equally appealing and are still a good size.

★**Yann's at Glenearn House**　FRENCH ££
(☑ 01764-650111; www.yannsatglenearnhouse.com; Perth Rd; mains £13-21; ⊙ 6-9pm Wed-Sun, noon-2pm Sun; P🐾🍽) On the main road heading east out of town, Crieff's most popular restaurant is run by the eponymous Savoyard who believes in keeping the menu straightforward and traditional, serving French comfort-food classics such as steak-frites, fondue and onion soup with a touch of contemporary flair. There's also luxury B&B **accommodation** (r £95; P🐾🍽) available.

Delivino　CAFE, DELI ££
(www.delivino.net; 6 King St; mains £8-12, sharing platters £16; ⊙ 9am-6pm Mon-Thu, to 9pm Fri & Sat, noon-4pm Sun) Delivino is an elegant cafe just down from the square on the main street. It offers something for everyone, from Crieff ladies-who-lunch to travellers looking for a light bite. An extensive selection of antipasti allows you to graze several flavours at a time, while delicious bruschetta and pizza, accompanied by a glass of Italian red, make this Crieff's best lunch option.

★**Barley Bree**　SCOTTISH £££
(☑ 01764-681451; www.barleybree.com; 6 Willoughby St, Muthill; mains lunch £11-15, dinner £20-25; ⊙ noon-2pm & 6.45-9pm Wed-Sat, noon-3pm & 6-9pm Sun; P🐾) 🌱 Set in the pretty village of Muthill (pronounced *mooth*-il), 3 miles south of Crieff, the Barley Bree is a delightfully rustic restaurant with rooms. Wooden floorboards, stone fireplace, stacked logs

and deer antlers set the scene for dishes of fine Scottish seafood, beef and game, and half a dozen luxurious bedrooms (double from £110) tempt you to stay the night.

ℹ Information

Crieff Tourist Office (☑ 01764-652578; www.perthshire.co.uk; ⊙ 10am-4pm Mon, Tue, Fri & Sat Apr-Sep, to 3pm Oct-Mar)

ℹ Getting There & Away

Hourly buses link Crieff with Perth (£2.90, 40 minutes), less frequently on Sunday; and Stirling (£3.30, one hour, four to 10 daily).

Blairgowrie & Around

Blairgowrie is a compact market town on the banks of the River Ericht, famed for its salmon fishing. Formerly a flax spinning centre, the town today is the hub of Scotland's soft fruits industry – the fields for miles around are ripe with raspberries and strawberries, for sale in season from kiosks on the edge of town.

About 5 miles east of Blairgowrie, **Alyth** is a charming historic village clustered along the banks of the Alyth Burn, which is crisscrossed picturesquely by several stone and iron footbridges. Ask at Blairgowrie's tourist office for the *Walk Auld Alyth* leaflet.

Off the A94 and 8 miles east of Blairgowrie, **Meigle** is well worth the trip for those with a fascination for Pictish sculptured stones, which can be viewed at the **Meigle Museum** (HS; ☑ 01828-640612; www.historicenvironment.scot; Dundee Rd, Meigle; adult/child £4.50/2.70; ⊙ 9.30am-5.30pm Apr-Sep, closed Oct-Mar).

Blairgowrie is the start and finish point for the Cateran Trail (www.caterantrail.org), a circular 64-mile waymarked path that leads you through the mountains around Glenshee on the southern fringe of the Cairngorms National Park. The first mile or so along the banks of the River Ericht, as far as the waterfall at Cargill's Leap and the former flax mill at Keathbank, makes an excellent short walk.

Blairgowrie's prosperous past has left a legacy of spacious Victorian villas. Many, like Gilmore House (☎01250-872791; www.gilmorehouse.co.uk; Perth Rd; d £70-84; P🐾), have been turned into B&Bs, but few as successfully as this welcoming haven. There are three gorgeously fitted-out en suite bedrooms, two guest lounges and a hearty breakfast built around seasonal local produce.

One of Blaigowrie's most popular eateries, the Dalmore Inn (☎01250-871088; www.dalmoreinn.com; Perth Rd, Blairgowrie; mains £10-25; ⊙10am-9pm; P🐾) 🌿 finds inventive ways to present the best of local produce, with dishes such as Arbroath smokie and smoked trout risotto, and venison and black pudding sausages with spring onion mash and onion gravy. The inn is on the southern edge of town, on the A93 towards Perth.

Buses run to Blairgowrie from Perth (£3.40, 50 minutes, half-hourly) and from Dundee (£3.60, one hour, hourly), and there are hourly buses between Blairgowrie and Alyth (£1.80, 17 minutes), and Blairgowrie and Meigle (£2.40, 30 minutes).

Northeast Scotland

Why Go?

Many visitors pass by this corner of the country in their headlong rush to the tourist honeypots of Loch Ness and Skye. But they're missing out on a part of Scotland that's just as beautiful and diverse as the more obvious attractions of the west.

Within its bounds you'll find two of Scotland's four largest cities: Dundee, the city of jute, jam and journalism, cradle of some of Britain's favourite comic characters, and home to Captain Scott's Antarctic research ship, the *Discovery;* and Aberdeen, the granite city, an economic powerhouse fuelled by the riches of North Sea oil.

Angus is a region of rich farmland and scenic glens dotted with the mysterious stones left behind by the ancient Picts, while Aberdeenshire and Moray are home to the greatest concentration of Scottish Baronial castles in the country, and dozens of distilleries along the River Spey.

Best Places to Eat

➡ Drouthy Cobbler (p236)

➡ Castlehill (p215)

➡ Parlour Cafe (p214)

➡ Tolbooth Restaurant (p233)

➡ Café 52 (p228)

Best Places to Sleep

➡ Dutch Mill Hotel (p228)

➡ 24 Shorehead (p233)

➡ Globe Inn (p227)

➡ Malmaison (p213)

➡ The Jays (p228)

When to Go
Aberdeen

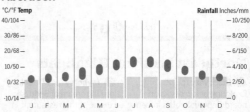

Jun/Jul Classic boats large and small fill Portsoy harbour for the Scottish Traditional Boat Festival.

Sep Revellers gather for a whisky and music festival in Dufftown.

Dec Spectacular fireball ceremony in Stonehaven on Hogmanay (New Year's Eve).

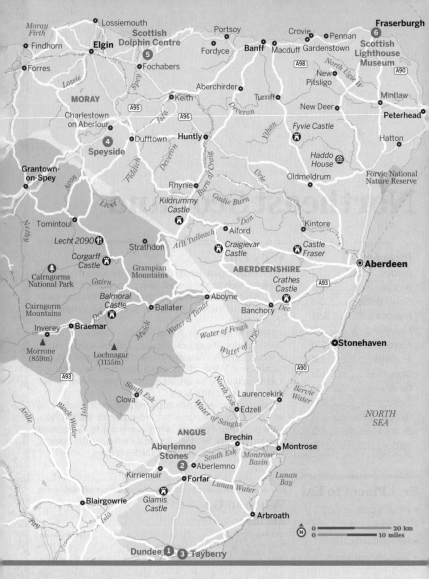

Northeast Scotland Highlights

1 Discovery (p212) Exploring below decks on board Captain Scott's famous polar exploration vessel in Dundee.

2 Aberlemno Stones (p220) Meditating on the meaning of the mysterious Pictish stones of Angus.

3 Tayberry (p217) Tucking into the cream of Scottish cuisine at this restaurant in Broughty Ferry.

4 Speyside (p237) Being initiated into the mysteries of malt whisky on a Speyside distillery tour.

5 Scottish Dolphin Centre (p234) Learning about the Moray Firth's bottlenose dolphins at Spey Bay.

6 Scottish Lighthouse Museum (p233) Discovering the heritage of Scotland's maritime tradition.

ℹ Getting Around

You can pick up a public transport map from tourist offices and bus stations. For timetable information, call **Traveline** (☎ 0871-200 2233; www.travelinescotland.com).

BUS

The Dundee to Aberdeen route is served by **Scottish Citylink** (www.citylink.co.uk) buses. **Stagecoach** (www.stagecoachbus.com) is the main regional bus operator, with services linking all the main towns and cities.

Stagecoach offers a **Moray Megarider ticket** (£29.50) that gives seven days unlimited bus travel around Elgin as far as Findhorn, Dufftown and Fochabers, and an **Aberdeen Zone 6 Megarider ticket** (£42.50) that allows seven days unlimited travel on all its services in Aberdeenshire, as far as Montrose, Braemar and Huntly.

TRAIN

The Dundee–Inverness railway line passes through Arbroath, Montrose, Stonehaven, Aberdeen, Huntly and Elgin.

DUNDEE & ANGUS

Angus is a fertile farming region stretching north from Dundee – Scotland's fourth-largest city – to the Highland border. It's an attractive area of broad straths (valleys) and low, green hills contrasting with the rich, red-brown soil of freshly ploughed fields. The romantic Angus Glens finger their way into the foothills of the Grampian Mountains, while the scenic coastline ranges from the red-sandstone cliffs of Arbroath to the long, sandy beaches around Montrose. This was the Pictish heartland of the 7th and 8th centuries, and many interesting Pictish symbol stones survive here.

Apart from the crowds visiting newly confident Dundee and the coach parties shuffling through Glamis Castle, Angus is a bit of a tourism backwater and a good place to escape the crowds.

Dundee

POP 147,300

London's Trafalgar Sq has Nelson on his column, Edinburgh's Princes St has its monument to Sir Walter Scott and Belfast has a statue of Queen Victoria outside City Hall. Dundee's City Sq, on the other hand, is graced – rather endearingly – by the bronze figure of Desperate Dan. Familiar to generations of British school children, Dan is one of the best-loved cartoon characters from the children's comic the *Dandy*, published by Dundee firm DC Thomson since 1937.

Dundee enjoys perhaps the finest location of any Scottish city, spreading along the northern shore of the Firth of Tay, and boasts tourist attractions of national importance in Discovery Point and the Verdant Works museum. Add in the attractive seaside town of Broughty Ferry and the Dundonians themselves – among the friendliest, most welcoming and most entertaining people you'll meet – and Dundee is definitely worth a stopover.

The waterfront around Discovery Point was undergoing a massive redevelopment at time of research, centred around the construction of the **V&A Museum of Design** (a branch of London's Victoria & Albert Museum, scheduled to open in summer 2018). In the meantime, be prepared for construction sites, temporary street layouts and traffic diversions on the approach to the Tay Bridge.

History

During the 19th century Dundee grew from its trading port origins to become a major player in the shipbuilding, whaling, textile and railway engineering industries. Dundonian firms owned and operated most of the jute mills in India (jute is a natural fibre used to make ropes and sacking), and the city's textile industry employed as many as 43,000 people – little wonder Dundee earned the nickname 'Juteopolis'.

Dundee is often called the city of the 'Three Js' – jute, jam and journalism. According to legend, it was a Dundee woman, Janet Keillor, who invented marmalade in the late 18th century; her son founded the city's famous Keillor jam factory. Jute is no longer produced, and when the Keillor factory was taken over in 1988, production was transferred to England. Journalism still thrives, however, led by the family firm of DC Thomson. Best known for children's comics such as the *Beano* and the *Dandy*, and regional newspapers including the *Press and Journal*, Thomson is now the city's largest employer.

In the late 19th and early 20th centuries Dundee was one of the richest cities in the country – there were more millionaires per head of population here than anywhere else in Britain – but the textile and engineering industries declined in the second half of the 20th century, leading to high unemployment and urban decay.

In the 1960s and '70s Dundee's cityscape was scarred by ugly blocks of flats, office buildings and shopping centres linked by unsightly concrete walkways and most visitors passed it by. Since the mid-1990s, however, Dundee has reinvented itself as a tourist destination, and a centre for banking, insurance and high-tech industries, while its waterfront is undergoing a major redevelopment. It also has more university students – one in seven of the population – than any other town in Europe, except Heidelberg.

◉ Sights

★ V&A Museum of Design   MUSEUM
(🖉 01382-305665; www.vandadundee.org; Riverside Esplanade) FREE The centrepiece of Dundee's revitalised waterfront is this stunning new building designed by Japanese architect Kengo Kuma. When it opens (scheduled in summer 2018) it will house an outpost of London's V&A museum of art and design. Exhibitions will showcase the work of Scottish designers past and present, from famous names such as Charles Rennie Mackintosh to modern creatives such as fashion designer Holly Fulton, alongside the best of art and design from around the world.

★ Discovery Point   MUSEUM
(www.rrsdiscovery.com; Discovery Quay; adult/child/family £9.25/5.50/27; ⊘10am-6pm Mon-Sat, 11am-6pm Sun Apr-Oct, to 5pm Nov-Mar; P ♿) The three masts of Captain Robert Falcon Scott's famous polar expedition vessel the RRS *Discovery* provide a historic counterpoint to the modern architecture of the V&A Design Museum. Exhibitions and audiovisual displays in the neighbouring visitor centre provide a fascinating history of both the ship and Antarctic exploration, but *Discovery* herself is the star attraction. You can visit the bridge, the galley and the mahogany-panelled officers' wardroom, and poke your nose into the cabins used by Scott and his crew.

The ship was built in Dundee in 1900, with a wooden hull at least half a metre thick to survive the pack ice, and sailed for the Antarctic in 1901 where it spent two winters trapped in the ice. From 1931 it was laid up in London where its condition steadily deteriorated, until it was rescued by the efforts of Peter Scott (Robert's son) and the Maritime Trust, and restored to its 1925 condition. In 1986 the ship was given a berth in its home port of Dundee, where it became a symbol of the city's regeneration.

A joint ticket that gives entry to both Discovery Point and the Verdant Works costs £16/9/43 per adult/child/family.

★ Verdant Works   MUSEUM
(www.verdantworks.com; West Henderson's Wynd; adult/child/family £9.25/5.50/27; ⊘10am-6pm Mon-Sat, 11am-6pm Sun Apr-Oct, shorter hours Nov-Mar; ♿) One of the finest industrial museums in Europe, the Verdant Works explores the history of Dundee's jute industry. Housed in a restored jute mill, complete with original machinery still in working condition, the museum's interactive exhibits and computer displays follow the raw material from its origins in India through to the manufacture of a wide range of finished products, from sacking to rope to wagon covers for the pioneers of the American West. The museum is 250m west of the city centre.

McManus Galleries   MUSEUM
(www.mcmanus.co.uk; Albert Sq; ⊘10am-5pm Mon-Sat, 12.30-4.30pm Sun) FREE Housed in a solid Victorian Gothic building designed by Gilbert Scott in 1867, the McManus Galleries are a city museum on a human scale – you can see everything there is to see in a single visit, without feeling rushed or overwhelmed. The exhibits cover the history of the city from the Iron Age to the present day, including relics of the Tay Bridge Disaster and the Dundee whaling industry.

Computer geeks will enjoy the Sinclair ZX81 and Spectrum (pioneering personal computers with a whole 16K of memory!) which were made in Dundee in the early 1980s.

HM Frigate Unicorn   MUSEUM
(www.frigateunicorn.org; Victoria Dock; adult/child £5/3; ⊘10am-5pm Apr-Oct, shorter hrs Nov-Mar) Dundee's second floating tourist attraction – unlike the polished and much-restored RRS *Discovery* – retains the authentic atmosphere of a salty old sailing ship. Built in 1824, the 46-gun *Unicorn* is the oldest British-built ship still afloat – she was mothballed soon after launching and never saw action. Wandering around below deck gives you an excellent impression of what it must have been like for the crew forced to live in such cramped conditions.

By the mid-19th century sailing ships were outclassed by steam and the *Unicorn* served as a gunpowder store, then later as a training vessel. When it was proposed to break up the ship for scrap in the 1960s, a preservation society was formed. The ship is berthed in Victoria Dock, just northeast of the Tay Road Bridge. The entry price includes a self-guided tour (also available in French and German).

Dundee Contemporary Arts ARTS CENTRE
(www.dca.org.uk; Nethergate; ⊙11am-6pm Tue, Wed & Fri-Sun, 11am-8pm Thu) **FREE** Pioneering the development of the city's Cultural Quarter from its opening in 1999, Dundee Contemporary Arts is a centre for modern art, design and cinema. The galleries here exhibit work by contemporary UK and international artists, and there are printmakers' studios where you can watch artists at work, or even take part in craft demonstrations and workshops. There's also the **Jute Cafe-Bar** (✆01382-909246; www.jutecafebar.co.uk; 152 Nethergate; mains £9-16; ⊙10am-9.30pm; 🛜👶).

City Square SQUARE
The heart of Dundee is City Sq, flanked to the south by the 1930s facade of **Caird Hall**, which was gifted to the city by a textile magnate and is now home to the City Chambers. A more recent addition to the square, unveiled in 2001, is a bronze statue of **Desperate Dan**, the lantern-jawed hero of children's comic the *Dandy* (he's clutching a copy in his right hand).

Dundee Law PARK
It's worth making the climb up Dundee Law (174m) for great views of the city, the two Tay bridges, and across to Fife. The **Tay Rail Bridge** – at just over 2 miles long, it was the world's longest when it was built – was completed in 1887. The 1.5-mile **Tay Road Bridge** was opened in 1966. Dundee Law is a short walk northwest of the city centre, along Constitution Rd.

The railway bridge replaced an earlier structure whose stumps can be seen alongside. The original bridge collapsed during a storm in 1879 less than two years after it was built, in the infamous **Tay Bridge Disaster**, taking a train and 75 lives along with it.

🛏️ Sleeping

Most of Dundee's city-centre hotels are business oriented and offer lower rates on weekends. B&Bs are concentrated along Broughty Ferry Rd and Arbroath Rd east of the city centre, and on Perth Rd to the west. If you don't fancy a night in the city, consider staying at the nearby seaside town of Broughty Ferry.

Accommodation in Dundee is usually booked solid when the Open golf tournament is staged at Carnoustie or St Andrews – check www.theopen.com for future dates and venues (it'll be in St Andrews in 2020).

Dundee Backpackers HOSTEL £
(✆01382-224646; www.hoppo.com/dundee; 71 High St; dm £17, s/tw from £25/45; @🛜) Set in a beautifully converted historic building, with clean, modern kitchen, pool room, and an ideal location right in the city centre. Can get a bit noisy at night, but that's because it's close to pubs and nightlife.

Athollbank B&B £
(✆01382-801118; www.athollbank.com; 19 Thomson St; s/d £27/46; 🛜🐾) A great-value B&B set on a quiet side street in the city's West End, Athollbank has smart, good-sized bedrooms (none are en suite, though) and is close to local pubs and restaurants.

Aabalree B&B £
(✆01382-223867; www.aabalree.com; 20 Union St; s/d £30/50; 🐾) This is a pretty basic B&B – there are no en suites, and no lift to the three floors – but the owners are welcoming (don't be put off by the dark entrance) and it couldn't be more central, close to both the train and bus stations. This makes it popular, so book ahead.

★ Malmaison BOUTIQUE HOTEL ££
(✆01382-339715; www.malmaison.com; 44 Whitehall Cres; r from £75; 🐾) Housed in a Victorian hotel building, this place has been refurbished in typical Malmaison style with period features such as intricate wrought-iron balustrades complemented by delightfully over-the-top modern decor. The rooms on the south side overlook the new waterfront development and, when that's complete, will have gorgeous views. Room rates are excellent value; check website for special offers.

Apex City Quay Hotel HOTEL ££
(✆0845-365 0000; www.apexhotels.co.uk; 1 West Victoria Dock Rd; r from £89; 🅿🛜🏊) Though it looks plain and boxy from the outside, the Apex sports the sort of stylish, spacious, sofa-equipped rooms that make you want to lounge around all evening munching chocolate in front of the TV. If you can drag yourself away from your room, there are spa treatments, saunas and Japanese hot tubs to enjoy.

The hotel is just east of the city centre, overlooking the city's redeveloping waterfront and close to the HM Frigate *Unicorn*.

Dundee

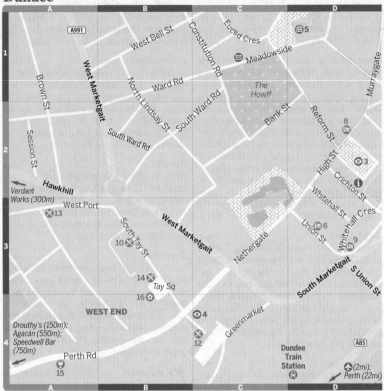

The map shows:
A991; West Bell St; Constitution Rd; Euclid Cres; 5; Meadowside; Murraygate; West Marketgait; North Lindsay St; Ward Rd; South Ward Rd; The Howff; Bank St; Reform St; 8; Brown St; Session St; Hawkhill; South Ward Rd; High St; 3; Crichton St; Verdant Works (300m); West Port; 13; West Marketgait; Whitehall St; Whitehall Cres; Union St; 6; Nethergate; 9; 10; South Tay St; 14; Tay Sq; 16; South Marketgait; S Union St; WEST END; 4; Greenmarket; Drouthy's (150m); Agacán (550m); Speedwell Bar (750m); Perth Rd; 15; 12; Dundee Train Station; (2mi); Perth (22mi); A85

Shaftesbury Lodge   HOTEL ££

(☎01382-669216; www.shaftesburylodge.co.uk; 1 Hyndford St; s/d from £60/80; �) The family-run, 12-room Shaftesbury was a Victorian mansion built for a jute baron and has many authentic period features, including a fine marble fireplace in the dining room. It's 1.5 miles west of the city centre, just off Perth Rd.

✕ Eating

★ Parlour Cafe   CAFE £

(☎01382-203588; theparlourcafe.co.uk; 58 West Port; mains £6-8; ☉8am-6pm Mon-Fri, to 4pm Sat, 10am-3pm Sun; ☜✐) ✿ Tiny but terrific, this friendly neighbourhood cafe is bursting with good things to eat including filled tortillas, savoury tarts, bean burgers, bagels and homemade soup, all freshly prepared using seasonal produce. Great coffee and cakes too, but be prepared to wait for a table or squeeze in among the locals.

Bridgeview Station   SCOTTISH £

(☎01382-660066; www.bridgeviewstation.com; Riverside Dr; lunch mains £7-10, 3-course dinner £22; ☉8am-6pm Sun-Tue, to 10pm Wed-Sat; P☜) Bridgeview enjoys a lovely setting in a red-brick Victorian railway station building on the western fringes of Dundee, with a view across the Firth of Tay. Covering everything from breakfast to dinner, the menu majors on fresh local produce with the lunch platters (seafood, vegetarian, or cheese and charcuterie) offering unbeatable value.

Pacamara   CAFE ££

(☎01382-527666; www.pacamara.co.uk; 302 Perth Rd; mains £12-21; ☉9am-5pm Mon-Fri, 9.30am-5pm Sat, 10am-4pm Sun; ☜✐) ✿ Lots of locals will tell you that this cool cafe serves the best coffee in Dundee, but it also does a roaring trade in tasty and offbeat breakfasts (£3.50 to £7, served till 11.30am) such as wild garlic scrambled egg with avocado and sourdough toast, and near-gourmet lunch

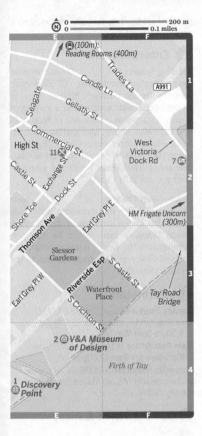

(İskender kebab is a favourite), it's no wonder that you have to book ahead at this colourful little restaurant, a 20-minute walk up Perth Rd from the centre. If you can't get a table, you can settle for takeaway.

★ **Castlehill**　　　　　　MODERN SCOTTISH **£££**
(☑ 01382-220008; www.castlehillrestaurant.co.uk; 22 Exchange St; 3-course lunch/dinner £19/36; ⊘ noon-2.30pm & 5.30-10pm Tue-Sat) Thought by many to be on its way to earning Dundee's first Michelin star, the Castlehill is passionate about Scottish produce (the chef is a keen forager for wild herbs and fungi) and invests a lot of imagination into turning out beautifully presented dishes made with Angus lamb, Perthshire pork and Shetland scallops – art on a plate.

Playwright　　　　　　　　　BISTRO **£££**
(☑ 01382-223113; www.theplaywright.co.uk; 11 Tay Sq; mains £25-27; ⊘ noon-2.30pm & 5-9.30pm Mon-Sat) ✐ Next door to the Dundee Rep Theatre (p216), and decorated with photos of Scottish actors, this innovative bistro serves a set lunch (two courses £13), pre-theatre menu (two/three courses £17/20, 5pm to 6.30pm) and a gourmet à la carte menu that concentrates on fine Scottish produce.

dishes such as tamarind-glazed roast lamb with squash purée and caramelised onions. Best to book a table.

Avery & Co　　　　　　　　　　CAFE **££**
(☑ 01382-201533; averyandco.co.uk; 34 South Tay St; mains £7-15; ⊘ 9am-9pm Mon-Fri, 10am-10pm Sat, 10am-4pm Sun; 🛜 ✐) Fresh, natural and local (with the occasional dash of Mexican) is the mantra at this utilitarian cafe (they make their own muesli), which serves everything from breakfast burritos to lunch platters of roast vegetable and hummus wholemeal wraps, to dinner dishes such as roast Scottish lamb on a bed of spiced quinoa, purple sprouting broccoli and salsa verde.

Agacán　　　　　　　　　　TURKISH **££**
(☑ 01382-644227; www.agacan.co.uk; 113 Perth Rd; mains £11-18; ⊘ 5-9.30pm Tue-Sun; 🌶) With a charismatic owner, quirky decor and wonderfully aromatic Turkish specialities

Drinking & Nightlife

Dundee has many lively pubs, especially in the West End and along West Port. The city's nightlife may not be as hot as Glasgow's, but there are plenty of places to go – pick up a free what's-on guide from the tourist office, or check out the What's On section of www.dundee.com. Tickets for most events are on sale at the Dundee Contemporary Arts centre (p213).

The Braes BAR
(☑ 01382-226344; www.braesdundee.co.uk; 14-18 Perth Rd; ☉ 10am-midnight Mon-Sat, 11am-midnight Sun; ☎) Students from the nearby university crowd the tables at this modern bar with its cute, Scandinavian-style decor (lots of colourfully painted wood panelling) and views across the rooftops to the Tay Bridge. A good range of craft beers and coffee are complemented by a decent choice of pub grub (mains £8 to £13, good vegetarian options).

Drouthy's PUB
(☑ 01382-202187; www.drouthysdundee.co.uk; 142 Perth Rd; ☉ 10am-midnight; ☎) A perfectly unpretentious local pub, serving a wide range of Scottish and international craft beers and an all-day menu of tempting pub grub (mains £7 to £11), including irresistible gourmet burgers. Live music in the basement club.

Speedwell Bar PUB
(www.mennies.co.uk; 165-167 Perth Rd; ☉ 11am-11pm Mon-Sat, 12.30pm-11pm Sun; ☎) Known to generations of Dundonians as 'Mennie's', this university district pub, 1½ miles west of the city centre, is the city's best preserved Edwardian bar, complete with acres of

polished mahogany, real ale on tap, and a choice of 150 malt whiskies.

☆ Entertainment

Reading Rooms LIVE MUSIC
(www.readingroomsdundee.com; 57 Blackscroft; admission free-£8) Dundee's hippest venue is an arty, bohemian hang-out in a run-down former library that hosts some of Scotland's best indie club nights. Live gigs have ranged from island singer-songwriter Colin MacIntyre (aka Mull Historical Society) to Glasgow guitar band Franz Ferdinand and Ayrshire rockers Biffy Clyro.

Dundee Rep Theatre DRAMA
(☑ 01382-223530; www.dundeereptheatre.co.uk; Tay Sq; ☉ box office 10am-6pm or start of performance) Dundee's main venue for the performing arts, the Rep is home to Scotland's only full-time repertory company and to the Scottish Dance Theatre.

ⓘ Information

Dundee Tourist Office (☑ 01382-527527; www.angusanddundee.co.uk; 16 City Sq; ☉ 9.30am-5pm Mon-Sat)
Main Post Office (4 Meadowside; ☉ 9am-5.30pm Mon-Fri, 9am-12.30pm Sat)
Ninewells Hospital (☑ 01382-660111; www.nhstayside.scot.nhs.uk) At Menzieshill, west of the city centre.

ⓘ Getting There & Away

AIR

Two and a half miles west of the city centre, **Dundee Airport** (www.hial.co.uk/dundee-airport) has daily scheduled services to London Stansted airport, Jersey and Amsterdam. A taxi from the city centre to the airport takes 10 minutes and costs around £5.

BUS

The bus station is northeast of the city centre. Some Aberdeen buses travel via Arbroath, others via Forfar.
Aberdeen £17.40, 1½ hours, hourly
Edinburgh £16.60, 1½ hours, hourly, some change at Perth
Glasgow £16.60, 1¾ hours, hourly
London £40, 11 hours; National Express, daily
Perth £7.70, 35 minutes, hourly
Oban £36.50, 5½ hours, three daily

TRAIN

Trains from Dundee to Aberdeen travel via Arbroath and Stonehaven.
Aberdeen £19.80, 1¼ hours, twice an hour

THE FORFAR BRIDIE

Forfar, the county town of Angus, is the home of Scotland's answer to the Cornish pasty: the famous Forfar bridie. A shortcrust pastry turnover filled with cooked minced beef, onion and gravy, it was invented in Forfar in the early 19th century. If you fancy trying one, head for **James McLaren & Son** (☑ 01382-462762; mclarenbakers.co.uk; 8 The Cross, Forfar; ☉ 8am-4.30pm Mon-Wed, Fri & Sat, 8am-1pm Thu), a family bakery bang in the centre of Forfar, which has been selling tasty, home-baked bridies since 1893.

Edinburgh £17.90, 1¼ hours, at least hourly

Glasgow £22, 1½ hours, hourly

Perth £7.90, 25 minutes

ⓘ Getting Around

The city centre is compact and is easy to get around on foot. For information on local public transport, check **Dundee Travel Info** (www. dundeetravelinfo.com).

BUS

City bus fares cost £1.50 to £2 depending on distance; buy your ticket from the driver (exact fare only – no change given).

CAR

Rental agencies include:

Arnold Clark (☑ 01382-225382; www.arnold clarkrental.com; East Dock St; ⊙ 8am-6pm Mon-Fri, 8am-4pm Sat, 9am-4pm Sun)

Europcar (☑ 01382-373939; www.europcar. co.uk; 45-53 Gellatly St)

TAXI

Tele Taxis (☑ 01382-825825; www.tele-taxis. co.uk)

Broughty Ferry

Dundee's attractive seaside suburb, known locally as 'The Ferry', lies 4 miles east of the city centre. It has a castle, a long, sandy beach and a number of good places to eat and drink. It's also handy for the golf courses at nearby Carnoustie.

◉ Sights

Broughty Castle Museum   MUSEUM

(www.leisureandculturedundee.com; Castle Green; ⊙ 10am-4pm Mon-Sat, 12.30-4pm Sun, closed Mon Oct-Mar; P) FREE A 16th-century tower that looms imposingly over the harbour, guarding the entrance to the Firth of Tay, houses a fascinating exhibit on Dundee's whaling industry, and the view from the top offers the chance of spotting seals and dolphins offshore.

🛏 Sleeping & Eating

Broughty Ferry is a more attractive place to stay than central Dundee, and has a good choice of B&Bs and hotels. There are campsites too, a few miles further east at Monifeith.

Fisherman's Tavern   B&B ££

(☑ 01382-775941; www.fishermanstavern-broughty ferry.co.uk; 10-16 Fort St; s/d from £50/76; 🛜) A delightful 17th-century terraced cottage just

a few paces from the seafront, the Fisherman's was converted into a pub in 1827. It now has 12 stylishly modern rooms, most with en suite, and an atmospheric pub.

Ashley House   B&B ££

(☑ 01382-776109; www.ashleyhousebroughtyferry. com; 15 Monifieth Rd; s/d £48/74; P 🛜 😊) This spacious and comfortable guesthouse has long been one of Broughty Ferry's best. Its five cheerfully decorated bedrooms come equipped with hotel-grade beds and DVD players; one has a particularly grand bathroom.

Hotel Broughty Ferry   HOTEL ££

(☑ 01382-480027; www.hotelbroughtyferry.com; 16 W Queen St; s/d from £79/88; P 🛜 😊) It may not look like much from the outside, but this is the Ferry's swankiest place to stay, with 16 beautifully decorated bedrooms, a sauna, a solarium and a small heated pool. It's only a five-minute stroll from the waterfront.

★ **Tayberry**   MODERN SCOTTISH ££

(☑ 01382-698280; www.tayberryrestaurant.com; cnr Brook St & Esplanade; 3-course lunch/dinner £22/36; ⊙ noon-2pm & 6-9pm Tue-Sat, noon-4pm Sun) 🍃 Neutral tones of cream and grey enriched with splashes of berry purple create a cool and understated atmosphere in which up-and-coming chef Adam Newth presents gorgeous and colourful confections using fresh and foraged local produce – dishes such as salmon with wild garlic, beetroot and cuttlefish dressing, or pork belly with carrot risotto, nasturtium and cumin, delight the eye as much as the palate.

Ship Inn   PUB FOOD ££

(☑ 01382-779176; www.theshipinn-broughtyferry. co.uk; 121 Fisher St; mains £10-19; ⊙ food served noon-2.30pm & 5-7.30pm) The Ship Inn is a snug, wood-panelled, 19th-century pub on the waterfront, which serves top-notch dishes ranging from gourmet haddock and chips to venison steaks; you can eat in the upstairs restaurant, or down in the bar (bar meals £8 to £10). It's always busy, so get there early to grab a seat.

ⓘ Getting There & Away

Dundee city bus 5 and Stagecoach bus 73 run from Dundee High St to Broughty Ferry (£2, 20 minutes) several times an hour from Monday to Saturday, and hourly on Sunday.

There are five trains daily from Dundee (£1.50, five to 10 minutes).

Glamis Castle

Looking every inch the Scottish Baronial castle, with its roofline sprouting a forest of pointed turrets and battlements, **Glamis Castle** (www.glamis-castle.co.uk; adult/child £11/8; 10am-5.30pm Apr-Oct, last entry 4.30pm; **P**) claims to be the legendary setting for Shakespeare's Macbeth. A royal residence since 1372, it is the family home of the earls of Strathmore and Kinghorne – the Queen Mother (born Elizabeth Bowes-Lyon; 1900–2002) spent her childhood at Glamis (pronounced 'glams') and Princess Margaret (the Queen's sister; 1930–2002) was born here.

The five-storey, L-shaped castle was given to the Lyon family in 1372, but was significantly altered in the 17th century. Inside, the most impressive room is the **drawing room**, with its vaulted plasterwork ceiling. There's a display of armour and weaponry in the haunted crypt and frescoes in the chapel (also haunted). **Duncan's Hall** is named for the murdered King Duncan from Macbeth (though the scene actually takes place in Macbeth's castle in Inverness). As with Cawdor Castle, the claimed Shakespeare connection is fictitious – the real Macbeth had nothing to do with either castle, and died long before either was built.

You can also look around the **royal apartments**, including the Queen Mother's bedroom. Hour-long guided tours (included in admission) depart every 15 minutes; the last tour is at 4.30pm.

Glamis Castle is 12 miles north of Dundee. There are two to four buses a day from Dundee (£6.45, 1½ hour) to Glamis; change at Forfar.

Arbroath

POP 23,900

Arbroath is an old-fashioned seaside resort and fishing harbour, home of the famous Arbroath smokie (a form of smoked haddock). The humble smokie achieved European Union 'Protected Geographical Indication' status in 2004 – the term 'Arbroath smokie' can only be used legally to describe haddock smoked in the traditional manner within an 8km radius of Arbroath.

👁 Sights

Arbroath Abbey   HISTORIC BUILDING
(HS; www.historicenvironment.scot; Abbey St; adult/child £5.50/3.30; 9.30am-5.30pm Apr-

Sep, 10am-4pm Oct-Mar) The picturesque, red-sandstone ruins of Arbroath Abbey, founded in 1178 by King William the Lion, dominate the town of Arbroath. It is thought that Bernard of Linton, the abbot here in the early 14th century, wrote the famous Declaration of Arbroath in 1320, asserting Scotland's right to independence; an exhibition in the beautifully preserved Abbot's House includes a replica of the declaration. You can climb part way up one of the towers for a grand view over the ruins.

St Vigeans Museum   MUSEUM
(HS; 01241-878756; www.historicenvironment. scot; St Vigeans Lane; adult/child £4.50/2.70; by appointment) About a mile north of Arbroath town centre, this cottage museum houses a superb collection of Pictish and medieval sculptured stones. The museum's masterpiece is the **Drosten Stone**, beautifully carved with animal figures and hunting scenes on one side, and an interlaced Celtic cross on the other (look for the devil perched in the top left corner). Phone ahead or ask at Arbroath Abbey to arrange a visit.

Signal Tower Museum   MUSEUM
(Ladyloan; 10am-5pm Tue-Sat; **P**) **FREE** This museum has displays dedicated to Arbroath's maritime heritage and the Bell Rock Lighthouse, which was built between 1807 and 1811 by the famous engineer Robert Stevenson (grandfather of writer Robert Louis Stevenson). It is housed in the elegant Signal Tower that was once used to communicate with the construction team working on the Bell Rock Lighthouse 12 miles offshore.

🏃 Activities

The coast northeast of Arbroath consists of dramatic red-sandstone cliffs riven by inlets, caves and natural arches. An excellent **clifftop walk** (pick up a leaflet from the tourist office) follows the coast for 3 miles to the quaint fishing village of **Auchmithie**, which claims to have invented the Arbroath smokie.

If you fancy catching your own fish, the **Marie Dawn** (07836 770609), **MV Ardent** (07543-005908; www.arbroathangling.co.uk) and **Girl Katherine II** (07752-470621; www. sea-angling.net) offer three-hour sea-angling trips (usually from 2pm to 5pm) out of Arbroath harbour for £15 to £20 per person, including tackle and bait.

🛏 Sleeping

Harbour Nights Guest House
B&B ££

(📞 01241-434343; www.harbournights-scotland. com; 4 The Shore; r from £75; 🛜) With a superb location overlooking the harbour, four stylishly decorated bedrooms and a gourmet breakfast menu, Harbour Nights is our favourite place to stay in Arbroath. Rooms 2 and 3, with harbour views, are a bit more expensive (from £80), but well worth asking for when booking.

Townhouse Hotel
HOTEL ££

(📞 01241-431577; townhousehotelarbroath.co.uk; 99 High St; r from £88; 🛜) The Townhouse, set in a restored Georgian-style building on Arbroath's main street, offers stylishly decorated if somewhat smallish rooms but with a superb location just a few minutes walk from Arbroath Abbey.

Old Vicarage
B&B ££

(📞 01241-430475; www.theoldvicaragebandb.co.uk; 2 Seaton Rd; s/d £80/100; 🅿🛜) 🍽 The three five-star bedrooms in this attractive Victorian villa have a pleasantly old-fashioned atmosphere, and the extensive breakfast menu includes Arbroath smokies. The house is on a quiet street close to the start of the clifftop walk to Auchmithie. Two-night minimum stay.

✕ Eating

But'n'Ben Restaurant
SCOTTISH ££

(📞 01241-877223; www.thebutnben.com; 1 Auchmithie; mains £8-26; ⏰ noon-2pm Wed-Mon, 6-9pm Mon & Wed-Sat, 4-5.30pm Sun; 👶) 🍽 Above the harbour in Auchmithie, this cosy cottage restaurant with open fireplace, rustic furniture and sea-themed art serves the best of local seafood – the Arbroath smokie pancakes are recommended – plus great homemade cakes and desserts, and high teas on Sunday (£16). Best to book ahead.

Old Brewhouse
SCOTTISH ££

(📞 01241-879945; www.oldbrewhousearbroath. co.uk; 1 High St; mains £8-13; 🛜) Located on the seafront east of the harbour, the Old Brewhouse has the scent of the North Sea in its nostrils, and also on its menu – choose from a pot of prawns, crab salad, haddock

---

PICTISH SYMBOL STONES

The mysterious carved stones that dot the landscape of eastern Scotland are the legacy of the warrior tribes who inhabited these lands 2000 years ago. The Romans occupied the southern half of Britain from AD 43 to 410, but the region to the north of the firths of Forth and Clyde – known as Caledonia – was abandoned as being too dangerous, and sealed off behind the ramparts of the Antonine Wall and Hadrian's Wall.

Caledonia was the homeland of the Picts, a collection of tribes named by the Romans for their habit of painting or tattooing their bodies. In the 9th century they were culturally absorbed by the Scots, leaving behind only a few archaeological remains, a scattering of Pictish place names beginning with 'Pit', and hundreds of mysterious carved stones decorated with intricate symbols, mainly in northeast Scotland. The capital of the ancient Southern Pictish kingdom is said to have been at Forteviot in Strathearn; Pictish symbol stones are found throughout this area and all the way up the eastern coast of Scotland into Sutherland and Caithness.

It is thought that the stones were set up to record Pictish lineages and alliances, but no-one is sure exactly how the system worked. They are decorated with unusual symbols, including z-rods (a lightning bolt?), circles (the sun?), double discs (a hand mirror?) and fantastical creatures, as well as figures of warriors on horseback, hunting scenes and (on the later stones) Christian symbols.

Local museums provide a free leaflet titled the *Angus Pictish Trail,* which will guide you to the main sites (there are similar leaflets for Aberdeenshire and Moray), while Historic Environment Scotland's **Pictish Stones** (www.pictishstones.org.uk) website details all the sites in Scotland. The finest assemblage of stones in their natural outdoor setting is at Aberlemno (p220), while there are excellent indoor collections at St Vigeans Museum (p218) and the Meigle Museum (p207).

The Pictish Trail by Anthony Jackson lists 11 driving tours, while *The Symbol Stones of Scotland* by the same author provides more detail on the history and meaning of the Pictish stones.

and chips, or Arbroath smokie done half a dozen ways (speciality of the house is a ramekin of Arbroath smokie and bacon topped with cheese).

Also offers B&B at £90 for a double room.

Gordon's Restaurant SCOTTISH **£££**
(☑ 01241-830364; www.gordonsrestaurant.co.uk; Main St, Inverkeillor; 3-course lunch £34, 4-course dinner £55; ⊙ 12.30-1.30pm Wed-Fri & Sun, 7-8.30pm Tue-Sun) ✐ Six miles north of Arbroath, in the tiny and unpromising-looking village of Inverkeillor, lies this hidden gem – an intimate and rustic eatery serving gourmet-quality Scottish cuisine. There are five comfortable bedrooms (single/double from £85/110) for those who don't want to drive after dinner.

ℹ Information

Visitor Centre & Tourist Office (☑ 01241-872609; Fishmarket Quay; ⊙ 10am-6pm Mon-Sat, noon-4pm Sun Apr-Oct, shorter hours Nov-Mar) Beside the harbour.

ℹ Getting There & Away

BUS

Bus 140 runs from Arbroath to Auchmithie (£2, 15 minutes, six daily Monday to Friday, three daily on Saturday and Sunday).

TRAIN

Trains from Dundee to Arbroath (£5.60, 20 minutes, two per hour) continue to Aberdeen (£19.40, 55 minutes) via Montrose and Stonehaven.

ABERLEMNO PICTISH STONES

The mysterious **Aberlemno Stones** (⊙ Apr-Oct) are among Scotland's finest Pictish carved stones. By the roadside there are three 7th- to 9th-century slabs with various symbols, including the z-rod and double disc; in the churchyard at the bottom of the hill there's a magnificent 8th-century stone displaying a Celtic cross, interlace decoration, entwined beasts and, on the reverse, scenes of the Battle of Nechtansmere (where the Picts vanquished the Northumbrians in 685). The site is 5 miles northeast of Forfar, on the B9134.

The stones are covered up from November to March; otherwise there's free access at all times.

Kirriemuir

POP 6100

Known as the Wee Red Town because of its close-packed, red-sandstone houses, Kirriemuir is famed as the birthplace of JM Barrie (1860–1937), writer and creator of the much-loved *Peter Pan*. A bronze statue of the 'boy who wouldn't grow up' graces the intersection of Bank and High Sts.

◉ Sights

JM Barrie's Birthplace MUSEUM
(NTS; www.nts.org.uk; 9 Brechin Rd; adult/child £6.50/5; ⊙ noon-5pm Thu-Mon Jul & Aug, Sat-Mon Apr-Jun & Sep) This is Kirriemuir's big attraction, a place of pilgrimage for *Peter Pan* fans from all over the world. The two-storey house where Barrie was born has been furnished in period style, and preserves Barrie's writing desk and the wash house at the back that served as his first 'theatre'.

Camera Obscura HISTORIC BUILDING
(www.kirriemuircameraobscura.com; admission by donation; ⊙ noon-4pm Sat-Mon Jun-Oct) This 1930s cricket pavilion on the hilltop northeast of the town centre was gifted to the town by JM Barrie himself, and is now managed by local volunteers. The camera obscura incorporated into the pointed turret uses a lens to project live images of the surrounding countryside onto a viewing table, and is one of only four in Scotland.

Gateway to the Glens Museum MUSEUM
(32 High St; ⊙ 10am-5pm Tue-Sat) **FREE** The old Town House opposite the Peter Pan statue dates from 1604 and houses the Gateway to the Glens Museum, a useful introduction to local history, geology and wildlife for those planning to explore the Angus Glens. It also contains a shrine to local boy made good, Bon Scott (1946–80), former lead singer of rock band AC/DC.

✕ Eating

★ **88 Degrees** CAFE, DELI **£**
(☑ 07449-345089; 17 High St; mains £3-7; ⊙ 9.30am-5pm Wed-Fri, 9.30am-4pm Sat, 10am-4pm Sun; ☑) ✐ This tiny deli serves the best cafe cuisine in the county – superb coffee (the cafe is named for the ideal temperature of an espresso), delicious cakes and traybakes, and handmade chocolates. Breakfast (served till 10.30am) includes mouth-watering omelettes made with free-range eggs.

Shopping

Star Rock Shop FOOD & DRINKS

(☑ 01575-572579; 27-29 Roods; ⊘ 10am-4.15pm Tue-Sat) For generations of local school kids, the big treat when visiting Kirriemuir was a trip to the Star Rock Shop. Established in 1833, it still specialises in traditional Scottish 'sweeties', arranged in colourful jars along the walls – including humbugs, cola cubes, pear drops, and the original Star Rock candy, still made to an 1833 recipe.

ℹ Information

The tourist office is in the Gateway to the Glens Museum.

ℹ Getting There & Away

Stagecoach bus 20 runs from Dundee to Kirriemuir (£4.30, one hour, hourly Monday to Saturday, every two hours Sunday) via Forfar (25 minutes; change here for Glamis).

Edzell

POP 900

The picturesque village of Edzell, with its broad main street and grandiose monumental arch, dates from the early 19th century when Lord Panmure decided that the original medieval village, a mile to the west, spoiled the view from Edzell Castle. The old village was razed and the villagers moved to this pretty, planned settlement.

Two miles north of Edzell, the B966 to Fettercairn crosses the River North Esk at Gannochy Bridge. From the lay-by just over the bridge, a wooden door in the stone wall gives access to a delightful footpath that leads along the wooded river gorge for 1.5 miles to a scenic spot known as the Rocks of Solitude.

The Lindsay earls of Crawford, Lord Panmure's predecessors as owners of Edzell Castle (HS; www.historicenvironment.scot; adult/child £5.50/3.30; ⊘ 9.30am-5.30pm Apr-Sep; ℙ), built the L-plan tower house in the 16th century. Sir David Lindsay, a cultured and well-travelled man, laid out this castle's beautiful pleasance in 1604 as a place of contemplation and learning. Unique in all of Scotland, this Renaissance walled garden is lined with niches for nesting birds, and sculptured plaques illustrating the cardinal virtues, the arts and the planetary deities.

Stagecoach bus 21 or 21A from Dundee (via Forfar and Brechin) stop at Edzell

(£6.85, 1½ hours, seven daily Monday to Friday, five on Saturday).

Brechin

POP 7480

The name of the local football team, Brechin City, proclaims this diminutive town's main claim to fame – as the seat of Brechin Cathedral (now demoted to a parish church) it has the right to call itself a city, albeit the smallest one in Scotland. Adjacent to the cathedral is a 32m-high round tower built around 1000 as part of a Celtic monastery. It is of a type often seen in Ireland, but one of only three that survive in Scotland. Its elevated doorway, 2m above the ground, has carvings of animals, saints and a crucifix.

Bus 140 goes from Arbroath to Brechin (£4.20, six daily Monday to Friday, three daily on Saturday and Sunday). Travelling north from Brechin requires a change of bus at Montrose.

Brechin's picturesque Victorian train station dates from 1897 and is now the terminus of the restored Caledonian Railway (www.caledonianrailway.com; 2 Park Rd; adult/child £8/6; ♿ 🚂), which runs steam trains along a 3.5-mile stretch of track to Bridge of Dun. Steam trains run on Sunday from June to August, and diesels on Saturday in July and August; check website for other dates.

From Bridge of Dun, it's a 15-minute sign-posted walk to the House of Dun (NTS; www.nts.org.uk; adult/child £10.50/7.50; ⊘ noon-5pm Sat-Wed Apr-Sep, noon-2.30pm Sat & Sun Oct-Nov; ℙ), a beautiful Georgian country house built in 1730.

ABERDEENSHIRE

Since medieval times Aberdeenshire and its northwestern neighbour Moray have been the richest and most fertile regions of the Highlands. Aberdeenshire is famed for its Aberdeen Angus beef cattle, its many fine castles and the prosperous 'granite city' of Aberdeen.

North of Aberdeen, the Grampian Mountains fall away to rolling agricultural plains pocked with small, craggy volcanic hills. This fertile lowland corner of northeastern Scotland is known as Buchan; the old Scots dialect called the Doric lives on in everyday use here (if you think the Glaswegian accent

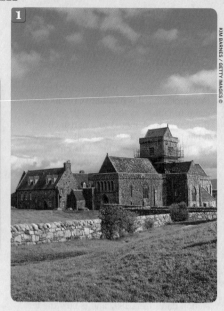

KIM BARNES / GETTY IMAGES ©

1. Iona Abbey (p288), Iona 2. Puffins in the Hebrides (p386)
3. Lochranza (p273), Arran 4. Sea stack, Orkney (p399)

MARK CAUNT / SHUTTERSTOCK ©

Scotland's Islands

Scotland's sweeping array of islands – 790 at last count, around a hundred of which are inhabited – defines the country's complex coastline. Ruins, from prehistoric religious centres to staunch castles, overlook landscapes where sheep crop lush grass, the scant remaining fisherfolk take on powerful seas, and urban professionals looking for a quieter life battle with unreliable wi-fi.

Geography & History

Though in the modern world these islands might seem remote outposts, Scotland's complex geography has meant that, from Celts through to Vikings and the Lords of the Isles, transport, trade and power are intimately tied to the sea. Today's lonely island stronghold was yesteryear's hub of connections spreading right across western and northern Britain and beyond.

Sights & Activities

For the visitor, there's bewildering scope. The once-Norse islands of Orkney and Shetland are Britain's northernmost parts, while the Hebrides guard the west coast like a storm shield against the mighty Atlantic. The choice is yours: for scenic splendour with hills to climb and memorable walks you might choose spectacular Skye, diverse Mull, accessible Arran or lonely Jura. Neolithic villages, standing stones, evocative prehistoric monuments? Head to far-flung Orkney, Shetland or the Outer Hebrides. Abbeys, castles or stately homes? Magical Iona, Bute, Coll, Barra or Westray. Beaches? Pick Harris or Tiree. Birdlife? Unst, the Uists, Fair Isle, Noss, North Ronaldsay or Staffa. Whisky? It's got to be Islay. A convivial pub, local seafood and a warm welcome? Take your pick of any and find yourself a snug cottage with a scent of the salty breeze and call it home for a day or three.

is difficult to understand, just try listening in on a conversation in Fraserburgh).

The Buchan coast alternates between rugged cliffs and long, long stretches of sand, dotted with picturesque little fishing villages such as Pennan, where parts of the film *Local Hero* were shot.

Aberdeen

POP 195,000

Aberdeen is the powerhouse of northeast Scotland, fuelled by the North Sea petroleum industry. Oil money has made the city as expensive as London and Edinburgh, and there are hotels, restaurants and clubs with prices to match the depth of oil-wealthy pockets. Fortunately, most of the cultural attractions, such as the excellent Maritime Museum and the Aberdeen Art Gallery, are free.

Known throughout Scotland as the granite city, much of the town was built using silvery-grey granite hewn from the now abandoned Rubislaw Quarry, at one time the biggest artificial hole in the ground in Europe. On a sunny day the granite lends an attractive glitter to the city, but when low, grey rain clouds scud in off the North Sea it can be hard to tell where the buildings stop and the sky begins.

Royal Deeside is easily accessible to the west, Dunnottar Castle to the south, sandy beaches to the north and whisky country to the northwest.

◉ Sights & Activities

◉ City Centre

Union St is the city's main thoroughfare, lined with solid, Victorian granite buildings. The oldest area is Castlegate, at the eastern end, where the castle once stood. When it was captured from the English for Robert the Bruce, the password used by the townspeople was 'Bon Accord' (good fellowship), which is now the city's motto.

In the centre of Castle St stands the 17th-century **Mercat Cross** (Castle St), bearing a sculpted frieze of portraits of Stuart monarchs. The Baronial heap towering over the eastern end of Castle St is the **Salvation Army Citadel** (Castle St), which was modelled on Balmoral Castle.

On the northern side of Union St, 200m west of Castlegate, is 17th-century **Provost Skene's House** (www.aagm.co.uk; Guestrow;

⊙10am-5pm Mon-Sat) FREE, one of the city's oldest buildings (at time of research closed to the public until completion of the surrounding Marischal Sq redevelopment). Another 100m to the west is **St Nicholas Church**, the so-called 'Mither Kirk' (Mother Church) of Aberdeen. The granite spire dates from the 19th century, but there has been a church on this site since the 12th century; the early 15th-century **St Mary's Chapel** survives in the eastern part of the church.

Aberdeen Maritime Museum　MUSEUM
(☑01224-337700; www.aagm.co.uk; Shiprow; ⊙10am-5pm Mon-Sat, noon-3pm Sun) FREE Overlooking the nautical bustle of Aberdeen harbour is the Maritime Museum, centred on a three-storey replica of a North Sea oil production platform, which explains all you ever wanted to know about the petroleum industry. Other galleries, some situated in **Provost Ross's House**, the oldest building in the city and part of the museum, cover the shipbuilding, whaling and fishing industries.

Sleek and speedy Aberdeen clippers were a 19th-century shipyard speciality, used by British merchants for the importation of tea, wool and exotic goods (opium, for instance) to Britain, and, on the return journey, the transportation of emigrants to Australia.

Aberdeen Art Gallery　GALLERY
(☑01224-523700; www.aagm.co.uk; Schoolhill; ⊙10am-5pm Tue-Sat, 2-5pm Sun) FREE Behind the grand facade of Aberdeen Art Gallery (at time of writing closed for refurbishment until winter 2017) is a cool, marble-lined space exhibiting the work of contemporary Scottish and English painters, such as Gwen Hardie, Stephen Conroy, Trevor Sutton and Tim Ollivier. There are also several landscapes by Joan Eardley, who lived in a cottage on the cliffs near Stonehaven in the 1950s and '60s and painted tempestuous oils of the North Sea and poignant portraits of slum children.

Among the Pre-Raphaelite works upstairs, look out for the paintings by Aberdeen artist William Dyce (1806–64), ranging from religious works to rural scenes.

Marischal College　HISTORIC BUILDING
(Broad St) Marischal College, founded in 1593 by the 5th Earl Marischal, merged with King's College (founded 1495) in 1860 to create the modern University of Aberdeen. The college's huge and impressive facade overlooking Broad St, in Perpendicular Gothic

style – unusual in having such elaborate masonry hewn from notoriously hard-to-work granite – dates from 1906 and is the world's second-largest granite structure (after L'Escorial near Madrid).

A recent renovation project saw the facade returned to its original silvery grey glory, and the building now houses Aberdeen City Council's headquarters; outside, Marischal Sq is undergoing redevelopment as a pedestrian plaza, creating controversy over plans for modern architecture juxtaposed with the college's neogothic facade.

Gordon Highlanders Museum MUSEUM
(www.gordonhighlanders.com; St Lukes, Viewfield Rd; adult/child £7/3.50; ⊙10am-4.30pm Tue-Sat Feb-Nov; P) This excellent museum records the history of one of the British Army's most famous fighting units, described by Winston Churchill as 'the finest regiment in the world'. Originally raised in the northeast of Scotland by the 4th Duke of Gordon in 1794, the regiment was amalgamated with the Seaforths and Camerons to form the Highlanders regiment in 1994. The museum is about a mile west of the western end of Union St – take bus 11 or X17 from Union St.

⊙ Aberdeen Harbour

Aberdeen has a busy, working harbour crowded with survey vessels and supply ships servicing the offshore oil installations, and car ferries bound for Orkney and Shetland. Despite all this traffic, the waters outside the harbour are rich in marine life – in summer dolphins, porpoises and basking sharks can be seen from cruise boats or from the headland of Girdle Ness, south of the harbour entrance.

Clyde Cruises WILDLIFE WATCHING
(01475-721281; www.clydecruises.com; Aberdeen Harbour; adult/child from £16/8; ⊙daily Jul-late Aug, Thu-Sun late Aug–mid Sep) Operates 45-minute cruises around Aberdeen's bustling commercial harbour, and 1¼-hours trips (adult/child £25/12) outside the harbour to look for dolphins and other marine wildlife. If you're driving, park in Union Sq car park (two hours £3) and walk across Market St to the harbour.

⊙ Aberdeen Beach

Just 800m east of Castlegate is a spectacular 2-mile sweep of clean, golden sand stretching between the mouths of the Rivers Dee and Don. At one time Aberdeen Beach was a good, old-fashioned British seaside resort, but the availability of cheap package holidays has lured Scottish holidaymakers away from its somewhat chilly delights. On a warm summer's day, though, it's still an excellent beach; when the waves are right, a small group of dedicated **surfers** ride the breaks at the south end.

The Esplanade sports several traditional seaside attractions, including **Codona's Amusement Park** (01224-595910; www.codonas.com; Beach Blvd; day pass per person £15; ⊙11am-6pm Jul & Aug, check website rest of year, closed Nov-Easter), complete with stomach-churning waltzers, dodgems, a roller coaster, log flume and haunted house. The adjacent **Sunset Boulevard** (www.codonas.com; Beach Blvd; day pass per person £15; ⊙10am-midnight year-round) is the indoor alternative, with tenpin bowling, dodgems, arcade games and pool tables.

Halfway between the beach and the city centre is **Aberdeen Science Centre** (01224-640340; www.aberdeensciencecentre.org/; 179 Constitution St; adult/child £5.75/4.50; ⊙10am-4pm Mon & Wed-Fri, to 5pm Sat & Sun;), a hands-on, interactive science centre.

You can get away from the funfair atmosphere by walking north towards the more secluded part of the beach. There's a **birdwatching hide** on the south bank of the River Don, between the beach and King St, which leads back south towards Old Aberdeen.

Bus 15 (eastbound) from Union St goes to the beach; or you can walk from Castlegate in 10 minutes.

⊙ Old Aberdeen

Just over a mile north of the city centre is the district called Old Aberdeen. The name is misleading – although Old Aberdeen is certainly old, the area around Castlegate in the city centre is older still. This part of the city was originally called Aulton, from the Gaelic for 'village by the stream', and this was Anglicised in the 17th century to Old Town.

Bus 20 from Littlejohn St (just north of Marischal College) runs to Old Aberdeen every 15 to 20 minutes.

St Machar's Cathedral CATHEDRAL
(www.stmachar.com; The Chanonry; ⊙9.30am-4.30pm) FREE The 15th-century St Machar's, with its massive twin towers, is a rare

Aberdeen

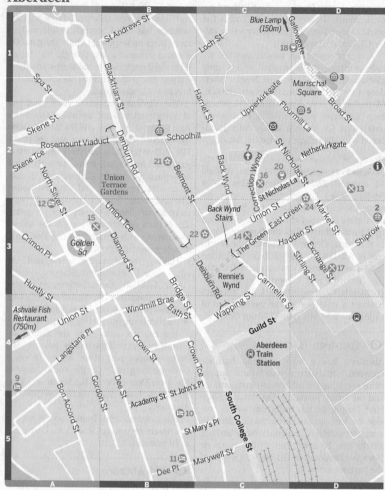

example of a fortified cathedral. According to legend, St Machar was ordered to establish a church where the river takes the shape of a bishop's crook, which it does just here. The cathedral is best known for its impressive **heraldic ceiling**, dating from 1520, which has 48 shields of kings, nobles, archbishops and bishops. Sunday services are held at 11am and 6pm.

King's College Chapel HISTORIC BUILDING
(College Bounds; ⊙10am-3.30pm Mon-Fri) FREE
It was here that Bishop Elphinstone established King's College, Aberdeen's first university (and Scotland's third), in 1495.

The 16th-century college chapel is easily recognised by its crown spire; the interior is largely unchanged since it was first built, with impressive stained-glass windows and choir stalls.

Festivals & Events

Held over the last weekend in September, **True North** (www.aberdeenperformingarts.com/truenorth) is a new four-day festival celebrating the balladeer tradition of northeast Scotland with a programme devoted to singer-songwriters from Scotland and all around the world.

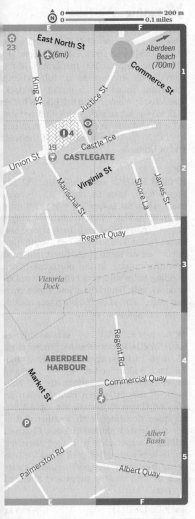

Aberdeen SYHA HOSTEL **£**

(SYHA; ☑ 01224-646988; www.syha.org.uk; 8 Queen's Rd; dm/d £20/50; @ 🛜) This unexceptional but good-value hostel, set in a granite Victorian villa, is a mile west of the train station. Walk west along Union St and take the right fork along Albyn Pl until you reach a roundabout; Queen's Rd continues on the western side of the roundabout.

⌂ Sleeping

There are clusters of B&Bs on Bon Accord St and Springbank Tce (both 400m southwest of the train station) and along Great Western Rd (the A93, a 25-minute walk southwest of the city centre). They're usually more expensive than the Scottish average and, with so many oil industry workers staying the night before flying offshore, single rooms are at a premium. Another side-effect of the industry is that rates tend to be significantly lower at weekends.

★ **Globe Inn** B&B **££**

(☑ 01224-624258; www.the-globe-inn.co.uk; 13-15 North Silver St; s/d £70/75) This popular pub has seven appealing, comfortable guest bedrooms upstairs, done out in dark wood with burgundy bedspreads. There's live music in the pub on weekends so it's not a place for early-to-bed types, but the price vs location factor can't be beaten. No dining room, so breakfast is continental, served on a tray in your room. Cheaper at weekends.

★ **The Jays** B&B **££**

(☏ 01224-638295; www.jaysguesthouse.co.uk; 422 King St; s/d from £50/100; P ﹇) Located halfway between the city centre (15 minutes walk) and Old Aberdeen (10 minutes walk), this elegantly decorated Edwardian villa is a cosy nest of hospitality, with welcoming owners who seemingly can't do enough to help their guests enjoy their stay. Popular, so book well in advance.

★ **Dutch Mill Hotel** HOTEL **££**

(☏ 01224-322555; www.dutchmill.co.uk; 7 Queens Rd; s/d £105/125; P ﹇) The grand, granite-hewn, Victorian-era mansions that line Queens Rd house financial offices, private schools, medical practices and the occasional hotel – this one has nine bedrooms with beautifully understated modern decor, a popular bar and a conservatory restaurant. Rates are almost halved at weekends.

Bauhaus Hotel BOUTIQUE HOTEL **££**

(☏ 01224-212122; www.thebauhaus.co.uk; 52-60 Langstane Pl; d/suite from £85/185; ﹇) Decor of exposed brick and leather wall panels, slate-lined bathrooms, and Corbusier armchairs in the more expensive suites, add a designer-ish touch to this centrally located, good-value hotel. Rates vary hugely, so check the website for special offers.

Butler's Guest House B&B **££**

(☏ 01224-212411; www.butlersguesthouse.com; 122 Crown St; s/d from £55/65; ﹇) Butler's is a cosy place with a big breakfast menu that includes fresh fruit salad, kippers and kedgeree as alternatives to the traditional fry-up (rates include a continental breakfast – cooked breakfast is £6.50 extra per person). There are cheaper rooms with shared bathrooms.

Brentwood Hotel HOTEL **££**

(☏ 01224-595440; www.brentwood-hotel.co.uk; 101 Crown St; s £45-85, d £59-95; P ﹇) The friendly and flower-bedecked Brentwood, set in a granite town house, is one of the most attractive hotels in the city centre. It's comfortable and conveniently located, but often busy during the week – weekend rates (Friday to Sunday) are much cheaper.

Adelphi Guest House B&B **££**

(☏ 01224-583078; www.adelphiguesthouse.com; 8 Whinhill Rd; s/d from £45/70; ﹇) A granite town house on a quiet street 400m south of the western end of Union St, the Adelphi offers clean, comfortable and brightly decorated rooms, just a 10-minute walk from the city centre.

✖ Eating

Ashvale Fish Restaurant FISH & CHIPS **£**

(www.theashvale.co.uk; 42-48 Great Western Rd; takeaway £5-10, sit-in £9-15; ⊙ 11.45am-10pm; ﹗) This is the flagship, 200-seat branch of the Ashvale, an award-winning fish-and-chip restaurant famed for its quality haddock. The Ashvale Whale – a 1lb fish fillet in batter (£12.45) – is a speciality; finish it off and you get a second one free (as if you'd want one by then!). It's 300m southwest of the west end of Union St.

★ **Café 52** BISTRO **££**

(☏ 01224-590094; www.cafe52.co.uk; 52 The Green; mains lunch £5, dinner £13; ⊙ noon-midnight Mon-Sat, to 4pm Sun; ﹇ ﹍) This little haven of laid-back industrial chic – a high, narrow space lined with bare stonework, rough plaster and exposed ventilation ducts – serves some of the finest and most inventive cuisine in the northeast (black pudding with wine-poached pear, smoked haddock with fennel, basil and lemon crayfish sauce), and at incredible prices considering the quality on offer.

★ **Adelphi Kitchen** MODERN SCOTTISH **££**

(☏ 01224-211414; www.theadelphikitchen.co.uk; 28 Adelphi Ln, Union St; mains £10-28; ⊙ noon-2.30pm & 5-10pm Tue-Sat; ﹇) ﹍ Cool and clever flavour combinations are the hallmark of this little gem hidden down an alley off Union St, a small but sophisticated space decorated with weathered timber and muted natural colours. Charcoal grilling is a speciality, with aged Aberdeen Angus beef and pulled pork given the barbecue treatment alongside seafood treats such as west coast scallops and Shetland mussels.

Sand Dollar Café CAFE **££**

(☏ 01224-572288; www.sanddollarcafe.com; 2 Beach Esplanade; mains £8-22; ⊙ 7.30am-9pm Mon-Wed, to 4pm Thu-Sat, to 6pm Sun, also 6-9pm Thu-Sat; ﹗) A cut above your usual seaside cafe – on sunny days you can sit at the wooden tables on the prom and share a bottle of chilled white wine, or choose from a menu that includes pancakes with maple syrup, homemade burgers and chocolate brownie with Orkney ice cream.

An evening bistro menu (mains £16 to £27) offers steak and seafood dishes; best to book for this. The cafe is on the esplanade, 800m northeast of the city centre.

Granite Park
MODERN SCOTTISH ££

(☎01224-478004; www.granitepark.co.uk; 8 Golden Sq; 2-/3-course lunch £16.50/20, dinner mains £17-32; ⊙noon-2.30pm & 5-9.30pm Mon-Sat, noon-8pm Sun) ✸ This smart and sophisticated restaurant and cocktail bar is a hidden gem, taking Scottish favourites such as venison, haddock and smoked salmon and giving them an Asian or Mediterranean twist. Gluten-free and dairy-free menus are also available. Best to book.

Musa Art Cafe
MODERN SCOTTISH ££

(☎01224-571771; www.musaaberdeen.com; 33 Exchange St; mains lunch £9-14, dinner £13-25; ⊙noon-11pm Tue-Sat; ☎✸) ✸ The bright paintings on the walls match the vibrant furnishings and smart gastronomic creations at this great cafe-restaurant, set in a former church. As well as a menu that focuses on quality local produce cooked in a quirky way – think haggis spring rolls with chilli and red-pepper jam – there are Brewdog beers from Fraserburgh, and interesting music, sometimes live.

Moonfish Café
MODERN SCOTTISH £££

(☎01224-644166; www.moonfishcafe.co.uk; 9 Correction Wynd; 2-/3-course dinner £33/38; ⊙noon-2pm & 6-9.30pm Tue-Sat) ✸ The menu of this funky little eatery tucked away on a back street concentrates on good-quality Scottish produce but draws its influences from cuisines all around the world, from simple smoked haddock with charred leeks and toasted rice, to mussels with saffron, chorizo and orange. Two-course lunch £14.

Silver Darling
SEAFOOD £££

(☎01224-576229; www.thesilverdarling.co.uk; Pocra Quay, North Pier; 2-/3-course lunch £19.50/25.50, dinner mains £17-26; ⊙noon-4pm & 6.30-9.30pm Mon-Sat) ✸ The Silver Darling (an old Scottish nickname for herring) is the place for a special meal, housed in a former Customs office at the entrance to Aberdeen harbour with picture windows overlooking the sea. Here you can enjoy fresh Scottish seafood prepared by a top French chef while you watch the porpoises playing in the harbour mouth. Bookings are recommended.

🍺 Drinking & Nightlife

Aberdeen is a great city for a pub crawl – it's more a question of knowing when to stop than where to start. There are lots of pre-club bars in and around Belmont St, with more traditional pubs scattered throughout the city centre.

BrewDog
BAR

(www.brewdog.com/bars/aberdeen; 17 Gallowgate; ⊙noon-midnight Mon-Thu, to 1am Fri & Sat, 12.30pm-midnight Sun; ☎) The original flagship bar of northeast Scotland's most innovative craft brewery brings a bit of industrial chic to Aberdeen's pub scene along with a vast range of guest beers from around the world.

Globe Inn
PUB

(www.the-globe-inn.co.uk; 13-15 North Silver St; ⊙11am-midnight, to 1am Fri & Sat) This lovely Edwardian-style pub with wood panelling, marble-topped tables and walls decorated with old musical instruments is a great place for a quiet lunchtime or afternoon drink. It serves good coffee, as well as real ales and malt whiskies, and has live music (rock, blues, soul) Friday to Sunday. It's also got probably the poshest pub toilets in the country.

Prince of Wales
PUB

(www.princeofwales-aberdeen.co.uk; 7 St Nicholas Lane; ⊙10am-midnight Mon-Thu, to 1am Fri & Sat, 11am-midnight Sun; ♿) Tucked down an alley off Union St, Aberdeen's best-known pub boasts the longest bar in the city, a great range of real ales and good-value pub grub. Quiet in the afternoons, but standing-room only in the evenings.

Blue Lamp
PUB

(www.jazzatthebluelamp.com; 121 Gallowgate; ⊙11am-midnight Mon-Thu, to 1am Fri & Sat, 12.30-11pm Sun) A long-standing feature of the Aberdeen pub scene, the Blue Lamp is a favourite student hang-out – a cosy drinking den with good beer, good *craic* (lively conversation) and regular sessions of live jazz and stand-up comedy. The pub is 150m north of the city centre, along Broad St.

Old Blackfriars
PUB

(www.oldblackfriars-aberdeen.co.uk; 52 Castlegate; ⊙11am-midnight Mon-Thu, 11am-1am Fri, 10am-1am Sat, 10am-11pm Sun; ☎) One of the most attractive traditional pubs in the city, with a lovely stone and timber interior, stained-glass windows and a relaxed atmosphere – a great place for an afternoon pint. Live folk music on Thursday from 9pm.

⭐ Entertainment

Belmont Filmhouse
CINEMA

(www.belmontfilmhouse.com; 49 Belmont St; ☎) The Belmont is a great little art-house cinema, with a lively programme of cult classics, director's seasons, foreign films and mainstream movies.

Cafe Drummond
LIVE MUSIC

(www.cafedrummond.com; 1 Belmont St) A long-established stalwart of Aberdeen's alternative music scene, Drummond is a crowded, grungy, student hang-out offering live gigs from up-and-coming local talent, and regular club nights extending into the wee hours of the night.

Tunnels
LIVE MUSIC

(www.thetunnels.co.uk; Carnegie's Brae) This cavernous, subterranean club – the entrance is in a road tunnel beneath Union St – is a great live-music venue, with a packed programme of up-and-coming Scottish bands. It also hosts regular DJ nights – check its Facebook page for the latest events.

Lemon Tree Theatre
PERFORMING ARTS

(www.aberdeenperformingarts.com; 5 West North St) Hosts an interesting programme of dance, music and drama, and often has live rock, jazz and folk bands playing. There are also children's shows, ranging from comedy to drama to puppetry.

ℹ Information

Aberdeen Royal Infirmary (☎ 0345-456 6000; www.nhsgrampian.org; Foresterhill) Medical services. About a mile northwest of the western end of Union St.

Aberdeen Tourist Office (☎ 01224-269180; www.aberdeen-grampian.com; 23 Union St; ⊙ 9am-6.30pm Mon-Sat, 10am-4pm Sun Jul & Aug, 9.30am-5pm Mon-Sat Sep-Jun; 🖥) Handy for general information; has internet access (£1 per 20 minutes).

Books & Beans (www.booksandbeans.co.uk; 22 Belmont St; per 15min £1; ⊙ 7.45am-4.30pm Mon-Sat, 9.45am-4pm Sun; 🖥) Internet access; also fair-trade coffee and secondhand books.

Main Post Office (St Nicholas Shopping Centre, Upperkirkgate; ⊙ 9am-5.30pm Mon-Sat, 1-5pm Sun) In the WH Smith shop.

ℹ Getting There & Away

AIR

Aberdeen Airport (p463) is at Dyce, 6 miles northwest of the city centre. There are regular flights to numerous Scottish and UK destinations, including Orkney and Shetland, and international flights to the Netherlands, Norway, Denmark, Germany and France.

Stagecoach Jet bus 727 runs regularly from Aberdeen bus station to the airport (single £2.90, 35 minutes). A taxi from the airport to the city centre takes 25 minutes and costs around £15.

BOAT

Car ferries from Aberdeen to Orkney and Shetland are run by **Northlink Ferries** (www.north-linkferries.co.uk). The ferry terminal is a short walk east of the train and bus stations.

BUS

The **bus station** (Guild St) is next to Jurys Inn, close to the train station.

Braemar £11.25, 2¼ hours, every two hours; via Ballater and Balmoral

Dundee £17.40, 1½ hours, hourly

Edinburgh £31, three hours, three daily direct, more frequent changing at Perth

Glasgow £31, three hours, at least hourly

Inverness £12.75, four hours, hourly; via Huntly, Keith, Fochabers, Elgin and Nairn

London £46, 12 hours, twice daily; National Express

Perth £24.70, two hours, hourly

TRAIN

The train station is south of the city centre, next to the massive Union Sq shopping mall.

Dundee £19.80, 1¼ hours, twice an hour

Edinburgh £35, 2½ hours, hourly

Glasgow £35, 2¾ hours, hourly

Inverness £28.20, 2¼ hour, eight daily

London King's Cross £150, eight to 11 hours, hourly; some direct, most change at Edinburgh

ℹ Getting Around

BUS

The main city bus operator is **First Aberdeen** (www.firstgroup.com/aberdeen). Local fares cost from £1.40 to £2.60; pay the driver as you board the bus. A FirstDay ticket (£4) allows unlimited travel from the time of purchase until midnight on all First Aberdeen buses. Information, route maps and tickets are available from the **First Travel Centre** (47 Union St; ⊙ 9am-5.30pm Mon-Fri, to 4.30pm Sat).

The most useful services for visitors are buses 15 and 19 from Union St to Great Western Rd (for B&Bs); bus 11 from Union St to Aberdeen SYHA and the airport; and bus 20 from Marischal College to Old Aberdeen.

CAR

Car rental companies include:

Arnold Clark (☎ 01224-622714; www.arnold clarkrental.com; Canal Rd; ⊙ 8am-7pm Mon-Fri, 8am-4.30pm Sat, 9am-4.30pm Sun)

Enterprise Car Hire (☎ 01224-642642; www.enterprise.co.uk; 80 Skene Sq; ⊙ 7am-7pm Mon-Fri, 8am-4pm Sat, 10am-3pm Sun).

TAXI

The main city-centre taxi ranks are at the train station and on Back Wynd, off Union St. To order

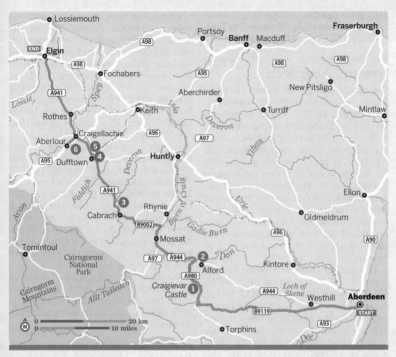

🚗 Driving Tour
Aberdeen to Elgin

START ABERDEEN
END ELGIN
LENGTH 80 MILES; ONE DAY

Head out of Aberdeen on the A944 and, just before Westhill, bear left on the B9119 towards Tarland. As you leave behind the fringes of the city you enter the sheep pastures, woods and barley fields of rural Aberdeenshire, with the foothills of the Cairngorm Mountains rising ahead.

Follow signs for Tarland for 18 miles, then turn right on the A980 towards Alford. A few miles along this road you'll see ① **Craigievar Castle** (p235) across the fields to your left; stop for an hour's visit (time your departure to arrive for opening time at 11am). Continue four miles north to the village of ② **Alford** (p234) where you can explore the Grampian Transport Museum, and have lunch at the Alford Bistro.

From Alford take the A944 and A97 west and north for 10 miles then turn left on the B9002 (signposted Craig and Cabrach). This

minor road climbs across heather-clad hills to reach the A941; turn left towards Cabrach and Dufftown. This is remote country, but a few miles beyond the tiny hamlet of Cabrach you'll find the ③ **Grouse Inn** (open Easter to October), a pub and tearoom famed for its whisky collection – there are more than 220 bottles behind the bar, all different.

Continue on the A941 as it climbs through a narrow pass in the hills and descends into the glen of the River Fiddich – the name tells you that you are now entering whisky country. Eight miles after the Grouse Inn you reach ④ **Dufftown** (p236), the whisky capital of Speyside. Visit the town's whisky museum or, better yet, take a tour of ⑤ **Glenfiddich Distillery** (p237).

From Dufftown, head north on the A941 for four miles to Craigellachie, and detour west for a mile and a half on the A95 to ⑥ **Aberlour** (p236) to round off your trip with a stroll along the banks of the River Spey, and perhaps a meal at the Mash Tun before driving the last 15 miles north to Elgin.

a taxi, phone **ComCab** (☎ 01224-353535; www.comcab-aberdeen.co.uk) or **Rainbow City Taxis** (☎ 01224-878787; www.rainbowcitytaxis.com).

Around Aberdeen

The atmospheric, 16th-century Crathes Castle (NTS; ☎ 01330-844525; www.nts.org.uk; adult/child £12.50/9; ⊙ 10.30am-5pm daily Apr-Oct, 11am-3.45pm Sat & Sun Nov-Mar; P ⓗ) is famous for its Jacobean painted ceilings, magnificently carved canopied beds, and the 'Horn of Leys', reputedly presented to the Burnett family by Robert the Bruce in the 14th century. The beautiful formal gardens include 300-year-old yew hedges and colourful herbaceous borders. The castle is signposted off the A93; Stagecoach buses 201 and 202 from Aberdeen stop at the castle entrance (£4.90, 45 minutes, every 30 minutes).

Designed in Georgian style by William Adam in 1732, **Haddo House** (NTS; ☎ 0844-493 2179; www.nts.org.uk; adult/child £10.50/7.50; ⊙ tours 11.30am, 1.30pm & 3pm Sun-Tue Jun-Aug, Sun & Mon Apr-May & Sep; P) is best described as a classic English stately home transplanted to Scotland. Home to the Gordon family, it has sumptuous Victorian interiors with wood-panelled walls, Persian rug–scattered floors and a wealth of period antiques. The beautiful grounds and terraced gardens are open all year (9am to dusk); guided tours of the house are best booked in advance. Haddo is 19 miles north of Aberdeen, near Ellon.

Buses run hourly Monday to Saturday from Aberdeen to Tarves/Methlick (£6, one hour), stopping at the end of the Haddo House driveway; it's a 1-mile walk from bus stop to house.

Though a magnificent example of Scottish Baronial architecture, Fyvie Castle (NTS; www.nts.org.uk; Fyvie; adult/child £12.50/9; ⊙ 11am-5pm Jul & Aug, noon-5pm Jun, noon-5pm Sat-Wed Apr, May, Sep & Oct; P) is probably more famous for its ghosts, including a phantom trumpeter and the mysterious Green Lady, and its art collection, which displays portraits by Thomas Gainsborough and Sir Henry Raeburn. The grounds are open all year (9am to dusk).

The castle is 25 miles north of Aberdeen on the A947 towards Turriff. A bus runs hourly from Aberdeen to Banff and Elgin via Fyvie village (£7.70, 1½ hours), a mile from the castle.

Stonehaven

POP 11,430

Originally a small fishing village, Stonehaven has been the county town of Kincardineshire since 1600 and is now a thriving family-friendly seaside resort.

◉ Sights & Activities

From the lane beside the tourist office, a boardwalk leads south along the shoreline to the picturesque cliff-bound harbour, where you'll find a couple of appealing pubs and the town's oldest building, the Tolbooth, built about 1600 by the Earl Marischal. It now houses a small local history museum (www.stonehaventolbooth.co.uk; Old Quay; ⊙ 1.30-4.30pm Wed-Mon Apr-Sep) FREE and a restaurant.

Dunnottar Castle   CASTLE
(☎ 01569-762173; www.dunnottarcastle.co.uk; adult/child £7/3; ⊙ 9am-6pm Apr-Sep, 10am-5pm or dusk Oct-Mar; P) A pleasant, 20-minute walk along the clifftops south of Stonehaven harbour leads to the spectacular ruins of Dunnottar Castle, spread out across a grassy promontory 50m above the sea. As dramatic a film set as any director could wish for, it provided the backdrop for Franco Zeffirelli's

NORTHEAST SCOTLAND AROUND ABERDEEN

SAND DUNES & SAND TRAPS

Coastal sand dunes extend north from Aberdeen for more than 14 miles, one of the largest areas of dunes in the UK, and the least affected by human activity. Forvie National Nature Reserve (www.nnr-scotland.org.uk/forvie; P) has wildlife hides and waymarked trails through the dunes to an abandoned medieval village where only the ruins of the church survive. The dunes form an important nesting and feeding area for birds – don't wander off the trails during the nesting season (April to August).

American tycoon and Republican presidential nominee Donald Trump sparked off a major controversy when he opened Trump International Golf Links in 2012, amid a 'protected' area of sand dunes just four miles south of Forvie. The development has split the community between those who welcome the potential economic benefits, and those worried about the environmental damage.

Hamlet (1990), starring Mel Gibson. The original fortress was built in the 9th century; the keep is the most substantial remnant, but the drawing room (restored in 1926) is more interesting.

Open-Air Swimming Pool SWIMMING
(☎ 01569-762134; www.stonehavenopenairpool.co. uk; adult/child £5/3; ⊙ 10am-7.30pm Mon-Fri, to 6pm Sat & Sun Jul–mid-Aug, 1-7.30pm Mon-Fri, 10am-6pm Sat & Sun Jun & late Aug; ♿) This Olympic-size (50m), heated, sea-water pool was built in 1934 in art-deco style, and sits on the seafront to the north of Stonehaven town centre. The pool is also open for 'midnight swims' from 10pm to midnight on Wednesday from the end of June to mid-August.

✵ Festivals & Events

Fireball Ceremony CULTURAL
(www.stonehavenfireballs.co.uk) Stonehaven's famous Fireball Ceremony takes place on Hogmanay (31 December), when people parade along the High St at midnight swinging blazing fireballs around their heads before throwing them into the harbour.

**Stonehaven Midsummer
Beer Happening** BEER
(www.midsummerbeerhappening.co.uk/) Home to the Six Degrees North craft brewery and several excellent real ale pubs, Stonehaven makes a great setting for this convivial three-day celebration of artisan beers, held in June.

Stonehaven Folk Festival MUSIC
(www.stonehavenfolkfestival.co.uk) The town fills with musicians for this lively four-day folk festival in mid-July.

🛏 Sleeping & Eating

★ 24 Shorehead B&B ££
(☎ 01569-767750; www.twentyfourshorehead. co.uk; 24 Shorehead; s/d £80/90; 📶) Location makes all the difference, and the location of this former cooperage offering peaceful and very stylish B&B accommodation can't be beaten – it's the last house at the end of the road, overlooking the harbour with lovely sea views. Using the binoculars provided, you can even spot seals from your bedroom. No credit cards.

Beachgate House B&B ££
(☎ 01569-763155; www.beachgate.co.uk; Beachgate Lane; s/d £60/75; 🅿) This luxurious mod-

WORTH A TRIP

SCOTTISH LIGHTHOUSE MUSEUM

The fascinating **Scottish Lighthouse Museum** (☎ 01346-511022; www.light housemuseum.org.uk; Kinnaird Head; adult/ child £7.70/3.30; ⊙ 10am-5pm Tue-Sun Apr-Oct, to 4pm Nov-Mar; 🅿) provides an insight into the network of lights that have safeguarded the Scottish coast for over 100 years, and the men and women who built and maintained them (plus a sobering fact – that *all* the world's lighthouses are to be decommissioned by 1 January 2080). A guided tour takes you to the top of the old Kinnaird Head lighthouse, built on top of a converted 16th-century castle.

The engineering is so precise that the 4.5-ton light assembly can be rotated by pushing with a single finger. The anemometer here measured the strongest wind speed ever recorded in the UK, with a gust of 123 knots (142mph) on 13 February 1989.

Buses 67 and 68 run to Fraserburgh from Aberdeen (£9.25, 1½ hours, every 30 minutes Monday to Saturday, hourly on Sunday) via Ellon.

ern bungalow is right on the seafront, just a few paces from the tourist office; two of its five rooms have sea views, as does the lounge/dining room.

★ Tolbooth Restaurant SEAFOOD ££
(☎ 01569-762287; www.tolbooth-restaurant.co.uk; Old Pier; mains £18-25; ⊙ noon-3pm & 6-9.30pm Wed-Sat year-round, noon-4pm Sun May-Sep) 🍴 Set in the 17th-century Tolbooth building overlooking the harbour, and decorated with local art and crisp white linen, this is one of the best seafood restaurants in the region. Daily specials include dishes such as scallops with crispy bacon and pea purée. From Wednesday to Saturday you can get a two-/three-course lunch for £16/20. Reservations recommended.

★ Creel Inn SEAFOOD ££
(☎ 01569-750254; www.thecreelinn.co.uk; Catterline; mains £13-19, 2-course lunch £14.50; ⊙ noon-2pm & 6-9pm Mon-Fri, noon-9.30pm Sat, noon-8.30pm Sun; 🅿♿) 🍴 Set in the tiny fishing village of Catterline, 5 miles south of Stonehaven,

WORTH A TRIP

SPEY BAY

Based in a historic ice house that was once used to store ice for preserving local salmon catches, the Scottish Dolphin Centre (☑01343-820339; www.wdcs.org/connect/wildlife_centre; Tugnet Ice House, Spey Bay; ⊙10.30am-5pm Apr-Oct, shorter hrs Nov-Mar; P) is one of the best land-based dolphin-spotting places in the country. The indoor attractions include feeds from nearby wildlife cameras, a 'dry dive' audio visual experience that takes you beneath the waves of the Moray Firth, and a pleasant cafe. Outdoors, you can watch for dolphins, seals and other marine creatures at the mouth of the River Spey, or join a guided wildlife walk.

The centre is located in the tiny village of Spey Bay, 4 miles north of Fochabers, at the mouth of the River Spey.

the Creel is a rustic pub with thick stone walls, low ceilings and open fireplaces, famous for its menu of locally caught fish and shellfish – the lobster and crab come from the bay below the village.

Carron Restaurant SCOTTISH ££
(☑01569-760460; www.carron-restaurant.co.uk; 20 Cameron St; mains £9-15; ⊙noon-2pm & 6-9.30pm Wed-Sat, noon-6pm Sun; ☑) This beautiful art-deco restaurant is a remarkable survivor from the 1930s, complete with bow-fronted terrace, iron fanlights, deco mirrors, player piano and original ceramic-tiled toilets. The Mediterranean-influenced menu (there's a separate vegetarian menu) makes the most of local produce, matching the elegance of the surroundings.

❶ Information

There's a **tourist office** (☑01569-762806; 66 Allardice St; ⊙10am-6pm Mon-Sat, 11am-4pm Sun Jul & Aug, 10am-1pm & 2-5pm Mon-Sat Apr-Jun, Sep & Oct) near Market Sq in the town centre.

❶ Getting There & Away

Stonehaven is 15 miles south of Aberdeen and is served by frequent buses travelling between Aberdeen (£4.90, 45 minutes, hourly) and Dundee (£4.15, 1¾ hours).

Trains to Dundee are faster (£15.20, 55 minutes, hourly) and offer a more scenic journey.

Strathdon

Strathdon – the valley of the River Don – is home to several of Aberdeenshire's finest castles, and stretches westward from Kintore, 13 miles northwest of Aberdeen, taking in the villages of Kemnay, Monymusk, Alford (ah-ford) and the tiny hamlet of Strathdon. The A944 parallels the lower valley; west of Alford, the A944, A97 and A939 follow the river's upper reaches.

The A939, known as the Cockbridge–Tomintoul road – a magnificent roller coaster of a route much loved by motorcyclists – runs from Strathdon across the Lecht pass (637m), where there's a small skiing area with lots of short easy and intermediate runs.

Stagecoach bus X18 runs from Aberdeen to Alford (£9.50, 1¼ hours, six a day Monday to Friday, three on Saturday).

The route between Alford and Strathdon is covered by the Strathdon A2B Dial-a-Bus (☑01224-664747) service (£6.50, 50 minutes, two a day on Thursdays only). Timetables are liable to change – call between 9.00am and 5.00pm, Monday to Friday, to confirm timings.

◉ Sights

Grampian Transport Museum MUSEUM
(☑01975-562292; www.gtm.org.uk; Alford; adult/child £9.50/1; ⊙10am-5pm Apr-Sep, 10am-4pm Oct; P⋒) The Grampian Transport Museum in Alford houses a fascinating collection of vintage motorbikes, cars, buses and trams, including a Triumph Bonneville in excellent nick, a couple of Model T Fords (including one used by Drambuie), a Ferrari F40 and an Aston Martin V8 Mk II. More unusual exhibits include a 19th-century horse-drawn sleigh from Russia, a 1942 Mack snowplough and the Craigievar Express, a steam-powered tricycle built in 1895 by a local postman.

Next to the museum is the terminus of the narrow-gauge Alford Valley Steam Railway (☑01975-562811; www.alfordvalleyrailway.org.uk; adult/child £4.50/3.50; ⊙12.30-4pm Jul & Aug, Sat & Sun only Apr-Jun & Sep; P).

Castle Fraser CASTLE
(NTS; www.nts.org.uk; adult/child £10.50/7.50; ⊙11am-5pm daily Jul & Aug, Wed-Sun Apr-Jun, Sep & Oct; P) The impressive 16th- to 17th-century Castle Fraser, 16 miles west of Aberdeen, is the ancestral home of the Fraser family. The largely Victorian interior includes the great hall (with a hidden open-

ing where the laird could eavesdrop on his guests), the library, various bedrooms and an ancient kitchen, plus a secret room for storing valuables. Fraser family relics on display include needlework hangings and a 19th-century artificial leg. The 'Woodland Secrets' area in the castle grounds is designed as an adventure playground for kids.

Craigievar Castle
CASTLE

(NTS; adult/child £12.50/9; ⊘11am-5.30pm daily Jul & Aug, Fri-Tue Apr-Jun & Sep; P) A superb example of the original Scottish Baronial style, Craigievar has managed to survive pretty much unchanged since its completion in the 17th century. The lower half is a plain tower house, the upper half sprouts corbelled turrets, cupolas and battlements – an extravagant statement of its builder's wealth and status (last admission 4.45pm). It's 6 miles south of Alford.

✕ Eating

Alford Bistro
CAFE £

(☑01975-563154; thealfordbistro@btconnect.com; 40 Main St; mains £5-10; ⊘9am-5pm Mon & Tue, 9am-8pm Wed-Sat, 10am-8pm Sun; ♦) ✐ This great-value family bistro is always crowded, and it's easy to see why – bright, modern decor in muted shades of pale green and grey, friendly service, and a menu of lovingly prepared, classic comfort food – yellow pea soup, macaroni cheese, beef stew with skirlie (oatmeal and onion fried in butter), homemade sausage rolls... be sure to wear trousers with an elasticated waistband.

MORAY

The old county of Moray (*murr*-ay), centred on the county town of Elgin, lies at the heart of an ancient Celtic earldom and is famed for its mild climate and rich farmland – the barley fields of the 19th century once provided the raw material for the Speyside whisky distilleries, one of the region's main attractions for present-day visitors.

Elgin

POP 23,130

Elgin has been the provincial capital of Moray for over eight centuries and was an important town in medieval times. Dominated by a hilltop monument to the 5th Duke of Gordon, Elgin's main attraction is its impressive ruined cathedral, where the tombs of the duke's ancestors lie.

◉ Sights

Elgin Cathedral
CATHEDRAL

(HS; www.historicenvironment.scot; King St; adult/child £5.50/3.30; ⊘9.30am-5.30pm Apr-Sep, 10am-4pm Sat-Wed Oct-Mar) Many people think that the ruins of Elgin Cathedral, known as the 'lantern of the north', are the most beautiful and evocative in Scotland; its octagonal chapter house is the finest in the country. Consecrated in 1224, the cathedral was burned down in 1390 by the infamous Wolf of Badenoch, the illegitimate son of Robert II, following his excommunication by the Bishop of Moray. Guided tours are available on weekdays.

Elgin Museum
MUSEUM

(www.elginmuseum.org.uk; 1 High St; donations accepted; ⊘10am-5pm Mon-Fri, 11am-4pm Sat Apr-Oct) FREE Scotland's oldest independent museum is an old-fashioned cabinet of curiosities, a captivating collection artfully displayed in a beautiful, purpose-built Victorian building. Exhibits range from Ecuadorian shrunken heads to Peruvian mummies, and include internationally important fish and reptile fossils discovered in local rocks, and mysterious Pictish carved stones.

🛏 Sleeping & Eating

Moraydale
B&B ££

(☑01343-546381; www.moraydaleguesthouse.com; 276 High St; s/d/f from £55/75/85; P🛜) The Moraydale is a spacious Victorian mansion filled with period features – check out the stained glass and the cast-iron and tile fireplaces. The bedrooms are all en suite and equipped with modern bathrooms – the three large family rooms are particularly good value.

Southbank Guest House
B&B ££

(☑01343-547132; www.southbankguesthouse.co.uk; 36 Academy St; s/d/f from £55/90/140; P🛜) The family-run, 15-room Southbank is set in a large Georgian town house in a quiet street south of Elgin's centre, just five minutes' walk from the cathedral and other sights.

Johnstons Coffee Shop
CAFE £

(Newmill; mains £5-10; ⊘10am-5pm Mon-Sat, 11am-4.30pm Sun; P🛜♦) The coffee shop at Johnstons woollen mill is one of the best places to eat in town, serving breakfast till

WORTH A TRIP

PENNAN

Pennan is a picturesque harbour village tucked beneath red-sandstone cliffs, 12 miles west of Fraserburgh. It featured in the 1983 film *Local Hero,* and fans of the film still come to make a call from the red telephone box that played a prominent part in the plot (the box in the film was just a prop, and it was only later that film buffs and locals successfully campaigned for a real one to be installed).

The interior of the village hotel, the Pennan Inn, also appeared in the film, though one of the houses further along the seafront to the east doubled for the exterior of the fictional hotel. The beach scenes were filmed on the other side of the country, at Camusdarach Beach (p342) in Arisaig.

11.45am, hot lunches noon to 3pm (crepes with a range of fillings, including smoked salmon with cream cheese and dill), and cream teas.

★ **Drouthy Cobbler** CAFE, BAR **££**
(☑ 01343-596000; thedrouthycobbler.co.uk; 48a High St; mains £11-15; ⊙ food served 8am-10pm; �ⓢ) This brand new cafe-bar is an all-day venue serving everything from breakfast to dinner, with a bistro-style menu that changes regularly but includes dishes such as carpaccio of beef, Caesar salad, scallops and pancetta, and homemade burgers. It's tucked away up a side alley, and also hosts live music and comedy gigs in the evenings.

🛍 Shopping

Gordon & MacPhail FOOD & DRINKS
(☑ 01343-545110; www.gordonandmacphail.com; 58-60 South St; ⊙ 8.30am-5pm Mon-Sat, alcohol on sale from 10am) Gordon & MacPhail is the world's largest specialist malt-whisky dealer. Over a century old and offering around 450 different varieties, its Elgin shop is a place of pilgrimage for whisky connoisseurs, as well as housing a mouth-watering delicatessen.

Johnstons of Elgin FASHION & ACCESSORIES
(☑ 01343-554009; www.johnstonscashmere.com; Newmill; ⊙ 9am-5.30pm Mon-Sat, 11am-5pm Sun) Founded in 1797, Johnstons is famous for its cashmere woollen clothing, and is the only UK woollen mill that still sees the manu-

facturing process through from raw fibre to finished garment. There's a retail outlet and coffee shop, and free guided tours of the works.

ⓘ Information

The **Tourist Office** (☑ 01343-562608; Elgin Library, Cooper Park; ⊙ 10am-5pm Mon-Sat, 10am-4pm Sun) has internet access upstairs.

ⓘ Getting There & Away

The bus station is a block north of High St, and the train station is 900m south of the town centre.

BUS
Aberdeen £12.75, 2½ hours, hourly
Banff & Macduff £10.40, 1¾ hours, hourly
Dufftown £5.80, 50 minutes, hourly Monday to Saturday
Inverness £10.40, 1½ hours, hourly

TRAIN
Aberdeen £18.90, 1¾ hours, five daily
Inverness £12.30, 40 minutes, five daily

Dufftown & Aberlour

Rome may be built on seven hills, but Dufftown's built on seven stills, say the locals. Founded in 1817 by James Duff, 4th Earl of Fife, Dufftown is 17 miles' south of Elgin and lies at the heart of the Speyside whisky-distilling region. With seven working distilleries nearby, Dufftown has been dubbed Scotland's malt-whisky capital and is host to the biannual Spirit of Speyside (p237) whisky festival. Ask at the whisky museum about the Malt Whisky Trail (www.maltwhisky trail.com), a self-guided tour around the local distilleries.

Aberlour (www.aboutaberlour.co.uk) – or Charlestown of Aberlour, to give it its full name – is prettier than Dufftown, straggling along the banks of the River Spey. It is famous as the home of Walkers Shortbread, and has Aberlour Distillery right on the main street. Attractions include salmon fishing on the Spey, nearby Knockando Woolmill, and some lovely walks along the Speyside Way.

◉ Sights & Activities

Knockando Woolmill MUSEUM
(www.knockandowoolmill.org.uk; Knockando; ⊙ 10am-4pm Easter-Nov; ℗) 🖉 **FREE** Hidden in a fold of the hills 5 miles west of Aberlour, Knockando is a rare survival of an 18th-century woollen mill that has been lovingly restored to full

working order. The ancient looms clank away Monday to Friday, turning out plaid and tweed textiles that can be purchased in the neighbouring shop. Guided tours cost £5.

Whisky Museum MUSEUM
(☑ 01340-821097; www.whisky.dufftown.co.uk; 12 Conval St; ☉1-4pm Mon-Fri May-Sep) `FREE`
As well as housing a selection of distillery memorabilia (try saying that after a few drams), the Whisky Museum holds 'nosing and tasting evenings' in the Commercial Hotel, where you can learn what to look for in a fine single malt (£10 per person; 8pm Wednesday in July and August).

You can then test your new-found skills at the nearby **Whisky Shop** (☑ 01340-821097; www.whiskyshopdufftown.co.uk; 1 Fife St; ☉ 10am-6pm Mon-Sat, to 5pm Sun), which stocks hundreds of single malts.

Keith & Dufftown Railway HERITAGE RAILWAY
(☑ 01340-821181; www.keith-dufftown-railway.co.uk; Dufftown Station; adult/child return £11/5; P 🐾)
A line running for 11 miles from Dufftown to Keith sees trains hauled by 1950s diesel motor units running on weekends from May to September, plus Fridays in July and August. There are also two 1930s 'Brighton Belle' Pullman coaches, and a cafe housed in a 1957 British Railways cafeteria car.

🛏 Sleeping & Eating

Davaar B&B B&B ££
(☑ 01340-820464; www.davaardufftown.co.uk; 17 Church St; d/f £65/80; 🐾) Davaar is a sturdy Victorian villa with three smallish but comfy rooms; the breakfast menu is superb, offering the option of Portsoy kippers as well as the traditional fry-up (which uses eggs from the owners' own chickens).

Mash Tun B&B ££
(☑ 01340-881771; www.mashtun-aberlour.com; 8 Broomfield Sq; s/d from £75/110; 🐾) Housed in a curious stone building made for a sea captain in the outline of a ship, this luxurious B&B is famous for its whisky bar – a place of pilgrimage for whisky enthusiasts – which has a collection of old and rare single malts. There's also an excellent restaurant (mains £10 to £20, lunch and dinner daily) that serves posh pub grub.

BLAZE YOUR OWN WHISKY TRAIL

Visiting a distillery can be memorable, but only hardcore malthounds will want to go to more than one or two. Some are great to visit; others are depressingly corporate.

Aberlour (☑ 01340-881249; www.aberlour.com; tours from £14; ☉ tours 10am & 2pm daily Apr-Oct, by appointment Mon-Fri Nov-Mar; P) Has an excellent, detailed tour with a proper tasting session. It's on the main street in Aberlour.

Glenfarclas (☑ 01807-500257; www.glenfarclas.co.uk; admission £7.50; ☉ 10am-4pm Mon-Fri Oct-Mar, to 5pm Mon-Fri Apr-Sep, 10am-4pm Sat Jul-Sep; P) Small, friendly and independent, Glenfarclas is 5 miles south of Aberlour on the Grantown road; the last tour leaves 90 minutes before closing. The in-depth Connoisseur's Tour (Fridays only, July to September) is £40.

Glenfiddich (☑ 01340-820373; www.glenfiddich.co.uk; admission free, tours from £10; ☉ 9.30am-4.30pm Apr-Oct, 11am-3pm Nov-Mar; P) It's big and busy, but handiest for Dufftown and foreign languages are available. The standard tour (£10) starts with an overblown video, but it's fun and informative. An in-depth half-day Pioneer's Tour (£50) must be prebooked.

Macallan (☑ 01340-872280; www.themacallan.com; Easter Elchies, Craigellachie; tours £15; ☉ 9.30am-6pm Mon-Sat Easter-Oct, to 5pm Mon-Fri Nov-Mar; P) Macallan makes an excellent sherry-casked malt. The 1¾-hour tours (maximum group of 10) should be prebooked. Lovely location 1 mile west of Craigellachie.

Speyside Cooperage (☑ 01340-871108; www.speysidecooperage.co.uk; adult/child £3.50/2; ☉ 9am-5pm Mon-Fri, closed late Dec-early Jan) Here you can see the fascinating art of barrel-making in action. It's a mile from Craigellachie on the Dufftown road.

The biannual **Spirit of Speyside** (www.spiritofspeyside.com) whisky festival in Dufftown has a number of great events. It takes place in early May and late September; both accommodation and events should be booked well ahead.

Craigellachie Hotel
HOTEL £££

(☎01340-881204; www.craigellachiehotel.co.uk; Craigellachie; r from £175; P ☎) The Craigellachie has a wonderfully old-fashioned, hunting-lodge atmosphere, from the wood-panelled lobby to the opulent drawing room where you can sink into a sofa in front of the log fire. But the big attraction for whisky connoisseurs is the Quaich Bar, a cosy nook filled with green leather armchairs and lined with almost 700 varieties of single malt whisky.

The hotel is a mile northeast of Aberlour, overlooking the River Spey.

Spey Larder
FOOD & DRINKS

(☎01340-871243; www.speylarder.com; 96-98 High St; ⊙9.30am-5pm Mon-Sat) This deli is the place to shop for picnic goodies to eat on the banks of the River Spey – a great selection of Scottish artisan cheeses, smoked salmon, venison charcuterie, delicious home-baked bread, and local craft beers.

❶ Getting There & Away

Buses link Elgin to Dufftown (£5.80, 50 minutes) hourly Monday to Saturday, continuing to Huntly and Aberdeen.

On summer weekends, you can take a train from Aberdeen or Inverness to Keith (£17, one hour, five daily), and then ride the Keith and Dufftown Railway to Dufftown.

There are hourly buses to Aberlour from Elgin (£5.50, 40 minutes), and from Dufftown (£2.70, 15 minutes).

Banff & Macduff
POP 9100

The handsome Georgian town of Banff and the busy fishing port of Macduff lie on either side of Banff Bay, separated only by the mouth of the River Deveron. Banff Links – 800m of clean golden sand stretching to the west – Duff House and Macduff's impressive aquarium pull in the holiday crowds.

Bus 35 runs from Banff to Elgin (£12.75, 1¾ hours, every two hours) and Aberdeen (£12.75, two hours), while bus 272 runs to Fraserburgh (£8.70, 55 minutes, three daily) on weekdays only.

One of Scotland's hidden gems, Duff House (☎01261-818181; www.duffhouse.org.uk; adult/child £7.10/4.30; ⊙11am-5pm Apr-Oct, 11am-4pm Thu-Sun Nov-Mar; P) is home to an art gallery that displays a superb collection of Scottish and European art, including important works by Raeburn and Gainsborough. The house is an impressive baroque mansion on the southern edge of Banff, built between 1735 and 1740 as the seat of the Earls of Fife. It was designed by William Adam and bears similarities to that other Adam masterpiece, Hopetoun House (p98) near Edinburgh.

The centrepiece of Macduff Marine Aquarium (www.macduff-aquarium.org.uk; 11 High Shore, Macduff; adult/child £6.65/3.45; ⊙10am-5pm Mon-Fri, 11am-5pm Sat & Sun Apr-Oct, 11am-4pm Sat-Wed Nov-Mar; P ♿) is a 400,000L open-air tank, complete with kelp-coated reef and wave machine. Marine oddities on view include the brightly coloured cuckoo wrasse, the warty-skinned lumpsucker and the vicious-looking wolf fish. There's also a live CCTV feed from the seabird nesting colonies at the RSPB's Troup Head nature reserve.

With a central location right on the main street, and an outlook over the old castle grounds, Trinity Manse (☎01261-812244; www.trinitymanseguesthouse.co.uk; 21 Castle St, Banff; s/d from £45/70; ☎) is a fine old Georgian house that provides a clean and comfortable place to lay your head. No credit cards.

Portsoy
POP 1750

The pretty fishing village of Portsoy has an atmospheric 17th-century harbour and a maze of narrow streets lined with picturesque cottages. An ornamental stone known as Portsoy marble – actually a beautifully patterned green-and-pale-pink serpentine – was quarried near Portsoy in the 17th and 18th centuries, and was reputedly used in the decoration of some rooms in the Palace of Versailles.

Portsoy is 8 miles west of Banff; the hourly bus between Banff (£4.90, 25 minutes) and Elgin (£10.25, 1½ hours) stops here.

Each year on the last weekend in June or first weekend in July, Portsoy harbour is home to the Scottish Traditional Boat Festival (www.stbfportsoy.com) . It's a lively gathering of historic wooden sailing boats accompanied by sailing races, live folk music, crafts demonstrations, street theatre and a food festival.

The Shore Inn (☎01261-842831; www.facebook.com/TheShoreInn; 49 Church St; mains £6-12; ⊙food served noon-8pm) is a characterful real-ale pub overlooking the harbour, with a kitchen that turns out hearty and warming pub grub such as soup, burgers and fish and chips.

Southern Highlands & Islands

Best Places to Eat

➡ Monachyle Mhor (p252)

➡ Lake of Menteith Hotel (p249)

➡ Calgary Farmhouse (p286)

➡ Iona Hostel (p288)

➡ Colonsay Hotel (p270)

Best Places to Sleep

➡ Ninth Wave (p287)

➡ Café Fish (p285)

➡ Callander Meadows (p251)

➡ Starfish (p260)

➡ The Pierhouse (p292)

Why Go?

The impossibly complex coastline of Scotland's southwest harbours some of its most inspiring corners. Here, sea travel is key – dozens of ferries, happily now subsidised with cheaper fares, allow you to island-hop from the scenic splendour of Arran to majestic Mull or Tiree's lonely sands, via the whisky distilleries of Islay, the wild mountains of Jura, the scenic delights of diminutive Colonsay and Oban's sustainable seafood scene.

On fresh water too, passenger ferries, vintage steamboats, canoes and kayaks ply Loch Lomond and the Trossachs National Park, a memorable concentration of scenic splendour that's very accessible but possessed of a wild beauty.

Wildlife experiences are a highlight here, from the rasping spout of a minke whale to the 'krek-krek' of a corncrake. Spot otters tumbling in the kelp, watch sea eagles snatch fish from a lonely loch and thrill to the sight of dolphins riding the bow-wave of your boat.

When to Go
Oban

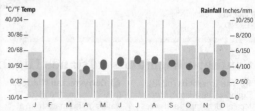

May Fèis Ìle (Islay Festival) celebrates traditional Scottish music and whisky.

Jun Roadsides and gardens become a blaze of colour with deep-pink rhododendron blooms.

Aug The best month of the year for whale-watching off the west coast.

Southern Highlands & Islands Highlights

❶ The Trossachs (p248)
Exploring the region's spectacular lochscapes and accessible walking and cycling routes.

❷ Islay (p262) Visiting the heavyweights of the whisky world on their peaty home turf.

❸ Arran (p270) Blowing away the cobwebs on this scenic, activity-packed island.

❹ Corryvreckan Whirlpool (p268) Visiting the white waters of this maelstrom at the north end of lonely Jura.

❺ Iona (p288) Journeying through wildlife-rich Mull to reach this holy emerald isle.

❻ West Highland Way (p241) Hiking along the eastern shore of Loch Lomond.

❼ Seafood Restaurants Tucking into a platter of fresh local langoustines at Ee-Usk (p279) or one of Oban's other eateries.

❽ Machrihanish (p261) Teeing off on the great-value old and new golf courses down the Kintyre peninsula.

LOCH LOMOND & AROUND

The 'bonnie banks' and 'bonnie braes' of Loch Lomond have long been Glasgow's rural retreat – a scenic region of hills, lochs and healthy fresh air within easy reach of Scotland's largest city. Today the loch's popularity shows no sign of decreasing.

Loch Lomond became the heart of Loch Lomond & the Trossachs National Park (www.lochlomond-trossachs.org) – Scotland's first national park, created in 2002. The park extends over a huge area, from Balloch north to Tyndrum and Killin, and from Callander west to the forests of Cowal. The length of Loch Lomond means that access between the western part of the park and the Trossachs is either in the far north of the region via Crianlarich or the far south via Drymen.

Loch Lomond

Loch Lomond is mainland Britain's largest lake and, after Loch Ness, the most famous of Scotland's lochs. Its proximity to Glasgow (20 miles away) means that the tourist honeypots of Balloch, Loch Lomond Shores and Luss get pretty crowded in summer. The eastern shore, which is followed by the West Highland Way long-distance footpath, is quieter and offers a better chance to appreciate the loch away from the busy main road.

Loch Lomond straddles the Highland border. The southern part is broad and island-studded, fringed by woods and Lowland meadows. However, north of Luss the loch narrows, occupying a deep trench gouged out by glaciers during the Ice Age, with 900m mountains crowding either side

🏃 Activities

The West Highland Way (www.west-highland-way.co.uk) runs along the loch's eastern shore, while the Rob Roy Way (www.robroyway.com) heads from Drymen to Pitlochry via the Trossachs. The Three Lochs Way (www.threelochsway.co.uk) loops west from Balloch through Helensburgh and Arrochar before returning to Loch Lomond at Inveruglas. There are numerous shorter walks around: get further information from tourist offices.

Rowardennan is the starting point for ascents of Ben Lomond (974m), a popular and relatively straightforward (if strenuous) climb.

The mostly traffic-free Clyde and Loch Lomond Cycle Way links Glasgow to Balloch (20 miles), where it joins the West Loch Lomond Cycle Path, which continues along the loch shore to Tarbet (10 miles). The park website (www.lochlomond-trossachs.org) details some other local routes.

Loch Lomond Golf Club GOLF
(📞 01436-655555; www.lochlomond.com; Luss) On the shores of the famous loch, this course – not a links – has a picturesque, romantic location, including an impressive clubhouse and a ruined castle by the 18th green. Nevertheless, it's a real test, with plenty of water hazards and cunningly placed sand traps. You have to be a member or be invited by one.

CanYou Experience OUTDOOR
(📞 01389-756251; www.canyouexperience.com; Loch Lomond Shores; ⊙10am-5.30pm Easter-Oct) Offers a huge range of activities on water and land from various bases around Loch Lomond. Hire mountain bikes (£13/17 per half-/full day), canoes and kayaks, or go abseiling, canoeing, paddleboarding or more. The six-hour canoe safari (£50) explores the loch's islands. The website gives a full rundown.

Loch Lomond Seaplanes SCENIC FLIGHTS
(📞 01436-675030; www.lochlomondseaplanes.com; flights from £129) Leaving from the Cameron House Hotel just north of Balloch, this offers a variety of scenic flights over the loch and western Scotland.

👉 Tours

Balmaha Boatyard BOATING
(📞 01360-870214; www.balmahaboatyard.co.uk; Balmaha; adult/child trip £10/5) The operator runs a lovely old wooden mailboat from Balmaha to loch islands, departing at 11.30am and returning at 2pm, with a one-hour stop on Inchmurrin. Trips depart daily (except Tuesday and Sunday) in July and August; and on Monday, Thursday and Saturday in May, June and September. There are also various other low-priced cruises in summer.

It also rents out rowing boats (£10/40 per hour/day) and motorboats (£60 per day).

Sweeney's Cruises BOATING
(📞 01389-752376; www.sweeneyscruiseco.com; Balloch Rd) Offers a range of trips including a one-hour return cruise to Inchmurrin (adult/child £10.20/7, five times daily April to October, twice daily November to March)

and a two-hour cruise (£18/10.20 twice daily May to September plus weekends April and October) around the islands. The quay is directly opposite Balloch train station. It also runs trips from a dock at Loch Lomond Shores (p243).

Piped commentary is by Neil Oliver.

Cruise Loch Lomond
BOATING

(☑ 01301-702356; www.cruiselochlomond.co.uk; Tarbet/Luss; ⊙ 8.30am-5.30pm early Apr-late Oct) With departures from Tarbet and Luss, this operator offers short cruises and two-hour trips to Arklet Falls and Rob Roy's Cave (adult/child £15/8). There are several options. You can also be dropped off at Rowardennan to climb Ben Lomond (£15/9), getting picked up in the afternoon, or get picked up at Inversnaid after a 9-mile hike along the West Highland Way (£15/9).

From its Tarbet office, it also rents out boats (half/full day £95/150) and bikes (£13/17).

❶ Information

Balloch Tourist Office (☑ 01389-753533; www.visitscotland.com; Balloch Rd; ⊙ 9.30am-6pm Jul & Aug, 9.30am-5.30pm Jun & Sep, 10am-5pm Oct-May) Opposite Balloch train station.

Balmaha National Park Centre (☑ 01389-722100; www.lochlomond-trossachs.org; Balmaha; ⊙ 9.30am-4pm Apr-Jun & Sep-Oct, 9.30am-6pm Jul & Aug, 9.30am-4pm Sat & Sun Nov-Mar) Has maps showing local walking routes.

National Park Gateway Centre (☑ 01389-751035; www.lochlomondshores.com; Loch Lomond Shores, Balloch; ⊙ 10am-6pm Apr-Sep, 10am-5pm Oct-Mar; ☎) At Loch Lomond Shores by Balloch, with a shop and cafe. Being refurbished at last visit and due to reopen in 2017.

❶ Getting There & Away
BUS

First Glasgow (www.firstglasgow.com) Bus 1/1A runs from Argyle St in central Glasgow to Balloch (£5, 1½ hours, at least two per hour)

LOCH LOMOND WATER BUS

From April to October a network of boats criss-crosses Loch Lomond, allowing you to explore the loch's hiking and biking trails using public transport. A Loch Lomond Water Bus timetable is available from tourist offices and online (www.lochlomond-trossachs.org/waterbus).

Arden to Inchmurrin (www.inchmurrin-lochlomond.com; return £5) On demand.

Ardlui to Ardleish (☑ 01301-704243; per person £3 or £5 for solo passengers; ⊙ 9am-7pm May-Sep, to 6pm Apr & Oct) On demand; operated by Ardlui Hotel.

Balloch to Luss (☑ 01389-752376; www.sweeneyscruises.com; single/return £11/18.50; ⊙ 3 daily May-Sep) Three daily May to September.

Balmaha to Inchcailloch (☑ 01360-870214; www.balmahaboatyard.co.uk; return £5; ⊙ 9.30am-5pm mid-Mar-Oct) On demand.

Inveruglas to Inversnaid (☑ 01301-702356; www.cruiselochlomond.co.uk; single/return £8/11.50; ⊙ mid-Mar-Oct) Must be booked.

Loch Lomond Shores to Inchmurrin and Inchcailloch (☑ 01475-722204; www.clydecruises.com; £12-14 return; ⊙ Wed-Sun Jul & Aug) Runs three sailings from Loch Lomond Shores to Inchmurrin, then Inchcailloch.

Luss to Balmaha (☑ 01389-752376; www.sweeneyscruises.com; single/return £7/9.50; ⊙ May-Sep) Four to five daily May to September.

Luss to Inchcailloch (☑ 01301-702356; www.cruiselochlomond.co.uk; single/return £8/11.50; ⊙ mid-Mar-Oct) Four daily.

Rowardennan to Luss (☑ 01301-702356; www.cruiselochlomond.co.uk; single/return £8/11.50; ⊙ mid-Mar-Oct) One daily; must be booked.

Tarbet to Inversnaid (☑ 01301-702356; www.cruiselochlomond.co.uk; single/return £8/11.50; ⊙ mid-Mar-Oct) Five to six daily.

Tarbet to Rowardennan (☑ 01301-702356; www.cruiselochlomond.co.uk; single/return £8/11.50; ⊙ mid-Mar-Oct) One daily.

and bus C8 runs to Drymen (£5.20, 1¼ hours, two daily).

Scottish Citylink (www.citylink.co.uk) Coaches from Glasgow stop at Luss (£8.80, 55 minutes, 17 daily), Tarbet (£8.80, 65 minutes, 17 daily) and Ardlui (£16, 1¼ hours, nine daily).

TRAIN

Glasgow–Balloch £5.30, 45 minutes, every 30 minutes

Glasgow–Arrochar & Tarbet £11.80, 1¼ hours, seven daily, four Sunday

Glasgow–Ardlui £15.50, 1½ hours, seven daily, four Sunday, continuing to Oban or Fort William

ℹ Getting Around

McGill's (☏ 08000-515651; www.mcgillsbuses.co.uk) bus 309 runs from Balloch to Drymen and Balmaha (£2.60, 25 minutes, nine to 10 daily), while bus 305 heads to Luss (£2.60, 20 minutes, nine to 10 daily). **McColl's** (☏ 01389-754321; www.mccolls.org.uk) bus 207 connects Balloch with Loch Lomond Shores and Alexandria. An **SPT Daytripper ticket** gives a family group unlimited travel for a day on most bus and train services in the Glasgow, Loch Lomond and Helensburgh area. Buy the ticket (£11.60 for one adult and two children, £20.50 for two adults and up to four children) from any train station or Glasgow bus station.

Tarbet and Ardlui are accessible by train and by Citylink buses between Glasgow and north-western destinations.

Local buses run from Helensburgh to Arrochar via Luss and Tarbet four times daily Monday to Friday.

Western Shore

Balloch, straddling the River Leven at Loch Lomond's southern end, is the loch's main population centre and transport hub. A Victorian resort once thronged by day trippers transferring between the train station and the steamer quay, it is now a 'gateway centre' for Loch Lomond and the Trossachs National Park. Visitors still arrive in abundance. On its edge, the overblown Loch Lomond Shores complex provides family-friendly attractions, boat trips, eateries and lots of retail.

Leaving Balloch behind, the road along the western shore offers great views of the loch and busy traffic along what is a major route to north and west Scotland.

Some would say that the western shore of the loch serves a purpose: to take one for the team, accept the tour coaches and leave other parts of the area and country comparatively traffic-free.

Head first for the picture-postcard village of **Luss**. Stroll among the pretty cottages, built by the local laird in the 19th century for his estate workers, and admire the loch-side vistas. You won't be alone: to live in one of these cute cottages must occasionally feel like being a celeb with paparazzi camped outside the door.

Beyond Luss, **Tarbet** sits at the junction where you choose between Argyll and Kintyre or Oban and the Highlands. Following the shore brings you to **Ardlui** and thence Crianlarich.

◉ Sights & Activities

Loch Lomond Shores   LEISURE COMPLEX
(☏ 01389-751031; www.lochlomondshores.com; ⊙ 9.30am-6pm) Loch Lomond Shores, a major tourism development situated a half-mile north of Balloch, sports a national park information centre plus various visitor attractions, outdoor activities and boat trips. In keeping with the times, the heart of the development is a large shopping mall.

Maid of the Loch   HISTORIC SHIP
(www.maidoftheloch.com; ⊙ 11am-5pm school holidays & weekends Easter-Oct) **FREE** The vintage paddle steamer *Maid of the Loch*, built in 1953, is moored at Loch Lomond Shores while awaiting full restoration – you can nip aboard for a look around.

🛏 Sleeping & Eating

Glenview   B&B ££
(☏ 01436-860606; www.glenview-luss.co.uk; Luss; d £90-110; ℗ 🛜) In the centre of things on the road through the village of Luss, this white house offers a genuine welcome and highly appealing rooms. Both are showroom-spotless: one is plush and cosy, the other contemporary and stylish, with a modish four-poster bed. Both have swish bathrooms and a sitting area. Single occupancy of either room costs £80 to £90.

Luss Seafood Bar   SEAFOOD ££
(☏ 01436-860420; www.luss-seafoodbar.com; Church Rd, Luss; dishes £8-20; ⊙ 9am-6pm; 🛜) It's curious that the eateries in Luss are tucked safely away from the lake; this is no exception, behind a shop on the main street. But it's a light, cheerful place serving tasty fresh oysters, potted fish and salmon smoked a few paces away. Prices are on the high side, but the produce is good.

Loch Lomond & the Trossachs NP

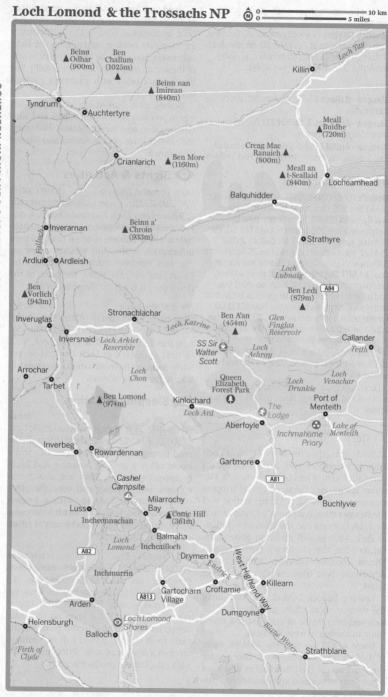

Drover's Inn
PUB FOOD ££

(☑ 01301-704234; www.thedroversinn.co.uk; Ardlui; bar meals £9-14; ⊙ 11.30am-10pm Mon-Sat, 11.30am-9.30pm or 10pm Sun; Ⓟ ⑧) Don't miss this low-ceilinged howff (drinking den) just north of Ardlui with its smoke-blackened stone, kilted bartenders, and walls festooned with moth-eaten stags' heads and stuffed birds. The bar, where Rob Roy allegedly dropped by for pints, serves hearty hill-walking fuel and hosts live folk music at weekends. Recommended more as an atmospheric place to eat and drink than somewhere to stay.

Rooms could do with an upgrade. Singles cost £35 to £55, doubles £75 to £90.

Eastern Shore

Away from the busy western road, the loch's eastern shore is a quieter spot populated mostly by walkers and campers. Nevertheless, the narrow road gets busy. It runs from **Drymen** through attractive **Balmaha**, where you can hire boats or take a cruise.

There are several lochside picnic areas; **Millarochy Bay** (1.5 miles north of Balmaha), has a nice gravel beach and superb views across the loch to the Luss hills.

The road ends at **Rowardennan**, but the West Highland Way (p241) hiking trail continues north along the shore of the loch. It's 7 miles to **Inversnaid**, reachable by road from the Trossachs, and 15 miles to **Inverarnan** at the loch's northern end.

In Balmaha, a short but steep climb from the car park leads up **Conic Hill** (361m), a superb viewpoint (2.5 miles round trip; allow two to three hours). The **Millennium Forest Path** is a 40-minute introduction to the area's tree and plant life.

🛏 Sleeping & Eating

Book your accommodation ahead in the walking season, as it packs out. There are hostel, hotel and camping options as well as B&Bs along this stretch.

From March to October, wild camping is banned on the eastern shore of Loch Lomond between Drymen and Ptarmigan Lodge (just north of Rowardennan Youth Hostel). There are campsites at Millarochy, Cashel and Sallochy. See also the hostel at Inversnaid.

Rowardennan SYHA
HOSTEL £

(☑ 01360-870259; www.syha.org.uk; Rowardennan; dm/tw/q £21/52/96; ⊙ late Mar-late Oct; Ⓟ ⑧) Where the road ends on the eastern side of the loch, this is a postcard-quality retreat in an elegant ex-hunting lodge with lawns stretching right down to the water's edge. Whether you're walking the West Highland Way, climbing Ben Lomond or just putting your feet up, it's a great choice with a huge lounge whose windows overlook Loch Lomond. Meals are available but the food is better in the nearby hotel.

Inversnaid Bunkhouse
HOSTEL £

(☑ 01877-386249; www.inversnaid.com; Inversnaid; dm £19-22, tw & d with shared bathroom £46-57, d £73, tent site per person £10; ⊙ Mar-Oct; Ⓟ ⑧ ⑧) Fifteen miles from Aberfoyle by road, a ferry across Loch Lomond from the western side, or an 8-mile walk north from Rowardennan on the West Highland Way, this former church is now a remote welcoming hostel in a peaceful streamside location. It's very popular with walkers and offers simple accommodation in crowded dorms, very pleasant doubles and grassy campsites (pre-pitched tents available).

A hot tub is great for aching muscles and the cafe offers simple meals (noon to 4pm and 6pm to 8pm), packed lunches and decent beers; you can also self-cater evening meals. It's a 15-minute uphill trudge from the lakeshore and trail, but they offer free transfers. A modern self-catering cabin is also available.

CLIMBING BEN LOMOND

Standing guard over the eastern shore of Loch Lomond is Ben Lomond (974m), Scotland's most southerly Munro. It's a popular climb: most follow the **Tourist Route** up and down from Rowardennan car park. It's a straightforward climb on a well used and maintained path; allow five hours for the 7-mile (11km) round trip.

The **Ptarmigan Route** is less crowded and has better views, following a narrow but clearly defined path up the western flank, directly overlooking the loch, to a curving ridge leading to the summit. You can descend via the tourist route, making a satisfying circuit.

To find the start of the Ptarmigan path, head north from Rowardennan car park 600m, past the youth hostel; cross the bridge after Ben Lomond Cottage and immediately turn right along a path through the trees. The route is then easy to follow.

Cashel Campsite CAMPSITE £

(☑ 01360-870234; www.campingintheforest.co.uk; Rowardennan; tent site for 2 £24.15; ☺ Mar-late Oct; P 🐾) The most attractive campsite in the area is 3 miles north of Balmaha, on the loch shore.

★ **Passfoot Cottage** B&B ££

(☑ 01360-870324; www.passfoot.com; Balmaha; s/d £70/80; ☺ Apr-Sep; P 🛜) Pretty Passfoot is a whitewashed cottage with colourful flower baskets, and enjoys a lovely location over-looking Balmaha Bay. The bright bedrooms have a homely feel, the bathrooms are Scandinavian-style wet rooms, and there's a cosy lounge with a wood-burning stove and loch view, and a wee garden down by the shore. The cheery owner makes you feel right at home.

Oak Tree Inn INN ££

(☑ 01360-870357; www.theoaktreeinn.co.uk; Balmaha; dm/s/d £30/70/90; P 🛜) An attractive traditional inn built in slate and timber, this offers bright modern guest bedrooms for pampered hikers, plus super-spacious superior chambers, self-catering cottages and two four-bed bunkrooms for hardier souls. The rustic restaurant brings locals, tourists and walkers together and dishes up hearty meals that cover lots of bases (mains £9 to £12; food noon to 9pm). There's lots of outdoor seating.

But it doesn't end there; the Oak Tree is an impressive set-up that brews its own beers, makes its own ice cream (and sells it in an adjacent cafe), and smokes its own fish.

Crianlarich & Tyndrum

POP 400

Surrounded by spectacular hillscapes at the northern edge of the Loch Lomond and the Trossachs National Park, these villages are popular pit stops on the main A82 road for walkers on the West Highland Way and Munro-baggers. Crianlarich has a train station and more community atmosphere, while Tyndrum (*tyne*-drum), 5 miles up the road, has two stations, a bus interchange, a petrol station, late-opening motorists' cafes and a **tourist office** (☑ 01838-400246; www.visitscotland.com; 6 Main St; ☺ 10am-5pm Apr-Jun & Sep-Oct, 9am-6pm Jul & Aug) – a good spot for route information and maps for ascents of Munros Cruach Ardrain (1046m), Ben More (1174m) and magnificent Ben Lui (1130m).

🛏 Sleeping & Eating

There are decent budget options in both places and lots of B&Bs. Crianlarich makes a marginally more appealing base than Tyndrum, with fewer vehicles speeding through town and better views.

By the Way HOSTEL, CAMPSITE £

(☑ 01838-400333; www.tyndrumbytheway.com; Lower Station Rd, Tyndrum; dm/s/d £18/28/42, camping per person £8; ☺ campsites Apr-Oct, hostel & cabins year-round; P 🛜🐾) This walkers' hostel offers ideal comfort on the West Highland Way. It's got a pleasant setting in a woodsy, grassy area away from the main road. The hostel building features snug, compact, comfortable rooms set around a

---

LOCH LOMOND'S ISLANDS

There are around 60 islands, large and small, in Loch Lomond. Most are privately owned, and only two (Inchcailloch and Inchmurrin) can be reached without your own boat or canoe. Four of the most interesting:

Inchcailloch A nature reserve reached by passenger ferry from Balmaha or Luss. The most accessible island, with nature trails and a small bookable campsite. See www.lochlomond-trossachs.org.

Inchmurrin Privately owned, reached by passenger ferry from Arden on the loch's western shore. Has walking trails, beaches, self-catering cottages and a restaurant that is open from Easter to October. See www.inchmurrin-lochlomond.com.

Inchconnachan Privately owned. Only accessible by boat or canoe. Has an unlikely wallaby population; the rare capercaillie nests here too.

Island I Vow Privately owned. Only accessible by boat or canoe. The loch's most northerly island is home to a ruined castle; Wordsworth visited in 1814 and found a hermit living in it, inspiring his poem *The Brownie's Cell*.

good large kitchen and dining area. Shared showers are good. The grassy adjacent campsite offers cabins and pods as well as tent and motorhome pitches.

Crianlarich SYHA HOSTEL £

(☑ 01838-300260; www.syha.org.uk; Station Rd, Crianlarich; dm/tr/q £18/65/86; P@🛜) Well run and comfortable, with a spacious kitchen, dining area and lounge, this is a real haven for walkers or anyone passing through. Dorms vary in size – there are some great en suite family rooms that should be prebooked – but all are clean and roomy.

Ewich House B&B ££

(☑ 01838-300536; www.ewich.co.uk; A82, Strathfillan; s/d £45/85; P🛜) This lovely Swiss-run stone farmhouse is just below the main road between Crianlarich and Tyndrum, but has a fabulous outlook over a valley, with uplifting views and a large garden. It's very handy for walking and cycling routes and boasts great rooms with cheerful fabrics and wooden floors. Breakfast has home-laid eggs; walker-friendly features like packed lunches, laundry and a drying room are also available.

Real Food Café CAFE £

(☑ 01838-400235; www.therealfoodcafe.com; A82, Tyndrum; mains £7-10; ⏱ 7.30am-8pm Nov-Mar, to 8.30pm Oct, to 9pm Apr-Sep; 🛜🍴) 🌿 Hungry hillwalkers throng the tables in this justifiably popular eatery. The menu looks familiar – with fish and chips, soups, salads and burgers – but the owners make an effort to source sustainably and locally, and the quality shines through.

❶ Getting There & Away

Scottish Citylink (www.citylink.co.uk) runs several **buses** daily to Glasgow (£17.60, 1¾ hours, 10 daily), Fort William (£14.80, 1¼ hours, eight daily) and Skye (£39, four hours, three daily) from both villages. One bus a day goes to Oban in summer (£12, one hour).

Trains run to Tyndrum and Crianlarich from Fort William (£20, 1¾ hours, four daily Monday to Saturday, two on Sunday), Oban (£12.10, 1¼ hours, four or six daily) and Glasgow (£20, two hours, three to seven daily).

Helensburgh

POP 13,700

With the coming of the railway in the mid-19th century, Helensburgh – named after the wife of Sir James Colquhoun of Luss –

became a popular seaside retreat for wealthy Glaswegian families. Their spacious Victorian villas now populate the hillside above the Firth of Clyde, but none can compare with splendid Hill House.

Built in 1902 for Glasgow publisher Walter Blackie, Hill House (NTS; ☑ 01436-673900; www.nts.org.uk; Upper Colquhoun St; adult/child £10.50/7.50; ⏱ 11.30am-5.30pm Apr-Oct) is perhaps architect Charles Rennie Mackintosh's finest creation – its timeless elegance still feels chic today. Mackintosh was keen not to cast his pearls before swine: he once chided Mrs Blackie for putting the wrong-coloured flowers in a vase in the hall. You can stay here – check the NTS website. The Hill House is near Upper Helensburgh station, but not all trains stop there.

Helensburgh has frequent trains to Glasgow (£6.30, 45 minutes, two per hour). Hill House is near Upper Helensburgh station, but not all trains stop there.

Regular buses head to Balloch, or you can change trains down the line in Dumbarton.

Arrochar

POP 700

The village of Arrochar has a wonderful location, looking across the head of Loch Long to the jagged peaks of the Cobbler (Ben Arthur; 884m). The mountain takes its name from the shape of its north peak (the one on the right, seen from Arrochar), which looks like a cobbler hunched over his bench. The village makes a picturesque overnight stop.

To climb the Cobbler, start from the roadside car park at Succoth near the head of Loch Long. A steep uphill hike through woods is followed by an easier section heading into the valley below the triple peaks. Then it's steeply uphill again to the saddle between the north and central peaks.

The central peak is higher, but awkward to get to – scramble through the hole and along the ledge to reach the airy summit. The north peak to the right is an easy walk. Allow five to six hours for the 5-mile round trip.

The black-and-white, 19th-century Village Inn (☑ 01301-702279; www.villageinnarrochar.co.uk; s/d £85/100; ⏱ food 10am-9pm; P🛜) is a gloriously convivial pub that boasts a beer garden with a great view of the Cobbler. There are 14 en suite bedrooms, lovely renovated chambers, some with loch views and most with decent bathrooms. Meals – bar standards supplemented by more ambitious blackboard specials – are somewhat over-priced (mains £10 to £17) but tasty enough.

Citylink (www.citylink.co.uk) buses from Glasgow to Inveraray and Campbeltown call at Arrochar (£8.80, 1¼ hours, nine daily). There are also three or four trains a day from Glasgow to Arrochar & Tarbet station (£11.80, 1¼ hours), continuing to Oban or Fort William.

THE TROSSACHS

The Trossachs region has long been a favourite weekend getaway, offering outstanding natural beauty and excellent walking and cycling routes within easy reach of the southern population centres. With thickly forested hills, romantic lochs, national-park status and an interesting selection of places to stay and eat, its popularity is sure to continue.

The Trossachs first gained cachet in the early 19th century, when curious visitors came from across Britain, drawn by the romantic language of Walter Scott's poem 'Lady of the Lake', inspired by Loch Katrine.

ROB ROY

Nicknamed Red ('*ruadh*' in Gaelic, anglicised to 'roy') for his ginger locks, Robert MacGregor (1671–1734) was the wild leader of the wildest of Scotland's clans, outlawed by powerful neighbours, hence their sobriquet, Children of the Mist. Incognito, Rob became a prosperous livestock trader, before a dodgy deal led to a warrant for his arrest.

A legendary swordsman, the fugitive from justice then became notorious for daring raids into the Lowlands to carry off cattle and sheep. Forever hiding from potential captors, he was twice imprisoned, but escaped dramatically on both occasions. He finally turned himself in and received his liberty and a pardon from the king. He lies buried – perhaps – in the churchyard at Balquhidder; his uncompromising later epitaph reads 'MacGregor despite them'. His life has been glorified over the years due to Walter Scott's novel and the 1995 film. Many Scots see his life as a symbol of the struggle of the common folk against the inequitable ownership of vast tracts of the country by landed aristocrats.

---

and Rob Roy, about the derring-do of the region's most famous son.

In summer, the Trossachs can be over-burdened with coach tours, but many of these are day trippers – peaceful, long evenings gazing at the reflections in the nearest loch are still possible. If you can, it's worth timing your visit not to coincide with a weekend.

Aberfoyle & Around

POP 700

Crawling with visitors on most weekends and dominated by a huge car park, little Aberfoyle is easily overwhelmed by day trippers. Callander or other Trossachs towns appeal more as places to stay, but Aberfoyle has lots to do close at hand and has great accommodation options nearby. It's also a stop on the Rob Roy Way (p241).

⊙ Sights & Activities

Inchmahome Priory RUINS
(HES; www.historicenvironment.scot; Lake of Menteith; adult/child incl ferry £5.50/3.30; ⊙10am-5pm Apr-Sep, 10am-4pm Oct, last ferry to island 45min before closing) From the Lake of Menteith (called lake not loch due to a mistranslation from Gaelic), 3 miles east of Aberfoyle, a ferry takes visitors to these substantial ruins. Mary, Queen of Scots was kept safe here as a child during Henry VIII's 'Rough Wooing'. Henry attacked Stirling trying to force Mary to marry his son in order to unite the kingdoms. Ongoing renovation may mean certain areas are closed and the admission fee reduced.

★ Loch Katrine Circuit CYCLING
An excellent 20-mile circular cycle route from Aberfoyle starts on the Lochs & Glens Cycle Way on the forest trail. Following the southern shore of Loch Achray, you reach the pier on Loch Katrine. The 10.30am boat (or afternoon sailings in summer) takes you to the western shore, from where you can follow the beautiful B829 via Loch Ard back to Aberfoyle.

Instead of getting the boat, you could bike it along the loch's northern shore, adding an extra 14 miles to the trip. An alternative to the forest trail from Aberfoyle is taking the A821 over Duke's Pass.

The Lodge NATURE CENTRE
(David Marshall Lodge; ☑0300 067 6615; www.forestry.gov.uk; A821; car park £1-3; ⊙10am-4pm Oct-Dec & Mar-Apr, to 3pm Jan & Feb, to 5pm May-

Jun & Sep, to 6pm Jul & Aug) **FREE** Half a mile north of Aberfoyle, this nature centre has info about the many walks and cycle routes in and around the **Queen Elizabeth Forest Park**. There are live wildlife cameras offering a peek at osprey and barn owl nests among others. The centre is worth visiting solely for the views.

Picturesque but busy waymarked trails start from here, ranging from a light 20-minute stroll to a nearby waterfall – with great interactive play options for kids – to a hilly 4-mile circuit. The centre has a popular cafe. Also here, **Go Ape!** (☑0333 920 4859; www.goape.co.uk; Queen Elizabeth Forest Park; adult/child £33/25; ☉Sat & Sun Nov & Feb-Easter, Wed-Mon Easter-Oct) will bring out the monkey in you on its exhilarating adventure course of long zip lines, swings and rope bridges through the forest.

Sleeping

Bield B&B **££**

(☑01877-382351; www.thebield.net; Trossachs Rd, Aberfoyle; s/d £45/65; P☎) With a kind, genuine welcome, the Bield is exactly the sort of place you want to fetch up after a long day's walking or cycling. This striking sandstone house has large, comfortable rooms, a sociable breakfast table and views from its hillside location just above the centre. Prices are very reasonable.

★**Duchray Castle** B&B **£££**

(☑01877-389333; www.duchraycastle.com; Aberfoyle; d £140-195; P☎) Splendidly set in secluded rural surrounds, all forest and stream, but just three miles from Aberfoyle, this castle is a treat, with four sumptuous rooms, a noble great hall and a cosier lounge space with games, DVDs and books. It's good for a luxurious romantic break, but also for families – children will love the spiral stairs, castle atmosphere and acres to romp in.

Breakfast is a treat, with quality produce served in an atmospheric stone-vaulted chamber. To get here, head across the stone bridge in Aberfoyle, take the third turning on the right (past a post box) and keep going. For part of the year, it is self-catering only.

★**Lake of Menteith Hotel** HOTEL **£££**

(☑01877-385258; www.lake-hotel.com; Port of Menteith; s £115, d £138-240; P☎) Soothingly situated on a lake (yes, it's the only non-loch in Scotland) 3 miles east of Aberfoyle, this makes a great romantic getaway. Though all rooms are excellent, with a handsome con-

TROSSACHS TRANSPORT

In a bid to cut public transport costs, **Demand Responsive Transport** (DRT; ☑01786-404040; www.stirling.gov.uk) now covers the Trossachs area. It sounds complex, but basically it means you get a taxi to where you want to go, for the price of a bus. There are various zones. Taxis should preferably be booked 24 hours in advance; call ☑01786-404040.

temporary feel, it's worth the upgrade to the enormous 'lake heritage' ones with a view of the water: it really is a sensational outlook.

Even if you're not staying, head down to the waterside bar-restaurant (mains £10 to £17; open noon to 2.30pm and 5.30pm to 9pm). Check the website for packages.

Information

The **Aberfoyle Tourist Office** (☑01877-381221; www.visitscotland.com; Main St, Aberfoyle; ☉10am-5pm Apr-Oct, 10am-4pm Nov-Mar; ☎) is large, and has a good selection of walking information.

Getting There & Away

First (www.firstgroup.com) has six daily buses (Monday to Saturday) from Stirling (£4.60, 45 minutes).

Demand Responsive Transport (DRT) operates in the Aberfoyle area.

Lochs Katrine & Achray

This rugged area, 7 miles north of Aberfoyle and 10 miles west of Callander, is the heart of the Trossachs. **Boats** (☑01877-376315; www.lochkatrine.com; Trossachs Pier; 1hr cruise adult £11-13, child £5.50-6.50; ☉Easter-Oct) run cruises from Trossachs Pier at the eastern tip of Loch Katrine. One of these is the fabulous centenarian steamship *Sir Walter Scott;* check the website departures, as it's worth coinciding with this veteran if you can. There are various one-hour afternoon sailings, and at 10.30am (plus additional summer departures) there's a departure to Stronachlachar at the other end of the loch (single/return adult £13/16, child £6.50/8, two hours return). From Stronachlachar (accessible by car via a 12-mile road from Aberfoyle), you can reach the eastern shore of Loch Lomond at isolated Inversnaid. A tarmac path links Trossachs Pier with Stronachlachar, so you can take the boat out and walk/cycle back (14 miles). At Trossachs Pier, Katrinewheelz (☎01877-376366; www.katrinewheelz.co.uk; Trossachs Pier, Loch Katrine; hire per half/full day from £15/20; ☺9am-5pm Apr-Oct, 11am-3pm Sat & Sun Nov-Dec & Feb-Mar) hires out good bikes and even electric buggies. Bring a picnic; the cafe is mediocre.

Two good walks start from nearby Loch Achray. The path to the rocky cone called Ben A'an (454m) begins at a car park just east of the Loch Katrine turnoff. It's easy to follow and the return trip is just under 4 miles. A tougher walk is up rugged Ben Venue (727m). Start walking from the signed car park just south of the Loch Katrine turnoff. The return trip is 7.5 miles.

Loch Katrine is within the Demand Responsive Transport (DRT; p249) zone and can be reached by prebooked transport from either Callander or Aberfoyle.

Callander

POP 3100

Callander, the principal Trossachs town, has been pulling in tourists for over 150 years, and has a laid-back ambience along its main thoroughfare that quickly lulls visitors into lazy pottering. There's an excellent array of accommodation options here, and some intriguing places to eat.

◉ Sights & Activities

★ **Hamilton Toy Collection**   MUSEUM
(☎01877-330004; www.thehamiltontoycollection.co.uk; 111 Main St; adult/child £3/1; ☺10am-5pm Mon-Sat, noon-5pm Sun Apr-Oct) The Hamilton Toy Collection is a powerhouse of 20th-century juvenile memorabilia, chock-full of dolls houses, puppets and toy soldiers. It's an amazing collection and a guaranteed nostalgia trip. Phone in winter as it opens some weekends.

Bracklinn Falls & Callander Crags   WALKING
Impressive Bracklinn Falls are reached by track and footpath from Bracklinn Rd (30 minutes each way from the car park). Also off Bracklinn Rd, a woodland trail leads up to Callander Crags, with great views over the surroundings; a return trip from the car park is about 4 miles.

Wheels Cycling Centre   CYCLING
(☎01877-331100; http://scottish-cycliing.com; bike per hour/day/week from £8/20/90; ☺10am-6pm Mar-Oct) The Trossachs is a lovely area to cycle around. On a cycle route, excellent Wheels Cycling Centre has a wide range of hire bikes. To get there, take Bridge St off Main St, turn right onto Invertrossachs Rd and continue for a mile.

🛏 Sleeping

★ **Callander Hostel**   HOSTEL £
(☎01877-331465; www.callanderhostel.co.uk; 6 Bridgend; dm £18.50-23.50, d £60-70; P@🛜) This hostel in a mock-Tudor building has been a major labour of love by a local youth project and is now a top-class facility. Well-furnished dorms offer bunks with individual light and USB charge ports, while en suite doubles have super views. Staff are welcoming and friendly, and it has a spacious common area and share kitchen as well as a cafe and garden.

White Shutters   B&B £
(☎01877-330442; www.incallander.co.uk/directory/white-shutters-bb; 6 South Church St; s/d £26/46; 🛜) A cute little house just off the main street, White Shutters offers pleasing rooms with shared bathroom and a friendly welcome. The large double is particularly appealing, but it's all clean and comfortable and offers exceptional value.

Roslin Cottage   B&B ££
(☎01877-339787; www.roslincottage.com; Stirling Rd; s £45, d £55-80; P🛜) A cottage that's a haven of good hospitality holds three snug en suite rooms that make an enticing Trossachs base. They all have charm: we love the Kirtle room with the original 17th-century wall exposed. Other delights include a lovely big back garden, a log fire in the lounge and sociable chef-cooked breakfasts.

It's on the right as you enter Callander from the east, before the petrol station. It was up for sale at time of research so may change.

Abbotsford Lodge   HOTEL ££
(☎01877-330066; www.abbotsfordlodge.com; Stirling Rd; s/d £65/80; ☺Mar-Nov; P🛜) This friendly Victorian house offers something different from the norm, with tartan and florals consigned to the bonfire, replaced by stylish, comfortable contemporary design that enhances the building's original features. There are fabulous, spacious superiors (from £125) with modish grey fabrics as well as cheaper top-floor rooms – shared bathroom – with lovably offbeat under-roof

shapes. Room-only and continental breakfast rates are available.

Arden House
B&B ££

(☑ 01877-339405; www.ardenhouse.org.uk; Bracklinn Rd; s from £75, d £80-100; ☺ Mar-Oct; ⊞ ☎) This elegant home has a fabulous hillside location with verdant garden and lovely vistas; close to the centre but far from the crowds. The commodious rooms are impeccable, with lots of natural light. They include large upstairs doubles with great views. Welcoming owners, noble architectural features – super bay windows – and a self-catering studio make this a top option.

There's a two-night minimum stay in summer.

★ Roman Camp Hotel
HOTEL £££

(☑ 01877-330003; www.romancamphotel.co.uk; off Main St; s/d/superior £110/160/220; ⊞ ☎ ☷) Callander's best hotel is centrally located but feels rural, set by the river in beautiful grounds. Endearing features include a lounge with blazing fire and a library with a tiny secret chapel. It's an old-fashioned warren of a place with four grades of room; standards are certainly luxurious, but superiors are even more appealing, with period furniture, excellent bathrooms, armchairs and fireplace.

The upmarket restaurant is open to the public. Reassuringly, the name refers not to toga parties but to a ruin in the adjacent fields.

✖ Eating & Drinking

Mhor Bread
CAFE, BAKERY £

(www.mhor.net; 8 Main St; light meals £2-6; ☺ 7am-5pm Mon-Sat, 8am-5pm Sun; ☎) ✦ Great bread for picnics – think sourdough, think seeds, think local – is baked at this high-street spot, which is also a good stop for decent coffee, pies and filled rolls. The steak and haggis pie is a treat.

★ Venachar Lochside
SEAFOOD ££

(Harbour Cafe; ☑ 01877-330011; www.venachar-lochside.com; Loch Venachar; mains £9-15; ☺ lunch noon-4pm Jan-Nov, plus dinner 5.30-8.30pm Fri & Sat Jun-Sep; ☎ ❸) On lovely Loch Venachar, 4½ miles west of Callander, this cafe-restaurant has a stunning waterside setting and does a nice line in delicious fresh seafood. It opens from 10am to 5pm daily for coffees, teas and baked goods. You can also hire boats and tackle to go fishing for trout on the loch here.

★ Callander Meadows
SCOTTISH ££

(☑ 01877-330181; www.callandermeadows.co.uk; 24 Main St; 2-/3-course lunch £12/17, mains £13-17; ☺ 10am-9pm Thu-Mon; ☎) Informal and cosy, this well-loved restaurant in the centre of Callander occupies the front rooms of a main street house. It's truly excellent; there's a contemporary flair for presentation and unusual flavour combinations, but a solidly British base underpins the cuisine. There's a great beer/coffee garden out the back, where you can also eat. Opens daily from June to September.

Lunch is offered from noon to 2.30pm, and dinner from 6pm to 9pm. At other times, it does teas, light meals, breakfasts and the like.

Mhor Fish
SEAFOOD ££

(☑ 01877-330213; www.mhor.net; 75 Main St; mains £8-18; ☺ noon-9pm Tue-Sun; ☎) ✦ This simply decorated spot, with formica tables and a hodgepodge of chairs, sources brilliant sustainable seafood. Browse the fresh catch then eat it pan-seared in the dining area accompanied by a decent wine selection, or fried and wrapped in paper with chips to take away. It's all great – calamari and oysters are wonderfully toothsome starters.

Lade Inn
PUB

(www.theladeinn.com; Kilmahog; ☺ noon-11pm Mon-Thu, noon-1am Fri & Sat, 12.30-10.30pm Sun; ☎ ⊞) Callander's best pub isn't in Callander – it's a mile west of town. It pulls a good pint (with its own real ales), and next door it has a shop with a dazzling selection of Scottish beers. There's low-key live music here at weekends. The food (noon to 9pm, from 12.30pm Sunday; mains £9 to £14) is solid rather than spectacular.

ℹ Information

Callander Tourist Office (☑ 01877-330342; www.lochlomond-trossachs.org; 52 Main St; ☺ 9.30am-5pm Apr-Oct, to 4pm Nov-Mar; ☎) is very helpful for information on the region and national park.

ℹ Getting There & Away

First (www.firstgroup.com) operates buses from Stirling (£5.20, 45 minutes, hourly Monday to Saturday, every two hours Sunday).

Kingshouse (☑ 01877-384768; www.kingshousetravel.com) buses run from Killin (£5.70, 40 minutes, six Monday to Saturday).

For Aberfoyle, use DRT (p249) or get off a Stirling-bound bus at Blair Drummond safari park and cross the road.

Balquhidder & Around

North of Callander, you'll skirt past the shores of gorgeous Loch Lubnaig. Not as famous as some of its cousins, it's still well worth a stop for its sublime views of forested hills.

In the small village of Balquhidder (bal-whidder), 9 miles north of Callander off the A84, there's a churchyard with – perhaps – Rob Roy's grave. It's an appropriately beautiful spot in a deep, winding glen in big-sky country. The uncompromising later epitaph reads 'MacGregor despite them'. In the church itself is the 8th-century St Angus' stone, probably a marker to the original tomb of St Angus, an 8th-century monk who built the first church here.

At the A84 junction, 18th-century inn Mhor 84 (☑01877-384646; www.mhor.net; A84, Kingshouse; r without breakfast £80; P 🛜 🐾) 🖉 has been given a modern-retro revamp and is now a great place with bags of facilities, simple, good-value rooms and a delicious menu of hearty, nourishing meals with the Mhor philosophy of local and sustainable. A great pit stop for drivers, walkers and cyclists. Some rooms are in a rear cottage; there's also a self-catering one.

There are three menus served: breakfast from 8am to noon, day from noon to 6pm and dinner from 6pm to 9pm.

Monachyle Mhor (☑01877-384622; www.mhor.net; d £195-265; ☉Feb-Dec; P 🛜 🐾) 🖉 is a luxury hideaway with a fantastically peaceful location overlooking two lochs. It's a great fusion of country Scotland and contemporary attitudes to design and food. Rooms are superb and feature quirkily original decor, particularly the fabulous 'feature rooms'; you might get your own steam room or a wonderful double bathtub. The restaurant is excellent.

Local buses between Callander and Killin stop at the main road turn-off to Balquhidder, as do daily Citylink (www.citylink.co.uk) buses between Edinburgh and Oban/Fort William.

Balquhidder is part of the DRT (p249) scheme, which you can use to get to Monachyle Mhor from the main road.

Killin

POP 800

A fine base for the Trossachs or Perthshire, this lovely village sits at the western end of Loch Tay and has a spread-out, relaxed feel, particularly around the scenic Falls of Dochart, which tumble through the centre. On a sunny day people sprawl over the rocks by the bridge, pint or picnic in hand. Killin offers fine walking around the town, and mighty mountains and glens close at hand.

🏃 Activities

Five miles northeast of Killin, Ben Lawers (1214m) rises above Loch Tay. Walking routes abound; one rewarding circular walk heads up into the Acharn forest south of town, emerging above the treeline to great views of Loch Tay and Ben Lawers. Killin Outdoor Centre offers walking advice.

Glen Lochay runs westwards from Killin into the hills of Mamlorn. You can take a mountain bike up the glen; the scenery is impressive and the hills aren't too difficult. It's possible, on a nice summer day, to climb over the top of Ben Challum (1025m) and descend to Crianlarich, but it's hard work. A potholed road, not maintained and no longer suitable for cars, also connects Glen Lochay with Glen Lyon.

Killin is on the Lochs & Glens Cycle Way from Glasgow to Inverness. Hire bikes from helpful Killin Outdoor Centre (☑01567-820652; www.killinoutdoor.co.uk; Main St; bike £25 per 24hr, kayak/canoe £25/30 per 2hr; ☉9am-5.30pm), which also has canoes and kayaks or, in winter, crampons and snowshoes.

🛏 Sleeping & Eating

High Creagan CAMPSITE £
(☑01567-820449; Aberfeldy Rd; per person tent/caravan sites £5/8; ☉Apr-Oct; P 🐾) This long-established favourite has a good-humoured boss and a well kept, sheltered campsite with plenty of grass set high on the slopes overlooking sparkling Loch Tay, 3 miles east of Killin. Kids aren't allowed in the tent area (for insurance reasons), as there's a stream running through it.

Old Bank B&B ££
(☑01567-829317; www.theoldbankkillin.co.uk; Manse Rd; s/d £55/80; P 🛜) This solid

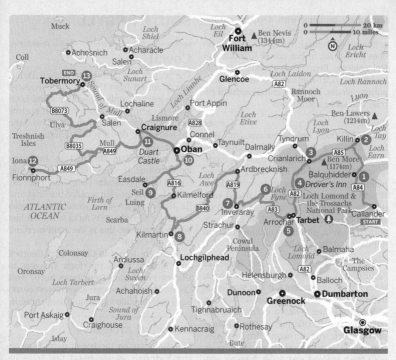

Driving Tour
Callander to Tobermory

START CALLANDER
END TOBERMORY
LENGTH 240 MILES; TWO TO FOUR DAYS

Having explored the southern part of the Trossachs, head north out of Callander on the A84, following pretty Loch Lubnaig before optional detours of a few miles to see Rob Roy's grave at **1 Balquhidder** (p252)and the Falls of Dochart at pretty **2 Killin** (p252).

Continue on the A85 to **3 Crianlarich** (p246), surrounded by Highland majesty, then turn left on the A82 to follow the western shore of Loch Lomond. Stop for a look and/or pint at the quirky **4 Drover's Inn** (p245), then deviate right at Tarbet onto the A83 – shortly thereafter, **5 Arrochar** (p247) makes a scenic lunch stop.

Head through scenic Glen Croe, over the pass and into Glen Kinglas, then follow the shore of Loch Fyne – stops at the **6 brewery** (p258) and/or oyster bar obligatory! – to picturesque **7 Inveraray** (p257). Go right through the arch here on the A819, then

left onto the B840, a lonely road following stiletto-like Loch Awe. You'll eventually reach **8 Kilmartin** (p259), with its great museum and evocative prehistoric sights.

Follow the A816 north to **9 Oban** (p275), where good accommodation options, a handsome harbour and delicious seafood awaits. You may want to deviate to see the island of **10 Seil** (p280) en route: from here, great boat trips can take you out to the Corryvreckan whirlpool. Catch a ferry from Oban to Mull and follow the A849 southwest via **11 Duart Castle** (p282) to the island's tip at Fionnphort, where you cross to the emerald jewel of **12 Iona** (p288) and can take a boat trip to the spectacular rock formations of Staffa.

Retrace your steps, then follow Mull's winding west coast on the B8035 and B8073 via spectacular coastline and the beach at Calgary to arrive at the colourful shorefront houses of the main town, **13 Tobermory** (p283).

foursquare building with a pretty garden stands proud above the main street. It's a genuinely welcoming place, with a host who does everything in her power to make you feel welcome. Breakfast is abundant and the rooms are super-comfortable, with contemporary colours, hill views and thoughtful extras. Two share a bathroom.

Courie Inn
INN ££

(☑ 01567-831000; www.thecourieinn.com; Main St; d £90-110; P ඁ) An excellent all-round choice on the Killin scene, this has quality, comfortable rooms in a variety of sizes, including a sumptuous suite with views. It artfully blends the traditional and contemporary. Downstairs, the restaurant does smart bistro food (mains £11 to £15; daily 5pm to 8.45pm, plus noon to 3pm Friday to Sunday) and there's a bar.

Falls of Dochart Inn
PUB FOOD ££

(☑ 01567-820270; www.falls-of-dochart-inn.co.uk; mains £10-16; ⊘ noon-3pm & 6-9pm Mon-Thu, to 9.30pm Fri, noon-9.30pm Sat, noon-8.30pm Sun; P ඁ) In a prime position overlooking the falls, this is a terrific pub: a snug, atmospheric space with a roaring fire, real ales, personable service and decent pub grub, with fresh seafood and Asian flavours adding a dimension to tasty staples and daily specials. The outside tables are great spots on a sunny day.

The rooms (single/double from £60/80) are handsome, but a few glitches like poor heating let some of them down.

ℹ Information

Old Mill (☑ 01567-820628; www.killinwatermill.co.uk; Pier Rd; ⊘ 10am-4pm Mar-Oct, reduced hours in winter; ඁ) is a picturesque old mill building by the falls. It houses a thrift shop whose volunteers also give out tourist information.

ℹ Getting There & Away

Kingshouse (p251) Runs six buses Monday to Saturday to Callander (£5.70, 40 minutes), where you can change for Stirling.

Summer bus service, **Ring of Breadalbane Explorer** (www.breadalbane.org; ⊘ Tue, Wed & Sun Jul-Sep), does a hop-on hop-off Breadalbane circuit around Crieff, Comrie, St Fillans, Lochearnhead, Killin, Kenmore, Acharn and Aberfeldy.

SOUTH ARGYLL

Cowal

The remote and picturesque Cowal Peninsula is cut off from the rest of the country by the lengthy fjords of Loch Long and Loch Fyne. It comprises rugged hills and narrow lochs, with only a few small villages and the old-fashioned, down-at-heel holiday resort of Dunoon.

From Arrochar, the A83 to Inveraray loops around the head of Loch Long and climbs into spectacular Glen Croe. The pass at the head of the glen is called the Rest and Be Thankful. As you descend Glen Kinglas on the far side, the A815 forks to the left just before Cairndow; this is the main overland route into Cowal.

There are ferries to Cowal from Gourock and Tarbert. Buses run from Glasgow to Dunoon via the ferry. Other buses run by West Coast Motors (www.westcoastmotors.co.uk) head overland into and around the peninsula.

Dunoon & Around

Like Rothesay on the Isle of Bute, Dunoon is a Victorian seaside resort that owes its existence to the steamers that once carried thousands of Glaswegians on pleasure trips 'doon the watter' in the 19th and 20th centuries. Fortunes declined when cheap foreign holidays stole the market and Dunoon is still a bit down in the dumps. Bypass its ugly town centre and take in the magnificent perspectives along the long waterfront.

The town's main attraction is still, as it was in the 1950s, strolling along the promenade, licking an icecream cone and watching the yachts at play in the Firth of Clyde.

◉ Sights

Benmore Botanic Garden
GARDENS

(☑ 01369-706261; www.rbge.org.uk; A815; adult/child £6.50/free; ⊘ 10am-6pm Apr-Sep, to 5pm Mar & Oct) This garden, 7 miles north of Dunoon, contains Scotland's finest collection of flowering trees and shrubs, including impressive displays of rhododendrons and azaleas, and is entered along a spectacular avenue of giant redwoods. A highlight is the Victorian fernery, nestled in an unlikely hold in the crags. The year-round cafe here appeals for lunch or coffee. Buses run between Dunoon and the gardens.

Festivals & Events

Cowal Highland Gathering HIGHLAND GAMES
(www.cowalgathering.com; ⊘late Aug) Held in
Dunoon. The spectacular finale features over
a thousand bagpipers saluting the chieftain.

ⓘ Information

Dunoon Tourist Office (🖉 01369-703785;
www.visitcowal.co.uk; 7 Alexandra Pde;
⊘10am-4pm Nov-Mar, 10am-5pm Apr–mid-Jun
& Sep-Oct, 9am-5pm mid-Jun–Aug) is on the
waterfront 100m north of the pier.

ⓘ Getting There & Away

BOAT
Dunoon is served by two competing ferry services from Gourock (near Greenock). Argyll Ferries
is better if you are travelling on foot and want to
arrive in the town centre.

Argyll Ferries (www.argyllferries.co.uk; adult/
child £4.50/2.25; 25 minutes; half-hourly
Monday to Saturday, hourly Sunday.)

Western Ferries (www.western-ferries.co.uk;
adult/child/car £4.40/2.10/12.40; 20 minutes;
two to three hourly.) Arrives at a pier just over
a mile from the centre of Dunoon. Departs from
McInroy's Point, 2 miles south of Gourock train
station on the Irvine road; Scottish Citylink
buses run to here.

BUS
McGill's run buses from Glasgow to Dunoon
(£9.50, two hours, five to seven daily) via the
ferry. It's quicker between Gourock and Glasgow
to jump on the train.

Buses around the Cowal Peninsula, to
Inveraray (£3.90) and to Rothesay on Bute
(£3.50), are operated by West Coast Motors
(www.westcoastmotors.co.uk).

Tighnabruaich
POP 200

Sleepy little seaside Tighnabruaich (tinna-
broo-ach) is one of the most attractive villages on the Firth of Clyde and by far the
most appealing place at which to overnight
on the Cowal Peninsula.

West Coast Motors (www.westcoastmo-
tors.co.uk) runs three to four buses Monday
to Saturday to Tighnabruaich from Dunoon
(£2.80, 35 minutes), most continuing to the
ferry at Portavadie.

🛏 Sleeping & Eating

Kames Hotel INN ££
(🖉 01700-811489; www.kames-hotel.com; Kames;
s £50, d £75-120; ⊘food noon-2.30pm & 6-8.30pm;
🛜) A mile south of Tighnabruaich, in the

village of Kames, this has a variety of comfortable rooms, including cute low-bedded
ones under the sloping roof on the top floor.
The bar downstairs, popular with yachties
and locals, has great atmosphere, killer water views and serves good-value bar meals
(mains £8 to £12), which are well presented
and generous in size. Wi-fi is fast.

★**Botanica** BISTRO ££
(🖉 01700-811186; www.botanicafood.co.uk; Main
St; dinner mains £12-17; ⊘10am-3.30pm Wed &
Thu, 10am-3.30pm & 6-11pm Fri & Sat, 10am-6pm
Sun Jun-Aug, reduced hours low season; 🛜🖉) In
the centre of Tighnabruaich village, this offers a touch of eclecticism focused on solid
British ingredients, with simple classics like
asparagus with Bearnaise sauce a lovely
lunchtime treat, and a changing dinner
menu featuring things like lamb tagine. Un-
derstandably, it tends to pack out for dinner,
so it's best to book.

Bute
POP 6500

Bute lies pinched between the thumb and
forefinger of the Cowal Peninsula, separated from the mainland by a narrow, scenic
strait. The Highland Boundary Fault cuts
through the middle of the island so that,
geologically speaking, the northern half is
in the Highlands and the southern half is in
the central Lowlands.

ⓘ Information

In the centre of Rothesay, **Isle of Bute Discovery Centre** (🖉 01700-507043; www.
visitscotland.com; Victoria St, Rothesay;
⊘9.30am-5.30pm Jul & Aug, 9.30am-5pm Apr-
Jun & Sep, 10am-5pm Oct, 10am-4pm Nov-Mar;
🛜) is in the Winter Gardens building.

> **GONE FISHIN'...**
>
> A lifetime's experience of exploring his
> native rivers, lochs and coastline means
> there isn't much that professional
> guide Duncan Pepper doesn't know
> about Scottish fishing. Though based
> in Argyll, he leads fishing trips all over
> Scotland for salmon, trout, pike, pollack
> and more. **Fishinguide Scotland**
> (🖉 07714-598848; www.fishinguide.co.uk;
> daily per person from £150; 🖪) packages
> include travel, instruction, permits,
> tackle and a lavish picnic lunch.

ℹ Getting There & Away

Buses run by **West Coast Motors** (☎01586-559135; www.westcoastmotors.co.uk) cross to Bute from the Cowal Peninsula.

CalMac ferries (☎0800-066 5000; www.calmac.co.uk) travel between Wemyss Bay and Rothesay (adult/car £3.05/10.95, 35 minutes, roughly hourly). Another crosses the short stretch of water between Rhubodach in the north of the island and Colintraive (adult/car £1.10/5.75, five minutes, half-hourly) in Cowal.

Rothesay

POP 4500

From the mid-19th century until the 1960s, Rothesay was one of Scotland's most popular holiday resorts, bustling with day trippers disembarking from numerous steamers crowded around the pier. Its hotels were filled with elderly holidaymakers and convalescents taking advantage of the famously mild climate.

Cheap foreign holidays saw Rothesay's fortunes decline, but a nostalgia-fuelled resurgence of interest has seen many Victorian buildings restored. The grassy, flowery waterfront and row of noble villas is a lovely place to be once again.

◉ Sights

Victorian Toilets HISTORIC BUILDING
(Rothesay Pier; adult/child 40p/free; ⊙9am-4.45pm daily Oct-Apr, 8am-5.45pm Mon-Thu, 8am-7.30pm Fri-Sun May-Sep) Dating from 1899, these are a monument to lavatorial luxury – a disinfectant-scented temple of green and black marbled stoneware, glistening white enamel, glass-sided cisterns and gleaming copper pipes. The attendant will escort ladies into the hallowed confines of the gents for a look around when unoccupied. You can shower here too.

Rothesay Castle CASTLE
(HES; www.historicenvironment.scot; King St; adult/child £4.50/2.70; ⊙9.30am-5.30pm Apr-Sep, 10am-4pm Sat-Wed Oct-Mar) Splendid ruined 13th-century Rothesay Castle, with seagulls and jackdaws nesting in the walls, was once a favourite residence of the Stuart kings. It is unique in Scotland in having a circular plan, with four stocky round towers. The landscaped moat, with manicured turf, flower gardens and lazily cruising ducks, makes a picturesque setting.

🛏 Sleeping

Roseland Holiday Park CAMPSITE, BUNGALOWS £
(☎01700-501840; www.roselandlodgepark.co.uk; Roslin Rd; tent site for 1/2 £10/12, pod s/d £30/36; ⊙Mar-Oct; P🐾❃) Take the steep climb up the eccentric hairpins of Serpentine Rd to this small but pleasant grassy area, where you can pitch a tent amid the static caravans and a handful of campervan sites. Adjacent, the holiday-park section (open year-round) has bungalows and cute little pods for glamping that sleep up to four. Showers cost £1.

Bute Backpackers Hotel HOSTEL £
(☎01700-501876; www.butebackpackers.co.uk; 36 Argyle St; s/tw/d £25/45/50, s without bathroom £20; P❃) An appealing budget option on Rothesay's main thoroughfare, this large, well-equipped place offers private rooms of various sizes at a bargain price. Some are en suite, but shared bathrooms are modern and spotless, with power showers. The kitchen is huge, and there's a barbecue too.

Boat House B&B £
(☎01700-502696; www.theboathouse-bute.co.uk; 15 Battery Pl; s/d £60/80; ❃) Boat House brings a touch of class to Rothesay's guesthouse scene, with quality fabrics and furnishings and an eye for design that makes it feel like a boutique hotel, without the expensive price tag. Rooms are very swish, with a kitchenette and breakfast provided. Other features include a garden, sea views, a central location and a ground-floor room kitted out for wheelchair users. There's a two-night minimum stay at weekends.

St Ebba B&B ££
(☎01700-500059; www.rothesayaccommodation.co.uk; s/d £45/70; P❃) Turn left from the ferry and follow the shoreline to reach this typically noble Victorian lodge, divided into two B&Bs. This, entered down the right, takes full advantage of the lovely views with spacious rooms with big windows. Courteous hosts.

🍴 Eating

★ **Musicker** CAFE £
(☎01700-502287; www.musicker.co.uk; 11 High St; mains £3-7; ⊙10am-5pm Mon-Sat; ❃🖘) This cool little cafe serves Bute's best coffee, alongside a range of homebaking, soup and sandwiches with imaginative fillings. It also sells CDs, books and guitars, and sports an old-fashioned jukebox.

Squat Lobster FISH & CHIPS **£**

(meals £6-10; ⊘ noon-8pm Wed-Sun Apr-Oct) This small shack by the putting green next to the ferry terminal is friendly and well above average, sourcing fresh fish for its tasty fish and chips and other seafoody offerings. Opening hours are variable.

Harry Haw's BISTRO **££**

(☑ 01700-505857; www.harryhaws.com; 23 High St; mains £8-15; ⊘ noon-9pm; 🛜 ⊿) Great scenes at this welcoming modern bistro, whose moderate prices and pleasing range of deli-style fare plus burgers, local roast meat and tasty pastas make it a standout. The interior is attractive, with views over the castle. Staff are very friendly and so cheerful you wonder if there's something in the water.

Around Bute

In the southern part of the island you'll find the haunting 12th-century ruin of St Blane's Chapel and a sandy beach at Kilchattan Bay. There are more good beaches: Scalpsie Bay has a fantastic outlook to Arran, while Ettrick Bay is bigger, and has a tearoom (ugly outside but great chat and snacks inside).

Cycling is excellent: you can hire a bike from the Bike Shed (☑ 01700-505515; david. thebikeshed@btinternet.com; 23-25 East Princes St; ⊘ 9.30am-5.30pm Mon-Sat) in Rothesay.

The family seat of the Stuart Earls of Bute, Mount Stuart (☑ 01700-503877; www. mountstuart.com; adult/child £11.50/6.75, grounds only £6.50/3.50; ⊘ 11am-2.30pm Apr, 11am-4pm May-Oct, grounds 10am-6pm Apr-Oct) is one of Britain's more magnificent 19th-century stately homes, the first to have a telephone, underfloor heating and heated pool. Its eclectic interior, with a imposing central hall and chapel in Italian marble, is heavily influenced by the third Marquess's interests in Greek mythology and astrology. The drawing room has paintings by Titian and Tintoretto among other masters. Mount Stuart is 5 miles south of Rothesay; bus 490 runs hourly.

Buy tickets at the visitor centre (last sale at 3pm), from where it's a 15-minute stroll through lovely grounds to the house. Entry is either by guided tour or free visit, depending on the time. A shuttle bus runs the route. Private tours (£20 or £40) offer glimpses of the pool and more bedrooms.

There's a cafe serving famously opulent afternoon teas here.

Discounted ferry-plus-entrance tickets are available from CalMac (www.calmac. co.uk).

Inveraray

POP 600

There's no fifty shades of grey around here: this historic planned village is all black and white – even logos of high street chain shops conform. Spectacularly set on the shores of Loch Fyne, Inveraray was built by the Duke of Argyll in Georgian style when he revamped his nearby castle in the 18th century.

◎ Sights & Activities

Inveraray Castle CASTLE

(☑ 01499-302203; www.inveraray-castle.com; adult/child/family £10/7/29; ⊘ 10am-5.45pm Apr-Oct) This visually stunning castle on the north side of town has been the seat of the Dukes of Argyll – chiefs of Clan Campbell – since the 15th century. The 18th-century building, with its fairytale turrets and fake battlements, houses an impressive armoury hall, its walls patterned with more than 1000 pole-arms, dirks, muskets and Lochaber axes.

Inveraray Jail MUSEUM

(☑ 01499-302381; www.inverarayjail.co.uk; Church Sq; adult/child £10.95/6.50; ⊘ 9.30am-6pm Apr-Oct, 10am-5pm Nov-Mar; 🖼) At this entertaining interactive tourist attraction you can sit in on a trial, try out a cell and discover the harsh tortures that were meted out to unfortunate prisoners. The attention to detail – including a life-sized model of an inmate squatting on a 19th-century toilet – more than makes up for the sometimes tedious commentary.

⭐ Festivals & Events

FyneFest BEER, MUSIC

(www.fynefest.com; ⊘ mid-Jun) Held over three days by the Fyne Ales brewery (p258), this has craft beer, quality food stalls and bands. What's not to like?

🛏 Sleeping & Eating

Claonairigh House B&B **£**

(☑ 01499-302160; www.inverarraybandb.co.uk; A83, Bridge of Douglas; s/tw/d £45/55/60; 🅿 @ 🛜) This attractive 18th-century house, built for the Duke of Argyll in 1745, is set in 3 hectares of grounds on a riverbank complete with waterfall and salmon fishing. There are three homely en suite rooms, one with

---

DON'T MISS

FYNE FOOD & DRINK

Eight miles north of Inveraray, at the head of Loch Fyne, it pays to stop by two great local establishments.

Fyne Ales (☑01499-600120; www.fyneales.com; Achadunan, Cairndow; tours £5; ☺10am-6pm) These friendly folk do a great range of craft beers in an attractive modern brewery off the A83. There's a lovely bar-cafe here (with outdoor seating) where you can taste them all: the light, citrussy Jarl is a standout. Tours run at least twice daily – call for times. A range of walks tackle the pretty glen from a car park nearby.

Loch Fyne Oyster Bar (☑01499-600236; www.lochfyne.com; Clachan, Cairndow; mains £11-22; ☺9am-5pm; ☎) The success of this cooperative is such that it now lends its name to dozens of restaurants throughout the UK. But the original is still the best, with salty oysters straight out of the lake, and fabulous salmon dishes. The atmosphere and decor is simple, friendly and unpretentious; it also has a shop and deli. Expect to queue if you haven't booked.

---

a four-poster bed, others compact and cute with exposed stone and sloping ceiling. It's a cheerful country home with a resident menagerie, 4 miles south of town.

Inveraray Hostel HOSTEL £
(☑01499-302454; www.inverarayhostel.co.uk; Dalmally Rd; dm/tw £17/39; ☺Apr-Oct; ☐☎) To get to this hostel, housed in a comfortable, modern bungalow, go through the right hand one of the two arched entrances on the seafront. Metal bunk beds – rooms sleep only two or four – are comfortable, and there's a wee lounge and a kitchen with plenty of stoves. Inconveniently, the hostel is shut between 10am and 4pm.

George Hotel INN ££
(☑01499-302111; www.thegeorgehotel.co.uk; Main St E; d £85-115; ☐☎☺) The George boasts a magnificent choice of opulent, individual rooms complete with four-poster beds, period furniture, Victorian roll-top baths and private Jacuzzis (superior rooms cost £135 to £180 per double). Some are in an annexe opposite. The cosy wood-panelled bar, with rough stone walls, flagstone floor and peat fires, is a delightful place for all-day bar meals and has a beer garden.

Samphire SEAFOOD ££
(☑01499-302321; www.samphireseafood.com; 6a Arkland; dinner mains £12-23; ☺noon-2.30pm & 5-8.45pm; ☎) ✿ There's lots to like about this compact restaurant that makes an effort to source sustainable local seafood. There's a fairly light touch from the kitchen, which tends to let the natural flavours shine through, with very pleasing results.

🛈 Information

Inveraray Tourist Office (☑01499-302063; www.visitscotland.com; Front St; ☺9am-6pm Jul & Aug, 10am-5pm Apr-Jun & Sep-Oct, 10am-4pm Nov-Mar; ☎) On the seafront.

🛈 Getting There & Away

Scottish Citylink (www.citylink.co.uk) buses run from Glasgow to Inveraray (£12.40, 1¾ hours, nine daily). Five continue to Campbeltown (£13.40, 2½ hours); the others to Oban (£10.20, 1¼ hours, four daily). There are also buses to Dunoon (£3.90, 1¼ hours, three daily Monday to Saturday)

Crinan Canal

Completed in 1801, picturesque Crinan Canal runs for 9 miles from Ardrishaig to Crinan allowing seagoing vessels – mostly yachts, these days – to take a short cut from the Firth of Clyde and Loch Fyne to the west coast of Scotland, avoiding the long passage around the Mull of Kintyre. You can easily walk or cycle the canal towpath in an afternoon.

The Crinan end is overlooked by romantic **Crinan Hotel** (☑01546-830261; www.crinanhotel.com; Crinan; s/d from £150/220; ☺Mar-Dec; ☐☎☺), which boasts one of the west coast's most spectacular views.

Situated in the hotel, **Crinan Seafood Bar** (mains £11-20; ☺noon-2.30pm & 6-8.30pm Mar-Dec; ☎) has an appropriately nautical, old-fashioned feel. The menu includes excellent local mussels with lemon, thyme and garlic.

If you want to walk one way along the canal and take the bus there or back, West Coast Motors (www.westcoastmotors.co.uk) service 425/426 from Lochgilphead runs along it once to twice Monday to Friday.

Kilmartin Glen

This magical glen is the focus of one of the biggest concentrations of prehistoric sites in Scotland. Burial cairns, standing stones, stone circles, hill forts and cup-and-ring-marked rocks litter the countryside. Within a 6-mile radius of Kilmartin village there are 25 sites with standing stones and more than 100 rock carvings.

In the 6th century, Irish settlers arrived in this part of Argyll and founded the kingdom of Dál Riata (Dalriada), which eventually united with the Picts in 843 to create the first Scottish kingdom. Their capital was the hill fort of Dunadd, on the plain to the south of Kilmartin.

In Kilmartin village, **Kilmartin House Museum** (☑ 01546-510278; www.kilmartin. org; Kilmartin; adult/child £6/2; ☺ 10am-5.30pm Mar-Oct, 11am-4pm Nov-23 Dec) is a fascinating interpretive centre that provides a context for the ancient monuments you can go on to explore, alongside displays of artefacts recovered from various sites. Funding is being sought to further develop the museum and seek World Heritage status for Kilmartin. It also has a cafe and a good shop with handicrafts and books on Scotland.

The hill fort of **Dunadd**, 3.5 miles south of Kilmartin village, was the seat of power of the first kings of Dál Riata, and may have been where the Stone of Destiny was originally located. Faint rock carvings of a boar and two footprints with an Ogham inscription may have been used in inauguration ceremonies. The prominent little hill rises out of the boggy plain of Moine Mhor Nature Reserve. A slippery path leads to the summit where you can gaze out on much the same view that the kings of Dál Riata enjoyed 1300 years ago.

Kilmartin Museum Café (☑ 01546-510278; mains £5-9; ☺ 10am-5pm Mar-Oct, 11am-4pm Nov-23 Dec; 🛜🍴) has a lovely conservatory with a view across fields to a prehistoric cairn. Nourishing, delicious, home-style dishes include great vegetarian options, sandwiches, soup, cheeses and daily specials. The drinks menu ranges from espresso to craft beer. Lunches are served from noon to 2.30pm.

You can walk or cycle along the **Crinan Canal** from Ardrishaig, then turn north at Bellanoch on the minor B8025 road to reach Kilmartin (12 miles one way).

Bus 423 between Oban and Ardrishaig (three to five Monday to Friday, two on Saturday) stops at Kilmartin (from Oban £5.60, one hour).

Kintyre

The 40-mile long Kintyre peninsula is almost an island, with only a narrow isthmus at Tarbert connecting it to Knapdale. During the Norse occupation of the Western Isles, the Scottish king decreed that the Vikings could claim as their own any island they circumnavigated in a longship. So in 1098 the wily Magnus Barefoot stood at the helm while his men dragged their boat across this neck of land, validating his claim to Kintyre.

The coastline is spectacular on both sides, with stirring views of Arran, Islay, Jura and Northern Ireland. On a sunny day the water shimmers beyond the stony shore. Hiking the Kintyre Way is a nice means of experiencing the peninsula, which has a couple of cracking golf courses at Machrihanish near Campbeltown.

Tarbert

POP 1100

The attractive fishing village and yachting centre of Tarbert is the gateway to Kintyre, and is most scenic, with buildings strung around its excellent natural harbour. A crossroads for nearby ferry routes, it's a handy stepping stone to Arran or Islay, but is well worth a stopover on any itinerary.

The picturesque harbour is overlooked by the crumbling, ivy-covered ruins of **Tarbert Castle** (☺ 24hr) FREE, rebuilt by Robert the Bruce in the 14th century. You can hike up via a signposted footpath beside **Loch Fyne Gallery** (www.lochfynegallery.com; Harbour St; ☺ 10am-5pm Mon-Sat, 10.30am-5pm Sun) FREE, which showcases the work of local artists.

Tarbert is the starting point for the 103-mile **Kintyre Way** (www.kintyreway.com), a walking route that runs the length of the peninsula to Southend at the southern tip. It's very scenic, with wonderful coastal views nearly the whole way.

ARGYLL SEA KAYAK TRAIL

The 96-mile route of the **Argyll Sea Kayak Trail** (www.paddleargyll.org.uk), promoted by the local government, runs from Oban to Helensburgh via sea lochs and the Crinan canal. It's a spectacular paddle; the only annoyance is not being able to traverse the canal's locks: bookable trolleys are provided for easy portage. Paddlers are encouraged to register online.

RETURN OF THE BEAVER

Beavers had been extinct in Britain since the 16th century. But in 2009 they returned to Scotland, when a population of Norwegian beavers was released into the hill lochs of Knapdale, Argyll. After a broadly successful trial, a Scottish government decision in late 2016 will decide on the future of the beaver project and the status of another feral beaver population in Tayside.

If the beavers are still present, you can try to get a glimpse of them on the Beaver Detective Trail. This circular walk starts from the Barnluasgan forestry car park on the B8025 road to Tayvallich, about 1.5 miles south of the Crinan Canal. There's an information centre here. The trail is 3 miles, but you might glimpse them at pretty Dubh Loch just half a mile down the track.

Festivals & Events

Tarbert Music Festival　　　　　MUSIC
(www.tarbertfestivals.co.uk; ⊘3rd weekend Sep) Live folk, blues, beer, jazz, rock, *ceilidhs* (evenings of traditional Scottish entertainment), more beer...

Tarbert Seafood Festival　　FOOD & DRINK
(www.tarbertfestivals.co.uk; ⊘1st weekend Jul) Food stalls, cooking demonstrations, music and family entertainment.

Sleeping & Eating

Moorings　　　　　　　　　　　B&B **££**
(☑01880-820756; www.themooringsbb.co.uk; Pier Rd; s £45, d £80-110; P🛜) Follow the harbour just past the centre to this spot, which is recently renovated and beautifully maintained and decorated by one man and his dogs. It has great views over the water and an eclectic menagerie of ceramic and wooden animals and offbeat artwork.

Knap Guest House　　　　　　B&B **££**
(☑01880-820015; www.knapguesthouse.co.uk; Campbeltown Rd; d £75-99; 🛜) A flight of stairs lit by Edwardian stained glass leads to this 1st-floor flat with three spacious en suite bedrooms sporting an attractive blend of Scottish and Far Eastern decor. The welcome is warm, and there are great harbour views from the lounge (leather sofas, log fire and a small library) and breakfast room.

★**Starfish**　　　　　　　　SEAFOOD **££**
(☑01880-820733; www.starfishtarbert.com; Castle St; mains £11-19; ⊘6-9pm Sun-Thu, noon-2pm & 6-9pm Fri & Sat; 🛜) 🌱 Simple but stylish describes not only the decor in this friendly restaurant but the seafood too. A great variety of specials – anything from classic French fish dishes to Thai curries – are prepared with whatever's fresh off the Tarbert boats that day. Best to book. It may open for lunch daily in summer. It has got some sweet rooms too.

ℹ Information

Tarbert Tourist Office (☑01880-739138; www.visitscotland.com; Harbour St; ⊘10am-5pm Mon-Sat, 11am-5pm Sun Apr-Jun & Sep-Oct, 9am-6pm Mon-Sat, 10am-5pm Sun Jul & Aug, 10am-2pm Tue-Sat Nov-Mar) Good-natured office by the water with information on the whole Kintyre peninsula.

ℹ Getting There & Away

BOAT

CalMac (☑0800 066 5000; www.calmac.co.uk) (www.calmac.co.uk) operates a car ferry from Tarbert to Portavadie on the Cowal Peninsula (adult/car £2.60/8.15, 25 minutes, hourly). From late October to March there are also ferries to Lochranza on Arran (adult/car £2.80/9.40, 1¼ hours, one daily).

Ferries to Islay and Colonsay depart from Kennacraig ferry terminal, 5 miles southwest.

BUS

Tarbert is served by five daily Scottish Citylink (www.citylink.co.uk) coaches between Campbeltown (£7.90, one hour) and Glasgow (£16.80, three hours).

Skipness

POP 100

Tiny Skipness, 13 miles south of Tarbert, is pleasant and quiet with great views of Arran. Beyond the village rise the substantial remains of 13th-century Skipness Castle (HES; www.historicenvironment.scot; ⊘24hr, tower Apr-Sep only) FREE, a former possession of the Lords of the Isles.

A shop in the village does tea and baking, but the summer seafood scene at Skipness Seafood Cabin (☑01880-760207; www.skipnessseafoodcabin.co.uk; dishes £3-20; ⊘11am-7pm Sun-Fri Whit Sunday-Sep) is the place to be. Look out, too, for Creelers: Arran's famous seafood restaurant was in the process of relocating here at time of last research.

Local bus 448 runs from Tarbert (£3.35, 35 minutes, three daily Monday to Saturday) via the Claonaig ferry.

At Claonaig, 2 miles southwest, there's a ferry to Lochranza on Arran (adult/car £2.80/9.40, 30 minutes, seven to nine daily April to October).

Gigha

POP 200

Gigha (*ghee*-ah; www.gigha.org.uk) is a low-lying island, 6 miles long by about 1 mile wide, famous for its sandy beaches, pristine turquoise water and mild climate – subtropical plants thrive in Achamore Gardens (☑ 01583-505275; www.gigha.org.uk/gardens; Achamore House; suggested donation adult/child £6/4; ☺ dawn-dusk). Other highlights include the ruined church at Kilchattan, the bible garden at the manse, and Gigha's picturesque northern end.

The island was famously purchased by its residents in 2002, though they have had some financial problems since. Local Gigha cheeses include goat's-milk cheese and oak-smoked cheddar.

You can hire bikes, paddleboards, sea kayaks and rowing boats from Gigha Boats Activity Centre (☑ 07876-506520; www.gigha. net/gighaboats; ☺ 9am-6pm Mon-Sat, 11am-6pm Sun Easter-Oct) near the ferry slip.

The friendly island shop, Ardminish Stores Yurt (☑ 01583-505251; www.facebook. com/ardminishstores; yurt £80; ℗), offers this appealing glamping option: a white yurt in the garden with a double mattress and two singles, as well as a wood stove and cute furniture, but no power.

The Gigha Hotel (☑ 01583-505254; www. gigha.org.uk; s £45, d £78-95; ☺ food noon-2pm & 6-8pm; ℗ 🛜 🐾), 100m south of the post office, has a variety of cosy rooms, some with view. It also serves up bar meals or, if you're feeling peckish, four-course dinners.

Near the ferry slip, Boat House Café Bar (☑ 01583-505123, 07841-335841; www.boathouse gigha.co.uk; mains £10-20; ☺ 11.30am-9pm Easter-Sep; 🛜) does simple dishes as well as quality fresh local seafood, with sustainable, organic Gigha-farmed halibut a highlight. You can also camp here (£4/2 per adult/child), but space is limited so call in advance.

CalMac (www.calmac.co.uk) runs from Tayinloan in Kintyre (adult/car £2.50/7.35, 20 minutes, roughly hourly). Five daily Citylink (www.citylink.co.uk) buses in each direction between Glasgow/Tarbert and Campbeltown stop at the terminal.

Campbeltown

POP 4800

Blue-collar Campbeltown, set around a beautiful harbour, still suffers from the decline of its fishing and whisky industries and the closure of the nearby air-force base, but is rebounding on the back of golf tourism and a ferry link to Ayrshire. The spruced-up seafront backed by green hills lends the town a distinctly optimistic air.

⊙ Sights & Activities

Springbank   DISTILLERY
(☑ 01586-552009; www.springbankwhisky.com; 85 Longrow; tours from £7; ☺ tours 10am & 1.30pm Mon-Sat) There were once no fewer than 32 distilleries around Campbeltown, but most closed in the 1920s. Today this is one of only three operational. It is also one of the few around that distills, matures and bottles all its whisky on the one site, making for an interesting tour. It's a quality malt, one of Scotland's finest.

Davaar Cave   CAVE
(☺ 24hr) FREE A very unusual sight awaits in this cave on the southern side of Davaar island, at the mouth of Campbeltown Loch.

> ### GOLF AT MACHRIHANISH
>
> Machrihanish, 5 miles northwest of Campbeltown, is home to a couple of classic golf courses.
>
> Machrihanish Golf Club (☑ 01586-810277; www.machgolf.com; Machrihanish; green fee £65) is a classic links course, designed by Old Tom Morris. It's remarkably good value compared to courses of a similar standard in Scotland. The famous first hole requires a very decent drive across the bay, or you'll literally end up on the beach. Nearby is an upmarket hotel and restaurant, as well as self-catering villas.
>
> Much newer than its venerable neighbour Machrihanish Golf Club, Machrihanish Dunes (☑ 01586-810000; www. machrihanishdunes.com; Machrihanish; green fee around £75) is an impressive seaside experience and commendably light on snobbery: the clubhouse is a convivial little hut, kids play free and there are always website offers. Good packages are available including accommodation.

MULL OF KINTYRE

A narrow winding road, 15 miles long, leads south from Campbeltown to the Mull of Kintyre, passing some good sandy beaches near Southend. This remote headland was immortalised in Paul McCartney's famous song – the former Beatle owns a farmhouse in the area. From where the road ends, a 30-minute steep downhill walk leads to a clifftop lighthouse, with Northern Ireland, only 12 miles away, visible across the channel. Don't leave the road when the frequent mists roll in as it's easy to become disoriented.

On the wall of the cave is an eerie painting of the Crucifixion by local artist Archibald MacKinnon, dating from 1887. You can walk to the island on low tide: check tide times with the tourist office.

Mull of Kintyre Seatours   BOATING
(☑07785-542811; www.mull-of-kintyre.co.uk; ☉Apr-Sep) Operates high-speed boat trips out of Campbeltown harbour to the spectacular sea cliffs of the Mull of Kintyre, Arran, Ailsa Craig (£35; gannet colony and puffins), or Sanda Island (£30; seals, puffins and other seabirds) as well as whalewatching (£35, best late July to early September). Book in advance by phone or at the tourist office. Operates from the pontoon next to the pier.

✴ Festivals & Events

Mull of Kintyre Music Festival   FOLK MUSIC
(☑01586-552056; www.mokfest.com; ☉late Aug) Held in Campbeltown, this is a popular event featuring traditional Scottish and Irish music.

⌦ Sleeping & Eating

★ **Campbeltown Backpackers**   HOSTEL £
(☑01586-551188; www.campbeltownbackpackers.co.uk; Big Kiln St; dm £20; ⓟ🛜) ◗ This beautiful hostel occupies a central former school building: it's great, with a modern kitchen, disabled access and state-of-the-art wooden bunks. Profits go to maintain the Heritage Centre that runs it. Rates are £2 cheaper if you prebook.

Royal Hotel   HOTEL £££
(☑01586-810000; www.machrihanishdunes.com; Main St; r £142-172; ☉food noon-9pm Sun-Thu, noon-10pm Fri & Sat; ⓟ🛜) Historically Campbeltown's best address, this reddish sandstone hotel opposite the harbour is looking swish again. It caters mostly to yachties and golfers; though rack rates feel overpriced, there are often online specials and rooms are very spacious and attractive. There are some excellent midweek specials that include golf at Machrihanish Dunes and a couple of extras.

ℹ Information

Helpful **Campbeltown Tourist Office** (☑01586-556162; www.visitscotland.com; the Pier; ☉10am-5pm Mon-Sat & noon-4pm Sun Apr-Jun & Sep, 9am-6pm Mon-Sat & 11am-5pm Sun Jul & Aug, 10am-5pm Mon-Sat Oct, 10am-4pm Mon-Fri Nov-Mar) is beside the harbour.

ℹ Getting There & Away

AIR

Loganair/FlyBe (www.loganair.co.uk) flies six days a week between Glasgow and Campbeltown's mighty runway at Machrihanish.

BOAT

Kintyre Express (☑01586-555895; www.kintyreexpress.com) operates a small, high-speed passenger ferry from Campbeltown to Ballycastle in Northern Ireland (£45/80 one way/return, 1½ hours, daily June to August, four weekly April and September). You must book in advance.

CalMac (www.calmac.co.uk) runs thrice-weekly May to September between Ardrossan in Ayrshire and Campbeltown (adult/car £7.65/40.50, 2¾ hours); the Saturday return service stops at Brodick on Arran.

BUS

Scottish Citylink (www.citylink.co.uk) runs from Campbeltown to Glasgow (£20.50, four to 4¼ hours, five daily) via Tarbert, Inveraray and Loch Lomond. Change at Inveraray for Oban.

Islay

POP 3200

The home of some of the world's greatest and peatiest whiskies, whose names reverberate on the tongue like a pantheon of Celtic deities, Islay (*eye*-lah) is a wonderfully friendly place whose welcoming inhabitants offset its lack of scenic splendour compared to Mull or Skye. The distilleries are well geared-up for visits; even if you're not a fan of single malt, the birdlife, fine seafood, turquoise bays and basking seals are ample reason to visit. Locals are among Britain's

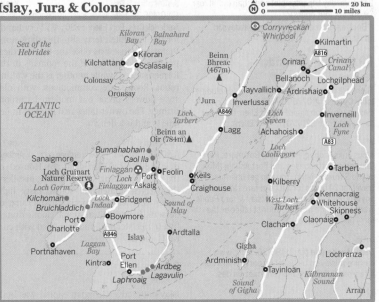

most genial: a wave or cheerio to passersby is mandatory, and you'll soon find yourself unwinding to relaxing island pace. The only drawback is that the waves of well-heeled whisky tourists have induced many sleeping and eating options to raise prices to eye-watering levels.

Tours

Islay Sea Safaris   BOATING
(☑ 01496-840510; www.islayseasafari.co.uk) Customised tours (£25 to £30 per person per hour) by sea from Port Ellen to spot some or all of Islay and Jura's distilleries in a single day, as well as birdwatching trips, coastal exploration, and trips to Jura's remote west coast and the Corryvreckan whirlpool.

Festivals & Events

★ Fèis Ìle   MUSIC, WHISKY
(Islay Festival; www.islayfestival.com; ⊙ late May) A week-long celebration of traditional Scottish music and whisky. Events include *ceilidhs* (evenings of traditional Scottish entertainment), pipe-band performances, distillery tours, barbecues and whisky tastings.

Islay Jazz Festival   MUSIC
(www.islayjazzfestival.co.uk; ⊙ 2nd weekend Sep) This three-day festival features a varied line-up of international talent playing at various venues across the island.

Information

Bowmore Tourist Office (☑ 01496-305165; www.islayinfo.com; the Square, Bowmore; ⊙ 10am-5pm Mon-Sat, noon-3pm Sun Apr-Jun, 9.30am-5.30pm Mon-Sat, noon-3pm Sun Jul & Aug, 10am-5pm Mon-Sat Sep-Oct, 10am-3pm Mon-Fri Nov-Mar) is one of the nation's best tourist offices. Staff bend over backwards to find you a bed if things are full up.

Getting There & Away

AIR

Loganair/FlyBe (www.loganair.co.uk) flies up to three times daily from Glasgow to Islay, while **Hebridean Air Services** (p464) operates twice daily Tuesday and Thursday from Oban to Colonsay and Islay.

BOAT

There are two ferry terminals: Port Askaig on the east coast, and Port Ellen in the south. Islay airport lies midway between Port Ellen and Bowmore.

    CalMac (www.calmac.co.uk) runs ferries from Kennacraig to Port Ellen or Port Askaig (adult/car £6.50/32.50, two to 2¼ hours, three to five daily). On Wednesdays and Saturdays in summer you can travel to Colonsay (adult/car £4/16.80,

1¼ hours, day trip possible) and Oban (adult/car £9.30/50, four hours).

Book car space on ferries several days in advance.

ⓘ Getting Around

BICYCLE

There are various places to hire bikes, including **Islay Cycles** (☑ 07760-196592; www.islaycycles.co.uk; 2 Corrsgeir Pl, Port Ellen; bikes per day/week from £20/70) in Port Ellen.

BUS

A bus links Ardbeg, Port Ellen, Bowmore, Port Charlotte, Portnahaven and Port Askaig (Monday to Saturday only). You can get unlimited travel for 24 hours for £10, but fares are low anyway. Pick up a copy of the *Islay & Jura Public Transport Guide* from the tourist office or the ferry on the way over.

CAR

D&N MacKenzie (☑ 01496-302300; www.carhireonislay.co.uk; Islay Airport) offers car hire from £35 a day and can meet ferries.

TAXI

There are various taxi services on Islay; **Carol's Cabs** (☑ 07775-782155, 01496-302155; www.carols-cabs.co.uk) is one that can take bikes.

Port Ellen & Around

Port Ellen is Islay's principal entry point. The coast stretching northeast is one of the loveliest parts of the island, where within 3 miles you'll find three of whisky's biggest names: Laphroaig, Lagavulin and Ardbeg.

The kelp-fringed skerries (small rocky islands or reefs) of the **Ardmore Islands**, near Kildalton, are a wildlife haven and home to Europe's second-largest colony of common seals.

A pleasant drive or ride leads past the distilleries to ruined **Kildalton Chapel**, 8 miles from Port Ellen. In the kirkyard is the exceptional late-8th-century Kildalton Cross. There are carvings of biblical scenes on one side and animals on the other.

🛏 Sleeping & Eating

Kintra Farm CAMPSITE, B&B £
(☑ 01496-302051; www.kintrafarm.co.uk; tent site £6-8, plus adult/child £4/2, s/d £50/80; ☺ May-Sep; 🅿🐾) At the southern end of Laggan Bay, 3.5 miles northwest of Port Ellen, Kintra is a basic but beautiful campsite on buttercup-sprinkled turf amid the dunes, with a sunset view across the beach. There's also B&B available.

Askernish B&B B&B ££
(☑ 01496-302536; www.askernishbandb.co.uk; 49 Frederick Cres, Port Ellen; r £90; 🛜) Very handy for the Port Ellen ferry slip, this dark-stone Victorian house was once the local medical practice; indeed, one of the rooms is in the former surgery, while another is the waiting room. Rooms are commodious, with old-style flowery decor but modern bathroom fittings. The owner takes real interest in her guests and is a delight.

Old Kiln Café CAFE £
(☑ 01496-302244; www.ardbeg.com; Ardbeg; mains £8-15; ☺ 10.30am-4pm; 🛜) Housed in the former malting kiln at Ardbeg distillery, this serves homemade soups, tasty light meals, heartier daily specials and a range of desserts, including traditional clootie dumpling (a rich steamed pudding filled with currants and raisins).

Bowmore
POP 700

Islay's attractive Georgian capital was built in 1768 to replace the village of Kilarrow, which just had to go – it was spoiling the view from the laird's house. Its centrepieces are the Bowmore distillery (p265) and distinctive **Round Church** at the top of Main St, built in circular form to ensure that the devil had no corners to hide in. He was last seen in one of the island's distilleries.

🛏 Sleeping & Eating

Bowmore distillery offers a tempting range of self-catering cottages around the centre. Accommodation fills fast in Bowmore, so book ahead. The tourist office usually knows who's still got rooms available.

⭐**Lambeth House** B&B ££
(☑ 01496-810597; lambethguesthouse@tiscali.co.uk; Jamieson St; s/d £65/96; 🛜) Cheerily welcoming, and with smart modern rooms with top-notch en suite bathrooms, this is a sound option in the centre of town. The host is a longtime expert in making guests feel welcome, and her breakfasts are reliably good. Rooms vary substantially in size, so ask for a larger one when booking, as the price is the same.

Island Bear B&B ££
(☑ 01496-810375; www.islandbear.co.uk; Shore St; s/d £85/100; 🛜) As central as you can be in Bowmore, this house is compact and curious, built very vertically. The three rooms

ISLAY'S DISTILLERIES

Islay has eight working distilleries, with a ninth, Ardnahoe, near Bunnahabhain, on the way. All welcome visitors and run tours. It's worth booking visits by phone, as they have maximum numbers. More expensive, specialised tours let you taste more malts and take you further behind the scenes. Pick up the invaluable pamphlet listing tour times from the tourist office. Five of the eight can be reached by the island's buses, and a bit of walking, hitching or cabbing will easily get you to the others.

Ardbeg (☑ 01496-302244; www.ardbeg.com; tours from £5; ⊙ 9.30am-5pm Mon-Fri, plus Sat & Sun Apr-Oct) Ardbeg's iconic peaty whiskies start with their magnificent 10-year-old. The basic tour is good, and it also offers longer tours involving walks, stories and extended tastings. Three miles northeast of Port Ellen. There's a good cafe for lunch here.

Bowmore (☑ 01496-810441; www.bowmore.com; School St; tours from £7; ⊙ 9am-5pm Mon-Fri & 9am-12.30pm Sat Oct-Mar, 9am-5pm Mon-Sat & noon-4pm Sun Apr-Sep) In the centre of Bowmore, this distillery malts its own barley. The tour begins with an overblown marketing video, but is redeemed by a look at (and taste of) the germinating grain laid out in golden billows on the floor of the malting shed. Various premium tours are available.

Bruichladdich (☑ 01496-850190; www.bruichladdich.com; Bruichladdich; tours £5; ⊙ 9am-6pm Mon-Fri, 9.30am-4pm Sat, 12.30-3pm Sun Apr-Sep, 9am-5pm Mon-Fri, 9.30am-4pm Sat Oct-Mar) A couple of miles from Port Charlotte, Bruichladdich (brook-laddy) is an infectiously fun place to visit and produces a mind-boggling range of bottlings; there's always some new experiment cooking. They also make a gin here, the Botanist, infused with local herbs.

Bunnahabhain (☑ 01496-840557; www.bunnahabhain.com; tours from £7; ⊙ 10am-5pm Mon-Sat, 11am-4pm Sun Apr-Oct, 10am-4pm Mon-Sat, noon-4pm Sun Nov-Mar) Pronounced 'boona-hah-ven', this is 4 miles north of Port Askaig down a narrow road. It enjoys a wonderful location with great views across to Jura. The standard malt is basically unpeated, though they are producing some peaty bottlings now too. The 18-year-old, sweet as a Speyside malt, is a standout dram. It's not as geared up to tourism here – don't expect a cafe or structured parking – but the guided visit is good. What you pay depends on how many drams you taste.

Caol Ila (☑ 01496-302769; www.discovering-distilleries.com; tours from £6; ⊙ 9am-5pm Mon-Sat, 10am-4pm Sun Mar-Oct, 10am-4pm Tue-Sat Nov-Feb) Pronounced 'cull ee-lah', this is a mile north of Port Askaig. It's a big, industrial set-up but enjoys a wonderful location with great views across to Jura. Some 95% of Caol Ila's production goes to blends, but its big production capacity means there's still plenty of single malt. Tours are free if you sign up to the mailing list on arrival.

Kilchoman (☑ 01496-850011; www.kilchomandistillery.com; Rockfield Farm, Kilchoman; tours from £6; ⊙ 9.45am-5pm Mar-Oct, closed Sat & Sun Nov-Feb) Likeable Kilchoman, set on a farm, is Scotland's second smallest distillery, going into production in 2005. It grows and malts some of its own barley here and does its own bottling by hand. It has got a wide variety of attractively packaged expressions: the 100% Islay whiskies are the ones produced from the home-grown barley. The tour is informative and the tasting generous. There's also a good cafe.

Lagavulin (☑ 01496-302749; www.discovering-distilleries.com; tours from £6; ⊙ 9am-6pm Mon-Fri, to 5pm Sat & Sun Jun-Aug, hours vary outside of summer) Peaty and powerful, this is one of the triumvirate of southern distilleries near Port Ellen. The standard tours are free if you sign up to the mailing list on arrival. The Core Range tour (£15) is a good option, cutting out much of the distillery mechanics that you might have already experienced elsewhere, and replacing it with an extended tasting.

Laphroaig (☑ 01496-302418; www.laphroaig.com; tours from £6; ⊙ 9.45am-5pm daily Mar-Oct, 9.45am-4.30pm daily Nov & Dec, 9.45am-4.30pm Mon-Fri Jan-Feb) Laphroaig produces famously peaty whiskies just outside Port Ellen. Of the various premium tastings that it offers, the 'Water to Whisky' tour (£90) is recommended – you see the water source, dig peat, have a picnic and try plenty of drams.

are cosy and enchanting, decorated with nautical fittings with tartan cushions and modern bathrooms. There are views from two of them, an inviting guest lounge and tasty breakfasts. The owner was looking to sell, so things may change.

Bowmore House B&B £££
(☑ 01496-810324; www.thebowmorehouse.co.uk; Shore St; s/d from £85/135; 🅿🛜) This stately former bank offers plenty of character and super water views. It's top-level B&B here, with coffee machines in the rooms, an honesty minibar with bottles of wine and local ales, and plush king-sized beds. Rooms are spacious, high-ceilinged and light. Further rooms are in a nearby cottage.

Harbour Inn BOUTIQUE HOTEL £££
(☑ 01496-810330; www.harbour-inn.com; the Square; s/d from £120/155; 🛜) The plush seven-room Harbour Inn, owned by Bowmore distillery, offers friendly service, a good restaurant, snug bar and prime location a few steps from the water in Islay's capital. The chambers are well appointed with modern comforts, quality amenities – including whisky soaps and gels – and plush fabrics, though some are on the small side for this price.

⭐**Harbour Inn** BRITISH ££
(☑ 01496-810330; www.harbour-inn.com; the Square; mains £15-20; ⊙ noon-2.30pm & 6-9.30pm; 🛜) Owned by the Bowmore distillery, this restaurant has changed in philosophy a few times in recent years. We enjoyed our last visit, with plates strong on presentation, with just a whiff of molecular and forage trends but based on solid mostly Scottish produce. Local oysters are an obvious choice. The conservatory-style dining area offers wonderful sunset views over the water.

It's open in the morning for pretty good breakfasts (£11.95) and all afternoon for sandwiches and light meals.

Port Charlotte & Around

Eleven miles from Bowmore, on the opposite shore of Loch Indaal, is attractive Port Charlotte, a former distillery town that appeals as a base. Museums in town and distilleries close by mean there's plenty to do.

Six miles southwest of Port Charlotte the road ends at **Portnahaven**, a picturesque fishing village. For seal-spotting, you can't do better; there are frequently dozens of the portly beasts basking in the small harbour.

◉ Sights & Activities

Museum of Islay Life MUSEUM
(☑ 01496-850358; www.islaymuseum.org; Port Charlotte; adult/child £3.50/1; ⊙ 10.30am-4.30pm Mon-Fri Apr-Oct) Islay's long history is lovingly recorded in this museum, housed in the former Free Church. Prize exhibits include an illicit still, 19th-century crofters' furniture, and a set of leather boots once worn by the horse that pulled the lawnmower at Islay House (so it wouldn't leave hoof prints on the lawn!).

Islay Natural History Centre NATURE DISPLAY
(☑ 01496-850288; www.islaynaturalhistory.org; Port Charlotte; adult/child £3.50/1.50; ⊙ 10am-4.30pm Mon-Fri May-Sep) Next to the youth hostel in Port Charlotte itself, this centre has displays explaining the island's natural history, with advice on where to see wildlife and lots of interesting hands-on exhibits for kids.

Loch Gruinart Nature Reserve BIRDWATCHING
(www.rspb.org.uk; Loch Gruinart) Seven miles north of Port Charlotte is Loch Gruinart Nature Reserve, where you can hear corncrakes in summer and see huge flocks of migrating ducks, geese and waders in spring and autumn; there's a hide with wheelchair access.

🛏 Sleeping & Eating

Anchorage B&B £
(☑ 01496-850540; http://anchoragebandb.blogspot.com; Bruichladdich; s/d without bathroom £40/60; 🅿🛜🐾) Spacious rooms at this four-square white house near Bruichladdich distillery have a super view across Loch Indaal to Bowmore opposite. It's run by a friendly couple and their white terriers, and it's an easygoing place that happily harks back to traditional B&B, with tea cosies, generosity and unlocked doors (though you can request a key). Rooms share good bathrooms.

Islay SYHA HOSTEL £
(☑ 01496-850385; www.syha.org.uk; Main St, Port Charlotte; dm/tw/q £19/45/85; ⊙ Apr-Oct; @🛜) This clean and modern brick hostel has spotless dorms with washbasin and a large kitchen and living room. It's housed in a former distillery building with views over the loch. The bus stops nearby. Breakfast and heatable dinners are available.

Port Mòr Campsite CAMPSITE £
(☑ 01496-850441; www.islandofislay.co.uk; tent sites per adult/child £8/4; 🅿@🛜) The sports field in Port Charlotte has a campsite – there

are toilets, showers, laundry and a children's play area in the main building, which also has a licensed cafe-bistro. Open all year.

Distillery House
B&B ££

(☎ 01496-850495; mamak@btinternet.com; Main St, Port Charlotte; s £40, d £80-84, tw without bathroom £75; P 🛜) For genuine islander hospitality at a fair price, head directly to this homey B&B on the right as you enter Port Charlotte. Set in part of the former Lochindaal distillery, it's run by a kindly local couple who make their own delicious marmalade and oatcakes. Rooms are well kept and most comfortable. The cute single has sea views. Rates drop slightly for two-night stays.

Port Charlotte Hotel
HOTEL £££

(☎ 01496-850360; www.portcharlottehotel.co.uk; Main St, Port Charlotte; s/d £135/210; P 🛜 🐾) This lovely old Victorian hotel has stylish, individually decorated bedrooms with sea views. It's a friendly, old-style place with a plush lounge, cosy bar and quality restaurant. Rooms are in modern classic style with tartan throws, crisp white sheets and quality toiletries.

Yan's Kitchen
BISTRO ££

(☎ 01496-850230; www.yanskitchen.co.uk; Main St, Port Charlotte; lunches £8-11, dinner mains £12-18; ⊙ food noon-2.30pm & 5.30-8.30pm Tue-Sun) On the left as you enter Port Charlotte, this cabin-like restaurant offers confident bistro cuisine using ingredients like duck breast and local scallops to create satisfying, well-presented plates. The appealing wooden-floored interior takes full advantage of the coastal views. It's open from 10am to noon for coffee and scones.

Port Askaig & Around

Port Askaig is little more than a hotel, shop (with ATM), petrol pump and ferry pier, set in a picturesque nook halfway along the Sound of Islay. There are two distilleries (with a third on the way) within reach and ferry connections to the mainland and Jura, just across the strait.

Three miles southwest, lush meadows swathed in buttercups and daisies slope down to reed-fringed Loch Finlaggan. This bucolic setting was once the most important settlement in the Hebrides, the central seat of power of the Lords of the Isles from the 12th to the 16th centuries.

Three miles from Port Askaig, Finlaggan (☎ 01496-840644; www.finlaggan.org; adult/child £4/2; ⊙ ruins 24hr, museum 10.30am-4.15pm Mon-Sat Apr-Oct) was once the stronghold of the Lords of the Isles. Little remains now except tumbledown ruins of houses and a chapel on an islet in a shallow loch. A wooden walkway leads over the reeds and water lilies to the island, where information boards describe the remains. Start your exploration at the visitor centre, which has some good explanation of the site's history and archaeology and a video featuring Tony Robinson. The island itself is open at all times.

Buses between Bowmore and Port Askaig stop at the road junction, from where it's a 15-minute walk to the loch.

Jura
POP 200

Jura lies long, dark and low off the coast like a vast Viking longship, its billowing sail the distinctive triple peaks of the Paps of Jura. A magnificently wild and lonely island, it's the perfect place to get away from it all – as George Orwell did in 1948. Orwell wrote his masterpiece *1984* while living at the remote farmhouse of Barnhill in the north of the island, describing it in a letter as 'a very un-get-at-able place'.

Jura takes its name from the Old Norse *dyr-a* (deer island) – an apt appellation, as the island supports a population of around 6000 red deer, outnumbering their human cohabitants by about 30 to one.

◉ Sights

Jura Distillery
DISTILLERY

(☎ 01496-820385; www.jurawhisky.com; Craighouse; tours from £6; ⊙ 10am-4.30pm Mon-Sat Mar-Oct, 10am-4pm Mon-Fri Nov-Feb) Apart from the superb wilderness walking and wildlife-watching, there's not a whole lot to do on the island of Jura except for visiting the Isle of Jura Distillery. The standard tour runs twice a day, while specialist tours (£15 to £25) take you deeper into the production process and should be prebooked.

🏃 Activities

There are few proper footpaths, and off-path exploration often involves rough going through giant bracken, knee-deep bogs and thigh-high tussocks. Most of the island is occupied by deer-stalking estates, and hill access may be restricted during the stalking season (July to February); the Jura Hotel (p269) can provide details.

Look out for adders – the island is infested with them, but they're shy snakes and will move away as you approach.

Evans' Walk
HIKING

This is a stalkers' path leading 6 miles from the main road through a pass in the hills to a hunting lodge above the remote sandy beach at Glenbatrick Bay. The path leaves the road 4 miles north of Craighouse (just under a mile north of the bridge over the River Corran). Allow six hours for the 12-mile round trip.

The first 0.75 miles is hard going along an interwoven braid of faint, squelchy trails through lumpy bog; aim just left of the cairn on the near horizon. The path firms up and is easier to follow after you cross a stream. On the descent on the far side of the pass, look out for wild orchids and sundews, and keep an eye out for adders.

Corryvreckan Viewpoint
HIKING

A good Jura walk is to a viewpoint for the Corryvreckan Whirlpool. From the northern end of the public road (a 16-mile return trip from here) hike past Barnhill to Kinuachdrachd Farm (6 miles). Just before the farm a footpath forks left and climbs before traversing rough and boggy ground, a natural grandstand for viewing the turbulent waters of the Gulf of Corryvreckan.

If you have timed it right (check tide times at the Jura Hotel), you will see the whirlpool as a writhing mass of white water.

Paps of Jura
HIKING

Climbing the Paps is a truly tough hill-walk over ankle-breaking scree requiring good fitness and navigational skills. It's 11 hard miles (allow eight hours). The first peak you reach is Beinn a'Chaolais (734m), the second Beinn an Oir (784m), then Beinn Shiantaidh (755m). Most hikers also climb Corra Bheinn (569m), before joining Evans' Walk to return.

The most popular starting place is by the bridge over the River Corran, 3 miles north of Craighouse. If you succeed in bagging all four, you can reflect on the fact that the record for the annual Paps of Jura fell race is just three hours!

Jura Island Tours
BUS

(☑ 01496-820314; www.juraislandtours.co.uk; short/long tour from Craighouse £15/25, from Feolin £25/35) Alex runs informative tours of the island in a modern minibus. Minimum numbers apply, but it's worth calling as he can put groups together.

THE SCOTTISH MAELSTROM

The Gulf of Corryvreckan – the channel (0.6 miles wide) between the northern end of Jura and the island of Scarba – is home to one of the most notorious tidal whirlpools in the world.

On Scotland's west coast, the rising tide – the flood tide – flows northwards. As it moves up the Sound of Jura, to the east of the island, it is forced into a narrowing bottleneck jammed with islands and builds up to a greater height than the open sea to the west of Jura. As a result, millions of tonnes of sea water pour westwards through the Gulf of Corryvreckan at speeds of up to 8 knots – an average sailing yacht is going fast at 6 knots.

The Corryvreckan Whirlpool forms where this mass of moving water hits an underwater pinnacle, which rises from the 200m-deep sea bed to within just 28m of the surface, and swirls over and around it. The turbulent waters create a magnificent spectacle, with white-capped breakers, standing waves, bulging boils and overfalls, and countless miniature maelstroms whirling around the main vortex.

Corryvreckan is at its most violent when a flooding spring tide, flowing west through the gulf, meets a westerly gale blowing in from the Atlantic. In these conditions, standing waves up to 5m high can form and dangerously rough seas extend more than 3 miles west of Corryvreckan, a phenomenon known as the Great Race.

You can see the whirlpool by making the long hike to the northern end of Jura (p268), or by taking a boat trip from Islay, Ardfern or the Isle of Seil.

For tide times, see www.whirlpool-scotland.co.uk.

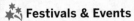 Festivals & Events

Isle of Jura Fell Race
SPORTS

(www.jurafellrace.org.uk; ⊙late May) This impressive feat of endurance tackles seven hill summits, including the Paps, over 17 miles of rough terrain. The record is around three hours...some feat.

Jura Music Festival
MUSIC

(www.juramusicfestival.com; ⊙late Sep) This pleasing folk festival is a popular drawcard.

🛏 Sleeping & Eating

Places to stay are very limited, so book ahead – don't rely on just turning up. As well as the hotel, there's a handful of B&B options and several self-catering cottages that are let by the week (see www.juradevelopment.co.uk). One of these is Barnhill (☑01786-850274; www.escapetojura.com; from £1000 per week; P🐾), where Orwell stayed, at the far north of the island.

You can camp (£5 per person) in the field below the Jura Hotel; there's a toilet and shower block (small charge) that walkers, yachties and cyclists can also use. From July to February, check on the deer-stalking situation before wild camping.

Jura Hotel
HOTEL ££

(☑01496-820243; www.jurahotel.co.uk; Craighouse; s £50-60, d £94-125; P🛜) The heart of Jura's community is this hotel, which is warmly welcoming and efficiently run. Rooms vary in size and shape, but all are renovated and feel inviting. The premier rooms – all of which have sea view – are just lovely, with understated elegance and polished modern bathrooms. Eat in the elegant restaurant or the convivial pub.

Antlers
CAFE £

(☑01496-820496; www.juradevelopment.co.uk; Craighouse; light meals £4-8; ⊙10am-4pm Easter-Oct, plus 6.30-8.30pm Fri) 🌱 This community-owned cafe has a craft shop and displays on Jura heritage. It does tasty home baking, sandwiches and the like, and is also open for more elaborate dinners on Fridays. Not licensed – £3 corkage.

ℹ Getting There & Around

A **car ferry** (☑01496-840681) shuttles between Port Askaig on Islay and Feolin on Jura (adult/car/bicycle £1.70/9.05/free, five minutes, hourly Monday to Saturday, every two hours Sunday). There is no direct car-ferry connection to the mainland.

From April to September, **Jura Passenger Ferry** (☑07768-450000; www.jurapassengerferry.com; one way £20; ⊙Apr-Sep) runs from Tayvallich on the mainland to Craighouse on Jura (one hour, one or two daily except Wednesday). Booking recommended.

The island's only **bus service** (☑01436-810200; www.garelochheadcoaches.co.uk) runs between the ferry slip at Feolin and Craighouse (20 minutes, six to seven Monday to Saturday), timed to coincide with ferry arrivals and departures. Some of the runs continue north as far as Inverlussa.

Hire bikes from **Jura Bike Hire** (☑07768-450000; bike hire per day £15) in Craighouse.

Colonsay

POP 100

Legend has it that when St Columba set out from Ireland in 563, his first landfall was Colonsay. But on climbing a hill he found he could still see the distant coast of his homeland, and pushed on north to Iona, leaving behind only his name (Colonsay means 'Columba's Isle').

Colonsay is a little jewel-box of varied delights, none exceptional but each exquisite – an ancient priory, a woodland garden, a golden beach – set amid a Highland landscape in miniature: rugged, rocky hills, cliffs and sandy strands, machair and birch woods, even a trout loch.

👁 Sights & Activities

There are several good sandy beaches, but Kiloran Bay in the northwest, a scimitar-shaped strand of dark golden sand, is outstanding.

★ Oronsay Priory
RUINS

(⊙24hr) FREE If tides are right, don't miss walking across the half-mile of cockle-shell-strewn sand that links Colonsay to smaller Oronsay. Here you can explore the 14th-century ruins of one of Scotland's best-preserved medieval priories. There are two beautiful 15th-century stone crosses in the kirkyard, but the highlight is the collection of carved grave slabs in the Prior's House. The island is accessible on foot for about 1½ hours either side of low tide; there are tide tables at the ferry terminal and hotel.

Colonsay House Gardens
GARDENS

(☑01951-200316; www.colonsayholidays.co.uk; Kiloran; ⊙gardens dawn-dusk, walled garden noon-5pm Wed & Fri, 2.30-5pm Sat Easter-Sep) FREE

Situated at Colonsay House, 1.5 miles north of Scalasaig, this garden is tucked in an unexpected fold of the landscape and is famous for its outstanding collection of hybrid rhododendrons and unusual trees. The formal walled garden around the mansion has a terrace cafe.

🛏 Sleeping & Eating

Accommodation is limited and should be booked before coming to the island. Wild camping is allowed. See www.colonsay.org. uk for self-catering listings.

Backpackers Lodge   HOSTEL £
(☑ 01951-200211; www.colonsayholidays.co.uk; Kiloran; dm/tw £20/52; P 🛜) Set in a former gamekeeper's house, this lodge is a 30-minute walk from the ferry (you can arrange to be picked up). Smart refurbished twin rooms are a great deal and are set in the house, with bunk rooms in a smaller stone building alongside. There's a kitchen in another building.

★ Colonsay Hotel   HOTEL ££
(☑ 01951-200316; www.colonsayholidays.co.uk; s/d from £75/105; P 🛜 🐾) ⟋ This wonderfully laid-back hotel is set in an atmospheric old inn dating from 1750, a short walk uphill from the ferry pier. It's a plush 18th-century place with well-appointed rooms, some with lovely views and four-poster beds. The bar and restaurant are the island's main social centres.

ℹ Information

The ferry pier is at **Scalasaig**, the main village, with a shop but no ATM. General information is available at the ferry waiting room, and at www. colonsay.org.uk.

ℹ Getting There & Around

On Wednesdays, a **minibus service** (☑ 01951-200141; adult/child £10/5) aimed at day trippers makes two circuits of the island to meet the arriving and departing ferries – you can be dropped off/picked up at any point on the circuit.

You can hire bikes from **Archie McConnell** (☑ 01951-200355; www.colonsaycottage. co.uk; Colnatarun Cottage, Kilchattan; per day £8-10) – book in advance and he'll deliver to the aerodrome or ferry.

Hebridean Air Services (p464) operates flights from Oban Airport (at North Connel) to Colonsay and Islay twice daily Tuesday and Thursday.

BOAT
CalMac (www.calmac.co.uk) runs from Oban to Colonsay (passenger/car £7.15/36.50, 2¼ hours, seven weekly summer, three winter). From April to October, on Wednesday and Saturdays, the ferry from Kennacraig to Islay continues to Colonsay (adult/car £4/16.80, 1¼ hours) and on to Oban. A day trip from Islay allows you six to seven hours on the island.

ARRAN
POP 4600

Enchanting Arran is a jewel in Scotland's scenic crown. The island is a visual feast, and boasts culinary delights, its own brewery and distillery, and stacks of accommodation options. The variations in Scotland's dramatic landscape can all be experienced on this one island, best explored by pulling on the hiking boots or jumping on a bicycle. Arran offers some challenging walks in the mountainous north, while the island's circular coastal road is very popular with cyclists.

🏃 Activities

The 55-mile coastal circuit is popular with cyclists and has few serious hills – more in the south than the north. There are plenty of walking booklets and maps available and trails are clearly signposted around the island. Several leave from Lochranza, including the spectacular walk to the island's northeast tip, the **Cock of Arran**, finishing in the village of Sannox (8 miles one way).

Goatfell   HIKING
The walk up and down Goatfell (874m), the island's highest point, is 8 miles return (up to eight hours), with trailheads at Brodick and Brodick Castle among others. In fine weather there are superb views to Ben Lomond and Northern Ireland. It can, however, be very cold and windy up there; take the appropriate maps (available at the tourist office), waterproofing and a compass.

Arran Bike Club   MOUNTAIN BIKING
(www.arranbikeclub.com) This local club has established and partially signposted various excellent mountain-biking routes around the island. Check its website for descriptions and maps.

Arran Adventure Company OUTDOORS
(☑ 01770 303349; www.arranadventure.com;
Auchrannie Rd) Run out of the Auchrannie
Resort, this company offers loads of activities, including sea kayaking (half/full
day £49/90), gorge walking (£49), abseiling (£49) and mountain biking (half/full
day £35/60). Most activities run for about
three hours and are cheaper for teens/kids.
Drop in to see what's available while you're
around. It also hires out mountain bikes
(£6/15/20 per hour/day/24 hours).

ℹ Information

The main **tourist office** (☑ 01770-303774; www.
visitarran.com; ☺9am-5pm Mon-Sat Mar-Oct,
plus 10am-5pm Sun Apr-Sep, 10am-4pm Mon-
Sat Nov-Feb) is in Brodick; the ferry from Ardrossan also has an information counter. Useful
websites include www.visitarran.com.

ℹ Getting There & Away

Calmac ferries (www.calmac.co.uk) run between
Ardrossan and Brodick (adult/car £3.75/15.10,
55 minutes, four to nine daily). From April to late
October services also run between Claonaig on
the Kintyre peninsula and Lochranza (adult/car
£2.80/9.40, 30 minutes, seven to nine daily).
In winter this service runs to Tarbert (1¼ hours)
once daily and must be reserved.

ℹ Getting Around

BICYCLE

Several places hire out bicycles, with three in
Brodick alone:

Arran Adventure Company Good mountain
bikes.

Arran Bike Hire (☑ 07825-160668; www.
arranbikehire.com; the Shorehouse, Shore Rd;
per half/full day/week £10/15/50; ☺Apr-Oct)
On the waterfront in Brodick. Trail bikes and
hybrids and can offer mountain-biking route
advice.

Boathouse Cycle Hire (☑ 01770-302868;
Beach; per hr/half/full day £7.50/9.50/14;
☺10am-6pm Easter-Christmas) By the beach
in Brodick.

BUS

Four to seven buses daily go from Brodick pier
to Lochranza (£3, 45 minutes), and many head
the other way to Lamlash (£2.10) and Whiting
Bay (£3, 30 minutes), then on to Kildonan and
Blackwaterfoot. Pick up a timetable from the
tourist office. An Arran Dayrider costs £5.60
from the driver, giving a day's travel. Download a
bus timetable from www.spt.co.uk.

Arran

CAR

Island of Arran Car Hire (☑ 01770-302839;
Pier, Brodick; car part-day/24hr £30/40) is at
the service station by Brodick ferry pier.

Brodick & Around

POP 800

Most visitors arrive in Brodick, the beating
heart of the island, and congregate along the
coastal road to admire the town's long curving bay. On a clear day it's a spectacular vista, with Goatfell looming over the forested
shore. Several of Brodick's main attractions
are just out of town, off the Lochranza road.

◉ Sights

Brodick Castle CASTLE
(NTS; Map p271; ☑ 01770-302202; www.nts.
org.uk; castle & park adult/child £12.50/9, park
only £6.50/5.50; ☺castle 11am-4pm May-Aug,
11am-3pm Apr & Sep, park 9.30am-sunset year-
round) This elegant castle 2 miles north of
Brodick evolved from 13th-century origins
into a stately home and hunting lodge for
the Dukes of Hamilton and was used until
the 1950s. You enter via the hunting gallery, wallpapered with deer heads. The rest
of the interior is characterised by fabulous
19th-century wooden furniture and an array

of horses 'n' hounds paintings. Helpful guides and laminated sheets – the kids' ones are more entertaining – add info.

The extensive grounds, now a country park with various trails among the rhododendrons, justify the steep entry fee.

Isle of Arran Brewery　BREWERY
(Map p271; ☑01770-302353; www.arranbrewery.com; tour £5; ☺10am-5pm Mon-Sat, 12.30-5pm Sun Apr-Sep, 10am-3.30pm Mon & Wed-Sat Oct-Mar) This brewery, 1.5 miles from town off the Lochranza road, produces the excellent Arran beers, which include the addictive Arran Dark. Tours run daily: call for times as they vary by season. They last about 45 minutes and include a tasting of all the beers.

✦✦ Festivals & Events

Arran Folk Festival　FOLK MUSIC
(www.arranevents.com) A four-day festival in June with concerts and great atmosphere. Held in Brodick and right across the island.

🛏 Sleeping

Brodick Bunkhouse　HOSTEL £
(☑01770-302897; www.brodickbunkhouse.co.uk; Alma Rd; dm £25; ⓟ�🛜) A short stroll from the ferry, behind the Douglas Hotel, this recently opened hostel has attractive, comfortable triple-decker bunks with individual plugs and USB ports. It's generally unstaffed, with keycode access. It has a simple kitchen and disabled access. No under-18s are admitted.

Glen Rosa Campsite　CAMPSITE £
(☑07985-566004; www.visitarran.com; Glen Rosa; site per adult/child £5/2.50; ⓟ🛜🐾) In a lush glen 2 miles from Brodick, this offers picturesque but basic camping in a large grassy riverside meadow, with cold water and toilets only. Take String Rd, then turn right almost immediately. After 400m, you'll see a white house on the left, where you register; the campsite is 400m further.

Broomage　B&B ££
(☑01770-302115; www.facebook.com/the.broomage; s £45-55, d £75-80; ⓟ🛜) Sparklingly clean and luminous, this well-kept place just back from the shorefront in Brodick offers an attractive modern environment with state-of-the-art bathrooms and eye-catching modern fabrics. The upstairs en suite has heaps of space, and there's a large lounge. There's a self-catering apartment available downstairs. It's fairly discreet; turn down the road by the Royal Bank of Scotland.

Glenartney　B&B ££
(☑01770-302220; www.glenartney-arran.co.uk; Mayish Rd; d £86-94; ☺Easter-Sep; ⓟ🛜🐾) ⚐ Uplifting bay views and genuine, helpful hosts make this a cracking option. Airy, stylish rooms make the most of the natural light available at the top of the town. Cyclists will appreciate bike wash, repair and storage facilities, while hikers can benefit from drying rooms and expert trail advice. It makes big efforts to be sustainable.

Belvedere Guest House　B&B ££
(☑01770-302397; www.vision-unlimited.co.uk; Alma Rd; s £40, d £80-95; ⓟ@🛜) Overlooking town, bay and surrounding mountains, this has pleasant hosts and very well-presented rooms with comfortable mattresses. Make sure you pay the extra and grab room 1 or 2, each of which is spacious and has fabulous vistas over the water. Breakfast has plenty of choice; there's also a self-catering cottage as well as reiki and healing packages available. A solid Brodick choice.

★Kilmichael Country House Hotel　HOTEL £££
(☑01770-302219; www.kilmichael.com; Glen Cloy; s £98, d £163-205; ☺Apr-Oct; ⓟ🛜🐾) The island's best hotel is also the oldest building – one bit dates from 1650. Luxurious and tastefully decorated, it's a mile outside Brodick but seems a world away in deep countryside. With just eight spacious, very individual rooms and excellent four-course dinners (£45, open to nonguests), it's an ideal, utterly relaxing hideaway that feels very classy without being overly formal.

In the grounds, patrolled by a sizeable muster of peacocks, there are also five self-catering cottages.

🍴 Eating & Drinking

Ormidale Hotel　PUB FOOD £
(☑01770-302293; www.ormidale-hotel.co.uk; Glen Cloy; mains £8-11; ☺food 5-9pm daily & 12.30-2.30pm Sat & Sun; 🛜🍽🦮) This hotel has decent bar food. Dishes change regularly, but there are always some good vegetarian options, and daily specials. Quantities and value-for-money are high, and Arran beers are on tap.

★Brodick Bar & Brasserie　BRASSERIE ££
(☑01770-302169; www.brodickbar.co.uk; Alma Rd; mains £13-26; ☺noon-2.30pm & 5.30-9pm Mon-Sat; 🛜) Though prices have soared in recent years, this is still one of Arran's most

enjoyable eating experiences. The regularly changing blackboard menu brings modern French flair to this Brodick pub, with great presentation, efficient service and delicious flavour combinations. You'll have a hard time choosing, as it's all brilliant. It's very buzzy on weekend evenings.

Douglas
BISTRO, PUB ££

(☑ 01770-302968; www.thedouglashotel.co.uk; Shore Rd; bistro mains £13-19, bar meals £9-14; ⊙ bistro 6-9.30pm, bar noon-9.30pm; 🛜🚲) Attractive and with upbeat service, the Douglas offers cleanly presented meals to complement its magic view from near the ferry dock. The bar zone serves upmarket versions of classic sandwiches and meals, while the bistro goes a step further in an equally appealing ambience. High-quality local produce from land and sea is used throughout.

Fiddlers' Music Bar
CAFE ££

(☑ 01770-302579; www.fiddlersmusicbar.com; Shore Rd; mains £9-16; ⊙ meals 10am-9pm; 🛜) A likeable little place with a really cheerful vibe, this is run by local musicians and does an all-round job as pub, venue, cafe and bistro. It hosts live folk music every day and a range of tasty food, including Sunday curry nights. Check out the appropriate toilet seats.

Corrie to Lochranza

The coast road heads north from Brodick to small, pretty Corrie, where there's a Goatfell trailhead. After Sannox, with sandy beach and great mountain views, the road cuts inland. Heading to the very north, on the island's main road, visitors weave through lush glens flanked by Arran's towering mountain splendour. This is perhaps the most beautiful section of the whole Arran coastal circuit.

Lochranza

The village of Lochranza has a stunning location in a small bay on the island's north coast. It's characterised by the ruined 13th-century Lochranza Castle, a ruin standing proud on a little promontory. The nearby distillery produces a light, aromatic single malt. The Lochranza area bristles with red deer, who wander insouciantly into the village to crop the grass.

◉ Sights

Isle of Arran Distillery
DISTILLERY

(Map p271; ☑ 01770-830264; www.arranwhisky.com; tours adult/child £7.50/free; ⊙ 10am-5.30pm Mar-Oct, 10.30am-4pm Nov-Feb) The Isle of Arran Distillery produces a light, aromatic single malt. The tour is a good one; it's a small distillery and the whisky-making process is thoroughly explained. There are three to five tours daily. You can opt for just a tutored tasting of several malts (£15) or a film and a dram (£3.50). There are also tours of the warehouse available.

Lochranza Castle
CASTLE

(HES; www.historicenvironment.scot; ⊙ 24hr) **FREE** The 13th-century Lochranza Castle is said to have been the inspiration for the castle in *The Black Island,* Hergé's Tintin adventure. Standing on a promontory, it's now basically a draughty shell inside, with interpretative signs to help you decipher the layout.

🛏 Sleeping & Eating

★ Lochranza SYHA
HOSTEL £

(☑ 01770-830631; www.syha.org.uk; dm/d/q £22/58/96; ⊙ mid-Mar–Oct plus Sat & Sun year-round; 🅿@🛜🐾) ✦ An excellent hostel in a charming place, with lovely views. Rooms sport chunky wooden furniture, keycards and lockers. Rainwater toilets, energy-saving heating solutions and a wheelchair-accessible room show thoughtful design, while plush lounging areas, a kitchen you could run a restaurant out of, a laundry, a drying room, red deer in the garden and welcoming management combine for a top option.

Castlekirk
B&B ££

(☑ 01770-830202; www.castlekirkarran.co.uk; s/d £45/75; ⊙ Mar-Oct; 🅿🛜🐾) This unusual and warmly welcoming place is a converted church chock-full of excellent artworks; there's a gallery downstairs, and paintings decorate the passageways and rooms. The breakfast area is dignified by a rose window, and there are great views of the castle opposite. Rooms are cosy under the sloping ceiling.

Stags Pavilion
BISTRO ££

(☑ 01770-830600; www.stagspavilion.com; mains £11-18; ⊙ 5.30-8.15pm Mon, Tue & Thu, 11am-2.30pm & 5.30-8.15pm Fri-Sun; 🛜) The best restaurant up this end of the island, this is unassumingly set in the former clubhouse of the rustic Lochranza golf course. There's a strong emphasis on local seafood, and dishes are created with a marked Italian influence. You'll likely see red deer munching the grass nearby. It's open for tea and baking all day.

West Coast

Blackwaterfoot is the west coast's largest village, with a shop and hotel. It's pleasant enough, though not the most scenic of Arran's settlements. You can walk to **King's Cave** (Map p271; ⏱24hr) FREE from here (6 miles); this walk can easily be extended to the Machrie Moor Stone Circle, the highlight of the area.

Machrie Moor Stone Circle (Map p271; ⏱24hr) FREE is on the western side of the island, a pleasant 1.2-mile stroll from the parking area on the coastal road. There are actually several separate groups of stones of varying sizes, erected around 4000 years ago. You pass a Bronze Age burial cairn along the path.

At the Old Byre Visitor Centre, **Cafe Thyme** (☑01770-840227; www.oldbyre.co.uk; Old Byre Visitor Centre, Machrie; dishes £8-12; ⏱10am-5pm, reduced hours winter; 🛜🅿) is a very pleasant spot, with chunky wooden tables, outdoor seating and sweeping views from its elevated position. It has home baking, a wide tea selection and decent coffee, but a less predictable food menu with great Turkish pizza, meze boards and smartly priced daily specials.

South Coast

The landscape in the south of Arran is gentler than in the north; the road drops into little wooded valleys, and it's particularly lovely around **Lagg**, where a 10-minute walk goes to **Torrylinn Cairn** (Map p271), a chambered tomb over 4000 years old. **Kildonan** has pleasant sandy beaches, a gorgeous water outlook, a hotel, a campsite and an ivy-clad ruined castle.

In genteel **Whiting Bay**, strung out along the water, you'll find small sandy beaches and easy one-hour walks through the forest to the **Giant's Graves** and **Glenashdale Falls** – keep an eye out for golden eagles and other birds of prey.

🛏 Sleeping & Eating

⭐ **Sealshore Campsite** CAMPSITE £
(☑01770-820320; www.campingarran.com; Kildonan; 1-/2-person tent £8/16, pods for 2 people £35; ⏱Apr-Oct; 🅿🛜🐾) Living up to its name, this excellent small campsite is right by the sea (and the Kildonan Hotel) with one of Arran's finest views from its grassy camping area. There's a good washroom area with heaps of showers, kitchen facilities and the breeze keeps the midges away. Cosy camping pods or a fabulously refurbished Roma caravan offer non-tent choices.

Kildonan Hotel HOTEL ££
(☑01770-820207; www.kildonanhotel.com; Kildonan; s/d/ste £75/99/125; 🅿@🛜🐾) Appealing rooms and a grounded attitude – dogs and kids are made very welcome – combine at one of Arran's better options. Oh, and it's right by the water, with seals basking on the rocks. Standard rooms are decent; the suites – with private terrace or small balcony – are just great. Nearly all rooms have sea views; other attractions include friendly staff, a bar and a restaurant.

Lagg Hotel INN ££
(☑01770-870255; www.lagghotel.com; Lagg, Kilmory; s/d £50/95, budget d £70; ⏱Apr-Oct; 🅿🛜🐾) This 18th-century coaching inn has a beautiful location and is the perfect place for a romantic weekend away from the cares of modern life. Rooms are smart; grab a superior one (£110) with garden views. There's also a cracking beer garden, a fine bar with a log fire and an elegant restaurant (mains £9 to £13) with good veggie options.

Coast BISTRO ££
(☑01770-700308; www.coastarran.co.uk; Shore Rd, Whiting Bay; mains £10-19; ⏱10am-4pm & 5-9pm Wed-Sun, hours vary by season; 🛜🅿) Offering a sun-drenched conservatory on the water's edge, this serves grills, seafood and salads in the evening, with lighter offerings during the day. There are several appealing vegetarian choices. It closes Wednesday and Sunday evenings outside of summer.

Lamlash

POP 1000

Lamlash, just 3 miles south of Brodick, is in a dazzling setting, strung along the beachfront. The bay was used as a safe anchorage by the navy during WWI and WWII.

◉ Sights

Holy Island
ISLAND

Just off Lamlash, this island is owned by the Samye Ling Tibetan Centre and used as a retreat, but day visits are allowed. A tide-dependent passenger **ferry** (☑01770-600998; tomin10@btinternet.com; adult/child return £12/6; ⊙daily May-Sep; by arrangement Tue & Fri winter) zips across from Lamlash. No dogs, bikes, alcohol or fires are allowed on Holy Island. A good walk to the top of the hill (314m), takes two or three hours return. You can stay at the **Holy Island Centre for World Peace & Health** (☑01770-601100; www.holyisle.org; dm/s/d £29/49/74; ⊙Apr-Oct). Prices include full (vegetarian) board.

🛏 Sleeping & Eating

Lilybank Guest House
B&B ££

(☑01770-600230; www.lilybank-arran.co.uk; Shore Rd; s/d £50/80; P🐾🛜) Built in the 17th century, Lilybank retains its heritage but has been refurbished for 21st-century needs. Rooms are clean and comfortable, with one adapted for disabled use. The front ones have great views over Holy Island. Breakfast includes organic porridge, oak-smoked kippers and other Arran goodies.

★ Glenisle Hotel
HOTEL £££

(☑01770-600559; www.glenislehotel.com; Shore Rd; s/d/superior d £90/139/172; 🛜) This stylish hotel offers great service and high comfort levels. Rooms are decorated with contemporary fabrics; 'cosy' rooms under the sloping roof are a little cheaper. All feel fresh and include binoculars for scouring the seashore; upgrade to a superior for the best water views. Downstairs is excellent pub food (mains £10 to £15) with Scottish classics and a good wine list.

★ Drift Inn
PUB FOOD ££

(☑01770-600608; www.driftinnarran.com; Shore Rd; mains £10-18; ⊙food noon-9pm; 🛜) In our more-or-less humble opinion, this is the island's best pub, offering a plush interior with leather chairs and a fireplace, as well as a fabulous beer garden – enjoy magnificent views from both across to Holy Island. Great bar food is on offer – upmarket, inventive fare with thoughtful vegetarian options – plus Arran ales on tap and blues on the stereo.

OBAN, MULL, TIRE & COLL

Oban
POP 8600

Oban, the main gateway to many of the Hebridean islands, is a peaceful waterfront town on a delightful bay, with sweeping views to Kerrera and Mull. OK, that first bit about peaceful is true only in winter; in summer the town centre is jammed with traffic and crowded with holidaymakers and travellers headed for the archipelago. But the setting is still lovely, and Oban's brilliant seafood restaurants are marvellous places to be as the sun sets over the bay.

◉ Sights

Dunollie Castle
CASTLE

(☑01631-570550; www.dunollie.org; Dunollie Rd; adult/child £5.50/2.80; ⊙10am-4pm Mon-Sat & 1-4pm Sun Apr-Oct) A pleasant 1-mile stroll along the coast road leads to Dunollie Castle, built by the MacDougalls of Lorn in the 13th century and unsuccessfully besieged for a year during the 1715 Jacobite rebellion. It's ruined, but you can enter the ground floor, and work is underway to restore the staircase. The nearby 1745 House – seat of Clan MacDougall – is an intriguing museum of local and clan history, and there are pleasant wooded grounds and a cafe. Free tours run twice daily.

Oban Distillery
DISTILLERY

(☑01631-572004; www.discovering-distilleries.com; Stafford St; tour £8; ⊙noon-4.30pm Dec-Feb, 9.30am-5pm Mar-Jun & Oct-Nov, 9.30am-7.30pm Mon-Fri & 9.30am-5pm Sat & Sun Jul-Sep) This handsome distillery has been producing since 1794. The standard guided tour leaves regularly (worth booking) and includes a dram, a take-home glass and a taste straight from the cask. Specialist tours (£40) run once Mondays to Fridays in summer. Even without a tour, it's still worth a look at the small exhibition in the foyer.

Pulpit Hill
VIEWPOINT

An excellent viewpoint to the south of Oban Bay; the footpath to the summit starts by Maridon B&B on Dunuaran Rd.

McCaig's Tower
HISTORIC BUILDING

(cnr Laurel & Duncraggan Rds; ⊙24hr) Crowning the hill above town is this Colosseum-like Victorian folly, commissioned in 1890 by

Oban

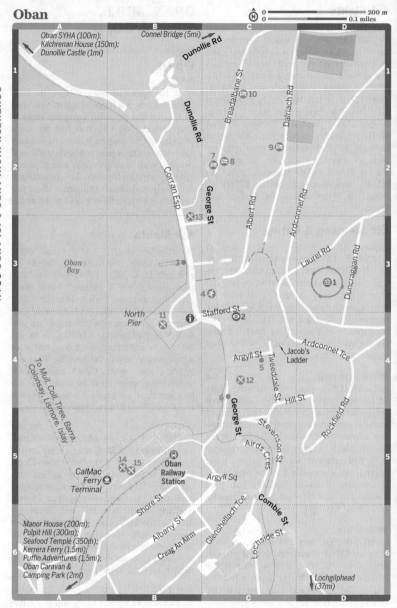

Oban SYHA (100m);
Kilchrenan House (150m);
Dunollie Castle (1mi)

Connel Bridge (5mi)

Dunollie Rd

Dunollie Rd

Breadalbane St

Dalriach Rd

Corran Esp

George St

Albert Rd

Ardconnel Rd

Oban
Bay

Laurel Rd

Duncraggan Rd

North
Pier

Stafford St

Ardconnel Tce

Argyll St

Jacob's
Ladder

Tweeddale St

Hill St

George St

Stevenson St

Rockfield Rd

Airds Cres

To Mull, Coll, Tiree, Barra,
Colonsay, Lismore, Islay

CalMac
Ferry
Terminal

**Oban
Railway
Station**

Argyll Sq

Combie St

Shore St

Glenshellach Tce

Manor House (200m);
Pulpit Hill (300m);
Seafood Temple (350m);
Kerrera Ferry (1.5mi);
Puffin Adventures (1.5mi);
Oban Caravan &
Camping Park (2mi)

Albany St

Creag An Airm

Lochside St

Lochgilphead
(37mi)

local worthy John Stuart McCaig, with the philanthropic intention of providing work for unemployed stonemasons. To reach it on foot, make the steep climb up Jacob's Ladder (a flight of stairs) from Argyll St; the bay views are worth the effort.

Activities

Hire a **bike** (☎ 01631-566033; www.obancycle scotland.com; 87 George St; per day/week £25/125; ⊙10am-5pm Tue-Sat) and pedal one of the local bike rides listed in a leaflet at the tourist office, including a 16-mile route to the Isle

Oban

of Seil. Various operators offer **boat trips** (adult/child £10/5) to spot seals and other marine wildlife, departing from North Pier.

Puffin Adventures DIVING
(☑01631-566088; www.puffin.org.uk; Port Gallanach) If you fancy exploring the underwater world, Puffin Adventures offers a two-hour package (£90) for complete beginners often available same-day – and four-day diving courses – as well as training services and excursions for more experienced divers. It is located south of town, near the Kerrera ferry. It's a serious professional set-up.

Sea Kayak Oban KAYAKING
(☑01631-565310; www.seakayakoban.com; Argyll St; ⊙10am-5pm Mon-Fri, 9am-5pm Sat, 10am-4pm Sun) Has a well-stocked shop, great route advice and sea-kayaking courses, including an all-inclusive two-day intro for beginners (£170 per person). Also full equipment rental for experienced paddlers – trolley your kayak from the shop to the ferry (kayaks carried free) to visit the islands. Three-hour excursions (adult/child £60/35) leave regularly in season.

Tours

Basking Shark Scotland BOATING
(☑07975-723140; www.baskingsharkscotland.co.uk; ⊙Apr-Oct) Runs entertaining boat trips with optional snorkelling, focused on finding and observing basking sharks – the world's second largest fish – and other notable marine species.

Coastal Connection BOATING
(☑01631-565833; www.coastal-connection.co.uk) Runs wildlife-spotting trips, fast day trips to Tobermory and custom excursions to many west coast islands in a speedy, comfortable boat.

West Coast Tours TOURS
(☑01631-566809; www.westcoasttours.co.uk; 1 Queens Park Pl; ⊙Apr-Oct) Offers a Three Isles day trip (adult/child £60/30, 10 hours, daily) from Oban that visits Mull, Iona and Staffa. The crossing to Staffa is weather dependent. Without Staffa, the trip is £35/17.50 and takes eight hours. Also runs various trips on Mull and other combinations with Staffa and the Treshnish Islands.

Festivals & Events

Highlands and Islands Music & Dance Festival MUSIC
(www.obanfestival.org; ⊙early May) An exuberant celebration of traditional Scottish music and dance. The town packs out.

West Highland Yachting Week SAILING
(www.whyw.co.uk; ⊙late Jul or early Aug) Oban becomes the focus of one of Scotland's biggest yachting events. Hundreds of yachts cram into the harbour and the town's bars are jammed with thirsty sailors.

Argyllshire Gathering HIGHLAND GAMES
(www.obangames.com; adult/child £10/5; ⊙late Aug) A key event in the highland-games calendar and includes a prestigious pipe-band competition.

Sleeping

Despite having lots of B&B accommodation, Oban's beds can still fill up quickly in July and August, so try to book ahead. Avoid the B&Bs south of the roundabout on Dunollie Road. If you can't find a bed in Oban, consider Connel, 4 miles north.

Backpackers Plus HOSTEL £
(☑01631-567189; www.backpackersplus.com; Breadalbane St; dm/s/tw with breakfast £20/29/52; @🛜) This is a friendly place with a good vibe and a large and attractive communal

lounge with lots of sofas and armchairs. Buffet breakfast is included in the price, plus there's free tea and coffee, a laundry service and powerful showers. Private rooms are available in a separate building (also with kitchen) just up the road: they are a very good deal.

Oban Backpackers
HOSTEL £

(☑ 01631-562107; www.obanbackpackers.com; Breadalbane St; dm £17.50-19.50; @⊚) Simple, colourful, relaxed and casual, this has plenty of atmosphere. Dorms are simple, with high ceilings and plenty of space; price varies according to size. Top bunks are wall-mounted. There's a sociable downstairs lounge with big windows and zebrapard couches, plus a sizeable kitchen. Breakfast is available for £2 and a safe is on hand (no lockers).

Oban SYHA
HOSTEL £

(☑ 01631-562025; www.syha.org.uk; Corran Esplanade; dm/tw £24/54; P@⊚) Set in a grand Victorian villa on the Esplanade, 0.75 miles north of the train station, this is modernised to a high standard with comfy wooden bunks, lockers, good showers and a lounge with great views across Oban Bay. All dorms are en suite; the neighbouring lodge has three- and four-bedded rooms. Breakfast available.

Oban Caravan & Camping Park
CAMPSITE £

(☑ 01631-562425; www.obancaravanpark.com; Gallanachmore Farm; tent/campervan site £16/20; ☺ Apr-Oct; P⊚⏾) This spacious campsite has a superb location overlooking the Sound of Kerrera, 2.5 miles south of Oban (two buses on school days). A one-person tent with no car is £8. No prebooking – it's first-come, first-served. There are also bungalows and camping pods that sleep up to four (for two/four £40/50).

★ Old Manse Guest House
B&B ££

(☑ 01631-564886; www.obanguesthouse.co.uk; Dalriach Rd; s/d £75/88; P⊚) Set on the hillside above town, this commands magnificent views over to Kerrera and Mull. It's run with genuine enthusiasm, and the owners are constantly adding thoughtful new features to the bright, cheerful rooms – think binoculars, DVDs, poetry, corkscrews and tartan hot-water bottles. There are breakfast menus, with special diets catered for.

★ Elderslie Guest House
B&B ££

(☑ 01631-570651; www.obanbandb.com; Soroba Rd; s £50-55, d £72-85; P⊚) B&B is a difficult balancing act: making things modern without losing cosiness; being friendly and approachable without sacrificing privacy. At this spot a mile south of town the balance is absolutely right, with a big variety of commodious rooms with big showers, large towels and lovely outlooks over greenery. Breakfast is great, there's outdoor lounging space and the hosts are really excellent.

Sandvilla Guesthouse
B&B ££

(☑ 01631-564483; www.holidayoban.co.uk; Breadalbane St; d £75-90; P⊚) Upbeat, colourful and modern, the rooms in this welcoming spot are lovely, bright and very well kept. Enthusiastic owners guarantee a personal welcome and service with a smile. It's our favourite of several options on this street.

Kilchrenan House
B&B ££

(☑ 01631-562663; www.kilchrenanhouse.co.uk; Corran Esplanade; s £50, d £70-110; P⊚) You'll get a warm welcome at the Kilchrenan, an elegant Victorian villa built for a textile magnate in 1883. Most of the rooms have views across Oban Bay, but rooms 5 and 9 are the best: the former has a huge freestanding bath tub, perfect for soaking weary bones.

Manor House
HOTEL £££

(☑ 01631-562087; www.manorhouseoban.com; Gallanach Rd; r £180-250; P⊚⏾) Built in 1780 for the Duke of Argyll, the old-fashioned Manor House is now one of Oban's finest hotels. It has small but elegant Georgian-style rooms – some with sea views – a posh bar frequented by yachties, and a fine restaurant serving Scottish and French cuisine (table d'hôte dinner £42). Rates include gym access and free golf at a nearby course. No under-12s.

✗ Eating

Oban Seafood Hut
SEAFOOD £

(www.obanseafoodhut.co.uk; Railway Pier; mains £3-13; ☺ 10am-6pm Mar-Oct) If you want to savour superb Scottish seafood without the expense of an upmarket restaurant, head for Oban's famous seafood stall – it's the green shack on the quayside near the ferry terminal. Here you can buy fresh and cooked seafood to take away – excellent prawn sandwiches, dressed crab and fresh oysters for a pittance.

Kitchen Garden DELI, CAFE £
(📞01631-566332; www.kitchengardenoban.co.uk;
14 George St; light meals £3-8; ⊙9am-5pm Mon-
Sat, 10.30am-4.30pm Sun; 🛜) A deli packed
with delicious picnic food, including some
great cheeses. Also has a great little cafe –
good coffee, scones, cakes, homemade soups
and sandwiches.

Oban Chocolate Company CHOCOLATE £
(📞01631-566099; www.obanchocolate.co.uk; 34
Corran Esplanade; hot chocolate £3; ⊙10am-5pm
Feb-Dec; 🛜♿) Specialises in hand-crafted
chocolates (you can watch them being
made) and also has a cafe serving excellent
coffee and hot chocolate (try the chilli chocolate for a kick in the tastebuds), with big
leather sofas in a window with a view of the
bay. Open to 9pm Thursday to Saturday in
July and August, when there's sometimes
live music.

**Waterfront Fishouse
Restaurant** SEAFOOD ££
(📞01631-563110; www.waterfrontfishouse.co.uk; 1
Railway Pier; mains £12-20; ⊙noon-2pm & 5.30-
9pm, extended hours Jun-Aug; 🛜♿) Housed on
the top floor of a converted seamen's mission, the Waterfront's stylish, unfussy decor,
bathed by the summer evening sun, does
little to distract from the seafood freshly
landed at the quay just a few metres away.
The menu ranges from classic haddock and
chips to fresh oysters, scallops and langoustines. Best to book for dinner.

★**Ee-Usk** SEAFOOD £££
(📞01631-565666; www.eeusk.com; North Pier;
mains £14-24; ⊙noon-3pm & 5.45-9.30pm; 🛜)
🐟 Bright and modern Ee-Usk (how you
pronounce *iasg*, Gaelic for fish) occupies
a prime pier location. Floor-to-ceiling windows allow diners on two levels to enjoy
sweeping views while sampling local sustainable seafood ranging from fragrant fish
cakes to langoustines and succulent fresh
fish. A bevy of serving staff make it swift and
efficient, and they'll try to give you the best
view available.

Both food and location are first class.
Closes 2.30pm and 9pm in winter.

🛈 Information

Lorn & Islands District General Hospital
(📞01631-567500; www.obanhospital.com;
Glengallan Rd) At the southern end of town.
Oban Library (📞01631-571444; www.argyll
-bute.co.uk; 77 Albany St; ⊙10am-1pm & 2-7pm

Mon & Wed, to 6pm Thu, to 5pm Fri, 10am-1pm
Sat; 🛜) Free internet and wi-fi.
Oban Tourist Office (📞01631-563122; www.
oban.org.uk; 3 North Pier; ⊙10am-5pm
Mon-Sat, 11am-4pm Nov-Mar Sun, 9am-6pm
Mon-Sat, 10am-5pm Sun Apr-May & Sep-Oct,
9am-6pm Jun, 9am-7pm Jul & Aug) Helpful; on
the waterfront.

🛈 Getting There & Away

AIR
Hebridean Air Services (p464) Flies from
Connel airfield to the islands of Coll, Tiree,
Colonsay and Islay.

BOAT
Oban is a major gateway to the Hebrides. CalMac
ferries run from here to Mull, Islay, Colonsay,
Coll, Tiree, Barra and Lismore. The **ferry terminal** (📞01631-562244; www.calmac.co.uk;
Railway Pier) is in the centre, close to the train
station.

BUS
Four to five Citylink (www.citylink.co.uk) buses
connect Glasgow (£19.40, three hours) with
Oban. Most of these travel via Tarbet and Inveraray; in summer, one goes via Crianlarich.
Three daily buses head north to Fort William
(£9.40, 1½ hours).

TRAIN
Scotrail trains run to Oban from Glasgow
(£23.90, three hours, five to six daily). Change at
Crianlarich for Fort William.

🛈 Getting Around

Hazelbank Motors (📞01631-566476; www.
obancarhire.co.uk; Lynn Rd; per day/week
from £40/225; ⊙8.30am-5pm Mon-Sat) Hires
out cars. You might get a van cheaper than a
hatchback.
Lorn Taxis (📞01631-564744)

Around Oban

South of Oban, the islands of Kerrera and
Seil and their subsidiary islets offer contrasting off-the-beaten-track experiences.

Kerrera
POP 50

Some of the area's best walking is on Kerrera, which faces Oban across the bay.
There's a 6-mile circuit (allow three hours),
which follows tracks or paths and offers the
chance to spot wildlife such as Soay sheep,
wild goats, otters, golden eagles, peregrine

falcons, seals and porpoises. At the island's southern end, there's a **ruined castle.**

The **Kerrera Bunkhouse** (☑01631-566367; www.kerrerabunkhouse.co.uk; Lower Gylen; dm £15; ☉Easter-Sep; 🐾) offers dormitory accommodation, self-catering bunkhouse hire and a luxurious tent. You can camp on the island with permission of local landowners.

The **Tea Garden** (☑01631-566367; www.kerrerabunkhouse.co.uk; Lower Gylen; light meals £3-9; ☉10.30am-4.30pm Easter-Sep) is the island's only eatery.

There's a daily passenger **ferry** (☑01631-563665; www.kerrera-ferry.co.uk; adult/child return £4.50/2; ☉half-hourly 10.30am-12.30pm & 2-6pm Easter-Oct, plus 8.45am Mon-Sat; 6-7 daily Nov-Easter) from Gallanach, 2 miles southwest of Oban town centre.

Seil

POP 600

The small island of Seil, 10 miles southwest of Oban, is best known for its connection to the mainland – the graceful **Bridge over the Atlantic**, designed by Thomas Telford and opened in 1793.

On the west coast is the pretty conservation village of **Ellenabeich**, with whitewashed cottages and rainwater barrels backed by a wee harbour and rocky cliffs. It was built to house local slate workers, but the industry collapsed in 1881 when the sea broke into the main quarry – the flooded pit can still be seen.

Just offshore is small **Easdale Island**, which has more old slate-workers' cottages and an interesting **folk museum** (☑01852-300370; www.easdalemuseum.org; Easdale; suggested donation £3; ☉11am-4pm Apr-Oct) with displays about the slate industry and social history. Once housing 450 people, the island's population fell to just seven oldtimers by 1950, but now has a healthier 48 after a program welcoming incomers.

Confusingly Ellenabeich is also referred to as Easdale, so 'Easdale Harbour', for example, is on the Seil side.

◉ Sights

Scottish Slate Islands Heritage Trust   MUSEUM
(☑01852-300449; www.slateislands.org.uk; Ellenabeich; ☉10.30am-4.30pm Apr-Oct, call for winter opening) **FREE** The Scottish Slate Islands Heritage Trust displays fascinating old photographs illustrating life in the village in the 19th and early 20th centuries.

Highland Arts   ARTS & CRAFTS
(☑01852-300273; www.highlandarts.co.uk; Ellenabeich; ☉9am-7pm Apr-Sep, 9am-5pm Oct-Mar) **FREE** Coach tours flock to this crafts and gift shop, which is a shrine to the eccentric output of the late 'poet, artist and composer' C John Taylor. Please, try to keep a straight face. Not browsing his booklets of poetry is a good way to accomplish this.

🏃 Activities

Sea Kayak Scotland   KAYAKING
(☑01852-300770; www.seakayakscotland.com; courses per person £85) Hire, instruction and guided sea-kayaking trips run by an experienced operator.

★ Sealife Adventures   BOATING
(☑01631-571010; www.sealife-adventures.com; 3/4/5hr trip £49/59/69) Exciting boat trips, based on the eastern side of the island near the bridge. It has a large, comfortable boat offering wildlife cruises with knowledgeable guides and trips to the Corryvreckan whirlpool.

★ Seafari Adventures   BOATING
(☑01852-300003; www.seafari.co.uk; Ellenabeich; ☉Apr-Oct) Runs a series of exciting boat trips in high-speed rigid inflatables to Corryvreckan whirlpool (adult/child £42/32; call for dates of 'Whirlpool Specials', when the tide is strongest), as well as three-hour summer whale-watching trips (£53/40). There are also day-long cruises to Iona and Staffa (£80/59), a weekly day trip to Colonsay (£53/40), plus trips to the remote Garvellach Islands (£53/40).

There's a minimum of six passengers required for out-of-season departures.

🎉 Festivals & Events

World Stone-Skimming Championships   SPORTS
(www.stoneskimming.com; ☉Sep) Anyone who fancies their hand at ducks and drakes should try to attend a flooded slate quarry in Easdale on the last Sunday in September. There's no use boasting about the number of skips: once it's hit the water a minimum of three times it's all about the distance reached. The laird's charge of £1000 to hold the event has been locally controversial.

ℹ Getting There & Around

West Coast Motors (www.westcoastmotors.co.uk) Bus 418 runs four to five times a day, except Sunday, from Oban to Ellenabeich (£3,

45 minutes) and on to North Cuan (£3, 53 minutes) at Seil's southern tip for the ferry to Luing.

Easdale Ferry (☑ 01631-562125; www.argyll -bute.gov.uk) Daily passenger-only ferry service from Ellenabeich to Easdale island (£2 return, bicycles free, five minutes, shuttle service at busy times, otherwise every 30 minutes).

Luing Ferry (www.argyll-bute.gov.uk; North Cuan; return per person/car £1.85/7.40) Departs every 30 minutes from Seil's southern tip for the three-minute trip.

Mull

POP 2800

From the rugged ridges of Ben More and the black basalt crags of Burg to the blinding white sand, rose-pink granite and emerald waters that fringe the Ross, Mull can lay claim to some of the finest and most varied scenery in the Inner Hebrides. Noble birds of prey soar over mountain and coast, while the western waters provide good whale-watching. Add a lovely waterfront 'capital', an impressive castle, the sacred island of Iona and easy access from Oban, and you can see why it's sometimes impossible to find a spare bed on the island.

☞ Tours

Mull's varied landscapes and habitats offer the chance to spot some of Scotland's rarest and most dramatic wildlife, including sea eagles, golden eagles, otters, dolphins and whales. Numerous operators offer walking or road trips to see them.

Mull Eagle Watch   BIRDWATCHING

(☑ 01680-812556;   www.mulleaglewatch.com; adult/child £8/4; ⊘ Apr-Sep) Britain's largest bird of prey, the white-tailed eagle, or sea eagle, has been successfully reintroduced to Mull, and the island is crowded with birdwatchers raptly observing the raptor. Two-hour tours to observe this bird are held in the mornings and afternoon, and must be prebooked.

Turus Mara   BOATING

(☑ 08000 858786; www.turusmara.com; ⊘ Easter-Oct) Offers trips from Ulva Ferry in central Mull to Staffa and the Treshnish Isles (adult/child £60/30, six hours), with an hour ashore on Staffa and two hours on Lunga, where you can see seals, puffins, kittiwakes, razorbills and many other species of seabird. There are also trips to Staffa alone (adult/child £30/15, 3¾ hours, Sunday to Friday).

SOUTHERN HIGHLANDS & ISLANDS MULL

Mull, Coll & Tiree

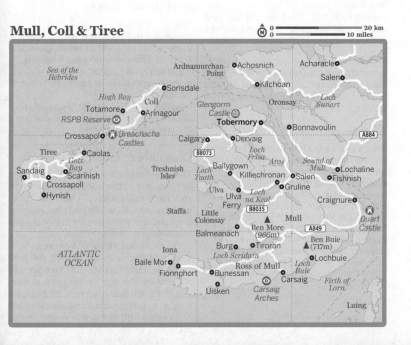

There is also transfer available from the Craignure ferry terminal, allowing you to visit as a day trip from Oban.

Mull Wildlife Expeditions WILDLIFE
(☑ 01688-500121; www.scotlandwildlife.com; adult/child £44.50/39.50) Six-hour Land Rover tours of the island with the chance of spotting red deer, golden eagles, peregrine falcons, white-tailed sea eagles, hen harriers, otters and perhaps dolphins and porpoises. Cost includes pick-up from accommodation or ferry, picnic lunch and binoculars. Possible as a day trip from Oban.

Staffa Tours BOATING
(☑ 07831-885985; www.staffatours.com) Runs boat trips from Fionnphort & Iona to Staffa (adult/child £30/15, three hours, daily April to October), or Staffa plus the Treshnish Isles (£60/30, five hours, Sunday to Friday May to July). The latter tour is also available from Tobermory and Ardnamurchan; there are also connection-plus-tour options leaving from Oban.

Festivals & Events

Mendelssohn on Mull MUSIC
(www.mendelssohnonmull.com; ⊘ early Jul) A week-long festival of classical music.

Mull Music Festival MUSIC
(www.mishnish.co.uk; ⊘ last weekend Apr) Four days of foot-stomping traditional Scottish and Irish folk music at Tobermory's pubs.

Mull Rally SPORTS
(www.mullrally.org; ⊘ Oct) Part of the Scottish Rally Championship, with around 150 cars involved. Public roads are closed for parts of the October weekend.

ⓘ Information

There's a bank with ATM in Tobermory; otherwise you can get cashback with a purchase from Co-op food stores.

Craignure Tourist Office (☑ 01680-812377; www.visitscotland.com; Craignure; ⊘ 9am-6pm Mon-Sat, 10am-6pm Sun Apr-Jun & Sep-Oct, 9am-7.30pm Mon-Sat, 10am-7.30pm Sun Jul & Aug) Opposite the ferry slip.

Explore Mull (☑ 01688-302875; www.isle-of-mull.net; Ledaig; ⊘ 9am-5pm Easter-Oct, to 7pm Jul-Aug; 🖥) In Tobermory car park. Local information, books all manner of island tours and hires bikes.

ⓘ Getting There & Away

Three **CalMac** (☑ 0800 066 5000; www.calmac.co.uk) (www.calmac.co.uk) car ferries link Mull with the mainland:

Oban to Craignure (adult/car £3.45/13, 40 minutes, every two hours) The busiest route – booking advised for cars.

Lochaline to Fishnish (adult/car £2.30/6.90, 15 minutes, at least hourly) On the east coast of Mull.

Tobermory to Kilchoan (adult/car £2.65/8.40, 35 minutes, seven daily Monday to Saturday, plus five Sunday May to August) Links to the Ardnamurchan peninsula.

ⓘ Getting Around

BICYCLE

You can hire bikes for around £20 per day from various places around the island, including **Explore Mull** in Tobermory.

BUS

West Coast Motors (☑ 01680-812313; www.westcoastmotors.co.uk) connects ferry ports and main villages. Its Discovery Day Pass (adult/child £15/7.50) is available from April to October and grants a day's unlimited bus travel.

The routes useful for visitors are bus 495 from Craignure to Tobermory, bus 496 from Craignure to Fionnphort, and bus 494 from Tobermory to Dervaig and Calgary.

CAR

Almost all of Mull's road network consists of single-track roads. There are petrol stations at Craignure, Fionnphort, Salen and Tobermory.

Mull Self Drive (☑ 01680-300402; www.mullselfdrive.co.uk; 1 day/3 days £45/117) rents out small cars.

Mull Taxi (☑ 07760-426351; www.mulltaxi.co.uk) is based in Tobermory and has a vehicle that is wheelchair accessible.

Craignure & Around

There's not much to see at Craignure, where the principal ferries from the mainland arrive, but 3 miles south is Duart Castle, the ancestral seat of the Maclean clan, enjoying a spectacular position on a rocky outcrop overlooking the Sound of Mull.

Originally built in the 13th century, **Duart Castle** (Map p281; ☑ 01680-812309; www.duartcastle.com; adult/child £6/3; ⊘ 10.30am-5pm daily May–mid-Oct, 11am-4pm Sun-Thu Apr) was abandoned for 160 years before a 1912 restoration. As well as the dungeons, courtyard and battlements with memorable views, there's a lot of clan history – pantomime boos go to Lachlan Cattanach, who took his wife on an outing to an island in the strait, then left her there to drown when the tide came in.

There's a handful of places to stay within 10 minutes' walk of the ferry, including a camping/glamping option and an excellent hostel.

Craignure Bunkhouse (☑ 01680-812043; www.craignure-bunkhouse.co.uk; Craignure; dm/q £20/75; P ☎ 🔊) 🏊 is an excellent hostel near the ferry slip, this purpose-built accommodation features excellent en suite dorms fetchingly decked out in wood. Bunks have lots of headroom and individual USB chargers, lamps and powerpoints. There are also double bunks for families. The ecologically minded design means sustainable sleeping, and the hostel has a great kitchen, sociable common area and enthusiastic staff.

A bus to the castle meets some of the incoming ferries at Craignure, but it's a pretty walk too.

Tobermory

POP 1000

Mull's main town is a very picturesque little fishing and yachting port with brightly painted houses arranged around a sheltered harbour. The children's TV program *Bal-* *amory* was set here, and while the series stopped filming in 2004, regular repeats mean that the town still swarms in summer with toddlers (and nostalgic teenagers) towing parents around (you can get a *Balamory* info sheet from tourist offices).

👁 Sights & Activities

Whale-watching boat trips run out of Tobermory harbour. A range of tours can be booked at the Explore Mull (p282) office in the waterfront car park.

Hebridean Whale & Dolphin Trust WILDLIFE EXHIBITION
(☑ 01688-302620; www.whaledolphintrust.co.uk; 28 Main St; ⏰ 10.30am-4.30pm) 🏊 **FREE** This has displays, videos and interactive exhibits on whale and dolphin biology and ecology, and is a great place for kids to learn about sea mammals. It also provides information about volunteering and reporting sightings of whales and dolphins. Opening is rather variable.

Mull Museum MUSEUM
(☑ 01688-301100; www.mullmuseum.org.uk; Main St; admission by donation; ⏰ 10am-4pm Mon-Fri Easter–mid-Oct) Places to go on a rainy day include Mull Museum, which records the history of the island. There are interesting exhibits on crofting, and on the *Tobermory*

WALKING ON MULL
....

There's some standout walking on Mull, including the popular climb of **Ben More** and the spectacular trip to **Carsaig Arches**. More information on these and other walks can be obtained from the tourist offices in Oban (p279), Craignure (p282) and Tobermory (p282).

Mull's highest peak, and the only island Munro outside Skye, Ben More (p283) (966m) offers spectacular views of surrounding islands. A trail leads up from Loch na Keal, by the bridge on the B8035 8 miles southwest of Salen. Return the same way or continue down the narrow ridge to the eastern top, A'Chioch, then descend to the road via Gleann na Beinn Fhada.

See Ordnance Survey (OS) 1:50,000 map sheet 49. The glen can be wet and there's not much of a path. The return trip is 6.5 miles; allow five hours.

One of the most adventurous walks (p283) is along the coast west of Carsaig Bay to the natural rock formation of Carsaig Arches at Malcolm's Point. There's a good path below the cliffs most of the way, but near the arches the route climbs and then traverses a very steep slope above a vertical drop into the sea (not for the unfit or faint-hearted).

You'll see spectacular rock formations on the way, culminating in the arches themselves: the 'keyhole', a freestanding rock stacks and the 'tunnel', a huge natural arch. The western entrance is hung with curtains of columnar basalt – an impressive place. The return trip is 8 miles – allow three to four hours' walking time plus at least an hour at the arches.

Galleon, a ship from the Spanish Armada that sank in Tobermory Bay in 1588 and has been the object of treasure seekers ever since.

Tobermory Distillery DISTILLERY

(☑ 01688-302647; www.tobermorymalt.com; Ledaig; tour £8; ☉ 10am-5pm) This bijou distillery was established in 1798. It doesn't always open winter weekends; phone to check or book. There are two lines here: the standard Tobermory and the lightly peated Ledaig. The standard tour lets you taste one of them; for £10, you can try them both.

Sea Life Surveys WILDLIFE

(☑ 01688-302916; www.sealifesurveys.com; Ledaig) Whale-watching trips head from Tobermory harbour to the waters north and west of Mull. An all-day whale-watch gives up to seven hours at sea (£80), and has a 95% success rate for sightings. The five-hour Family Whalewatch cruise (adult/child £50/40) is better for young kids. Shorter seal-spotting excursions are also available (adult/child £30/20, two hours).

🛏 Sleeping

Tobermory has dozens of B&Bs, but the place can still be booked solid any time from May through to August, especially at weekends.

Tobermory SYHA HOSTEL £

(☑ 01688-302481; www.syha.org.uk; Main St; dm/q £20/92; ☉ Mar-Oct; @ 🛜) This hostel has a great location in a Victorian house right on the waterfront. It's got an excellent kitchen and spotless, if somewhat austere dorms, as

well as good triples and quads for families. It books out fast in summer.

Tobermory Campsite CAMPSITE £

(☑ 01688-302624; www.tobermory-campsite.co.uk; Newdale, Dervaig Rd; tent site per adult/child £7.50/3; ☉ Mar-Oct; P 🛜 💥) 🍴 A quiet, family-friendly campsite 1 mile west of town on the road to Dervaig. It also has a self-catering house, cute little glamping huts and static caravans available. Credit/debit cards not accepted.

Harbour View B&B ££

(☑ 01688-301111; www.tobermorybandb.com; 1 Argyll Tce; s £80-90, d £90-100; 🛜) This beautifully renovated fisherman's cottage is perched on the edge of Tobermory's 'upper town'. Exposed patches of original stone walls add a touch of character, while an extension provides the family suite (two adjoining rooms with shared bathroom, sleeps four) with an outdoor terrace that enjoys breathtaking views across the harbour.

Sonas House B&B ££

(☑ 01688-302304; www.sonashouse.co.uk; the Fairways, Erray Rd; apt & s/d £90/125; P 🛜 💥) Here's a first – a B&B with a heated, indoor 10m swimming pool! Sonas is a large, modern house – follow signs to the golf course – offering luxury B&B in a beautiful setting with superb views over Tobermory Bay; ask for the 'Blue Poppy' bedroom, which has its own balcony. There's also a self-contained studio apartment with double bed.

THAR SHE BLOWS!

The North Atlantic Drift – a swirling tendril of the Gulf Stream – carries warm water into the cold, nutrient-rich seas off the Scottish coast, resulting in huge plankton blooms. Small fish feed on the plankton, and bigger fish feed on the smaller fish; this huge seafood smorgasbord attracts large numbers of marine mammals, from harbour porpoises and dolphins to minke whales and even – though sightings are rare – humpback and sperm whales.

There are dozens of operators around the coast offering whale-watching boat trips lasting from a couple of hours to all day; some have sighting success rates of 95% in summer.

While seals, porpoises and dolphins can be seen year-round, minke whales are migratory. The best time to see them is from June to August, with August being the peak month for sightings. The website of the Hebridean Whale & Dolphin Trust (www.whaledolphin trust.co.uk) has lots of information on the species you are likely to see, and how to identify them.

Cuidhe Leathain
B&B **££**

(✉ 01688-302504; www.cuidhe-leathain.co.uk; Breadalbane St; r £100; 🐾) A handsome 19th-century house in the upper town, Cuidhe Leathain (coo-lane), which means Maclean's Corner, exudes a cosily cluttered Victorian atmosphere. The rooms are beautifully plush, with plunger coffee and decent teas. Breakfasts will set you up for the rest of the day, and the owners are a fount of knowledge about Mull and its wildlife. Minimum two-night stay.

★ Highland Cottage
HOTEL **£££**

(✉ 01688-302030; www.highlandcottage.co.uk; Breadalbane St; d £155-170; ⊙ Apr–mid-Oct; P 🐾🐾) Antique furniture, four-poster beds, embroidered bedspreads, fresh flowers and candlelight lend this small hotel (only six rooms) an appealingly old-fashioned cottage atmosphere, but with all mod cons, including cable TV, full-size baths and room service. There's also an excellent restaurant here (dinner £42.50), and the personable owners are experts in guest comfort.

✗ Eating & Drinking

Fish & Chip Van
FISH & CHIPS **£**

(✉ 01688-301109; www.tobermoryfishandchipvan. co.uk; Main St; fish & chips £6-10; ⊙ 12.30-9pm Mon-Sat Apr-May, 12.30-9pm daily Jun-Sep, 12.30-7pm Mon-Sat Oct-Mar) If it's takeaway you're after, you can tuck into some of Scotland's best gourmet fish and chips down on the waterfront. And where else will you find a chip van selling freshly cooked scallops?

Pier Café
CAFE **£**

(✉ 07786-197377; the Pier; light meals £6-9; ⊙ 10am-5pm Mon-Thu, 10am-9pm Fri & Sat; 🐾) A cosy wee corner with local art on the walls, tucked beneath Café Fish at the north end of the village, the Pier serves great coffee and breakfast rolls, top baguettes that might feature local squat lobster or other seafood, plus tasty lunches such as haddock and chips, pasta, and sandwiches.

★ Café Fish
SEAFOOD **££**

(✉ 01688-301253; www.thecafefish.com; the Pier; mains £13-24; ⊙ noon-3pm & 5.30-11.30pm Mar–Oct; 🐾) 🍴 Seafood doesn't come much fresher than the stuff served at this warm and welcoming little restaurant overlooking Tobermory harbour – as its motto says, 'The only thing frozen here is the fisherman'! Crustaceans go straight from boat to kitchen to join rich seafood stew, fat scallops, fish pie and catch-of-the-day on the daily-changing menu, where confident use of Asian ingredients adds an extra dimension. Book ahead.

★ Mishnish Hotel
PUB

(✉ 01688-302009; www.mishnish.co.uk; Main St; 🐾) 'The Mish', near the pier on the harbourfront, is a favourite hang-out for visiting yachties and a great place for a pint, with a very convivial atmosphere. Wood-panelled and flag-draped, this is a good old traditional pub where you can listen to live folk music, toast your toes by the open fire, or challenge the locals to a game of pool.

North Mull

The road from Tobermory west to Calgary cuts inland, leaving most of Mull's north coast wild and inaccessible. It continues through the settlement of Dervaig to the glorious beach at Calgary. From here onwards you are treated to spectacular coastal views; it's worth doing the route in reverse from Grunart for the best vistas.

◉ Sights

Glengorm Castle
GALLERY, PARK

(Map p281; ✉ 01688-302321; www.glengorm castle.co.uk; Glengorm; ⊙ 10am-5pm Easter-Oct) **FREE** A long, single-track road leads north for 4 miles from Tobermory to majestic Glengorm Castle, with views across the sea to Ardnamurchan, Rum and the Outer Hebrides. The castle outbuildings house an **art gallery** featuring local artists, a **farm shop** and an excellent cafe (p286). The castle, which offers upmarket B&B (p286), is not open to the public, but you're free to explore the beautiful grounds, where several good walks are signposted. Guided nature walks also run from here; check the website for times.

Calgary Beach
BEACH

Mull's best (and busiest) silver-sand beach, flanked by cliffs and with views out to Coll and Tiree, is about 12 miles west of Tobermory. And yes – this is the place from which Canada's more famous Calgary takes its name.

Old Byre Heritage Centre
MUSEUM

(✉ 01688-400229; www.old-byre.co.uk; Dervaig; adult/child £4/2; ⊙ 10.30am-6.30pm Mon-Fri Easter-late Oct) The curious and cheerful Old Byre brings Mull's heritage and natural history to life through a series of tableaux and half-hour film shows. The prize for most bizarre exhibit goes to the 40cm-long model of a midge. The centre's **tearoom** serves good, inexpensive snacks, and there's a kids' outdoor play area.

🛏 Sleeping & Eating

Calgary Bay Campsite CAMPSITE
(Calgary) FREE You can camp for free in a lovely setting at the southern end of the beach at Calgary Bay. There are no facilities other than the public toilets across the road; water comes from the stream.

Dervaig Hostel HOSTEL £
(☑ 01688-400491; www.mull-hostel-dervaig.co.uk; Dervaig; dm/q £18/60; P 🛜) Basic but very comfortable bunkhouse accommodation in Dervaig's village hall, with self-catering kitchen and sitting room.

★ Calgary Farmhouse SELF-CATERING ££
(☑ 01688-400256; www.calgary.co.uk; Calgary; apt & cottages per week summer £480-1750, studios & cabin 3 days £180; P 🛜 🐕) 🍴 This brilliant complex near Calgary Beach offers a number of fantastic apartments, cottages and houses, beautifully designed and fitted out with timber furniture and wood-burning stoves. The Hayloft is spectacular, with noble oak and local art, while the wood-clad longhall-like Beach House offers luxury and dreamy views. Romantic Kittiwake, a beautiful wooden camping cabin among trees, has bay views and a boat ceiling.

There are options sleeping from two to 10. The larger ones go by the week in summer, but smaller ones are available for shorter stays. There's a good on-site cafe that sells some foodstuffs too. Bikes available for hire.

Tigh na Mara B&B ££
(☑ 01688-400278; www.mullbandb.co.uk; Dervaig; d £70-80) With a great location just where Dervaig meets the sea loch, this is ultra-friendly and offers views over the water, where you might be lucky enough to spot an otter. Breakfast features homemade eggs and the modernised rooms are spotless and comfortable with good bathrooms. It books out fast in summer.

Glengorm Castle B&B £££
(☑ 01688-302321; www.glengormcastle.co.uk; r £135-250; ⊙ mid-Feb–mid-Dec; P 🛜 🐕) Bristling with turrets as a real castle should, this enjoys an unforgettable location; huge windows frame green fields sloping down to the water. The attractive interior has 20th-century art instead of stags' heads. Bedrooms are all different, with lots of space and character. It's got lively, genuinely friendly owners, and kids will have a ball running around the grounds.

There are also various self-catering cottages available (£495 to £920 per week).

Glengorm Coffee Shop CAFE £
(☑ 01688-302321; www.glengormcastle.co.uk; Glengorm; light meals £3-9; ⊙ 10am-5pm Easter-Oct; 🛜 🐕) 🍴 Set in a cottage courtyard in the grounds of Glengorm Castle, this licensed cafe serves superb lunches (from noon to 4.30pm) – the menu changes daily, but includes sandwiches and salads (much of the salad veg is grown on the Glengorm estate), soups and tasty specials.

Am Birlinn SCOTTISH ££
(☑ 01688-400619; www.ambirlinn.com; Penmore, Dervaig; mains £13-23; ⊙ noon-2.30pm & 5-9pm Wed-Sun; 🛜) 🍴 Occupying a spacious modern wooden building between Dervaig and Calgary, this is an interesting dining option. Locally caught crustaceans and molluscs are the way to go here, though there are burgers, venison and other meat dishes available. Free pick-up and drop-off from Tobermory or other nearby spots is offered.

Central Mull

The central part of the island, between the Craignure–Fionnphort road and the narrow isthmus between Salen and Gruline, contains the island's highest peak, **Ben More** (966m) and some of its wildest scenery.

The narrow B8035 along the southern shore of Loch na Keal squeezes past impressive cliffs before cutting south towards Loch Scridain. About 1 mile along the shore from Balmeanach, where the road climbs away from the coast, is **Mackinnon's Cave**, a deep spooky fissure in basalt cliffs that was once used as a refuge by Celtic monks. A big, flat rock inside, known as **Fingal's Table**, may have been their altar.

South Mull

The road from Craignure to Fionnphort climbs through wild and desolate scenery before reaching the southwestern part of the island, which consists of a long peninsula called the **Ross of Mull**. The Ross has a spectacular south coast lined with black basalt cliffs that give way further west to

WORTH A TRIP

STAFFA

Felix Mendelssohn, who visited the uninhabited island of Staffa, off Mull, in 1829, was inspired to compose his 'Hebrides Overture' after hearing waves echoing in the impressive and cathedral-like **Fingal's Cave**. The cave walls and surrounding cliffs are composed of vertical, hexagonal basalt columns that look like pillars (Staffa is Norse for 'Pillar Island'). You can land on the island and walk into the cave via a causeway. Nearby **Boat Cave** can be seen from the causeway, but you can't reach it on foot. Staffa also has a sizable puffin colony, north of the landing place.

Northwest of Staffa lies a chain of uninhabited islands called the Treshnish Isles. The two main islands are the curiously shaped **Dutchman's Cap** and **Lunga**. You can land on Lunga, walk to the top of the hill, and visit the shag, puffin and guillemot colonies on the west coast at Harp Rock.

Unless you have your own boat, the only way to reach Staffa and the Treshnish Isles is on an organised boat trip from Fionnphort, Iona, Tobermory, Ardnamurchan, Seil or the Ulva ferry slip. Operators include: Turus Mara (p281), Staffa Tours (p282), Staffa Trips (p288) and Seafari Adventures (p280).

white-sand beaches and pink granite crags. The cliffs are highest at Malcolm's Point, near the superb **Carsaig Arches**.

The village of **Bunessan** is home to a cottage museum; a minor road leads south from here to the beautiful white-sand bay of **Uisken**, with views of the Paps of Jura.

At the western end of the Ross, 35 miles from Craignure, is **Fionnphort** (*finn*-a-fort) and the Iona ferry. The coast here is a beautiful blend of pink granite rocks, white sandy beaches and vivid turquoise sea.

The little village of Bunessan is home to the **Ross of Mull Historical Centre** (☑ 01681-700659; www.romhc.org.uk; Bunessan; admission by donation; ⊙ 10am-4pm Mon-Fri Easter-Oct, 10am-1pm Mon-Thu Nov-Easter), a cottage museum by a ruined mill that houses displays on local history, geology, archaeology, genealogy and wildlife.

🛏 Sleeping & Eating

Fidden Farm
CAMPSITE **£**

(☑ 01681-700427; Fidden, Fionnphort; site per adult/child £7/4; ⊙ Easter-Aug; 🅿 🐕) A basic but popular and beautifully situated campsite, with views over pink granite reefs to Iona and Erraid. It's 1.25 miles south of Fionnphort. Opening months vary a little year to year.

★ Seaview
B&B **££**

(☑ 01681-700235; www.iona-bed-breakfast-mull. com; Fionnphort; s 59, d £80-95; 🅿 🛜 🐕) 🍴 Just up from the ferry, this has beautifully decorated bedrooms and a breakfast conservatory with grand views across to Iona. The

owners are incredibly helpful and also offer tasty three-course dinners (not in summer), often based around local seafood. Breakfasts include locally sourced produce and the rooms are compact and charming, with gleaming modern bathrooms. Bikes available for guests to hire.

Staffa House
B&B **££**

(☑ 01681-700677; www.staffahouse.co.uk; Fionnphort; s/d £53/76; ⊙ Mar-Oct; 🅿 🛜) 🍴 This charming and hospitable B&B is packed with antiques and period features, and offers breakfast in a conservatory with a view of Iona. Solar panels top up the hot-water supply, and the hearty breakfasts and packed lunches make use of local and organic produce where possible. Rooms are designed for relaxation, with no TVs. Two-night minimum.

★ Ninth Wave
SCOTTISH **£££**

(☑ 01681-700757; www.ninthwaverestaurant. co.uk; Bruach Mhor, Fionnphort; 3-/4-course dinner £46/54; ⊙ from 7pm Wed-Sun May-Oct) 🍴 This croft restaurant is owned and operated by a lobster fisherman and his Canadian wife. The daily menu makes use of locally landed shellfish and crustaceans, vegetables and salad grown in the garden, and quality local meats with a nose-to-tail ethos, all served in a stylishly converted bothy. It's excellent. Advance booking (think a couple of weeks at least) essential. No under-12s.

It's worth going for the excellent cheeseboard if you've got room. Don't miss the handmade chocolates infused with locally foraged flavours.

Iona

POP 200

Like an emerald teardrop off Mull's western shore, enchanting, idyllic Iona, holy island and burial ground of kings, is a magical place that lives up to its lofty reputation. From the moment you embark on the ferry towards its sandy shores and green fields, you'll notice something different about it. To appreciate its charms, spend the night: there are some excellent places to do it. Iona has declared itself a fair-trade island and actively promotes ecotourism.

History

St Columba sailed from Ireland and landed on Iona in 563, establishing a monastic community with the aim of Christianising Scotland. It was here that the *Book of Kells* – the prize attraction of Dublin's Trinity College – is believed to have been transcribed. It was taken to Ireland for safekeeping from 9th-century Viking raids.

The community was re-founded as a Benedictine monastery in the early 13th century and prospered until its destruction during the Reformation. The ruins were given to the Church of Scotland in 1899, and by 1910 a group of enthusiasts called the Iona Community Council had reconstructed the abbey. It's still a flourishing spiritual community offering regular courses and retreats.

◉ Sights & Activities

Past the abbey, look for a footpath on the left signposted Dun I (dun-ee). An easy 15-minute walk leads to Iona's highest point, with fantastic 360-degree views.

★ Iona Abbey   HISTORIC BUILDING
(HES; ☑ 01681-700512; www.historicenvironment. scot; adult/child £7.10/4.30; ☺ 9.30am-5.30pm Apr-Sep, 10am-4.30pm Oct-Mar) Iona's ancient but heavily reconstructed abbey is the spiritual heart of the island. The spectacular nave, dominated by Romanesque and early Gothic vaults and columns is a powerful space; a door on the left leads to the beautiful cloister, where medieval grave slabs sit alongside modern religious sculptures. Out the back, the museum displays fabulous carved high crosses and other inscribed stones, along with lots of background information. A replica of the intricately carved St John's Cross stands outside the abbey

Next to the abbey is an ancient graveyard where there's an evocative Romanesque chapel as well as a mound that marks the burial place of 48 of Scotland's early kings, including Macbeth. Former Labour party leader John Smith is also buried in this cemetery. The ruined nunnery nearby was established at the same time as the Benedictine abbey.

Iona Heritage Centre   MUSEUM
(☑ 01681-700576; www.ionaheritage.co.uk; adult/child £3.40/1.70; ☺ 10am-5.15pm Mon-Sat Easter-Oct) Covers the history of Iona, crofting and lighthouses; there's a craft shop and a cafe serves delicious home baking.

☞ Tours

Staffa Trips   BOATING
(MV Iolaire; ☑ 01681-700358; www.staffatrips. co.uk; ☺ Apr-Oct) Runs three-hour boat trips to Staffa (adult/child £30/15) on the MV *Iolaire*, departing Iona pier at 9.45am and 1.45pm, and from Fionnphort at 10am and 2pm, with one hour ashore on Staffa.

Alternative Boat Hire   BOATING
(☑ 01681-700537; www.boattripsiona.com; ☺ Mon-Thu Apr-Oct) Offers cruises in a traditional wooden sailing boat for fishing, birdwatching, picnicking or just admiring the scenery. Three-hour afternoon trips cost £25/10 per adult/child; on Wednesday there's a full day cruise (10am to 5pm, £45/20). Booking essential.

🛏 Sleeping & Eating

There are B&B options, camping, a hostel and a pair of hotels on the island. It's imperative to book accommodation well ahead in spring and summer.

★ Iona Hostel   HOSTEL £
(☑ 01681-700781; www.ionahostel.co.uk; dm adult/child £21/17.50; P 🤶) 🍃 This wonderful ecological croft and environmentally sensitive hostel is one of Scotland's most rewarding and tranquil places to stay. Lovable black Hebridean sheep surround the building, which features pretty, practical, and comfy dorms and an excellent kitchen-lounge. There's a fabulous beach nearby, and a hill to climb for views. It's just over a mile from the ferry, past the abbey.

Iona Campsite   CAMPSITE £
(☑ 07747-721275; www.ionacampsite.co.uk; tent site per adult/child £7.50/4; ☺ Apr-Oct; 🐾) This

basic, welcoming grassy campsite is about 1 mile west of the ferry. Sleeping bags and mats are available for hire.

★ Argyll Hotel
HOTEL **££**

(☑ 01681-700334; www.argyllhoteliona.co.uk; s £76, d £95-114; ☺ Mar-Oct; 🛜🏠) 🍴 This loveable, higgledy-piggledy warren of a hotel has great service and appealing snug rooms (a sea view costs more – £167 for a double), including good-value family options. The rooms offers simple comfort and relaxation rather than luxury. Most look out to the rear, where a huge organic garden supplies the restaurant. This is a relaxing and amiably run Iona haven.

ℹ️ Getting There & Around

The ferry from Fionnphort to Iona (£3.30 adult return, five minutes, hourly) runs daily. Cars can only be taken with a permit. There are also various day trips available to Iona from Tobermory and Oban.

Iona Taxi (☑ 07810-325990) is useful for lugging bags in the rain.

Tiree

POP 700

Low-lying Tiree (tye-*ree*; from the Gaelic *tiriodh*, meaning 'land of corn') is a fertile sward of lush, green machair liberally sprinkled with yellow buttercups, much of it so flat that, from a distance, the houses seem to rise out of the sea. It's one of the sunniest places in Scotland, but also one of the windiest – cyclists soon find that, although it's flat, heading west usually feels like going uphill. One major benefit – the constant breeze keeps away the midges.

The surf-lashed coastline here is scalloped with broad, sweeping beaches of white sand, hugely popular with windsurfers and kite-surfers. Most visitors, however, come for the birdwatching, beachcombing and lonely coastal walks.

◉ Sights & Activities

In the 19th century Tiree had a population of 4500, but poverty, food shortages and overcrowding led the Duke of Argyll to introduce a policy of assisted emigration. Between 1841 and 1881, more than 3600 left, many emigrating to Canada, the USA, Australia and New Zealand.

An Iodhlann
LIBRARY

(☑ 01879-220793; www.aniodhlann.org.uk; Scarinish; adult/child £3/free; ☺ 9am-1pm Mon & Wed-Thu, 11am-3.30pm Tue & Fri Sep-Jun, 11am-5pm Mon-Fri Jul & Aug) A historical and genealogical library and archive, where some of the tens of thousands of descendants of Tiree emigrants come to trace their ancestry. The centre stages summer exhibitions on island life and history.

Skerryvore Lighthouse Museum
MUSEUM

(☑ 01879-220726; www.hebrideantrust.org; Hynish; ☺ 9am-5pm May-Sep) **FREE** The picturesque harbour and hamlet of Hynish, near Tiree's southern tip, was built in the 19th century to house workers and supplies for the construction of lonely Skerryvore Lighthouse, 10 miles offshore. This museum occupies the old workshops by the sand-filled but flushable harbour; up the hill is the signal tower once used to communicate by semaphore with the lighthouse.

Tiree Wave Classic
SPORTS

(www.tireewaveclassic.co.uk; ☺ Oct) Reliable wind and big waves have made Tiree one of Scotland's top windsurfing venues. The annual Tiree Wave Classic competition is held here.

Wild Diamond
WATER SPORTS

(☑ 01879-220399; www.wilddiamond.co.uk; Cornaig) Professional and friendly, this outfit runs courses in windsurfing (£30/100 per session/day), kitesurfing (£70/120 per half/full day), surfing, sand-yachting and stand-up paddleboarding, and rents out equipment including kayaks and surfboards.

🛏️ Sleeping & Eating

Millhouse Hostel
HOSTEL **£**

(☑ 01879-220892; www.tireemillhouse.co.uk; Cornaig; dm/s/tw £21/35/48; 🅿️🛜) Housed in a converted barn next to an old ruined water mill, this small but comfortable hostel is 5 miles west of the ferry pier. The dorms have beds rather than bunks, there's a common area and it's cheaper if you stay more than one night.

Balinoe Croft Campsite
CAMPSITE **£**

(☑ 01879-220399; www.wilddiamond.co.uk; Balinoe; tent site adult/child £12/6; 🅿️🛜🏠) A sheltered site with full facilities in the southwest of the island, near Balemartine, with great views of Mull. It's cheaper for multinight stays or in the off-season.

★ Rockvale Guest House
B&B ££

(☑ 01879-220675; www.rockvaletiree.co.uk; Balephetrish; s £65, d £85-96; ☏ 🛜 🐾) Smart, comfortable, modern accommodation and a genuine welcome make this easily Tiree's best midrange accommodation choice. It's situated in the north of the island and does things with real panache. Breakfast is way above average, with smoothies, fruit skewers, poached egg with spinach and pesto or banana mash featuring.

Kirkapol House
B&B ££

(☑ 01879-220729; www.kirkapoltiree.co.uk; Kirkapol; s/d £38/70; ⊘ Apr-Sep; ☏ 🛜 🐾) Set in a converted 19th-century church overlooking the island's biggest beach, the Kirkapol has six homely rooms within earshot of the soothing sounds of waves, and a big lounge with a leather sofa. It's 2 miles north of the ferry terminal.

Ceàbhar
SCOTTISH ££

(☑ 01879-220684; www.ceabhar.com; Sandaig; mains £8-15; ⊘ 7-8.30pm Wed-Sat Easter-Oct, plus Tue Jul & Aug; ☏ 🛜 🐾) 🍴 At Tiree's western end, this attractive restaurant looks out over the Atlantic towards the sunset. The cordial owners have the right attitude; they grow their own salads, eschew chips and have a nice line in good Fyne ales. The menu runs to handmade pizzas, soups, fish of the day and local lamb. A snug cottage sleeps up to eight people in five bedrooms.

ⓘ Information

There's a bank (without ATM), post office and supermarket in Scarinish, the main village, half a mile south of the ferry pier. You can get cashback with debit-card purchases at the Co-op.

Some tourist information is available in the ferry terminal. A useful website is www.isleoftiree.com.

ⓘ Getting There & Around

AIR

Loganair/FlyBe flies from Glasgow to Tiree daily. **Hebridean Air** (☑ 0845 805 7465; www.hebrideanair.co.uk) operates from Oban to Tiree via Coll (one way from Oban/Coll £65/10, twice daily Monday and Wednesday).

BICYCLE

Rent bicycles and cars from **MacLennan Motors** (☑ 01879-220555; www.maclennanmotors.com; Pierhead, Scarnish; per day car £45, bicycle £10) at the ferry pier. **Tiree Fitness** (☑ 07867-304640; www.tireefitness.co.uk; Sandaig; per day £15) has better bikes and will deliver them to the ferry (£5 extra).

BOAT

A CalMac (www.calmac.co.uk) ferry runs from Oban to Tiree (adult/car £10.30/56, four hours, one daily) via Coll, except on Friday when the boat calls at Tiree first (three hours 20 minutes). The one-way fare from Coll to Tiree (one hour) is £3.35/15.15 per adult/car.

On Wednesdays, the ferry continues to Barra in the Outer Hebrides (adult/car £8.75/45.50 one way, three hours), and stops again on the way back to Oban, allowing a long day trip to Tiree from the mainland. In high summer, a day trip is also possible on Saturdays.

Coll

POP 200

Coll is Tiree's more rugged, less populous neighbour. The northern part of the island is a mix of bare rock, bog and lochans (small lochs), while the south is swathed in golden shell-sand beaches and machair dunes up to 30m high. It's a gloriously relaxing place.

The island's main attraction is the peace and quiet – empty beaches, bird-haunted coastlines, and long walks along the shore. The biggest and most beautiful sandy beaches are at **Crossapol** in the south, and **Hogh Bay** and **Cliad** on the west coast.

In summer the corncrake's 'krek-krek' is heard at the **RSPB Reserve** at Totronald in the southwest of the island. From Totronald a sandy 4WD track runs north past the dunes backing Hogh Bay to the road at Totamore, allowing walkers and cyclists to make a circuit back to Arinagour rather than backtracking.

There are two castles about 6 miles southwest of Arinagour, both known as **Breachacha Castle**, built by the Macleans. The older, ruined towerhouse was replaced by a mid-18th-century palace alongside, now gradually being restored.

ⓘ Information

Arinagour, 0.5 miles from the ferry pier, is Coll's only village, home to a shop, post office (with ATM), craft shops and aged petrol station. Pride of the island is the new phone mast; there was virtually no signal until 2015. For more information, see www.visitcoll.co.uk.

ⓘ Getting There & Around

AIR

Hebridean Air operates from Oban to Coll (one way £65, twice daily Monday and Wednesday) and on to Tiree (£10).

BICYCLE

There is no public transport. Mountain bikes can be hired from the post office in Arinagour for £10 per day.

BOAT

A **CalMac** (p256) ferry (www.calmac.co.uk) runs from Oban to Coll (adult/car £10.30/56, 2¾ hours, one daily) and on to Tiree, except on Friday when the boat calls at Tiree first. The one-way fare between Coll and Tiree (one hour) is £3.35/15.15 per adult/car.

On Wednesdays, the ferry continues to Barra in the Outer Hebrides (adult/car £8.75/45.50 one way, four hours), and stops again on the way back to Oban, allowing a long day trip to Coll from the mainland. In high summer, a day trip is also possible on Saturdays.

NORTH ARGYLL

Loch Awe

Loch Awe is one of Scotland's most beautiful lochs, with rolling forested hills around its southern end and spectacular mountains in the north. It lies between Oban and Inveraray and is the longest loch in Scotland – about 24 miles – but is less than 1 mile wide for most of its length. At its northern end, it escapes to the sea through the narrow **Pass of Brander**, where Robert the Bruce defeated the MacDougalls in 1309.

At the northern end of Loch Awe are the scenic ruins of the strategically situated and much-photographed **Kilchurn Castle** (HES; www.historicenvironment.scot; Dalmally; ◷9am-5pm Apr-Sep) FREE. Built in 1440, it enjoys one of Scotland's finest settings. At time of research, ownership issues meant that the castle wasn't open to the public, though you could still enjoy the scenic stroll to it. It's a half-mile walk from a car park on the A85 road, just west of the Inveraray turnoff between Dalmally and Lochawe.

The castle is situated on a tiny peninsula guarding the northern tip of the loch. Long held by the Campbell clan, it was enlarged in 1693 to garrison government troops during the Jacobite uprising; it was then abandoned in the 1750s after a fire ran through most of it. Nowadays it's just a shell, although a very picturesque one. When it's open, you can climb to the top of the four-storey castle tower for impressive views of Loch Awe and the surrounding hills.

In the Pass of Brander, by the A85, you can visit **Cruachan Power Station** (☐0141-614-9105; www.visitcruachan.co.uk; A85; adult/child £7/2.50; ◷9.30am-4.45pm Apr-Oct, 10am-3.45pm Mon-Fri Nov-Dec & Feb-Mar). Electric buses take you more than half a mile inside Ben Cruachan, allowing you to see the pump-storage hydroelectric scheme, which occupies a vast cavern hollowed out of the mountain.

Connel & Taynuilt

Hemmed in by dramatic mountain scenery, **Loch Etive** stretches 17 miles from Connel to Kinlochetive (accessible by road from Glencoe). Three very different but worthwhile sights complement the beautiful scenery around here.

Bonawe Iron Furnace (HS; ☐01866-822432; www.historicenvironment.scot; Taynuilt; adult/child £4.50/2.70; ◷9.30am-5.30pm Apr-Sep) is one of the region's most unusual historical sights. Near Taynuilt, and dating from 1753, it was built by an iron-smelting company from Cumbria because of the abundance of birch and oak in the area. The coppiced wood was made into the charcoal that was needed for smelting the iron. It's now a tranquil, beautiful place, the old buildings picturesquely arranged around a green hillside. There's great background information on the iron industry. Take a picnic!

Dunstaffnage Castle (HES; ☐01631-562465; www.historicenvironment.scot; adult/child £5.50/3.30; ◷9.30am-5.30pm Apr-Sep, 10am-4pm Sat-Wed Oct-Mar), 2 miles west of Connel, looks like a child's drawing of what a castle should be – square and massive, with towers at the corners, and perched on top of a rocky outcrop. It was built around 1260 and was captured by Robert the Bruce during the Wars of Independence in 1309. The haunted ruins of the nearby 13th-century **chapel** contain lots of Campbell tombs decorated with skull-and-crossbone carvings.

At Connel Bridge, 5 miles north of Oban, the loch joins the sea via a narrow channel partly blocked by an underwater rock ledge. When the tide flows in and out water pours through this bottleneck, creating spectacular white-water rapids known as the **Falls of Lora**. Park near the north end of the bridge and walk back into the middle to have a look.

Appin & Around

The Appin region, once ruled over by the Stewarts from their stronghold at Castle Stalker, stretches north from the rocky shores of Loch Creran to the hills of Glencoe. Port Appin, a couple of miles off the main road, is a pleasant spot with a passenger ferry to the island of Lismore.

North of Loch Creran, at Portnacroish, there's a wonderful view of **Castle Stalker** (✆ 01631-730354; www.castlestalker.com; adult/child/family £20/10/50; ⊘ tours Mar-Oct) perched on a tiny offshore island – Monty Python buffs will recognise it as the castle that appears in the final scenes of the film *Monty Python and the Holy Grail*. Visits are by two-hour guided tour, which can be booked by email or the website, and leaves from a boat dock just off the A828. There's a maximum of one a day, so it's wise to arrange your visit in advance.

The **Scottish Sea Life Sanctuary** (✆ 01631-720386; www.visitsealife.com; Barcaldine; adult/child £13.20/10.80; ⊘ 10am-4pm Nov-Mar, 10am-5pm Apr-Oct) ✆, 10 miles north of Oban on the shores of Loch Creran, provides a haven for orphaned seal pups. As well as the seal pools, there are tanks housing herrings, rays and flatfish, touch pools for children, an otter sanctuary and displays on Scotland's marine environment. An outdoor nature trail is aimed at young 'uns. You save a significant amount if you prebook online. There's a pleasant cafe here by the water.

The excellent **restaurant** (✆ 01631-730302; www.pierhousehotel.co.uk; Port Appin; restaurant mains £18-30, bar mains £9-16; ⊘ restaurant 12.30-2.30pm & 6.30-9.30pm, bar meals noon-2.30pm & 6-9pm; 🐾) at the **Pierhouse Hotel** (r £165-195; P 🐾 🐕) enjoys a view across the water to Lismore, and specialises in local seafood and game. The bar menu also focuses on quality fishy fare.

Lismore

POP 200

The island of Lismore (in Gaelic *Lios Mór* means 'Big Garden') is all lush grassland sprinkled with wildflowers, with grey blades of limestone breaking through the soil. And that's the secret – limestone is rare in the Highlands, but it weathers to a very fertile soil.

Lismore is long and narrow – 10 miles long by 1 mile wide – with a road running almost its full length. There's a shop on the island.

In the middle of the island, **Lismore Gaelic Heritage Centre** (✆ 01631-760030; www.lismoregaelicheritagecentre.org; suggested donation £3; ⊘ 11am-4pm Apr-Oct) ✆ has a museum with a fascinating exhibition on Lismore's history and culture; alongside stands a reconstruction of a crofter's cottage. The **cafe** (✆ 01631-760020; light meals £4-8; ⊘ 11am-4pm Apr-Oct; 🐾 🐕) ✆ here has an outdoor deck with a stunning view of the mainland mountains.

The romantic ruins of 13th-century **Castle Coeffin** have a lovely setting on the west coast. **Tirefour Broch**, a defensive tower with double walls reaching 4m in height, is directly opposite on the east coast.

❶ Getting There & Around

You can hire **bikes** (✆ 01631-730391; Port Appin; per day adult/child £15/10) in Port Appin to bring across on the ferry.

A CalMac car ferry (www.calmac.co.uk) runs from Oban to Achnacroish, with four to five sailings Monday to Saturday, two on Sunday (adult/car £2.65/11.50, 55 minutes).

Argyll & Bute Council (✆ 01631-730356; www.argyll-bute.gov.uk) operates the passenger ferry from Port Appin to Point (£1.70, 10 minutes, hourly). Bicycles are free.

Inverness & the Central Highlands

Best Places to Eat

➡ Lime Tree (p337)

➡ Café 1 (p299)

➡ Cross (p315)

➡ Lochleven Seafood Cafe (p335)

➡ Old Forge (p345)

Best Places to Sleep

➡ Rocpool Reserve (p299)

➡ Grange (p337)

➡ Lovat (p308)

➡ Milton Eonan (p331)

➡ Trafford Bank (p298)

Why Go?

From the subarctic plateau of the Cairngorms to the rolling hills of Highland Perthshire and the rugged, rocky peaks of Glen Coe, the central mountain ranges of the Scottish Highlands are testimony to the sculpting power of ice and weather. Here the landscape is at its grandest, with soaring hills of rock and heather bounded by wooded glens and rushing waterfalls.

Not surprisingly, this part of the country is an adventure playground for outdoor-sports enthusiasts. Aviemore, Glen Coe and Fort William draw hill walkers and climbers in summer, and skiers, snowboarders and ice climbers in winter. Inverness, the Highland capital, provides urban rest and relaxation, while nearby Loch Ness and its elusive monster add a hint of mystery.

From Fort William, base camp for climbing Ben Nevis, the Road to the Isles leads past the beaches of Arisaig and Morar to Mallaig, jumping-off point for the isles of Eigg, Rum, Muck and Canna.

When to Go
Inverness

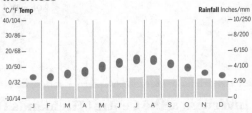

Apr–May Mountain scenery is at its most spectacular, with snow lingering on the higher peaks.

Jun Fort William hosts the UCI Mountain Bike World Cup, pulling huge crowds.

Sep Ideal for hiking and hill walking: midges are dying off, but weather is still reasonably good.

Inverness & the Central Highlands Highlights

1 Glen Affric (p304)
Hiking among the hills, lochs and forests of Scotland's most beautiful glen.

2 Rothiemurchus Estate (p309) Wandering through

ancient Caledonian forest in the heart of the Cairngorms.

3 Ben Nevis (p339)
Making it to the summit of the UK's highest mountain – and being able to see the view.

4 Glen Lyon (p331)
Exploring the woods and mountains around this gorgeous and romantic glen.

5 Rannoch Moor (p328)
Keeping right on to the end

of the road at this bleak but beautiful moor.

6 **Nevis Range** (p339) Rattling your teeth loose on this championship downhill mountain-bike course.

7 **Sgurr of Eigg** (p346) Taking in the stunning panorama from the summit of this dramatic island peak.

8 **Glen Coe** (p331) Soaking up the moody but magnificent scenery (when you can see it!).

9 **Knoydart Peninsula** (p344) Venturing into the country's most remote and rugged wilderness.

❶ Getting There & Around

BUS

Scottish Citylink (p334) Runs buses from Perth and Glasgow to Inverness and Fort William, and links Inverness to Fort William along the Great Glen.

Stagecoach (www.stagecoachbus.com) The main regional bus company, with offices in Aviemore, Inverness and Fort William. Dayrider tickets are valid for a day's unlimited travel on Stagecoach buses in various regions, including Inverness (£3.50), Aviemore and around (£6.70) and Fort William (£3.40).

TRAIN

Two railway lines serve the region: the Perth–Aviemore–Inverness line in the east, and the Glasgow–Fort William–Mallaig line in the west.

INVERNESS & THE GREAT GLEN

Inverness, one of the fastest growing towns in Britain, is the capital of the Highlands. It's a transport hub and jumping-off point for the central, western and northern Highlands, the Moray Firth coast and the Great Glen.

The Great Glen is a geological fault running in an arrow-straight line across Scotland from Fort William to Inverness. The glaciers of the last ice age eroded a deep trough along the fault line, which is now filled by a series of lochs – Linnhe, Lochy, Oich and Ness. The glen has always been an important communication route – General George Wade built a military road along the southern side of Loch Ness in the early 18th century, and in 1822 the various lochs were linked by the Caledonian Canal to create a cross-country waterway. The modern A82 road along the glen was completed in 1933 – a date that coincides neatly with the first modern sightings of the Loch Ness Monster.

Inverness

POP 61,235

Inverness has a great location astride the River Ness at the northern end of the Great Glen. In summer it overflows with visitors intent on monster hunting at nearby Loch Ness, but it's worth a visit in its own right for a stroll along the picturesque River Ness, a cruise on Loch Ness, and a meal in one of the city's excellent restaurants.

Inverness was probably founded by King David in the 12th century, but thanks to its often violent history few buildings of real age or historical significance have survived – much of the older part of the city dates from the period following the completion of the Caledonian Canal in 1822. The broad and shallow River Ness, famed for its salmon fishing, runs through the heart of the city.

◉ Sights

★ Ness Islands
PARK

The main attraction in Inverness is a leisurely stroll along the river to the Ness Islands. Planted with mature Scots pine, fir, beech and sycamore, and linked to the river banks and each other by elegant Victorian footbridges, the islands make an appealing picnic spot. They're a 20-minute walk south of the castle – head upstream on either side of the river (the start of the Great Glen Way), and return on the opposite bank.

On the way you'll pass the red-sandstone towers of **St Andrew's Cathedral** (11 Ardross St), dating from 1869, and the modern Eden Court Theatre (p300), which hosts regular art exhibits, both on the west bank.

Inverness Museum & Art Gallery
MUSEUM

(☑ 01463-237114; www.inverness.highland.museum; Castle Wynd; ☺ 10am-5pm Tue-Sat Apr-Oct, noon-4pm Thu-Sat Nov-Mar) **FREE** Inverness Museum & Art Gallery has wildlife dioramas, geological displays, period rooms with historic weapons, Pictish stones and exhibitions of contemporary Highland arts and crafts.

Victorian Market
MARKET

(Academy St; ☺ 9am-5pm Mon-Sat) If the rain comes down, you could opt for a spot of retail therapy in the Victorian Market, a shopping mall that dates from the 1890s and has rather more charm than its modern equivalents.

Inverness Castle
CASTLE

(Castle St) The hill above the city centre is topped by the picturesque Baronial turrets of Inverness Castle, a pink-sandstone confection dating from 1847 that replaced a medieval castle blown up by the Jacobites in 1746; it serves today as the Sheriff's Court. It's not open to the public, but there are good views from the surrounding gardens.

Inverness

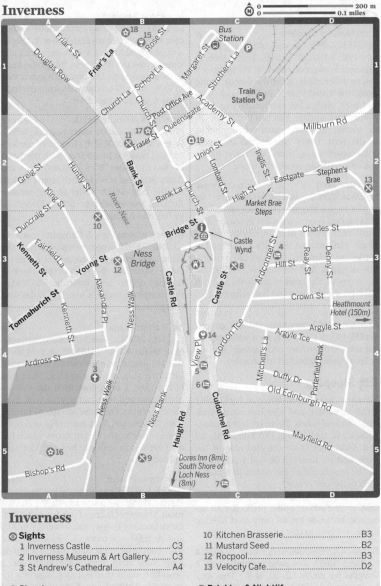

Inverness

⊚ Sights
1	Inverness Castle	C3
2	Inverness Museum & Art Gallery	C3
3	St Andrew's Cathedral	A4

🛏 Sleeping
4	Ardconnel House	C3
5	Bazpackers Backpackers Hotel	C4
	Glenmoriston Town House Hotel	(see 9)
6	Inverness Student Hotel	C4
7	Rocpool Reserve	C5

⊗ Eating
8	Café 1	C3
9	Contrast Brasserie	B5
10	Kitchen Brasserie	B3
11	Mustard Seed	B2
12	Rocpool	B3
13	Velocity Cafe	D2

⊙ Drinking & Nightlife
14	Castle Tavern	C4
15	Phoenix	B1

⊛ Entertainment
16	Eden Court Theatre	A5
17	Hootananny	B2
18	Ironworks	B1

⊙ Shopping
19	Victorian Market	C2

☞ Tours

Loch Ness by Jacobite
BOATING

(☎ 01463-233999; www.jacobite.co.uk; Glenurquhart Rd; adult/child £33/26) From June to September, boats depart from Tomnahurich Bridge twice daily for a three-hour cruise along the Caledonian Canal to Loch Ness and back, with a live commentary on local history and wildlife. You can buy tickets at the tourist office and catch a free minibus to the boat. Other cruises and combined cruise/coach tours, from one to 6½ hours, are also available, some year-round.

Dolphin Spirit
WILDLIFE WATCHING

(☎ 07544-800620; www.dolphinspirit.co.uk; Inverness Marina, Longman Dr; adult/child £16/10; ☺ Easter-Oct) Four times a day in season, this outfit runs cruises from Inverness into the Moray Firth to spot the UK's largest pod of bottlenose dolphins – around 130 animals. The dolphins feed on salmon heading for the rivers at the head of the firth, and can often be seen leaping and bow-surfing.

Happy Tours
WALKING

(☎ 07828-154683; www.happy-tours.biz; per person £10) Offers 1¼-hour guided walks exploring the town's history and legends, starting at 7pm (must be booked in advance).

🛏 Sleeping

Inverness has a good range of backpacker accommodation, and also has some excellent boutique hotels. There are lots of guesthouses and B&Bs along Old Edinburgh Rd and Ardconnel St on the east side of the river, and on Kenneth St and Fairfield Rd on the west bank; all are within 10 minutes' walk of the city centre.

The city fills up quickly in July and August, so you should either prebook your accommodation or get an early start looking for somewhere to stay.

Bazpackers Backpackers Hotel
HOSTEL £

(☎ 01463-717663; www.bazpackershostel.co.uk; 4 Culduthel Rd; dm/tw £18/50; @ 🛜) This may be Inverness' smallest hostel (34 beds), but it's hugely popular. It's a friendly, quiet place – the main building has a convivial lounge centred on a wood-burning stove, and a small garden and great views (some rooms are in a separate building with no garden). The dorms and kitchen can be a bit cramped, but the showers are great.

Inverness Student Hotel
HOSTEL £

(☎ 01463-236556; www.scotlands-top-hostels. com; 8 Culduthel Rd; dm £18.50; P @ 🛜) Set in a rambling old house with comfy beds and views across the River Ness, this hostel has a party atmosphere, and organises pub crawls in town. It's a 10-minute walk from the train station, just past the castle.

Inverness Millburn SYHA
HOSTEL £

(SYHA; ☎ 01463-231771; www.syha.org.uk; Victoria Dr; dm/tw £22/55; P @ 🛜) Inverness' modern 166-bed hostel is 10 minutes' walk northeast of the city centre. With its comfy beds and flashy stainless-steel kitchen, some reckon it's the best SYHA hostel in the country. Booking is essential, especially at Easter and in July and August.

Bught Caravan Park & Campsite
CAMPSITE £

(☎ 01463-236920; www.invernesscaravanpark.com; Bught Lane; tent site per person £10, campervan £18; ☺ Easter-Sep; 🛜) A mile southwest of the city centre near Tomnahurich Bridge, this camping ground is hugely popular with backpackers.

★ Trafford Bank
B&B ££

(☎ 01463-241414; www.traffordbankguesthouse. co.uk; 96 Fairfield Rd; d £120-140; P 🛜) Lots of word-of-mouth rave reviews for this elegant Victorian villa, which was once home to a bishop, just a mitre-toss from the Caledonian Canal and 10 minutes' walk west from the city centre. The luxurious rooms include fresh flowers and fruit, bathrobes and fluffy towels – ask for the Tartan Room, which has a wrought-iron king-size bed and Victorian roll-top bath.

Ardconnel House
B&B ££

(☎ 01463-240455; www.ardconnel-inverness.co.uk; 21 Ardconnel St; r per person £36-45; 🛜) The six-room Ardconnel is one of our favourites (advance booking is essential, especially in July and August) – a terraced Victorian house with comfortable en suite rooms, a dining room with crisp white table linen, and a breakfast menu that includes Vegemite for homesick Antipodeans. Kids under 10 not allowed.

Ach Aluinn
B&B ££

(☎ 01463-230127; www.achaluinn.com; 27 Fairfield Rd; r per person £40-45; P) This large, detached Victorian house is bright and homely, and offers all you might want from a B&B – private bathroom, TV, reading lights, comfy beds with two pillows each, and an excellent breakfast. Less than 10 minutes' walk west from the city centre.

Heathmount Hotel
BOUTIQUE HOTEL ££

(☑ 01463-235877; www.heathmounthotel.com; Kingsmills Rd; s/d from £75/105; P �***) Small and friendly, the Heathmount combines a popular local bar and restaurant with eight designer hotel rooms, each one different, ranging from a boldly coloured family room in purple and gold to a slinky black velvet four-poster double. Five minutes' walk east of the city centre.

MacRae Guest House
B&B ££

(☑ 01463-243658; joycemacrae@hotmail.com; 24 Ness Bank; s/d from £45/66; P �***) This pretty, flower-bedecked Victorian house on the eastern bank of the river has smart, tastefully decorated bedrooms (one is wheelchair accessible), and vegetarian breakfasts are available. Minimum two-night bookings in July and August.

★ Rocpool Reserve
BOUTIQUE HOTEL £££

(☑ 01463-240089; www.rocpool.com; Culduthel Rd; s/d from £195/230; P �***) Boutique chic meets the Highlands in this slick and so-phisticated little hotel, where an elegant Georgian exterior conceals an oasis of contemporary cool. A gleaming white entrance hall lined with red carpet and contemporary art leads to designer rooms in shades of chocolate, cream and gold; a restaurant by Albert Roux completes the luxury package.

Expect lots of decadent extras in the more expensive rooms, ranging from two-person showers to balcony hot tubs with aqua-vision TV.

Glenmoriston
Town House Hotel
BOUTIQUE HOTEL £££

(☑ 01463-223777; www.glenmoristontownhouse. com; 20 Ness Bank; r from £180; P �***) Luxurious boutique hotel on the banks of the River Ness, where spacious bedrooms are decorated in rustic colours with touches of tweed; it's worth paying a bit extra for the luxury rooms with river views. Can organise golfing and fishing for guests.

✗ Eating

Velocity Cafe
CAFE £

(☑ 01463-419956; http://velocitylove.co.uk; 1 Crown Ave; mains £4-7; ⊙9am-5pm Mon, Wed, Fri & Sat, 9am-9pm Thu, 11am-5pm Sun; �) ✔ This cyclists' cafe serves soups, sandwiches and salads prepared with organic, locally

sourced produce, as well as yummy cakes and coffee. There's also a workshop where you can repair your bike or book a session with a mechanic.

★ Café 1
BISTRO ££

(☑ 01463-226200; www.cafe1.net; 75 Castle St; mains £13-25; ⊙noon-2.30pm & 5-9.30pm Mon-Fri, noon-2.30pm & 6-9.30pm Sat; ☏) ✔ Café 1 is a friendly, appealing bistro with candle-lit tables amid elegant blonde-wood and wrought-iron decor. There is an international menu based on quality Scottish produce, from Aberdeen Angus steaks to crisp pan-fried sea bass and meltingly tender pork belly. The set lunch menu (two courses for £12) is served noon to 2.30pm Monday to Saturday.

Contrast Brasserie
BRASSERIE ££

(☑ 01463-223777; www.glenmoristontownhouse. com; 20 Ness Bank; mains £14-21; ⊙noon-2.30pm & 5-10pm) Book early for what we think is one of the best-value restaurants in Inverness – a dining room that drips designer style, with smiling professional staff and truly delicious food prepared using fresh Scottish produce. The two-/three-course lunch menu (£11/14) and three-course early-bird menu (£16, 5pm to 6.30pm) are bargains.

Mustard Seed
BISTRO ££

(☑ 01463-220220; www.mustardseedrestaurant. co.uk; 16 Fraser St; mains £13-21; ⊙noon-3pm & 5.30-10pm) ✔ The menu at this bright and bustling bistro changes weekly, but focuses on Scottish and French cuisine with a modern twist. Grab a table on the upstairs balcony if you can – it's the best outdoor lunch spot in Inverness, with a great view across the river. And a two-course lunch for £9 – yes, that's right – is hard to beat.

Kitchen Brasserie
MODERN SCOTTISH ££

(☑ 01463-259119; www.kitchenrestaurant.co.uk; 15 Huntly St; mains £9-20; ⊙noon-3pm & 5-10pm; ☏☕) This spectacular glass-fronted restaurant offers a great menu of top Scottish produce with a Mediterranean or Asian touch, and a view over the River Ness – try to get a table upstairs. Great value two-course lunch (£9, noon to 3pm) and early-bird menu (£13, 5pm to 7pm).

Rocpool
MEDITERRANEAN £££

(☑ 01463-717274; www.rocpoolrestaurant.com; 1 Ness Walk; mains £13-23; ⊙noon-2.30pm & 5.45-10pm Mon-Sat) ✔ Lots of polished wood, crisp white linen and leather booths and banquettes lend a nautical air to this relaxing bistro, which offers a Mediterranean-influenced menu that makes the most of quality Scottish produce, especially seafood. The two-course lunch is £16.

Drinking & Nightlife

Clachnaharry Inn   PUB
(☑ 01463-239806; www.clachnaharryinn.co.uk; 17-19 High St, Clachnaharry; ⊙ 11am-11pm Mon-Thu, 11am-1am Fri & Sat, noon-11pm Sun; 🐾) Just over a mile northwest of the city centre, on the bank of the Caledonian Canal just off the A862, this is a delightful old coaching inn (with beer garden out the back) serving an excellent range of real ales and good pub grub.

Phoenix   PUB
(☑ 01463-233685; 108 Academy St; ⊙ 11am-1am Mon-Sat, noon-midnight Sun) Beautifully refurbished, this is the most traditional of the pubs in the city centre, with a mahogany horseshoe bar and several real ales on tap, including beers from the Cairngorm, Cromarty and Isle of Skye breweries.

Castle Tavern   PUB
(☑ 01463-718718; www.castletavern.net; 1-2 View Pl; ⊙ 11am-11pm) Offering a tempting selection of craft beers, this pub has a wee suntrap of a terrace out the front. It's a great place for a pint on a summer afternoon.

☆ Entertainment

Hootananny   LIVE MUSIC
(☑ 01463-233651; www.hootananyinverness.co.uk; 67 Church St) Hootananny is the city's best live-music venue, with traditional folk-and/or rock-music sessions nightly, including big-name bands from all over Scotland (and, indeed, the world). The bar is well stocked with a range of beers from the local Black Isle Brewery.

Ironworks   LIVE MUSIC, COMEDY
(☑ 0871-789 4173; www.ironworksvenue.com; 122 Academy St) With live bands (rock, pop, tribute) and comedy shows two or three times a week, the Ironworks is the town's main venue for big-name acts.

Eden Court Theatre   THEATRE
(☑ 01463-234234; www.eden-court.co.uk; Bishop's Rd; 🐾) The Highlands' main cultural venue – with theatre, art-house cinema and a conference centre – Eden Court stages a busy program of drama, dance, comedy, music, film and children's events, and has a good bar and restaurant. Pick up a program from the foyer or check the website.

ℹ Information

Inverness Tourist Office (☑ 01463-252401; www.visithighlands.com; Castle Wynd; internet access per 20min £1; ⊙ 9am-5pm Mon-Sat, 10am-3pm Sun, longer hours Mar-Oct) Bureau de change and accommodation booking service; also sells tickets for tours and cruises. Opening hours limited November to March.

ℹ Getting There & Away

AIR
Inverness Airport (INV; ☑ 01667-464000; www.hial.co.uk/inverness-airport) is at Dalcross, 10 miles east of the city, off the A96 towards Aberdeen. There are scheduled flights to Amsterdam, London, Manchester, Dublin, Orkney, Shetland and the Outer Hebrides, as well as other places in the UK.

BUS
Services depart from **Inverness bus station** (Margaret St). Most intercity routes are served by **Scottish Citylink** (☑ 0871-266 3333; www.citylink.co.uk).

Aberdeen (Stagecoach, p301) £12.75, 3¾ hours, hourly

Aviemore £10.20, 45 minutes, eight daily

Edinburgh £31, 3½ to 4½ hours, hourly

Fort William £11.60, two hours, five daily

Glasgow £31, 3½ to 4½ hours, hourly

London (**National Express** (☑ 08717-818181; www.nationalexpress.com)) £45, 13 hours, one daily; more frequent services requiring a change at Glasgow.

Portree £25, 3¼ hours, three daily

Thurso (Stagecoach) £19.80, three hours, three to five daily

Ullapool £13.20, 1½ hours, two daily except Sunday

If you book far enough in advance, **Megabus** (☑ 0141-352 4444; www.megabus.com) offers fares from as little as £1 for buses from Inverness to Glasgow and Edinburgh, and £10 to London.

TRAIN
Aberdeen £21, 2¼ hours, eight daily

Edinburgh £38, 3½ hours, eight daily

Glasgow £38, 3½ hours, eight daily

Kyle of Lochalsh £18, 2½ hours, four daily Monday to Saturday, two Sunday; one of Britain's great scenic train journeys

London £120, eight to nine hours, one daily direct; others require a change at Edinburgh

Wick £16, 4½ hours, four daily Monday to Saturday, one or two on Sunday; via Thurso

ℹ Getting Around

TO/FROM THE AIRPORT

Stagecoach (📞01463-233371; www.stage coachbus.com) bus 11/11A runs from the airport to Inverness bus station (£4, 20 minutes, every 30 minutes).

BICYCLE

Ticket to Ride (📞01463-419160; www.ticket toridehighlands.co.uk; Bellfield Park; per day from £25; ⏰9am-6pm Apr-Oct) Hires out mountain bikes, hybrids and tandems; can be dropped off in Fort William. Will deliver bikes free to local hotels and B&Bs.

BUS

City services and buses to places around Inverness, including Nairn, Forres, the Culloden battlefield, Beauly, Dingwall and Lairg, are operated by Stagecoach. An Inverness City Dayrider ticket costs £3.50 and gives unlimited travel for a day on buses throughout the city.

CAR

The big boys charge from around £50 to £65 per day, but **Focus Vehicle Rental** (📞01463-709517; www.focusvehiclerental.co.uk; 6 Harbour Rd) has cheaper rates starting at £40 per day.

TAXI

Inverness Taxis (📞01463-222222; www.inverness-taxis.com) There's a taxi rank outside the train station.

Around Inverness

Culloden Battlefield

The Battle of Culloden in 1746 – the last pitched battle ever fought on British soil – saw the defeat of Bonnie Prince Charlie and the end of the Jacobite dream when 1200 Highlanders were slaughtered by government forces in a 68-minute rout. The Duke of Cumberland, son of the reigning King George II and leader of the Hanoverian army, earned the nickname 'Butcher' for his brutal treatment of the defeated Jacobite forces. The battle sounded the death knell for the old clan system, and the horrors of the Clearances soon followed. The sombre moor where the conflict took place has scarcely changed in the ensuing 260 years.

Culloden is 6 miles east of Inverness. Bus 5A runs from Eastgate shopping centre in Inverness to Culloden battlefield (£2.45, 30 minutes, hourly except Sunday).

The impressive **Culloden Visitor Centre** (NTS; www.nts.org.uk/culloden; adult/child £11/8.50; ⏰9am-6pm Jun-Aug, to 5.30pm Apr, May, Sep & Oct, 10am-4pm Nov-Mar; 🅿) has everything you need to know about the Battle of Culloden in 1746, including the lead-up and the aftermath, with perspectives from both sides. An innovative film puts you on the battlefield in the middle of the mayhem, and a wealth of other audio presentations must have kept Inverness' entire acting community in business for weeks. The admission fee includes an audioguide for a self-guided tour of the battlefield itself.

Fort George

The headland guarding the narrows in the Moray Firth opposite Fortrose is occupied by the magnificent and virtually unaltered 18th-century artillery fortification of Fort George.

One of the finest artillery fortifications in Europe, **Fort George** (HS; 📞01667-462777; adult/child £8.50/5.10; ⏰9.30am-5.30pm Apr-Sep, 10am-4pm Oct-Mar; 🅿) was established in 1748 in the aftermath of the Battle of Culloden, as a base for George II's army of occupation in the Highlands. By the time of its completion in 1769 it had cost the equivalent of around £1 billion in today's money. It still functions as a military barracks; public areas have exhibitions on 18th-century soldiery, and the mile-plus walk around the ramparts offers fine views out to sea and back to the Great Glen.

Given its size, you'll need at least two hours to do the place justice. The fort is off the A96 about 11 miles northeast of Inverness; there is no public transport.

Nairn

POP 9775

Nairn is a popular golfing and seaside resort with good sandy beaches. You can spend many pleasant hours wandering along the **East Beach**, one of the finest in Scotland.

The most interesting part of town is the old fishing village of **Fishertown**, down by the harbour, a maze of narrow streets lined with picturesque cottages.

◉ Sights

Nairn Museum MUSEUM
(📞01667-456791; www.nairnmuseum.co.uk; Viewfield House; adult/child £3/50p; ⏰10am-4.30pm Mon-Fri, to 1pm Sat Apr-Oct) Nairn Museum, a

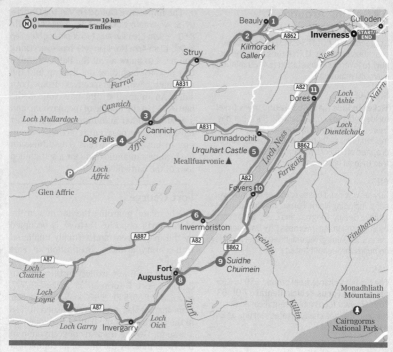

Driving Tour
A Loch Ness Circuit

START INVERNESS
END INVERNESS
LENGTH 130 MILES; SIX TO SEVEN HOURS

Head out of Inverness on the A862 to Beauly, arriving in time for breakfast at **1 Corner on the Square** (p303). Backtrack a mile and turn right on the A831 to Cannich, passing **2 Kilmorack Gallery**, which exhibits contemporary art in a converted church. The scenery gets wilder as you approach **3 Cannich**; turn right and follow the single-track road to the car park at **4 Dog Falls**. Take a stroll along the rushing river, or hike to the viewpoint (about one-hour round trip; 2.5 miles) for a glimpse of remote Glen Affric.

Return to Cannich and turn right on the A831 to Drumnadrochit, then right on the A82 past picturesque **5 Urquhart Castle** (p307) and along the shores of Loch Ness. At **6 Invermoriston**, pause to look at the old bridge, built by Telford in 1813, then head west on the A887 towards Kyle of Lochalsh; after 16 miles go left on the A87 towards Invergarry. You are now among some of the finest mountain scenery in the Highlands; as the road turns east above Loch Garry, stop at the famous **7 viewpoint** (layby on right, signposted Glengarry Viewpoint). Through a quirk of perspective, the lochs to the west appear to form the map outline of Scotland.

At Invergarry, turn left on the A82 to reach **8 Fort Augustus** and a late lunch at the Lovat (p308) or Lock Inn (p309). Take the B862 out of town, following the line of General Wade's 18th-century military road, to another viewpoint at **9 Suidhe Chuimein**. A short (800m) walk up the well-worn path to the summit affords an even better panorama.

Ahead, you can choose the low road via the impressive **10 Falls of Foyers**, or stay on the the high road (B862) for more views; both converge on Loch Ness at **11 Dores**, at the Dores Inn (p308), where you can sip a pint with a view along Loch Ness, and even stay for dinner before returning to Inverness.

few minutes' walk from the tourist office, has displays on the history of the harbour community of Fishertown, as well as on local archaeology, geology and natural history.

⚡ Festivals & Events

The big events in the town's calendar are the **Nairn Highland Games** (www.nairnhighlandgames.co.uk; ⊙mid-Aug) and the **Nairn Book and Arts Festival** (www.nairnfestival.co.uk; ⊙Sep).

🛏 Sleeping & Eating

Glebe End   B&B ££
(☑01667-451659; www.glebe-end.co.uk; 1 Glebe Rd; r per person £35-50; P🕸) It's people as much as place that make a good B&B, and the owners here are all you could wish for – helpful and welcoming. The house is lovely too, a spacious Victorian villa with home-away-from-home bedrooms and a sunny conservatory where breakfast is served.

Boath House Hotel   HOTEL £££
(☑01667-454896; www.boath-house.com; Auldearn; s/d from £190/295; P🕸) This beautifully restored Regency mansion, set in private woodland gardens 2 miles east of Nairn on the A96, is one of Scotland's most luxurious country-house hotels, and includes a spa offering holistic treatments and a Michelin-starred restaurant (three-/six-course dinner £45/70).

Classroom   GASTROPUB ££
(☑01667-455999; www.theclassroombistro.com; 1 Cawdor St; mains £14-27; ⊙noon-4.30pm & 5-10pm) 🍃 Done up in an appealing mixture of modern and traditional styles – lots of richly glowing wood with designer detailing – the Classroom doubles as cocktail bar and gastropub, with a tempting menu that ranges from Cullen skink (soup made with smoked haddock, potato, onion and milk) to Highland steak with peppercorn sauce.

ℹ Information

Tourist information point (☑01667-453476; Nairn Community Centre, King St; ⊙9am-5pm)

ℹ Getting There & Away

Buses run hourly (less frequently on Sunday) from Inverness to Nairn (£5.60, 30 minutes) and on to Aberdeen. The bus station is just west of the town centre.

The town also lies on the Inverness–Aberdeen railway line, with five to seven trains a day from Inverness (£6, 15 minutes).

Cawdor Castle

Five miles southwest of Nairn, **Cawdor Castle** (☑01667-404615; www.cawdorcastle.com; Cawdor; adult/child £10.70/6.70; ⊙10am-5.30pm May-Sep; P), was once the seat of the Thane of Cawdor, one of the titles bestowed on Shakespeare's *Macbeth*. The real Macbeth – an ancient Scottish king -- couldn't have lived here though, since he died in 1057, 300 years before the castle was begun. Nevertheless the tour gives a fascinating insight into the lives of the Scottish aristocracy.

Cawdor Tavern (www.cawdortavern.co.uk; mains £11-19; ⊙11am-11pm Mon-Thu, 11am-midnight Fri & Sat, noon-11pm Sun), in the village close to Cawdor Castle, is worth a visit, though it can be difficult deciding what to drink as it stocks over 100 varieties of whisky. There's also excellent pub food (served noon to 9pm), with tempting daily specials.

West of Inverness

Beauly

POP 1365

Mary, Queen of Scots is said to have given this village its name in 1564 when she visited, exclaiming in French: '*Quel beau lieu!*' (What a beautiful place!). Founded in 1230, the red-sandstone **Beauly Priory** is now an impressive ruin, haunted by the cries of rooks nesting in a magnificent centuries-old sycamore tree.

Buses 28 and 28A from Inverness run to Beauly (£4.90, 30 to 45 minutes, hourly Monday to Saturday, five on Sunday), and the town lies on the Inverness–Thurso railway line.

The **Priory Hotel** (☑01463-782309; www.priory-hotel.com; The Square; s/d £85/130; P🕸), on Beauly's central square, has bright, modern rooms and serves good bar meals.

Beauly's best lunch spot is **Corner on the Square** (☑01463-783000; www.corneronthesquare.co.uk; 1 High St; mains £7-13; ⊙8.30am-5.30pm Mon-Fri, 8.30am-5pm Sat, 9.30am-5pm Sun), a superb little delicatessen and cafe that serves breakfast (till 11.30am), daily lunch specials (11.30am to 4.30pm) and excellent coffee.

Strathglass & Glen Affric

The broad valley of Strathglass extends about 18 miles inland from Beauly, followed by the A831 to Cannich (the only village in the area), where there's a grocery store and a post office.

Glen Affric (www.glenaffric.org), one of the most beautiful glens in Scotland, extends deep into the hills beyond Cannich. The upper reaches of the glen, now designated as **Glen Affric Nature Reserve** (www. nnr-scotland.org.uk/glen-affric), is a scenic wonderland of shimmering lochs, rugged mountains and native Scots pine forest, home to pine marten, wildcat, otter, red squirrel and golden eagle.

About 4 miles southwest of Cannich is **Dog Falls**, a scenic spot where the River Affric squeezes through a narrow, rocky gorge. A circular walking trail (red waymarks) leads from Dog Falls car park to a footbridge below the falls and back on the far side of the river (2 miles, allow one hour).

The road continues beyond Dog Falls to a parking area and picnic site at the eastern end of **Loch Affric**, where there are several short walks along the river and the loch shore. The circuit of Loch Affric (10 miles, allow five hours walking, two hours by mountain bike) follows good paths right around the loch and takes you deep into the heart of some very wild scenery.

It's possible to walk all the way from Cannich to Glen Shiel on the west coast (35 miles) in two days, spending the night at the remote Glen Affric Youth Hostel. The route is now part of the newly waymarked **Affric-Kintail Way** (www.affrickintailway. com), a 56-mile walking or mountain-biking trail leading from Drumnadrochit to Kintail via Cannich.

A minor road on the east side of the River Glass leads to the pretty little conservation village of **Tomich**, 3 miles southwest of Cannich, built in Victorian times as accommodation for estate workers. The road continues (unsurfaced for the last 2 miles) to a forestry car park, the starting point for a short (800m) walk to pretty **Plodda Falls**. A restored Victorian viewing platform extends over the top of the falls like a diving board, giving a dizzying view straight down the cascade into a remote and thickly forested river gorge. Keep your eyes peeled for red squirrels and crossbills.

🛏️ Sleeping & Eating

Glen Affric SYHA
HOSTEL £

(SYHA; 📞 bookings 0845-293 7373; www.syha. org.uk; Allt Beithe; dm £23; ☉ Apr–mid-Sep) This remote and rustic hostel is set amid magnificent scenery at the halfway point of the cross-country walk from Cannich to Glen Shiel, 8 miles from the nearest road. Facilities are basic and you'll need to take all supplies with you (and all litter away). Book in advance. There is no phone, internet or mobile phone signal at the hostel.

Cannich Caravan & Camping Park
CAMPSITE £

(📞 01456-415364; www.highlandcamping.co.uk; sites per adult/child £8/4, pods s/d £22/34; 📶) Good, sheltered site, with option of wooden camping 'pods' and on-site cafe. Mountain bikes for hire from £17 a day.

★ Struy Inn
HOTEL ££

(📞 01463-761308; www.thestruy.co.uk; Struy Village; d £95; ☉ Wed-Sun; 🅿️📶) Set in the heart of lovely Strathglass, on the road between Cannich and Beauly, this fine old Victorian inn is a haven of old-fashioned charm. It has just two guest bedrooms and a top-quality restaurant (mains £17 to £27, served from 5.30pm) serving the finest Scottish cuisine. Booking essential.

★ Kerrow House
B&B ££

(📞 01456-415243; www.kerrow-house.co.uk; Cannich; per person £40-45; 🅿️📶) 🍴 This wonderful Georgian hunting lodge has bags of old-fashioned character – it was once the home of Highland author Neil M Gunn – and has spacious grounds with 3.5 miles of private trout fishing. It's a mile south of Cannich on the minor road along the east side of the River Glass.

Tomich Hotel
HOTEL ££

(📞 01456-415399; www.tomichhotel.co.uk; Tomich; s/d from £75/120; 🅿️📶🏊) About 3 miles southwest of Cannich on the southern side of the River Glass, this Victorian hunting lodge has a blazing log fire; an intimate, candlelit restaurant and eight comfortable en suite rooms. It can organise trout fishing on local waters.

ℹ️ Getting There & Away

Stagecoach buses 17 and 117 (www.stage coachbus.com) run from Inverness to Cannich (£5.30, one hour, three a day Monday to Saturday) via Drumnadrochit, and continue from Cannich to Tomich (10 minutes).

From the first Monday in July to the 2nd Friday in September, **Ross's Minibuses** (www.ross-minibuses.co.uk) runs a service from Inverness bus station to the Glen Affric car park via Drumnadrochit and Cannich (£8.50, 1½ hours, once daily Monday, Wednesday and Friday). It shuttles between Cannich and Glen Affric (30 minutes) twice more on the same days. Check the website for the latest timetables.

Black Isle

The Black Isle – a peninsula rather than an island – is linked to Inverness by the Kessock Bridge. Bypassed by the main A9 road, it's a peaceful backwater of wooded hills, picturesque villages and dramatic coastlines, with the added attraction of Scotland's best mainland dolphin-watching spot.

ⓘ Getting There & Away

Stagecoach (p301) buses 26 and 26A run from Inverness to Fortrose and Rosemarkie (£3.80, 30 to 40 minutes, twice hourly Monday to Saturday); half of them continue to Cromarty (£4.80, one hour).

Fortrose & Rosemarkie

The neighbouring towns of Fortrose and Rosemarkie make up the main population centre of the Black Isle. Between the two, the long gravel spit of **Chanonry Point** is the best land-based dolphin-spotting area in the country – one-hour dolphin-watching cruises depart from the harbour at Avoch (pronounced 'auch'), 3 miles southwest.

At **Fortrose Cathedral** you'll find the vaulted crypt of a 13th-century chapter house and sacristy, and the ruinous 14th-century south aisle and chapel, while Rosemarkie's **Groam House Museum** (☑ 01381-620961; www.groamhouse.org.uk; High St; ⊙11am-4.30pm Mon-Fri, 2-4.30pm Sat & Sun Easter-Oct) **FREE** has a superb collection of Pictish stones.

From the northern end of Rosemarkie's High St, a short but pleasant signposted walk leads you through the gorges and waterfalls of the **Fairy Glen**.

The **Anderson Hotel** (☑ 01381-620236; www.theanderson.co.uk; Union St, Fortrose; ⊙4-11pm, closed Sun-Tue Nov-Mar) serves good pub grub, a range of real ales (including Belgian beers and Somerset cider) and more than 200 single malt whiskies.

Cromarty

POP 725

The pretty village of Cromarty at the north-eastern tip of the Black Isle has lots of 18th-century red-sandstone houses, and a lovely green park beside the sea for picnics and games. An excellent walk, known as the **100 Steps**, leads from the north end of the village to the headland viewpoint of South Sutor (4 miles round trip).

The 18th-century **Cromarty Courthouse** (☑ 01381-600418; www.cromarty-courthouse.org.uk; Church St; ⊙noon-4pm May–mid-Oct) **FREE** is now a museum chronicling the town's history using contemporary references. Kids will love the talking mannequins.

Near the courthouse is **Hugh Miller's Cottage & Museum** (NTS; www.hughmiller.org; Church St; adult/child £6.50/5; ⊙noon-5pm daily Apr-Sep, also Thu, Fri & Fri only Oct). This thatch-roofed cottage is the birthplace of Hugh Miller (1802–56), a local stonemason and amateur geologist who pioneered the study of fossil fishes in Scotland; he later moved to Edinburgh and became a famous journalist and newspaper editor. The Georgian villa next door is home to a museum celebrating his life and achievements.

Ecoventures (☑ 01381-600323; www.ecoventures.co.uk; Cromarty Harbour; adult/child £28/21) runs two-hour boat trips from Cromarty harbour into the Moray Firth to see bottlenose dolphins and other wildlife.

Also at the harbour, **Sutor Creek** (☑ 01381-600855; www.sutorcreek.co.uk; 21 Bank St; mains £12-22; ⊙5-9pm Wed, noon-9pm Thu-Sun; 🅿) 🍝 is an excellent little cafe-restaurant serves wood-fired pizzas and fresh local seafood – the Cromarty langoustines with garlic and chilli butter are recommended.

Loch Ness

Deep, dark and narrow, Loch Ness stretches for 23 miles between Inverness and Fort Augustus. Its bitterly cold waters have been extensively explored in search of Nessie, the elusive Loch Ness monster, but most visitors see her only in the form of a cardboard cut-out at Drumnadrochit's monster exhibitions. The busy A82 road runs along the northwestern shore, while the more tranquil and picturesque B862 follows the southeastern shore. A complete circuit of the loch is about 70 miles – travel anticlockwise for the better views.

⭐ Activities

The 79-mile **Great Glen Way** (www.greatglen way.com) long-distance footpath stretches from Inverness to Fort William, where walkers can connect with the **West Highland Way**. It is described in detail in *The Great Glen Way*, a guide by Jacquetta Megarry and Sandra Bardwell.

The Great Glen Way can also be ridden (strenuous!) by mountain bike, while the **Great Glen Mountain Bike Trails** at Nevis Range and Abriachan Forest offer challenging cross-country and downhill trails. You can hire a mountain bike in Fort William (p338) and drop it off in Inverness (p301), and vice versa.

The **South Loch Ness Trail** (www.visit invernesslochness.com) links a series of footpaths and minor roads along the less-frequented southern side of the loch. The 28 miles from Loch Tarff near Fort Augustus to Torbreck on the fringes of Inverness can be done on foot, by bike or on horseback.

There's also the option of the **Great Glen Canoe Trail** (www.greatglencanoetrail.info), a series of access points, waymarks and informal campsites that allow you to travel the length of the glen by canoe or kayak.

The climb to the summit of **Meallfuarvonie** (699m), on the northwestern shore of Loch Ness, makes an excellent short hill walk: the views along the Great Glen from the top are superb. It's a 6-mile round trip, so allow about three hours. Start from the car park at the end of the minor road leading south from Drumnadrochit to Bunloit.

MONSTERS, MYTHS & LOCH NESS

Highland folklore is filled with tales of strange creatures living in lochs and rivers, notably the kelpie (water horse) that lures unwary travellers to their doom. The use of the term 'monster', however, is a relatively recent phenomenon, whose origins lie in an article published in the *Inverness Courier* on 2 May 1933, entitled 'Strange Spectacle on Loch Ness'.

The article recounted the sighting of a disturbance in the loch by Mrs Aldie Mackay and her husband: 'There the creature disported itself, rolling and plunging for fully a minute, its body resembling that of a whale, and the water cascading and churning like a simmering cauldron.'

The story was taken up by the London press and sparked a flurry of sightings that year, including a notorious on-land encounter with London tourists Mr and Mrs Spicer on 22 July 1933, again reported in the *Inverness Courier*:

'It was horrible, an abomination. About 50 yards ahead, we saw an undulating sort of neck, and quickly followed by a large, ponderous body. I estimated the length to be 25 to 30 feet, its colour was dark elephant grey. It crossed the road in a series of jerks, but because of the slope we could not see its limbs. Although I accelerated quickly towards it, it had disappeared into the loch by the time I reached the spot. There was no sign of it in the water. I am a temperate man, but I am willing to take any oath that we saw this Loch Ness beast. I am certain that this creature was of a prehistoric species.'

The London newspapers couldn't resist. In December 1933 the *Daily Mail* sent Marmaduke Wetherall, a film director and big-game hunter, to Loch Ness to track down the beast. Within days he found 'reptilian' footprints in the shoreline mud (soon revealed to have been made with a stuffed hippopotamus foot). Then in April 1934 came the famous 'long-necked monster' photograph taken by the seemingly reputable Harley St surgeon Colonel Kenneth Wilson. The press went mad and the rest, as they say, is history.

In 1994, however, Christian Spurling – Wetherall's stepson, by then 90 years old – revealed that the most famous photo of Nessie ever taken was in fact a hoax, perpetrated by his stepfather with Wilson's help. Today, of course, there are those who claim that Spurling's confession is itself a hoax. And, ironically, the researcher who exposed the surgeon's photo as a fake still believes wholeheartedly in the monster's existence.

There have been regular sightings of the monster through the years (see www.lochnesssightings.com), with a peak in 1996–97 (the Hollywood movie *Loch Ness* was released in 1996), but reports have tailed off in recent years.

Hoax or not, the bizarre mini-industry that has grown up around Loch Ness and its mysterious monster since that eventful summer last century is a spectacle in itself.

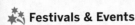 Festivals & Events

Groove Loch Ness   MUSIC

(www.groovefestival.co.uk; ⊘Aug) A vast loch-side field at the village of Dores hosts this successor to the now-defunct Rock Ness Festival, a one-day smorgasbord of the best in Scottish and international DJs.

Drumnadrochit

POP 1100

Seized by monster madness, its gift shops bulging with Nessie cuddly toys, Drumnadrochit is a hotbed of beastie fever, with two monster exhibitions battling it out for the tourist dollar.

⊙ Sights & Activities

Urquhart Castle   CASTLE

(HS; ☑01456-450551; adult/child £8.50/5.10; ⊘9.30am-6pm Apr-Sep, to 5pm Oct, to 4.30pm Nov-Mar; P) Commanding a superb location 1.5 miles east of Drumnadrochit, with outstanding views (on a clear day), Urquhart Castle is a popular Nessie-hunting hot spot. A huge visitor centre (most of which is beneath ground level) includes a video theatre (with a dramatic 'reveal' of the castle at the end of the film) and displays of medieval items discovered in the castle. The site includes a huge gift shop and a restaurant, and is often very crowded in summer.

The castle was repeatedly sacked and rebuilt (and sacked and rebuilt) over the centuries; in 1692 it was blown up to prevent the Jacobites from using it. The five-storey tower house at the northern point is the most impressive remaining fragment and offers wonderful views across the water.

Loch Ness Centre & Exhibition   INTERPRETATION CENTRE

(☑01456-450573; www.lochness.com; adult/child £7.95/4.95; ⊘9.30am-6pm Jul & Aug, to 5pm Easter-Jun, Sep & Oct, 10am-3.30pm Nov-Easter; P⧗) This Nessie-themed attraction adopts a scientific approach that allows you to weigh the evidence for yourself. Exhibits include the original equipment – sonar survey vessels, miniature submarines, cameras and sediment coring tools – used in various monster hunts, as well as original photographs and film footage of sightings. You'll find out about hoaxes and optical illusions, as well as learning a lot about the ecology of Loch Ness – is there enough food in the loch to support even one 'monster', let alone a breeding population?

Nessieland   EXHIBITION

(www.nessieland.co.uk; adult/child £6/3; ⊘9am-7pm Apr-Oct, to 5pm Nov-Mar; P) This attraction is a miniature theme park aimed squarely at the kids, though we suspect its main function is to sell you Loch Ness monster souvenirs.

Nessie Hunter   BOATING

(☑01456-450395; www.lochness-cruises.com; adult/child £15/10; ⊘Easter-Oct) One-hour monster-hunting cruises, complete with sonar and underwater cameras. Cruises depart from Drumnadrochit hourly (except 1pm) from 9am to 6pm daily.

🛏 Sleeping & Eating

BCC Loch Ness Hostel   HOSTEL £

(☑07780-603045; www.bcclochnesshostel.co.uk; Glen Urquhart; tr/q £75/90, tent site per person £5, 2-person pod £70; P⧖) Clean, modern, high-quality budget accommodation located halfway between Cannich and Loch Ness; advance booking recommended. There's also a good campsite with the option of luxury glamping pods.

Drumbuie Farm   B&B ££

(☑01456-450634; www.loch-ness-farm.co.uk; s/d from £54/68; P) A B&B in a modern house on a working farm surrounded by fields full of sheep and highland cattle, with views over Urquhart Castle and Loch Ness. Walkers and cyclists are welcome.

Loch Ness Inn   INN ££

(☑01456-450991; www.staylochness.co.uk; Lewiston; s/d/f £89/112/145; P⧖) The Loch Ness Inn ticks all the weary traveller's boxes, with comfortable bedrooms (the family suite sleeps two adults and two children), a cosy bar pouring real ales from the Cairngorm and Isle of Skye breweries, and a rustic restaurant (mains £10 to £20) serving hearty, wholesome fare.

It's conveniently located in the quiet hamlet of Lewiston, between Drumnadrochit and Urquhart Castle.

🍷 Drinking

Benleva Hotel   MICROBREWERY

(☑01456-450080; www.benleva.co.uk; Kilmore Rd; ⊘noon-midnight Mon-Thu, to 1am Fri, to 12.45am Sat, 12.30-11pm Sun; ⧖) Set in an 18th-century manse a half-mile east of the main road, the Benleva is a rough diamond of a pub – a bit frayed around the edges but with a heart of gold. The beer is the main event, with a

WORTH A TRIP

DORES INN

While crowded tour coaches pour down the west side of Loch Ness to the hot spots of Drumnadrochit and Urquhart Castle, the narrow B862 road along the eastern shore is relatively peaceful. It leads to the village of Foyers, where you can enjoy a pleasant hike to the **Falls of Foyers**.

But it's worth making the trip just for the **Dores Inn** (📞01463-751203; www.thedoresinn. co.uk; Dores; mains £11-24; ⏲ pub 10am-11pm, food served noon-2pm & 6-9pm; 🅿🛜), a beautifully restored country pub furnished with recycled furniture, local landscape paintings and fresh flowers. The menu specialises in quality Scottish produce, from haggis, turnips and tatties (potatoes), and haddock and chips, to steaks, scallops and seafood platters.

The pub garden enjoys a stunning view along Loch Ness, and even has a dedicated monster-spotting vantage point. The nearby campervan, emblazoned with Nessie-Serry Independent Research, has been home to dedicated Nessie hunter Steve Feltham (www. nessiehunter.co.uk) since 1991; in 2015 he finally concluded that Nessie was in fact a giant catfish!

selection of real ales from around the country, including those from their own Loch Ness Brewery, located nearby.

ℹ Getting There & Away

Stagecoach buses (p301) run from Inverness to Drumnadrochit (£3.30, 30 minutes, six to eight daily, five on Sunday) and Urquhart Castle car park (£3.60, 35 minutes).

Fort Augustus

POP 620

Fort Augustus, at the junction of four old military roads, was originally a government garrison and the headquarters of General George Wade's road-building operations in the early 18th century. Today it's a neat and picturesque little place bisected by the Caledonian Canal, and often overrun by coach-tour crowds in summer.

◉ Sights & Activities

Caledonian Canal   CANAL
(www.scottishcanals.co.uk) At Fort Augustus, boats using the Caledonian Canal are raised and lowered 13m by a 'ladder' of five consecutive locks. It's fun to watch, and the neatly landscaped canal banks are a great place to soak up the sun or compare accents with fellow tourists. The **Caledonian Canal Centre** (📞01320-366493; Ardchattan House, Canalside; ⏲10am-4pm) FREE, beside the lowest lock, has information on the history of the canal.

Cruise Loch Ness   BOATING
(📞01320-366277; www.cruiselochness.com; adult/child £14/8; ⏲hourly 10am-4pm Apr-Oct, 1 & 2pm only Nov-Mar) One-hour cruises on Loch Ness

are accompanied by the latest high-tech sonar equipment so you can keep an underwater eye open for Nessie. There are also one-hour evening cruises, departing 8pm daily (except Friday) April to August, and 90-minute speedboat tours.

🛏 Sleeping & Eating

Morag's Lodge   HOSTEL £
(📞01320-366289; www.moragslodge.com; Bunoich Brae; dm/tw/f from £23/54/76; 🅿@🛜) This large, well-run hostel is based in a big Victorian house with great views of Fort Augustus' hilly surrounds, and has a convivial bar with open fire. It's hidden away in the trees up the steep side road just north of the tourist office car park.

Cumberland's Campsite   CAMPSITE £
(📞01320-366257; www.cumberlands-campsite.com; Glendoe Rd; sites per adult/child £10/3; ⏲ Apr-Sep) Spacious site with smart, modern facilities, including its own bar and restaurant. Southeast of the village on the B862 towards Whitebridge; entrance beside Stravaigers Lodge.

Lorien House   B&B ££
(📞01320-366576; www.lorien-house.co.uk; Station Rd; s/d £64/74; 🅿) Lorien is a cut above your usual B&B – the bathrooms come with bidets and the breakfasts with smoked salmon. There's a library of walking, cycling and climbing guides in the lounge. No children under 12.

★Lovat   HOTEL £££
(📞01456-459250; www.thelovat.com; Main Rd; d from £135; 🅿🛜🐾) 🍃 A boutique-style makeover has transformed this former

huntin'-and-shootin' hotel into a luxurious but eco-conscious retreat set apart from the tourist crush around the canal. The bedrooms are spacious and stylishly furnished, while the lounge is equipped with a log fire, comfy armchairs and grand piano.

It has an informal brasserie and a highly acclaimed restaurant (five-course dinner £50), which serves top-quality cuisine (open 7pm to 9pm, Wednesday to Saturday, Easter to October).

Lock Inn PUB FOOD ££
(☑ 01320-366302; Canal Side; mains £10-14; ⊘ meals noon-8pm) A superb little pub right on the canal bank, the Lock Inn has a vast range of malt whiskies and a tempting menu of bar meals, which includes Orkney salmon, Highland venison and daily seafood specials; the house speciality is beer-battered haddock and chips.

ℹ Information

There's an ATM and bureau de change in the post office beside the canal.

Fort Augustus Tourist Office (☑ 01320-345156; ⊘ 9.30am-5pm Mon-Sat & 10am-4pm Sun Apr-Sep, shorter hours Oct-Mar) is in the main car park.

ℹ Getting There & Away

Scottish Citylink (www.citylink.co.uk) and **Stagecoach** (www.stagecoachbus.com) buses from Inverness to Fort William stop at Fort Augustus (£7 to £10.60, one hour, five to eight daily Monday to Saturday, five on Sunday).

THE CAIRNGORMS

The Cairngorms National Park (www.cairngorms.co.uk) is the largest national park in the UK, more than twice the size of the Lake District. It stretches from Aviemore in the north to the Angus Glens in the south, and from Dalwhinnie in the west to Ballater and Royal Deeside in the east.

The park encompasses the highest landmass in Britain – a broad mountain plateau, riven only by the deep valleys of the Lairig Ghru and Loch Avon, with an average altitude of over 1000m and including five of the six highest summits in the UK. This wild mountain landscape of granite and heather has a sub-Arctic climate and supports rare alpine tundra vegetation and high-altitude bird species, such as snow bunting, ptarmigan and dotterel.

The harsh mountain environment gives way lower down to scenic glens softened by beautiful open forests of native Scots pine, home to rare animals and birds such as pine martens, wildcats, red squirrels, ospreys, capercaillies and crossbills.

This is prime hill-walking territory, but even couch potatoes can enjoy a taste of the high life by taking the Cairngorm Mountain Railway up to the edge of the Cairngorm plateau.

Aviemore

POP 3150

The gateway to the Cairngorms, Aviemore is the region's main centre for transport, accommodation, restaurants and shops. It's not the prettiest town in Scotland by a long stretch – the main attractions are in the surrounding area – but when bad weather puts the hills off-limits, Aviemore fills up with hikers, cyclists and climbers (plus skiers and snowboarders in winter) cruising the outdoor-equipment shops or recounting their latest adventures in the cafes and bars. Add in tourists and locals and the eclectic mix makes for a lively little town.

Aviemore is on a loop off the A9 Perth–Inverness road; almost everything of note is to be found along the main drag, Grampian Rd; the train station and bus stop are towards its southern end.

The Cairngorm Mountain funicular railway and ski area lie 10 miles southeast of Aviemore along the B970 (Ski Rd) and its continuation, past Coylumbridge and Glenmore.

◎ Sights

★ **Rothiemurchus Estate** FOREST
(www.rothiemurchus.net) The Rothiemurchus Estate, which extends from the River Spey at Aviemore to the Cairngorm summit plateau, is famous for having one of Scotland's largest remnants of **Caledonian forest**, the ancient forest of Scots pine that once covered most of the country. The forest is home to a large population of red squirrels, and is one of the last bastions of the capercaillie and the Scottish wildcat.

The **Rothiemurchus Estate visitor centre** (☑ 01479-812345; Ski Rd, Inverdruie; ⊘ 9.30am-5.30pm; P) FREE, a mile southeast of Aviemore along the B970, sells an *Explorer Map* detailing more than 50 miles of **footpaths** and **cycling trails**, including the

The Cairngorms

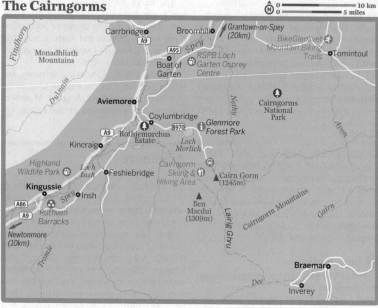

wheelchair-accessible 4-mile trail around **Loch an Eilein**, with its ruined castle and peaceful pine woods.

Strathspey Steam Railway HERITAGE RAILWAY
(☑ 01479-810725; Station Sq; return ticket per adult/child £14.25/7.15; 🅿) Strathspey Steam Railway runs steam trains on a section of restored line between Aviemore and Broomhill, 10 miles to the northeast, via Boat of Garten. There are four or five trains daily from June to August, and a more limited service in April, May, September, October and December, with the option of enjoying afternoon tea, Sunday lunch or a five-course dinner on board.

An extension to Grantown-on-Spey is under construction (see www.railstograntown.org); in the meantime, you can continue from Broomhill to Grantown-on-Spey by bus.

Craigellachie Nature Reserve NATURE RESERVE
(www.nnr-scotland.org.uk/craigellachie; Grampian Rd) **FREE** This reserve is a great place for short hikes across steep hillsides covered in natural birch forest where you can spot wildlife such as the peregrine falcons that nest on the crags from April to July. A trail leads west from Aviemore Youth Hostel and passes under the A9 into the reserve.

🏃 Activities

Bothy Bikes MOUNTAIN BIKING
(☑ 01479-810111; www.bothybikes.co.uk; 5 Granish Way, Dalfaber; per half-/full day from £16/20; ⊙ 9am-5.30pm) Located in northern Aviemore on the way to the golf course, this place rents out mountain bikes and can also advise on routes and trails; a good choice for beginners is the **Old Logging Way**, which runs from Aviemore to Glenmore, where you can make a circuit of Loch Morlich before returning. For experienced bikers, the whole of the Cairngorms is your playground. Booking recommended.

Rothiemurchus Fishery FISHING
(☑ 01479-810703; www.rothiemurchus.net; Rothiemurchus Estate; ⊙ 9.30am-5pm Sep-May, 9.30am-dusk Jun-Aug; 🖐) Cast for rainbow trout at this loch at the southern end of the village; buy permits (from £10 for two hours to £30 per day, plus £5 for tackle hire) at the Fish Farm Shop. If you're a fly-fishing virgin, there's a beginner's package, including tackle hire, one hour's instruction and one hour's fishing, for £45 per person.

For experienced anglers, there's also salmon and sea-trout fishing on the River Spey – a day permit costs around £20; numbers are limited, so it's best to book in advance.

Cairngorm Sled-Dog Centre DOG SLEDDING
(☑ 07767-270526; www.sled-dogs.co.uk; Ski Rd; ♿) This outfit will take you on a 30-minute sled tour (adult/child £60/40) of local forest trails in the wake of a team of huskies, or a three-hour sled-dog safari (£175 per person). The sleds have wheels, so snow's not necessary. There are also one-hour guided tours of the kennels (adult/child £8/4). The centre is 3 miles east of Aviemore, signposted off the road to Loch Morlich.

Alvie & Dalraddy Estate ADVENTURE SPORTS
(☑ 01479-810330; www.alvie-estate.co.uk; Dalraddy Holiday Park; per person £45) Join an hour-long cross-country quad-bike trek at this estate, 3 miles south of Aviemore on the B9152 (call first).

🛏 Sleeping

Aviemore SYHA HOSTEL £
(SYHA; ☑ 01479-810345; www.syha.org.uk; 25 Grampian Rd; dm £21; P @ 🛜) Upmarket hostelling in a spacious, well-equipped modern building, five minutes' walk south of the village centre. There are four- and six-bed rooms, and a comfortable lounge with views of the mountains.

Rothiemurchus Camp & Caravan Park CAMPSITE £
(☑ 01479-812800; www.rothiemurchus.net; Coylumbridge; sites per adult/child £11/3) The nearest campsite to Aviemore is this year-round park, beautifully sited among Scots pines at Coylumbridge, 1.5 miles along the B970.

Aviemore Bunkhouse HOSTEL £
(☑ 01479-811181; www.aviemore-bunkhouse.com; Dalfaber Rd; dm/d/f from £19/50/65; P @ 🛜) This independent hostel provides accommodation in bright, modern six- or eight-bed dorms, each with private bathroom, and one twin/family room. It has a drying room, secure bike storage and wheelchair-accessible dorms. From the train station, cross the pedestrian bridge over the tracks, turn right and walk south on Dalfaber Rd.

Ardlogie Guest House B&B £
(☑ 01479-810747; www.ardlogie.co.uk; Dalfaber Rd; s/d £60/80, bothy per 3 nights £270; P 🛜) Handy to the train station, the five-room Ardlogie has great views over the River Spey towards the Cairngorms. There's also self-catering accommodation in the Bothy, a cosy, two-person timber cabin. Facilities include a boules pitch in the garden.

Ravenscraig Guest House B&B ££
(☑ 01479-810278; www.aviemoreonline.com; Grampian Rd; s/d £55/88; P 🛜) Ravenscraig is a large, flower-bedecked Victorian villa with six spacious en suite rooms, plus another six in a modern chalet at the back (one wheelchair accessible). It serves traditional and veggie breakfasts in an attractive conservatory dining room.

Cairngorm Hotel HOTEL ££
(☑ 01479-810233; www.cairngorm.com; Grampian Rd; s/d from £72/104; P 🛜) Better known as 'the Cairn', this long-established hotel is set in the fine old granite building with the pointy turret opposite the train station. It's a welcoming place with comfortable rooms and a determinedly Scottish atmosphere, with tartan carpets and stags' antlers. There's live music on weekends, so it can get a bit noisy – not for early-to-bedders.

Old Minister's House B&B £££
(☑ 01479-812181; www.theoldministershouse.co.uk; Ski Rd, Inverdruie; s/d £125/140; P 🛜) This former manse dates from 1906 and has five rooms with a luxurious, country-house atmosphere. It's in a lovely setting amid Scots pines on the banks of the River Druie, southeast of Aviemore.

🍴 Eating & Drinking

★ Mountain Cafe CAFE £
(www.mountaincafe-aviemore.co.uk; 111 Grampian Rd; mains £7-12; ⏱ 8.30am-5pm Tue-Thu, to 5.30pm Fri-Mon; P 🖉 ♿) The Mountain Cafe offers freshly prepared local produce with a Kiwi twist (the owner is from New Zealand) – healthy breakfasts of muesli, porridge and fresh fruit (till 11.30am); hearty lunches of seafood chowder, burgers and imaginative salads; and home-baked breads, cakes and biscuits. Vegan, coeliac and nut-allergic diets catered for.

Roo's Leap AMERICAN ££
(☑ 01479-811161; www.roosleap.com; Station Sq; mains £7-14, steaks £20-30; ⏱ noon-2.30pm & 5-9pm Mon-Fri, noon-9pm Sat & Sun; 🛜 ♿) Friendly service, cold bottled beer and great barbecue contribute to the antipodean atmosphere at this lively restaurant set in the old railway station building. However, the menu is more like classic American and Tex Mex – sizzling steaks, juicy burgers, buffalo wings and nachos.

Ski-ing Doo
STEAK ££

(☑ 01479-810392; 9 Grampian Rd; mains £8-13, steaks £18-21; ☺ noon-9.30pm; ☎ ♨) A long-standing Aviemore institution, the child-friendly Ski-ing Doo (it's a pun...ask the waiter!) is a favourite with family skiers and hikers. It's an informal place offering a range of hearty, homemade burgers, chicken dishes and juicy steaks; the Doo Below cafe-bar is open from 3pm to 11pm.

Winking Owl
PUB

(www.thewinkingowl.co; Grampian Rd; ☺ 11am-11pm Mon-Thu, 11am-1am Fri & Sat, 12.30-11pm Sun; ☎) Lively local pub, recently taken under the wing of the Cairngorm Brewery, popular with hikers and climbers and serving a good range of real ales and malt whiskies.

ⓘ Information

There are ATMs outside the Tesco supermarket, and currency exchange at the post office and the tourist office, all located on Grampian Rd.

Aviemore Tourist Office (☑ 01479-810930; www.visitaviemore.com; The Mall, Grampian Rd; ☺ 9am-5pm Mon-Sat, 10am-4pm Sun year-round, longer hours Jul & Aug)

ⓘ Getting There & Away

BUS
Buses stop on Grampian Rd opposite the train station; buy tickets at the **tourist office**. Services include the following:

Edinburgh £27, four hours, five daily
Glasgow £27, 2¾ hours, five daily
Grantown-on-Spey £3.60, 35 minutes, five daily weekdays, two Saturday
Inverness £10.20, 45 minutes, eight daily
Perth £19.80, 2¼ hours, five daily

TRAIN
The train station is on Grampian Rd.
Edinburgh £40, three hours, six daily
Glasgow £40, three hours, six daily
Inverness £12.10, 40 minutes, 12 daily

ⓘ Getting Around

Several places in Aviemore, Rothiemurchus Estate and Glenmore have mountain bikes for hire. An off-road cycle track links Aviemore with Glenmore and Loch Morlich.

Bothy Bikes (p310) charges £20 a day for a quality bike with front suspension and disc brakes.

Bus 31 links Aviemore to Cairngorm Mountain car park (£2.55, 30 minutes, hourly) via Coylumbridge and Glenmore. A Strathspey Dayrider/Megarider ticket (£6.70/17) gives one/seven days unlimited bus travel from Aviemore as far as Cairngorm, Carrbridge and Kingussie; buy them from the bus driver.

Around Aviemore

Cairngorm Mountain

Cairngorm Mountain (1245m), 10 miles southeast of Aviemore, is the sixth-highest summit in the UK and home to Scotland's biggest ski area. A funicular railway ferries skiers almost to the top of the mountain, and continues to operate throughout the summer so that visitors can get a taste of the high mountain plateau.

The national park's most popular attraction is the **funicular railway** (☑ 01479-861261; www.cairngormmountain.org; adult/child return £11.50/7.50; ☺ every 20min 10am-4pm May-Nov, 9am-4.30pm Dec-Apr; ⓟ) that will whisk you to the edge of the Cairngorm plateau (altitude 1085m) in just eight minutes. The bottom station is at the Coire Cas car park at the end of Ski Rd; at the top is an exhibition, a shop (of course) and a restaurant. Unfortunately, for environmental and safety reasons, you're not allowed out of the top station in summer unless you book a guided walk or mountain-bike descent.

From May to October, a 90-minute **guided walk** (£20) to the summit of Cairn Gorm departs twice a day, while a five-hour guided hill walk runs twice a week. There's also the option of a four-hour guided **mountain-bike descent** (£35 incl bike hire), from the top station all the way to Aviemore. Check the website for details.

Aspen or Val d'Isère it ain't, but with 19 runs and 23 miles of piste Cairngorm is Scotland's biggest **ski area** (www.cairngormmountain.org; 1-day ski pass per adult/child £35/21). When the snow is at its best and the sun is shining you can close your eyes and imagine you're in the Alps; sadly, low cloud, high winds and horizontal sleet are more likely. Ski or snowboard hire is around £25/19 per adult/child per day; there are lots of hire outlets at Coire Cas, Glenmore and Aviemore.

The season usually runs from December until the snow melts, which may be as late as the end of April, but snowfall here is unpredictable – in some years the slopes can be open in November, but closed for lack of snow in February. During the season the tourist office in Aviemore displays snow conditions and avalanche warnings. You can check the latest snow conditions at www.cairngormmountain.org/lifts-pistes and www.winterhighland.info.

Loch Morlich

Six miles east of Aviemore, Loch Morlich is surrounded by some 8 sq miles of pine and spruce forest that make up the Glenmore Forest Park. Its attractions include a sandy beach (at the east end) and a water-sports centre.

Activities

The visitor centre at Glenmore has a small exhibition on the Caledonian forest and sells the *Glenmore Forest Park Map,* detailing local walks. The **circuit of Loch Morlich** (one hour) makes a pleasant outing; the trail is pram- and wheelchair-friendly.

★ Glenmore Lodge ADVENTURE SPORTS
(☑ 01479-861256; www.glenmorelodge.org.uk; Glenmore; one-day courses from £75) One of Britain's leading adventure-sports training centres, offering courses in hill walking, rock climbing, ice climbing, canoeing, mountain biking and mountaineering. The centre's comfortable **B&B accommodation** (☑ 01479-861256; www.glenmorelodge.org.uk; Glenmore; s/tw £60/80; ℗ ☎) is available to all, even if you're not taking a course, as is the indoor climbing wall, gym and sauna.

Cairngorm Reindeer Centre TOURS
(www.cairngormreindeer.co.uk; Glenmore; adult/child £14/8; ☺ closed early Jan–mid-Feb;) The warden here will take you on a guided walk to see and feed Britain's only herd of reindeer, who are very tame and will even eat out of your hand. Walks take place at 11am daily year-round (weather-dependent), plus another at 2.30pm from May to September, and a third at 3.30pm Monday to Friday in July and August.

Loch Morlich Watersports Centre WATER SPORTS
(☑ 01479-861221; www.lochmorlich.com; ☺ 9am-5pm Easter-Oct) This popular outfit rents out Canadian canoes (£21 an hour), kayaks (£9), sailboards (£17.50), sailing dinghies (£25) and stand-up paddle boards (£11), and also offers instruction.

🛌 Sleeping

There is a hostel and campsite, as well as accommodation at Glenmore Lodge.

Cairngorm Lodge SYHA HOSTEL £
(☑ 01479-861238; www.syha.org.uk; Glenmore; dm/tw £17/45; ☺ closed Nov & Dec; ℗ @ ☎) Set in a former shooting lodge that enjoys a great location at the east end of Loch Morlich; prebooking is essential.

Glenmore Campsite CAMPSITE £
(☑ 01479-861271; www.campingintheforest.co.uk; tent & campervan sites £27; ☺ year-round) Campers can set up base at this attractive lochside site with pitches amid the Scots pines; rates include up to four people per tent/campervan.

❶ Getting There & Away

Bus 31 links Aviemore with Loch Morlich and Glenmore (£2.55, 20 minutes, hourly).

Kincraig & Glen Feshie

At Kincraig, 6 miles southwest of Aviemore, the Spey widens into Loch Insh, home of the **Loch Insh Outdoor Centre** (☑ 01540-651272; www.lochinsh.com; Kincraig; day ticket incl all activities per adult/child £35/25; ☺ 8.30am-5.30pm;), which offers canoeing, windsurfing, sailing, mountain biking and fishing, as well as B&B accommodation.

Beautiful, tranquil **Glen Feshie** extends south from Kincraig, deep into the Cairngorms, with Scots pine woods in its upper reaches surrounded by big, heathery hills. The 4WD track to the head of the glen makes a great mountain-bike excursion (25-mile round trip).

Highland Wildlife Park (☑ 01540-651270; www.highlandwildlifepark.org; Kincraig; adult/child £15.40/11.55; ☺ 10am-6pm Jul & Aug, to 5pm Apr-Jun & Sep-Oct, to 4pm Nov-Mar; ℗) features a drive-through safari park as well as animal enclosures offering the chance to view rarely seen native wildlife, such as wildcats, capercaillies, pine martens, white-tailed sea eagles and red squirrels, as well as species that once roamed the Scottish hills but have long since disappeared, including the wolf, lynx, wild boar, beaver and European bison.

Visitors without cars get driven around by staff (at no extra cost). Last entry is two hours before closing.

❶ Getting There & Around

Buses link Aviemore with Kincraig village (£2, 10 minutes, five to seven daily except Sunday). There is no public transport in Glen Feshie.

Carrbridge

POP 700

Carrbridge, 7 miles north of Aviemore, is a good alternative base for exploring the region. It takes its name from the graceful old bridge (spotlit at night), built in 1717, over the thundering rapids of the River Dulnain.

Set in a forest of Scots pines, Landmark Forest Adventure Park (✆0800 731 3446; www.landmarkpark.co.uk; adult/child £17.95/15.95; ⊙10am-7pm mid-Jul–Aug, to 5pm or 6pm Apr–mid-Jul & Sep, to 5pm Oct-Mar; ▮) is a theme park with a difference; the theme is timber. The main attractions are the Ropeworx highwire adventure course, the Red Squirrel Nature Trail (a raised walkway through the forest canopy that allows you to view red squirrels, crossbills and crested tits), and the steam-powered sawmill.

Bus 34 runs from Inverness to Carrbridge (£4.80, 45 minutes, six daily Monday to Friday, three on Saturday) and onwards to Grantown-on-Spey (£2.55, 20 minutes). Bus 32 links with Aviemore (£2.55, 15 minutes, five daily except Sunday).

Boat of Garten

Boat of Garten is known as the Osprey Village because these rare and beautiful birds of prey nest nearby at the RSPB Loch Garten Osprey Centre.

There is flexible, good-quality homestay accommodation at Fraoch Lodge (✆01479-831331; www.scotmountainholidays.com; Deshar Rd; per person £25-30; ▣🖥) , along with a wide range of outdoor activities, while the Boat Hotel (✆01479-831258; www.boathotel.co.uk; s/d from £75/95; ▣🖥🖥) offers luxurious accommodation and a superb restaurant.

Ospreys migrate to RSPB Loch Garten Osprey Centre (✆01479-831694; www.rspb.org.uk/lochgarten; Tulloch; osprey hide adult/child £5/2; ⊙osprey hide 10am-6pm Apr-Aug) each spring from Africa and nest in a tall pine tree beside Loch Garten – you can watch from a hide as the birds feed their young. The centre is signposted about 2 miles east of Boat of Garten village.

Boat of Garten is 6 miles northeast of Aviemore. The most interesting way to get here is on the Strathspey Steam Railway (p310) from Aviemore.

Grantown-on-Spey

POP 2430

Grantown (*gran*-ton) is an elegant Georgian town with a grid of streets and a broad, tree-lined main square. It is a fine example of a planned settlement, founded by Sir Ludovic Grant in 1766 as a centre for the linen industry, and later becoming a tourist town after Queen Victoria's visit in 1860.

Thronged with visitors in summer, a favoured haunt of anglers and the tweed-cap-and-green-wellies brigade, it reverts to a quiet backwater in winter. Most hotels can kit you out for a day of fly-fishing on the Spey, or put you in touch with someone who can.

◉ Sights & Activities

Grantown Museum MUSEUM
(✆01479-872478; www.grantownmuseum.co.uk; Burnfield Ave; adult/child £4/free; ⊙10am-5pm Mon-Sat Apr-Oct; ▣▮) A small museum that chronicles the history of the town and its relationship to Clan Grant; also houses a tourist information centre.

Craggan Fishery FISHING
(✆01479-873283; www.cragganoutdoors.co.uk; Craggan Outdoors; per person £15; ▮) This rainbow trout fishery, just over one mile south of Grantown, offers the chance to hone your fly-fishing skills (tackle hire £5).

🍽 Sleeping & Eating

★**Brooklynn** B&B ££
(✆01479-873113; www.woodier.com; Grant Rd; r per person £40-45; ▣🖥) ✹ This beautiful Victorian villa features original stained glass and wood panelling, and seven spacious, luxurious rooms (all doubles have en suites). The food – dinner is available, as well as breakfast – is superb, too.

No 7 Bistro SCOTTISH ££
(✆01479-872087; www.no7thesquare.co.uk; 7 The Square; mains £10-19; ⊙10am-9pm Tue-Sat) ✹ Soothing moss-green decor and friendly service create a relaxed atmosphere in this busy bistro, whose menu includes hearty favourites from seafood chowder and haddock and chips to chicken curry and sizzling steaks. Daily specials regularly include dressed Aberdeenshire crab and Scottish seafood platters.

ℹ Getting There & Away

Bus 34 runs from Inverness to Aviemore via Grantown-on-Spey (£6, 1¼ hours, six daily Monday to Friday, three on Saturday).

Kingussie & Newtonmore

The old Speyside towns of Kingussie (kin-*yew*-see) and Newtonmore sit at the foot of the great heather-clad humps known as the Monadhliath Mountains. Newtonmore is best known as the home of the excellent Highland Folk Museum; Kingussie for one of the Highlands' best restaurants.

The road west from Newtonmore to Spean Bridge passes Ardverikie Estate and Loch Laggan, famous as the setting for the BBC TV series *Monarch of the Glen*.

⊙ Sights & Activities

Ruthven Barracks RUINS
(HS; ⊙24hr; P) FREE Ruthven Barracks was one of four garrisons built by the British government after the first Jacobite rebellion of 1715, as part of a Hanoverian scheme to take control of the Highlands. Ironically the barracks were last occupied by Jacobite troops awaiting the return of Bonnie Prince Charlie after the Battle of Culloden. Perched dramatically on a river terrace and clearly visible from the main A9 road near Kingussie, the ruins are spectacularly floodlit at night.

Highland Folk Museum MUSEUM
(☑01540-673551; www.highlandfolk.museum; Kingussie Rd, Newtonmore; ⊙10.30am-5.30pm Apr-Aug, 11am-4.30pm Sep & Oct; P) FREE This open-air museum comprises a collection of historical buildings and artefacts revealing many aspects of Highland culture and lifestyle. Laid out like a farming township, it has a community of traditional thatch-roofed cottages, a sawmill, a schoolhouse, a shepherd's bothy (hut) and a rural post office. Actors in period costume give demonstrations of woodcarving, woolspinning and peat-fire baking. You'll need at least two to three hours to make the most of a visit here.

Laggan Wolftrax MOUNTAIN BIKING
(http://scotland.forestry.gov.uk/visit/laggan-wolftrax; Strathmashie Forest; trails free, parking £3; ⊙10am-6pm Mon, 9.30am-5pm Tue, Thu & Fri, 9.30am-6pm Sat & Sun) Ten miles southwest of Newtonmore, on the A86 road towards Spean Bridge, this is one of Scotland's top mountain-biking centres with purpose-built trails ranging from open-country riding to black-diamond downhills with rock slabs and drop-offs. Includes bike hire outlet and a good cafe (open 11am to 4pm Friday to Sunday).

Highland All Terrain ADVENTURE
(☑01528-544358; http://quadbiketours.co.uk; Old Filling Station, Kinloch Laggan; per person from £50) Join an off-road quad-bike tour of Ardverikie Estate, which appears as Glen Bogle in the TV series *Monarch of the Glen*. Tours range from one hour to 3½ hours, and take in many of the TV locations.

🍽 Sleeping & Eating

★**Eagleview Guest House** B&B ££
(☑01540-673675; Perth Rd, Newtonmore; r per person from £39; P🅿📶🐕) Welcoming Eagleview is one of the best places to stay in the area, with beautifully decorated bedrooms, super-king-size beds, spacious bathrooms with power showers (except room 4, which has a Victorian slipper bath!), and nice little touches such as cafetières (coffee plungers) with real coffee – and fresh milk – on your hospitality tray, and Scottish kippers on the breakfast menu.

Hermitage B&B ££
(☑01540-662137; www.thehermitage-scotland.com; Spey St, Kingussie; s/d from £72/82; P📶) The five-bedroom Hermitage is a lovely old house with plenty of character, filled with Victorian period features – ask for room 5 (Feshie), with double bed, Chesterfield sofa, and a view of the hills. The lounge has deep sofas ranged by a log fire, and there are good views of the Cairngorms from the breakfast room and garden.

★**Cross** SCOTTISH £££
(☑01540-661166; www.thecross.co.uk; Tweed Mill Brae, off Ardbroilach Rd, Kingussie; 3-course lunch/dinner £25/55; ⊙noon-2pm & 7-8.30pm; P📶) 🍴 Housed in a converted watermill, the Cross is one of the finest restaurants in the Highlands. The intimate, low-raftered dining room has an open fire and a patio overlooking the stream, and serves a daily-changing menu of fresh Scottish produce accompanied by a superb wine list (booking essential).

If you want to stay the night, there are eight stylish rooms (double or twin £110 to £180) to choose from.

1. Kilchurn Castle, Loch Awe (p291) 2. Loch Tummel from Queen's View (p327) 3. Ben Nevis (p339) 4. Urquhart Castle (p307) and Loch Ness (p305)

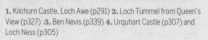

DAVID C TOMLINSON / GETTY IMAGES ©

Lochs & Mountains

Since the 19th century, when the first tourists started to arrive, the Scottish Highlands have been famed for their wild nature and majestic scenery, and today the country's biggest draw remains its magnificent landscape. At almost every turn is a vista that will stop you in your tracks – keep your camera close at hand.

Ben Nevis

Scotland's highest peak is a perennial magnet for hillwalkers and ice climbers, but it's also one of the country's most photographed mountains. The classic viewpoints for the Ben include Corpach Basin at the entrance to the Caledonian Canal, and the B8004 road between Banavie and Gairlochy, from where you can see the precipitous north face.

Loch Ness

Scotland's largest loch by volume (it contains more water than all the lakes in England and Wales added together) may be most famous for its legendary monster, but it is also one of Scotland's most scenic. The minor road along the southeastern shore reveals a series of classic views.

Schiehallion

From the Gaelic *Sìdh Chailleann* (Fairy Hill of the Caledonians), this is one of Scotland's most distinctive mountains, its conical peak a prominent feature of views along Loch Tummel and Loch Rannoch. It's also one of the easier Munros, and a hike to the summit is rewarded with a superb panorama of hills and lochs.

Loch Awe

Loch Awe is a little off the beaten track, but is well worth seeking out for its gorgeous scenery. Dotted with islands and draped with native woodlands of oak, birch and alder, its northern end is dominated by the evocative ruins of Kilchurn Castle, with the pointed peaks of mighty Ben Cruachan reflected in its shifting waters.

ⓘ Getting There & Away

BUS

Kingussie and Newtonmore are served by **Scottish Citylink** (☑ 0871-266 3333; www.citylink.co.uk) buses:

Aviemore £7.90, 25 minutes, twice daily

Inverness £13.80, one hour, twice daily

Perth £16.50, 1¾ hours, twice daily

TRAIN

Kingussie and Newtonmore are on the Edinburgh/Glasgow to Inverness railway line.

Edinburgh £36, 2½ hours, seven a day Monday to Saturday, two Sunday

Inverness £12.10, one hour, eight a day Monday to Saturday, four Sunday

Tomintoul & Around

POP 320

Tomintoul (tom-in-towel) is a pretty, stone-built village with a grassy, tree-lined main square. It was built by the Duke of Gordon in 1775 on the old military road that leads over the Lecht pass from Corgarff, a route now followed by the A939 (usually the first road in Scotland to be blocked by snow when winter closes in). The duke hoped that settling the dispersed population of his estates in a proper village would help to stamp out cattle stealing and illegal distilling.

🏃 Activities

The **Glenlivet Estate** (now the property of the Crown) has lots of **walking and cycling trails** – the estate's **information centre** (☑ 01479-870070; www.glenlivetestate.co.uk; Main St; ⊘ 9am-5pm Mon-Fri) distributes free maps of the area – and a spur of the **Speyside Way** long-distance footpath runs between Tomintoul and **Ballindalloch**, 15 miles to the north.

There's excellent mountain-biking at **BikeGlenlivet** (www.glenlivetestate.co.uk; trails free, parking £3) trail centre, 4.5 miles north of Tomintoul, off the B9136 road. Custom-built trails range from the 9km blue run for beginners to the 22km red route for more experienced riders. Cafe and bike hire on site.

🛏 Sleeping & Eating

Accommodation for walkers includes the **Smugglers Hostel** (☑ 01807-580364; www.thesmugglershostel.co.uk; Main St; dm/tw £17/50; 🛜), housed in the old village school; the highly recommended **Argyle Guest House** (☑ 01807-580766; www.argyletomintoul.co.uk; 7

Main St; d/f from £65/115; 🛜 🐾) is a more comfortable alternative (best porridge in the Cairngorms!).

For something to eat, try the **Coffee Still** (☑ 07599-973845; BikeGlenlivet Trail Centre; mains £6-8; ⊘ 11am-5pm Tue-Fri, 10am-5.30pm Sat & Sun; 🅿) , a cosy coffee house with an open fire. It specialises in home baking and mouth-watering homemade burgers.

ⓘ Getting There & Away

There is a very limited bus service to Tomintoul, once a week from either Aberlour (£6.70, 40 minutes, two on Thursdays only) or Dufftown (£6.70, 30 minutes, two on Tuesdays only); check with the tourist office in Elgin for the latest timetables. Outside these times, there is a **Dial-a-Bus** (☑ 0300-123 4565) service; call Monday to Friday to book a seat.

Royal Deeside

The upper valley of the River Dee stretches west from Aboyne and Ballater to Braemar, closely paralleled by the A93 road. Made famous by its long association with the monarchy – today's royal family still holiday at Balmoral Castle, built for Queen Victoria in 1855 – the region is often called Royal Deeside.

The River Dee, renowned world-over for its salmon fishing, has its source in the Cairngorm Mountains west of Braemar, the starting point for long walks into the hills. The FishDee website (www.fishdee.co.uk) has all you need to know about fishing on the river.

Ballater

POP 1530

The attractive little village of Ballater owes its 18th-century origins to the curative waters of nearby Pannanich Springs (now bottled commercially as Deeside Natural Mineral Water), and its prosperity to nearby Balmoral Castle.

The village recently received a double dose of misfortune when the Old Royal Station (its main tourist attraction) burned down in May 2015, followed by the worst flooding in living memory in January 2016. The station may remain closed until 2018.

👁 Sights & Activities

Note the crests on the shop fronts along the main street proclaiming 'By Royal Appointment' – the village is a major supplier of provisions to Balmoral (p319).

As you approach Ballater from the east the hills start to close in, and there are many pleasant walks in the surrounding area. The steep woodland walk up **Craigendarroch** (400m) takes just over one hour. **Morven** (871m) is a more serious prospect, taking about six hours, but offers good views from the top; ask at the tourist office for more info.

You can hire bikes from **CycleHighlands** (☑ 01339-755864; www.cyclehighlands.com; The Pavilion, Victoria Rd; bicycle hire per half-day/day £12/18; ☉ 9am-6pm) and **Bike Station** (☑ 01339-754004; www.bikestationballater.co.uk; Station Sq; bicycle hire per 3hr/day £12/18; ☉ 9am-6pm), which also offer guided bike rides and advice on local trails.

🛏 Sleeping & Eating

Habitat HOSTEL **£**
(☑ 01339-753752; www.habitat-at-ballater.com; Bridge Sq; dm/tw from £22/55; 🛜) 🚲 Tucked up a lane near the bridge over the River Dee, Habitat is an attractive, ecofriendly hostel with two bunk rooms (with personal lockers and reading lamps), three en suite private rooms (sleeping one to four) and a comfortable lounge with big, soft sofas and a wood-burning stove.

⭐ Auld Kirk HOTEL **££**
(☑ 01339-755762; www.theauldkirk.com; Braemar Rd; s/d from £80/115; 🅿🛜🍽) Here's something a little out of the ordinary – a seven-bedroom hotel housed in a converted 19th-century church. The interior blends original features with sleek modern decor – the pulpit now serves as the reception desk, while the breakfast room is bathed in light from leaded Gothic windows.

Rock Salt & Snails CAFE **£**
(☑ 07834-452583; 2 Bridge St; mains £4-9; ☉ 10am-6pm Sun-Thu, to 9pm Fri & Sat May-Sep, 10am-5pm Mon-Sat, 11am-5pm Sun Oct-Apr; 🛜🍽) A great little cafe serving excellent coffee and tempting lunch platters featuring locally sourced deli products (cheese, ham, salads etc), including a kids' platter.

ⓘ Getting There & Away

Bus 201 runs from Aberdeen to Ballater (£11.25, 1¾ hours, hourly Monday to Saturday, six on Sunday) via Crathes Castle, and continues to Braemar (£5.80, 30 minutes) every two hours.

Balmoral Castle

Built for Queen Victoria in 1855 as a private residence for the royal family, **Balmoral Castle** (☑ 01339-742534; www.balmoralcastle.com; Crathie; adult/child £11.50/5; ☉ 10am-5pm Apr-Jul, last admission 4.30pm; 🅿) kicked off the revival of the Scottish Baronial style of architecture that characterises so many of Scotland's 19th-century country houses. The admission fee includes an interesting and well thought-out audioguide, but the tour is very much an outdoor one through garden and grounds.

As for the castle itself, only the ballroom, which displays a collection of Landseer paintings and royal silver, is open to the public. Don't expect to see the Queen's private quarters! The main attraction is learning about Highland estate management, rather than royal revelations.

You can buy a booklet that details several waymarked walks within Balmoral Estate; the best is the climb to **Prince Albert's Cairn**, a huge granite pyramid that bears the inscription 'To the beloved memory of Albert the great and good, Prince Consort. Erected by his broken hearted widow Victoria R. 21st August 1862'.

The massive pointy-topped mountain that looms to the south of Balmoral is **Lochnagar** (1155m), immortalised in verse by Lord Byron, who spent his childhood years in Aberdeenshire:

England, thy beauties are tame and domestic
To one who has roamed o'er the mountains afar.
Oh! for the crags that are wild and majestic:
The steep frowning glories of dark Lochnagar.

Lord Byron, Lochnagar

Balmoral is eight miles west of Ballater, and can be reached on the Aberdeen–Braemar bus.

Braemar

POP 450

Braemar is a pretty little village with a grand location on a broad plain ringed by mountains where the Dee valley and Glen Clunie meet. In winter this is one of the coldest places in the country – temperatures as low as -29°C have been recorded – and during spells of severe cold, hungry deer wander the streets looking for a bite to eat. Braemar is an excellent base for hill walking, and there's also skiing at nearby Glenshee.

Sights & Activities

An easy walk from Braemar is up **Creag Choinnich** (538m), a hill to the east of the village above the A93. The 1-mile route is waymarked and takes about 1½ hours. For a longer walk (4 miles; about three hours) and superb views of the Cairngorms, head for the summit of **Morrone** (859m), southwest of Braemar. Ask at the tourist office for details of these and other walks.

Braemar Castle   CASTLE
(www.braemarcastle.co.uk; adult/child £8/4; ⊙10am-4pm daily Jul & Aug, Wed-Sun Apr-Jun, Sep & Oct; **P**) Just north of Braemar village, turreted Braemar Castle dates from 1628 and served as a government garrison after the 1745 Jacobite rebellion. It was taken over by the local community in 2007, which now offers guided tours of the historic castle apartments. There's a short walk from the car park to the castle.

Braemar Mountain Sports   CYCLING
(☑ 01339-741242; www.braemarmountainsports. com; 5 Invercauld Rd; bike hire per day £18; ⊙9am-6pm) You can hire bikes from Braemar Mountain Sports. They also rent skiing and mountaineering equipment.

Festivals & Events

Braemar Gathering   HIGHLAND GAMES
(☑ 01339-755377; www.braemargathering.org; adult/child from £12/2) There are Highland games in many towns and villages throughout the summer, but the best known is the Braemar Gathering (www.braemargathering.org), which takes place on the first Saturday in September. It's a major occasion, organised every year since 1817 by the Braemar Royal Highland Society

Events include Highland dancing, pipers, tug-of-war, a hill race up Morrone, tossing the caber, hammer- and stone-throwing and the long jump. International athletes are among those who take part. These kinds of events took place informally in the Highlands for many centuries as tests of skill and strength, but they were formalised around 1820 as part of the rise of Highland romanticism initiated by Sir Walter Scott and King George IV. Queen Victoria attended the Braemar Gathering in 1848, starting a tradition of royal patronage that continues to this day.

Sleeping

Rucksacks Bunkhouse   HOSTEL £
(☑ 01339-741517; 15 Mar Rd; bothy £7, dm £12-15, tw £36; **P**) This appealing cottage has a comfy dorm, and cheaper beds in an alpine-style bothy (shared sleeping platform for 10 people; bring your own sleeping bag). Extras include a drying room (for wet-weather gear), a laundry and even a sauna (£10 an hour). The friendly owner is a fount of knowledge about the local area.

Braemar SYHA   HOSTEL £
(☑ 01339-741659; www.syha.org.uk; 21 Glenshee Rd; dm/tw £21/48; ⊙Feb-Oct; **P @ 🖥 🐾**) This hostel is housed in a grand former shooting lodge just south of Braemar village centre on the A93 to Perth. It has a comfy lounge with pool table, and a barbecue in the garden.

Braemar Caravan & Camping Park   CAMPSITE £
(☑ 01339-741373; www.braemarcaravansite.co.uk; tent sites incl 2 people £20.50; ⊙closed mid-Oct–mid-Dec; 🐾) There is good camping here, in a sheltered spot surrounded by mountains, with hot showers, a laundry and a small shop selling caravan and camping essentials.

Craiglea   B&B ££
(☑ 01339-741641; www.craigleabraemar.com; Hillside Dr; d/f from £76/105; **P** 🐾) Craiglea is a homely B&B set in a pretty stone cottage with three en suite bedrooms. Vegetarian breakfasts are available and the owners can rent you a bike and give advice on local walks.

St Margarets   B&B ££
(☑ 01339-741697; soky37@hotmail.com; 13 School Rd; s/tw £34/56; 🐾) Grab this place if you can, but there's only one room: a twin with a serious sunflower theme. The genuine warmth in the welcome is delightful. It's tucked behind the church on the south side of the A93 road.

Braemar Lodge Hotel   HOTEL, BUNKHOUSE ££
(☑ 01339-741627; www.braemarlodge.co.uk; Glenshee Rd; dm/s/d from £15/80/120; **P**) This Victorian shooting lodge on the southern outskirts of Braemar has bags of character, not least in the wood-panelled Malt Room bar, which is as well stocked with mounted deer heads as it is with single malt whiskies. There's a good restaurant with views of

the hills, plus a 12-berth hikers' bunkhouse (book in advance) in the hotel grounds.

Eating

The Bothy   CAFE **£**
(Invercauld Rd; mains £4-6; ⏰9am-5.30pm)
An appealing little cafe tucked behind the Mountain Sports shop, with a sunny terrace out front and a balcony at the back overhanging the river.

Taste   CAFE **£**
(☏01339-741425; www.taste-braemar.co.uk; Airlie House, Mar Rd; mains £4-8; ⏰10am-5pm Tue-Sat; 📶) 🍴 Taste is a relaxed little cafe with armchairs in the window bays, serving homemade soups, sandwiches, coffee and cakes.

ℹ️ Information

The **tourist office** (☏01399-741600; The Mews, Mar Rd; ⏰9am-6pm Aug, 9am-5pm Jun, Jul, Sep & Oct, shorter hours Nov-May), opposite the Fife Arms Hotel, has lots of useful info on walks in the area.

ℹ️ Getting There & Away

Bus 201 runs from Aberdeen to Braemar (£11.50, 2¼ hours, every two hours Monday to Saturday, five on Sunday). The 50-mile drive from Perth to Braemar is beautiful, but there's no public transport on this route.

Mar Lodge Estate

West of Braemar spreads the National Trust for Scotland's **Mar Lodge Estate** (www.nts. org.uk/property/mar-lodge-estate; ⏰24hr year-round) **FREE**, one of the country's most important nature conservation areas, covering 7% of the Cairngorms National Park. The £4 million legacy that allowed the trust to purchase the property in 1995 stipulated that, as well as promoting conservation and public access, the trust should continue to run Mar Lodge as a sporting estate. So alongside walking trails and forest regeneration there is salmon fishing and deer stalking.

Several easy, waymarked walks start from the Linn of Dee car park, 6.5 miles west of Braemar, including the **Linn of Dee**, a narrow gorge that extends downstream from the road bridge, and **Glen Lui**. Numerous long mountain walks (for experienced hill walkers only) also start from here, including the adventurous 24-mile walk through the **Lairig Ghru** pass to Aviemore.

Another short walk (3 miles, 1½ hours) begins 4 miles beyond the Linn of Dee at the **Linn of Quoich** – a waterfall that thunders through a narrow slot in the rocks. Head uphill on a footpath on the east bank of the stream, past the Punch Bowl (a giant pothole) to a modern bridge that spans the narrow gorge, and return via a 4WD road on the far bank. A longer walk (10 miles) is to follow the 4WD road up **Glen Quoich** to a beautiful remnant of Caledonian pine forest (return the same way).

The Angus Glens

Five scenic glens – Isla, Prosen, Clova, Lethnot and Esk – cut into the hills along the southern fringes of the Cairngorms National Park, accessible from Kirriemuir in Angus. All have attractive scenery, but Glen Clova and Glenesk are the most beautiful and most frequented. You can get detailed information on walks in the Angus Glens from the tourist office in Kirriemuir and from the Glen Clova Hotel in Glen Clova.

There is no public transport to the Angus Glens other than a limited school-bus service along Glen Clova; ask at the tourist office in Kirriemuir for details.

Glen Clova

The longest and loveliest of the Angus Glens stretches north from Kirriemuir for 20 miles, broad and pastoral in its lower reaches but growing narrower and craggier as the steep, heather-clad Highland hills close in around its head.

The minor road beyond the Glen Clova Hotel ends at a Forestry Commission car park at Glen Doll with a **visitor centre** (☏01575-550233; Glen Doll; admission free, parking £2; ⏰9am-6pm Apr-Sep, to 4.30 Oct-Mar) and picnic area, which is the trailhead for a number of strenuous walks through the hills to the north.

Jock's Road is an ancient footpath that was much used by cattle drovers, soldiers, smugglers and shepherds in the 18th and 19th centuries; 700 Jacobite soldiers passed this way during their retreat in 1746, en route to defeat at Culloden. From the car park the path strikes west along Glen Doll, then north across a high plateau (900m) before descending steeply into Glen Callater and on to Braemar (15 miles; allow five to seven hours). The route is hard going and should not be attempted in winter; you'll need OS 1:50,000 maps numbers 43 and 44.

An easier walk leads from Glen Doll car park to **Corrie Fee**, a spectacular glacial hollow in the edge of the mountain plateau (4.5-mile round trip, waymarked).

The **Glen Clova Hotel** (☏ 01575-550350; www.clova.com; s/d from £65/90, bunkhouse per person £20; 🅿) is a lovely old drover's inn near the head of the glen, and a great place to get away from it all. As well as 10 comfortable, country-style, en suite rooms (one with a four-poster bed), it has a bunkhouse, a rustic, stone-floored climbers' bar with a roaring log fire, and a **restaurant** (mains £11-25; ⊙ noon-7.45pm Sun-Thu, to 8.45pm Fri & Sat, shorter hours Nov-Mar; 🐾). No mobile phone reception.

Glenesk

The most easterly of the Angus Glens, Glenesk runs for 15 miles from Edzell to lovely **Loch Lee**, surrounded by beetling cliffs and waterfalls.

Fifteen miles up the glen from Edzell, the public road ends near **Invermark Castle**, an impressive ruined tower. From the car park, good hiking trails lead to a 17th-century kirkyard beside Loch Lee (1 mile), the monument at **Queen's Well** (a spring once visited by Queen Victoria; 2 miles), and the summit of **Mt Keen** (939m; 5 miles).

Ten miles up Glenesk from Edzell is **Glenesk Retreat & Folk Museum** (www.glenesk retreat.co.uk; admission by donation; ⊙ 10am-5pm Mon-Fri, to 6pm Sat & Sun Apr-Oct; 🅿🐾) 🐾, a former shooting lodge that houses a fascinating collection of antiques and artefacts documenting everyday life in the glen from the 17th to the early 20th centuries – 860 people once lived here; today the population is less than 100.

There's also a restaurant (mains £7 to £8) serving superb fish and chips, a gift shop and public internet access.

HIGHLAND PERTHSHIRE

The Highland border cuts diagonally across Scotland from Dumbarton to Stonehaven, dividing the county of Perthshire into two distinctive regions. Highland Perthshire, spreading north of a line from Comrie to Blairgowrie, is a land of mountains, forest and lochs, with some of the finest scenery in the UK. The ancient city of Dunkeld, on the main A9 road from Perth to Inverness, is the main gateway to the region.

❶ Getting Around

Away from the main A9 Perth-to-Inverness road, public transport is thin on the ground, and often geared to the needs of local schools. On Tuesdays, Wednesdays and Sundays from July to September, the **Ring of Breadalbane Explorer** (☏ 01764-681231; www.breadalbane.org/ring-of-breadalbane-explorer) bus service operates on a circular route taking in Crieff, Comrie, Lochearnhead, Killin, Kenmore and Aberfeldy, with four circuits a day in each direction. The £10 fare allows unlimited hop-on hop-off travel for one day.

Dunkeld & Birnam

POP 1005

The Tay runs like a storybook river through the heart of Perthshire's Big Tree Country, where the twin towns of Dunkeld and Birnam are linked by Thomas Telford's graceful bridge of 1808. As well as Dunkeld's ancient cathedral, there's much walking to be done in this area of magnificent forested hills. These same walks were one of the inspirations for Beatrix Potter to create her children's tales.

There's less to see in Birnam, a name made famous by Macbeth. There's not much left of Birnam Wood, but a riverside path leads to the Birnam Oak, a venerable 500-year-old survivor from Shakespeare's time, its ageing boughs propped up with timber supports. Nearby is the 300-year-old Birnam Sycamore.

◉ Sights & Activities

Dunkeld Cathedral CHURCH
(HS; www.dunkeldcathedral.org.uk; High St; ⊙ 10am-6.30pm Apr-Sep, to 4pm Oct-Mar) **FREE** Situated on the grassy banks of the River Tay, Dunkeld Cathedral is one of the most beautifully sited churches in Scotland; don't miss it on a sunny day, when there are few lovelier places to be. Half the cathedral is still in use as a church; the rest is a romantic ruin. It partly dates from the 14th century, having suffered damage during the Reformation and the battle of Dunkeld (Jacobites vs government) in 1689.

The Wolf of Badenoch, a fierce 14th-century noble who burned towns and abbeys to the ground in protest at his excommunication, is buried here – undeservedly – in a fine medieval tomb behind the wooden screen in the church.

Dunkeld House Grounds GARDENS

(⏰24hr) FREE Waymarked walks lead upstream from Dunkeld Cathedral through the gorgeous grounds of Dunkeld House Hotel, formerly a seat of the dukes of Atholl. In the 18th and early 19th centuries the 'planting dukes', as they became known, planted more than 27 million conifers on their estates 'for beauty and profit', introducing species such as larch, Douglas fir and sequoia, and sowing the seeds of Scottish forestry.

The abundance of vast, ancient trees here has given rise to the nickname Big Tree Country (www.perthshirebigtreecoun try.co.uk). Just west of the cathedral is the 250-year-old 'parent larch', the lone survivor of several planted in 1738, and said to have provided the seed stock for all Scottish larch trees. On the far side of the river is Niel Gow's Oak, another ancient tree, said to have provided inspiration for legendary local fiddler Niel Gow (1727–1807).

Beatrix Potter Exhibition & Garden EXHIBITION

(www.birnaminstitute.com; Station Rd; admission £3; ⏰10am-5pm mid-Mar–Oct, 10am-4.30pm Nov–mid-Mar; P🚸) In the middle of Birnam village is the small, leafy Beatrix Potter Garden; the children's author, who wrote the evergreen story of *Peter Rabbit*, spent her childhood holidays in the area. Next to the park, in the Birnam Arts Centre, is a small exhibition on Potter and her characters.

Loch of the Lowes Wildlife Centre WILDLIFE RESERVE

(☎01350-727337; www.swt.org.uk; adult/child £4/50p; ⏰10am-5pm Mar-Oct, 10.30am-4pm Fri-Sun Nov-Feb; P) Loch of the Lowes, 2 miles east of Dunkeld off the A923, has a visitor centre devoted to red squirrels and the majestic osprey. There's a birdwatching hide (with binoculars provided), where you can see the birds nesting during breeding season (late April to August), complete with a live video link to the nest.

🛏 Sleeping & Eating

★ Jessie Mac's HOSTEL, B&B £

(☎01350-727324; www.jessiemacs.co.uk; Murthly Tce, Birnam; dm/d £18/70; 🖥🐾) 🍴 Set in a Victorian manse complete with baronial turret, Jessie Mac's is a glorious cross between B&B and luxury hostel, with three gorgeous doubles and four shared or family rooms with bunks. Guests make good use of the country-style lounge, sunny dining room

DUNKELD WALKS: THE HERMITAGE

One of the most popular walks is The Hermitage, just outside Dunkeld, where a well-marked trail follows the River Braan to Ossian's Hall, a quaint folly built by the Duke of Atholl in 1758 overlooking the spectacular Falls of Braan (salmon can be seen leaping here, especially in September and October).

and well-equipped kitchen, and breakfasts are composed of local produce, from organic eggs to Dunkeld smoked salmon.

Erigmore Estate LODGE ££

(☎01350-727236; www.erigmore.co.uk; Birnam; d for 3 nights from £294; P🚸🐾) Scattered around the wooded, riverside grounds of Erigmore House, the former country retreat of a wealthy clipper ship's captain, these luxury timber lodges provide cosseted comfort complete with outdoor deck and – at the more expensive end of the range – a private hot tub. The house itself contains shared facilities, including a bar, restaurant and swimming pool.

There's a three-night minimum stay.

★ Taybank PUB FOOD ££

(☎01350-727340; www.thetaybank.co.uk; Tay Tce; mains £9-12; ⏰food served noon-9pm; P) 🍴 Top choice for a sun-kissed pub lunch by the river is the Taybank, a regular meeting place and performance space for folk musicians and a wonderfully welcoming bar serving ales from the local Strathbraan Brewery. There's live music several nights per week, and the menu features local produce with dishes such as smoked venison or grilled sea trout.

ⓘ Information

Dunkeld Tourist Office (☎01350-727688; www.dunkeldandbirnam.org.uk; The Cross; ⏰10.30am-4.30pm Mon-Sat, 11am-4pm Sun Apr-Oct, longer hours Jul & Aug, Fri-Sun only Nov-Mar) has information on local hiking and biking trails.

ⓘ Getting There & Away

Citylink (p300) buses running between Glasgow/Edinburgh and Inverness stop at the Birnam Hotel (£17, two hours, two daily). **Stagecoach** (www.stagecoachbus.com) runs hourly buses (only five on Sunday) between Perth and Dunkeld (£2.50, 40 minutes), continuing to Aberfeldy.

There are also buses from Dunkeld to Blairgowrie (£2.60, 40 minutes, twice daily except Sunday).

Pitlochry

POP 2780

Pitlochry, with the scent of the Highlands already in the air, is a popular stop on the way north. In summer the main street can be a conga line of tour groups, but linger a while and it can still charm – on a quiet spring evening it's a pretty place with salmon leaping in the Tummel and good things brewing at the Moulin Hotel.

Sights

One of Pitlochry's attractions is its beautiful riverside; the River Tummel is dammed here, and if you're lucky you might see salmon swimming up the fish ladder to Loch Faskally above (May to November; best month is October).

★ Edradour Distillery   DISTILLERY
(01796-472095; www.edradour.co.uk; Moulin Rd; tour adult/child £7.50/2.50; 10am-5pm Mon-Sat late Apr-late Oct; P) This is proudly Scotland's smallest and most picturesque distillery and one of the best to visit: you can see the whole process, easily explained, in one building. It's 2.5 miles east of Pitlochry by car, along the Moulin road, or a pleasant 1-mile walk.

Blair Athol Distillery   DISTILLERY
(01796-482003; www.discovering-distilleries. com; Perth Rd; standard tour £7; 10am-5pm Apr-Oct, to 4pm Nov-Mar) Tours here focus on whisky making and the blending of this well-known dram. More detailed private tours give you greater insights and superior tastings.

Explorers Garden   GARDENS
(01796-484600; www.explorersgarden.com; Foss Rd; adult/child £4/1; 10am-5pm Apr-Oct; P) This gem of a garden is based around plants brought to Scotland by 18th- and 19th-century Scottish botanists and explorers such as David Douglas (after whom the Douglas fir is named), and celebrates 300 years of collecting and the 'plant hunters' who tracked down these exotic species.

Wild Space   GALLERY
(www.jmt.org/wildspace.asp; Tower House, Station Rd; 10am-4.30pm Mon & Wed-Sat May-Sep, shorter hours winter) FREE This combined art gallery, interpretation centre and bookshop is run by environmental charity the John Muir Trust. It stages exhibitions of contemporary landscape art, and sells maps, walking guides, and wildlife- and environment-related books.

Festivals & Events

Winter Words   LITERATURE
(www.pitlochry.org/whats_on; Feb) A 10-day literary festival, with a packed program of talks by authors, poets and broadcasters. Past guests have ranged from novelist Louis de Bernières to mountaineer/author Sir Chris Bonington.

Étape Caledonia   SPORTS
(www.etapecaledonia.co.uk; mid-May) This 81-mile charity cycling event brings competitors of all standards onto the beautiful Highland roads between Pitlochry and Tummel Bridge. It's grown into a huge event, with more than 5000 participants; you'll have to prebook accommodation when its on.

Enchanted Forest   LIGHT SHOW
(www.enchantedforest.org.uk; adult £14-20, child £7-10; Oct) This spectacular three-week sound-and-light show staged in Faskally Wood near Pitlochry is a major family hit.

Sleeping

Ashleigh   B&B
(01796-470316; www.ashleighbedandbreakfast. com; 120 Atholl Rd; s/d £30/57;) Genuine welcomes don't come much better than Nancy's and her place on the main street makes a top Pitlochry pit stop. Two comfortable doubles share an excellent bathroom, and there's an open kitchen stocked with goodies where you make your own breakfast in the morning. A home away from home and a standout budget choice. Cash only; no kids.

She also has a good self-catering apartment with great views, available by the night.

Pitlochry Backpackers Hotel   HOSTEL
(01796-470044; www.scotlands-top-hostels. com; 134 Atholl Rd; dm/tw £20/53; Apr–mid Nov; P@) Friendly, laid-back and very comfortable, this is a cracking hostel smack bang in the middle of town, with three- to eight-bed dorms that are in mint condition.

KILLIECRANKIE

The beautiful, rugged **Pass of Killiecrankie** (NTS; parking £2; ⊙24hr; P) FREE, 3.5 miles north of Pitlochry, where the River Garry tumbles through a narrow gorge, was the site of the 1689 **Battle of Killiecrankie** that ignited the Jacobite rebellion.

Located near the site of the Battle of Killiecranki the **visitor centre** (NTS; ✆01796-473233; www.nts.org.uk; parking £2; ⊙10am-5.30pm Apr-Oct; P) FREE has great interactive displays on Jacobite history and local flora and fauna. There's plenty to touch, pull and open – great for kids. There are some stunning **walks** along the wooded gorge, too; keep an eye out for red squirrels.

For somewhere to stay the **Killiecrankie Hotel** (✆01796-473220; www.killiecrankiehotel. co.uk; d incl dinner £300; ⊙Mar-Dec; P🅿🐾) is a standout choice offering faultless hospitality in a peaceful setting, with interesting art on the walls, and relaxing rooms with views over the lovely gardens. The best things about the Scottish country-house experience are here, without the musty feel that sometimes goes with it; the food is also excellent. Two-night minimum stay at busy times; B&B-only rates are sometimes available.

There are also good-value en suite twins and doubles, with beds, not bunks. Cheap breakfast and a pool table add to the convivial party atmosphere. No extra charge for linen.

Pitlochry SYHA HOSTEL £
(✆01796-472308; www.syha.org.uk; Knockard Rd; dm/tw £18/48; ⊙Mar-Oct; P@🛜) Great location overlooking the town centre. Popular with families and walkers.

Tir Aluinn B&B £
(✆01796-473811; www.tiraluinn.co.uk; 10 Higher Oakfield Rd; per person £35-39; P🛜) Tucked away above the main street, this is a little gem of a place with bright rooms, easy-on-the-eye furniture, and a warm personal welcome. Breakfasts are a pleasure too.

★**Craigatin House** B&B ££
(✆01796-472478; www.craigatinhouse.co.uk; 165 Atholl Rd; d £98-108, ste £125; P@🛜) Several times more tasteful than the average Scottish B&B, this elegant house and garden is set back from the main road. Chic contemporary fabrics covering expansive beds offer a standard of comfort above and beyond the reasonable price; the rooms in the converted stable block are particularly inviting. A fabulous breakfast and lounge area gives views over the lush garden.

Breakfast choices include whisky-laced porridge, smoked-fish omelettes and apple pancakes. Kids not allowed.

★**Fonab Castle Hotel** HISTORIC HOTEL £££
(✆01796-470140; www.fonabcastlehotel.com; Foss Rd; r from £195; P🛜) This Scottish Baronial fantasy in red sandstone was built in 1892 as the country house of Lt Col George Sande-

man, a scion of the famous port and sherry merchants. Opened as a luxury hotel and spa in 2013, it has a tasteful modern extension with commanding views over Loch Faskally, and a superb restaurant serving the finest Scottish venison, beef and seafood.

🍴 Eating & Drinking

★**Moulin Hotel** PUB FOOD ££
(✆01796-472196; www.moulinhotel.co.uk; Kirkmichael Rd; mains £9-16; P🛜) A mile away from town but a world apart, this atmospheric inn has low ceilings, ageing wood and snug booths. It's a wonderfully romantic spot for a home-brewed ale (there's a microbrewery out back) and a portion of Highland comfort food: try the mince and tatties, or venison stew. It's a pleasant uphill stroll from Pitlochry, and an easy roll down afterwards.

Port-na-Craig Inn BAR, BISTRO ££
(✆01796-472777; www.portnacraig.com; Port-na-Craig; mains £13-22, 2-/3-course lunch £13/15; ⊙11am-8.30pm; P🛜) Across the river from the town centre, this cute little cottage sits in what was once a separate hamlet. Top-quality main meals are prepared with confidence and panache; there are also simpler sandwiches, kids' meals and light lunches. Or you could just sit outdoors by the river with a pint and watch the anglers.

☆ Entertainment

★**Pitlochry Festival Theatre** THEATRE
(✆01796-484626; www.pitlochryfestivaltheatre. com; Port-na-Craig; tickets £26-35) Founded in 1951 (in a tent!), this famous and much-loved theatre is the focus of Highland Perthshire's

cultural life. The summer season, from May to mid-October, stages a different play each night of the week except Sunday.

ℹ Information

Pitlochry Tourist Office (☎ 01796-472215; www.perthshire.co.uk; 22 Atholl Rd; ⊙ 9.30am-5.30pm Mon-Sat, 10am-4pm Sun Mar-Oct, longer hours Jul & Aug, shorter hours Nov-Feb) has good information on local walks.

ℹ Getting There & Away

BUS

Citylink (www.citylink.co.uk) Buses run two to four times daily to Inverness (£17.20, 1¾ hours), Perth (£11.10, 50 minutes), Edinburgh (£17, two to 2½ hours) and Glasgow (£17, 2¼ hours).

Megabus (☎ 0871-266 3333; www.megabus.com) Offers discounted fares to Inverness, Perth, Edinburgh and Glasgow.

Stagecoach (www.stagecoachbus.com) Buses run to Aberfeldy (£3.50, 40 minutes, hourly Monday to Saturday, three Sunday), Dunkeld (£2.50, 40 minutes, hourly Monday to Saturday) and Perth (£3.70, 1¼ hours, hourly Monday to Saturday).

TRAIN

Pitlochry is on the main railway line from Perth (£13.60, 30 minutes, nine daily Monday to Saturday, five on Sunday) to Inverness (£22, 1½ hours, same frequency).

ℹ Getting Around

Local buses between Pitlochry and Blair Atholl stop at Killiecrankie (£1.60, 10 minutes, three to seven daily).

Escape Route (☎ 01796-473859; www.escape-route.co.uk; 3 Atholl Rd; bike hire per half-/full day from £14/24; ⊙ 9am-5.30pm Mon-Sat, 10am-5pm Sun) Rents out bikes and provides advice on local trails; it's worth booking ahead at weekends.

Blair Atholl

The village of Blair Atholl dates only from the early 19th century, springing up along the main road to the north after a new bridge was thrown across the River Tilt in 1822 (the original 16th-century Black Bridge, upgraded by General Wade in 1730, still stands just under a mile upstream at Old Bridge of Tilt).

Blair Castle is the main attraction here, but there's also the Atholl Country Life Museum, the old watermill, and many superb walks in the surrounding countryside, from short strolls through the castle grounds and longer walks to various viewpoints, to day-long hikes along Glen Tilt and up into the surrounding mountains (details from the information point in the museum).

◉ Sights

★ **Blair Castle**   CASTLE
(☎ 01796-481207; www.blair-castle.co.uk; Family/adult/child £28.90/10.70/6.40; ⊙ 9.30am-5.30pm Easter-Oct, 10am-4pm Sat & Sun Nov-Mar; P ♿) One of the most popular tourist attractions in Scotland, magnificent Blair Castle – and its surrounding estates – is the seat of the Duke of Atholl, head of the Murray clan. (The current duke visits the castle every May to review the **Atholl Highlanders**, Britain's only private army.) It's an impressive white heap set beneath forested slopes above the River Garry. Thirty rooms are open to the public and they present a wonderful picture of upper-class Highland life from the 16th century on.

The original tower was built in 1269, but the castle underwent significant remodelling in the 18th and 19th centuries. Highlights include the second-floor **Drawing Room** with its ornate Georgian plasterwork and Zoffany portrait of the 4th duke's family, complete with a pet lemur (yes, you read that correctly) called Tommy; and the **Tapestry Room** draped with 17th-century wall hangings created for Charles I. The **dining room** is sumptuous – check out the 9-pint wine glasses – and the **ballroom** is a vast oak-panelled chamber hung with hundreds of stag antlers.

Atholl Country Life Museum   MUSEUM
(www.athollcountrylifemuseum.org.uk; Main Rd; adult/child £3/free; ⊙ 10am-5pm Jul-Aug, 1.30-5pm Jun & Sep, 1.30-5pm Sat & Sun May; P) This eccentric collection housed in the old village school celebrates local life through the ages, with exhibits ranging from a letter from a Canadian emigrant written on birch bark to a reconstruction of a 1930s post office. The museum also houses a Cairngorms National Park information point.

🛏 Sleeping & Eating

Atholl Arms Hotel   HOTEL **££**
(☎ 01796-481205; www.athollarms.co.uk; r from £90; P 🕾 🐾) This hotel, near Blair Atholl train station, is convenient for the castle, with rooms of a high standard; book ahead

on weekends. The Bothy Bar here is the sibling pub of the Moulin Hotel in Pitlochry, snug with booth seating, an enormous fireplace and bucket-loads of character; there's no better place to be when the rain is lashing down outside.

Blair Atholl Watermill
CAFE £

(☎01796-481321; www.blairathollwatermill.co.uk; Ford Rd; mains £4-8; ⊗9.30am-5pm late Mar-Oct; P🗐🖟) 🖉 This working watermill grinds its own flour and bakes its own bread, and serves it up in this atmospheric cafe as deliciously fresh sandwiches and toasties. You can watch the mill at work, and even sign up for bakery courses.

❶ Getting There & Away

Local buses run between Pitlochry and Blair Atholl (£2.25, 25 minutes, three to seven daily). Three buses a day (Monday to Saturday) go directly to the castle, which is nearly a mile from the village.

There are trains from Perth (£13.60, 40 minutes, nine daily Monday to Saturday, five on Sunday).

Lochs Tummel & Rannoch

The scenic route along Lochs Tummel and Rannoch (www.rannochandtummel.co.uk) is worth doing any way you can – by foot, bicycle or car. Hillsides shrouded with ancient birchwoods and forests of spruce, pine and larch make up the fabulous **Tay Forest Park**, whose wooded hills roll into the glittering waters of the lochs; a visit in autumn is recommended, when the birch leaves are at their finest.

The **Queen's View** at the eastern end of Loch Tummel is a magnificent viewpoint with a vista along the loch to the prominent mountain of Schiehallion. The nearby **visitor centre** (www.forestry.gov.uk; admission free, parking £2; ⊗10am-4pm; P) provides parking and houses a cafe and gift shop.

Kinloch Rannoch is a great base for walks and cycle trips, or for fishing on Loch Rannoch for brown trout, Arctic char and pike; you can get permits (£8 per day) at the Country Store in the village. Walking trails lead into the wildlife-rich **Black Wood of Rannoch**, a remnant of Caledonian pine forest on the south shore of the loch.

Schiehallion (1083m), whose conical peak dominates views from Loch Rannoch, is a relatively straightforward climb from Braes of Foss car park (6.5 miles return),

and is rewarded by spectacular views. See www.jmt.org/east-schiehallion-estate.asp for more information.

Eighteen miles west of Kinloch Rannoch the road ends at romantic and isolated **Rannoch Station**, which lies on the Glasgow–Fort William railway line. Beyond sprawls the desolate expanse of **Rannoch Moor**. There's an excellent tearoom on the station platform, and a welcoming small hotel alongside.

Be aware that Rannoch Station is a dead-end, and the nearest service station is at Aberfeldy.

🛏 Sleeping & Eating

There are useful accommodation listings at www.rannochandtummel.co.uk.

Kilvrecht Campsite
CAMPSITE £

(☎01350-727284; Kilvrecht; tent site with/without car £8/5; ⊗Apr–mid-Oct) This basic but beautiful campsite (toilet block, but no electricity or hot water) is 2 miles west of Kinloch Rannoch on the south shore of the loch. Hiking and mountain-biking trails begin from the site.

Moor of Rannoch Hotel
HOTEL ££

(☎01882-633238; www.moorofrannoch.co.uk; Rannoch Station; s/d £80/114; ⊗mid-Feb–Oct; P🏵) At the end of the road beside Rannoch train station, this is one of Scotland's most isolated places (no internet, no TV, only fleeting mobile-phone reception), but luckily this hotel is here to keep your spirits up with cosy rooms and expansive views – a magical getaway. It does good dinners (6.30pm to 8pm, three courses £30), and can prepare a packed lunch.

Gardens B&B
B&B ££

(☎01882-632434; www.thegardensdunalastair. co.uk; Dunalastair; per person £40-45; P) Off the beaten track between Kinloch Rannoch and Tummel Bridge, this place has just two rooms – a double and a twin. But what rooms they are: effectively suites, each with its own bathroom and sitting room. The conservatory space is great for soaking up the sun and contemplating the stunning view of Schiehallion.

Look for the signpost at the crest of the hill just east of Dunalastair Reservoir.

Rannoch Station Tea Room
CAFE £

(☎01882-633247; www.rannochstationtearoom. co.uk; Rannoch Station; mains £4-6; ⊗8.30am-4pm Mon-Thu & Sat, 10am-4.30pm Sun, closed Fri; P) This superb little tearoom sits on the

RANNOCH MOOR

Beyond Rannoch Station, civilisation fades away and Rannoch Moor begins. This is the largest area of moorland in Britain, stretching west for eight barren, bleak and uninhabited miles to the A82 Glasgow–Fort William road. A triangular plateau of blanket bog occupying more than 50 sq miles, the moor is ringed by high mountains and puddled with countless lochs, ponds and peat hags. Water covers 10% of the surface, and it has been canoed across, swum across, and even skated across in winter.

Despite the appearance of desolation, the moor is rich in wildlife, with curlew, golden plover and snipe darting among the tussocks, black-throated diver, goosander and merganser on the lochs, and – if you're lucky – osprey and golden eagle overhead. Herds of red deer forage alongside the railway, and otters patrol the loch shores. And keep an eye out for the sundew, a tiny, insect-eating plant with sticky-fingered leaves.

A couple of excellent (and challenging) walks start from Rannoch Station – north to Corrour Station (11 miles, four to five hours) from where you can return by train; and west along the northern edge of the moor to the Kings House Hotel (p333) at the eastern end of Glen Coe (11 miles, four hours).

platform at remote Rannoch Station, serving coffee, sandwiches and cake to visiting hikers, mountain bikers and railway excursionists. Next door, in the former waiting room, is a fascinating exhibition on Rannoch Moor and the history of the railway.

ⓘ Getting There & Away

Broons Buses (☑ 01882-632418; www.broonsbusesandtaxis.co.uk) runs a demand-responsive minibus service (ie you have to phone and book it) between Kinloch Rannoch and Rannoch Station (£3, 35 minutes).

Elizabeth Yule Coaches (☑ 01796-472290) operates a bus service from Pitlochry to Kinloch Rannoch (£3.70, 50 minutes, three to five a day Monday to Saturday, April to October) via Queen's View and the Inn at Loch Tummel.

There are two to four **trains** daily from Rannoch Station north to Fort William (£10.50, one hour) and Mallaig, and south to Glasgow (£24, 2¾ hours).

Aberfeldy

POP 1895

Aberfeldy is the gateway to Breadalbane (the historic region surrounding Loch Tay), and a good base: adventure sports, angling, art and castles all feature on the menu here. It's a peaceful, pretty place on the banks of the Tay, but if it's moody lochs and glens that steal your heart, you may want to push a little further west.

The B846 road towards Fortingall crosses the Tay via the elegant **Wade's Bridge**, built in 1733 as part of the network of military roads designed to tame the Highlands.

◉ Sights & Activities

The **Birks of Aberfeldy**, made famous by a Robert Burns poem, offer a great short walk from the centre of town, following a vigorous burn upstream past several picturesque cascades.

Aberfeldy Distillery　　　DISTILLERY
(www.dewars.com; tour adult/child £9.50/4.50; ⊙10am-6pm Mon-Sat, noon-4pm Sun Apr-Oct, 10am-4pm Mon-Sat Nov-Mar; ℗) At the eastern end of Aberfeldy, the home of the famous Dewar's blend offers a good 90-minute tour. After the usual overblown film, there's a museum section with audioguide, and an entertaining interactive blending session, as well as the tour of the whisky-making process. More expensive tours allow you to try venerable Aberfeldy single malts and others.

Castle Menzies　　　CASTLE
(www.castlemenzies.org; adult/child £6.50/3; ⊙10.30am-5pm Mon-Sat, 2-5pm Sun Easter-Oct; ℗) Castle Menzies is the 16th-century seat of the chief of clan Menzies (*ming*-iss), magnificently set against a forest backdrop. Inside it reeks of authenticity, despite extensive restoration work. Check out the fireplace in the dungeon-like kitchens, and the gaudy Great Hall with windows revealing a ribbon of lush, green countryside extending into wooded hills beyond the estate. It's about 1.5 miles west of Aberfeldy, off the B846.

The Watermill　　　GALLERY, BOOKSHOP
(www.aberfeldywatermill.com; Mill St; ⊙10am-5pm Mon-Sat & 11am-5pm Sun Oct-Apr, to 5.30pm May-Sep) FREE You could while away several hours at this converted watermill, which

houses a cafe, bookshop and art gallery exhibiting contemporary works of art. The shop has the biggest range of titles in the Highlands, with a great selection of books on Scottish history, landscape and wildlife.

Highland Safaris TOURS
(📞01887-820071; www.highlandsafaris.net; ⊘9am-5pm, closed Sun Nov-Jan; 🚻) This outfit offers an ideal way to spot some wildlife or simply enjoy Perthshire's magnificent countryside. Standard trips include the 2½-hour Mountain Safari (adult/child £40/25), which includes whisky and shortbread in a mountain bothy; and the four-hour Safari Trek (adult/child £75/45), culminating with a walk in the mountains and a picnic. You may spot wildlife such as golden eagles, osprey and red deer. There's also gold panning for kids (£5) and mountain-bike hire (per day £20).

Splash RAFTING
(📞01887-829706; www.rafting.co.uk; Dunkeld Rd; ⊘9am-9pm; 🚻) Splash offers family-friendly white-water rafting on the River Tay (adult/child £40/30, Wednesday to Sunday year-round) and more advanced adult trips on the Tummel (Grade III/IV, June to September) and the Orchy (Grade III/V, October to March). It also offers pulse-racing descents on river bugs (£60), canyoning (£55) and mountain-bike hire (per half/full day £15/20).

🛏 Sleeping & Eating

Balnearn Guest House B&B ££
(📞01887-820431; www.balnearnhouse.com; Crieff Rd; s/d/f from £48/69/80; 🅿🛜🏊) Balnearn is a sedate and luxurious mansion near the centre of town, with space to spare. Most rooms have great natural light, and there's a particularly good family room downstairs. Breakfast has been lavishly praised by guests, and the attentive, cordial hosts are helpful while respecting your privacy.

Tigh'n Eilean Guest House B&B ££
(📞01887-820109; www.tighneilean.com; Taybridge Dr; s/d from £48/78; 🅿🛜🏊) Everything about this property screams comfort. It's a gorgeous place overlooking the Tay, with individually designed rooms – one has a Jacuzzi, while another is set on its own in a cheery yellow summer house in the garden, giving you a bit of privacy. The garden itself is fabulous, with hammocks for lazing in, and the riverbank setting is delightful.

⭐**Inn on the Tay** PUB FOOD ££
(📞01887-840760; www.theinnonthetay.co.uk; Grandtully; mains £11-18; ⊘food served noon-2.45pm & 5-8.45pm; 🅿🛜🚻) This convivial pub, with its modern bistro-style dining room, make a great pit stop on the way west to Loch Tay. The menu is simple – salads, burgers, fish and chips – but top quality, and there's an outdoor deck above the river where you can enjoy a drink while watching rafters and canoeists descend the Grandtully rapids.

ℹ Information
Aberfeldy Tourist Office (📞01887-829010; The Square; ⊘9.30am-5pm Apr-Oct, closed Thu & Sun Nov-Mar) is in an old church on the central square.

ℹ Getting There & Away
Stagecoach bus 23 (www.stagecoachbus.com) runs from Perth to Aberfeldy (£3.70, 1½ hours, hourly Monday to Saturday, fewer on Sunday) via Pitlochry (£3.50, 40 minutes), you'll need to change buses at Ballinluig. There's no regular bus link west to Killin, but the Ring of Breadalbane Explorer (p322) operates on a circular route taking in Crieff, Comrie, Lochearnhead, Killin, Kenmore and Aberfeldy, with four circuits a day in each direction, on Tuesdays, Wednesdays and Sundays from July to September.

Local buses run a circular route from Aberfeldy through Kenmore, Fortingall and back to Aberfeldy once each way on school days only.

Kenmore
The picturesque village of Kenmore lies at Loch Tay's eastern end, 6 miles west of Aberfeldy. Dominated by a striking archway leading to Taymouth Castle (not open to the public), it was built by the 3rd Earl of Breadalbane in 1760 to house his estate workers.

◉ Sights & Activities
⭐**Scottish Crannog Centre** INTERPRETATION CENTRE
(📞01887-830583; www.crannog.co.uk; tours adult/child £8.75/6.50; ⊘10am-5.30pm Apr-Oct; 🅿🚻) Less than a mile south of Kenmore on the banks of Loch Tay is the fascinating Scottish Crannog Centre, perched on stilts above the loch. Crannogs – effectively artificial islands – were a favoured form of defensive dwelling from the 3rd millennium BC onwards. This superb re-creation (based on studies of Oakbank crannog, one of 18

discovered in Loch Tay) offers a guided tour that includes an impressive demonstration of fire making and Iron Age crafts.

Loch Tay Boat House OUTDOORS
(☏ 07923 540826; www.loch-tay.co.uk; Pier Rd; ☉ mid-Mar–mid-Oct) Kenmore is a good activity base, and Loch Tay Boating Centre can have you speeding off on a mountain bike (£20 per day) or out on the loch itself in anything from a canoe (£10 to £15 per hour) to a cabin cruiser (£50 per hour) that'll take a whole family.

🛏 Sleeping & Eating

Kenmore Hotel HOTEL ££
(☏ 01887-830205; www.kenmorehotel.com; The Square; r from £79; P @ 🅿 🛜 🐾) The heart of Kenmore, this hotel has a bar with a roaring fire and some verses scribbled on the chimney by Robert Burns in 1787, when the inn was already a couple of centuries old. There's also a riverbank beer garden and a wide variety of rooms that sport modern conveniences; the nicest have bay windows and river views.

Prices plummet off-season and midweek. There are also upmarket self-catering lodges available.

Taymouth Marina SCOTTISH ££
(☏ 01887-830450; http://taymouthmarinarestaurant.co.uk; mains £13-17, steaks £25; P 🛜 🐾) This appealing modern restaurant has a prime position on the banks of Loch Tay, with window tables making the most of the gorgeous views. Service is friendly and the menu runs from Scottish mussels and Cullen skink to seafood platters and sirloin steaks.

❶ Getting There & Away

Local buses run from Aberfeldy to Kenmore (£2.50, 15 minutes) twice a day on school days only.

Loch Tay & Ben Lawers

Loch Tay is the heart of the ancient region known as Breadalbane (from the Gaelic Bràghad Albainn, 'the heights of Scotland') – mighty **Ben Lawers** (1214m), looming over the loch, is the highest peak outside the Ben Nevis and Cairngorms regions. Much of the land to the north of Loch Tay falls within the **Ben Lawers National Nature Reserve** (www.nnr-scotland.org.uk/ben-lawers), known for its rare alpine flora.

The main access point for the **ascent of Ben Lawers** is the car park 1½ miles north of the A827, on the minor road from Loch Tay to Bridge of Balgie. The climb is 6.5 miles and can take up to five hours (return): pack wet-weather gear, water and food, and a map and compass. There's also an easier nature trail here.

Loch Tay is famous for its fishing – salmon, trout and pike are all caught here. **Fish'n'Trips** (☏ 07967 567347; www.lochtayfishntrips.co.uk) can kit you out for a day's fishing with boat, tackle and guide for £95 per person, or rent you a boat for £60 a day.

The main road from Kenmore to Killin (p252) runs along the north shore of Loch Tay. The minor road along the south shore is narrow and twisting (unsuitable for large vehicles), but offers great views of the hills to the north.

Fortingall

Fortingall is one of the prettiest villages in Scotland, with 19th-century thatched cottages in a tranquil setting beside an ancient church with impressive wooden beams and a 7th-century monk's bell.

The famous Fortingall Yew Tree in the churchyard is estimated to be between 2000 and 3000 years old, one of the oldest living organisms in Europe. Its girth was measured at 16m in 1769, but since then souvenir hunters and natural decay have reduced it to a few gnarly but thriving boughs – in 2015

SALMON FISHING ON THE TAY

The Tay is Scotland's longest river (117 miles) and the most powerful in Britain, discharging more water into the sea each year than the Thames and Severn combined. It is also Europe's most famous salmon river, attracting anglers from all over the world (the season runs from 15 January to 15 October). The British record rod-caught salmon, weighing in at 64lb (29kg), was hooked in the Tay near Dunkeld in 1922, by local girl Georgina Ballantine.

Salmon fishing has an air of exclusivity, and can be expensive, but anyone, even complete beginners, can have a go. There is lots of information on the FishTay website (www.fishtay.co.uk), but novices will do best to hire a guide – check out Fishinguide (p255).

it produced berries for the first time on record. It was almost certainly around when the Romans camped in the meadows by the River Lyon in the 1st century AD; popular, if unlikely, tradition says that Pontius Pilate was born here.

Glen Lyon

The 'longest, loneliest and loveliest glen in Scotland', according to Sir Walter Scott, stretches for 32 unforgettable miles of rickety stone bridges, native woodland and heather-clad hills, becoming wilder and more uninhabited as it snakes its way west. The ancients believed it to be a gateway to Faerieland, and even the most sceptical of visitors will be entranced by the valley's magic.

From Fortingall, a narrow road winds up the glen, while another steep and spectacular route from Loch Tay crosses the hills to meet it at **Bridge of Balgie**. The road continues west as far as the dam on Loch Lyon, passing a memorial to Robert Campbell (1808–94; a Canadian explorer and fur trader, who was born in the glen).

There are no villages in the glen – the majestic scenery is the main reason to be here – just a cluster of houses at Bridge of Balgie and the **Bridge of Balgie Tearoom** (☑ 01887-866221; Bridge of Balgie; snacks £3-5; ☉ 10am-5pm Apr-Oct; ⓟ 🛜 🐾) ✔.

There are several waymarked **woodland walks** beginning from a car park a short distance beyond Bridge of Balgie, and more challenging hill walks into the surrounding mountains (see www.walkhighlands.co.uk/perthshire). **Cycling** is an ideal way to explore the glen, and fit riders can complete a loop over to Glen Lochay via a potholed road (motor vehicles not permitted) leading south from the Loch Lyon dam.

Milton Eonan (☑ 01887-866337; www.milton eonan.com; Bridge of Balgie; per person £39-43; ⓟ 🛜 🐾) ✔ is a must for those seeking tranquillity. On a bubbling stream where a watermill once stood, it's a working rarebreed croft with a romantic one-bedroom cottage at the bottom of the garden (available as B&B or self-catering). It can sleep three at a pinch. The helpful owners offer packed lunches and evening meals using local and homegrown produce. After crossing the bridge at Bridge of Balgie, you'll see Milton Eonan signposted to the right.

WEST HIGHLANDS

This region extends from the bleak blanket-bog of the Moor of Rannoch to the west coast beyond Glen Coe and Fort William, and includes the southern reaches of the Great Glen. The scenery is grand throughout, with high, rocky mountains rising above wild glens. Great expanses of moor alternate with lochs and patches of commercial forest. Fort William, at the inner end of Loch Linnhe, is the only sizeable town in the area.

Since 2007 the region has been promoted as Lochaber Geopark (www.lochaber geopark.org.uk), an area of outstanding geology and scenery.

Glen Coe

Scotland's most famous glen is also one of its grandest and – in bad weather – its grimmest. The approach to the glen from the east is guarded by the rocky pyramid of **Buachaille Etive Mor** – the Great Shepherd of Etive – and the lonelyKings House Hotel (p333), on the old military road from Stirling to Fort William (now followed by the West Highland Way). After the Battle of Culloden in 1745 it was used as a Hanoverian garrison – hence the name.

The modern road leads over the Pass of Glencoe and into the narrow upper glen. The southern side is dominated by three massive, brooding spurs, known as the **Three Sisters**, while the northern side is enclosed by the continuous steep wall of the knife-edged **Aonach Eagach** ridge, a classic mountaineering challenge. The road threads its way past deep gorges and crashing waterfalls to the more pastoral lower reaches of the glen around Loch Achtriochtan and the only settlement here, **Glencoe village**.

A few miles east of Glen Coe, on the south side of the A82, is Glencoe Mountain Resort (p333), where commercial skiing in Scotland first began back in 1956. Two miles west of the ski centre, a minor road leads along peaceful and beautiful **Glen Etive**, which runs southwest for 12 miles to the head of Loch Etive. On a hot summer's day the River Etive contains many tempting pools for swimming in, and there are lots of good picnic sites.

Glen Coe was written into the history books in 1692 when the resident MacDonalds were murdered by Campbell soldiers in what became known as the Glencoe Massacre (p332).

⚡ Activities

There are several short, pleasant walks around **Glencoe Lochan**, near the village. To get there, turn left off the minor road to the youth hostel, just beyond the bridge over the River Coe. There are three walks (40 minutes to an hour), all detailed on a signboard at the car park. The artificial lochan was created by Lord Strathcona in 1895 for his homesick Canadian wife, Isabella, and is surrounded by a North American–style forest.

A more strenuous hike, but well worth the effort on a fine day, is the climb to the **Lost Valley**, a magical mountain sanctuary still haunted by the ghosts of MacDonalds who died here while escaping the Glencoe Massacre in 1692 (only 2.5 miles round trip, but allow three hours). A rough path from the car park at Allt na Reigh (on the A82, 6 miles east of Glencoe village) bears left down to a footbridge over the river, then climbs up the wooded valley between Beinn Fhada and Gearr Aonach. The route leads steeply up through a maze of giant, jumbled, moss-coated boulders before emerging – quite unexpectedly – into a broad, open valley with an 800m-long meadow as flat as a football pitch. Back in the days of clan warfare, the valley – invisible from below – was used for hiding stolen cattle; its Gaelic name, Coire Gabhail, means 'corrie of capture'.

The summits of Glen Coe's mountains are for experienced mountaineers only. The Cicerone guidebook *Ben Nevis & Glen Coe*

THE GLENCOE MASSACRE

Glen Coe – Gleann Comhann in Gaelic – is sometimes (wrongly) said to mean 'the glen of weeping', a romantic mistranslation that gained popularity in the wake of the brutal murders that took place here in 1692 (the true origin of the name is pre-Gaelic, its meaning lost in the mists of time).

Following the Glorious Revolution of 1688, in which the Catholic King James VII/II (VII of Scotland, II of England) was replaced on the British throne by the Protestant King William II/III, supporters of the exiled James – known as Jacobites – most of them Highlanders, rose up against William in a series of battles. In an attempt to quash Jacobite loyalties, King William offered the Highland clans an amnesty on the condition that all clan chiefs took an oath of loyalty to him before 1 January 1692.

Maclain, the elderly chief of the MacDonalds of Glencoe, had long been a thorn in the side of the authorities. Not only was he late in setting out to fulfil the king's demand, but he mistakenly went first to Fort William before travelling slowly through winter mud and rain to Inveraray, where he was three days late in taking the oath before the Sheriff of Argyll.

The secretary of state for Scotland, Sir John Dalrymple, decided to use the fact that Maclain had missed the deadline to punish the troublesome MacDonalds, and at the same time set an example to other Highland clans, some of whom had not bothered to take the oath.

A company of 120 soldiers, mainly from the Campbell territory of Argyll, were sent to the glen under cover of collecting taxes. It was a long-standing tradition for clans to provide hospitality to travellers and, since their commanding officer was related to Maclain by marriage, the troops were billeted in MacDonald homes.

After they'd been guests for 12 days, the government order came for the soldiers to 'fall upon the rebels the MacDonalds of Glencoe and put all to the sword under 70. You are to have a special care that the Old Fox and his sons do upon no account escape'. The soldiers turned on their hosts at 5am on 13 February, killing Maclain and 37 other men, women and children. Some of the soldiers alerted the MacDonalds to their intended fate, allowing them to escape; many fled into the snow-covered hills, where another 40 people perished in the cold.

The ruthless brutality of the incident caused a public uproar, and after an inquiry several years later Dalrymple lost his job. There's a monument to Maclain in Glencoe village, and members of the MacDonald clan still gather here on 13 February each year to lay a wreath.

by Ronald Turnbull, available in most book-shops and outdoor equipment stores, details everything from short easy walks to chal-lenging mountain climbs.

Steven Fallon Mountain Guides OUTDOORS
(📞 0131-466 8152; www.stevenfallon.co.uk; per person from £50) If you lack the experience or confidence to tackle Glen Coe's challenging mountains alone, then you can join a guided hill walk or hire a private guide from this outfit.

Glencoe Mountain Resort OUTDOORS
(📞 01855-851226; www.glencoemountain.com; Kingshouse; chairlift adult/child £10/5; ⊙9am-4.30pm) Scotland's oldest ski area, estab-lished in the 1950s, is also one of the best, with grand views across the wild expanse of Rannoch Moor. The chairlift continues to operate in summer providing access to mountain-biking trails. The **Lodge Café-Bar** (open 9am to 8.30pm) at the base sta-tion has comfy sofas where you can soak up the view through the floor-to-ceiling win-dows. In winter a lift pass costs £32 a day; equipment hire is £25.

There are **tent pitches** (£6 per person), **camping pods** (£50 a night) and **camp-ervan hookups** (£15 a night) beside the car park.

🛏 Sleeping

Kings House Hotel HOTEL ££
(📞 01855-851259; www.kingshousehotel.co.uk; Kingshouse; s/d £45/100; 🅿) This remote ho-tel claims to be one of Scotland's oldest li-censed inns, dating from the 17th century. It has long been a favourite meeting place for climbers, skiers and walkers (it's on the West Highland Way); accommodation is basic, but there is good pub grub and real ale. Plans to redevelop the hotel in 2016-17 include the addition of a hostel.

The rustic **Climbers Bar** (open 11am to 11pm) around the back is more relaxed than the lounge, and there's free **wild camping** across the wee bridge behind the hotel – no facilities, but you're allowed to use the toilets in the Climbers Bar.

Glencoe Village

The little village of Glencoe stands on the south shore of Loch Leven at the west-ern end of the glen, 16 miles south of Fort William.

💿 Sights & Activities

Glencoe Folk Museum MUSEUM
(📞 01855-811664; www.glencoemuseum.com; adult/child £3/free; ⊙10am-4.30pm Mon-Sat East-er-Oct) This small, thatched cottage houses a varied collection of farm equipment, tools of the woodworking, blacksmithing and slate-quarrying trades, and military mem-orabilia, including a riding boot that once belonged to Robert Campbell of Glenlyon (who took part in the Massacre of Glencoe).

Glencoe Visitor Centre INTERPRETATION CENTRE
(NTS; 📞 01855-811307; www.glencoe-nts.org.uk; adult/child £6.50/5; ⊙9.30am-5.30pm Easter-Oct, 10am-4pm Thu-Sun Nov-Easter; 🅿) 🐾 The centre provides comprehensive informa-tion on the geological, environmental and cultural history of Glen Coe via high-tech interactive and audiovisual displays, charts the history of mountaineering in the glen, and tells the story of the Glencoe Massacre in all its gory detail. It's 1.5 miles east of Glencoe village.

Action Glen WATER SPORTS
(📞 01764-651582; http://glencoe.actionglen.com; Ballachulish; ⊙9.30am-5pm Apr-Oct) You can take a guided sea kayaking trip (£40 per person) or a beginner's kayak taster session (£15 per person), or have a go at stand-up paddle-boarding (£35 per person) at the water-sports centre next to the Isles of Glencoe Hotel.

🛏 Sleeping & Eating

Invercoe Caravan & Camping Park CAMPSITE £
(📞 01855-811210; www.invercoe.co.uk; Invercoe; tent sites without car per person £9, campervan site £23; 🐾) This place has great views of the surrounding mountains and is equipped with anti-midge machines. There's a covered cooking area for campers.

Glencoe SYHA HOSTEL £
(📞 08155-811219; www.syha.org.uk; dm £22.50; 🅿 @ 🛜 🐾) Very popular with hikers, though the atmosphere can be a little institution-al. It's a 1.5-mile walk from Glencoe village along the minor road on the northern side of the river.

Glencoe Independent Hostel HOSTEL £
(📞 01855-811906; www.glencoehostel.co.uk; dm/bunkhouse £17/15; 🅿 @ 🛜) This handily locat-ed hostel, just 1.5 miles southeast of Glen-coe village, is set in an old farmhouse with six- and eight-bed dorms, and a bunkhouse

with another 16 bed spaces in communal, alpine-style bunks. There's also a cute little wooden cabin that sleeps up to three (£80 per night).

Clachaig Inn HOTEL £££
(☑ 01855-811252; www.clachaig.com; s/d £53/106; ℗ 🛈) The Clachaig, 2 miles east of Glencoe village, has long been a favourite haunt of hill walkers and climbers. As well as comfortable en suite accommodation, there's a smart, modern lounge bar with snug booths and high refectory tables, mountaineering photos and bric-a-brac, and climbing magazines to leaf through.

Climbers usually head for the lively **Boots Bar** on the other side of the hotel – it has log fires, serves real ale and good pub grub (mains £9 to £18, served noon to 9pm), and has live Scottish music on Saturday nights.

★ **Glencoe Café** CAFE £
(☑ 01855-811168; www.glencoecafe.co.uk; Glencoe village; mains £4-8; ⊙ 10am-4pm daily, to 5pm May-Sep, closed Nov; ℗ 🛈) This friendly cafe is the social hub of Glencoe village, serving breakfast fry-ups till 11.30am (including vegetarian versions), light lunches based around local produce (think Cullen skink, smoked salmon quiche, venison burgers), and the best cappuccino in the glen.

Crafts & Things CAFE £
(☑ 01855-811325; www.craftsandthings.co.uk; Annat; mains £3-7; ⊙ 9.30am-5pm Mon-Fri, to 5.30pm Sat & Sun; ℗ 🛈 ♿) Just off the main road between Glencoe village and Ballachulish, the tearoom in this craft shop is a good spot for a lunch of homemade lentil soup with crusty rolls, ciabatta sandwiches, or just coffee and carrot cake. There are tables outdoors and a box of toys to keep the little ones occupied.

🛈 Getting There & Away

Scottish Citylink (☑ 0871-266 3333; www.citylink.co.uk) buses run between Fort William and Glencoe (£8, 30 minutes, four to eight daily) and from Glencoe to Glasgow (£22, 2½ hours, four to eight daily). Buses stop at Glencoe village, Glencoe Visitor Centre and Glencoe Mountain Resort.

Stagecoach bus 44 (www.stagecoachbus.com) links Glencoe village with Fort William (£3.80, 35 minutes, hourly Monday to Saturday, three on Sunday) and Kinlochleven (£2, 15 minutes).

Kinlochleven
POP 900

Kinlochleven is hemmed in by high mountains at the head of beautiful Loch Leven, about 7 miles east of Glencoe village. The aluminium smelter that led to the town's development in the early 20th century has long since closed, and the opening of the Ballachulish Bridge in the 1970s allowed the main road to bypass it completely. Decline was halted by the opening of the West Highland Way, which now brings a steady stream of hikers through the village.

The final section of the **West Highland Way** stretches for 14 miles from Kinlochleven to Fort William. The village is also the starting point for easier walks up the glen of the River Leven, through pleasant woods to the **Grey Mare's Tail** waterfall, and harder mountain hikes into the **Mamores**.

🏃 Activities

Via Ferrata ADVENTURE SPORTS
(☑ 01855-413200; www.glencoeactivities.com; per person/family £55/170) Scotland's first via ferrata – a 500m climbing route equipped with steel ladders, cables and bridges – snakes through the crags around the Grey Mare's Tail waterfall, allowing non-climbers to experience the thrill of climbing (you'll need a head for heights, though!).

Ice Factor ADVENTURE SPORTS
(☑ 01855-831100; www.ice-factor.co.uk; Leven Rd; ⊙ 9am-10pm Tue & Thu, to 7pm Mon, Wed & Fri-Sun; ♿) If you fancy trying your hand at ice-climbing, even in the middle of summer, the world's biggest indoor ice-climbing wall offers a one-hour beginner's 'taster' session for £30. You'll also find a rock-climbing wall, an aerial adventure course, a soft-play area for kids, and a cafe (open 9am to 5.30pm) and bar-bistro (food served 6pm to 9pm).

🛏 Sleeping & Eating

Blackwater Hostel HOSTEL, CAMPSITE £
(☑ 01855-831253; www.blackwaterhostel.co.uk; Lab Rd; tw £46, tent sites per person £8, pods from £55; ℗ 🛈) This 39-bed hostel (preference given to groups – individual travellers should check availability in advance) has spotless dorms with en suite bathrooms and TV, and a well-sheltered campsite with the option of wooden 'glamping' pods.

★ **Lochleven Seafood Cafe** SEAFOOD ££
(☎ 01855-821048; www.lochlevenseafoodcafe.co.uk; mains £11-23, whole lobster £40; ☺ meals noon-3pm & 6-9pm, coffee & cake 10am-noon & 3-5pm mid-Mar–Oct; P 🐾) This outstanding place serves superb shellfish freshly plucked from live tanks – oysters on the half shell, razor clams, scallops, lobster and crab – plus a daily fish special and some non-seafood dishes. For warm days, there's an outdoor terrace with a view across the loch to the Pap of Glencoe, a distinctive conical mountain.

🛈 Getting There & Away

Stagecoach bus 44 (www.stagecoachbus.com) runs from Fort William to Kinlochleven (£4.80, 50 minutes, hourly Monday to Saturday, three on Sunday) via Ballachulish and Glencoe village.

Fort William

POP 9910

Basking on the shores of Loch Linnhe amid magnificent mountain scenery, Fort William has one of the most enviable settings in the whole of Scotland. If it weren't for the busy dual carriageway crammed between the less-than-attractive town centre and the loch, and one of the highest rainfall records in the country, it would be almost idyllic. Even so, the Fort has carved out a reputation as 'Outdoor Capital of the UK' (www.outdoorcapital.co.uk), and easy access by rail and bus makes it a good place to base yourself for exploring the surrounding mountains and glens.

Magical Glen Nevis begins near the northern end of the town and wraps itself around the southern flanks of Ben Nevis (1345m) – Britain's highest mountain and a magnet for hikers and climbers. The glen is also popular with movie makers – parts of *Braveheart*, *Rob Roy* and the Harry Potter movies were filmed there.

History

There is little left of the fort from which the town takes its name. The first castle here was constructed by General Monck in 1654 and called Inverlochy, but the meagre ruins by the loch are those of the fort built in the 1690s by General Mackay and named after King William II/III. In the 18th century it became part of a chain of garrisons (along with Fort Augustus and Fort George) that controlled the Great Glen in the wake of the Jacobite rebellions; it was pulled down in the 19th century to make way for the railway.

Originally a tiny fishing village called Gordonsburgh, the town adopted the name of the fort after the opening of the railway in 1901 (in Gaelic it is known as An Gearasdan, 'the garrison'). The juxtaposition of the railway and the Caledonian Canal saw the town grow into a major tourist centre. Its position has been consolidated in the last three decades by the huge increase in popularity of climbing, skiing, mountain biking and other outdoor sports.

⊙ Sights

★ **Jacobite Steam Train** HERITAGE RAILWAY
(☎ 0844 850 4685; www.westcoastrailways.co.uk; day return adult/child £34/19; ☺ daily Jul & Aug, Mon-Fri mid-May–Jun, Sep & Oct) The Jacobite Steam Train, hauled by a former LNER K1 or LMS Class 5MT locomotive, travels the scenic two-hour run between Fort William and Mallaig. Classed as one of the great railway journeys of the world, the route crosses the historic Glenfinnan Viaduct, made famous in the Harry Potter films – the Jacobite's owners supplied the steam locomotive and rolling stock used in the film.

Trains depart from Fort William train station in the morning and return from Mallaig in the afternoon. There's a brief stop at Glenfinnan station, and you get 1½ hours in Mallaig.

West Highland Museum MUSEUM
(☎ 01397-702169; www.westhighlandmuseum.org.uk; Cameron Sq; ☺ 10am-5pm Mon-Sat Apr-Oct, to 4pm Mar & Nov-Dec, closed Jan & Feb) FREE This small but fascinating museum is packed with all manner of Highland memorabilia. Look out for the secret portrait of Bonnie Prince Charlie – after the Jacobite rebellions, all things Highland were banned, including pictures of the exiled leader, and this tiny painting looks like nothing more than a smear of paint until viewed in a cylindrical mirror, which reflects a credible likeness of the prince.

☞ Tours

Crannog Cruises WILDLIFE
(☎ 01397-700714; www.crannog.net/cruises; adult/child £15/7.50; ☺ 11am, 1pm & 3pm daily Easter-Oct) Operates 1½-hour wildlife cruises on Loch Linnhe, visiting a seal colony and a salmon farm.

THE CALEDONIAN CANAL

Running for 59 miles from Corpach, near Fort William, to Inverness via lochs Lochy, Oich and Ness, the **Caledonian Canal** (www.scottishcanals.co.uk) links the east and west coasts of Scotland, avoiding the long and dangerous sea passage around Cape Wrath and through the turbulent Pentland Firth. Designed by Thomas Telford and completed in 1822 at a cost of £900,000 – a staggering sum then – the canal took 20 years to build, including 29 locks, four aqueducts and 10 bridges.

Conceived as a project to ease unemployment and bring prosperity to the Highlands in the aftermath of the Jacobite rebellions and the Clearances, the canal proved to be a commercial failure – the locks were too small for the new breed of steamships that came into use soon after its completion. But it proved to be a success in terms of tourism, especially after it was popularised by Queen Victoria's cruise along the canal in 1873. Today the canal is used mainly by yachts and pleasure cruisers, though since 2010 it has also been used to transport timber from west-coast forestry plantations to Inverness.

Much of the **Great Glen Way** (p306) follows the line of the canal; it can be followed on foot, by mountain bike or on horseback, and 80% of the route has even been done on mobility scooters. An easy half-day hike or bike ride is to follow the canal towpath from Corpach to Gairlochy (10 miles), which takes you past the impressive flight of eight locks known as Neptune's Staircase (p337), and through beautiful countryside with grand views to the north face of Ben Nevis.

If you're cycling the length of the Great Glen Way, you can hire mountain bikes from **Nevis Cycles** (p338) in Fort William and drop them off at **Ticket to Ride** (p301) in Inverness, or vice versa.

The glen can also be explored by water, by following the **Great Glen Canoe Trail** (www.greatglencanoetrail.info).

Festivals & Events

UCI Mountain Bike
World Cup
MOUNTAIN BIKING
(www.fortwilliamworldcup.co.uk) In June, Fort William pulls in crowds of more than 18,000 spectators for this World Cup downhill mountain-biking event. The gruelling downhill course is at nearby Nevis Range ski area.

Sleeping

It's best to book well ahead in summer, especially for hostels.

Calluna
APARTMENT £
(☑ 01397-700451; www.fortwilliamholiday.co.uk; Heathercroft, Connochie Rd; dm/tw £17/40, 6- to 8-person apt per week £575; P 🖨) Run by well-known mountain guide Alan Kimber and wife Sue, the Calluna offers self-catering apartments geared to groups of hikers and climbers, but also takes individual travellers prepared to share; there's a fully equipped kitchen and an excellent drying room for your soggy hiking gear.

Fort William Backpackers
HOSTEL £
(☑ 01397-700711; www.scotlands-top-hostels.com; Alma Rd; dm/tw £18.50/47; P @ 🖨) A 10-minute walk from the bus and train stations, this lively and welcoming hostel is set in a grand Victorian villa, perched on a hillside with great views over Loch Linnhe.

Ashburn House
B&B ££
(☑ 01397-706000; www.ashburnhouse.co.uk; Achintore Rd; r per person £55; ⊘ Mar-Oct; P 🖨) Gorgeously bright and spacious bedrooms – some with views over Loch Linnhe – are the norm at this grand Victorian villa south of the centre. The leather sofas in the residents lounge and the breakfast tables in the dining room enjoy sea views. No children under 12.

Lime Tree
HOTEL ££
(☑ 01397-701806; www.limetreefortwilliam.co.uk; Achintore Rd; s/d from £110/120; P 🖨 🐾) Much more interesting than your average guesthouse, this former Victorian manse overlooking Loch Linnhe is an 'art gallery with rooms', decorated throughout with the artist-owner's atmospheric Highland landscapes. Foodies rave about the restaurant, and the gallery space – a triumph of sensitive design – stages everything from serious exhibitions (works by David Hockney and Andy Goldsworthy have appeared) to folk concerts.

No 6 Caberfeidh
B&B ££

(☑ 01397-703756; www.6caberfeidh.com; 6 Caberfeidh, Fassifern Rd; d/f £75/120; ☏) Friendly owners and comfortable accommodation make a great combination; add a good central location and you're all set. Choose from one of two family rooms (one double and one single bed) or a romantic double with four-poster. Freshly prepared breakfasts include scrambled eggs with smoked salmon.

St Andrew's Guest House
B&B ££

(☑ 01397-703038; www.standrewsguesthouse. co.uk; Fassifern Rd; s/d £57/70; P☏) Set in a lovely 19th-century building that was once a rectory and choir school, St Andrew's retains period features such as carved masonry, wood panelling and stained-glass windows. It has six spacious bedrooms; those at the front have stunning views.

★ Grange
B&B £££

(☑ 01397-705516; www.grangefortwilliam.com; Grange Rd; d £145; P☏) An exceptional 19th-century villa set in its own landscaped grounds, the Grange is crammed with antiques and fitted with log fires, chaise lounges and Victorian roll-top baths. The Turret Room, with its window seat in the turret overlooking Loch Linnhe, is our favourite. It's 500m southwest of the town centre. No children.

✗ Eating & Drinking

Delicraft
DELI £

(☑ 01397-698100; www.delicraft.co.uk; 61 High St; mains £2.50-5; ☑) A welcome new deli serving great coffee and delicious sandwiches to eat in or take away, including deli classics such as pastrami on rye, as well as a range of Scottish cheeses, craft beers and gins.

★ Lime Tree
SCOTTISH ££

(☑ 01397-701806; www.limetreefortwilliam.co.uk; Achintore Rd; mains £16-20; ⏱ 6.30-9.30pm; P☏) ✐ Fort William is not over-endowed with great places to eat, but the restaurant at this small hotel and art gallery has put the UK's Outdoor Capital on the gastronomic map. The chef turns out delicious dishes built around fresh Scottish produce, ranging from Loch Fyne oysters to Loch Awe trout and Ardnamurchan venison.

Bayleaf
SCOTTISH ££

(Cameron Sq; mains lunch £5-11, dinner £13-20; ⏱) ✐ A great new addition to the town's restaurant scene, this place combines crisp, modern decor, friendly service (the chef often comes out to chat with customers), and the best of Scottish beef, lamb and seafood freshly and simply prepared. If Scotland's national dish hasn't appealed, try a haggis fritter with Drambuie mayonnaise!

Crannog Seafood Restaurant
SEAFOOD ££

(☑ 01397-705589; www.crannog.net; Town Pier; mains £15-23; ⏱ noon-2.30pm & 6-9pm) ✐ The Crannog wins the prize for the best location in town – perched on the Town Pier, giving window-table diners an uninterrupted view down Loch Linnhe. Informal and unfussy, it specialises in fresh local fish – there are three or four daily fish specials plus the main menu – though there are lamb, venison and vegetarian dishes, too. Two/three-course lunch £15/19.

Grog & Gruel
PUB

(☑ 01397-705078; www.grogandgruel.co.uk; 66 High St; ⏱ noon-midnight; ☏) The Grog & Gruel is a traditional-style, wood-panelled pub with an excellent range of cask ales from regional Scottish and English microbreweries.

① Information

Belford Hospital (☑ 01397-702481; Belford Rd) Opposite the train station.

Fort William Tourist Office (☑ 01397-701801; www.visithighlands.com; 15 High St; internet per 20min £1; ⏱ 9am-5pm Mon-Sat, 10am-3pm Sun, longer hrs Jun-Aug) Has internet access.

Post Office (☑ 0845-722 3344; 5 High St; ⏱ 9am-5.30pm Mon-Sat, noon-4pm Sun) In WH Smith shop.

① Getting There & Away

The bus and train stations are next to the huge Morrisons supermarket, reached from the town centre via an underpass next to the Nevisport shop.

NEPTUNE'S STAIRCASE

Three miles north of Fort William, at Banavie, is Neptune's Staircase, an impressive flight of eight locks that allows boats to climb 20m to the main reach of the Caledonian Canal (p308). The B8004 road runs along the west side of the canal to Gairlochy at the south end of Loch Lochy, offering superb views of Ben Nevis; the canal towpath on the east side makes a great walk or bike ride (6.5 miles).

BUS

Shiel Buses (☑ 01397-700700; www.shielbuses. co.uk) service 500 runs to Mallaig (£6.10, 1½ hours, three daily Monday to Friday, plus one daily weekends April to September) via Glenfinnan (£3.30, 30 minutes) and Arisaig (£5.60, one hour).

Scottish Citylink (☑ 0871-266 3333; www. citylink.co.uk) buses link Fort William with other major towns and cities.

Edinburgh £35, five hours, seven daily with a change at Glasgow; via Glencoe and Crianlarich

Glasgow £24, three hours, eight daily

Inverness £11.60, two hours, six daily

Oban £9.40, 1½ hours, two daily

Portree £311, three hours, three daily

TRAIN

The spectacular West Highland line runs from Glasgow to Mallaig via Fort William. The overnight **Caledonian Sleeper** (www.sleeper.scot) service connects Fort William and London Euston (from £125 sharing a twin-berth cabin, 13 hours).

There's no direct rail connection between Oban and Fort William – you have to change at Crianlarich, so it's faster to take the bus.

Edinburgh £35, five hours; change at Glasgow's Queen St station, three daily, two on Sunday

Glasgow £26, 3¾ hours, three daily, two on Sunday

Mallaig £12.20, 1½ hours, four daily, three on Sunday

❶ Getting Around

BICYCLE

Located a half-mile northeast of the town centre, **Nevis Cycles** (☑ 01397-705555; www. neviscycles.com; cnr Montrose Ave & Locheil Rd, Inverlochy; per day from £25; ⊙ 9am-5.30pm) rents everything from hybrid bikes and mountain bikes to full-suspension downhill racers. Bikes can be hired here and dropped off in Inverness.

BUS

A Zone 2 Dayrider ticket (£8.60) gives unlimited travel for one day on Stagecoach bus services in the Fort William area, as far as Glencoe and Fort Augustus. Buy from the bus driver.

CAR

Fort William is 146 miles from Edinburgh, 104 miles from Glasgow and 66 miles from Inverness. The tourist office has listings of car-hire companies.

Easydrive Car Hire (☑ 01397-701616; www. easydrivescotland.co.uk; North Rd) hires out small cars from £36/165 a day/week, including tax and unlimited mileage, but not Collision Damage Waiver (CDW).

TAXI

There's a taxi rank on the corner of High St and the Parade.

Around Fort William

Glen Nevis

Scenic Glen Nevis – used as a filming location for *Braveheart* and the Harry Potter movies – lies just an hour's walk from Fort William town centre. The **Glen Nevis Visitor Centre** (☑ 01397-705922; www. bennevisweather.co.uk; ⊙ 8.30am-6pm Jul & Aug, 9am-5pm Apr-Jun, Sep & Oct, 9am-3pm Nov-Mar; 🅿) is situated 1.5 miles up the glen, and provides information on hiking, weather forecasts, and specific advice on climbing Ben Nevis.

From the car park at the far end of the road along Glen Nevis, there is an excellent 1.5-mile walk through the spectacular Nevis Gorge to **Steall Meadows**, a verdant valley dominated by a 100m-high bridal-veil waterfall. You can reach the foot of the falls by crossing the river on a wobbly, three-cable wire bridge – one cable for your feet and one for each hand – a real test of balance!

🛌 Sleeping & Eating

Glen Nevis Caravan & Camping Park CAMPSITE £
(☑ 01397-702191; www.glen-nevis.co.uk; tent sites £9, incl car £11, campervan £13 plus per person £3.50; ⊙ mid-Mar–early Nov; 🛜) This big, well-equipped site is a popular base camp for Ben Nevis and the surrounding mountains. The site is 2.5 miles from Fort William, along the Glen Nevis road.

Glen Nevis SYHA HOSTEL £
(SYHA; ☑ 01397-702336; www.syha.org.uk; dm/ tw £19.50/56; 🅿@🛜) Large, impersonal and slightly reminiscent of a school camp, this hostel is 3 miles from Fort William, right beside one of the starting points for the tourist track up Ben Nevis.

Achintee Farm B&B, HOSTEL ££
(☑ 01397-702240; www.achinteefarm.com; Achintee; B&B d £90-100, hostel tw/tr £50/75; ⊙ B&B May-Sep, hostel year-round; 🅿🛜) This attractive farmhouse offers excellent B&B accommodation and also has a small hostel attached. It's at the start of the path up Ben Nevis.

★ Ben Nevis Inn SCOTTISH ££
(☑ 01397-701227; www.ben-nevis-inn.co.uk; Achintee; mains £9-16; ⊙ noon-11pm daily Apr-Oct, Thu-Sun only Nov-Mar; 🅿) This great barn of a pub serves real ale and tasty bar meals, and

has a comfy 24-bed bunkhouse downstairs (beds £16.50 per person). It's at the start of the path from Achintee up Ben Nevis, and only a mile from the end of the West Highland Way.

❶ Getting There & Away

Bus 41 runs from Fort William bus station to the Glen Nevis SYHA Hostel (£2, 15 or 20 minutes, two daily year-round, five daily Monday to Saturday June to September). Check at the tourist office for the latest timetable, which is liable to alteration.

Nevis Range

Six miles to the north of Fort William lies Nevis Range ski area, where a gondola gives access to the upper part of Aonach Mor mountain. The facility operates year-round, allowing visitors to access mountain paths and downhill mountain-biking trails outside of the ski season.

🏃 Activities

Nevis Range Downhill & Witch's Trails
MOUNTAIN BIKING

(☑ 01397-705825; http://bike.nevisrange.co.uk; single/multitrip ticket £14/32; ☺ downhill course 10.15am-3.45pm mid-May–mid-Sep, forest trails 24hr year-round) A world championship **downhill mountain-bike trail** – for experienced riders only – runs from the Snowgoose restaurant at the Nevis Range ski area to the base station; bikes are carried up on a rack on the gondola cabin. A multitrip ticket gives unlimited uplift for a day; full-suspension bike hire costs from £40/70 per single run/full day.

There's also a 4-mile **XC red trail** that begins at the Snowgoose, and the **Witch's Trails** – 25 miles of waymarked forest road and singletrack in the nearby forest, including a 5-mile world championship loop.

Nevis Range
OUTDOORS

(☑ 01397-705825; www.nevisrange.co.uk; gondola return trip per adult/child £12.50/7.25; ☺ 10am-5pm summer, 9.30am-dusk winter, closed mid-Nov–

CLIMBING BEN NEVIS

As the highest peak in the British Isles, Ben Nevis (1345m) attracts many would-be ascensionists who would not normally think of climbing a Scottish mountain – a staggering (often literally) 100,000 people reach the summit each year.

Although anyone who is reasonably fit should have no problem climbing Ben Nevis on a fine summer's day, an ascent should not be undertaken lightly; every year people have to be rescued from the mountain. You will need proper walking boots (the path is rough and stony, and there may be snow on the summit), warm clothing, waterproofs, a map and compass, and plenty of food and water. And don't forget to check the weather forecast (www.bennevisweather.co.uk).

Here are a few facts to mull over before you go racing up the tourist track: the summit plateau is bounded by 700m-high cliffs and has a sub-Arctic climate; at the summit it can snow on any day of the year; the summit is wrapped in cloud nine days out of 10; in thick cloud, visibility at the summit can be 10m or less; and in such conditions the only safe way off the mountain requires careful use of a map and compass to avoid walking over those 700m cliffs.

The tourist track (the easiest route to the top) was originally called the Pony Track. It was built in the 19th century for the pack ponies that carried supplies to a meteorological observatory on the summit (now in ruins), which was in use continuously from 1883 to 1904.

There are three possible starting points for the tourist track ascent – Achintee Farm; the footbridge at Glen Nevis SYHA Hostel; and, if you have a car, the car park at Glen Nevis Visitor Centre. The path climbs gradually to the shoulder at Lochan Meall an t-Suidhe (known as the Halfway Lochan), then zigzags steeply up beside the Red Burn to the summit plateau. The highest point is marked by a trig point on top of a huge cairn beside the ruins of the old observatory; the plateau is scattered with countless smaller cairns, stones arranged in the shape of people's names and, sadly, a fair bit of litter.

The total distance to the summit and back is 8 miles; allow at least four or five hours to reach the top, and another 2½ to three hours for the descent. Afterwards, as you celebrate in the pub with a pint, consider the fact that the record time for the annual Ben Nevis Hill Race is just under 1½ hours – up *and* down. Then have another pint.

mid-Dec) The Nevis Range ski area, 6 miles north of Fort William, spreads across the northern slopes of Aonach Mor (1221m). The gondola that gives access to the bottom of the ski area at 655m operates year-round (15 minutes each way). At the top there's a restaurant and a couple of hiking trails through nearby Leanachan Forest, as well as excellent mountain-biking trails.

During the ski season a one-day lift pass costs £32/20 per adult/child; a one-day package, including equipment hire, lift pass and two hours' instruction, costs £71.

❶ Getting There & Away

Bus 41 runs from Fort William bus station to Nevis Range (£2, 15 minutes, five daily Monday to Saturday, limited service on Sunday, limited service October to April). Check at the tourist office for the latest timetable, which is liable to alteration.

Ardnamurchan

Ten miles south of Fort William, a car ferry makes the short crossing to Corrran Ferry. The drive from here to **Ardnamurchan Point** (www.ardnamurchan.com), the most westerly point on the British mainland, is one of the most beautiful in the western Highlands, especially in late spring and early summer when much of the narrow, twisting road is lined with the bright pink and purple blooms of rhododendrons.

The road clings to the northern shore of Loch Sunart, going through the pretty villages of **Strontian** – which gave its name to the element strontium, first discovered in ore from nearby lead mines in 1790 – and **Salen**.

The mostly single-track road from Salen to Ardnamurchan Point is only 25 miles long, but it'll take you 1½ hours each way. It's a dipping, twisting, low-speed roller coaster of a ride through sun-dappled native woodlands draped with lichen and fern. Just when you're getting used to the views of Morvern and Mull to the south, it makes a quick detour to the north for a panorama over the islands of Rum and Eigg.

◉ Sights

Ardnamurchan Natural History & Visitor Centre   INTERPRETATION CENTRE

(☑ 01972-500209; www.ardnamurchannaturalhist orycentre.com; Glenmore; adult/child £5/2.50; ☺ 9am-5pm Mon-Sat, 10am-4pm Sun; ⏸) This fascinating centre – midway between Salen and Kilchoan – was originally devised by a wildlife photographer and tries to bring you face to face with the flora and fauna of the Ardnamurchan peninsula. The Living Building exhibit is designed to attract local wildlife, with a mammal den that is occasionally occupied by hedgehogs or pine martens, an owl nest-box, a mouse nest and a pond.

If the beasties are not in residence, you can watch recorded video footage of the animals. There's also seasonal live CCTV coverage of local wildlife, ranging from nesting herons to a golden eagle feeding site.

Ardnamurchan Distillery   DISTILLERY

(☑ 01972-500285; www.adelphidistillery.com; Glenbeg; tours per person from £7; ☺ 10am-6pm Mon-Fri, 11am-5pm Sun Easter-Oct, phone for winter hours) This brand new whisky distillery went into production in 2014, complete with visitor centre and tasting room. Although you will be able to see the whisky-making process, the finished product will be matured in casks until at least 2020 before being bottled as a single malt.

Ardnamurchan Lighthouse   LIGHTHOUSE

(☑ 01972-510210; www.ardnamurchanlighthouse. com; Ardnamurchan Point; visitor centre adult/child £3/2, guided tour £6/4; ☺ 10am-5pm Apr-Oct; ⏸) The final 6 miles of road from Kilchoan to Ardnamurchan Point end at this 36m-high, grey granite tower, built in 1849 by the 'Lighthouse Stevensons' – family of Robert Louis – on the westernmost point of the British mainland. There's a tearoom, and the visitor centre will tell you more than you'll ever need to know about lighthouses, with lots of hands-on stuff for kids.

The guided tour (every half-hour 11am to 4pm) includes a trip to the top of the lighthouse. But the main attraction here is the expansive view over the ocean – this is a superb sunset viewpoint, provided you don't mind driving back in the dark.

Kilchoan   VILLAGE

The scattered crofting village of Kilchoan, the only village of any size west of Salen, is best known for the scenic ruins of 13th-century **Mingary Castle**. The village has a tourist office (p341), a shop, a hotel and a campsite, and there's a ferry to Tobermory on the Isle of Mull.

🛏 Sleeping & Eating

Ardnamurchan Campsite   CAMPSITE £

(☑ 01972-510766; www.ardnamurchanstudycentre. co.uk; Kilchoan; sites per adult/child £9/4; ☺ May-

Sep; 🛜) Basic but beautifully situated camp-site, with the chance of seeing otters from your tent. It's along the Ormsaig road, 2 miles west of Kilchoan village.

★ Ard Daraich
B&B ££

(📞 01855-841384; www.ardgour-selfcatering.co.uk; Sallachan, Ardgour; s/d from £60/75; 🅿 🛜) 🚗 Set back from the main road about 3 miles southwest of Corran Ferry, this handsome West Highland house once belonged to florist Constance Spry (who arranged flowers for Queen Elizabeth II's coronation), and is set in beautiful gardens filled with rhodo-dendrons, azaleas and heathers. Breakfast includes eggs from the owners' hens, and there's a chance of seeing otters and pine martens nearby.

Inn at Ardgour
INN ££

(📞 01855-841225; www.ardgour.biz; Corran Ferry; d/tr/f £115/155/175; 🅿 🛜) This pretty, white-washed coaching inn, draped in colourful flower baskets, makes a great place for a lunch break or an overnight stop. The res-taurant (food served 5pm to 8pm, mains £10 to £18) is set in the row of cottages once oc-cupied by the Corran ferrymen, and serves traditional, homemade Scottish dishes.

Lochview Tearoom
CAFE £

(Ardnamurchan Natural History & Visitor Centre, Glenmore; mains £4-7; ⊙10am-5pm Mon-Sat, 11am-4pm Sun; 🅿 🛜 ♿) The cafe at this wildlife cen-tre (p340) serves coffee, home-baked goods and lunch dishes, including fresh salads and sandwiches and homemade soup.

ℹ Information

Kilchoan Tourist Office (📞 01972-510222; Pier Rd, Kilchoan; ⊙9am-5pm Mon-Sat East-er-Nov) Near the pier; has information and leaflets on walking and wildlife.

ℹ Getting There & Away

Shiel Buses (📞 01397-700700; www.shiel buses.co.uk) bus 506 runs from Fort William to Acharacle, Salen and Kilchoan (£7.60, 3½ hours, one daily Monday to Saturday) via **Corran Ferry** (car £8.20, bicycle & foot passenger free; ⊙every 30min). There's a car ferry between Kilchoan and Tobermory on the Isle of Mull.

Road to the Isles

The 46-mile A830 road from Fort William to Mallaig is traditionally known as the Road to the Isles, as it leads to the jump-ing-off point for ferries to the Small Isles and Skye, itself a stepping stone to the Outer Hebrides. This is a region steeped in Jacobite history, having witnessed both the beginning and the end of Bonnie Prince Charlie's doomed attempt to regain the Brit-ish throne in 1745–46.

The final section of this scenic route, be-tween Arisaig and Mallaig, has been upgrad-ed to a fast straight road. Unless you're in a hurry, opt instead for the more scenic old road (signposted Alternative Coastal Route).

Between the A830 and the A87 far to the north lie Knoydart and Glenelg – Scotland's 'Empty Quarter'.

ℹ Getting There & Around

Shiel Buses bus 500 runs from Fort William to Mallaig (£6.10, 1½ hours, four daily Monday to Friday, one on Saturday) via Glenfinnan (30 minutes), Arisaig (one hour) and Morar (1¼ hours).

The Fort William–Mallaig railway line has four trains a day (three on Sunday), with stops at many points along the way, including Corpach, Glenfinnan, Lochailort, Arisaig and Morar.

Glenfinnan

POP 100

Glenfinnan is hallowed ground for fans of Bonnie Prince Charlie; the monument here marks where he raised his Highland army. It is also a place of pilgrimage for steam train enthusiasts and Harry Potter fans – the fa-mous railway viaduct features in the Potter films, and is regularly traversed by the Jaco-bite Steam Train (p335).

◎ Sights & Activities

Glenfinnan Monument
MONUMENT

FREE This tall column, topped by a statue of a kilted Highlander, was erected in 1815 on the spot where Bonnie Prince Charlie first raised his standard and rallied the Jacobite clans on 19 August 1745, marking the start of his ill-fated campaign, which would end in disaster at Culloden 14 months later. The setting, at the north end of Loch Shiel, is hauntingly beautiful.

Glenfinnan Visitor Centre
INTERPRETATION CENTRE

(NTS; adult/child £3.50/2.50; ⊙9.30am-5pm Jul & Aug, 10am-5pm Easter-Jun, Sep & Oct; 🅿) This centre recounts the story of the '45, as the Jacobite rebellion of 1745 is known, when Bonnie Prince Charlie's loyal clansmen

WORTH A TRIP

GLENUIG INN

Set on a peaceful bay on the Arisaig coast, halfway between Lochailort and Acharacle on the A830, the **Glenuig Inn** (☎01687-470219; www.glenuig.com; Glenuig; B&B s/d/f from £70/110/135, bunkhouse per person £30; P 🖥) ✦ is a great place to get away from it all. As well as offering comfortable accommodation, good food (mains £10 to £25, served noon to 9pm) and real ale on tap, it's a great base for exploring Arisaig, Morar and the Loch Shiel area.

Rockhopper Sea Kayaking (☎07739-837344; www.rockhopperscotland.co.uk; half-/full day £45/80) can take you on a guided kayak tour along the wild and beautiful coastline, starting and finishing at the inn.

marched and fought their way from Glenfinnan south via Edinburgh to Derby, then back north to final defeat at Culloden.

Glenfinnan

Station Museum   MUSEUM

(www.glenfinnanstationmuseum.co.uk; admission by donation, suggested £1; ⊘9am-5pm Easter-Oct; P) This fascinating little museum records the epic tale of building the West Highland railway line. The famous 21-arch **Glenfinnan viaduct**, just east of the station, was built in 1901, and featured in several Harry Potter movies. A pleasant walk of around 0.75 miles east from the station (signposted) leads to a viewpoint for the viaduct and for Loch Shiel.

Loch Shiel Cruises   CRUISE

(☎07801-537617; www.highlandcruises.co.uk; per person £10-19; ⊘Apr-Sep) Offers boat trips along Loch Shiel, with the opportunity for spotting golden eagles and other wildlife. There are one- to 2½-hour cruises Monday, Tuesday, Thursday and Friday. On Wednesday the boat goes the full length of the loch to **Acharacle** (one way/return £18/26), calling at Polloch and Dalilea, allowing for a range of walks and bike rides using the forestry track on the eastern shore. The boat departs from a jetty near Glenfinnan House Hotel.

🛏 Sleeping & Eating

Sleeping Car Bunkhouse   HOSTEL £

(☎01397-722295; www.glenfinnanstationmuseum.co.uk; Glenfinnan Station; per person £15, entire coach £130; ⊘May-Oct; P) Two converted railway carriages at Glenfinnan Station house this unusual 10-berth bunkhouse and the atmospheric **Dining Car Tearoom** (☎01397-722300; mains £6-10; ⊘9am-4.30pm May-Oct; P).

⭐**Prince's House Hotel**   INN £££

(☎01397-722246; www.glenfinnan.co.uk; s/d from £85/140; P) A delightful old coaching inn dating from 1658, the Prince's House is a great place to pamper yourself – ask for the spacious, tartan-clad Stuart Room (£225), complete with four-poster bed, if you want to stay in the oldest part of the hotel. The relaxed but well-regarded restaurant specialises in Scottish produce (four-course dinner £44).

There's no documented evidence that Bonnie Prince Charlie actually stayed here in 1745, but it was the only sizeable house in Glenfinnan at that time, so...

Arisaig & Morar

The 5 miles of coast between Arisaig and Morar is a fretwork of rocky islets, inlets and gorgeous silver-sand beaches backed by dunes and machair, with stunning sunset views across the sea to the silhouetted peaks of Eigg and Rum. The **Silver Sands of Morar**, as they are known, draw crowds of bucket-and-spade holidaymakers in July and August, when the many campsites scattered along the coast are filled to overflowing.

👁 Sights

Camusdarach Beach   BEACH

(P) Fans of the movie *Local Hero* still make pilgrimages to Camusdarach Beach, just south of Morar, which starred in the film as Ben's beach. To find it, look for the car park 800m north of Camusdarach campsite; from here, a wooden footbridge and a 400m walk through the dunes lead to the beach. (The village that featured in the film is on the other side of the country, at Pennan.)

Land, Sea & Islands Visitor Centre MUSEUM

(www.arisaigcommunitytrust.org.uk; ⊘10am-6pm Mon-Sat, noon-5pm Sun Apr-Oct, shorter hours Sat-Mon only Nov-Mar; P) **FREE** This centre in Arisaig village houses exhibits on the cultural and natural history of the region. A small but fascinating exhibition explains the part played by the local area as a base for training spies for the Special Operations Executive (SOE, forerunner of MI6) during WWII, including famous names such as Violette Szabo (made famous by the 1958 film *Carve Her Name With Pride*) and the Czech paratroopers who assassinated Nazi leader Reinhard Heydrich in Prague in 1942.

Arisaig Marine CRUISE
(🖉01687-450224; www.arisaig.co.uk; Arisaig Harbour; ☺late Apr-Sep) Runs cruises from Arisaig harbour to Eigg, Rum and Muck, with four hours ashore on Eigg, or two to three hours on Rum or Muck. The trips include whale-watching, with up to an hour for close viewing.

🛏 Sleeping & Eating

There are at least a half-dozen campsites between Arisaig and Morar; all are open in summer only, and are often full in July and August, so book ahead.

Camusdarach Campsite CAMPSITE **£**
(🖉01687-450221; www.camusdarach.co.uk; Arisaig; tent/campervan sites £10/15, plus per person £5; ☺Mar-Oct; 🛜🐾) 🏊 A small and nicely landscaped site with good facilities, only three minutes' walk from the *Local Hero* beach (p342) via a gate in the northwest corner.

Leven House B&B **££**
(🖉01687-450238; www.thelevenhouse.co.uk; Arisaig; s/d from £45/60; 🅿) Set back from the main road, three miles east of Arisaig village, this peaceful farmhouse offers a warm welcome and gorgeous views over the sea towards the Small Isles. Breakfasts include homemade bread and marmalade, and the friendly host is a mine of information about local history and wildlife. There's also a lovely two-bedroom, self-catering cottage (£400 a week).

Old Library Lodge & Restaurant SCOTTISH **££**
(🖉01687-450651; www.oldlibrary.co.uk; Arisaig; mains £10-19; 🅿🐾) 🏊 The Old Library is a charming restaurant with rooms (single/double £75/120) set in converted 200-year-old stables overlooking the waterfront in Arisaig village. The lunch menu concentrates on soups, burgers and smoked fish or meat platters, while dinner is a more sophisticated affair offering local seafood, beef and lamb.

Mallaig
POP 800

If you're travelling between Fort William and Skye, you may find yourself overnighting in the bustling fishing and ferry port of Mallaig (*mahl*-ig). Indeed, it makes a good base for a series of day trips by ferry to the Small Isles and Knoydart.

◉ Sights & Activities

Mallaig Heritage Centre MUSEUM
(🖉01687-462085; www.mallaigheritage.org.uk; Station Rd; adult/child £2.50/1; ☺11am-4pm Mon-Fri, noon-4pm Sat Apr-Oct, longer hours Jul & Aug, shorter hours Nov-Mar) The village's rainy-day attractions are limited to this heritage centre, which covers the archaeology and history of the region, including the heart-rending tale of the Highland Clearances in Knoydart.

Sea.fari Adventures BOATING
(🖉01471-833316; adult/child £42/34; ☺Easter-Sep) Sea.fari runs three-hour whale-watching cruises in a high-speed inflatable boat. These trips have a high success rate for spotting minke whales in summer (an average of 180 sightings a year), with rarer sightings of bottlenose dolphins and basking sharks.

🛏 Sleeping & Eating

Seaview Guest House B&B **££**
(🖉01687-462059; www.seaviewguesthousemallaig.com; Main St; r per person £35-40, cottage per week £400-495; ☺Mar–mid-Nov; 🅿) This comfortable B&B has grand views over the harbour, not only from the upstairs bedrooms but also from the breakfast room. There's also a cute little cottage next door that offers self-catering accommodation (www.selfcateringmallaig.com; one double and one twin room).

Springbank Guest House B&B **££**
(🖉01687-462459; www.springbank-mallaig.co.uk; East Bay; s/d £35/65; 🐾) The Springbank is a traditional West Highland house with six homely guest bedrooms, with superb views across the harbour to the Cuillin of Skye.

Jaffy's FISH & CHIPS **£**
(www.jaffys.co.uk; Station Rd; mains £4-8; ☺noon-2pm & 5-8pm Mon-Sat May-Nov, 5-8pm Thu-Sat only Dec-Apr) 🏊 Owned by a third-generation fish merchant's family, Mallaig's chippy serves superbly fresh fish and

chips, as well as kippers, prawns and other seafood.

Fish Market Restaurant SEAFOOD **££**
(☑ 01687-462299; www.thefishmarketrestaurant.co.uk; Station Rd; mains £10-22; ☺ noon-3pm & 6-9pm) 🥢 At least half-a-dozen signs in Mallaig advertise 'seafood restaurant', but this bright, modern, bistro-style place next to the harbour is our favourite, serving simply prepared scallops, smoked salmon, mussels, and fresh Mallaig haddock fried in breadcrumbs, as well as the tastiest Cullen skink on the west coast.

Upstairs is a **coffee shop** (Station Rd; mains £6-8; ☺ 11am-5pm, to 6pm Jun-Aug).

❶ Information

Mallaig has a **tourist office** (☑ 01687-462170; East Bay; ☺ 10am-5.30pm Mon-Fri, 10.15am-3.45pm Sat, noon-3.30pm Sun), a post office, a bank with ATM and a **co-op supermarket** (Station Rd; ☺ 8am-10pm Mon-Sat, 9am-9pm Sun).

❶ Getting There & Away

BOAT

A passenger ferry operated by Western Isles Cruises (p345) links Mallaig to Inverie on the Knoydart Peninsula (25 to 40 minutes) four times daily Monday to Saturday from April to October.

CalMac (p345) operates the passenger-only ferry from Mallaig to the following destinations in the Small Isles:

Canna £10.50 return, two hours, six a week

Eigg £7.70 return, 1¼ hours, five a week

Muck £8.90 return, 1½ hours, five a week

Rum £8.30 return, 1¼ hours, five a week

There are Calmac car ferry services to Armadale in Skye (car/passenger £9.40/2.80, 30 minutes, eight daily Monday to Saturday, five to seven on Sunday), and Lochboisdale in South Uist (car/passenger £56/10.15, 3½ hours, one a day).

BUS

Shiel Buses (p338) bus 500 runs from Fort William to Mallaig (£6.10, 1½ hours, three daily Monday to Friday, plus one daily weekends April to September) via Glenfinnan (£3.30, 30 minutes) and Arisaig (£5.60, one hour).

TRAIN

The West Highland line runs between Fort William and Mallaig (£12.20, 1½ hours, four daily, three on Sunday).

Knoydart Peninsula

POP 150

The Knoydart peninsula – a rugged landscape of wild mountains and lonely sea lochs – is the only sizeable area in Britain that remains inaccessible to the motor car, cut off by miles of rough country and the embracing arms of Lochs Nevis and Hourn – Gaelic for the lochs of Heaven and Hell. The main reasons for visiting are to climb the remote 1020m peak of **Ladhar Bheinn** (laar-ven), which affords some of the west coast's finest views, or just to enjoy the feeling of being cut off from the rest of the world. There are no shops, no TV and no mobile-phone reception (although there is internet access); electricity is provided by a private hydroelectric scheme – truly 'off the grid' living!

No road penetrates this wilderness of rugged hills – **Inverie**, its sole village, can only be reached by ferry from Mallaig, or on foot from the remote road's end at Kinloch Hourn (a tough 16-mile hike). A 4WD track leads northwest from Inverie for 7 miles to the outposts of **Doune** and **Airor**, which offer even more remote accommodation options. For more information and full list of places to stay – some of them surprisingly luxurious – see www.visitknoydart.co.uk.

🛏 Sleeping & Eating

Knoydart Foundation Bunkhouse HOSTEL **£**
(☑ 01687-462163; www.knoydart-foundation.com; Inverie; dm adult/child £17/10; @ 🤶) 🥢 A 15-minute walk east of Inverie ferry pier, this is a cosy hostel with wood-burning stove, kitchen and drying room.

Long Beach Campsite CAMPSITE **£**
(Inverie; per tent & 1 person £4, per extra person £3) A basic but beautiful campsite, a 10-minute walk east of the ferry; there's a water supply, fire pits and composting toilet, but no showers. Ranger comes around to collect fees; firewood available for £4.50 a bundle.

Knoydart Lodge B&B **££**
(☑ 01687-460129; www.knoydartlodge.co.uk; Inverie; lodge per week from £800, apt from £200; 🤶🤶🐾) This must be some of the most spacious and luxurious accommodation on the whole west coast, let alone in Knoydart. The fantastic, modern timber-built lodge – reminiscent of an Alpine chalet – sleeps up to eight in four large, stylish bedrooms just

a short stroll from the beach. There's also a studio apartment for two.

★ Old Forge   PUB FOOD ££

(☑ 01687-462267; www.theoldforge.co.uk; Inverie; mains £10-23; ☺ 2.30pm-midnight Thu-Tue Apr-Oct, 4-11pm Thu-Tue Nov-Mar; 🖥️ 🍴) 🍴 The Old Forge is listed in the *Guinness Book of Records* as Britain's most remote pub. It's surprisingly sophisticated – as well as having real ale on tap, there's an Italian coffee machine for those wilderness lattes and cappuccinos. Food is served till 10pm; the house special is a seafood platter (£35), all ingredients sourced within 7 miles of the pub.

In the evening you can sit by the fire, pint of beer in hand and join the impromptu *ceilidh* (an evening of traditional Scottish entertainment including music, song and dance) that seems to take place just about nightly.

❶ Getting There & Away

Western Isles Cruises (☑ 01687-462233; westernislescruises.co.uk; one-way/day return £10/18, bike £2) runs a asenger ferry linking Mallaig to Inverie (25 to 40 minutes) four times daily Monday to Saturday from April to October. Taking the morning boat gives you up to 5½ hours ashore in Knoydart before the return trip (first and last boats of the day should be booked in advance). There's also an afternoon sailing between Inverie and Tarbet on the south side of Loch Nevis, allowing walkers to hike along the northern shore of Loch Morar to Tarbet and return by boat (£15 Tarbet–Inverie–Mallaig).

It's also possible to join the boat just for the cruise, without going ashore (£20 for Mallaig–Inverie–Tarbet–Inverie–Mallaig).

SMALL ISLES

The scattered jewels of the Small Isles – Rum, Eigg, Muck and Canna – lie strewn across the silvery-blue Cuillin Sound to the south of Skye. Their distinctive outlines enliven the glorious views from the beaches of Arisaig and Morar.

Rum is the biggest and boldest of the four, a miniature Skye of pointed peaks and dramatic sunset silhouettes. Eigg is the most pastoral and populous, dominated by the miniature sugarloaf mountain of the Sgurr. Muck is a botanist's delight with its wildflowers and unusual alpine plants, and Canna is a craggy bird sanctuary made of magnetic rocks.

If your time is limited and you can only visit one island, choose Eigg or Rum; they have the most to offer on a day trip.

❶ Getting There & Away

The main ferry operator is **CalMac** (☑ 0800 066 5000; www.calmac.co.uk), which operates the passenger-only ferry from Mallaig.

Canna £10.50 return, two hours, six a week
Eigg £7.70 return, 1¼ hours, five a week
Muck £8.90 return, 1½ hours, five a week
Rum £8.30 return, 1¼ hours, five a week

You can also hop between the islands without returning to Mallaig, but the timetable is complicated and it requires a bit of planning – you would need at least five days to visit all four islands. Bicycles are carried for free.

In summer **Arisaig Marine** (p343) operates day cruises from Arisaig harbour to Eigg (£18 return, one hour, six a week), Rum (£25 return, 2½ hours, two or three a week) and Muck (£20 return, two hours, three a week). The trips include whale-watching, with up to an hour for close viewing. Sailing times allow four or five hours ashore on Eigg, and two or three hours on Muck or Rum.

Rum

POP 22

The Isle of Rum (www.isleofrum.com) – the biggest and most spectacular of the Small Isles – was once known as the Forbidden Island. Cleared of its crofters in the early 19th century to make way for sheep, from 1888 to 1957 it was the private sporting estate of the Bulloughs, a nouveau-riche Lancashire family who made their fortune in the textile industry. Curious outsiders who ventured too close to the island were liable to find themselves staring down the wrong end of a gamekeeper's shotgun.

The island was sold to the Nature Conservancy in 1957 and has since been a wildlife reserve noted for its deer, wild goats, ponies, golden and white-tailed eagles, and a 120,000-strong nesting colony of Manx shearwaters. Its dramatic, rocky mountains, known as the Rum Cuillin for their similarity to the peaks on neighbouring Skye, draw hill walkers and climbers.

◉ Sights & Activities

There's some great coastal and mountain walking on the island, including a couple of easy, waymarked nature trails in the woods around Kinloch. The first path on the left after leaving the pier leads to an otter hide (signposted).

The climb to the island's highest point, **Askival** (812m), is a strenuous hike and involves a bit of rock scrambling (allow six hours for the round trip from Kinloch).

Glen Harris is a 10-mile round trip from Kinloch, on a rough 4WD track – allow four to five hours' walking, or two hours by bike. You can hire bikes from **Rum Bike Hire** (☑ 01687-462744; www.rumbikehire.co.uk; per day £15) at the craft shop near Kinloch Castle.

★ Kinloch Castle CASTLE

(☑ 01687-462037; www.isleofrum.com; adult/child £9/4.50; ☺ guided tours daily Apr-Oct, to coincide with ferry times) When George Bullough – a dashing, Harrow-educated cavalry officer – inherited Rum along with half his father's fortune in 1891, he became one of the wealthiest bachelors in Britain. Bullough blew half his inheritance on building his dream bachelor pad – the ostentatious Kinloch Castle. Since the Bulloughs left, the castle has survived as a perfect time capsule of upper-class Edwardian eccentricity – the guided tour should not be missed.

Bullough shipped in pink sandstone from Dumfriesshire and 250,000 tonnes of Ayrshire topsoil for the gardens, and paid his workers a shilling extra a day to wear tweed kilts – just so they'd look more picturesque. Hummingbirds were kept in the greenhouses and alligators in the garden, and guests were entertained with an orchestrion, the Edwardian equivalent of a Bose hi-fi system (one of only six that were ever made).

⌂ Sleeping

Accommodation on Rum is strictly limited – there is only one B&B, the campsite and the bunkhouse. Booking is essential, except for campers. There are also two bothies (unlocked cottages with no facilities, for the use of hikers) on the island, and wild camping is permitted.

Rum Bunkhouse HOSTEL £

(☑ 01687-460318; www.rumbunkhouse.co.uk; Kinloch; dm/tw £23/50; ☎) This beautiful, Scandinavian-style timber building was purpose-built as a hostel in 2014, and now provides the island's main accommodation, complete with hot showers, a wood-burning stove and picture windows overlooking the sea.

Kinloch Village Campsite CAMPSITE £

(www.isleofrum.com; sites per adult/child £6/3, cabins £22) Situated between the pier and Kinloch Castle, this basic campsite has toilets, a water supply and hot showers (from April to October). There are also two wooden camping cabins (sleeping two persons), which must be booked in advance at rumka bins@gmail.com.

ⓘ Information

Kinloch, where the ferry lands, is the island's only settlement; it has a small **grocery shop** (☺ 5-7pm, also 10am-noon on ferry days), post office and public telephone, and a **tourist office** (☺ 8.30am-5pm Apr-Oct) near the pier where you can get information and leaflets on walking and wildlife. For more information see www.isleofrum.com.

Bring plenty of food supplies, as there is only one tearoom, and the grocery shop opening times are limited.

Eigg

POP 90

The island of Eigg (www.isleofeigg.net) made history in 1997 when it became the first Highland estate to be bought out by its inhabitants. The island is now owned and managed by the Isle of Eigg Heritage Trust, a partnership among the islanders, Highland Council and the Scottish Wildlife Trust.

The island takes its name from the Old Norse *egg* (meaning 'edge'), a reference to the Sgurr of Eigg (393m), an impressive minimountain that towers over Galmisdale, the main settlement. Ringed by vertical cliffs on three sides, it's composed of pitchstone lava with columnar jointing similar to that seen on the Isle of Staffa and at the Giant's Causeway in Northern Ireland.

⚡ Activities

The climb to the summit of the **Sgurr of Eigg** (4.5 miles round trip; allow three to four hours) begins on the road that leads steeply uphill from the pier, which continues through the woods to a red-roofed cottage. Go through the gate to the right of the cottage and turn left; just 20m along the road a cairn on the right marks the start of a boggy footpath that leads over the eastern shoulder of the Sgurr, then traverses beneath the northern cliffs until it makes its way up onto the summit ridge.

On a fine day the views from the top are magnificent – Rum and Skye to the north, Muck and Coll to the south, Ardnamurchan Lighthouse to the southeast and Ben Nevis shouldering above the eastern horizon. Take binoculars – on a calm summer's day there's a good chance of seeing minke whales feeding down below in the Sound of Muck.

A shorter walk (2 miles; allow 1½ hours round trip, and bring a torch) leads west from the pier to the spooky and claustrophobic **Uamh Fraing** (Massacre Cave). Start as for the Sgurr of Eigg, but 800m from the pier turn left through a gate and into a field. Follow the 4WD track and fork left before a white cottage to pass below it. A footpath continues across the fields to reach a small gate in a fence; go through it and descend a ridge towards the shore.

The cave entrance is tucked inconspicuously down to the left of the ridge. The entrance is tiny – almost a hands-and-knees job – but the cave opens out inside and runs a long way back. Go right to the back, turn off your torch, and imagine the cave packed shoulder to shoulder with terrified men, women and children. Then imagine the panic as your enemies start piling firewood into the entrance. Almost the entire population of Eigg – around 400 people – sought refuge in this cave when the MacLeods of Skye raided the island in 1577. In an act of inhuman cruelty, the raiders lit a fire in the narrow entrance and everyone inside died of asphyxiation. There are more than a few ghosts floating around in here.

🛏️ Sleeping & Eating

All accommodation should be booked in advance. Wild camping is allowed. For a full listing of self-catering accommodation, see www.iseleofeigg.net.

Eigg Organics   CAMPSITE £
(☑ 01687-482480; www.eiggorganics.co.uk; Cleadale; per tent £5, yurt £40-45; 🐾) This organic croft in the north of the island has a campsite with basic facilities, and also offers accommodation for two in a Mongolian yurt.

Glebe Barn   HOSTEL £
(☑ 01687-315099; www.glebebarn.co.uk; Galmisdale; dm/tw £20/45; 🐾) Excellent bunkhouse accommodation in the middle of the island, with a smart, maple-floored lounge with central fireplace, modern kitchen, laundry, drying room, and bright, clean dorms and bedrooms.

Lageorna   B&B ££
(☑ 01687-460081; www.lageorna.com; Cleadale; s/d £75/100, incl dinner £95/150; 🐾) 🍽 This converted croft house and lodge in the island's northwest is Eigg's most luxurious accommodation. Rooms are fitted with beautiful, locally made, 'driftwood-style' timber beds, and even have iPod docks (but no mobile-phone reception). Evening meals are available, with the menu heavy on locally grown vegetables, seafood and venison.

Galmisdale Bay   CAFE £
(☑ 01687-482487; www.galmisdale-bay.com; Galmisdale; mains £5-10; ⊗ 10.30am-5pm Sun-Thu, 10am-11pm Fri & Sat May-Sep, shorter hours Oct-Apr) 🍽 The cafe-bar above the ferry pier is the social hub of the community, and serves tasty, great-value food. Winter opening hours coincide with ferry arrivals and departures.

ℹ️ Information

The building above the pier, **An Laimhrig** (www.isleofeiggshop.co.uk; ⊗ 10am-5pm Mon, Tue & Fri, 11am-5pm Wed, 11am-3pm Thu, 1-5pm Sat & Sun May–mid-Oct, shorter hours & closed Wed winter), houses a grocery store, post office, craft shop and cafe. You can hire **bikes** (☑ 07855-363252; www.eiggadventures.co.uk; Galmisdale; per day £15) here, too.

Canna

POP 12

The island of Canna (www.theisleofcanna.com) is a moorland plateau of black basalt rock, just 5 miles long and 1.25 miles wide; it was gifted to the National Trust for Scotland in 1981 by its owner, the Gaelic scholar and author John Lorne Campbell. **Compass Hill** (143m), at the northeastern corner, contains enough magnetite (an iron oxide mineral) to deflect the navigation compasses in passing yachts.

The ferry arrives at the hamlet of **A'Chill** at the eastern end of the island, where visiting sailors have left extensive graffiti on the rock face south of the harbour. There's a tearoom and craft shop by the harbour, and a tiny post office in a hut. There is no mobile-phone reception.

You can walk to **An Coroghon**, just east of the ferry pier, a medieval stone tower perched atop a sea cliff, and continue to Compass Hill, or take a longer hike along the southern shore past **Canna House** (guided tour £5; ⊗ 1-2.30pm Wed, 4-5.30pm Sat May-Sep) (the former home of John Lorne Campbell) and an ornately decorated **early Christian stone cross**. In 2012 a *bullaun,* or 'cursing stone', with an inscribed cross was discovered nearby; these are common in Ireland, but this was the first to be found in Scotland.

Facilities are limited. **Tighard** (☑01687-462474; www.tighard.co.uk; s/d £80/130; �🖥) is the only B&B. **Canna Campsite** (☑01687-462477; www.cannacampsite.com/; tent sites £12, pod/caravan £35-55; 🖥) provides grassy pitches for tents, and accommodation in static caravans and timber glamping pods.

The only eating place on the island of Canna is **Cafe Canna** (☑01687-462251; www.cafecanna.co.uk; mains £10-15; ⊙1-9pm Sun-Fri Easter-Sep, longer hours incl 6-9pm Sat mid Jun-Aug; 🖥) 🍃. This cafe serves meal such as hadddock and chips (fish freshly landed at Mallaig) and Canna rabbit stew, in a lovely setting beside the harbour.

Muck
POP 40

The tiny island of Muck (www.isleofmuck.com), measuring just 2 miles by 1 mile, has exceptionally fertile soil, and the island is carpeted with wildflowers in spring and early summer. It takes its name from the Gaelic *muc* (pig), and pigs are still raised here.

Ferries call at the southern settlement of Port Mor. There's a tearoom and craft shop above the pier, which also acts as a tourist office.

Northern Highlands & Islands

Why Go?

Scotland's vast and melancholy soul is here: an epic land with a stark beauty that indelibly imprints the hearts of those who journey through the mist and mountains, rock and heather. Long, sun-blessed summer evenings are the pay-off for so many days of horizontal rain. It's simply magical.

Stone tells stories throughout. The chambered cairns of Caithness and structures of the Western Isles are testament to the skills of prehistoric builders; cragtop castles and broken walls of abandoned crofts tell of the Highlands' turbulent history.

Outdoors is the place to be, whatever the weather; there's nothing like comparing windburn or mud-ruined boots over a well-deserved dram by the crackling fire of a Highland pub. The landscape lends itself to activity, from woodland strolls to thrilling mountain-bike descents, from sea-kayaking to Munro-bagging, from beachcombing to birdwatching. Best are the locals, big-hearted and straight-talking; make it your business to get to know them.

When to Go

Portree

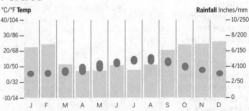

Jun Long evenings bathe achingly sublime landscapes in dreamy light.

Jul The Hebridean Celtic Festival is a top time to experience the culture of the Outer Hebrides.

Sep Less busy than summer, the midges have gone and temperatures are (maybe!) still OK.

Northern Highlands & Islands Highlights

1 **North Coast 500** (p360) Driving one of Europe's most spectacularly scenic road trips.

2 **Ullapool** (p367) Gorging on fresh, succulent seafood in this delightful town with its picture-perfect harbour.

3 **Harris** (p391) Dipping your toes in the water at some of the world's most beautiful beaches in the Western Isles.

4 **Cuillin Hills** (p381) Shouldering the challenge of these hills, with their rugged silhouettes brooding over the skyscape of Skye.

5 **Far Northwest** (p349) Picking your jaw up off the floor as you marvel at the epic Highland scenery.

6 **Cape Wrath** (p364) Taking the trip out to Britain's gloriously remote northwestern shoulder.

7 **Plockton** (p373) Relaxing in a postcard-pretty village where the Highlands meet the Caribbean.

8 **Skye** (p377) Launching yourself in a sea kayak to explore the otter-rich waters around the Isle of Skye.

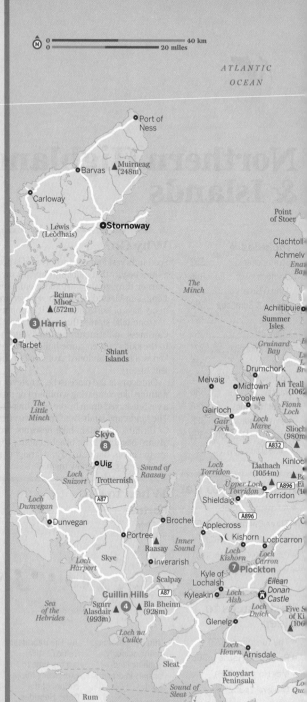

EAST COAST

In both landscape and character, the east coast is where the real barrenness of the Highlands begins to unfold. A gentle splendour and a sense of escapism mark the route along the twisting A9, as it heads north for the last of Scotland's far-flung, mainland population outposts. With only a few exceptions the tourism frenzy is left behind once the road traverses Cromarty Firth and snakes its way along wild and pristine coastline.

While the interior is dominated by the vast and mournful Sutherland mountain range, along the coast great heather-covered hills heave themselves out of the wild North Sea. Rolling farmland drops suddenly into the icy waters, and small, historic towns are moored precariously on the coast's edge.

Strathpeffer

POP 1100

Strathpeffer is a charming old Highland spa town, with creaking pavilions and grandiose hotels dripping with faded grandeur. It rose to prominence during Victorian times, when the fashionable flocked here in huge numbers to bathe in, wash with and drink the sulphurous waters. The tourist influx led to the construction of grand buildings and architectural follies.

Sights & Activities

Locals have put together excellent interactive tours of Strathpeffer. Download them to your phone at www.strathpeffer.org, or pick up a tablet from participating places around town.

There are many good signposted walking trails around Strathpeffer.

Highland Museum of Childhood MUSEUM
(☏01997-421031; www.highlandmuseumofchildhood.org.uk; Old Train Station; adult/child £3/1.75; ☺10am-5pm Mon-Sat, 2-4pm Sun Apr-Oct) Strathpeffer's former train station houses a wide range of social-history displays about childhood and also has activities for children, including a dressing-up box and toy train. In the complex there's also a gift shop for presents for a little somebody and a peaceful cafe. Call for winter hours, as it does open some days.

**Spa Pavilion &
Upper Pump Room** HISTORIC BUILDING
(www.strathpefferpavilion.org; Golf Course Rd; ☺Pump Room 10am-5pm Jun-Aug, 10am-5pm Tue-Thu & Sat, 1-5pm Mon, Fri & Sun Sep-Dec & Mar-May) FREE In Strathpeffer's heyday, the Pavilion was the social centre, venue for dances, lectures and concerts. These days it's been renovated as a performing arts venue. The neighbouring Upper Pump Room has some splendid displays showing the bizarre lengths Victorians went to for a healthy glow and local art exhibitions, as well as artisanal sweets and tourist information in the friendly shop. Opening hours vary.

Square Wheels Cycles CYCLING
(☏01997-421000; www.squarewheels.biz; The Square; half-/full day/2nd day £12/20/10; ☺10am-6pm Tue-Sat) Right in the centre of town. Hires out mountain bikes and gives route information; prices decrease with multiday hire.

🛌 Sleeping & Eating

★**Craigvar** B&B ££
(☏01997-421622; www.craigvar.com; The Square; s/d £65/98; 🅿🛜) Luxury living with a refined touch is what you'll find in this delightful Georgian house in the village's heart. Classy little extras are all here, including a welcome drink, Highland-Belgian chocolates, bathrobes and fresh fruit. The owner offers wonderfully genuine hospitality. Light, elegant rooms are great, with fabulous modern bathrooms and all sorts of thoughtful extras.

One double has a particularly pleasing outlook and a sensational bed – you'll need to collapse back into it after the gourmet breakfast.

Coul House Hotel HOTEL £££
(☏01997-421487; www.coulhousehotel.com; Contin; s/d from £95/175; 🅿@🛜🐾) At Contin, south of Strathpeffer on the A835, Coul House dates from 1821 but has a light, airy feel in contrast to many country houses of this vintage. It's family run, and very cordial. Beautiful dining and lounge areas are complemented by elegant rooms with views over the lovely gardens; superiors look out to the mountains beyond.

There are forest trails for walking or mountain biking right on the doorstep and a good restaurant. You can often find lower prices on the website.

Red Poppy BISTRO ££
(☏01997-423332; www.redpoppyrestaurant.co.uk; Main Rd; mains £13-18; ☺noon-3pm & 5-9pm Tue-Sat, noon-3pm Sun; 🛜) On the main road opposite the spa buildings, this is comfortably Strathpeffer's best eatery. The casual modern interior with its bright red chairs is the venue for confident, well-presented dishes

covering game and other classic British ingredients. It's a little cheaper at lunchtime, when set-priced menus are available.

ℹ Getting There & Away

Stagecoach operates from Inverness to Strathpeffer (£5.30, 40 minutes, hourly Monday to Saturday, four on Sunday). Inverness to Gairloch and Durness services, plus some Inverness to Ullapool buses, also drop in.

Tain

POP 3700

Scotland's oldest royal burgh, Tain is a proud sandstone town that rose to prominence as pilgrims descended to venerate the relics of St Duthac, who is commemorated by the 12th-century ruins of St Duthac's Chapel, and St Duthus Church.

◉ Sights

Tain Through Time   MUSEUM

(☑ 01862-894089; www.tainmuseum.org.uk; Tower St; adult/child £3.50/2.50; ⊘ 10am-5pm Mon-Fri Apr-Oct, plus Sat Jun-Aug) Set in the grounds of St Duthus Church is Tain Through Time, an entertaining heritage centre with a colourful and educational display on St Duthac, King James IV and key moments in Scottish history. Another building focuses on the town's fine silversmithing tradition. Admission includes an audioguided walk around town.

Glenmorangie   DISTILLERY

(☑ 01862-892477; www.glenmorangie.com; tours £7, special tour £30; ⊘ tours 10am-4pm Jun-Aug, 10am-3pm Mon-Sat Apr-May & Sep-Oct, by appointment Mon-Fri Nov-Mar) Located on Tain's northern outskirts, Glenmorangie (emphasis on the second syllable) produces a fine lightish malt, subjected to a number of different cask finishes for variation. The tour is less in-depth than some but finishes with a free dram.

🛏 Sleeping & Eating

Golf View House   B&B ££

(☑ 01862-892856; www.bedandbreakfasttain.co.uk; 13 Knockbreck Rd; s/d £65/90; 🅿 🛜) Set in an old manse in a secluded location just off the main drag, this spot offers magnificent views

NORTHERN HIGHLANDS & ISLANDS TAIN

CROFTING & THE CLEARANCES

The wild empty spaces up here are among Europe's least populated zones, but this wasn't always so. Ruins of cottages in desolate areas are mute witnesses to one of the most heartless episodes of Scottish history: the Highland Clearances.

Until the 19th century the most common form of farming settlement here was the *baile,* a group of a dozen or so families who farmed the land granted to them by the local chieftain in return for military service and a portion of the harvest. The arable land was divided into strips called *rigs,* which were allocated to different families by annual ballot so that each took turns at getting the poorer soils; this system was known as *runrig.* The families worked the land communally and their cattle shared grazing land.

After the Battle of Culloden, however, the king banned private armies and new laws made the clan chiefs actual owners of their traditional lands, often vast tracts of territory. With the prospect of unimagined riches allied to a depressing failure of imagination, the lairds decided that sheep were more profitable than agriculture and proceeded to evict tens of thousands of farmers. These desperate folk were forced to head for the cities in the hope of finding work or to emigrate to the Americas or southern hemisphere. Those who stayed were forced to eke a living from narrow plots of marginal agricultural land, often close to the coast. This form of smallholding became known as crofting. The small patch of land barely provided a living and had to be supplemented by other work such as fishing and kelp-gathering. It was always precarious, as rights were granted on a year-by-year basis, so at any moment a crofter could lose not only the farm but also the house they'd built on it.

The late 19th-century economic depression meant many couldn't pay their rent. This time, however, they resisted expulsion, instead forming the Highland Land Reform Association and their own political party. Their resistance led the government to accede to several demands, including security of tenure, fair rents and eventually the supply of land for new crofts. Crofters now have the right to purchase their farmland and 2004 laws finally abolished the feudal system, which created so much misery.

over fields and water. Impeccable rooms are very cheerful and bright, and there's an upbeat feel, with delicious breakfasts and welcoming hospitality. It's worth the extra for a room with a view.

Platform 1864
BISTRO, BAR ££

(☑01862-894181; 1 Station Rd; mains £11-20; ⊙12.30-2.30pm & 5.30-9.30pm; 🛜🚹) 🍴 Real love has gone into this excellent restoration of Tain's station building, which has become a handsome wood-clad bar and restaurant, open all day. The menu covers simple bar-style meals as well as local venison and daily specials. The enthusiastic owner and a beer garden make it a fine place to drop by for a drink or coffee at any time too.

❶ Getting There & Away

Stagecoach buses run from Inverness (£9.80, 1¼ hours) roughly hourly; some continue north as far as Thurso.

Trains run daily to Inverness (£13.90, 1¼ hours) and Thurso/Wick (£17.10, 2¾ hours).

Portmahomack
POP 600

Portmahomack is a former fishing village in a flawless spot – off the beaten track, gazing across the water at sometimes snowcapped peaks. It's a lovely place. There have been some fascinating Pictish finds here, and archaeologists believe it may have been the capital of a major Pictish kingdom.

Intriguing **Tarbat Discovery Centre** (☑01862-871351; www.tarbat-discovery.co.uk; Tarbatness Rd; adult/child £3.50/1; ⊙10am-5pm Mon-Sat May-Sep, 2-5pm Mon-Sat Apr & Oct, plus 2-5pm Sun Jun-Oct) has some excellent carved Pictish stones. When 'crop circles' appeared in aerial photos a few years ago, the foundations of an Iron Age settlement were discovered around the village church; ongoing investigation revealed a Pictish monastery and evidence of production of illuminated manuscripts. Archaeologists theorise that this could have been the nexus of a major Pictish kingdom, and a major excavation project is underway. The exhibition includes the church's spooky crypt.

Seafood aficionados shouldn't miss the **Oystercatcher** (☑01862-871560; www.the-oystercatcher.co.uk; Main St; mains £14-24; ⊙6-9pm Wed-Sat, 12.30-3pm Sun Apr-Oct; 🅿🛜), a quirky restaurant, which serves up excellent seafood in a small room on the Portmahomack waterfront. Lobster is a speciality and beau-

tifully done; other dishes have French roots and are served with rich sauces. Delicate amuse-bouche and sorbet servings add a lighter touch. Don't miss the duck-fat chips or madeira selection: just one part of a brilliant wine list.

It also offers three cosy rooms (doubles £85 to £112); the rate includes one of Scotland's most amazing breakfasts, with numerous gourmet options.

Stagecoach buses run from Portmahomack to Tain (£2.55, 25 minutes, four to five Monday to Friday).

Bonar Bridge & Around

While the main road north crosses Dornoch Firth near Tain, an alternative scenic route brings you to the almost-joined villages of Ardgay and Bonar Bridge. This is an area worth exploring, with reminders of the Clearances, fine old-growth forest and good scope for outdoor activities. The A836 to Lairg branches west at Bonar Bridge.

From Ardgay, a single-track road leads 10 miles up Strathcarron to **Croick**, the scene of notorious evictions during the 1845 Clearances. You can still see the evocative messages scratched by refugee crofters from Glencalvie on the eastern windows of Croick Church.

Near Croick, **Alladale Wilderness Reserve** (☑07770-419671; www.alladale.com; Ardgay; self-catering per week from £950; 🅿🛜🐾) lodge is part of a notable rewilding project. The main lodge (which includes meals) is for entire hire only, so you'd want a large group (it sleeps 12 to 14). Smaller buildings – a farmhouse and a cottage – accommodate up to four on a self-catering basis. See the website for details. The scope for outdoor activity here is superb.

Lairg & Around

Lairg is an attractive village, although the tranquillity can be rudely interrupted by the sound of military jets roaring overhead (the valley is frequently used by the RAF for low-flying exercises). Located at the southern end of Loch Shin, it's a remote but important Highlands crossroad, gateway to central Sutherland's remote mountains and loch-speckled bogs.

Four miles south of Lairg, the picturesque **Falls of Shin** (www.fallsofshin.co.uk; 🚹) FREE is one of the best places in the Highlands to see salmon leaping on their way upstream to spawn (June to September). A short, easy footpath leads to a viewing terrace overlooking the waterfall; there are waymarked forest trails here. A new visitor centre to replace the last one that burned down is in the pipeline; meanwhile, there are no facilities.

A really worthwhile stop by the loch, bustling **Pier Café** (☑ 01549-402971; www.pier-cafe-co.uk; Lochside, Lairg; lunch mains £8-11; ⏱ 10am-4pm Tue-Thu, 10am-4pm & 5.30-9pm Fri & Sat, 10am-6pm Sun; ☎ ♿) has pleasant views, art exhibitions on the walls and a friendly atmosphere. Great chalkboard specials augment a Mediterranean-influenced bistro menu that draws on local produce. The coffee is the best for some distance around and the cafe is licensed. There's a little craft shop too.

Dornoch

POP 1200

On the northern shore of Dornoch Firth, 2 miles off the A9, this attractive old market town, all elegant sandstone, is one of the east coast's most pleasant settlements. Dornoch is best known for its championship golf course, but there's a fine cathedral among other noble buildings. Other historical oddities: the last witch to be executed in Scotland was boiled alive in hot tar here in 1722 and Madonna married Guy Ritchie here in 2000.

◉ Sights & Activities

Have a walk along Dornoch's golden-sand beach, which stretches for miles. South of Dornoch, seals are often visible on the sandbars of Dornoch Firth.

Dornoch Cathedral CHURCH
(www.dornoch-cathedral.com; St Gilbert St; ⏱ 9am-7pm or later) **FREE** Consecrated in the 13th century, Dornoch Cathedral is an elegant Gothic edifice with an interior softly illuminated through modern stained-glass windows. The controversial first Duke of Sutherland, whose wife restored the church in the 1830s, lies in a sealed burial vault beneath the chancel.

Royal Dornoch GOLF
(☑ 01862-810219; www.royaldornoch.com; Golf Rd, Dornoch; summer green fee £130) One of Scotland's most famous links, described by Tom Watson as 'the most fun I have ever had on

a golf course'. It's public, and you can book a slot online. Twilight rates are the most economical. A golf pass (www.dornochfirthgolf.co.uk) lets you play several courses in the area at a good discount.

🛏 Sleeping & Eating

⭐ **2 Quail** B&B ££
(☑ 01862-811811; www.2quail.com; Castle St; r £105-115; ☎) Intimate and upmarket, 2 Quail offers a warm main street welcome. Tasteful, spacious chambers are full of old-world comfort, with sturdy metal bed frames, plenty of books and plump duvets. The downstairs guest lounge is an absolute delight, while the guest dinners (2-/3-courses £18/22) are a treat as one of the owners is a noted chef. It's best to book ahead.

Dornoch Castle Hotel HOTEL ££
(☑ 01862-810216; www.dornochcastlehotel.com; Castle St; s/d £75/129, superior/deluxe d £179/260; ℗ ☎) This 16th-century former bishop's palace makes a wonderful place to stay, particularly if you upgrade to a superior room, which has views, space, whisky and chocolates on the welcome tray and (some) a four-poster bed; the deluxe rooms are unforgettable. Add to this the convivial bar and restaurant and helpful staff and you have a very impressive package.

Sule Skerry

B&B ££

(📞 01862-810519; www.dornoch-bed-and-breakfast -com; 2 Castle St; s/d £55/80; 🛜) With a warm welcome and a cute sandstone cottage with climbing roses, this is a very homelike B&B experience. Two sweet rooms have every comfort, including modern bathroom, and chatting with the owner over excellent and the abundant breakfast in her kitchen is delightful.

Luigi

ITALIAN, CAFE £

(📞 01862-810893; www.luigidornoch.com; Castle St; lunch £7-11, dinner mains £13-21; ⊙10am-5pm daily, plus 6.45-9pm Fri & Sat Mar-Oct, daily Jul & Aug; 🛜) The clean lines of this contemporary Italian-American cafe make a break from the omnipresent heritage and history of this coastline. Ciabattas and salads stuffed with tasty deli ingredients make it a good lunch stop; more elaborate dinners usually include fine seafood choices. The coffee is the best in town.

ℹ️ Getting There & Away

There are buses roughly hourly from Inverness (£10.40, 1¼ hours), with some services continuing north to Wick or Thurso.

Golspie

POP 1400

Golspie is a pretty little village most visited for nearby Dunrobin Castle. It's a congenial place to spend a day or two, with good facilities and a pleasant beach.

◉ Sights & Activities

There are several good local walks, including the classic 3¾ mile (return) hike climbing steeply to the summit of **Ben Bhraggie** (394m), crowned by a massive monument to the Duke of Sutherland, notorious for his leading role in the Highland Clearances.

★ Dunrobin Castle

CASTLE

(📞 01408-633177; www.dunrobincastle.co.uk; A9, Golspie; adult/child £11/6.50; ⊙10.30am-4.30pm Mon-Sat, noon-4.30pm Sun Apr, May & Sep–mid-Oct, 10am-5pm daily Jun-Aug) Magnificent Dunrobin Castle, a mile past Golspie, is the Highlands' largest house. Although it dates to 1275, most of what you see was built in French style between 1845 and 1850. A home of the dukes of Sutherland, it's richly furnished and offers an intriguing insight into the aristocratic lifestyle. The beautiful castle inspires mixed feelings locally; it was once the seat of the first Duke of Sutherland, notorious for some of the cruellest episodes of the Highland Clearances.

Highland Wildcat

MOUNTAIN BIKING

(www.highlandwildcat.com; ⊙dawn-dusk) **FREE** The expert-only black trail at Highland Wildcat is famous for having the highest single-track descent in the country (a 390m drop over 7km). There's plenty for beginners and families too, with a scenic blue trail and easy forest routes. No facilities; grab the map off the website.

🛏️ Sleeping

Invicta House

B&B ££

(📞 01408-633097; www.invictahouse.co.uk; 10 Ferry Rd; s/d £35/70; 🛜📺) By the football pitch, behind a fabric shop, Invicta House has refurbished rooms with excellent en suite bathrooms away from the main road noise. The upstairs single has an exterior bathroom. The easygoing owner turns on a tasty breakfast, offers laundry facilities and lets dogs stay free.

Blar Mhor

B&B ££

(📞 01408-633609; www.blarmhor.co.uk; Drummuie Rd; s/d/f £35/70/90; 🅿️🛜📺) On the approach into Golspie from Dornoch, this excellent guesthouse with landscaped gardens has large, beautifully kept rooms with swish modern bathrooms in a towering Victorian mansion. The cheerful hosts will brighten your stay with little extras like chocolates on the bed.

ℹ️ Getting There & Away

Trains (£18.90, 2¼ hours) and buses (£11.80, 1½ hours) between Inverness and Wick/Thurso stop in Golspie and at Dunrobin Castle.

Helmsdale

POP 700

Surrounded by hills whose gorse explodes mad yellow in springtime, this sheltered fishing town, like many spots on this coast, was a major emigration point during the Clearances and also a booming herring port. It's surrounded by stunning, undulating coastline, and the River Helmsdale is one of the best salmon rivers in the Highlands.

In the centre of town, **Timespan** (📞01431-821327; www.timespan.org.uk; Dunrobin St; adult/child £4/2; ⊙10am-5pm Easter-Oct, 2-4pm Tue, 10am-3pm Sat & Sun Nov-Easter) heritage centre has an impressive display covering local history (including the Clearances and the 1869 gold rush) and Barbara Cartland, late queen of romance novels, who was a Helmsdale regular. There are also local art exhibitions, a geology garden and a cafe.

🛏 Sleeping & Eating

Helmsdale Hostel
HOSTEL £

(📞 07971 516287, 01431-821636; www.helmsdale hostel.co.uk; Stafford St; dm/tw/f £19/45/60; ⊗ Apr-Sep; 🛜🐾) This lovingly run hostel is in very good nick, well equipped and spotlessly clean, and makes a cheerful, comfortable budget base for exploring Caithness. Dorms have mostly cosy single beds rather than bunks; en suite rooms are great for families. The lofty central space has a lounge with wood stove and good kitchen. Closed for refurbishment at last visit but reopening for 2017.

Customs House
B&B £

(📞 01431-821648; Shore St; r per person £24; 🅿) Old-fashioned, cordial and top value, Customs House has a great location opposite the little harbour and fluffy, comfortable rooms with heaps of cushions and big cosy beds. Breakfast is great, with fresh fruit, cheese, abundant coffee and juice, plus cooked options.

La Mirage
BISTRO ££

(📞 01431-821615; www.lamirage.org; 7 Dunrobin St; mains £10-15; ⊗ 11am-8.45pm Mon-Sat, noon-8.45pm Sun; 🛜) Created in homage to Barbara Cartland, this is a '70s throwback with pink walls, kitschy installations and a retro menu. Meals aren't gourmet – think chicken Kiev – but portions are huge. Fish and chips are also available for takeaway so you can eat 'em by the pretty harbour. One portion feeds two.

CAITHNESS

Once you pass Helmsdale, you are entering Caithness, a place of jagged gorse-and-grass-topped cliffs hiding tiny fishing harbours. Scotland's top corner was once Viking territory, historically more connected to Orkney and Shetland than the rest of the mainland. It's a mystical, ancient land dotted with ancient monuments and peopled by folk who are proud of their Norse heritage.

Lybster & Around

This spectacular stretch of coast follows the folds of the undulating landscape through villages established on the shoreline when communities were evicted from the interior in the Highland Clearances in the early 19th century.

Seven miles north of Helmsdale is **Badbea**, an abandoned crofting village established at this time. The village of **Dunbeath** is spectacularly set in a deep glen. Lybster is a purpose-built fishing village dating from 1810, with a stunning harbour area surrounded by grassy cliffs. In its heyday, it was Scotland's third-busiest port. Things have changed – now there are only a couple of boats – but there are several interesting prehistoric sites in the area.

◎ Sights

Whaligoe Steps
HISTORIC SITE

(Ulbster; ⊗ 24hr) FREE At Ulbster, 5 miles north of Lybster, this staircase cut into the cliff provides access to a tiny natural harbour, with ideal grassy picnic spot, ringed by vertical cliffs and echoing with the cackle of nesting fulmars. The path begins at the end of the minor road opposite the road signposted 'Cairn of Get'. There's a cafe at the top, open Thursday to Sunday (10.30am to 5.30pm).

Grey Cairns of Camster
ARCHAEOLOGICAL SITE

(⊗ 24hr) FREE Dating from between 4000BC and 2500BC, these burial chambers are hidden in long, low mounds rising from an evocatively lonely moor. The Long Cairn measures 60m by 21m. You can enter the main chamber, but must first crawl into the well-preserved Round Cairn, which has a corbelled ceiling. From a turn-off a mile east of Lybster on the A99, the cairns are 4 miles north. You can continue 7 further miles to approach Wick on the A882.

Wick

POP 7100

More gritty than pretty, Wick has been down on its luck since the collapse of the herring industry. It was once the world's largest fishing port for the 'silver darlings', but when the market dropped off after WWII, job losses were huge and the town hasn't ever totally recovered. It's worth a visit though, particularly for its excellent museum and attractive, spruced-up harbour area.

◉ Sights & Activities

★ Wick Heritage Centre
MUSEUM

(☑ 01955-605393; www.wickheritage.org; 20 Bank Row; adult/child £4/50p; ☺ 10am-5pm Apr-Oct, last entry 3.45pm) Tracking the rise and fall of the herring industry, this great town museum displays everything from fishing equipment to complete herring boats. It's absolutely huge inside, and is crammed with memorabilia and extensive displays describing Wick's heyday in the mid-19th century. The Johnston collection is the star exhibit. From 1863 to 1977, three generations photographed everything that happened around Wick and the 70,000 photographs are an amazing record.

Old Wick Castle
RUINS

(☺ 24hr) **FREE** A path leads a mile south from town to the ruins of 12th-century Old Wick Castle, with the spectacular cliffs of the Brough and the Brig, as well as Gote o'Trams, a little further south. In good weather, it's a fine coastal walk to the castle, but take care on the final approach as there's a crevasse that you don't spot until you're quite close.

Old Pulteney
DISTILLERY

(☑ 01955-602371; www.oldpulteney.com; Huddart St; tours £7; ☺ 10am-4pm Mon-Fri Oct-Apr, 10am-5pm Mon-Fri, 10am-4pm Sat May-Sep) Though it's no longer the most northerly whisky distillery on mainland Scotland (that goes to the upstart Wolfburn in Thurso), Pulteney still runs excellent tours twice daily, with more expensive visits available for aficionados.

Castle Sinclair Girnigoe
RUINS

(☺ 24hr) **FREE** Three miles northeast of Wick is the magnificently located cliff-top ruin of Castle Sinclair. It's a short walk from a car park, with some interpretative signboards along the way.

Caithness Seacoast
BOATING

(☑ 01955-609200; www.caithness-seacoast.co.uk; ☺ Apr-Oct) This outfit will take you out to sea to inspect the rugged coastline of the northeast. Various options include a half-hour jaunt (adult/child £19/12), a 1½-hour tour (adult/child £30/22) and a three-hour return trip down to Lybster (adult/child £50/39).

🛏 Sleeping & Eating

Seaview
B&B ££

(☑ 01955-602735; www.wickbb.co.uk; 14 Scalesburn; s/d £45/65; P🐾🅿🐕) On the water, though not in its prettiest part, Seaview has genuine, bend-over-backwards hospitality from cheerful June. It's reliably comfortable, with compact rooms, two of which share a bathroom. The little conservatory lounge is a top spot for lazy moments with river views.

Mackays Hotel
HOTEL ££

(☑ 01955-602323; www.mackayshotel.co.uk; Union St; s/d £90/119; 🐾) Hospitable Mackays is Wick's best hotel by a long stretch. Attractive, mostly refurbished rooms vary in layout and size, so ask to see a few; prices are usually lower than the rack rates. On-site **No 1 Bistro** (mains £13-22; ☺ noon-2pm & 5-9pm; 🐾) is a fine option for lunch or dinner. The world's shortest street, 2.06m-long Ebenezer Place, is one side of the hotel.

Bord de l'Eau
FRENCH ££

(☑ 01955-604400; 2 Market St; mains £16-24; ☺ 6-9pm Tue-Fri, noon-2pm & 6-9pm Sun & Sat) This serene, relaxed French restaurant is Wick's best place to eat. It overlooks the river and serves a changing menu of mostly meat and game French classics, backed up by daily fish specials. Starters are great value, and mains include a huge assortment of vegetables, so you won't go hungry. The conservatory dining room with water views is lovely on a sunny evening.

ℹ Information

Wick Information Centre (☑ 01955-602547; 66 High St; ☺ 9am-5.30pm Mon-Sat) has a good selection of information. It's upstairs in McAllans Clothing Store.

ℹ Getting There & Away

AIR

Wick is a Caithness transport gateway. Flybe/Loganair flies to Edinburgh and **Eastern Airways** (☑ 0870 366 9100; www.easternairways.com) to Aberdeen (three daily, Monday to Friday).

BUS

Stagecoach and Citylink operate to/from Inverness (£19.80, three hours, six daily) and Stagecoach to Thurso (£3.80, 40 minutes, hourly). There's also connecting service to John O'Groats and Gills Bay (£3.40, 30 minutes, four to five Monday to Saturday) for the passenger and car ferries to Orkney.

TRAIN

Trains service Wick from Inverness (£20, 4¼ hours, four daily Monday to Saturday, one on Sunday).

John O'Groats

POP 300

Though not the northernmost point of the British mainland (that's Dunnet Head), John O'Groats still serves as the end point of the 874-mile trek from Land's End in Cornwall, a popular if arduous route for cyclists and walkers, many of whom raise money for charitable causes. Most of the settlement is taken up by a stylish modern self-catering complex.

◎ Sights & Activities

Duncansby Head VIEWPOINT
Two miles east of John O'Groats, Duncansby Head has a small lighthouse and 60m-high cliffs sheltering nesting fulmars. A 15-minute walk through a sheep paddock yields spectacular views of the sea-surrounded monoliths known as Duncansby Stacks.

Wildlife Cruises BOATING
(www.jogferry.co.uk; adult/child £18/9; ⊗ mid-Jun–Aug) The friendly folk who run the Orkney ferry also run 1½-hour wildlife cruises to the island of Stroma or Duncansby Head.

❶ Information

John O'Groats Information Centre (☑ 01955-611373; www.visitjohnogroats.com; ⊗10am-4pm Apr, to 5pm May & Sep-Oct, 9am-6pm Jun-Aug) has souvenirs plus a fine selection of local novels and nonfiction.

❶ Getting There & Away

Stagecoach (p301) runs between John O'Groats and Wick (£3.40, 30 minutes, four to five Monday to Saturday) or Thurso (£4.40 to £7.50, 40 minutes to one hour, five to eight Monday to Saturday).

From May to September, a passenger **ferry** (p399) shuttles across to Burwick in Orkney. Three miles west, a car ferry (p399) runs from Gills Bay to St Margaret's Hope in Orkney.

Mey

POP 200

West of John O'Groats, the small village of Mey has a major drawcard for lovers of the royal family in its pretty castle, formerly a residence of the Queen Mother.

The **Castle of Mey** (☑ 01847-851473; www.castleofmey.org.uk; adult/child £11/6.50; ⊗10.20am-5pm mid-May–Sep, last admission 4pm), a big crowd-puller for its Queen Mother connections, is 6 miles west of John O'Groats. The exterior is grand but inside it feels domestic and everything is imbued with the Queen Mum's character. The highlight is the genteel guided tour, with various anecdotes recounted by staff who once worked for her. In the grounds there's a farm zoo, an unusual walled garden that's worth a stroll and lovely views over the Pentland Firth.

The castle normally closes for a couple of weeks at the end of July for royal visits; Prince Charles often comes here in summer.

Just off the main road, **Mey House** (☑ 01847-851852; www.meyhouse.co.uk; East Mey; r £130 per night, for 2 or more nights £115; ⊗ Easter-Oct; ℗⊛) is beautifully situated among green fields running down to water and majestic views of Orkney, Dunnet Head and nearby Castle of Mey. This modern top-drawer sleep is a welcoming, sumptuous place to stay. They've thought it all through: the huge, luxurious rooms have arty designer decor, excellent custom-made beds, Nespresso machines, big flat-screen TVs, sound bar and stunning modern bathrooms with shower and tub.

Dunnet Head

Eight miles east of Thurso a minor road leads to dramatic Dunnet Head, the most northerly point on the British mainland. There are majestic cliffs dropping into the turbulent Pentland Firth, inspiring views of Orkney, basking seals and nesting seabirds below, and a lighthouse built by Robert Louis Stevenson's grandad. Just west, the excellent curving strand of Dunnet Bay is one of Scotland's finest beaches.

Thurso & Scrabster

POP 7600

Britain's most northerly mainland town, Thurso makes a handy overnight stop if you're heading west or across to Orkney. There's a pretty town beach, riverside strolls and a good museum. Ferries for Orkney leave from Scrabster, 2.5 miles away.

◎ Sights & Activities

Thurso is an unlikely surfing centre but the nearby coast has arguably the best and most regular surf on mainland Britain. There's an excellent right-hand reef break on the eastern side of town, directly in front of the castle (closed to the public), and another shallow reef break 5 miles west at Brimms

Ness. Drysuits are the way to go. The Thurso Surf (www.facebook.com/thursosurf) Facebook page has some info on the local scene.

Caithness Horizons MUSEUM
(☎01847-896508; www.caithnesshorizons.co.uk; High St; ⊙10am-6pm Mon-Fri, to 5pm Sat, plus noon-5pm Sun May-Aug) FREE This museum brings Caithness history and lore to life through excellent displays. Fine Pictish cross-slabs greet the visitor downstairs; the main exhibition is a wide-ranging look at local history using plenty of audiovisuals – check out the wistful account of the now-abandoned island of Stroma. There's also a gallery space, an exhibition on the Dounreay nuclear reactor, tourist information and a cafe.

Sleeping

Sandra's Backpackers HOSTEL £
(☎01847-894575; www.sandras-backpackers.co.uk; 24 Princes St; dm/d/f £18/42/65; P@) In the heart of town above a chip shop, this budget backpacker option offers en suite dorms, mostly four-berthers with aged mattresses, a spacious kitchen and traveller-friendly facilities such as help-yourself cereals and toast. It's not luxurious but it's a reliable cheap sleep.

★**Pennyland House** B&B ££
(☎01847-891194; www.pennylandhouse.co.uk; Thurso; s/d £78/98; P) A super conversion of a historic house, this is a standout B&B choice. It offers phenomenal value for this level of accommodation, with huge oak-furnished rooms named after golf courses: we especially loved St Andrews – super-spacious, with a great chessboard-tiled bathroom. Hospitality is enthusiastic and helpful, and there's an inviting breakfast space, garden and terraced area with views across to Hoy.

Two-night minimum stay in summer.

Camfield House B&B ££
(☎01847-891118; www.riversideaccommodation.co.uk; Janet St, Thurso; s £75, d £99-115; P) A Narnia-style portal leads from central Thurso through a gate and you're suddenly in what feels like an opulent rural estate. The garden is sumptuous and extravagantly features a manicured par-3 golf hole, complete with bunker and water hazard. The interior lacks nothing by comparison, with spacious rooms with huge TVs, quality linen and excellent bathrooms. There's even a full-sized billiard table.

Prices seem very reasonable for this standard of accommodation.

Marine B&B ££
(☎01847-890676; www.themarinethurso.co.uk; 38 Shore St, Thurso; s £80, d £90-105; P) Tucked away in Thurso's most appealing corner you'll find a top spot right by the pretty town beach, offering spectacular vistas over it and across to Orkney. Rooms are just fabulous, with a designer's touch and a subtle maritime feel, and surfers can study the breakers from the stunning conservatory-lounge. Two rooms in the adjacent house make a great family option.

Forss House Hotel HOTEL £££
(☎01847-861201; www.forsshousehotel.co.uk; s/d £125/175; P) Tucked into trees 5 miles west of Thurso is a Georgian mansion offering elegant accommodation with both character and style. Sumptuous upstairs rooms are preferable to basement rooms as they have lovely garden views. There are also beautifully appointed suites in the garden itself, providing both privacy and tranquillity. Thoughtful extras like CDs and books in every room add appeal.

It's right alongside a beautiful salmon river – the hotel can sort out permits and equipment – and if you've had a chilly day in the waders, some 300 malt whiskies await in the hotel bar. There are some cheaper rooms available (d £99) also.

NORTH COAST 500

The drive along Scotland's far northern coastline is one of Europe's finest road trips. Words fail to describe the sheer variety of the scenic splendour which unfolds before you as you cross this awe-inspiring landscape of desolate moorlands, brooding mountains, fertile coastal meadows and stunning white-sand beaches.

In a clever piece of marketing it's been dubbed the **North Coast 500** (www.northcoast500.com), as the round trip from Inverness is roughly that many miles, though you'll surely clock up a few more if you follow your heart down narrow byroads and seek perfect coastal vistas at the end of dead-end tracks.

✕ Eating

Holborn Hotel
BISTRO ££

(📞 01847-892771; www.holbornhotel.co.uk; 16 Princes St; bar meals £8-11, restaurant mains £13-20; ⊙ noon-2pm & 6-8pm Mon-Thu, noon-2pm & 6-9pm Fri, noon-2.30pm & 6-9pm Sat & Sun; 🛜) A trendy, comfortable place decked out in light wood, the Holborn contrasts stark-ly with more traditional Thurso watering holes. Uncomplicated but decent meals are available in the bar, while quality seafood – including delicious home-smoked salmon – is the mainstay of a short menu fleshed out by specials at the evening-only Red Pepper restaurant, where desserts are excellent too. Service can be slow when busy.

It also has decent accommodation (single/double £65/90).

★ Captain's Galley
SEAFOOD £££

(📞 01847-894999; www.captainsgalley.co.uk; Scrab-ster; 5-course dinner £53.50, with wine flight £77; ⊙ 6.30-11pm Tue-Sat, last orders 9pm) 🍴 Classy but friendly Captain's Galley, just by the Scrabster ferry, offers a short, seafood-based menu featuring local and sustainably sourced produce prepared in delicious ways that let the natural flavours shine through. The chef picks the best fish off the local boats, and the menu describes exactly which fishing grounds your morsel came from. It's worth scheduling a night in Thurso to eat here.

ℹ Information

Thurso Information Centre (📞 01847-893155; www.visitscotland.com; High St; ⊙ 10am-6pm Mon-Fri, to 5pm Sat, plus noon-5pm Sun May-Aug) is located in the Caithness Horizons museum.

ℹ Getting There & Away

Stagecoach/Citylink buses link Thurso/Scrabster with Inverness (£19.80, three hours, five daily). There are also buses roughly every hour to Wick (£3.80, 40 minutes), as well as every couple of hours to John O'Groats (£4.40 to £7.50, 40 minutes to one hour, five to eight Monday to Saturday).

There are four daily trains (one on Sunday) from Inverness (£20, 3¾ hours), with a connect-ing bus to Scrabster.

It's a 2-mile walk from Thurso train station to the ferry at Scrabster; there are buses on Olrig St.

NORTH & WEST COAST

Carving its way from Thurso to Kyle of Lochalsh, Scotland's north and northwest coastline is a feast of deep inlets, forgotten beaches and surging peninsulas. Within the rugged confines of the deep interior are vast, empty spaces, enormous lochs and some of Scotland's highest peaks.

Thurso to Durness

It's 80 winding – and utterly spectacular – coastal miles from Thurso to Durness.

Ten miles west of Thurso, the Dounreay nuclear power station was the first in the world to supply mains electricity; it's cur-rently being decommissioned. The clean-up is planned to be finished by 2025; it's still a major source of employment for the region.

Beyond, Melvich overlooks a fine beach and there are great views from Strathy Point (a 2-mile drive from the coast road, then a 15-minute walk).

Bettyhill is a pretty village overlooking a magnificent stretch of coastline, and the scenery just improves as you head west through Coldbackie and Tongue, with a succession of gorgeous sea lochs, stun-ning beaches and striking rock formations backed by imposing hills and mountains.

Bettyhill

POP 500

Bettyhill is a crofting community of resettled tenant farmers kicked off their land during the Clearances. The spectacular panorama of a sweeping, sandy beach backed by vel-vety green hills with rocky outcrops makes a sharp contrast to that sad history.

Housed in an old church, **Strathnaver Museum** (📞 01641-521418; www.strathnaver museum.org.uk; adult/child £2/1; ⊙ 10am-5pm Mon-Sat Apr-Oct) tells the sad story of the Strathnaver Clearances through posters written by local kids. The museum contains memorabilia of Clan Mackay, various items of crofting equipment and a 'St Kilda mail-boat', a small wooden boat-shaped container bearing a letter that was used by St Kildans to send messages to the mainland.

Outside the back door of the church is the **Farr Stone**, a fine carved Pictish cross-slab.

A good B&B option, **Farr Cottage** (📞 01641-521755; www.bettyhillbedandbreakfast. co.uk; Farr; s/d £50/70; 🅿🛜), a welcoming white bungalow amid the bleating of sheep

FORSINARD & STRATHNAVER

Though it's tough to tear yourself away from the coast, we recommend plunging down the A897 just east of Melvich. After 14 miles you reach the railway at Forsinard. On the platform is **Forsinard Flows Visitor Centre** (☑ 01641-571225; www.rspb.org.uk; Forsinard; ☉ 9am-5pm Apr-Oct) **FREE**, a small nature exhibition. There's a live hen-harrier cam, plus guided walks and 4x4 excursions available – phone for dates. A 1-mile trail introduces you to the Flows peatland; 4 miles north is a 4-mile trail crossing golden plover and dunlin nesting grounds. The deep peat blanket bog is a rare and important habitat, at risk from climate change. A larger visitor centre is in the works.

Past here, the epic peaty moorscapes stir the heart with their desolate beauty. Take a right at Kinbrace onto the B871, which covers more jaw-dropping scenery before arriving at **Syre**. Turn right to follow the Strathnaver (valley) back to the coast near Bettyhill, or left to reach the lonely outpost of Altnaharra. Strathnaver saw some of the worst of the Clearances; the **Strathnaver Trail** is a series of numbered points of interest along the valley relating to both this and various prehistoric sites.

Accommodation options on this lonely detour include **Cornmill Bunkhouse** (☑ 01641-571219; www.achumore.co.uk; A897; dm £15; P), a comfortable, modern hostel occupying a picturesque old mill on a working croft in the middle of nowhere; it's on the A897 4 miles south of the coast road. Turning left instead of right at Syre, you'll eventually reach the remote **Altnaharra Hotel** (☑ 01549-411222; www.altnaharra.com; Altnaharra; s £65, d £99-110, superior d £130-150; ☉ Mar-Dec; P 🐾 🐕).

and beautiful scenery and vistas a mile off the main road. There are two rooms, modern and compact, with sparkling bathrooms. The delightful owner is a seafood chef, so excellent dinners are a bargain at £15 for two courses. Packed lunches are also available. Follow signs to Farr.

In the nearby village of Kirtomy, **Côte du Nord** (☑ 01641-521773; www.cotedunord.co.uk; The School House, Kirtomy; degustation £39, with wine flight £75; ☉ 7-9pm Wed, Fri & Sat Apr-Sep) 🍴 is an extraordinary place to eat. Brilliantly innovative cuisine, wonderfully whimsical presentation and an emphasis on local ingredients are the highlights of the gastronomic degustation menu here. It's an unlikely spot to find such a gourmet experience; the chef is none other than the local GP who forages for wild herbs and flavours in between surgery hours. Top value. It's tiny, so reserve well ahead.

Kirtomy is signposted off the main road about 2½ miles east of Bettyhill; the restaurant is about a mile down this road.

From Monday to Saturday, there's one daily bus from Bettyhill to Thurso (1¼ hours) and one or two to Tongue (35 minutes). Timetables for these services change regularly.

Coldbackie & Tongue

POP 500

Coldbackie has outstanding views over sandy beaches, turquoise waters and offshore islands. Two miles further is Tongue, with the evocative 14th-century ruins of Castle Varrich, once a Mackay stronghold. To get to the castle, take the trail next to the Royal Bank of Scotland – it's an easy stroll.

🛏 Sleeping

Kyle of Tongue Hostel & Holiday Park   HOSTEL, CAMPSITE £

(☑ 01847-611789; www.tonguehostelandholidaypark.co.uk; A838, Tongue; dm £19, d £44-50; P 🐕) In a wonderful spot right by the causeway across the Kyle of Tongue, a mile west of town, this is the top budget option in the area, with clean, spacious dorms, great family rooms, views, a decent kitchen and a cosy lounge. It's bright and helpful, and there's a bikeshed and camping as well.

Camping is charged at £9 per person for showers and toilet use, or £12 for full hostel facilities.

★ **Cloisters**   B&B ££

(☑ 01847-601286; www.cloistersbandb.co.uk; Talmine; s/d £40/70; P 🐕) Superbly located Cloisters has three en suite twin rooms and absolutely brilliant views over the Kyle of Tongue and offshore islands. Breakfast is in the artistically converted church alongside, and it can do evening meals at weekends. From Tongue, cross the causeway and take the right-hand turn to Melness; Cloisters is a couple of miles down this road.

Tigh-nan-Ubhal
B&B **££**

(☑01847-611281; www.tigh-nan-ubhal.com; Main St; d £65-75; P🛜😿) In the middle of Tongue and within stumbling distance of two pubs is this charming B&B. There are snug, loft-style rooms with plenty of natural light, but the basement double with spa is the pick of the bunch – it's the biggest en suite we've seen in northern Scotland. There's also a caravan in the garden and a cheaper room that shares a bathroom.

Durness

POP 400

Scattered Durness (www.durness.org) is wonderfully located, strung out along cliffs rising from a series of pristine beaches. When the sun shines, the effects of blinding white sand, the cry of seabirds and the spring-green-coloured seas combine in a magical way.

◉ Sights & Activities

Walking around the sensational sandy coastline is a highlight, as is a visit to **Cape Wrath** (p364). Durness's beautiful beaches include **Rispond** to the east, **Sango Sands** below town and **Balnakeil** to the west. At Balnakeil, under a mile beyond Durness, a craft village occupies a onetime early-warning radar station. A walk along the beach to the north leads to **Faraid Head**, where you can see puffin colonies in early summer. You can hire bikes from a shed on the square.

A mile east of the centre is a path down to **Smoo Cave** (www.smoocave.org) `FREE`. From the vast main chamber, you can head through to a smaller flooded cavern where a waterfall sometimes cascades from the roof. There's evidence the cave was inhabited about 6000 years ago. You can take a **boat trip** (☑01971-511704; adult/child £4/2; ⊙11am-4pm Apr-May & Sep, 10am-5pm Jun-Aug) to explore a little further into the interior.

🛏 Sleeping

Lazy Crofter Bunkhouse
HOSTEL **£**

(☑01971-511202; www.durnesshostel.com; dm £19; 🛜) Durness' best budget accommodation is here, opposite the supermarket. A bothy vibe gives it a very Highland feel. Inviting dorms have plenty of room and lockers, and there's also a sociable shared table for meals and board games, and a great wooden deck with sea views, perfect for midge-free evenings.

Sango Sands Oasis
CAMPSITE **£**

(☑07838 381065; www.sangosands.com; sites per adult/child £8/6, 2nd child £3, others free; P🛜😿) You couldn't imagine a better location for a campsite: great grassy areas on the edge of cliffs, descending to two lovely sandy beaches. Facilities are good and very clean and there's a pub next door. Electric hookup is an extra £4. You can camp free from November to March but don't complain about the cold.

★Mackays Rooms
HOTEL **££**

(☑01971-511202; www.visitdurness.com; d standard £129, deluxe £139-149; ⊙May–mid-Oct; P🛜😿) You really feel you're at the furthest corner of Scotland here, where the road turns through 90 degrees. But whether heading south or east, you'll go far before you find a better place to stay than this haven of Highland hospitality. With big beds, contemporary colours and soft fabrics, it's a romantic spot with top service and numerous boutique details.

There's also a new self-contained cabin here, which can be rented on a self-catering or B&B basis. With two rooms, it sleeps up to four.

Morven
B&B **££**

(☑01971-511252; s/d £50/65; P🛜😿) Cheery owners, a handy next-to-pub location and a serious border collie theme are key features of this ultra-cosy place. Rooms, which are upstairs and share a downstairs bathroom, have been recently renovated and feel new and super-comfortable. One is especially spacious and has a top coastal vista.

Croft 103
SELF-CATERING **£££**

(☑01971-511202; www.croft103.com; Port na Con, Laid; per week £1600-1800; P🛜) 🌿 The owners of Mackays Rooms in Durness also run Croft 103, a stunning, modern self-catering option aimed at couples, 6 miles east, right on Loch Eriboll. There are two cottages, both immaculate.

WORTH A TRIP

CAPE WRATH

Though its name actually comes from the Norse word for 'turning point', there is something daunting and primal about Cape Wrath, the remote north-western point of the British mainland, crowned by a lighthouse built by the famous Stevenson family of engineers and close to the seabird colonies of **Clo Mor**, Britain's highest coastal cliffs. A **cafe** at the lighthouse serves soup and sandwiches.

Getting to Cape Wrath involves taking a **ferry** (☑ 07719 678729; www.capewrathferry.co.uk; single/return £4.50/6.50; ☉ Easter–Oct) – passengers and bikes only – across the Kyle of Durness (10 minutes). It connects with the **Cape Wrath Minibus** (☑ 01971-511284; www.visitcapewrath.com; single/return £7/12; ☉ Easter–Oct), which runs the 11 miles to the cape (40 minutes).

This combination is a friendly but eccentric and sometimes shambolic service with limited capacity, so plan on waiting in high season, and call ahead to make sure the ferry is running. The ferry leaves from 2 miles southwest of Durness, and runs twice or more daily from April to September. If you eschew the minibus, it's a spectacular 11-mile ride or hike from boat to cape over bleak scenery.

An increasingly popular but challenging walking route, the **Cape Wrath Trail** (www.capewrathtrail.org.uk) runs from Fort William up to Cape Wrath (200 miles). It's unmarked so buy the Cape Wrath Trail guidebook (www.cicerone.co.uk) or go with a guide – **C-n-Do** (☑ 01786-445703; www.cndoscotland.com) is one operator.

✖ Eating

★ Cocoa Mountain
CAFE £

(☑ 01971-511233; www.cocoamountain.co.uk; Balnakeil; hot chocolate £3.95, 10 truffles £9.90; ☉ 9am–6pm Easter–Oct) At the Balnakeil craft village, this upbeat cafe and chocolate maker offers handmade treats including a chilli, lemongrass and coconut white-chocolate truffle, plus many more unique flavours. Tasty espresso and hot chocolate warm the cockles on those blowy horizontal-drizzle days. It offers light lunches and home-baking too, plus chocolate-making workshops.

Smoo Cave Hotel
PUB FOOD ££

(www.smoocavehotel.co.uk; mains £9-15; ☉ kitchen 11.30am-9.30pm; 🛜) Signposted off the main road at the eastern end of town, this amiable local offers quality bar food in hefty portions. Haddock or daily seafood specials – plump scallops are a highlight – are an obvious and worthwhile choice; there's also a restaurant area with clifftop views.

❶ Information

Durness has full services, including shops, an ATM and petrol.

Durness Information Centre (☑ 01971-511368; www.visithighlands.com; ☉ 10am-5pm Mon-Sat, to 3pm Sun Easter-Oct, shorter hours in winter) is very helpful, and has good info on local walks and transport.

❶ Getting There & Away

From mid-May to mid-September, one **D & E Coaches** (☑ 01463-222444; www.decoaches.co.uk; ☉ mid-May–mid-Sep) service runs four to six times weekly from Durness to Inverness (£17, four hours) via Ullapool (£12.70, 1½ hours). You can take bikes (£6) but they must be prebooked (during office hours).

A year-round **Far North Bus** (☑ 07782 110007; www.thedurnessbus.com) heads daily to Lairg (£8.10, 2½ hours, Monday to Friday), where there is a train station. On Saturday buses head to Inverness (£11.80, three hours) or Thurso (£9.40, 2½ hours). All these services should be prebooked; you can do the Inverness and Thurso ones online.

There are also two Tuesday **services** (☑ 01847-601238; http://transportfortongue.co.uk) between Tongue and Durness.

Durness to Ullapool

Perhaps Scotland's most spectacular road, the 69 miles connecting Durness to Ullapool is a smorgasbord of dramatic scenery, almost too much to take in. From Durness you pass through a broad heathered valley with the looming grey bulk of Foinaven and Arkle to the southeast. Heather gives way to a rockier landscape of Lewisian gneiss pockmarked with hundreds of small lochans. This is the most interesting zone geologically in the UK, with Britain's oldest rock. Next come gorse-covered hills prefacing the magnificent Torridonian sandstone mountains of Assynt and Coigach, including Suilven's distinctive sugarloaf, ziggurat-like Quinag and pinnacled Stac Pollaidh. The area has been named as the **Northwest Highlands Geopark** (www.nwhgeopark.com).

Scourie & Handa Island

Scourie is a pretty crofting community with decent services, halfway between Durness and Ullapool.

A few miles north of Scourie Bay lies **Handa Island Nature Reserve** (www.scottishwildlifetrust.org.uk), a nature reserve run by the Scottish Wildlife Trust. The island's western sea cliffs provide nesting sites for important breeding populations of great skuas, arctic skuas, puffins, kittiwakes, razorbills and guillemots. Reach the island from Tarbet, 6 miles north of Scourie, via the **Handa Island Ferry** (☑ 07780 967800; www.handa-ferry.com; Tarbet Pier; adult/child return £12.50/5; ☺ outbound 9am-2pm Mon-Sat Apr-Aug, last ferry back 5pm); call for times and to book your spot.

By the ferry pier for Handa, **Shorehouse Seafood Restaurant** (☑ 01971-502251; www.shorehousetarbet.co.uk; Tarbet Pier; mains £9-18; ☺ noon-7pm Mon-Sat Easter-Sep) is in a lovely setting, looking across the sound to the sandy beach on Handa Island. There's a conservatory and outdoor terrace that make the most of the view, and a menu that concentrates on local seafood including crab and prawn salads and Achiltibuie smoked salmon.

Kylesku & Loch Glencoul

Hidden away on the shores of Loch Glencoul, tiny Kylesku served as a ferry crossing on the route north until it was made redundant by beautiful Kylesku Bridge in 1984. It's a good base for walks; you can hire bikes too.

Sights & Activities

Eas a'Chuil Aluinn   WATERFALL
Five miles southeast of Kylesku, in wild, remote country, lies 213m-high Eas a'Chuil Aluinn, Britain's highest waterfall. You can hike to the top of the falls from a parking area at a sharp bend in the main road 3 miles south of Kylesku; allow five hours for the 6 miles return trip. It can also be seen on boat trips from Kylesku.

Kylesku Boat Tours   BOATING
(☑ 01971-502231; www.kyleskuboattours.com; Kylesku; adult/child £25/18; ☺ Apr-Sep) By the Kylesku Hotel, this little boat runs trips out to see the Eas a'Chuil Aluinn waterfall and local seal colonies. The cruise lasts around 1½-hours and can be booked at the hotel. There are two daily departures in season, at midday and 2pm.

✕ Eating

★**Kylesku Hotel**   SEAFOOD ££
(☑ 01971-502231; www.kyleskuhotel.co.uk; Kylesku; mains £11-22; ☺ noon-2.30pm & 5.30-8.30pm mid-Feb–Apr & Oct-Nov, noon-9pm May-Sep; ☎) In this remote loch-side location, it's a real pleasure to gorge yourself on delicious sustainable seafood in this convivial restaurant, with a new extension offering extra water-view seating. Local langoustines, squat lobsters and mussels are the specialities. There's still a good atmosphere of mingling locals and visitors at the bar.

Lochinver & Assynt

With its otherworldly scenery of isolated peaks rising above a sea of crumpled, lochan-spattered gneiss, Assynt epitomises the northwest's wild magnificence. Glaciers have sculpted the hills of Suilven (731m), Canisp (846m), Quinag (808m) and Ben More Assynt (998m) into strange, wonderful silhouettes.

Lochinver is the main settlement, a busy little fishing port that's a popular port of call with its laid-back atmosphere, good facilities and striking scenery. Just north of Lochinver (or if coming from the north, not far south of Kylesku), a 23-mile detour on the narrow B869 rewards with spectacular views and fine beaches. From the lighthouse at Point of Stoer, a one-hour cliff walk leads to the Old Man of Stoer, a spectacular sea stack.

Activities

The limestone hills around Inchnadamph are famous for their caves. The Assynt Visitor Centre (p366) in Lochinver has plenty of information on walking and other activities.

NorWest Sea Kayaking   KAYAKING
(☑ 01571-844281; www.norwestseakayaking.com; 1-day introduction £85) This outfit offers introductory sea-kayaking courses and guided kayaking tours around the Summer Isles and in the Lochinver and Ullapool area. It also hires kayaks in Lochinver.

WORTH A TRIP

SANDWOOD BAY

South of Cape Wrath, **Sandwood Bay** boasts one of Scotland's best and most isolated beaches, guarded at one end by the spectacular rock pinnacle Am Buachaille. Sandwood Bay is about 2 miles north of the end of a track from Blairmore (approach from Kinlochbervie), or you could walk south from the cape (allow eight hours) and on to Blairmore. Sandwood House is a creepy ruin reputedly haunted by the ghost of a 16th-century shipwrecked sailor from the Spanish Armada.

🛏 Sleeping & Eating

An Cala Bunkhouse   HOSTEL £
(Lochinver Bunkhouse; ☑01571-844598; http://ancalacafeandbunkhouse.co.uk; Culag Park, Lochinver; s/d bunk £22/40; P ⚍) Housed near the harbour in the former fishermen's mission, this is an appealing modern hostel with three functional dorms and a good kitchen and lounge. Call ahead on Sunday when the cafe downstairs is closed and there's nobody on the premises.

Clachtoll Beach Campsite   CAMPSITE £
(☑01571-855377; www.clachtollbeachcampsite.co.uk; B869, Clachtoll; site £6-14, plus per adult/child £4/1; ⊘Apr-Sep; P ⚍) Set among the machair (grass- and wildflower-covered dunes) beside a lovely white-sand beach and emerald seas, Clachtoll is a divine coastal camping spot, though somewhat overwhelmed by the adjacent self-catering development. It's 6 miles north of Lochinver by road.

Achmelvich Beach SYHA   HOSTEL £
(☑01571-844480; www.syha.org.uk; dm/tw £20/50; ⊘Apr-Sep) Off the B869, this whitewashed cottage is set beside a great beach at the end of a side road. Dorms are simple, and there's a sociable common kitchen and eating area. Heat-up meals are available as well as a basic shop in summer; otherwise, there's a chip van at the adjacent campsite or take the 4-mile walk to Lochinver.

★ Albannach   HOTEL £££
(☑01571-844407; www.thealbannach.co.uk; Baddidarroch, Lochinver; s/d/ste incl dinner £240/320/385; ⊘Tue-Sun Mar-Dec; P ⚍) 🍴 One of the Highlands' top places to stay and eat, this hotel combines old-fashioned country-house elements – steep creaky stairs, stuffed animals, fireplaces and noble antique furniture – with strikingly handsome rooms that range from a sumptuous four-poster to more modern spaces with things like underfloor heating and, in one case, a private deck with outdoor spa.

The restaurant serves a table d'hôte (tailored to your needs) that's famed throughout Scotland (£70 for non-residents); the welcoming owners grow lots of their own produce and focus on organic and local ingredients. Glorious views, spacious grounds and great walks in easy striking distance make this a perfect place to base yourself.

Lochinver Larder & Riverside Bistro   CAFE, BISTRO ££
(☑01571-844356; www.lochinverlarder.co.uk; 3 Main St, Lochinver; pies £5, mains £11-15; ⊘10am-7.45pm Mon-Sat, to 5.30pm Sun; ⚍) An outstanding menu of inventive food made with local produce is on offer here. The bistro turns out delicious seafood dishes in the evening, while the takeaway counter sells tasty pies with a wide range of gourmet fillings (try the wild boar and apricot). It also does quality meals to take away and heat up: great for hostellers and campers.

ℹ Information

Assynt Visitor Centre (☑01571-844194; www.discoverassynt.co.uk; Main St, Lochin; ⊘10am-4.30pm Mon-Sat, 11am-3pm Sun Easter-Jun, Sep & Oct, 9.30am-5pm Mon-Sat, 10am-4pm Sun Jul & Aug) Has leaflets on hill walks in the area and a display on the story of Assynt.

ℹ Getting There & Away

There are buses from Ullapool to Lochinver (£5, one hour, two to three Monday to Saturday) and a summer bus that goes on to Durness.

Coigach

The region south of Assynt, west of the main A835 road from Ullapool to Ledmore Junction, is known as Coigach (www.coigach.com). A lone, single-track road penetrates this wilderness, leading through gloriously wild scenery to remote settlements. At the western end of Loch Lurgainn, a branch leads north to Lochinver, a scenic backroad so narrow and twisting that it's nicknamed the Wee Mad Road.

Coigach is a wonderland for walkers and wildlife enthusiasts, with a patchwork of sinuous silver lochs dominated by the isolated peaks of Cul Mor (849m), Cul Beag (769m), Ben More Coigach (743m) and Stac Pollaidh (613m). The main settlement is the straggling township of **Achiltibuie**, 15 miles from the main road, with the gorgeous Summer Isles moored just off the coast, and silhouettes of mountains skirting the bay.

🏃 Activities

Stac Pollaidh   HIKING
Despite its diminutive size, Stac Pollaidh provides one of the most exciting hill walks in the Highlands, with some good scrambling on its narrow sandstone crest.

Begin at the car park overlooking Loch Lurgainn, 5 miles west of the A835, and follow a clearly marked and well-made footpath around the eastern end of the hill to ascend from the far side; return by the same route (3 miles return, two to four hours).

Summer Isles Seatours   CRUISE
(☏07927 920592; www.summerisles-seatours. co.uk; adult/child £30/15; ☻Mon-Sat May-Sep) Cruises to the Summer Isles from Old Dornie pier, northwest of Achiltibuie. You get to spend some time ashore on Tanera Mòr.

🛌 Sleeping & Eating

Acheninver Hostel   HOSTEL £
(Achininver Hostel; http://acheninverhostel.com; ☻May-Aug) A half-mile walk off the main road, this basic hostel is ideal for walkers and outdoor enthusiasts. Formerly an SYHA hostel, it was due to reopen as an independent hostel just after our last visit; check the website for updates. Its remote, serene location has to be one of the country's best.

★ Summer Isles Hotel   HOTEL £££
(☏01854-622282; www.summerisleshotel.com; Achiltibuie; s £110-190, d £140-250; ☻Easter-Oct; 🅿🐕🛜🐾) This is a special place, with cracking views, wonderfully romantic, commodious rooms – one themed on Charlie Chaplin, who stayed here, plus others suites in separate cottages – and a snug bar with outdoor seating. 'Courtyard view' rooms are darkish; it's worth upgrading to one with vistas. It's the perfect spot for a romantic getaway or some quality time off life's treadmill.

The restaurant (noon to 3pm and 6pm to 9pm; dinner £49) is of high quality, with local lobster usually featuring and renowned cheese and dessert trolleys. There's also a great wine list considering you're in the middle of nowhere.

Salt Seafood Kitchen   SEAFOOD £
(☏01854-622434; www.saltseafood.com; 140 Badenscaillie; dishes £6-14; ☻noon-3pm & 6-9pm Tue-Sat, noon-3pm Sun May-Sep) 🐾 A mile past Achiltibuie, this sweet chalet offers views to the Summer Isles and fresh local seafood served with a smile. What's on offer varies according to availability, but expect to find mussels, langoustines and squat lobster among other denizens of the sea, as well as burgers, sandwiches and soups. Prices are very reasonable, and the seafood platter is an absolute feast for two.

Ullapool

POP 1500

This pretty port on the shores of Loch Broom is the largest settlement in Wester Ross and one of the most alluring spots in the Highlands, a wonderful destination in itself as well as a gateway to the Western Isles. Offering a row of whitewashed cottages arrayed along the harbour and special views of the loch and its flanking hills, the town has a very distinctive appeal. The harbour served as an emigration point during the Clearances, with thousands of Scots watching Ullapool recede behind.

◉ Sights & Activities

Ullapool Museum   MUSEUM
(www.ullapoolmuseum.co.uk; 7 West Argyle St; adult/child £3.50/free; ☻10am-5pm Mon-Fri, 11am-4pm Sat Apr-Oct) Housed in a converted Telford church, this museum relates the prehistoric, natural and social history of the town and Lochbroom area, with a particular focus on the emigration to Nova Scotia and other places. There's also a genealogy section if you want to trace your Scottish roots.

Shearwater Cruises   BOATING
(☏01854-612472; www.summerqueen.co.uk; ☻Mon-Sat May-Sep) Weather permitting, the catamaran *Shearwater* takes you out to the Summer Isles for a three-hour cruise (adult/child £35/25) or a shorter 1½-hour jaunt (£25/20).

🛌 Sleeping

There's a good selection of B&Bs, with some standout options. Note that during summer Ullapool is very busy and finding accommodation can be tricky – book ahead.

Broomfield Holiday Park
CAMPSITE £

(☎ 01854-612020; www.broomfieldhp.com; West Lane; 1-/2-person tent £8/15, car £2; ☺ Apr-Sep; 🅿 🛜 🐶) This campsite has a great grassy headland location, very close to the centre. Kids stay free, and there are midge-busting machines in action.

Ullapool SYHA
HOSTEL £

(☎ 01854-612254; www.syha.org.uk; Shore St; dm/tw/q £20/46/90; ☺ Apr-Oct; 🛜) You've got to hand it to the SYHA – it's chosen some very sweet locations for its hostels. This is right in the heart of town on the pretty waterfront; some rooms have harbour views and the busy dining area and little lounge are also good spots for contemplating the water.

★ Tamarin Lodge
B&B £

(☎ 01854-612667; www.tamarinullapool.com; 9 The Braes; s/d £43/86; 🅿 🛜 🐶) Effortlessly elegant modern architecture in this hilltop house is noteworthy in its own right, but the glorious vistas over the hills opposite and water far below are unforgettable. All rooms face the view; some have a balcony, and all are very spacious, quiet and utterly relaxing, with unexpected features and gadgets. The great lounge and benevolent hosts are a delight.

Follow signs for Braes from the Inverness road.

★ West House
B&B ££

(☎ 01854-613126; www.westhousebandb.co.uk; West Argyle St; s £70, d £80-90; ☺ May-Oct; 🅿 🛜) 🍴 Slap bang in the centre, this solid white house, once a manse, offers excellent rooms with contemporary style and great bathrooms. Breakfast is continental: you've got a fridge stocked with fresh fruit, cheeses, yoghurts, homemade bread, proper coffee and juice so you can eat at your leisure in your own chamber. Most rooms have great views, as well as lots of conveniences.

There's a minimum two-night stay. The genial owners also have tempting self-catering options in the Ullapool area.

House on the Point
B&B ££

(☎ 01854-613454; www.ullapoolpoint.com; 27 Shore St; r £85-90; ☺ Easter–mid-Oct; 🅿 🛜) At the end of the shorefront road, this has a prime position with wraparound water vistas. The large double has views both ways but there's a great outlook whichever room you pick. A good continental breakfast, including fruit compote and fresh croissants, is taken in your room, and Angus is a solicitous host.

★ Ceilidh Place
HOTEL £££

(☎ 01854-612103; www.theceilidhplace.com; 14 West Argyle St; s £66-92, d £140-172; ☺ Feb-Dec; 🅿 🛜 🐶) This hotel is a celebration of Scottish culture: we're talking literature and traditional music, not tartan and Nessie dolls. Rooms go for character over modernity; instead of a TV they come with a selection of books chosen by Scottish literati, eclectic artwork and cosy touches. The sumptuous lounge has sofas, chaises longues and an honesty bar. There's a bookshop here too.

It's one of the Highlands' more unusual and delightful places to stay.

🍴 Eating

West Coast Delicatessen
CAFE £

(☎ 01854-613450; www.westcoastdeli.co.uk; 5 Argyle St; light meals £3-7; ☺ 9am-5pm Mon-Sat; 🛜) A likeable venue for coffee or a snack, this upbeat modern place has tasty sub rolls, decent coffee and a variety of deli produce, including some very tasty cheeses. It also does a good soup, perfect for the windier Ullapool days.

Arch Inn
PUB FOOD ££

(☎ 01854-612454; www.thearchinn.co.uk; West Shore St; mains £10-18; ☺ kitchen noon-2.30pm & 5-9pm Mon-Sat, 12.30-2.30pm & 5-9pm Sun; 🛜) There's pleasing pub food to be had at this shorefront establishment, where the cosy bar and restaurant area dishes up generously proportioned, well-presented mains that range from tender chicken and fish dishes to more advanced blackboard specials with local seafood a highlight. Service is helpful and efficient. The outdoor tables right beside the lapping water are a top spot for a pint.

ℹ Information

Ullapool Information Centre (☎ 01854-612486; ullapool@visitscotland.com; 6 Argyle St; ☺ 9am-6pm Mon-Sat, 9.30am-4.30pm Sun Jul & Aug, 9.30am-5pm Mon-Sat, 10am-3pm Sun Jun & Sep, 9.30am-4.30pm Mon-Sat, 10am-3pm Sun Easter-May & Oct) can book ferries and buses.

ℹ Getting There & Away

Citylink has buses from Inverness to Ullapool (£13.20, 1½ hours, one to three daily), connecting with the Lewis ferry.

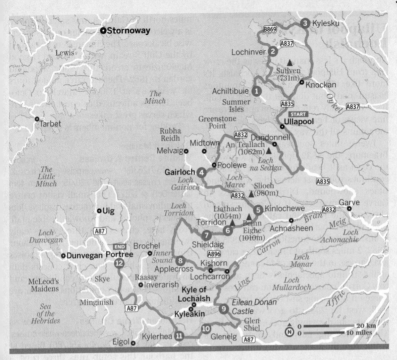

Driving Tour
Wee Roads & Mighty Mountains

START ULLAPOOL
END PORTREE
LENGTH 320 MILES; THREE TO FOUR DAYS

Starting in photogenic harbourside Ullapool, this drive takes in some of the lesser-known roads and the most majestic of Highland scenery, leaving you on the Isle of Skye.

Leave your bags in the hotel, because the first day is a long round-trip from Ullapool. Head north on the A835, and turn left to **1 Achiltibuie** (p366), where after gaping at impressive lochside Stac Pollaidh en route, you can admire the outlook over the Summer Isles. From here, backtrack 6 miles then turn left up the Wee Mad Road, a narrow, tortuous but scenic drive north to **2 Lochinver** (p365). From here, the B869 winds north past spectacular beaches at Achmelvich and Clachtoll to **3 Kylesku** (p365), where the hotel makes a great lunch stop. Return south to Ullapool on the main road (A894-A837-A835), with classic northwestern scenery and things to see along the way including Inchnadamph Caves, Ardvreck Castle and Knockan Crag.

The next day head inland along the A835 before taking the A832 **4 Gairloch** (p370) turn-off, following the coast road and its activity options, from whale-watching trips to a botanic garden and hill walking around Loch Maree. At **5 Kinlochewe** (p371) turn back coastwards on the A896, descending a spectacular pass to **6 Torridon** (p371), where the beauty is simply breathtaking. There are good overnight stops all along this route.

From **7 Shieldaig** (p371), take the coastal road to sublime little **8 Applecross** (p372), then brave the Bealach na Ba pass to get you back to the main road. A loop around Loch Carron will eventually bring you to the A87. Turn left, passing **9 Eilean Donan Castle** (p375) and, reaching Glen Shiel, take the right turn to **10 Glenelg** (p375), a scenic, out-of-the-way place with a wonderfully rustic summer ferry crossing to Skye. Disembark at **11 Kylerhea** (p378) and enjoy the vistas on one of the island's least-trafficked roads before hitting the A87 again. From here, **12 Portree** (p382) is an easy drive, but numerous picturesque detours – to Sleat or Elgol for example – mean you might take a while to reach it yet.

Ullapool to Kyle of Lochalsh

Although it's less than 50 miles as the crow flies from Ullapool to Kyle of Lochalsh, it's more like 150 miles along the circuitous coastal road – but don't let that put you off. It's a deliciously remote region and there are fine views of beaches and bays backed by mountains all the way along.

Twelve miles southeast of Ullapool at Braemore, the A832 doubles back towards the coast as it heads for Gairloch (the A835 continues southeast across the wild, sometimes snowbound, Dirrie More pass to Garve and Inverness). If you're hurrying to Skye, use the A835 and catch up with the A832 further south, near Garve.

Just west of the junction of the A835 and A832, 2 miles south of Braemore, a car park gives access to the **Falls of Measach**, which spill 45m into spectacularly deep and narrow Corrieshalloch Gorge. You can cross the gorge on a swaying suspension bridge, and walk west for 250m to a viewing platform that juts out dizzyingly above a sheer drop. The thundering falls and misty vapours rising from the gorge are very impressive.

Gairloch & Around

POP 1000

Gairloch is a group of villages (comprising Achtercairn, Strath and Charlestown) around the inner end of a loch of the same name. Gairloch is a good base for whale- and dolphin-watching excursions and the surrounding area has beautiful sandy beaches, good trout fishing and birdwatching. Hill walkers also use Gairloch as a base for the Torridon hills and An Teallach.

Sights & Activities

The B8056 runs along Loch Gairloch's southern shore, past the cute little harbour of **Badachro**, to end at the gorgeous pink-sand beach of **Red Point** – a perfect picnic spot. Another coastal road leads north from Gairloch 11 miles to the settlement of **Melvaig**. From here a private road (open to walkers and cyclists) continues 3 miles to **Rua Reidh Lighthouse** (building and grounds off-limits to nonguests).

★ Inverewe Garden GARDENS
(NTS; www.nts.org.uk; adult/concession £10.50/7.50; ◷9.30am-6pm Jun-Aug, 10am-5.30pm Sep, 10am-5pm Apr, May & Oct, 10am-3pm Nov-Mar) Six

miles north of Gairloch, this splendid place is a welcome splash of colour on this otherwise bleak coast. The climate here is warmed by the Gulf Stream, which allowed Osgood MacKenzie to create this exotic woodland garden in 1862. There are free guided tours on weekdays at 1.30pm (March to October). There's a licensed cafe-restaurant here which serves great cakes.

Parking for non-members is steep at £2.

Gairloch Marine Wildlife Centre & Cruises WILDLIFE
(☑01445-712636; www.porpoise-gairloch.co.uk; Pier Rd; cruises adult/child £20/15; ◷10am-4pm Easter-Oct) **FREE** This small visitor centre has audiovisual and interactive displays, lots of charts, photos and knowledgeable staff. From here, cruises run three times daily (weather permitting); during the two-hour trips you may see basking sharks, porpoises and minke whales. The crew collects data on water temperature and conditions, and monitors cetacean populations, so you are subsidising important research.

Hebridean Whale Cruises BOATING
(☑01445-712458; www.hebridean-whale-cruises.com; Pier Rd; cruises 2½/4hr £50/80) Based at the harbour, this setup runs three trips, a standard 2½ hour excursion, a three-hour visit to the seabird-rich Shiant Islands and a four-hour excursion to further-flung feeding grounds. As well as birds and seals, possible wildlife includes otters, dolphins, minke whales and orca. Trips are in a zippy rigid inflatable.

Sleeping & Eating

Rua Reidh Lighthouse LODGE ££
(☑01445-771263; www.stayatalighthouse.co.uk; d £85-95; ◷Easter-Oct; P🐾) Three miles down a private road beyond Melvaig (11 miles north of Gairloch), this simple yet excellent lodge gives a taste of a lighthouse keeper's life. It's a wild, lonely location great for walking and birdwatching. Breakfast is included and tasty evening meals are available. There's no mobile signal or wi-fi and there's usually a two-night minimum stay: book well ahead.

There's a separate self-catering apartment that's available year-round.

Gairloch View Guest House B&B ££
(☑01445-712666; www.gairlochview.com; Auchtercairn; s/d £55/80; P🛜) The unique selling point of this unassuming modern house is a patio with a stunning view over the sea

to Skye – a view you can also enjoy from your breakfast table. The three bedrooms, with plenty of natural light, are comfortably furnished in classic country style, and the lounge has satellite TV and a small library of books and games.

Mountain Coffee Company
CAFE £

(☑ 01445-712316; Strath Sq, Strath; light meals £4-7; ⊘ 9am-5.30pm, shorter hours low season) 🍴 More the sort of place you'd expect to find on the gringo trail in the Andes, this offbeat and cosy (if occasionally a touch brusque) spot is a shrine to mountaineering and travelling. It serves tasty savoury bagels, home baking and sustainably sourced coffees. The conservatory is the place to lap up the sun, while the attached Hillbillies Bookshop is worth a browse. There are rather sweet rooms available too.

Spiral
BISTRO ££

(☑ 01445-712397; www.facebook.com/spiralcafeand bistro; Strath Sq, Strath; mains £11-17; ⊘ noon-2pm & 6-8.30pm Tue-Sat; 🛜🍴) On the square in Strath, this place pleases locals and visitors alike with its upbeat, cheerful atmosphere and range of tasty bistro fare, with a variety of influences. Local seafood features; the monkfish curry is a signature dish. Vegetarian choices show more imagination than the norm.

Loch Maree & Around

Stretching 12 miles between Poolewe and Kinlochewe, Loch Maree is considered one of Scotland's prettiest lochs. At its southern end, tiny Kinlochewe makes a good base for outdoor activities.

Offering magnificent views over Loch Maree, **Beinn Eighe Mountain Trail** is a way-marked 4-mile return walk to a plateau and cairn on the side of Beinn Eighe. It's quite exposed up here, so take some warm clothing. It starts from a car park on the A832 about a mile and a half northwest of the Beinn Eighe visitor centre.

Kinlochewe Hotel (☑ 01445-760253; www. kinlochewehotel.co.uk; Kinlochewe; dm £16.50, s £50, d £90-98; 🅿🛜🐾) 🍴 is a welcoming place that's very walker-friendly. There are nice features like a handsome lounge well stocked with books, a great bar with several real ales on tap and a thoughtful menu of locally sourced food. There are 'economy' rooms that share a bath-only bathroom (£75) and also a bunkhouse with one no-frills 12-bed dorm, a decent kitchen and clean bathrooms.

A colourful presence in the former village hall, **Whistle Stop Cafe** (☑ 01445-760423; Kinlochewe; meals £8-16; ⊘ 9am-6pm Mar-Nov, check for evening opening hours) is a tempting place to drop by for anything from a coffee to enticing bistro fare. There are great daily specials and delicious home baking, juices and smoothies. It's very friendly, and used to pumping life back into chilled walkers and cyclists. It's unlicensed, but you can take your own wine (£1 corkage).

Torridon & Around

The road southwest from Kinlochewe passes through Glen Torridon, amid some of Britain's most beautiful scenery. Carved by ice from massive layers of ancient sandstone that takes its name from the region, the mountains here are steep, shapely and imposing, whether flirting with autumn mists, draped in dazzling winter snows, or reflected in the calm blue waters of Loch Torridon on a summer day.

The road reaches the sea at spectacularly sited Torridon village, then continues westwards to lovely Shieldaig, which boasts an attractive main street of whitewashed houses right on the water.

🏃 Activities

The Torridon Munros – **Liathach** (1054m; pronounced 'lee-agakh', Gaelic for 'the Grey One'), **Beinn Eighe** (1010m; 'ben *ay*', 'the File') and **Beinn Alligin** (986m; 'the Jewelled Mountain') – are big, serious mountains for experienced hill walkers only. Though not technically difficult, their ascents are long and committing, often over rough and rocky terrain. Information is available at the **Torridon Countryside Centre** (NTS; ☑ 01445-791221; www.nts.org.uk; Torridon; ⊘ 10am-5pm Sun-Fri Easter-Sep).

Torridon Sea Tours
BOATING

(☑ 01520-755353; www.torridonseatours.com; Shieldaig) Runs various trips from Shieldaig, including 1½-hour morning or evening cruises on Loch Torridon (adult/child £30/20) and half-day (£50/30) or full-day (£100/50) cruises around offshore islands. You're a good chance of seeing wildlife including sea eagles and porpoises.

🛏 Sleeping & Eating

There's a free campsite at the entrance to Torridon village and some excellent places to stay both here and in Shieldaig.

Torridon SYHA
HOSTEL **£**

(☑ 01445-791284; www.syha.org.uk; Torridon; dm/tw £20/52; ⊙ Mar-Oct, plus weekends Nov-Feb; P @ 🛜 🐾) This spacious hostel has enthusiastic, can-do management and sits in a magnificent location, surrounded by spectacular mountains. Spacious dorms and privates (twins have single beds) are allied to a huge kitchen and convivial lounge area, with ales on sale. It's a very popular walking base, with great advice from the in-house mountain rescue team, so book ahead.

As well as breakfasts, packed lunches and heat-up dinners are offered.

Torridon Inn
INN **££**

(☑ 01445-791242; www.thetorridon.com; Torridon; s/d/q £110/120/185; ⊙ daily May-Oct, Thu-Sun Nov, Mar & Apr, closed Dec-Feb; P 🛜 🐾) This convivial but upmarket walkers hangout offers excellent modern rooms that vary substantially in size and layout. Rooms for groups (up to six) offer more value than the commodious but overpriced doubles. The sociable bar offers all-day food.

★ The Torridon
HOTEL **£££**

(☑ 01445-791242; www.thetorridon.com; Torridon; r standard/superior/master £245/370/450; ⊙ closed Jan, plus Mon & Tue Nov, Dec, Feb & Mar; P @ 🛜 🐾) If you prefer the lap of luxury to the sound of rain beating on your tent, head for this lavish Victorian shooting lodge with a romantic lochside location. Sumptuous contemporary rooms with awe-inspiring views and top bathrooms and a cheery Highland cow atop the counterpane couldn't be more inviting. This is one of Scotland's top country hotels, always luxurious but never pretentious.

Master suites are lavish in size and comfort, with a more classic decor and bay windows making the most of the panoramas. Service is excellent, with muddy boots positively welcomed, and dinners are sumptuous affairs, open to nonguests (£60). Friendly staff can organise any number of activities on land or water.

Tigh an Eilean Hotel
HOTEL **£££**

(☑ 01520-755251; www.tighaneilean.co.uk; Shieldaig; s/d £70/140; ⊙ Feb-Dec; 🛜) With a lovely waterfront position, this is an appealing destination for a relaxing stay, offering not luxury but comfortable old-style rooms. Lochview rooms – with gloriously soothing vistas – are allocated on a first-come basis, so it's worth booking ahead. Service is very helpful, and there's a cosy lounge

with honesty bar. The restaurant's offering includes regional produce, local seafood and delicious Scottish cheeses.

The price drops for stays of three or more nights.

Shieldaig Bar & Coastal Kitchen
SEAFOOD **££**

(☑ 01520-755251; www.shieldaigbarandcoastalkitchen.co.uk; Shieldaig; mains £9-17; ⊙ noon-2.30pm & 6-8.30pm Sep-Jun, noon-8.30pm Jul & Aug; 🛜) This attractive pub has real ales and waterside tables plus a great upstairs dining room and outdoor deck for more casual dining, with an emphasis on local seafood and bistro-style meat dishes like steak-frites or sausages and mash. Blackboard specials feature the daily catch.

Applecross
POP 200

The delightfully remote seaside village of Applecross feels like an island retreat due to its isolation and the magnificent views of Raasay and the hills of Skye that set the pulse racing, particularly at sunset. On a clear day it's an unforgettable place. The campsite and pub fill to the brim in school holidays.

A road leads here 25 winding miles from Shieldaig, but more spectacular (accessed from further south on the A896) is the magnificent Bealach na Ba (626m; Pass of the Cattle), the third-highest motor road in the UK, and the longest continuous climb. Originally built in 1822, it climbs steeply and hair-raisingly via hairpin bends perched over sheer drops, with gradients up to 25%, then drops dramatically to the village with views of Skye.

Just above and behind the waterfront and inn, **Applecross Campsite** (☑ 01520-744268; www.applecross.uk.com; sites per adult/child £9/4.50, 2-person hut £45; ⊙ Mar-Oct; P 🛜 🐾) offers green grassy plots, cute little wooden cabins and a good greenhouse-like cafe.

With its spectacular vistas of Skye, Raasay and the sea, remote **Applecross Inn** (☑ 01520-744262; www.applecross.uk.com; Shore St; mains £9-18; ⊙ noon-9pm; P 🛜) 🍴 has the perfect shoreside location for a sunset pint and is deservedly famous for its food. Most of what's on offer are daily blackboard specials concentrating on local seafood and venison. It's all delicious but you should book your table ahead. Priority is given to room guests.

Lochcarron

POP 900

Appealing, whitewashed Lochcarron is a veritable metropolis in these parts, with two supermarkets, a bank with an ATM and a petrol station. A long shoreline footpath at the loch's edge provides the perfect opportunity for a stroll to walk off breakfast.

The **Old Manse** (☑ 01520-722208; www.the oldmanselochcarron.com; Church St; s/d £45/70, tw with loch view £80; ⓟ🛜🐾) is a top-notch Scottish guesthouse, beautifully appointed and in a prime, quiet lochside position. Rooms are traditional in style and simply gorgeous with elegant furniture. Those overlooking the water are larger and well worth the extra tenner.

On the main waterfront road, the excellent **Rockvilla Guest House** (☑ 01520-722379; www.therockvilla.com; Main St; s £65, d £78-88; ☺ Easter-Oct; ⓟ🛜) has very welcoming hosts and lovely modernised rooms with heaps of space and dreamy views over the water. The restaurant here is open to the public and serves good inventive bistro fare with an Asian twist at fair prices. The owners were looking to move on at last research so things may change.

Four miles west of Lochcarron, the **Kishorn Seafood Bar** (☑ 01529-733240; www. kishornseafoodbar.co.uk; A896, Kishorn; mains £7-16; ☺ 10am-5pm Sat-Thu, to 9pm Fri Easter–mid-Jul & mid-Sep–Nov, 10am-9pm Mon-Sat, to 5pm Sun mid-Jul–mid-Sep) 🍴 is a cute pale blue bungalow which serves the freshest of local seafood simply and well, with very fair prices. The baguettes are great, the views are spectacular, and you've got the satisfaction of knowing that much of what you eat was caught in Loch Kishorn just below. Book for dinner.

Plockton

POP 400

Idyllic little Plockton, with its perfect cottages lining a perfect bay, looks like it was designed as a film set. And it has indeed served as just that – scenes from *The Wicker Man* (1973) were filmed here, and the village became famous as the location for the 1990s TV series *Hamish Macbeth*.

With all this picture-postcard perfection, it's hardly surprising that Plockton is a tourist hot spot, crammed with day trippers and holidaymakers in summer. But there's no denying its appeal, with 'palm trees' (actually hardy New Zealand cabbage palms) lining the waterfront, a thriving small-boat sailing scene and several good places to stay, eat and drink. The big event of the year is the Plockton Regatta.

🏃 Activities

Hire canoes and rowboats on the waterfront to explore the bay.

Sea Kayak Plockton　KAYAKING
(☑ 01599-544422; www.seakayakplockton.co.uk; 1-day beginner course £85) Offers everything from beginner lessons to multiday trips around Skye and highly challenging odysseys right out to St Kilda.

Calum's Seal Trips　BOATING
(☑ 01599-544306; www.calums-sealtrips.com; adult/child £11.50/6; ☺ Apr-Oct) Seal-watching cruises visit swarms of the slippery fellas just outside the harbour. There's an excellent commentary and you may even spot otters too. Trips leave several times daily. There's also a longer dolphin-watching trip available.

🛏 Sleeping

Plockton Station Bunkhouse　HOSTEL £
(☑ 01599-544235; mickcoe@btinternet.com; dm £16; ⓟ🛜) Airily set in the former train station (the new one is opposite), this hostel has cosy four-bed dorms, a garden and kitchen-lounge with plenty of light and good perspectives over the frenetic comings-and-goings (OK, that last bit's a lie) of the platforms below. The owners also do good-value B&B accommodation (single/double £35/54) next door in the inaccurately named 'Nessun Dorma'.

★ Tigh Arran　B&B ££
(☑ 01599-544307; www.plocktonbedandbreakfast. com; Duirinish; s/d £60/70; ⓟ🛜🐾) It's hard to decide which is better at this sweet spot 2 miles from the Plockton shorefront – the warm personal welcome or the absolutely stunning views across to Skye. All three of the en suite rooms – with appealing family options – enjoy the views, as does the comfy lounge. A top spot, far from stress and noise; great value too.

Plockton Hotel　INN ££
(☑ 01599-544274; www.plocktonhotel.co.uk; 41 Harbour St; s/d £95/140, cottage s/d £60/90; 🛜) 🍴 Black-painted Plockton Hotel is one of those classic Highland spots that manages to make everyone happy, whether it's thirst, hunger or fatigue that brings you

knocking. Assiduously tended rooms are a delight, with excellent facilities and thoughtful touches. Those without a water view are consoled with more space and a balcony with rock-garden perspectives. The cottage nearby offers simpler comfort.

Duncraig Castle
B&B ££

(☑ 01599-544295; www.duncraigcastle.co.uk; ℗) Duncraig Castle offers luxurious, offbeat hospitality, as long as stuffed animals don't offend you. At the time of research it was closed for substantial renovation, but should open for the 2017 season. It's very close to Plockton but has its own train station.

🍴 Eating

★ Plockton Shores
SEAFOOD ££

(☑ 01599-544263; www.plocktonshoresrestaurant.com; 30 Harbour St; mains £11-19; ☉ noon-2.15pm & 6-9pm Tue-Sat, noon-2.30pm & 6-9pm Sun; ☍) ❋ This welcoming restaurant attached to a shop sports a tempting menu of local seafood, including good-value platters with langoustines, mussels, crab, squat lobster and more, or succulent hand-dived tempura scallops. There's also a very tasty line in venison, steaks and a small selection of tasty vegetarian dishes that are more than an afterthought. Breakfast, teas and snacks are served from morning until night.

Plockton Inn
SEAFOOD ££

(☑ 01599-544222; www.plocktoninn.co.uk; Innes St; mains £10-18; ☉ noon-2.15pm & 6-9pm; ☎) Offering a wide range of anything from haggis to toothsome local langoustines (Plockton prawns) and daily seafood specials, Plockton Inn covers lots of bases and offers genuinely welcoming service. A range of rooms – some substantially more spacious than others, and some in an annexe – are available at a decent price.

ℹ Getting There & Away

Trains running between Kyle of Lochalsh (£2.70, 15 minutes) and Inverness (£21.90, 2½ hours) stop in Plockton up to four times daily each way.

Kyle of Lochalsh

POP 700

Before the bridge was opened in 1995, this was Skye's principal mainland ferry port. Visitors now tend to buzz through town, but Kyle has some good boat trips if you're interested in marine life and there's some great seafood eating to be done here.

There's a string of B&Bs just outside of town on the road to Plockton.

🏃 Activities

Seaprobe Atlantis
BOATING

(☑ 0800 980 4846; www.seaprobeatlantis.com; adult/child from £13/7; ☉ Easter-Oct) A glass-hulled boat takes you on a spin around the kyle to spot seabirds, seals and maybe an otter. The basic trip includes entertaining commentary and plenty of beautiful jellyfish; longer trips also take in a WWII shipwreck. Book at the tourist office. At the time of research pickups were from Kyleakin, but should be back at Kyle by the time you read this.

🍴 Eating

Buth Bheag
SEAFOOD £

(Old Ferry Slip; salads £3-6; ☉ 10am-5pm Tue-Fri, to 3pm Sat Easter-Oct) This tiny place by the water near the tourist office has great takeaway fresh seafood salads and rolls for a pittance. Munch on them while sitting by the harbour.

★ Waterside
SEAFOOD ££

(☑ 01599-534813; www.watersideseafoodrestaurant.co.uk; mains £15-19; ☉ 6-9pm Mon-Sat, plus noon-2.30pm Wed) ❋ In a former waiting room on the station platform itself, this quaint little spot serves up reliably delicious fresh fish and shellfish. A big effort is made to source sustainably from local producers, and the quality is sky-high. The seafood platter (£23) is tops. In summer you nearly always have to book ahead.

ℹ Information

Next to the main seafront car park, **Kyle of Lochalsh Information Centre** (☑ 01471-822716; ☉ 9.30am-4.30pm Easter-Oct) has tourist information on Skye and the Lochalsh region. Next to it is one of Scotland's most lavishly decorated public toilets.

ℹ Getting There & Away

Citylink runs two to three daily buses from Inverness (£20.50, two hours) and three from Glasgow (£39, five to six hours).

The train route between Kyle of Lochalsh and Inverness (£22.80, 2½ hours, up to four daily) is marvellously scenic.

Kyle to the Great Glen

It's 55 miles southeast via the A87 from Kyle to Invergarry, which lies between Fort William and Fort Augustus, on Loch Oich. The road passes one of Scotland's most famous castles and through picturesque Glen Shiel, while a detour leads to the off-the-beaten-track Glenelg area.

Eilean Donan Castle

Photogenically sited at the entrance to Loch Duich, **Eilean Donan Castle** (📞01599-555202; www.eileandonancastle.com; A87, Dornie; adult/child/family £7/6/17; ⏱10am-6pm Apr-Oct, to 4pm Nov-Jan, to 5pm Feb-Mar) is one of Scotland's most evocative castles and must now be represented in millions of photo albums. It's on an offshore islet, elegantly linked to the mainland by a stone-arched bridge. It's very much a re-creation inside, with an excellent introductory exhibition. Citylink buses from Fort William and Inverness to Portree stop opposite the castle.

Glen Shiel & Glenelg

From Eilean Donan Castle, the A87 follows Loch Duich into spectacular Glen Shiel, with 1000m-high peaks soaring on either side of the road. Here, in 1719, a Jacobite army was defeated by Hanoverian government forces. Among those fighting on the rebel side were clansmen led by famous outlaw Rob Roy MacGregor and 300 soldiers loaned by the king of Spain; the mountain above the battlefield is still called Sgurr nan Spainteach (Peak of the Spaniard).

At Shiel Bridge, home to a famous wildgoat colony, a narrow side road goes over the Bealach Ratagain (pass), with great views of the Five Sisters of Kintail peaks, to Glenelg, where there's a community-run ferry to Skye. From palindromic Glenelg round to the road-end at Arnisdale, the scenery becomes even more spectacular, with great views across Loch Hourn to the remote Knoydart peninsula. Along this road are two fine ruined Iron Age brochs.

There are several good walks in the area, including the two-day, cross-country hike from Morvich to Cannich via scenic **Gleann Lichd** and Glen Affric SYHA (35 miles). The **Five Sisters of Kintail** hill-walking expedition is a classic but seriously challenging.

🛏 Sleeping & Eating

Ratagan SYHA HOSTEL £
(📞01599-511243; www.syha.org.uk; Ratagan; dm/tw £20/54; ⏱Apr–mid-Oct; ℗@🖥) This hostel has excellent facilities and a to-die-for spot on the southern shore of Loch Duich. Cheap meals are on offer and there's a licensed bar. A bus runs Monday to Friday from Kyle of Lochalsh; otherwise it's a 2-mile walk from Shiel Bridge on the main road.

Kintail Lodge Hotel INN, HOSTEL ££
(📞01599-511275; www.kintaillodgehotel.co.uk; Shiel Bridge; dm/s/d £17/70/140; ℗🖥🖥) With most of the fine rooms here facing the loch, you'd be unlucky not to get a decent outlook. There are also two bunkhouses with self-catering facilities, each sleeping six; linen is £6 extra. Tasty bar meals (£13 to £22), including local venison and seafood, are available for lunch (noon to 2.30pm) and dinner (6pm to 9pm).

Glenelg Inn INN ££
(📞01599-522273; www.glenelg-inn.com; Glenelg; mains £10-18; ⏱kitchen 12.30-3.30pm & 6.30-9.30pm; ℗🖥🖥) One of the Highlands' most picturesque places for a pint or a romantic away-from-it-all stay (doubles £110), the Glenelg Inn has tables in a lovely garden with cracking views of Skye. The elegant dining room and cosy bar area serves up posh fare, with the local catch always featuring.

ⓘ Getting There & Away

A picturesque community-owned vehicle **ferry** (www.skyeferry.com; foot passenger/bike/car with passengers £3/4/15; ⏱10am-6pm Easter–mid-Oct) runs from Glenelg across to Kylerhea on Skye. This is a highly recommended way of reaching the island; it runs every 20 minutes and doesn't need booking.

Citylink **buses** between Fort William/Inverness and Skye travel along the A87. One bus runs Monday to Friday from Kyle of Lochalsh to Arnisdale, via Shiel Bridge, Ratagan and Glenelg (£7.50, 1¼ hours).

SKYE

POP 10,000

The Isle of Skye (an t-Eilean Sgiathanach in Gaelic) takes its name from the old Norse *sky-a*, meaning 'cloud island', a Viking reference to the often-mist-enshrouded Cuillin Hills. It's the second-largest of Scotland's islands, a 50-mile-long patchwork of velvet

Skye & Outer Hebrides

moors, jagged mountains, sparkling lochs and towering sea cliffs.

The stunning scenery is the main attraction, but when the mist closes in there are plenty of castles, crofting museums and cosy pubs and restaurants; there are also dozens of art galleries and craft studios.

Along with Edinburgh and Loch Ness, Skye is one of Scotland's top-three tourist destinations. However, the crowds tend to stick to Portree, Dunvegan and Trotternish – it's almost always possible to find peace and quiet in the island's further-flung corners. Come prepared for changeable weather:

when it's fine it's very fine indeed, but all too often it isn't.

Activities

Walking

Skye offers some of the finest – and in places, the roughest and most difficult – walking in Scotland. There are many detailed guidebooks available, including a series of four walking guides by Charles Rhodes, available from the Aros Experience (p382) and the tourist office in Portree. You'll need Ordnance Survey (OS) 1:50,000 maps 23 and 32, or Harvey's 1:25,000 *Superwalker – The Cuillin*. Don't attempt the longer walks in bad weather or in winter.

Easy, low-level routes include: through **Strath Mor** from Luib (on the Broadford–Sligachan road) and on to Torrin (on the Broadford–Elgol road; allow 1½ hours, 4 miles); from **Sligachan to Kilmarie** via Camasunary (four hours, 11 miles); and from **Elgol to Kilmarie** via Camasunary (2½ hours, 6.5 miles). The walk from **Kilmarie to Coruisk** and back via Camasunary and the 'Bad Step' is superb but slightly harder (11 miles round trip, allow five hours). The **Bad Step** is a rocky slab poised above the sea that you have to scramble across; it's easy in fine, dry weather, but some walkers find it intimidating.

Skye Wilderness Safaris (☑ 01470-552292; www.skye-wilderness-safaris.com; per person £95-120; ⊙ May-Sep) runs one-day guided hiking trips for small groups (four to six people) through the Cuillin Hills, into the Quiraing or along the Trotternish ridge; transport to/from Portree included.

Climbing

The Cuillin Hills is a playground for rock climbers, and the two-day traverse of the **Cuillin Ridge** is the finest mountaineering expedition in the British Isles. There are several mountain guides in the area who can provide instruction and safely introduce inexperienced climbers to the more difficult routes.

Skye Guides (☑ 01471-822116; www.skyeguides.co.uk) offers a two-day introduction to rock climbing course for around £420; a private mountain guide can be hired for £260 a day (both rates are for two clients).

Sea Kayaking

The sheltered coves and sea lochs around the coast of Skye provide enthusiasts with magnificent sea-kayaking opportunities.

Skyak Adventures KAYAKING
(☑ 01471-820002; www.skyakadventures.com; 29 Lower Breakish, Breakish; 1-day course per person from £100) Expeditions and courses for both beginners and experienced paddlers to otherwise inaccessible places. Specialist courses include photography and tidal race paddling.

Whitewave Outdoor Centre KAYAKING
(☑ 01470-542414; www.white-wave.co.uk; 19 Linicro, Kilmuir; half-day kayak session per person £40-50; ⊙ Mar-Oct) Provides sea kayaking instruction and guiding for both beginners and experts; prices include equipment hire. Other activities include mountain-boarding, bushcraft and rock climbing.

Tours

There are several operators who offer guided minibus tours of Skye, covering history, culture and wildlife. Rates are from £150 to £200 for a six-hour tour for up to six people.

SkyeBus BUS
(☑ 01470-532428; www.realscottishjourneys.com; adult/child £43/38) Runs full-day minibus tours from Portree to remote parts of the island, including the Quiraing, Neist Point, and the Fairy Pools in Glenbrittle.

Skye Tours BUS
(☑ 01471-822716; www.skye-tours.co.uk; adult/child £35/30; ⊙ Mon-Sat) Five-hour sightseeing tours of Skye in a minibus, taking in the Old Man of Storr, Kilt Rock and Dunvegan Castle. Depart from Kyle of Lochalsh train station at 11.30am (connects with 8.55am train from Inverness, returns to Kyle by 4.45pm in time to catch the return train at 5.13pm).

ℹ Information

INTERNET ACCESS

Portree Tourist Office (☑ 01478-612992; www.visitscotland.com; Bayfield Rd; ⊙ 9am-6pm Mon-Sat, 10am-4pm Sun Jun-Aug, shorter hours Sep-May; 🛜)

Columba 1400 Community Centre (☑ 01478-611407; www.columba1400.com; Staffin; per hr £1; ⊙10am-8pm Mon-Sat Apr-Oct; 🛜)

MEDICAL SERVICES

Portree Community Hospital (☑ 01478-613200; Fancyhill) has a casualty department and dental surgery.

MONEY

Only Portree and Broadford have banks and ATMs. Portree's tourist office has a currency exchange desk.

TOURIST INFORMATION

Portree Tourist Office (p377) The only tourist office on the island; provides internet access and currency exchange. Ask for the free *Art Skye – Gallery & Studio Trails* booklet.

❶ Getting There & Away

BOAT

Despite the bridge, there are still a couple of ferry links between Skye and the mainland. Ferries also operate from Uig on Skye to the Outer Hebrides.

The **CalMac** (📞 0800 066 5000; www.calmac.co.uk; per person/car £2.80/9.40) ferry between Mallaig and Armadale (30 minutes, eight daily Monday to Saturday, five to seven on Sunday) is very popular on weekends and in July and August. Book ahead if you're travelling by car.

Skye Ferry (www.skyeferry.co.uk; car with up to 4 passengers £15; ⊙ Easter–mid Oct) runs a tiny vessel (six cars only) on the short Kylerhea to Glenelg crossing (five minutes, every 20 minutes). The ferry operates from 10am to 6pm daily (till 7pm June to August).

BUS

There are buses from Glasgow to Portree (£42, seven hours, three daily), and Uig (£42, 7½ hours, two daily) via Crianlarich, Fort William and Kyle of Lochalsh, plus a service from Inverness to Portree (£25, 3¼ hours, three daily).

CAR & MOTORCYCLE

The Isle of Skye became permanently tethered to the Scottish mainland when the Skye Bridge opened in 1995. The controversial bridge tolls were abolished in 2004 and the crossing is now free.

Much of the driving is on single-track roads – remember to use passing places to allow any traffic behind you to overtake. There are petrol stations at Broadford (open 24 hours), Armadale, Portree, Dunvegan and Uig.

❶ Getting Around

BUS

Getting around the island by public transport can be a pain, especially if you want to explore away from the main Kyleakin–Portree–Uig road. Here, as in much of the Highlands, there are fewer buses on Saturday and only a handful of Sunday services.

Stagecoach (www.stagecoachbus.com) operates the main bus routes on the island, linking all the main villages and towns. Its Skye Dayrider/Megarider ticket gives unlimited bus travel for one day/seven days for £8.50/32. For timetable info, call **Traveline** (📞 0871 200 22 33; www.travelinescotland.com).

TAXI

You can order a taxi or hire a car (arrange for the car to be waiting at Kyle of Lochalsh train station) from **Kyle Taxi Company** (📞 01599-534323; www.skyecarhire.co.uk; car hire day/week from around £40/240).

Kyleakin (Caol Acain)

POP 100

Poor wee Kyleakin had the carpet pulled from under it when the Skye Bridge opened and it went from being the gateway to the island to a backwater bypassed by the main road. It's now a pleasant, peaceful little place, with a harbour used by yachts and fishing boats.

About 3 miles southwest of Kyleakin, a minor road leads southwards to **Kylerhea**, where there's a 1½-hour nature trail to a shore-front otter hide, where you stand a good chance of seeing these elusive creatures. A little further on is the jetty for the car ferry to Glenelg on the mainland.

The community-run **Bright Water Visitor Centre** (📞 01599-530040; www.eileanban.org; The Pier; adult/child £1/free; ⊙ 10am-4pm Mon-Fri Easter-Sep) serves as a base for tours of Eilean Ban – the island used as a stepping stone by the Skye Bridge – where Gavin Maxwell (author of *Ring of Bright Water*) spent the last 18 months of his life in 1968–69, living in the lighthouse keeper's cottage. The island is now a nature reserve and tours (£7 per person) are available in summer; bookings are a must.

The visitor centre also houses a child-friendly exhibition on Maxwell, the lighthouse and the island's wildlife. Tours run twice daily on weekdays, at 11am and 2pm.

Broadford (An T-Ath Leathann)

POP 750

The long, straggling village of Broadford is a service centre for the scattered communities of southern Skye.

Broadford has a 24-hour petrol station, a bank and a large **Co-op supermarket** (⊙ 8am-10pm Mon-Sat, 9am-6pm Sun) with an ATM.

There are lots of B&Bs in and around Broadford and the village is well placed for exploring southern Skye by car.

🛏 Sleeping & Eating

★ Tigh an Dochais
B&B ££

(☑ 01471-820022; www.skyebedbreakfast.co.uk; 13 Harrapool; d £105; P 🤝) 🌊 A cleverly designed modern building, Tigh an Dochais is one of Skye's best B&Bs – a little footbridge leads to the front door, which is on the 1st floor. Here you'll find the dining room (gorgeous breakfasts) and lounge offering a stunning view of sea and hills; the bedrooms (downstairs) open onto an outdoor deck with that same wonderful view.

Luib House
B&B ££

(☑ 01471-820334; www.luibhouse.co.uk; Luib; r per person £36-38; P 🤝) This large, comfortable and well-appointed B&B, 6 miles north of Broadford, has a good-sized family room.

Berabhaigh
B&B ££

(☑ 01471-822372; www.isleofskye.net/berabhaigh; 3 Lime Park; r per person £38; ⊘ Mar-Oct; P 🤝) This lovely old croft house with bay views is located just off the main road at the eastern end of the village, not far from Creelers.

Broadford Hotel
HOTEL £££

(☑ 01471-822204; www.broadfordhotel.co.uk; Torrin Rd; s/d from £150/164; P 🤝) The Broadford Hotel is a stylish retreat with luxury fabrics and designer colour schemes. There's a formal restaurant and the more democratic **Gabbro Bar** (www.broadfordhotel.co.uk/drink; ⊘ kitchen noon-9pm; 🤝), where you can enjoy a bar meal of smoked haddock chowder or steak pie washed down with Isle of Skye Brewery ale.

★ Cafe Sia
CAFE, PIZZERIA ££

(☑ 01471-822616; www.cafesia.co.uk; mains £6-12; ⊘ 9.30am-9.30pm; 🤝 🍴) 🌊 Serving everything from eggs Benedict and cappuccino to cocktails and seafood specials, this appealing cafe specialises in wood-fired pizzas (also available to take away) and superb artisan coffee (yes, that's a coffee roaster sitting in the corner). There's also an outdoor deck with great views of the Red Cuillin.

★ Creelers
SEAFOOD ££

(☑ 01471-822281; www.skye-seafood-restaurant. co.uk; Lower Harrapool; mains £14-19; ⊘ noon-8.30pm Tue-Sat Mar-Oct; 🍴) 🌊 Broadford has several places to eat but one really stands out: Creelers is a small, bustling, no-frills restaurant that serves some of the best seafood on Skye. The house speciality is traditional Marseille *bouillabaisse* (a rich, spicy seafood stew). Best to book ahead.

Armadale & Sleat

If you cross over the sea to Skye on the ferry from Mallaig you arrive in Armadale, at the southern end of the long, low-lying peninsula known as Sleat (pronounced 'slate'). The landscape of Sleat itself is not exceptional, but it provides a grandstand for ogling the magnificent scenery on either side – take the steep and twisting minor road that loops through Tarskavaig and Tokavaig for stunning views of the Isle of Rum, the Cuillin Hills and Bla Bheinn.

Armadale, where the ferry from Mallaig arrives, is little more than a store, a post office, a cluster of craft shops and a scattering of houses.

◉ Sights & Activities

You can attend **cookery courses** (☑ 01471-833333; www.kinloch-lodge.co.uk; Kinloch, Sleat) run by Lady Claire Macdonald at Kinloch Lodge.

Museum of the Isles
MUSEUM

(☑ 01471-844305; www.clandonald.com; adult/child £8.50/6.95; ⊘ 9.30am-5.30pm Apr-Oct, occasionally shorter hours Oct; P 🐾) Just along the road from Armadale pier is the part-ruined Armadale Castle, former seat of Lord Mac-Donald of Sleat. The neighbouring museum will tell you all you ever wanted to know about Clan Donald, and also provides an easily digestible history of the Lordship of the Isles. Prize exhibits include rare portraits of clan chiefs, and a wine glass that was once used by Bonnie Prince Charlie. The ticket also gives admission to the lovely castle gardens.

🛏 Sleeping & Eating

The northern part of Sleat, around Isleornsay, has a cluster of fine-dining restaurants attached to luxury hotels.

Flora MacDonald Hostel
HOSTEL £

(☑ 01471-844272; www.skye-hostel.co.uk; The Glebe; dm/tw/q £18/40/72; P 🤝) Rustic accommodation 3 miles north of the Mallaig–Armadale ferry, on a farm full of Highland cattle and Eriskay ponies.

Shed
CAFE ££

(☑ 01471-844222; mains £8-15; ⊘ 9am-6pm; P) A cute little wooden shed at Armadale pier has some outdoor tables and serves good seafood salads, pizzas, fish and chips, and coffees. You can sit in or take away.

❶ Getting There & Away

There are six or seven buses a day Monday to Saturday (three on Sunday) from Armadale to Broadford (£3.60, 30 minutes) and Portree (£7, 1¼ hours).

Isleornsay

This pretty harbour, 8 miles north of Armadale, lies opposite Sandaig Bay on the mainland, where Gavin Maxwell lived and wrote his much-loved memoir *Ring of Bright Water*.

Gallery An Talla Dearg (www.eileaniarmain. co.uk; ⊘ 10am-6pm Mon-Fri, to 4pm Sat & Sun Apr-Oct; P) FREE exhibits the works of artists who were inspired by Scottish landscapes and culture.

Three miles south of Isleornsay, **Toravaig House Hotel** (☏ 01471-820200; www.toravaig. com; Toravaig; d £110-149; P 🛜) is one of those places where the owners know a thing or two about hospitality – as soon as you arrive you'll feel right at home, whether relaxing on the sofas by the log fire in the lounge or admiring the view across the Sound of Sleat from the lawn chairs in the garden.

The spacious bedrooms – ask for room 1 (Eriskay), with its enormous sleigh bed – are luxuriously equipped, from the crisp bed linen to the huge, high-pressure shower heads. The elegant restaurant serves the best of local fish, game and lamb. After dinner you can retire to the lounge with a single malt and flick through the yachting magazines – you can even arrange a day trip aboard the hotel's 50ft sailing yacht.

Charming old Victorian hotel, **Hotel Eilean Iarmain** (☏ 01471-833332; www.eilean -iarmain.co.uk; d from £180; P 🛜 🐾) with log fires, chintzy traditional decor, a candlelit restaurant and 12 luxurious rooms, many with sea views. The hotel's cosy, wood-panelled **Prában Bar** (☏ 01471-833332; www. eileaniarmain.co.uk; mains £10-16; ⊘ noon-2.30pm & 5.30-9pm) hosts live folk music and serves delicious, upmarket pub grub.

Elgol (Ealaghol)

On a clear day, the journey along the road from Broadford to Elgol is one of the most scenic on Skye. It takes in two classic postcard panoramas – the view of Bla Bheinn across Loch Slapin (near Torrin), and the superb view of the entire Cuillin range from Elgol pier. Elgol itself is a tiny settlement at the end of a long, single-track road.

The only places to eat is the cafe above the car park halfway down the hill towards the pier, and the restaurant at **Coruisk House** (☏ 01471-866330; http://coruiskhouse. com; r £130-150; ⊘ Mar-Oct; P 🛜). You can buy groceries and get takeaway soup and sandwiches at the **Elgol Shop** (www.elgolshop.com; ⊘ 10am-5pm Mon-Sat) nearby.

Just west of Elgol is the **Spar Cave**, famously visited by Sir Walter Scott in 1814 and mentioned in his poem 'Lord of the Isles'. The 80m-deep cave is wild, remote and filled with beautiful flowstone formations. It is a short walk from the village of Glasnakille, but the approach is over seaweed-covered boulders and is only accessible for one hour either side of low water. Check tide times and route information at the tearoom in Elgol.

❧ Tours

Bella Jane BOATING
(☏ 0800 731 3089; www.bellajane.co.uk; Elgol Pier; adult/child £26/14; ⊘ Apr-Oct) Bella Jane offers a three-hour cruise (three daily) from Elgol harbour to the remote Loch na Cuilce, an impressive inlet surrounded by soaring peaks. On a calm day, you can clamber ashore here to make the short walk to Loch

---

DINOSAUR FOOTPRINTS ON SKYE

The occasional dinosaur bone has been turning up in the Jurassic rocks of the Trotternish peninsula since 1982 – intriguing, but nothing very exciting. Then, following a storm in 2002, a set of fossilised dinosaur footprints was exposed at An Corran in Staffin Bay. Their interest piqued, geologists began taking a closer interest in the Trotternish rocks and, in 2015, a major discovery was made near Duntulm Castle – a 170-million-year-old trackway of footprints left by a group of sauropods. Skye is now a major focus for research into dinosaur evolution.

A collection of Jurassic fossils and further information on dinosaur sites in Skye can be found at the **Staffin Dinosaur Museum** (www.facebook. com/StaffinDinosaurMuseum; 3 Ellishadder, Staffin; adult/child £2/1; ⊘ 10.30am-1pm Mon, Tue, Thu & Fri Easter-Sep; P).

Coruisk in the heart of the Cuillin Hills. You get 1½ hours ashore and visit a seal colony en route.

Aquaxplore
BOATING

(☎0800 731 3089; www.aquaxplore.co.uk; Elgol Pier; ⊙Apr-Oct) Runs 1½-hour high-speed boat trips from Elgol to an abandoned shark-hunting station on the island of Soay (adult/child £30/22), once owned by *Ring of Bright Water* author Gavin Maxwell. There are longer trips (adult/child £56/46, four hours) to Rum, Canna and Sanday to visit breeding colonies of puffins, with the chance of seeing minke whales on the way.

🛏 Sleeping

★ Mary's Thatched Cottages   COTTAGE £££
(☎01471-866275; www.isleofskyecottages.com; 3/7 nights £575/995; ⊙Apr-Sep; P🐾🐕) This cluster of traditional thatch-roofed dwellings (each sleeping two to four people) by the roadside as you arrive in Elgol from Broadford must be the cutest accommodation on the island. Four beautifully reconstructed stone cottages have been designed with modern comforts in mind – the stone slab floors have underfloor heating. Minimum stay is three nights, Friday to Monday; book as far in advance as possible.

❶ Getting There & Away

Bus 55 runs from Broadford to Elgol (£3.80, 55 minutes, three daily Monday to Friday, two Saturday).

Cuillin Hills

The Cuillin Hills are Britain's most spectacular mountain range (the name comes from the Old Norse *kjöllen,* meaning 'keel-shaped'). Though small in stature – Sgurr Alasdair, the highest summit, is only 993m – the peaks are near-alpine in character, with knife-edge ridges, jagged pinnacles, scree-filled gullies and hectares of naked rock. While they are a paradise for experienced mountaineers, the higher reaches of the Cuillin are off limits to the majority of walkers.

The good news is that there are also plenty of good low-level hikes within the ability of most walkers. One of the best (on a fine day) is the steep climb from Glenbrittle campsite to Coire Lagan (6 miles round-trip; allow at least three hours). The impressive upper corrie contains a lochan for bathing (for the hardy!), and the surrounding cliffs are a playground for rock climbers – bring your binoculars.

Even more spectacular, but much harder to reach on foot, is Loch Coruisk (from the Gaelic Coir'Uisg, the Water Corrie), a remote loch ringed by the highest peaks of the Cuillin. Accessible by boat trip (p380) from Elgol, or via an arduous 5.5-mile hike from Kilmarie, Coruisk was popularised by Sir Walter Scott in his 1815 poem *Lord of the Isles.* Crowds of Victorian tourists and landscape artists followed in Scott's footsteps, including JMW Turner, whose watercolours were used to illustrate Scott's works.

There are two main bases for exploring the Cuillin – Sligachan to the north (on the Kyle of Lochalsh–Portree bus route), and Glenbrittle to the south (no public transport).

🛏 Sleeping & Eating

Glenbrittle Campsite   CAMPSITE £
(☎01478-640404; www.dunvegancastle.com; Glenbrittle; sites per adult/child incl car £10/6; ⊙Apr-Sep) Excellent site, close to mountains and sea, with a shop selling food and outdoor kit. The midges can be diabolical, though.

Sligachan Campsite   CAMPSITE £
(Sligachan; sites per person £7.50; ⊙Apr-Oct) This basic campsite is across the road from the Sligachan Hotel. Be warned – this spot is a midge magnet. No bookings.

Glenbrittle SYHA   HOSTEL £
(☎01478-640278; Glenbrittle; dm £20; ⊙Apr-Sep; P) Scandinavian-style timber hostel that quickly fills up with climbers on holiday weekends.

Sligachan Hotel   HOTEL £££
(☎01478-650204; www.sligachan.co.uk; Sligachan; per person from £70; P🐕) The Slig, as it has been known to generations of climbers, is a near village in itself, encompassing a comfortable hotel, a microbrewery, self-catering cottages, a small mountaineering museum, a big barn of a pub – Seamus Bar (Sligachan Hotel; mains £10-15; ⊙food served 11am-9.30pm; 🐕🍴) – and an adventure playground.

Minginish

Loch Harport, to the north of the Cuillin, divides the Minginish Peninsula from the rest of Skye. On its southern shore lies the village of Carbost, home to Talisker malt whisky, produced at Talisker Distillery.

Magnificent **Talisker Bay**, 5 miles west of Carbost, is framed by a sea stack and a waterfall.

There's one bus a day (school days only) from Portree to Carbost (£3.90, 40 minutes) via Sligachan.

Skye's only distillery, **Talisker** (☑ 01478-614308; www.discovering-distilleries.com/talisker; guided tour £8; ☺ 9.30am-5pm Mon-Sat, 11am-5pm Sun Jun-Aug, shorter hours Sep-May; ℗) produces smooth, sweet and smoky Talisker single-malt whisky. The guided tour includes a free dram.

Three miles northwest of Carbost, **Skyewalker Independent Hostel** (☑ 01478-640250; www.skyewalkerhostel.com; Fiskavaig Rd, Portnalong; dm £17-20; ℗) is housed in the old village school, with cosy lounge, well-equipped kitchen, and superb gardens with glamping huts (£60 for two people) and a glass-domed outdoor seating area. No wi-fi or mobile phone signal.

The **Old Inn** (☑ 01478-640205; www.theoldinnskye.co.uk; Carbost; bunkhouse per person from £18, s/d £55/84; ℗) is an atmospheric wee pub, offering accommodation in bright B&B bedrooms and an appealing chalet-style bunkhouse. The bar is a favourite with walkers and climbers from Glenbrittle, and serves excellent pub grub (£10 to £20, noon to 10pm), from fresh oysters to haddock and chips. There's an outdoor patio at the back with great views over Loch Harport.

The **Oyster Shed** (www.theoysterman.co.uk; Carbost; mains £4-9; ☺ 11am-6pm Mon-Sat, noon-5pm Sun Apr-Oct, shorter hours Nov-Mar) 🖉 is a farm shop that sells fresh local seafood to take away, including oysters, cooked mussels and scallops, lobster and chips, and seafood platters.

Portree (Port Righ)

POP 2490

Portree is Skye's largest and liveliest town. It has a pretty harbour lined with brightly painted houses, and there are great views of the surrounding hills. Its name (from the Gaelic for King's Harbour) commemorates James V, who came here in 1540 to pacify the local clans.

◉ Sights & Activities

Aros Centre   CULTURAL CENTRE
(☑ 01478-613750; www.aros.co.uk; Viewfield Rd, Portree; exhibition £5; ☺ 9am-5pm; ℗ 🖑) **FREE** On the southern edge of Portree, the Aros Centre is a combined visitor centre, book and gift shop, restaurant, theatre and cinema. The new St Kilda Exhibition details the history and culture of these remote rocky outcrops, and XBOX technology allows you to take a virtual tour of the islands.

The centre is a useful rainy-day retreat, with an indoor soft play area for children.

MV Stardust   BOATING
(☑ 07798 743858; www.skyeboat-trips.co.uk; Portree Harbour; adult/child £18/12) MV *Stardust* offers 1½-hour boat trips around Portree Bay, with the chance to see seals, porpoises and – if you're lucky – white-tailed sea eagles. There are longer two-hour cruises to the Sound of Raasay (£25/15). You can also arrange fishing trips, or to be dropped off for a hike on the Isle of Raasay and picked up again later.

✨ Festivals & Events

Isle of Skye
Highland Games   SPORTS
(www.skye-highland-games.co.uk) These annual games are held in Portree in early August.

🛏 Sleeping

Portree is well supplied with B&Bs, but accommodation fills up fast in July and August, so be sure to book ahead.

Portree Youth Hostel   HOSTEL £
(SYHA; ☑ 01478-612231; www.syha.org.uk; Bayfield Rd; dm/tw £24/66; ℗ 📶) This brand new SYHA hostel (formerly Bayfield Backpackers) has been completely renovated and offers brightly decorated dorms and private rooms, a stylish lounge with views over the bay, and outdoor seating areas, with an ideal location in the town centre just 100m from the bus stop.

Torvaig Campsite   CAMPSITE £
(☑ 01478-611849; www.portreecampsite.co.uk; Torvaig; sites per adult/child £8/3; ☺ Apr-Oct; 📶) An attractive, family-run campsite located 1.5 miles north of Portree, on the road to Staffin.

Ben Tianavaig B&B   B&B ££
(☑ 01478-612152; www.ben-tianavaig.co.uk; 5 Bosville Tce; r £78-90; ℗ 📶) 🖉 A warm welcome awaits from the Irish-Welsh couple who run this appealing B&B bang in the centre of town. All four bedrooms have a view across the harbour to the hill that gives the house its name and breakfasts include free-range eggs and vegetables grown in the garden.

Two-night minimum stay April to October; no credit cards.

Woodlands
B&B ££

(☑ 01478-612980; www.woodlands-portree.co.uk; Viewfield Rd; r £70; ⊙ Mar-Oct; P 🛜) A great location, with views across the bay, and unstinting hospitality make this modern B&B, a half-mile south of the town centre, a good choice.

Rosedale Hotel
HOTEL ££

(☑ 01478-613131; www.rosedalehotelskye.co.uk; Beaumont Cres; s/d from £60/90; ⊙ Easter-Oct; P 🛜) The Rosedale is a cosy, old-fashioned hotel delightfully situated down by the waterfront – you'll be welcomed with a glass of whisky when you check-in. Its three converted fishermen's cottages are linked by a maze of narrow stairs and corridors, the recently spruced-up bedrooms include a couple with four-poster beds, and the dining room has a view of the harbour.

Cuillin Hills Hotel
HOTEL £££

(☑ 01478-612003; www.cuillinhills-hotel-skye.co.uk; Scorrybreac Rd; r from £240; P 🛜) Located on the eastern fringes of Portree, this luxury hotel enjoys a superb outlook across the harbour towards the Cuillin mountains. The more expensive rooms cosset guests with four-poster beds and panoramic views, but everyone can enjoy the scenery from the glass-fronted restaurant and well-stocked whisky bar.

🍴 Eating

Café Arriba
CAFE £

(☑ 01478-611830; www.cafearriba.co.uk; Quay Brae; mains £6-12; ⊙ 7am-6pm daily May-Sep, 8am-5pm Thu-Sat Oct-Apr; 🖉) 🌱 Arriba is a funky little cafe, brightly decked out in primary colours and offering delicious flatbread melts (bacon, leek and cheese is a favourite), as well as the best choice of vegetarian grub on the island, ranging from a veggie breakfast fry-up to falafel wraps with hummus and chilli sauce. Also serves excellent coffee.

★ Scorrybreac
MODERN SCOTTISH ££

(☑ 01478-612069; www.scorrybreac.com; 7 Bosville Tce; 2-/3-course dinner £27.50/32.50; ⊙ 5-9.30pm Tue-Sat) 🌱 Set in the front rooms of what was once a private house, and with just eight tables, Scorrybreac is snug and intimate, offering fine dining without the faff. Chef Calum Munro (son of Donnie Munro, of Gaelic rock band Runrig fame) sources

as much produce as possible from Skye, including foraged herbs and mushrooms, and creates the most exquisite concoctions.

Dulse & Brose
MODERN SCOTTISH ££

(☑ 01478-612846; www.bosvillehotel.co.uk; Bosville Hotel, 7 Bosville Tce; mains £15-22; ⊙ noon-3pm & 6-10pm; 🛜) 🌱 This hotel restaurant sports a relaxed atmosphere, an award-winning chef and a menu that makes the most of Skye produce – including lamb, game, seafood, cheese, organic vegetables and berries – and adds a French twist to traditional dishes. The neighbouring **Merchant Bar** (food served noon to 10pm) serves tapas-style bar snacks through the afternoon.

Sea Breezes
SEAFOOD ££

(☑ 01478-612016; www.seabreezes-skye.co.uk; 2 Marine Buildings, Quay St; mains £13-21; ⊙ 12.30-2pm & 5.30-9pm Mon-Sat Apr-Oct) 🌱 Sea Breezes is an informal, no-frills restaurant specialising in local fish and shellfish fresh from the boat – try the impressive seafood platter, a small mountain of langoustines, crab, oysters and lobster (£50 for two). Book early, as it's often hard to get a table.

MADDENING MIDGES

Forget Nessie; the Highlands have a real monster. A voracious bloodsucking female fully 3mm long named the Highland midge (culicoides impunctatus). The bane of campers and as much a symbol of Scotland as the kilt or dram, they drive sane folk to distraction, descending in biting clouds.

Though normally vegetarian, the female midge needs a dose of blood in order to lay her eggs. And, like it or not, if you're in the Highlands between June and August, you just volunteered as a donor. Midges especially congregate near water, and are most active in the early morning, though squadrons also patrol in the late evening.

Repellents and creams are reasonably effective, though some walkers favour midge veils. Light-coloured clothing also helps. Many pubs and campsites have midge-zappers. Check www.midgeforecast.co.uk for activity levels by area, but don't blame us: we've been eaten alive when the forecast said moderate too.

❶ Getting There & Around

BUS

The main bus stop is at Somerled Sq. There are six Scottish Citylink buses every day from Kyle of Lochalsh to Portree (£6.70, one hour) continuing to Uig.

Local buses (mostly six to eight Monday to Saturday, three on Sunday) run from Portree to:

Armadale (£7, 1¼ hours) Connecting with the ferry to Mallaig.

Broadford (£5.30, 40 minutes)

Dunvegan Castle (£4.80, 40 minutes, one daily)

There are also three buses a day on a circular route around Trotternish (in both directions), taking in Flodigarry (£4.10, 35 minutes), Kilmuir (£4.80, 45 minutes) and Uig (£3.60, 30 minutes).

BICYCLE

Island Cycles (☑ 01478-613121; www.island cycles-skye.co.uk; The Green; hire bike per half-/full day £8.50/17.50; ☺ 9am-5pm Mon-Sat) You can hire bikes here.

Dunvegan (Dun Bheagain)

Dunvegan, an unremarkable village on the western side of Skye, is famous for its historic namesake castle which has links to Sir Walter Scott and Bonnie Prince Charlie.

Skye's most famous historic building, and one of its most popular tourist attractions, **Dunvegan Castle** (☑ 01470-521206; www.dun vegancastle.com; adult/child £12/9; ☺ 10am-5.30pm Apr–mid-Oct; P) is the seat of the chief of Clan MacLeod. In addition to the usual castle stuff – swords, silver and family portraits – there are some interesting artefacts, including the Fairy Flag, a diaphanous silk banner that dates from some time between the 4th and 7th centuries, and Bonnie Prince Charlie's waistcoat and a lock of his hair, donated by Flora MacDonald's granddaughter.

From the end of the minor road beyond Dunvegan Castle entrance, an easy 1-mile walk leads to the Coral Beaches – a pair of blindingly white beaches composed of the bleached exoskeletons of coralline algae known as *maerl*.

On the way to Dunvegan from Portree you'll pass **Edinbane Pottery** (☑ 01470-582234; www.edinbane-pottery.co.uk; Edinbane; ☺ 9am-6pm daily Easter-Oct, Mon-Fri Nov-Easter), one of the island's original craft workshops, established in 1971, where you can watch potters at work creating beautiful and colourful stoneware.

Duirinish & Waternish

The Duirinish peninsula to the west of Dunvegan, and Waternish to the north, boast some of Skye's most atmospheric hotels and restaurants, plus an eclectic range of artists studios and crafts workshops.

The sparsely populated Duirinish peninsula is dominated by the distinctive flat-topped peaks of Helabhal Mhor (469m) and Helabhal Bheag (488m), known locally as MacLeod's Tables. There are some fine walks from Orbost, including the summit of Helabhal Bheag (allow 3½ hours return) and the 5-mile trail from Orbost to MacLeod's Maidens, a series of pointed sea stacks at the southern tip of the peninsula.

It's worth making the long drive beyond Dunvegan to the western side of the Duirinish peninsula to see the spectacular sea cliffs of Waterstein Head and to walk down to Neist Point lighthouse with its views to the Outer Hebrides.

🛏 Sleeping & Eating

Eco Bells Glamping   CAMPSITE £
(☑ 01470-521461; Orbost, Duirinish; per tent £82; ☺ Apr-Sep; P) ✐ Tucked away in a remote corner of the island, on a minor road about 3 miles south of Dunvegan, this place offers accommodation in three large bell tents in a rural setting. Each tent sleeps up to three adults (or two adults and two children) and has beds, heating, a fire pit and barbecue.

★**Hillstone Lodge**   B&B ££
(☑ 01470-511434; www.hillstonelodge.com; 12 Colbost; s/d £110/120; P 🛜) ✐ You can't help notice the many new houses on Skye that bear the hallmarks of award-winning local architects Rural Design – weathered timber walls and modern materials used with traditional shapes and forms. Hillstone is one of the best, with tasteful modern styling and stunning views across Loch Dunvegan. It's about 1km north of the Three Chimneys, above the pier.

★**Red Roof Café**   CAFE ££
(☑ 01470-511766; www.redroofskye.co.uk; Glendale, Duirinish; mains £9-13; ☺ 11am-5pm Sun-Thu Easter-Oct; P 🛜 👪 🐾) ✐ Tucked away up a glen, a mile off the main road, this restored 250-year-old byre is a wee haven of home-grown grub. As well as great coffee and cake, there are lunch platters (noon to 3pm) of Skye seafood, game or cheese served with

salad leaves and edible flowers grown just along the road.

Stein Inn　　　　　PUB FOOD **££**

(☎01470-592362; www.steininn.co.uk; Stein, Waternish; mains £7-15; ⊙kitchen noon-4pm & 6-9.30pm Mon-Sat, 12.30-4pm & 6.30-9pm Sun Easter-Oct; **P**) This old country inn dates from 1790 and has a handful of bedrooms (per person £39 to £58), all with sea views, a lively little bar and a delightful beer garden beside the loch – a real suntrap on summer afternoons. The bar serves real ales from the Isle of Skye Brewery and excellent bar meals. Food is served in winter too, but call ahead to check hours.

★ Three Chimneys　　MODERN SCOTTISH **£££**

(☎01470-511258; www.threechimneys.co.uk; Colbost; 3-course lunch/dinner £38/65; ⊙12.15-1.45pm Mon-Sat mid-Mar–Oct, plus Sun Easter-Sep, 6.15-9pm daily year-round; **P**🛜) 🍴 Halfway between Dunvegan and Waterstein, the Three Chimneys is a superb romantic retreat combining a gourmet restaurant in a candlelit crofter's cottage with sumptuous five-star rooms (double £345) in the modern house next door. Book well in advance, and note that children are not welcome in the restaurant in the evenings.

Lochbay Seafood Restaurant　　SEAFOOD **£££**

(☎01470-592235; www.lochbay-seafood-restaurant. co.uk; Stein, Waternish; 3-course dinner £37.50; ⊙12.15-1.45pm Wed-Sun, 6.15-9pm Tue-Sat Apr-early Oct; **P**) 🍴 This is one of Skye's most romantic restaurants, a cosy farmhouse kitchen of a place with terracotta tiles and a woodburning stove, and a menu that includes most things that either swim in the sea or live in a shell. Best to book ahead.

🛍 Shopping

Shilasdair Yarns　　　　KNITWEAR

(☎01470-592297; www.theskyeshilasdairshop. co.uk; Carnach, Waternish; ⊙10am-6pm Apr-Oct) The couple who run this place, a few miles north of Stein, moved to Skye in 1971 and now raise sheep, hand-spin woollen yarn, and hand-dye a range of wools and silks using natural dyes. You can see the dyeing process and try hand-spinning in the exhibition area behind the studio, which sells finished knitwear as well as yarns.

Skye Weavers　　　　ARTS & CRAFTS

(☎01470-511201; www.skyeweavers.co.uk; 18 Fasach, Glendale, Duirinish; ⊙10am-6pm Tue-Sat Mar-Oct) Signposted off the main road, a wooden shed on an old croft houses a pedal-powered loom where the owners create hand-woven tweed and turn it into scarves, shawls, throws and other household and fashion items. You can watch the loom at work before browsing the shop.

Dandelion Designs　　　ARTS & CRAFTS

(☎01470-592218; www.dandelion-designs.co.uk; Captain's House, Stein, Waternish; ⊙11am-5pm Easter-Oct, shorter hours Nov-Mar; 👶) Dandelion Designs is an interesting little gallery with a good range of colour and monochrome landscape photography, lino prints by Liz Myhill and a range of handmade arts and crafts.

Trotternish

The Trotternish Peninsula to the north of Portree has some of Skye's most beautiful – and bizarre – scenery. A loop road allows a circular driving tour of the peninsula from Portree, passing through the village of Uig, where the ferry to the Outer Hebrides departs.

⊙ Sights & Activities

★ Quiraing　　　　ROCK FORMATION

Staffin Bay is dominated by the dramatic basalt escarpment of the Quiraing: its impressive land-slipped cliffs and pinnacles constitute one of Skye's most remarkable landscapes. From a parking area at the highest point of the minor road between Staffin and Uig you can walk north to the Quiraing in half an hour.

Old Man of Storr　　　ROCK FORMATION

The 50m-high, pot-bellied pinnacle of crumbling basalt known as the Old Man of Storr is prominent above the road 6 miles north of Portree. Walk up to its foot from the car park at the northern end of Loch Leathan (2-mile round-trip). This seemingly unclimbable pinnacle was first scaled in 1955 by English mountaineer Don Whillans, a feat that has been repeated only a handful of times since.

Fairy Glen　　　　OUTDOORS

Just south of Uig, a minor road (signposted 'Sheader and Balnaknock') leads in a mile or so to the Fairy Glen, a strange and enchanting natural landscape of miniature conical hills, rocky towers, ruined cottages and a tiny roadside lochan.

Skye Museum of Island Life MUSEUM
(📞01470-552206; www.skyemuseum.co.uk; Kilmuir; adult/child £2.50/50p; ⏱9.30am-5pm Mon-Sat Easter-late Sep; 🅿) The peat-reek of crofting life in the 18th and 19th centuries is preserved in the thatched cottages, croft houses, barns and farm implements of the Skye Museum of Island Life. Behind the museum is Kilmuir Cemetery, where a tall Celtic cross marks the grave of Flora MacDonald; the cross was erected in 1955 to replace the original monument, of which 'every fragment was removed by tourists'.

🛏 Sleeping & Eating

⭐**Cowshed Boutique Bunkhouse** HOSTEL £
(📞07917 536820; www.skyecowshed.co.uk; Uig; dm/tw £20/80, pod £70; 🅿🤗📶) This new hostel enjoys a glorious setting overlooking Uig Bay, with superb views from its ultra-stylish lounge. The dorms have custom-built wooden bunks that offer comfort and privacy, while the camping pods (sleeping up to four, but more comfortable with two) have heating and en suite shower rooms; there are even mini 'dog pods' for your canine companions.

Shulista Croft CAMPSITE £
(📞01470-552314; www.shulistacroft.co.uk; North Duntulm, Shulista; campervan sites £15, pod per night £80) 🌿 Set on a working croft amid sheep, lambs and chickens, Shulista has four luxury timber camping pods with great views (two night minimum stay; sleeps up to four, kids stay free). Each one is heated and insulated, and has an en suite shower room, basic kitchenette and even a TV. There are also pitches for campervans and motorhomes.

Dun Flodigarry Hostel HOSTEL £
(📞01470-552212; www.hostelflodigarry.co.uk; Flodigarry; dm/tw £19/45, tent sites per person £9.50; 🅿@📶) A bright and welcoming hostel that enjoys a stunning location overlooking the sea, with views across Raasay to the mainland mountains. A nearby hiking trail leads to the Quiraing rock formation (2.5 miles away), and there's a hotel bar barely 100m from the door. You can also camp nearby and use all the hostel facilities.

Single Track CAFE £
(www.facebook.com/SingleTrackSkye; Kilmaluag; snacks £3; ⏱10.30am-5pm Sun-Thu; 🅿📶) This turf-roofed, timber-clad art gallery and es-

presso bar will be familiar to fans of British TV's *Grand Designs* – it was featured on the Channel 4 series in 2012. The owners are serious about their coffee, and it's seriously good, as are the accompanying cakes and scones. Art by the owners and other Skye artists is on display, and for sale.

Raasay
POP 160

Raasay is the rugged, 10-mile-long island that lies off Skye's east coast. The island's fascinating history is recounted in the book *Calum's Road* by Roger Hutchinson.

There are several good walks here, including one to the flat-topped conical hill of **Dun Caan** (443m), and another to the extraordinary ruin of **Brochel Castle**, perched on a pinnacle at the northern end of Raasay. The Forestry Commission publishes a free leaflet (available in the ferry waiting room) with suggested walking trails.

Just a short walk from the ferry pier, beautifully renovated **Raasay House** (📞01478-660266; www.raasay-house.co.uk; dm £17, d £155; 🅿📶) 🌿 was originally the laird's residence. It provides outdoor activity courses and accommodation ranging from hostel bunks to luxury B&B. The bar and restaurant (mains £5 to £19) serves good quality pub grub and locally brewed beers.

Accommodation is very limited – don't turn up without a reservation unless you are planning to wild camp (there are plenty of places to do so in the east and north of the island).

CalMac (www.calmac.co.uk; return passenger/car £1.85/6.10) ferries run from Sconser, on the road from Portree to Broadford, to Raasay (25 minutes, nine daily Monday to Saturday, twice daily Sunday). There are no petrol stations (or public transport) on the island.

OUTER HEBRIDES

The Western Isles, or Na h-Eileanan an Iar in Gaelic – also known as the Outer Hebrides – are a 130-mile-long string of islands lying off the northwest coast of Scotland. There are 119 islands in total, of which the five main inhabited islands are Lewis and Harris (two parts of a single island, although often described as if they are separate islands), North Uist, Benbecula, South Uist and Barra. The middle three (often referred to simply as 'the Uists') are connected by road-bearing causeways.

The ferry crossing from Ullapool or Uig to the Western Isles marks an important cultural divide – more than a third of Scotland's registered crofts are in the Outer Hebrides, and no less than 60% of the population are Gaelic speakers. The rigours of life in the old island blackhouses are still within living memory.

Religion still plays a prominent part in public and private life, especially in the Protestant north, where shops and pubs close their doors on Sunday and some accommodation providers prefer guests not to arrive or depart on the Sabbath. The Roman Catholic south is a little more relaxed about these things.

If your time is limited, head straight for the west coast of Lewis with its prehistoric sites, preserved blackhouses and beautiful beaches. As with Skye, the islands are dotted with arts and crafts studios – the tourist offices can provide a list.

ℹ️ Information

INTERNET RESOURCES

CalMac (☎ 0800 066 5000; www.calmac. co.uk) Ferry timetables.

Visit Hebrides (www.visithebrides.com) Tourist information.

MEDICAL SERVICES

Uist & Barra Hospital (☎ 01870-603603; Balivanich, Benbecula)

Western Isles Hospital (☎ 01851-704704; MacAulay Rd)

MONEY

There are banks with ATMs in Stornoway (Lewis), Tarbert (Harris), Lochmaddy (North Uist), Balivanich (Benbecula), Lochboisdale (South Uist)

and Castlebay (Barra). Elsewhere, some hotels and shops offer cash-back facilities.

TOURIST INFORMATION

Castlebay Tourist Office (☎ 01871-810336; www.visithebrides.com; Main St, Castlebay; ⏱ 9.15am-1pm & 2-4.45pm Mon-Sat, noon-4pm Sun Jul & Aug, shorter hours Apr-May & Sep)

Stornoway Tourist Office (☎ 01851-703088; www.visithebrides.com; 26 Cromwell St, Stornoway; ⏱ 9am-6pm Mon-Sat year-round)

Tarbert Tourist Office (☎ 01859-502011; www.visithebrides.com; Pier Rd; ⏱ 9am-5pm Mon-Sat Apr-Oct)

ℹ️ Getting There & Away

AIR

There are airports at Stornoway (Lewis), Benbecula and Barra. Flights operate to Stornoway from Edinburgh, Inverness, Glasgow and Aberdeen. There are also two flights a day (Tuesday to Thursday only) between Stornoway and Benbecula.

There are daily flights from Glasgow to Barra, and from Tuesday to Thursday to Benbecula. At Barra, the planes land on the hard-sand beach at low tide, so the schedule depends on the tides.

Eastern Airways (☎ 0870 366 9100; www. easternairways.com)

FlyBe/Loganair (☎ 01857-873457; www. loganair.co.uk)

ℹ️ Getting Around

Despite their separate names, Lewis and Harris are actually one island. Berneray, North Uist, Benbecula, South Uist and Eriskay are all linked by road bridges and causeways. There are car ferries between Leverburgh (Harris) and Berneray and between Eriskay and Castlebay (Barra).

The local council publishes timetables of all bus and ferry services within the Outer

OUTER HEBRIDES FERRIES

There are two or three ferries a day to Stornoway, one or two a day to Tarbert and Lochmaddy, and one a day to Castlebay and Lochboisdale.

Advance booking for cars is recommended (essential in July and August); foot and bicycle passengers should have no problems. Bicycles are carried free.

Standard one-way fares on **CalMac** ferries:

CROSSING	DURATION (HOURS)	CAR (£)	DRIVER/PASSENGER (£)
Oban–Castlebay	4¾	66	14.30
Mallaig–Lochboisdale	3½	56	10.15
Uig–Lochmaddy	1¾	30	6.10
Uig–Tarbert	1½	30	6.10
Ullapool–Stornoway	2¾	49.50	9.20

Hebrides, which is available at tourist offices. Timetables can also be found online at www. cne-siar.gov.uk/travel.

BICYCLE

Bikes can be hired for around £12 to £15 a day or £60 to £80 a week in Stornoway (Lewis), Uig (Lewis), Leverburgh (Harris), Howmore (South Uist) and Castlebay (Barra).

BUS

The bus network covers almost every village in the islands, with around four to six buses a day on all the main routes; however, there are no buses at all on Sunday. You can pick up timetables from tourist offices, or call **Stornoway bus station** (p389) for information.

CAR & MOTORCYCLE

Apart from the fast, two-lane road between Tarbert and Stornoway, most roads are single track (p466). The main hazard is posed by sheep wandering about or sleeping on the road. Petrol stations are far apart (almost all of those on Lewis and Harris are closed on Sunday), and fuel is about 10% more expensive than on the mainland.

There are petrol stations at Stornoway, Barvas, Borve, Uig, Breacleit (Great Bernera), Ness, Tarbert and Leverburgh on Lewis and Harris; Lochmaddy and Cladach on North Uist; Balivanich on Benbecula; Howmore, Lochboisdale and Daliburgh on South Uist; and Castlebay on Barra.

Cars can be hired from around £35 per day.

Arnol Motors (☑ 018510-710548; www.arnol motors.com; Arnol, Lewis; per day from £40; ☉ 8am-5pm Mon-Sat)

Lewis Car Rentals (☑ 01851-703760; www. lewis-car-rental.co.uk; 52 Bayhead St; per day from £40; ☉ 8am-5pm Mon-Sat)

Lewis (Leodhais)

POP 19,000

The northern part of Lewis is dominated by the desolate expanse of the Black Moor, a vast, undulating peat bog dimpled with glittering lochans, seen clearly from the Stornoway–Barvas road. But Lewis' finest scenery is on the west coast, from Barvas southwest to Mealista, where the rugged landscape of hill, loch and sandy strand is reminiscent of the northwestern Highlands. The Outer Hebrides' most evocative historic sites – Callanish Standing Stones, Dun Carloway and Arnol Blackhouse Museum – are also to be found here.

Stornoway (Steornabhagh)

POP 5715

Stornoway is the bustling 'capital' of the Outer Hebrides and the only real town in the whole archipelago. It's a surprisingly busy little place, with cars and people swamping the centre on weekdays. Though set on a beautiful natural harbour, the town isn't going to win any prizes for beauty or atmosphere, but it's a pleasant enough introduction to this remote corner of the country.

◉ Sights

Lews Castle   CASTLE
(☑ 01851-822750; www.lews-castle.co.uk; ☉ 10am-5pm Mon-sat May-Sep, shorter hours Oct-Apr; P) **FREE** The Baronial mansion across the harbour from Stornoway town centre was built in the 1840s for the Matheson family, then owners of Lewis; it was gifted to the community by Lord Leverhulme in 1923. A major redevelopment sees the new **Museum nan Eilean** (Museum of the Isles) opening here from late 2016, covering the history of the Outer Hebrides and exploring traditional island life. It's hoped that some of the famous Lewis chessmen will be on display.

The beautiful wooded grounds, crisscrossed with walking trails, are open to the public and host the Hebridean Celtic Festival in July.

An Lanntair Arts Centre   ARTS CENTRE
(☑ 01851-708480; www.lanntair.com; Kenneth St; ☉ 10am-9pm Mon-Wed, to 10pm Thu, to midnight Fri & Sat) **FREE** The modern, purpose-built An Lanntair (Gaelic for 'lighthouse'), complete with art gallery, theatre, cinema and restaurant, is the centre of the town's cultural life. It hosts changing exhibitions of contemporary art and is a good source of information on cultural events.

✸ Festivals & Events

Hebridean Celtic Festival   MUSIC
(www.hebceltfest.com; ☉ Jul) A four-day extravaganza of folk, rock and Celtic music held in the second half of July.

⌂ Sleeping

Heb Hostel   HOSTEL £
(☑ 01851-709889; www.hebhostel.com; 25 Kenneth St; dm £18; @ 奈) The Heb is a friendly, easy-going hostel close to the ferry, with comfy wooden bunks, a convivial living room with peat fire and a welcoming owner

who can provide all kinds of advice on what to do and where to go.

Laxdale Holiday Park
CAMPSITE £

(☑ 01851-703234; www.laxdaleholidaypark.com; 6 Laxdale Lane; tent sites £9-11, plus per person £3.50; ☺ Mar-Oct; ⊚) This campsite, 1.5 miles north of town off the A857, has a sheltered woodland setting, though the tent area is mostly on a slope – get there early for a level pitch. There are also wooden camping pods (per night £36 to £42), and a bunkhouse (£18 per person) that stays open year-round.

Hal o' the Wynd
B&B ££

(☑ 01851-706073; www.halothewynd.com; 2 Newton St; s/d from £60/80; ⊚) Touches of tartan and Harris Tweed lend a traditional air to this welcoming B&B, conveniently located directly opposite the ferry pier. Most rooms have views over the harbour to Lews Castle. There's also a cafe on the premises.

Park Guest House
B&B ££

(☑ 01851-702485; www.the-parkguesthouse.com; 30 James St; s/d from £79/110; ⊚) A charming Victorian villa with a conservatory and six luxurious rooms (mostly en suite), the Park Guest House is comfortable and central and has the advantage of an excellent restaurant specialising in Scottish seafood, beef and game plus one or two vegetarian dishes (three-course dinner around £35). Rooms overlooking the main road can be noisy on weekday mornings.

Royal Hotel
HOTEL ££

(☑ 01851-702109; www.royalstornoway.co.uk; Cromwell St; s/d from £99/119; P ⊚) The 19th-century Royal is the most appealing of Stornoway's hotels – the rooms at the front retain period features such as wood panelling and enjoy a view across the harbour to Lews Castle. Ask to see your room first, though, as some are a bit cramped.

Braighe House
B&B £££

(☑ 01851-705287; www.braighehouse.co.uk; 20 Braighe Rd; s/d from £95/130; P ⊚) This spacious and luxurious guesthouse, 3 miles east of the town centre on the A866, has stylish, modern bedrooms and a great seafront location. Good bathrooms with powerful showers, hearty breakfasts and genuinely hospitable owners round off the perfect package.

Eating

Artizan Cafe
CAFE £

(☑ 01851-706538; www.facebook.com/artizan stornoway; 12-14 Church St; ☺ 10am-6pm Mon-Fri, 9am-11pm Sat; ⊚ ⊞) Recycled timber and cool colours mark out this cafe-gallery as one of Stornoway's hip hangouts, serving great coffee and cake and tapas-style lunches (noon to 2.30pm). Hosts cultural events, including poetry nights on Saturday.

An Lanntair Arts Centre
BISTRO ££

(http://lanntair.com/cafebar; Kenneth St; mains £6-15; ☺ kitchen 10am-8pm; ⊚ ⊘ ⊞) The stylish and family-friendly cafe-bar at the arts centre serves a broad range of freshly prepared dishes, from tasty bacon rolls at breakfast to burgers, salads or fish and chips for lunch and chargrilled steaks or local scallops for dinner.

★ Digby Chick
BISTRO ££

(☑ 01851-700026; www.digbychick.co.uk; 5 Bank St; mains £18-25, 2-course lunch £14.50; ☺ noon-2pm & 5.30-9pm Mon-Sat; ⊞) ⊘ A modern restaurant that dishes up bistro cuisine such as haddock and chips, slow-roast pork belly or roast vegetable panini at lunchtime, the Digby Chick metamorphoses into a candlelit gourmet restaurant in the evening, serving dishes such as grilled langoustines, seared scallops, venison and steak. Three-course early-bird menu (5.30pm to 6.30pm) for £22.

ⓘ Information

The only shop in town that's open on a Sunday, **Sandwick Rd Petrol Station** (Engebret Ltd; ☑ 01851-702304; www.engebret.co.uk; Sandwick Rd; ☺ 6am-11pm Mon-Sat, 10am-4pm Sun) sells groceries, alcohol, hardware, fishing tackle and outdoor kit. The Sunday papers arrive around 2pm.

ⓘ Getting There & Away

The **bus station** (☑ 01851-704327) is on the waterfront next to the ferry terminal (left luggage 25p to £1.30 per piece). Bus W10 runs from Stornoway to Tarbert (£4.80, one hour, four or five daily Monday to Saturday) and Leverburgh (£6.80, two hours).

The Westside Circular bus W2 runs a circular route from Stornoway through Callanish (£2.70, 30 minutes), Carloway, Garenin and Arnol; the timetable allows you to visit one or two of the sites in a day.

Arnol

One of Scotland's most evocative historic buildings, the **Arnol Blackhouse** (HS; ☑ 01851-710395; www.historicenvironment.scot; Arnol; adult/child £4.50/2.70; ☺ 9.30am-5.30pm Mon-Sat Apr-Sep, 10am-4pm Mon, Tue & Thu-Sat Oct-Mar; P) is not so much a museum as a perfectly preserved fragment of a lost world. Built in 1885, this traditional blackhouse – a combined byre, barn and home – was inhabited until 1964 and has not been changed since the last inhabitant moved out. The museum is about 3 miles west of Barvas.

The staff faithfully rekindle the central peat fire every morning so you can experience the distinctive peat-reek; there's no chimney, and the smoke finds its own way out through the turf roof, windows and door – spend too long inside and you might feel like you've been kippered!

At nearby Bragar, a pair of whalebones forms an arch by the road, with the rusting harpoon that killed the whale dangling from the centre.

Garenin (Na Gearrannan)

The picturesque and fascinating Gearrannan Blackhouse Village is a cluster of nine restored thatch-roofed blackhouses perched above the exposed Atlantic coast. One of the cottages is home to the **Blackhouse Museum** (☑ 01851-643416; www.gearrannan.com; adult/child £3/1; ☺ 9.30am-5.30pm Mon-Sat Apr-Sep; P), a traditional 1955 blackhouse with displays on the village's history, while another houses the **Taigh an Chocair Cafe** (mains £3-6; ☺ 9.30am-5.30pm Mon-Sat).

Carloway (Carlabagh)

Dun Carloway (Dun Charlabhaigh; P) is a 2000-year-old, dry-stone broch, perched defiantly above a beautiful loch with views to the mountains of North Harris. The site is clearly signposted along a minor road off the A858, a mile southwest of Carloway village. One of the best-preserved brochs in Scotland, its double walls (with internal staircase) still stand to a height of 9m and testify to the engineering skills of its Iron Age architects.

Callanish (Calanais)

Callanish, on the western side of Lewis, is famous for its prehistoric standing stones. One of the most atmospheric prehistoric sites in the whole of Scotland, its ageless mystery, impressive scale and undeniable beauty leave a lasting impression.

The **Callanish Standing Stones** (☑ 01851-621422; ☺ 24hr) FREE, 15 miles west of Stornoway on the A858 road, form one of the most complete stone circles in Britain. It is one of the most atmospheric prehistoric sites anywhere. Sited on a wild and secluded promontory overlooking Loch Roag, 13 large stones of beautifully banded gneiss are arranged, as if in worship, around a 4.5m-tall central monolith.

Some 40 smaller stones radiate from the circle in the shape of a cross, with the remains of a chambered tomb at the centre. Dating from 3800 to 5000 years ago, the stones are roughly contemporary with the pyramids of Egypt.

The **visitor centre** (☑ 01851-621422; www.callanishvisitorcentre.co.uk; admission free, exhibition £2.50; ☺ 9.30am-8pm Mon-Sat Jun-Aug, 10am-6pm Mon-Sat Apr, May, Sep & Oct, 10am-4pm Tue-Sat Nov-Mar; P) near the Callanish Standing Stones is a tour de force of discreet design. Inside is a small exhibition that speculates on the origins and purpose of the stones, and an excellent **cafe** (mains £4-7; ☺ 9.30am-8pm Mon-Sat Jun-Aug, 10am-6pm Mon-Sat Apr, May, Sep & Oct, 10am-4pm Tue-Sat Nov-Mar; P).

Great Bernera

This rocky island is connected to Lewis by a bridge built by the local council in 1953 – the islanders had originally planned to blow up a small hill with explosives and use the material to build their own causeway. Berneray's attractions include fine coastal walks, a remote sandy beach, and a fascinating reconstruction of an Iron Age house.

On a sunny day, it's worth making the long detour to the island's northern tip for a picnic at the perfect little sandy beach of **Bosta** (Bostadh). As an alternative to driving, there's a signposted 5-mile coastal walk from Breacleit, the island's only village, to Bosta.

In 1996 archaeologists excavated an entire Iron Age village at the head of Bosta beach. Afterwards, the village was reburied for protection, but a reconstruction of an **Iron Age House** (🖉 01851-612314; Bosta; adult/child £3/1; ⊙ noon-4pm Mon-Fri May-Sep; 🅿) now stands nearby. Gather round the peat fire, above which strips of mutton are being smoked, while the custodian explains the domestic arrangements – fascinating, and well worth the trip. Opening hours are provisional, so call ahead to check.

Western Lewis

The B8011 road (signposted Uig, on the A858 Stornoway–Callanish road) from Garrynahine to Timsgarry (Timsgearraidh) meanders through scenic wilderness to some of Scotland's most stunning beaches. At **Miavaig**, a loop road detours north through the Bhaltos Estate to the pretty, mile-long white strand of **Reef Beach**; there's a basic but spectacular **campsite** (Traigh na Beirigh; tent sites £10; ⊙ Apr-Oct) in the machair behind the beach.

From April to September, **SeaTrek** (🖉 01851-672469; www.seatrek.co.uk; Miavaig Pier) runs two-hour boat trips (adult/child £38/28, Monday to Saturday) in a high-speed rigid inflatable boat (RIB) to spot seals and nesting seabirds. In June and July it also runs more-adventurous, all-day trips (£125 per person, twice monthly) in a large motor boat to the **Flannan Isles**, a remote group of tiny, uninhabited islands 25 miles northwest of Lewis. Puffins, seals and a ruined 7th-century chapel are the main attractions, but the isles are most famous for the mystery of the three lighthouse keepers who disappeared without trace in December 1900. There's also a 12-hour round-trip to remote **St Kilda** (£190, once or twice weekly, May to September, weather permitting).

From Miavaig, the road continues west through a rocky defile to Timsgarry and the vast, sandy expanse of **Traigh Uige** (Uig Sands). The famous 12th-century **Lewis chess pieces**, made of walrus ivory, were discovered in the sand dunes here in 1831. Of the 78 pieces, 67 are in the British Museum in London, with 11 in Edinburgh's National Museum of Scotland (p58); some may end up in Stornoway's new museum.

There's a basic **campsite** (sites per person £2) on the southern side of the bay (signposted 'Ardroil Beach') and a superb guesthouse, **Baile-na-Cille** (🖉 01851-672242; www.bailenacille.co.uk; Timsgarry; per person £65; 🅿🛜), on the northern side.

At the southwestern end of Traigh Uige is **Auberge Carnish** (🖉 01851-672459; www.aubergecarnish.co.uk; Carnais; r from £130; 🅿), a beautifully designed timber building that houses a luxury B&B and restaurant (three-course dinner £36.50; booking essential) with a stunning outlook over the sands.

The minor road that continues south from Timsgarry to **Mealista** passes a few smaller, but still spectacular, white-sand and boulder beaches on the way to a remote dead end; on a clear day you can see St Kilda on the horizon.

Harris (Na Hearadh)

POP 2000

Harris, to the south of Lewis, is the scenic jewel in the necklace of islands that comprise the Outer Hebrides. It has a spectacular blend of rugged mountains, pristine beaches, flower-speckled machair and barren rocky landscapes. The isthmus at Tarbert splits Harris neatly in two: North Harris is dominated by mountains that rise forbiddingly above the peat moors to the south of Stornoway – Clisham (799m) is the highest point. South Harris is lower-lying, fringed by beautiful white-sand beaches in the west and a convoluted rocky coastline to the east.

Harris is famous for Harris Tweed, a high-quality woollen cloth still hand-woven in islanders' homes. The industry employs around 400 weavers; staff at Tarbert tourist office can tell you about weavers and workshops you can visit.

Tarbert (An Tairbeart)

POP 480

Tarbert is a harbour village with a spectacular location, tucked into the narrow neck of land that links North and South Harris. It is one of the main ferry ports for the Outer Hebrides, and home to the new Isle of Harris Distillery.

⊙ Sights

Isle of Harris Distillery   DISTILLERY
(🖉 01859-502212; www.harrisdistillery.com; Main St; tours £10; ⊙ 10am-5pm Mon-Sat; 🅿) This brand new distillery started production in 2015, so its first batch of single malt whisky won't be ready till 2019; meanwhile, they're producing Isle of Harris gin too. The modern building is very stylish – the lobby feels like a luxury hotel – and 75-minute tours depart

two or three times daily in summer (they're popular, so book in advance). There's a cafe here too.

Sleeping & Eating

Tigh na Mara
B&B £

(01859-502270; East Tarbert; per person £25-30; P) Excellent-value B&B (though the single room is a bit cramped) just five minutes from the ferry – head up the hill above the tourist office and turn right. The owner bakes fresh cakes every day, which you can enjoy in the conservatory with a view over the bay.

Harris Hotel
HOTEL ££

(01859-502154; www.harrishotel.com; s/d from £80/110; P🛜) Run since 1903 by four generations of the Cameron family, Harris Hotel is a 19th-century sporting hotel, built in 1865 for visiting anglers and deer stalkers, and retains a distinctly old-fashioned atmosphere. It has spacious, comfy rooms and a decent restaurant; look out for JM Barrie's initials scratched on the dining-room window (the author of *Peter Pan* visited in the 1920s).

Hotel Hebrides
HOTEL £££

(01859-502364; www.hotel-hebrides.com; Pier Rd; s/d/f £75/150/180; 🛜) The location and setting don't look promising – a nondescript building squeezed between the ferry pier and car park – but this modern establishment brings a dash of urban glamour to Harris, with flashy fabrics and wall coverings, luxurious towels and toiletries, and a stylish restaurant and lounge bar.

Kate's Canteen
CAFE £

(Harris Distillery, Main St; mains £5-6; ⊙10am-5pm Mon-Sat) The cafe at the Isle of Harris Distillery, with its communal, scrubbed-timber tables and chunky benches, is bright and convivial. The menu is not extensive – a choice of soups, cakes, home-baked bread, smoked salmon and crowdie (Scottish cream cheese) – but the quality of the food shines brightly, most of it sourced directly from Harris.

Hebscape
CAFE £

(www.hebscapegallery.co.uk; Ardhasaig; mains £3-7; ⊙10.30am-4.30pm Tue-Sat Apr-Oct; P🛜) This stylish cafe-cum-art-gallery, a couple of miles outside Tarbert on the road north towards Stornoway, occupies a hilltop site with breathtaking views over Loch A Siar.

Enjoy home-baked cakes or scones with Suki tea or freshly brewed espresso, or a hearty bowl of homemade soup, while admiring the gorgeous landscape photography of co-owner Darren Cole.

North Harris

Magnificent North Harris is the most mountainous region of the Outer Hebrides. There are few roads here, but many opportunities for climbing, walking and birdwatching.

The B887 leads west, from a point 3 miles north of Tarbert, to Hushinish, where there's a lovely silver-sand beach. Along the way the road passes an old whaling station, one of Lord Leverhulme's failed development schemes, and the impressive shooting lodge of Amhuinnsuidhe Castle, now an exclusive hotel.

Between the old whaling station and Amhuinnsuidhe Castle, at Miavaig, a parking area and gated track gives hikers access to a golden eagle observatory, a 1.3-mile walk north from the road. On Wednesday from April to September, local rangers lead a 3½-hour guided walk (£5 per person) in search of eagles; details from Tarbert tourist office (p387) or www.north-harris.org.

South Harris

The west coast of South Harris has some of the most beautiful beaches in Scotland. The blinding white sands and turquoise waters of Luskentyre and Scarasta would be major holiday resorts if they were transported to somewhere with a warm climate; as it is, they're usually deserted.

The east coast is a complete contrast to the west – a strange, rocky moonscape of naked gneiss pocked with tiny lochans, the bleakness lightened by the occasional splash of green around the few crofting communities. Film buffs will know that the psychedelic sequences depicting an alien landscape in *2001: A Space Odyssey* were shot from an aircraft flying low over the east coast of Harris.

The narrow, twisting road that winds its way along this coast is known locally as the Golden Road because of the vast amount of money it cost per mile. It was built in the 1930s to link all the tiny communities known as 'The Bays'.

◉ Sights

Clò Mòr   EXHIBITION
(☏01859-502040; Old School, Drinishader; ☺9am-5.30pm Mon-Sat Mar-Oct; P) FREE The Campbell family has been making Harris tweed for 90 years, and this exhibition (behind the family shop) celebrates the history of the fabric known in Gaelic as *clò mòr* (the 'big cloth'); ask about live demonstrations of tweed weaving on the 70-year-old Hattersley loom. Drinishader is 5 miles south of Tarbert on the east coast road.

St Clement's Church   HISTORIC BUILDING
(Rodel; ☺9am-5pm Mon-Sat) At the southernmost tip of the east coast of Harris stands the impressive 16th-century St Clement's Church, built by Alexander MacLeod of Dunvegan between the 1520s and 1550s, only to be abandoned after the Reformation. There are several fine tombs inside, including the cenotaph of Alexander MacLeod, finely carved with hunting scenes, a castle, a *birlinn* (the traditional longboat of the islands) and various saints, including St Clement clutching a skull.

Seallam! Visitor Centre INTERPRETATION CENTRE
(www.seallam.com; Northton; adult/child £2.50/2; ☺10am-5pm Mon-Sat; P♿) The culture and landscape of the Hebrides are celebrated in the fascinating exhibition at Seallam! Visitor Centre (*Seallam* is Gaelic for 'Let me show you'). The centre, which is in Northton, 3 miles north of Leverburgh, also has a genealogical research centre for people who want to trace their Hebridean ancestry.

🛏 Sleeping & Eating

Lickisto Blackhouse Camping   CAMPSITE £
(☏01859-530485; www.freewebs.com/vanvon; Liceasto; tent sites per adult/child £12/6, yurt £70; 🐾) 🍴 Remote and rustic campsite on an old croft, with pitches set among heather and outcrops with chickens running wild. Campers can use a communal kitchen-lounge in a converted blackhouse, and there are two yurts with woodburning stove and gas cooker (no electricity). Bus W13 from Tarbert to Leverburgh stops at the entrance.

Am Bothan   HOSTEL £
(☏01859-520251; www.ambothan.com; Ferry Rd, Leverburgh; dm £22.50; P🐾) An attractive, chalet-style hostel, Am Bothan has small, neat dorms and a great porch where you can enjoy morning coffee with views over the bay. The hostel offers bike hire and can arrange wildlife-watching boat trips.

Sorrel Cottage   B&B ££
(☏01859-520319; www.sorrelcottage.co.uk; 2 Glen, Leverburgh; s/d from £65/85; 🐾) Sorrel Cottage is a pretty crofter's house with beautifully modernised rooms, about 1.5 miles west of the ferry at Leverburgh. Vegetarians and vegans are happily catered for. Bike hire available.

★ Blue Reef Cottages   COTTAGE £££
(☏01859-550370; www.stay-hebrides.com; Scarista; per night £200-300; P🌐) These luxury self-catering cottages (sleeping two) were built to an award-winning architect's design using stone walls and a turf roof, with panoramic picture windows giving views of Scarista sands. Each is equipped with a fully fitted kitchen, under-floor heating and a spacious bathroom with sauna and Jacuzzi.

Rodel Hotel   INN £££
(☏01859-520210; www.rodelhotel.co.uk; Rodel; s/d from £90/140; ☺Apr-Oct; P🌐🐾) Don't be put off by the rather grey and grim-looking exterior of this remote hotel – the interior has been refurbished to a high standard and offers four large, luxurious bedrooms; the one called Iona (a twin room) has the best view, across the little harbour towards Skye. The hotel **restaurant** (mains lunch £9-11, dinner £16-20; ☺noon-3pm & 5.30-9.30pm) serves delicious local seafood, steak and venison.

★ Skoon Art Café   CAFE £
(☏01859-530268; www.skoon.com; Geocrab; mains £4-7; ☺10am-4.30pm Tue-Sat Apr-Sep, shorter hours Oct-Mar; P) 🍴 Set halfway along the Golden Road, this neat little art gallery doubles as an excellent cafe serving delicious homemade soups, sandwiches, cakes and desserts (try the marmalade and ginger cake).

Temple Cafe   CAFE £
(☏07876 340416; www.facebook.com/TheTemple Cafe; Northton; mains £5-9; ☺10.30am-5pm Tue-Sun Apr-Sep, shorter hours Oct-Mar; P♿) Set in a cute stone-and-timber 'hobbit house' that was originally a visitor centre, and strewn with cushions covered in Harris tweed, this rustic cafe serves homemade scones, soups, salads and hot lunch specials to a soundtrack of '70s tunes.

❶ Getting There & Away

A **CalMac** (p387) car ferry zigzags through the reefs of the Sound of Harris from Leverburgh to Berneray (pedestrian/car £3.45/13.15, one hour, three or four daily Monday to Saturday, two or three Sunday).

There are two to four buses a day (except Sunday) from Tarbert to Leverburgh; W10 takes the main road along the west coast (£3.20, 40 minutes), while W13 winds along the Golden Road on the east (£3.20, one hour).

Berneray (Bearnaraigh)

POP 138

Berneray was linked to North Uist by a causeway in October 1998, and that hasn't altered the peace and beauty of the island. The beaches on its west coast are some of the most beautiful and unspoilt in Britain, and seals and otters can be seen in Bays Loch on the east coast.

Accommodation on the island is limited to the **Gatliff Hostel** (www.gatliff.org.uk; dm adult/child £14/8, camping per person £9), one B&B, and half a dozen self-catering cottages (see the full listing at www.isleofberneray. com), so be sure to book ahead.

North Uist (Uibhist A Tuath)

POP 1255

North Uist, an island half-drowned by lochs, is famed for its trout fishing (www.nuac. co.uk) but also has some magnificent beaches on its north and west coasts. For birdwatchers this is an earthly paradise, with regular sightings of waders and wildfowl ranging from redshank to red-throated diver to red-necked phalarope. The landscape is less wild and mountainous than Harris but it has a sleepy, subtle appeal.

Little Lochmaddy is the first village you hit after arriving on the ferry from Skye.

◉ Sights

Balranald RSPB Reserve   WILDLIFE RESERVE
(P) FREE Birdwatchers flock to this Royal Society for the Protection of Birds (RSPB) nature reserve, 18 miles west of Lochmaddy, in the hope of spotting the rare red-necked phalarope or hearing the distinctive call of the corncrake. There's a visitor centre with a resident warden who offers 1½-hour guided walks (£5), departing at 10am Tuesday from May to September.

St Kilda Viewpoint   VIEWPOINT
(P) From the westernmost point of the road that runs around North Uist, a minor, drivable track leads for 1.5 miles to the summit of Clettraval hill where a lookout point with telescope affords superb views west to the distant peaks of St Kilda and the Monach Isles.

Bharpa Langass & Pobull Fhinn   HISTORIC SITE
(P) A waymarked path from a car park off the A867, 6 miles southwest of Lochmaddy, leads to the chambered Neolithic burial tomb of Bharpa Langass and the stone circle of Pobull Fhinn (Finn's People); both are reckoned to be around 5000 years old. There are lovely views over the loch, where you may be able to spot seals and otters.

Taigh Chearsabhagh   ARTS CENTRE, MUSEUM
(☎ 01870-603970; www.taigh-chearsabhagh.org; Lochmaddy; arts centre free, museum £3; ⊙ 10am-5pm Mon-Sat; P) Taigh Chearsabhagh is a museum and arts centre that preserves and displays the history and culture of the Uists, and is also a thriving community centre, post office and meeting place. The centre's cafe (mains £4 to £6, closes at 3pm) dishes up homemade soups, sandwiches and cakes.

🛏 Sleeping & Eating

Balranald Campsite   CAMPSITE £
(☎ 01876-510304; www.balranaldhebrideanholidays.com; Balranald Nature Reserve, Hougharry; tent sites £7-9, plus per person £2; ☜) You can birdwatch from your tent at this lovely campsite set on the machair alongside the RSPB's Balranald Nature Reserve, and listen to rare corncrakes calling as the sun goes down beyond the neighbouring white-sand beach.

★ Langass Lodge   HOTEL ££
(☎ 01876-580285; www.langasslodge.co.uk; Locheport; s/d £95/115; P☜) The delightful Langass Lodge Hotel is a former shooting lodge set in splendid isolation overlooking Loch Langais. Refurbished and extended, it now offers a dozen appealing rooms, many with sea views, as well as one of the Hebrides' best restaurants (mains £15-21, 3-course dinner £34; ⊙ 6-8.30pm), noted for its fine seafood and game.

Rushlee House   B&B ££
(☎ 01876-500274; www.rushleehouse.co.uk; Lochmaddy; s/d £50/75; P) A lovely modern bungalow with three luxuriously appointed

ST KILDA

About 45 miles west of North Uist, **St Kilda** (www.kilda.org.uk) is a collection of spectacular sea stacks and cliff-bound islands. The largest island, **Hirta**, measures only 2 miles by 1 mile, with huge cliffs along most of its coastline. Owned by National Trust for Scotland (NTS), the islands are a Unesco World Heritage Site and are the biggest seabird nesting site in the North Atlantic. They are home to more than a million birds.

In addition to watching the bird life, visitors can explore the remains of the settlement at Village Bay, where there's a ranger's office and small museum, and climb to the island's highest point.

Hirta was inhabited by a Gaelic-speaking population of around 200 until the 19th century, when the arrival of church missionaries and tourists began the gradual breakdown of St Kilda's traditional way of life. By the 1920s disease and emigration had seen the islands' economy collapse, and the 35 remaining islanders were evacuated, at their own request, in 1930. The people had survived here by keeping sheep, fishing, growing a few basic crops such as barley, and climbing the cliffs barefoot to catch seabirds and collect their eggs. Over the centuries this resulted in a genetic peculiarity – St Kilda men had unusually long big toes.

There is no accommodation on St Kilda other than a tiny campsite with toilets, showers and a drinking water supply; the maximum permitted stay is five nights.

Getting There & Away

Boat tours to St Kilda are a major undertaking – day trips are at least 12-hour affairs, involving a minimum three-hour crossing each way, often in rough seas; all must be booked in advance and are weather-dependent.

Tour operators include:

Go To St Kilda (☑ 07789 914144; www.gotostkilda.co.uk; Uig Pier; per person £248)

Kilda Cruises (☑ 01859-502060; www.kildacruises.co.uk; Leverburgh Pier, South Harris; per person £190)

SeaTrek (p391)

Uist Sea Tours (p396)

bedrooms and great views of the hills to the south. No evening meals, but it's just a short walk to the restaurant at Hamersay House. The B&B is 0.75 miles from the ferry pier; take the first road on the right, then first left.

Hamersay House   HOTEL £££
(☑ 01876-500700; www.hamersayhouse.co.uk; Lochmaddy; s/d £95/135; P 🕸) Hamersay is Lochmaddy's most luxurious accommodation, with eight designer bedrooms, a lounge with leather sofas set around an open fire, and a good restaurant (mains £13 to £21, open 6pm to 8.30pm) with sea views from the terrace.

🛈 Getting There & Around

Buses from Lochmaddy to Lochboisdale (£5.30, 1¾ hours), Eriskay Pier (£6.20, 2½ hours), Berneray, Langass, Clachan na Luib Benbecula and Daliburgh run five to eight times a day Monday to Saturday.

Benbecula (Beinn Na Faoghla)

POP 1305

Benbecula, which sits between North Uist and South Uist, and is connected to both by causeways, is a low-lying island with a flat, lochan-studded landscape that's best appreciated from the summit of Rueval (124m), the island's highest point. There's a path around the southern side of the hill (signposted from the main road; park beside the landfill site) that is said to be the route taken to the coast by Bonnie Prince Charlie and Flora MacDonald during the prince's escape in 1746.

The main village, Balivanich, has a bank with an ATM, a post office, a large **Co-op Supermarket** (Balivanich; ⊗ 8am-8pm Mon-Sat, 11am-6pm Sun) and a petrol station (open on Sunday). It is also the location of the Benbecula airport.

South Uist (Uibhist A Deas)

POP 1755

South Uist is the second-largest island in the Outer Hebrides and saves its choicest corners for those who explore away from the main north–south road. The low-lying west coast is an almost unbroken stretch of white-sand beach and flower-flecked machair – a waymarked hiking trail, the **Machair Way**, follows the coast – while the multitude of inland lochs provide excellent trout fishing (www.southuistfishing.com). The east coast, riven by four large sea lochs, is hilly and remote, with spectacular **Beinn Mhor** (620m) the highest point.

Driving south from Benbecula you cross from the predominantly Protestant northern half of the Outer Hebrides into the mostly Roman Catholic south, a religious transition marked by the granite statue of **Our Lady of the Isles** on the slopes of Rueval (the hill with the military radomes on its summit) and the presence of many roadside shrines.

The ferry port of **Lochboisdale** is the island's largest settlement.

◉ Sights & Activities

Kildonan Museum
MUSEUM

(☑ 01878-710343; www.kildonanmuseum.co.uk; Kildonan; adult/child £2.50/free; ⊙ 10am-5pm Apr-Oct; P) Six miles north of Lochboisdale, Kildonan Museum explores the lives of local crofters through its collection of artefacts, an absorbing exhibition of B&W photography and first-hand accounts of harsh Hebridean conditions. There's also an excellent tearoom (mains £4 to £8, open 11am to 4pm) and craft shop.

Amid Milton's ruined blackhouses, half a mile south of the museum, a cairn marks the site of Flora MacDonald's birthplace.

Loch Druidibeg National Nature Reserve
WILDLIFE RESERVE

FREE The northern part of North Uist is mostly occupied by the watery expanses of Loch Bee and Loch Druidibeg. Loch Druidibeg National Nature Reserve is an important breeding ground for birds such as dunlin, redshank, ringed plover, greylag goose and corncrake; you can take a 5-mile self-guided walk through the reserve. Ask for details at the Scottish Natural Heritage office on the main road beside the loch.

Uist Sea Tours
BOATING

(☑ 07810 238752; www.uistseatours.com; The Pier, Lochboisdale) This outfit runs two-hour boat trips (per person £40) from Lochboisdale pier to spot bottlenose dolphins in the Sound of Barra (Thursday) or sea eagles on the east coast of South Uist (Tuesday). On Sunday there are six-hour trips (per person £90) to see nesting puffins on the island of Mingulay.

🛏 Sleeping & Eating

Uist Storm Pods
CAMPSITE £

(☑ 01878-700845; www.uiststormpods.co.uk; Lochboisdale; per pod per night £60; P 🐾) This place has two Scandinavian-style timber camping pods set on a hillside on a working farm. Each has an outdoor deck and barbecue overlooking the sea; a mini-kitchen, fridge and chemical toilet; and can sleep up to four people. They are a short walk from the ferry; take the second road on the left, immediately before the RBS bank.

Wireless Cottage
B&B £

(☑ 01878-700660; www.wirelesscottage.co.uk; Lochboisdale; per person from £25; 🛜) This pretty little cottage, which once housed the local telephone exchange, is now a welcoming and good-value B&B with just two bedrooms (one double, one family). It's a short (300m) walk from the ferry.

Tobha Mor Crofters' Hostel
HOSTEL £

(www.gatliff.org.uk; Howmore; dm adult/child £14/8) An atmospheric hostel housed in a restored thatched blackhouse, about 12 miles north of Lochboisdale.

★ Polochar Inn
INN ££

(☑ 01878-700215; www.polocharinn.com; Polochar; s/d from £75/95; P 🛜) This 18th-century inn has been transformed into a stylish, welcoming hotel with a stunning location looking out across the sea to Barra. The excellent **restaurant** (mains £11 to £20; booking recommended) and bar menu includes seafood chowder, venison casserole, local salmon and scallops, and Uist lamb. Polochar is 7 miles southwest of Lochboisdale, on the way to Eriskay.

ℹ Getting There & Around

Bus W17 runs about four times a day (except Sunday) between Berneray and Eriskay via Lochmaddy, Balivanich and Lochboisdale. The trip from Lochboisdale to Lochmaddy (£5.20) takes 1¾ hours.

Rothan Cycles (☑ 07740 364093; www.rothan.com; Howmore; ⊙ 9am-5pm) offers a delivery and pick-up service at various points between Eriskay and Stornoway.

Barra (Barraigh)

POP 1175

With its beautiful beaches, wildflower-clad dunes, rugged little hills and strong sense of community, diminutive Barra – just 14 miles in circumference – is the Outer Hebrides in miniature. For a great view of the island, walk up to the top of Heaval (383m), a mile northeast of Castlebay (Bagh a'Chaisteil), the largest village.

Sights

Kisimul Castle CASTLE

(HS; 01871-810313; www.historicenvironment. scot; Castlebay; adult/child incl ferry £5.50/3.30; 9.30am-5.30pm Apr-Sep) Castlebay takes its name from the island fortress of Kisimul Castle, first built by the MacNeil clan in the 11th century. A short boat trip (weather permitting) takes you out to the island, where you can explore the fortifications and soak up the view from the battlements.

The castle was restored in the 20th century by American architect Robert MacNeil, who became the 45th clan chief; he gifted the castle to Historic Scotland in 2000 for an annual rent of £1 and a bottle of whisky (Talisker single malt, if you're interested).

Traigh Mor BEACH

This vast expanse of firm golden sand (the name means 'Big Strand') serves as Barra's airport (a mile across at low tide, and big enough for three 'runways'), the only beach airport in the world that handles scheduled flights. Watching the little Twin Otter aircraft come and go is a popular spectator sport. In between flights, locals gather cockles, a local seafood speciality, from the sands.

Sleeping & Eating

Accommodation on Barra is limited, so make a reservation before committing to a night on the island. Wild camping (on foot or by bike) is allowed almost anywhere; campervans and car campers are restricted to official sites – check www.isleofbarra.com for details.

Dunard Hostel HOSTEL £

(01871-810443; www.dunardhostel.co.uk; Castlebay; dm/tw from £18/40; P) Dunard is a friendly, family-run hostel just a five-minute walk from the ferry terminal. The owners can help to organise sea-kayaking trips.

Borve Camping & Caravan Site CAMPSITE £

(01871-810878; www.barracamping.co.uk; Borve; sites 2-person tent £16, campervan £19; Mar-Oct;) An attractive campsite on the west coast of the island, close to Barra's best sandy beaches, with basic facilities including toilets, showers and a laundry.

Tigh na Mara B&B ££

(01871-810304; www.tighnamara-barra.co.uk; Castlebay; per person £35-40; Apr-Oct; P) A lovely cottage B&B with a brilliant location just above the ferry pier, looking out over the bay and Kisimul Castle. Ask for the en suite double bedroom with bay view.

Castlebay Hotel HOTEL ££

(01871-810223; www.castlebayhotel.com; Castlebay; s/d from £69/115; P) The Castlebay Hotel offers spacious bedrooms decorated with a subtle tartan motif – it's worth paying a bit extra for a sea view – and there's a comfy lounge and conservatory with grand views across the harbour to the islands south of Barra. The hotel bar is the hub of island social life, with regular sessions of traditional music.

The restaurant specialises in local seafood and game (often rabbit)

Deck CAFE £

(www.hebrideantoffeecompany.com; Castlebay; mains £4-6; 10am-6pm Mon-Sat, noon-5pm Sun May-Sep) There are only outdoor seats at this cafe (attached to a toffee factory), on a wooden deck overlooking the bay, but it's worth waiting for a fine day to sample the freshly baked scones and homemade cakes.

Getting There & Around

There are two daily flights from Glasgow to Barra airport.

CalMac (p387) ferries link Eriskay with Ardmhor (pedestrian/car £2.95/10.25, 40 minutes, three to five daily) at the northern end of Barra. Ferries also run from Castlebay to Oban.

You can hire bikes from **Barra Cycle Hire** (01871-810846; Paduls's Island Store, Castlebay; per day/week £15/50; 9am-5pm Mon-Sat), at the western end of Castlebay.

A **bus service** links ferry arrivals and departures at Ardmhor with Castlebay (£1.80, 20 minutes). Bus W32 makes a circuit of the island up to five times daily (except Sunday), and also connects with flights at the airport.

Orkney & Shetland

Best Places to Eat

➡ Eastward Guest House (p407)

➡ Scalloway Hotel (p421)

➡ Foveran (p405)

➡ Hay's Dock (p419)

➡ Hamnavoe Restaurant (p411)

Best Places to Sleep

➡ Brinkies Guest House (p410)

➡ Scalloway Hotel (p421)

➡ Almara (p423)

➡ West Manse (p414)

➡ Albert Hotel (p404)

Why Go?

Up here at Britain's top end it can feel more Scandinavian than Scottish, and no wonder. For the Vikings, the jaunt across the North Sea from Norway was as easy as a stroll down to the local mead hall and they soon controlled these windswept, treeless archipelagos, laying down longhouses alongside the stony remains of ancient prehistoric settlements.

An ancient magic hovers in the air above Orkney and Shetland, endowing them with an allure that lodges firmly in the soul. It's in the misty seas, where seals, whales and porpoises patrol lonely coastlines; it's in the air, where squadrons of seabirds wheel above huge nesting colonies; and it's on land, where standing stones catch late summer sunsets and strains of folk music disperse in the air before the wind gusts shut the pub door. These islands reward the journey.

When to Go
Lerwick

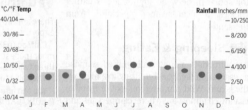

Jan Shetland's Up Helly Aa (p417): horned helmets and burning Viking ships on the beach.

Jun Orkney rocks to the St Magnus Festival (p403): book accommodation ahead.

Jul Summer sunlight and Scotland's longest daylight hours.

ORKNEY

POP 21.670

There's a magic to Orkney that you begin to feel as soon as the Scottish mainland slips astern. Only a few short miles of ocean separate the chain of islands from Scotland's north coast, but the Pentland Firth is one of Europe's most dangerous waterways, a graveyard of ships that adds an extra mystique to these islands shimmering in the sea mists.

An archipelago of mostly flat, green-topped islands stripped bare of trees and ringed with red sandstone cliffs, its heritage dates back to the Vikings whose influence is still strong today. Famed for ancient standing stones and prehistoric villages, for sublime sandy beaches and spectacular coastal scenery, it's a region whose ports tell of lives shared with the blessings and rough moods of the sea, and a destination where seekers can find melancholy wrecks of warships and the salty clamour of remote seabird colonies.

Tours

Orkney Archaeology Tours   TOURS
(☏ 01856-721450; www.orkneyarchaeologytours.co.uk) Specialises in all-inclusive multiday tours focusing on Orkney's ancient sites with an archaeologist guide. Also run customisable private tours.

Wildabout Orkney   BUS
(☏ 01856-877737; www.wildaboutorkney.com) Operates tours covering Orkney's history, ecology, folklore and wildlife. Day trips operate year-round and cost £59, with pick-ups in Stromness (to meet the morning ferry) and Kirkwall.

Great Orkney Tours   DRIVING
(☏ 01856-861443; www.greatorkneytours.co.uk) Readers rave about Jean's enthusiasm for the culture and archaeology of these islands on her flexible small-group tours.

ⓘ Getting There & Away

AIR

Flybe (☏ 0371-700 2000; www.flybe.com) flies daily from Kirkwall to Aberdeen, Edinburgh, Glasgow, Inverness and Sumburgh (Shetland). Most summers it also serves Bergen (Norway).

BOAT

During summer, book car spaces ahead. Peak-season fares are quoted here.

Northlink Ferries (☏ 0845 6000 449; www.northlinkferries.co.uk) Operates ferries from Scrabster to Stromness (passenger/car £19.40/59, 1½ hours, two to three daily), from Aberdeen to Kirkwall (passenger/car £31.50/111, six hours, three or four weekly) and from Kirkwall to Lerwick (passenger/car £24.65/103, six to eight hours, three or four weekly) on Shetland. Fares are up to 35% lower off-season.

Pentland Ferries (☏ 0800 688 8998; www.pentlandferries.co.uk; adult/child/car/bike £16/8/38/free) Leave from Gills Bay, 3 miles west of John O'Groats, and head to St Margaret's Hope on South Ronaldsay three to four times daily. The crossing takes an hour.

John O'Groats Ferries (☏ 01955-611353; www.jogferry.co.uk; single £17, incl bus to Kirkwall £18; ☉ May-Sep) Passenger-only service from John O'Groats to Burwick, on the southern tip of South Ronaldsay, with connecting bus to Kirkwall. Two to three departures daily. Forty-minute crossing.

BUS

Citylink (www.citylink.co.uk) Runs daily from Inverness to Scrabster, connecting with the Stromness ferries.

John O'Groats Ferries (☏ 01955-611353; www.jogferry.co.uk; ☉ May-Sep) Has summer-only 'Orkney bus' services from Inverness to Kirkwall. Tickets (one way £25, five hours) include bus-ferry-bus travel from Inverness to Kirkwall. There are two daily from June to August.

ⓘ Getting Around

The *Orkney Transport Guide* details all island transport and is free from tourist offices.

The largest island, Mainland, is linked by causeways to four southern islands; others are reached by air and ferry.

AIR

Loganair (☏ 01856-873457; www.loganair.co.uk) operates interisland flights from Kirkwall to Eday, Stronsay, Sanday, Westray, Papa Westray and North Ronaldsay. Fares are reasonable, with some special discounted tickets if you stay a night on the outer islands.

ⓘ ORKNEY EXPLORER PASS

The **Orkney Explorer Pass** (www.historicenvironment.scot; adult/child/family £18/10.80/36; ☉ Apr-Sep) covers all Historic Environment Scotland sites in Orkney, including Maeshowe, Skara Brae, the Broch of Gurness, the Brough of Birsay and the Bishop's Palace and Earl's Palace in Kirkwall.

Orkney & Shetlands Highlights

1 Skara Brae (p408) Shaking your head in astonishment at extraordinary prehistoric perfection that predates the pyramids.

2 Maeshowe (p407) Sensing the gulf of years in this ancient prehistoric tomb enlivened by later Viking graffiti.

3 Hoy (p411) Soaking up the glorious scenery and making the hike to the spectacular Old Man of Hoy.

4 Northern Islands (p412) Island-hopping through Orkney, where crystal azure waters lap against glittering white-sand beaches.

5 Scapa Flow (p412) Submerging yourself among the sunken warships of Scapa Flow.

6 Lerwick (p417) Discovering your inner Viking at the Up Helly Aa festival.

7 Hermaness Nature Reserve (p425) Capering with puffins and dodging dive-bombing skuas at Shetland's birdwatching centre.

8 Lighthouse Cottages Staying in one of Shetland's romantic lighthouse cottages; one of the best is at spectacular **Sumburgh** (p420).

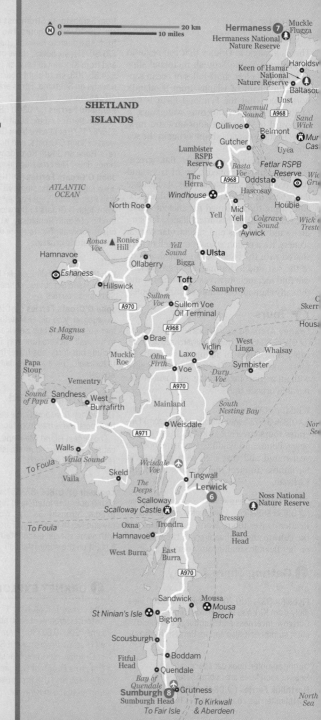

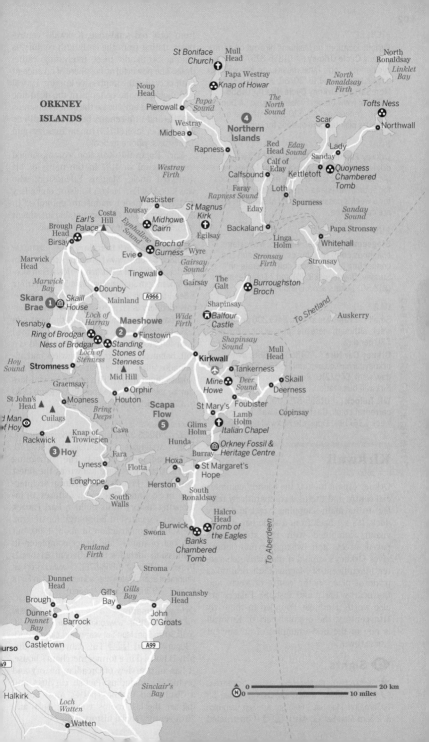

ORKNEY ISLANDS

St Boniface Church
Mull Head
North Ronaldsay
Linklet Bay
Papa Westray
Knap of Howar
North Ronaldsay Firth
Noup Head
Papa Sound
Pierowall
The North Sound
④ **Northern Islands**
Tofts Ness
Scar
Northwall
Westray
Midbea
Rapness
Red Head
Eday Sound
Lady
Sanday
Quoyness Chambered Tomb
Calf of Eday
Kettletoft
Westray Firth
Calfsound
Faray
Rapness Sound
Eday
Loth
Spurness
Sanday Sound
Wasbister
Rousay
St Magnus Kirk
Papa Stronsay
Whitehall
Costa Hill
Midhowe Cairn
Egilsay
Backaland
Linga Holm
Earl's Palace
Enhallow Sound
Broch of Gurness
Wyre
Stronsay
Brough Head
Birsay
Evie
Gairsay Sound
Stronsay Firth
Marwick Head
Tingwall
Gairsay
The Galt
Burroughston Broch
To Shetland
Auskerry
Marwick Bay
Dounby
Mainland
A966
Shapinsay
Balfour Castle
Skara Brae ①
Skaill House
Loch of Harray
Maeshowe
Wide Firth
Shapinsay Sound
Mull Head
Yesnaby
② Finstown
Ring of Brodgar
Ness of Brodgar
Standing Stones of Stenness
Loch of Stenness
Kirkwall
Tankerness
Skaill
Hoy Sound
Stromness
Mid Hill
Mine Howe
Deer Sound
Deerness
Graemsay
Orphir
Houton
Scapa Flow ⑤
St Mary's
Foubister
Copinsay
St John's Head
Moaness
Bring Deeps
Cava
Lamb Holm
Italian Chapel
d Man f Hoy
Cuilags
Glims Holm
Rackwick
Knap of Trowiegien
Hunda
Orkney Fossil & Heritage Centre
③ **Hoy**
Fara
Hoxa
Burray
Lyness
Flotta
St Margaret's Hope
Longhope
Herston
South Walls
South Ronaldsay
Halcro Head
Pentland Firth
Burwick
Swona
Tomb of the Eagles
Banks Chambered Tomb
To Aberdeen
Stroma
Dunnet Head
Brough
Gills Bay
Gills Bay
Duncansby Head
Dunnet
Dunnet Bay
Barrock
John O'Groats
Castletown
urso
A99
A99
Halkirk
Loch Watten
Sinclair's Bay
Watten

0   20 km
0   10 miles

BICYCLE

Various locations on Mainland hire out bikes, including **Cycle Orkney** (☑ 01856-875777; www.cycleorkney.com; Tankerness Lane, Kirkwall; per day/3 days/week £15/30/60; ⏰ 9am-5.30pm Mon-Sat) and **Orkney Cycle Hire** (☑ 01856-850255; www.orkneycyclehire.co.uk; 54 Dundas St, Stromness; per day £10-15). Both offer out-of-hours pick-ups and options for kids.

BOAT

Orkney Ferries (☑ 01856-872044; www.orkneyferries.co.uk) operates car ferries from Mainland to the islands. See individual islands for details. An Island Explorer pass costs £42 for a week's passenger travel in summer. Bikes are carried free.

BUS

Stagecoach (☑ 01856-870555; www.stagecoachbus.com) runs buses on Mainland and connecting islands. Most don't operate on Sunday. Dayrider (£8.30) and 7-Day Megarider (£18.50) tickets allow unlimited travel.

CAR

Small-car rates are around £40/200 per day/week, although there are specials for as low as £30 per day.

Orkney Car Hire (☑ 01856-872866; www.orkneycarhire.co.uk; Junction Rd, Kirkwall; per day/week £40/210) Recommended. Close to Kirkwall bus station.

WR Tullock (☑ 01856-875500; www.orkneycarrental.co.uk; Castle St, Kirkwall; per day/week £36/196) Opposite Kirkwall bus station.

Kirkwall

POP 7000

Orkney's main town is the islands' commercial centre and there's a comparatively busy feel to its main shopping street and ferry dock. It's set back from a wide bay, and its vigour, combined with the atmospheric paved streets and twisting wynds (lanes), gives Orkney's capital a distinctive character. Magnificent St Magnus Cathedral takes pride of place in the centre of town, and the nearby Earl's and Bishop's Palaces are also worth a ramble. Founded in the early 11th century, the original part of Kirkwall is one of the best examples of an ancient Norse town.

◉ Sights

★ **St Magnus Cathedral**   CATHEDRAL
(☑ 01856-874894; www.stmagnus.org; Broad St; ⏰ 9am-6pm Mon-Sat, 1-6pm Sun Apr-Sep, 9am-1pm & 2-5pm Mon-Sat Oct-Mar) **FREE** Constructed from local red sandstone, Kirkwall's centrepiece, dating from the early 12th century, is among Scotland's most interesting cathedrals. The powerful atmosphere of an ancient faith pervades the impressive interior. Lyrical and melodramatic epitaphs of the dead line the walls and emphasise the serious business of 17th- and 18th-century bereavement. Tours of the upper level (£7.75) run on Tuesdays and Thursdays; phone to book.

Earl Rognvald Brusason commissioned the cathedral in 1137 in the name of his martyred uncle, Magnus Erlendsson, who was killed by Earl Hakon Paulsson on Egilsay in 1117. Magnus's remains are entombed in an interior pillar. Another notable interment is that of the Arctic explorer John Rae.

★ **Highland Park Distillery**   DISTILLERY
(☑ 01856-874619; www.highlandpark.co.uk; Holm Rd; tour adult/child £7.50/free; ⏰ 10am-5pm Mon-Sat & noon-5pm Sun May-Aug, 10am-5pm Mon-Fri Apr & Sep, 1-5pm Mon-Fri Oct-Mar) South of the centre, this distillery is great to visit. They malt their own barley; you can see it and the peat kiln used to dry it on the excellent, well-informed hour-long tour. The standard 12-year-old is a soft, balanced malt, great for novices and aficionados alike; the 18-year-old is among the world's finest drams. This and older whiskies can be tasted on more specialised tours (£20 to £75), which you can prearrange.

Earl's Palace   RUINS
(HES; ☑ 01856-871918; www.historicenvironment.scot; Watergate; adult/child £4.50/2.70; ⏰ 9.30am-5.30pm Apr-Sep) The intriguing Earl's Palace was once known as the finest example of French Renaissance architecture in Scotland. One room features an interesting history of its builder, Earl Patrick Stewart, executed in Edinburgh for treason. He started construction in about 1600, but ran out of money and never completed it. Admission includes the adjacent **Bishop's Palace** (HES; ☑ 01856-871918; www.historicenvironment.scot; Watergate; admission incl in Earl's Palace; ⏰ 9.30am-5.30pm Apr-Sep).

Orkney Museum   MUSEUM
(☑ 01856-873191; www.orkney.gov.uk; Broad St; ⏰ 10.30am-5pm Mon-Sat year-round, closed 12.30-1.30pm Nov-Apr) **FREE** This labyrinthine display is housed in a former merchant's house. It has an overview of Orcadian history and prehistory, including Pictish carvings and a display on the Ba' (p404). Most engaging are the last rooms, covering 19th- and 20th-century social history.

Kirkwall

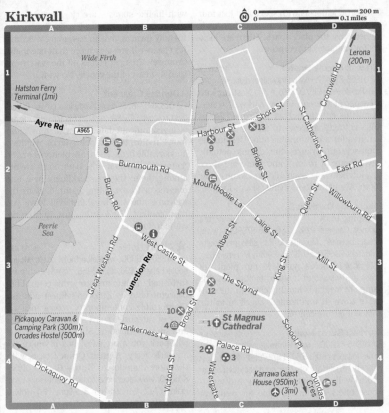

N 0 ——————— 200 m
0 ——————— 0.1 miles

Kirkwall

🎊 Festivals & Events

St Magnus Festival   ARTS, MUSIC
(☏ 01856-871445; www.stmagnusfestival.com;
⊙ late Jun) Running for a week over midsummer, this is a colourful celebration of music and the arts.

🛏 Sleeping

Orcades Hostel   HOSTEL £
(☏ 01856-873745; www.orcadeshostel.com; Muddisdale Rd; dm/s/d £20/40/52; P@⊚) Book ahead to get a bed in this cracking hostel on the western edge of town. It's a guesthouse conversion, so there's a very smart kitchen and lounge, and great-value doubles.

Comfortable dorms with space and just four bunks make for sound sleeping; enthusiastic owners give the place spark. There are lockers for valuables at reception.

Kirkwall Peedie Hostel
HOSTEL £

(✆ 01856-875477; www.kirkwallpeediehostel.com; Ayre Rd; dm/s/d £15/20/30; P ⊜) Nestling into a corner at the end of the Kirkwall waterfront, this cute hostel set in former fisherfolk's cottages squeezes in all the necessary features for a comfortable stay. Despite the compact appearance, the dorms actually have plenty of room – and there are three tiny kitchens, so you should find some elbow room. A separate bothy (hut) sleeps four.

Pickaquoy Caravan & Camping Park
CAMPSITE £

(Orkney Caravan Park; ✆ 01856-879900; www.pickaquoy.co.uk; Muddisdale Rd; sites per adult/child/tent £9.95/2.50/3.95; ⊙ early Mar–mid-Dec; P ⊜ ⊜ ⊜) There's no view, but plenty of grass and excellent modern facilities at this campsite, which is handily close to the centre of town. If unattended, check in at the adjacent leisure centre.

Karrawa Guest House
GUESTHOUSE ££

(✆ 01856-871100; www.karrawaguesthouseorkney.co.uk; Inganess Rd; s £64, d £72-76; P ⊜ ⊜) In a peaceful location on the southeastern edge of Kirkwall, this enthusiastically run guesthouse offers significant value for well-kept modern double rooms with comfortable mattresses. Breakfast is generously proportioned.

Lerona
B&B ££

(✆ 01856-874538; Cromwell Cres; s/d £35/70; P) Guests come first here, but the wee folk – a battalion of garden gnomes and clans of dolls

---

THE BA'

Every Christmas Day and New Year's Day, Kirkwall holds a staggering spectacle: a crazy ball game known as the ba'. Two enormous teams, the Uppies and the Doonies, fight their way, no holds barred, through the streets, trying to get a leather ball to the other end of town. The ball is thrown from the Market Cross to the waiting teams; the Uppies have to get the ba' to the corner of Main St and Junction Rd, the Doonies must get it to the water. Violence, skulduggery and other stunts are common, and the event, fuelled by plenty of strong drink, can last hours.

---

with lifelike stares – are close behind. The rooms, some en suite, are a good size, and friendly owners give an easygoing welcome. It's cheaper if you stay more than one night. Cromwell Crescent comes off the waterfront road just east of the centre. No wi-fi.

2 Dundas Crescent
B&B ££

(✆ 01856-874805; www.twodundas.co.uk; 2 Dundas Cres; s/d £45/80; P ⊜) This former manse is a magnificent building with four enormous rooms blessed with large windows and sizeable beds. There are plenty of period features, but the en suite bathrooms are not among them: they're sparklingly new, and one has a free-standing bathtub. Both the welcome and the breakfast will leave you most content. The location just up from the cathedral is great.

★ Albert Hotel
HOTEL £££

(✆ 01856-876000; www.alberthotel.co.uk; Mounthoolie Lane; s £96, d £142-158; ⊜) Stylishly refurbished in plum and grey, this central but peaceful hotel is Kirkwall's finest address. Comfortable contemporary rooms in a variety of categories sport super-inviting beds and smart bathrooms. Staff are helpful, and will pack you a breakfast box if you've got an early ferry. A great Orkney base, with the more-than-decent **Bothy Bar** (✆ 01856-876000; www.alberthotel.co.uk; Mounthoolie Lane; mains £7-12; ⊙ noon-2pm & 5-9pm; ⊜) downstairs. Walk-in prices are often cheaper.

Ayre Hotel
HOTEL £££

(✆ 01856-873001; www.ayrehotel.co.uk; Ayre Rd; s/d £95/135; P ⊜) Right on the waterfront, this 200-year-old hotel has been recently renovated, leaving its low-ceilinged, large-bedded rooms looking very spruce. It's definitely worth paying the extra few pounds to grab one with a sea view.

✕ Eating & Drinking

Judith Glue Real Food Cafe
CAFE £

(✆ 01856-874225; www.judithglue.com; 25 Broad St; light meals £7-14; ⊙ 9.30am-5.30pm Mon-Sat, 11am-5pm Sun Jan-Mar, 9am-6pm Mon-Sat, 11am-5pm Sun Apr-May & Oct-Dec, 9am-10pm Mon-Sat, 10am-6pm Sun Jun-Sep; ⊜) ✿ At the back of a lively craft shop opposite the cathedral, this licensed cafe-bistro serves toothsome sandwiches and salads, as well as daily specials and succulent seafood platters. There's a strong emphasis on sustainable and organic ingredients, but put the feel-good factor aside for a moment and fight for a table at lunchtime. Check Facebook for regular events.

Reel
CAFE £

(www.facebook.com/thereelkirkwall; Albert St; sandwiches £3-6; ⊙9am-6pm Mon-Sat, 10am-5pm Sun; 🗐) Part music shop and part cafe, Kirkwall's best coffee-stop sits alongside the cathedral, and bravely puts tables outside at the slightest threat of sunshine. It's a relaxed spot, good for a morning-after debriefing, a quiet Orkney ale, or lunchtime panini and musically named sandwiches (plus the cheese-and-mushroom Skara Brie). It's a local folk-musicians' centre, with regular evening sessions.

★ Foveran
SCOTTISH ££

(☑01856-872389; www.thefoveran.com; St Ola; mains £15-26; ⊙6.30-8.30pm mid-Apr–mid-Oct, Fri & Sat only plus other days by arrangement offseason; 🗐) 🍴 Three miles down the Orphir road, one of Orkney's best dining options is surprisingly affordable for the quality. Tranquilly located, with a cosy eating area overlooking the sea, it shines presenting classic Orcadian ingredients – the steak with haggis and whisky sauce is feted throughout, while North Ronaldsay lamb comes in four different, deliciously tender cuts.

Lynnfield Hotel
BRITISH ££

(☑01856-872505; www.lynnfield.co.uk; Holm Rd; dinner mains £16-23; ⊙noon-1.45pm & 6-8.30pm; 🗐) This sizeable hotel restaurant by the Highland Park distillery offers well-presented, rich cuisine that's long been a local favourite. The menu changes, but expect quality meat and fish, including North Ronaldsay lamb, all tasty and heavy on the butter and sauces.

Shore
GASTROPUB ££

(☑01856-872200; www.theshore.co.uk; 6 Shore St; bar meals £9-10, restaurant mains £10-15; ⊙food noon-2pm & 6-8.30pm Mon-Fri, 10am-5pm & 6-8.30pm Sat & Sun; 🗐) This popular harbourside eatery offers high-standard bar meals with a bit of local seafood added into the mix in the evening fare in the restaurant section. It's run with a customer-comes-first attitude and is a convivial spot.

Kirkwall Hotel
PUB, SCOTTISH ££

(☑01856-872232; www.kirkwallhotel.com; Harbour St; mains £9-16; ⊙noon-2pm & 6-9pm; 🗐) This grand old waterfront hotel is among Kirkwall's better dining places. The elegant bar and eating area packs out; it's a favourite spot for older couples or a clan evening out. A fairly standard pub-food list is comple-

> ### BLACKENINGS
> ··············
> An attractive Orcadian has caught your eye? Think twice, because weddings up here are traditionally preceded by a 'blackening'. The groom (and these days, often the bride) is stripped naked by friends, painted with treacle, floured, feathered and paraded around town before being bound to the Mercat Cross with clingfilm. You have been warned.

mented by a seasonal menu featuring local seafood and meat – the lamb is delicious. The more modern bar down the side, Skippers, also does pub grub.

Service gets patchy when the hotel is busy, which is often.

Helgi's
PUB FOOD ££

(www.helgis.co.uk; 14 Harbour St; mains £10-13; ⊙food noon-9pm, from 12.30pm Sun; 🗐) There's a traditional cosiness about this place, but the decor has moved beyond the time-honoured beer-soaked carpet to a comfortable contemporary slate floor and quotes from the *Orkneyinga Saga* (p413) plastering the walls. It's more find-a-table than jostle-at-the-bar and serves cheerful, well-priced comfort food – light bites only between 2pm and 5pm. Take your pint upstairs for quiet harbour contemplation.

🔒 Shopping

Kirkwall has some gorgeous jewellery and crafts along Albert St, as well as shops selling quality Orcadian food and drink.

Longship
JEWELLERY, CRAFT

(☑01856-888790; www.thelongship.co.uk; 7 Broad St; ⊙9am-5.30pm daily Jun-Aug, 10am-5pm Mon-Sat Sep-May) The Longship, established in 1859, has Orkney-made crafts, food, gifts and exquisite designer jewellery across adjacent shops.

ℹ️ Information

Follow Junction Rd south out of town and you'll see **Balfour Hospital** (☑01856-888000; www. ohb.scot.nhs.uk; New Scapa Rd) on your right. It's scheduled to be replaced with a bigger facility currently being built.

Kirkwall Information Centre (☑01856-872856; www.visitorkney.com; West Castle St; ⊙9am-5pm Mon-Sat Oct-Mar, 9am-5pm daily Apr-Sep) has a good range of Orkney info. Shares a building with the bus station.

ⓘ Getting There & Away

Kirkwall Airport (www.hial.co.uk) is located a few miles east of town and served regularly by bus 4 (15 minutes).

Ferries to the Northern Islands depart from the town harbour; however, ferries to Aberdeen and Shetland use the Hatston terminal, 1 mile northwest. Bus X10 shuttles out there regularly.

All bus services leave from the **bus station** (West Castle St):

Bus X1 Stromness (£3.10, 30 minutes, hourly, seven Sunday); in the other direction to St Margaret's Hope (£2.90).

Bus 2 Orphir and Houton (£2.55, 20 minutes, four or five daily Monday to Saturday, five on Sunday from mid-June to mid-August).

Bus 6 Evie (£3.40, 30 minutes, three to five daily Monday to Saturday) and Tingwall (Rousay ferry). Runs Sunday in summer to Tingwall only.

East Mainland to South Ronaldsay

After a German U-boat sank battleship HMS *Royal Oak* in 1939, Winston Churchill had causeways of concrete blocks erected across the channels on the eastern side of Scapa Flow, linking Mainland to the islands of Lamb Holm, Glims Holm, Burray and South Ronaldsay. The Churchill Barriers, flanked by rusting wrecks of blockships, now support the main road from Kirkwall to Burwick.

East Mainland

On a farm at Tankerness, the mysterious Iron Age site of **Mine Howe** is an eerie underground chamber, about 1.5m in diameter and 4m high. Its function is unknown; archaeologists from the TV series *Time Team* carried out a dig here and concluded that it may have had some ritual significance, perhaps as an oracle or shrine. At time of last research it was closed to the public, though some intrepid folk with torches still accessed it.

Lamb Holm

The **Italian Chapel** (☎ 01865-781268; Lamb Holm; adult/child £3/free; ☉ 9am-6.30pm Jun-Aug, 9am-5pm Mon-Sat, noon-5pm Sun May & Sep, 10am-4pm Mon-Sat, noon-3pm Sun mid-Mar–Apr & Oct, 11am-2pm Mon-Sat Nov–mid-Mar) is all that remains of a POW camp that housed the Italian soldiers who worked on the Churchill Barriers. They built the chapel in their spare time, using two Nissen huts, scrap metal and

their considerable artistic skills. One of the artists returned in 1960 to restore the paintwork. It's quite extraordinary inside and definitely worth seeing.

The **Orkney Wine Company** (☎ 01856-781736; www.orkneywine.co.uk; Lamb Holm; ☉ 10am-5pm Mon-Sat May-Sep, plus noon-4pm Sun Jul & Aug, reduced hours Mar-Apr & Oct-Dec) produces handmade wines made from berries, flowers and vegetables, all naturally fermented. Get stuck into some strawberry-rhubarb wine or blackcurrant port – unusual flavours but surprisingly delicious.

Burray
POP 400

This small island, a link in the chain joined by the Churchill Barriers, has a fine beach at Northtown on the east coast, where you may see seals. The village has a shop and places to stay, and there's a worthwhile museum on the island.

The eclectic **Fossil & Heritage Centre** (☎ 01856-731255; www.orkneyfossilcentre.co.uk; adult/child £4.50/3; ☉ 10am-5pm Apr-Oct) museum is a great visit, combining some excellent 360-million-year-old Devonian fish fossils found locally with a well-designed exhibition on the world wars and Churchill Barriers. Upstairs is a selection of household and farming implements. There's a good little gift shop and an enjoyable coffee shop here. It's on the left half a mile after crossing to Burray, coming from Kirkwall.

This commodious refurbished 19th-century herring station, **Sands Hotel** (☎ 01856-731298; www.thesandshotel.co.uk; s/d/ste £100/125/175; P 🛜) is right on the pier in Burray village. Rooms have stylish furnishings, and all have great water views. Families and groups should consider a suite: brilliant two-level self-contained flats that sleep four and have a kitchen. There's a good **restaurant** (noon to 2pm and 5pm to 9pm) with a genteel nautical feel.

South Ronaldsay
POP 900

South Ronaldsay's main village, pristine **St Margaret's Hope**, was named after the Maid of Norway, who died here in 1290 on her way to marry Edward II of England (strictly a political affair: Margaret was only seven years old). The island has some intriguing prehistoric tombs and fine places to stay and eat, and is also the docking point of two of the three mainland ferries.

◉ Sights

★ Tomb of the Eagles ARCHAEOLOGICAL SITE
(☑ 01856-831339; www.tomboftheeagles.co.uk; Cleat; adult/child £7.50/3.50; ⊙ 9.30am-5.30pm Apr-Sep, 10am-noon Mar, 9.30am-12.30pm Oct) Two significant archaeological sites were found here by a farmer on his land. The first is a Bronze Age stone building with a firepit, indoor well and plenty of seating; a communal cooking site or the original Orkney pub? Beyond, in a spectacular clifftop position, the neolithic tomb (wheel yourself in prone on a trolley) is an elaborate stone construction that held the remains of up to 340 people who died some five millennia ago.

An excellent personal explanation is given to you at the visitor centre; you meet a few spooky skulls and can handle some of the artefacts found, plus absorb information on the mesolithic period. It's about a mile's airy walk to the tomb from the centre, which is near Burwick.

Banks Chambered Tomb ARCHAEOLOGICAL SITE
(Tomb of the Otters; ☑ 01856-831605; www.bankschamberedtomb.co.uk; Cleat; adult/child £6/2.50; ⊙ 10.30am-5pm Apr-Sep) Discovered while digging a car park, this 5000-year-old chambered tomb has yielded a vast quantity of human bones, well preserved thanks to the saturation of the earth. The tomb is dug into bedrock and makes for an atmospheric if claustrophobic visit. The guided tour mixes homespun archaeological theories with astute observations. Within the adjacent bistro, you can handle finds of stones and bones, including the remains of otters, who presumably used this as a den. Follow signs for Tomb of the Eagles.

⊨ Sleeping & Eating

★ Eastward Guest House B&B ££
(The Missing Bell; ☑ 01956-831551; www.eastwardhouse.com; A961; d £90-105, dinner £40-60; P @ 🛜) 🍴 Not a bed-and-breakfast in any sense that the phrase is usually understood, this utterly captivating haven is a converted church that offers a foodie experience like few others. Patrick and Keiko aren't just passionate about food – they've taken it several steps beyond, to the realms of philosophy, of religion, of a messianic determination to cook the way they believe in.

★ Bankburn House B&B ££
(☑ 01856-831310; www.bankburnhouse.co.uk; A961, St Margaret's Hope; s/d £48.75/72.50, without bathroom £42.50/65; P @ 🛜 🐾) 🍴 This large rustic house does everything right, with smashing good-sized rooms and engaging owners who put on quality breakfasts and take pride in constantly innovating to improve guests' comfort levels. The huge lawn overlooks St Margaret's Hope and the bay – perfect for sunbathing on shimmering Orkney summer days. Prices drop substantially for multinight stays.

Robertson's CAFE £
(☑ 01856-831889; Church Rd; light meals £3-9; ⊙ food 10am-9pm; 🛜) Tastefully renovated, this characterful high-ceilinged space with chessboard tiles makes an atmospheric venue for a morning coffee and filled roll or light meals such as soups and cheeseboards with local varieties, also available for purchase. It also does cocktails and opens as a bar until midnight or later.

Skerries Bistro SEAFOOD ££
(☑ 01856-831605; www.skerriesbistro.co.uk; Cleat; lunches £5-9, dinner mains £10-18; ⊙ 11am-5pm & 6-9pm Wed-Mon, 11am-4pm Tue Mar-Oct) This cafe-bistro occupies a spectacular setting at the southern end of South Ronaldsay; it's a smart, modern glass-walled building with a deck and great clifftop views. Meals range from soups and sandwiches to daily fish and shellfish specials. Dinner should be booked ahead. A romantic little separate pod is available for private dining.

West & North Mainland

This part of the island is sprinkled with outstanding prehistoric monuments: the journey to Orkney is worth it for these alone. It would take a day to see all of them – if pushed for time, visit Skara Brae then Maeshowe, but book your visit to the latter in advance.

◉ Sights & Activities

★ Maeshowe ARCHAEOLOGICAL SITE
(HES; ☑ 01856-761606; www.historicenvironment.scot; adult/child £5.50/3.30; ⊙ 9.30am-5pm Apr-Sep, 10am-4pm Oct-Mar, tours hourly 10am-4pm, plus 6pm and 7pm Jul & Aug.) Egypt has pyramids, Scotland has Maeshowe. Constructed about 5000 years ago, it's an extraordinary place, a Stone Age tomb built from enormous sandstone blocks, some of which weighed many tons and were brought from several miles away. Creeping down the long stone passageway to the central chamber, you feel the indescribable gulf of years that separate us from the architects of this mysterious place.

Though nothing is known about who and what was interred here, the scope of the project suggests it was a structure of great significance.

In the 12th century, the tomb was broken into by Vikings searching for treasure. A couple of years later, another group sought shelter in the chamber from a three-day blizzard. Waiting out the storm, they carved runic graffiti on the walls. As well as the some-things-never-change "Olaf was 'ere" and 'Thorni bedded Helga', there are also more intricate carvings, including a particularly fine dragon and a knotted serpent.

Buy tickets in Tormiston Mill across the road. Oversized groups mean guides tend to only show a couple of the Viking inscriptions, but they'll happily show more if asked.

By chance or design, for a few weeks around the winter solstice the setting sun shafts up the entrance passage, and strikes the back wall of the tomb in spooky alignment. If you can't be there, check the webcams on www.maeshowe.co.uk.

Entry is by 45-minute guided tours on the hour: you must reserve your tour slot ahead by phone.

Standing Stones of Stenness
ARCHAEOLOGICAL SITE

(HES; www.historicenvironment.scot; ⊘ 24hr) **FREE** Within sight of Maeshowe, four mighty stones remain of what was once a circle of 12. Recent research suggests they were perhaps erected as long ago as 3300 BC, and they impose by their sheer size; the tallest measures 5.7m in height. The narrow strip of land they're on, the Ness of Brodgar, separates the Harray and Stenness lochs and was the site of a large settlement inhabited throughout the neolithic period (3500–1800 BC).

Barnhouse
Neolithic Village
ARCHAEOLOGICAL SITE

(HES; www.historicenvironment.scot; ⊘ 24hr) **FREE** Alongside the Standing Stones of Stenness are the excavated remains of a village thought to have been inhabited by the builders of Maeshowe. Don't skip this: it brings the area to life. The houses are well preserved and similar to Skara Brae with their stone furnishings. One of the buildings was entered by crossing a fireplace: possibly an act of ritual significance.

Ring of Brodgar
ARCHAEOLOGICAL SITE

(HES; www.historicenvironment.scot; ⊘ 24hr) **FREE** A mile northwest of Stenness is this wide circle of standing stones, some over 5m

tall. The last of the three Stenness monuments to be built (2500–2000 BC), it remains a most atmospheric location. Twenty-one of the original 60 stones still stand among the heather. On a grey day with dark clouds thudding low across the sky, the stones are a spine-tingling sight.

Orkney Folklore & Storytelling Visitor Centre
STORYTELLING

(🖉 01856-841207; www.orkneyattractions.com; A967) Located between Brodgar and Skara Brae, this offbeat centre focuses on the islands' folkloric tradition. The best way to experience it is on one of its atmospheric storytelling evenings, Peatfire Tales of Orkney (Sunday, Tuesday and Friday at 8.30pm March to October, adult/child £10/6) where local legends are told with musical accompaniment around a peat fire. It also runs interesting guided walks of the coastline and of Stromness (£7) and offers B&B.

★ Skara Brae
ARCHAEOLOGICAL SITE

(HES; www.historicenvironment.scot; adult/child £6.10/3.70, incl Skaill House adult/child £7.10/4.30; ⊘ 9.30am-5.30pm Apr-Sep, 10am-4pm Oct-Mar) Idyllically situated by a sandy bay 8 miles north of Stromness, and predating Stonehenge and the pyramids of Giza, extraordinary Skara Brae, one of the world's most evocative prehistoric sites, is northern Europe's best-preserved prehistoric village. Even the stone furniture – beds, boxes and dressers – has survived the 5000 years since a community lived and breathed here. It was hidden until 1850, when waves whipped up by a severe storm eroded the sand and grass above the beach, exposing the houses underneath.

There's an excellent interactive exhibit and short video, arming visitors with facts and theory, which will enhance the impact of the site. You then enter a reconstructed house, giving the excavation (which you head on to next) more meaning. The official guidebook, available from the visitor centre, includes a good self-guided tour.

The joint ticket also gets you into **Skaill House** (HES; www.historicenvironment.scot; incl Skara Brae adult/child £7.10/4.30; ⊘ Apr-Oct), a mansion built for the bishop in 1620. It's a bit anticlimactic catapulting straight from the neolithic to the 1950s decor, but you can see a smart hidden compartment in the library as well as the bishop's original 17th-century four-poster bed.

Buses run to Skara Brae from Kirkwall and Stromness a few times weekly in summer, but not all are useful to visit the site. It's possible to walk along the coast from Stromness to Skara Brae (9 miles), or it's an easy taxi (£15), hitch or cycle from Stromness.

Orkney Brewery BREWERY
(☑ 01856-841777; www.orkneybrewery.co.uk; Quoyloo; tour adult/child £6/3.50; ☺ 10am-4.30pm Mon-Sat, 11am-4.30pm Sun Apr–mid-Oct) These folk have been producing their brilliant Orcadian beers – Dark Island is a standout, while Skullsplitter lives up to its name – for years now, but this visitor centre is a great place to come and try them. Tours run regularly and explain the brewing process, while, fashionably decked out in local stone, the cafe-bar is atmospheric.

Birsay

The small village of Birsay is 6 miles north of Skara Brae, set amid peaceful countryside. It has some worthwhile attractions, and the Brough of Birsay makes a tempting picnic destination.

The ruins of **Earl's Palace** (☺ 24hr) FREE, built in the 16th century by the despotic Robert Stewart, earl of Orkney, dominate the village of Birsay. Today it's a mass of half walls and crumbling columns; the size of the palace is impressive, matching the reputed ego and tyranny of its former inhabitant.

At low tide – check tide times at any Historic Scotland site – you can walk out to windswept **Brough of Birsay** (HES; www.historicenvironment.scot; adult/child £4.50/2.70; ☺ 9.30am-5.30pm mid-Jun–Sep) island, the site of extensive Norse ruins, including a number of longhouses and 12th-century **St Peter's Church**. There's also a replica of a Pictish stone found here. St Magnus was buried here after his murder on Egilsay in 1117, and the island became a pilgrimage place. The attractive lighthouse has fantastic views. Take a picnic, but don't get stranded...

Birsay Hostel (☑ after hours 01856-721470, office hours 01856-873535; https://orkney.camp stead.com; A967; tent sites 1/2 people £7.65/11.80, dm/tw £17.65/48.75; [P][☎]), a former activity centre and school now has dorms that vary substantially in spaciousness – go for two- or four-bedded ones. There's a big kitchen and a grassy camping area; kids and families sleep substantially cheaper. Book via the website to avoid an admin fee. It's on the A967 south of Birsay village.

A pleasant spot with sweeping views over green grass, black cows and blue-grey sea, **Birsay Bay Tearoom** (☑ 01856-721399; www.birsay baytearoom.co.uk; Birsay; light meals £3-8; ☺ 11am-

NESS OF BRODGAR

Ongoing excavations on the **Ness of Brodgar** (www.nessofbrodgar.co.uk; ☺ tours 2-3 times daily early Jul-late Aug) FREE, between the Stenness standing stones and the Ring of Brodgar, are rapidly revealing that this was a neolithic site of huge importance. Probably a major power and religious centre and used for over a millennium, the settlement had a mighty wall, a large building (a temple or palace?) and as many as 100 other structures, some painted. Each dig season reveals new, intriguing finds.

4.30pm Wed-Sun Apr, 11am-6pm Wed-Mon May-Sep, 11am-3.30pm Fri-Sun Oct-Dec & Feb-Mar; ☎) serves tea, coffee, home-baking and light meals. It's a good spot to wait for the tide to go out before crossing to the Brough (in plain sight).

Evie

The **Broch of Gurness** (HES; www.historicenvironment.scot; Evie; adult/child £5.50/3.30; ☺ 9.30am-5.30pm Apr-Sep) is a fine example of the drystone fortified towers that were both a status symbol for powerful farmers and useful protection from raiders some 2200 years ago. The imposing entranceway and sturdy stone walls – originally 10m high – are impressive; inside you can see the hearth and where a mezzanine floor would have fitted. Around the broch are a number of well-preserved outbuildings, including a curious shamrock-shaped house. The visitor centre has some interesting displays on the culture that built these remarkable fortifications.

The broch is on an exposed headland at Aikerness, a 1.5-mile walk northeast from the strung-out village of Evie.

Stromness

POP 1800

This appealing grey-stone port has a narrow, elongated, flagstone-paved main street and tiny alleys leading down to the waterfront between tall houses. It lacks Kirkwall's size but makes up for that with bucketloads of character, having changed little since its heyday in the 18th century, when it was a busy staging post for ships avoiding the troublesome English Channel during European wars. Stromness is ideally located for trips to Orkney's major prehistoric sites.

◉ Sights

The main recreation in Stromness is simply strolling up and down the narrow, atmospheric main street, where cars and pedestrians move at the same pace.

★ Stromness Museum   MUSEUM

(☎01856-850025; www.stromnessmuseum.co.uk; 52 Alfred St; adult/child £5/1; ⊙10am-5pm daily Apr-Sep, 10am-5pm Mon-Sat Oct, 11am-3.30pm Mon-Sat Nov) This superb museum, run with great passion, is full of knick-knacks from maritime and natural-history exhibitions covering whaling, the Hudsons Bay Company and the sunk German fleet. There's always an excellent summer exhibition too. You can happily nose around for a couple of hours. Across the street is the house where local poet and novelist George Mackay Brown lived.

Pier Arts Centre   GALLERY

(☎01856-850209; www.pierartscentre.com; 30 Victoria St; ⊙10.30am-5pm Tue-Sat, plus Mon mid-Jun–Aug) FREE This gallery has really rejuvenated the Orkney modern-art scene with its sleek lines and upbeat attitude. It's worth a look as much for the architecture as for its high-quality collection of 20th-century British art and the changing exhibitions.

★☆ Festivals & Events

Orkney Folk Festival   MUSIC

(www.orkneyfolkfestival.com) A four-day event in late May, with folk concerts, *ceilidhs* (evenings of traditional Scottish entertainment) and casual pub sessions. Stromness packs out, and late-night buses from Kirkwall are laid on. Book tickets and accommodation ahead.

🛏 Sleeping

Hamnavoe Hostel   HOSTEL £

(☎01856-851202; www.hamnavoehostel.co.uk; 10a North End Rd; dm £20-22, s £22, tw £30-33; 🛜) This well-equipped hostel is efficiently run and boasts excellent facilities, including a fine kitchen and a lounge room with great perspectives over the water. The dorms are very commodious, with duvets, decent mattresses and reading lamps (bring a pound coin for the heating), and the showers are good. Ring ahead as the owner lives off-site.

Point of Ness Caravan & Camping Park   CAMPSITE £

(☎office hours 01856-873535, site 01856-850532; https://orkney.campstead.com; Ness Rd; tent sites 1/2 people £7.65/11.80; ⊙Apr-Sep; 🅿🛜🐾) This breezy, fenced-in campsite has a super loca-

tion overlooking the bay at the southern end of town and is as neat as a pin.

Brown's Hostel   HOSTEL £

(☎01856-850661; www.brownsorkney.com; 45 Victoria St; s £22.50, d £40-50; @🛜) On the main street, this handy, sociable place has cosy private rooms – no dorms, no bunks – at a good price. There's an inviting common area, where you can browse the free internet or swap pasta recipes in the open kitchen. There are en suite rooms in a house up the street, with self-catering options available.

★ Brinkies Guest House   B&B ££

(☎01856-851881; www.brinkiesguesthouse.co.uk; Brownstown Rd; s £50, d £80-90; 🅿🛜) Just a short walk from the centre, but with a lonely, king-of-the-castle position overlooking the town and bay, this exceptional place offers five-star islander hospitality. Compact, modern rooms are handsome, stylish and comfortable, public areas are done out most attractively in wood, but above all it's the charming owner's flexibility and can-do attitude that makes this so special.

Breakfast is 'continental Orcadian' – a stupendous array of local cheese, smoked fish and homemade wheat-barley bread. Take Outertown Rd off Back Rd, turn right on to Brownstown Rd, and keep going.

Burnside Farm   B&B ££

(☎01856-850723; www.burnside-farm.com; North End Rd/A965; s £60, d £85-90; 🅿🛜) On a working dairy farm on the edge of Stromness, this offers lovely views over green fields, town and harbour. Rooms are elegant and maintain the style from when the house was built in the late forties, with elegant period furnishings. The top-notch bathrooms, however, are sparklingly contemporary. Breakfast comes with views, and the kindly owner couldn't be more welcoming.

6 South End   SELF-CATERING ££

(☎01856-850215; www.orkneyholidaycottages.co.uk; 6 South End; per week £400-500; 🛜) Just off the main street near the museum and right by the water, this very cute fisherfolk's cottage seems to embody this nautical town. It's ideal for a couple or small family, with a double and single room and cosy lounge with fireplace. Decor is attractive and contemporary.

✕ Eating & Drinking

Bayleaf Delicatessen   DELI £

(☎01856-851605; www.bayleafdelicatessen.co.uk; 19 Graham Pl; snacks £2-5; ⊙10am-5pm Mon-Sat, plus 10am-4pm Sun Jun-Aug) 🍴 On one of the numerous little wynds off the main street through Stromness you'll find this very likeable little deli. Local cheeses and yoghurts are a highlight, alongside smoked fish, takeaway seafood salads and other tasty Orkney produce. There's good coffee too, though nowhere to sit down to sip it.

Ferry Inn
PUB FOOD £

(☑ 01856-850280; www.ferryinn.com; 10 John St; mains £7-15; ⊙ food noon-2pm & 5-9pm Mon-Fri, noon-9pm Sat & Sun; 🛜) Every port has its pub, and in Stromness it's the Ferry. Convivial and central, it warms the cockles with folk music, local beers and characters, and pub food that offers decent value in a dining area done out like the deck of a ship. The fish and chips are excellent, and a few blackboard specials fill things out. It's also open for breakfasts.

Hamnavoe Restaurant
SEAFOOD ££

(☑ 01856-851226, 01856-850606; 35 Graham Pl; mains £15-22; ⊙ 7-9pm Tue-Sun Jun-Aug) Tucked away off the main street, this Stromness favourite specialises in excellent local seafood in an intimate, cordial atmosphere. There's always something good off the boats, and the chef prides himself on his lobster. Booking is a must. It opens some weekends off-season; it's worth calling.

ℹ️ Information

Stromness Information Centre (☑ 01856-850716; www.visitorkney.com; Ferry Rd; ⊙ 10am-3pm Mon-Sat Apr-Sep) is in the ferry terminal.

ℹ️ Getting There & Around

Northlink Ferries (p399) runs services from Stromness to Scrabster on the mainland (passenger/car £19.40/59, 1½ hours, two to three daily).

Bus X1 runs regularly to Kirkwall (£3.10, 30 minutes, hourly, seven Sunday), with some going on to St Margaret's Hope (£5.75, 1¼ hours).

Orkney Cycle Hire (p402) offers family options include kids' bikes and child trailers.

Hoy
POP 400

Orkney's second-largest island, Hoy (meaning 'High Island'), got the lion's share of the archipelago's scenic beauty. Shallow turquoise bays lace the east coast and massive seacliffs guard the west, while peat and moorland cover Orkney's highest hills. Much of the north is a reserve for breeding seabirds.

👁️ Sights

Old Man of Hoy
ROCK FORMATION

Hoy's best-known sight is this spectacular 137m-high rock stack jutting from the ocean off the tip of an eroded headland. It's a tough ascent and for experienced climbers only, but the walk to see it is a Hoy highlight, revealing much of the island's most spectacular scenery. You can also spot the Old Man from the Scrabster–Stromness ferry.

The easiest approach to the Old Man is from Rackwick Bay, a 5-mile walk by road from Moaness Pier (in Hoy village on the east coast, where the ferries dock) through the beautiful Rackwick Glen. You'll pass the 5000-year-old **Dwarfie Stane**, the only example of a rock-cut tomb in Scotland. On your return you can take the path via the Glens of Kinnaird and Berriedale Wood, Scotland's most northerly tuft of native forest.

From Rackwick Bay, where there's a hostel, the most popular path climbs steeply westwards then curves northwards, descending gradually to the edge of the cliffs opposite the Old Man of Hoy. Allow seven hours for the return trip from Moaness Pier, or three hours from Rackwick Bay.

Scapa Flow
Visitor Centre & Museum
MUSEUM

(☑ 01856-791300; www.orkney.gov.uk; Lyness; ⊙ 10am-4.30pm Mon-Sat Mar-Apr & Oct, 9am-4.30pm Mon-Sat, 1st to last ferry Sun May-Sep) FREE Lyness was an important naval base during both world wars, when the British Grand Fleet was based in Scapa Flow. This fascinating museum and photographic display, located in an old pumphouse that once fed fuel to the ships, is a must-see for anyone interested in Orkney's military history. Take your time to browse the exhibits and have a look at the folders of supplementary information: letters home from a seaman lost when the *Royal Oak* was torpedoed are particularly moving.

It's just by the ferry slip at Lyness, so easily visited. There's a decent cafe here.

🛏️ Sleeping & Eating

Hoy Centre
HOSTEL £

(☑ office hours 01856-873535, warden 01856-791315; https://orkney.campstead.com; dm/tw £19.20/53.50; 🅿️🛜) This clean, bright modern hostel has an enviable location, around 15 minutes' walk from Moaness Pier, at the base of the rugged Cuilags. Rooms are all en suite and include good-value family options; it also has a spacious kitchen and DVD lounge. Book via the website to avoid an admin fee.

ORKNEY & SHETLAND HOY

Quoydale
B&B £

(☎01856-791315; www.orkneyaccommodation.co.uk; s/d £35/60; ℗🛜🏠) This welcoming B&B is nestled at the base of Ward Hill, on a working farm 1 mile south of the Moaness ferry terminal. It has spectacular views over Scapa Flow and offers tours and a taxi service. There's also a self-catering cottage available.

Stromabank Hotel
INN ££

(☎01856-701494; www.stromabank.co.uk; Longhope; s/d £55/90; ⊘food 6-8pm Fri-Wed, plus noon-2pm Sun; ℗🛜) Perched on the hill above Longhope, the small atmospheric Stromabank has very acceptable, refurbished en suite rooms, as well as tasty home-cooked meals, including seafood and steaks (£8 to £14) using lots of local produce. The owners were looking to sell, so details may change. They do meals for residents only on Thursdays and takeaways on Saturday evenings.

❶ Getting There & Away

Orkney Ferries (p402) runs a passenger/bike ferry (adult £4.25, 30 minutes, two to six daily) between Stromness and Moaness at Hoy's northern end, and a car ferry to Lyness (with one service to/from Longhope) from Houton on Mainland (passenger/car £4.25/13.60, 40 minutes, up to seven daily Monday to Friday, two or three Saturday and Sunday); book cars well in advance. Sunday service is May to September only.

The Moaness ferry also stops at **Graemsay**. The Houton one also links to **Flotta**.

Northern Islands

The group of windswept islands north of Mainland are a haven for birds, rich in archaeological sites and blessed with wonderful white-sand beaches and azure seas. Though some are hillier than others, all offer a broadly similar landscape of flattish green farmland running down to scenic coastline. Some give a real sense of what Orkney was like before the modern world impinged upon island life.

Accessible by reasonably priced ferry or plane, the islands are well worth exploring. Though you can see 'the sights' in a matter of hours, the key is to stay a day or two and relax into the pace of island life.

Note that the 'ay' at the end of island names (from the Old Norse for 'island') is pronounced closer to 'ee'.

Orkney Ferries (p402) and Loganair (p399) enable you to make day trips to many of the islands from Kirkwall. That said, it's really best to stay and soak up the slow, easy pace of life.

Rousay

POP 200

Just off the north coast of Mainland, hilly Rousay merits exploration for its fine assembly of prehistoric sites, great views and relaxing away-from-it-all ambience. Connected by regular ferry from Tingwall, it makes a great little day trip, but you may well feel a pull to

ORKNEY & SHETLAND NORTHERN ISLANDS

DIVING SCAPA FLOW

One of the world's largest natural harbours, Scapa Flow has been in near constant use by fleets from the time of the Vikings onwards. After WWI, 74 German ships were interned here; when the armistice dictated a severely reduced German navy, Admiral von Reuter, in charge of the fleet, took matters into his own hands. A secret signal was passed around and the British watched incredulously as every German ship began to sink. Fifty-two of them went to the bottom, with the rest left aground in shallow water.

Most were salvaged, but seven vessels remain to attract divers. There are three battleships – the *König*, the *Kronprinz Wilhelm* and the *Markgraf*. The first two were partially blasted for scrap, but the *Markgraf* is undamaged and considered one of Scotland's best dives. Numerous other ships rest on the sea bed. HMS *Royal Oak*, sunk by a German U-boat in October 1939 with the loss of 833 crew, is a war grave and diving is prohibited.

It's worth prebooking diving excursions far in advance. **Scapa Scuba** (☎01856-851218; www.scapascuba.co.uk; Lifeboat House, Stromness; beginner dive £80, 2 guided dives £140-160; ⊘noon-7pm Mon-Fri & 3-6pm Sat & Sun May-Sep) caters for both beginners – with 'try dives' around the Churchill barriers – and tried-and-tested divers. You'll need plenty of experience to dive the wrecks, some of which are 47m deep, plus have recent drysuit experience: this can be organised for you. **Diving Cellar** (☎01856-850055; www.dives capaflow.co.uk; Pierhead, Stromness; week diving incl B&B £500) offers intensive week-long packages, including accommodation, for experienced divers; it recommends 40 logged dives plus cold-water and 35m-plus depth experience to make the most of the week.

stay longer. A popular option is to hire a bike from Trumland Farm near the ferry and take on the 14-mile circuit of the island.

The major **prehistoric sites** (HES; www. historicenvironment.scot; ⊘24hr) FREE are clearly labelled from the road ringing the island. Heading west from the ferry, you soon come to **Taversoe Tuick**, an intriguing burial cairn constructed on two levels, with separate entrances – perhaps a joint tomb for different families; a semidetached solution in posthumous housing. Not far beyond are two other significant cairns; **Blackhammer**, then **Knowe of Yarso**, the latter a fair walk up the hill but with majestic views.

Six miles from the ferry, mighty **Midhowe Cairn** (HES; www.historicenvironment.scot; ⊘24hr) FREE has been dubbed the 'Great Ship of Death'. Built around 3500 BC and enormous, it's divided into compartments, in which the remains of 25 people were found. Covered by a protective stone building, it's nevertheless memorable. Adjacent **Midhowe Broch**, whose sturdy stone lines echo the rocky shoreline's striations, is a muscular Iron Age fortified compound with a mezzanine floor. The sites are on the water, a 10-minute walk downhill from the main road.

An easy stroll from the ferry (turn left at the main road), organic **Trumland Farm** (☑01856-821252; trumland@btopenworld.com; sites £6, dm £14-15; P ⊞) ✦ farm has a wee hostel with two dorms and a pretty little kitchen and common area. You can pitch tents and use the facilities; there's also well-equipped self-catering in a cottage and various farm buildings.

Two miles west from the ferry pier, the island's only hotel, **Taversoe** (☑01856-821325; www.taversoehotel.co.uk; s £40-55, d £80-95; P 🖱), is an attractively low-key place, with renovated rooms offering excellent bathrooms – one a disabled-friendly wet room – and beautiful water views. The best views are from the dining room, which serves good-value meals. The friendly owners will collect you from the ferry.

Food is served from noon to 5pm Monday, noon to 9pm Tuesday to Saturday and noon to 7.30pm Sunday May to September, with shorter hours in winter.

❶ Getting There & Around

A small **ferry** (☑01856-751360; www.orkney ferries.co.uk) connects Tingwall on Mainland with Rousay (passenger/bicycle/car £4.25/ free/13.60, 30 minutes, up to six daily) and the nearby islands of **Egilsay** and **Wyre**. Vehicle bookings are compulsory.

ORKNEYINGA SAGA

Written around AD1200, this saga is a rich tale of sorcery, political intrigue, and cunning and unscrupulous acts among the Viking earls of Orkney. Part myth and part historical fact, it begins with the capture of the islands by the king of Norway and recounts the tumultuous centuries until they become part of Scotland. It's a wonderful piece of medieval literature and well worth a read. Head to the **Orkneyinga Saga Centre** (Orphir; ⊘9am-6pm Apr-Oct) FREE in the south coast village of Orphir for more background.

Rousay Tours (☑01856-821234; www. rousaytours.co.uk; adult/child £32/10) offers taxi service and recommended guided tours of the island, including wildlife-spotting (seals and otters), visits to the prehistoric sites and optional tasty packed lunch.

Sanday
POP 500

Aptly named, blissfully quiet and flat, Sanday is ringed by Orkney's best beaches – with dazzling-white sand of the sort you'd expect in the Caribbean. It's a peaceful, green, pastoral landscape with the sea revealed at every turn.

There are several archaeological sites on Sanday, the most impressive being the **Quoyness chambered tomb** (⊘24hr) FREE, similar to Maeshowe and dating from the 3rd millennium BC. It has triple walls, a main chamber and six smaller cells.

Sanday Heritage Centre (www.sanday. co.uk; Lady; donations appreciated; ⊘9.30am-5pm May-Oct) FREE museum in the former temperance hall has intriguing displays on various aspects of island history, including fishing, the wars, archaeology and shipwrecks. In an adjacent field, a typical croft house is preserved.

Ayre's Rock Hostel & Campsite (☑01857-600410; www.ayres-rock-hostel-orkney. com; tent sites 1-/2-person £6/10, pods £20, dm/s/ tw £17.50/20/35; P 🖱⊞) is a super-friendly spot 6 miles north of the ferry by a beach that offers a cosy hostel with three rooms sleeping two or four in beds, and a sweet grassy campsite by the water. As well as tent pitches, there are heated two-person pods and a static caravan. It has a craft shop and Saturday chip shop on site, and hosts are extremely helpful.

Set on a working cattle farm by the sea, **Backaskaill** (☑ 01857-600305; www.bedandbreakfastsandayorkney.com; s/d £50/75; P ✿) offers comfortable accommodation in a stone farmhouse. The polished interior features an eclectic collection of art and curios and cordial, professional hospitality. Rooms feel light and modern, and there's a fabulous guest lounge. The island's best meals (mains £9 to £16) are here and can be booked by non-guests.

❶ Getting There & Away

There are **Loganair** (p399) flights from Kirkwall to Sanday (one way £37, 20 minutes, once or twice daily).

Orkney Ferries (p402) runs from Kirkwall (passenger/car £8.35/19.70, 1½ hours), with a link to Eday. A bus meets the boat.

Westray

POP 600

If you've time to visit only one of Orkney's Northern Islands, make Westray (www.westraypapawestray.co.uk) the one. The largest of the group, it has rolling farmland, handsome sandy beaches, great coastal walks and several appealing places to stay.

◉ Sights & Activities

★ Noltland Castle   CASTLE

(⊙ 8am-8pm) FREE A half-mile west of Pierowall stands this sturdy ruined towerhouse, built in the 16th century by Gilbert Balfour, aide to Mary, Queen of Scots. The castle is super-atmospheric and bristles with shot holes, part of the defences of the deceitful Balfour, who plotted to murder Cardinal Beaton and, after being exiled, the king of Sweden. Like a pantomime villain, he met a sticky end.

At the nearby Links of Noltland, archaeological investigation has resumed and interesting neolithic finds are being unearthed with regularity. Most intriguing has been a chamber built over a spring, which was possibly used as a sauna.

Noup Head   NATURE RESERVE

FREE This bird reserve at Westray's northwestern tip is a dramatic area of sea cliffs with vast numbers of breeding seabirds from April to July. You can walk here along the clifftops from a car park, passing the impressive chasm of Ramni Geo, and return via the lighthouse access road (4 miles).

Westray Heritage Centre   MUSEUM

(☑ 01857-677414; www.westrayheritage.co.uk; Pierowall; adult/child £3/50p; ⊙ 11.30am-5pm Mon,

9am-noon & 2-5pm Tue-Sat & 1.30-5pm Sun early May-late Sep) This has displays on local history, nature dioramas and archaeological finds, with some famous neolithic carvings (including the 5000-year-old 'Westray Wife'). These small sandstone figurines are the oldest known depictions of the human form so far found in the British Isles.

Westraak   DRIVING

(☑ 01857-677777; www.westraak.co.uk; Quarry Rd, Pierowall; adult £59) This husband-and-wife outfit runs informative and engaging trips around the island, covering everything from Viking history to puffin mating habits. It also runs the island's taxi service.

🛏 Sleeping & Eating

★ West Manse   B&B £

(☑ 01857-677482; www.westmanse.co.uk; Westside; r per person £25; P ✿🐾) ✎ No timetables reign at this imposing house with arcing coastal vistas; make your own breakfast when you feel like it. Your welcoming hosts have introduced a raft of green solutions for heating, fuel and more. Kids will love this unconventional place, with its play nooks and hobbit house, while art exhibitions, eclectic workshops, venerably comfortable furniture and clean air are drawcards for parents.

There's also a self-catering apartment, Brotchie (£300 per week), and soon a fabulous little waterside cottage in Pierowall totally designed for the needs of a disabled visitor accompanied by a carer.

Bis Geos   SELF-CATERING £

(☑ 01857-677420; www.bisgeos.co.uk; per week from £350; P) Stunning views at this spectacular, quirky and cosy self-catering option between Pierowall and Noup Head. There are three separate units here, with the largest sleeping eight and offering the finest vistas. Shorter stays are sometimes available.

Chalmersquoy & The Barn   B&B, HOSTEL £

(☑ 01857-677214; http://chalmersquoywestray.co.uk; Pierowall; dm/s/q £22/29/65, apt for 4/6 £60/100, tent sites £7-10 plus per adult/child £2/1; P ✿) This excellent, intimate, modern hostel is an Orcadian gem. It's heated throughout and has pristine kitchen facilities and an inviting lounge; rooms sleep two or three in comfort. Out the front, the lovely owners have top self-catering apartments with great views, and spacious en suite B&B rooms. It also has a campsite and a fabulous byre that hosts atmospheric concerts. A recommended all-round choice.

Braehead Manse
B&B ££

(The Reid Hall; ☑ 01857-677861; www.braehead manse.co.uk; Braehead; s/d £100/130; P 🛜) ✎ A top-notch conversion of a former village hall behind the church in the middle of the island, this has two luminous, high-ceilinged rooms with modern en suite bathrooms and a swish open-plan kitchen/living/dining area with excellent facilities. You can either take it as self-catering – perfect for a family of four – or B&B, with your hosts appearing in the morning to make breakfast.

Pierowall Hotel
PUB FOOD £

(☑ 01857-677472; www.pierowallhotel.co.uk; Piero wall; mains £8-11; ⏲ food noon-2pm & 5-8.30pm Mon-Thu, 6-9pm Fri & Sat, 1-2.30pm & 6-8pm Sun; 🛜) The heart of this island community, the refurbished local pub is famous through-out Orkney for its popular fish and chips – whatever has turned up in the day's catch by the hotel's boats is displayed on the black-board. There are also some curries available, but the sea is the way to go here. It also has rooms and hires bikes (£10 per day).

ⓘ Getting There & Away

There are daily Loganair (p399) flights from Kirkwall to Westray (one way £37, 20 minutes).

Orkney Ferries (p402) links Kirkwall with Rapness (passenger/car £8.35/19.70, 1½ hours, daily). A bus to the main town, Pierowall, meets the ferry.

Papa Westray

Known locally as Papay, this exquisitely peaceful, tiny island (4 miles by 1 mile) is home to possibly Europe's oldest domestic building, the 5500-year-old **Knap of Howar** (⏲24hr) FREE, and largest Arctic tern colony. Plus the two-minute hop from Westray is the world's shortest scheduled air service. It's a charming island with seals easily spotted while walking its coast.

Owned by the local community, **Beltane House** (☑ 01857-644224; www.papawestray. co.uk; Beltane; dm/s/d £20/28/44; P 🛜🐾) is the island's hub, with the only shop, and func-tions as a makeshift pub on a Saturday night. One wing is a hostel with bunks, the other a guesthouse with immaculate rooms with en suite. There are two kitchens, zippy wi-fi (when it works), a big lounge/eating area and views over grassy fields to the sea beyond.

It's just over a mile north of the ferry. You can also camp here (£8/4 per adult/child).

ⓘ Getting There & Away

There are two or three daily Loganair (p399) flights to North Ronaldsay (£18, 20 minutes) from Kirkwall. The £21 return offer (you must stay overnight) is great value. Some of the Kirk-wall flights go via Westray (£17, two minutes, the world's shortest scheduled flight) or North Ronaldsay (£17, 10 minutes).

A passenger-only Orkney Ferries (p402) ferry runs from Pierowall on Westray to Papa Westray (£4.15, 25 minutes, three to six daily in summer); the crossing is free if you've come straight from the Kirkwall–Westray ferry. From October to April the boat sails by arrange-ment (☑ 01857-677216). On Fridays a car ferry from Kirkwall makes the journey to Papa Westray.

North Ronaldsay
POP 70

North Ronaldsay is a real outpost surround-ed by rolling seas and big skies. Delicious peace and quiet and the island's excellent birdwatching lure visitors. There are enough semiferal sheep to seize power, but a 13-mile drystone wall running around the island keeps them off the grass; they make do with seaweed, which gives their meat a unique flavour.

Phone ahead to book a tour with **North Ronaldsay Tours** (☑ 01857-633257, 07703-112224; lighthouse or mill adult/child £6/4, com-bined £9/7), which will take you up the 176 steps to the top of the North Ronaldsay Lighthouse. You can combine this with a visit to the adjacent woollen mill workshop where you can see the yarn-working.

Powered by wind and solar energy, **Ob-servatory Guest House** (☑ 01857-633-200; www.nrbo.co.uk; campsites £5, dm/s/d £18.50/57.50/85; P @ 🛜) ✎ offers first-rate accommodation and ornithological activ-ities next to the ferry pier. There's a cafe-bar with lovely coastal views and convivial communal dinners (£15) in a sun-kissed (sometimes) conservatory; if you're lucky, local lamb might be on the menu. You can also camp here.

ⓘ Getting There & Away

There are two or three daily Loganair (p399) flights to North Ronaldsay (£18, 20 minutes) from Kirkwall. The £21 return offer (you must stay overnight) is great value.

Orkney Ferries (p402) runs from Kirk-wall on Tuesday and Friday (passenger/car £8.35/19.70, 2½ hours).

SHETLAND

Close enough to Norway geographically and historically to make nationality an ambiguous concept, the Shetland Islands are Britain's most northerly outpost. There's a Scandinavian lilt to the local accent, and streets named King Haakon or St Olaf remind that Shetland was under Norse rule until 1469, when it was gifted to Scotland in lieu of the dowry of a Danish princess.

The stirringly bleak setting – it's a Unesco geopark – still feels uniquely Scottish, though, with deep, naked glens flanked by steep hills, twinkling, sky-blue lochs and, of course, sheep on the roads.

Despite the famous ponies and woollens, it's no agricultural backwater. Offshore oil makes it quite a busy, well-heeled place, with hotels frequently block-booked for workers. Nevertheless nature still rules the seas and islands, and the birdlife (p426) is spectacular: pack binoculars.

ℹ Information

In the centre of the main town, **Lerwick Information Centre** (☏ 01595-693434; www.shetland.org; cnr Commercial & Mounthooly Sts; ☉9am-5pm Mon-Sat & 10am-4pm Sun Apr-Sep, 10am-4pm Mon-Sat Oct-Mar) has comprehensive information on the islands.

Sumburgh Airport Information Centre (☏ 01950-460905; www.shetland.org; Sumburgh Airport; ☉ 8.45am-4.45pm Mon-Fri, 10.15am-4pm Sat, 10.30am-5.30pm Sun, closed Sat Nov-Mar) has brochures available when the office is shut.

www.shetland.org is an excellent website with good info on accommodation, activities and more.

ℹ Getting There & Away

AIR

The main **airport** (LSI; ☏ 01950-461000; www.hial.co.uk) is at Sumburgh, 25 miles south of Lerwick. **Flybe** (☏ 0371 700 2000; www.flybe.com) runs daily services to Aberdeen, Kirkwall, Inverness, Edinburgh and Glasgow, and summer services to Bergen (Norway).

BOAT

Northlink Ferries (☏ 0845 600 0449; www.northlinkferries.co.uk; ☏) runs daily overnight car ferries between Aberdeen and Lerwick (high-season one way passenger/car £41/146, 12 to 15 hours), some stopping at Kirkwall, Orkney. With a basic ticket you can sleep in recliner chairs or the bar area. It's £36.50 for a berth in a shared cabin and £84 up to £137

for a comparatively luxurious double cabin. Sleeping pods (£18) are comfortable, reclinable seats. Ferries have a cafe, bar, paid lounge and cinema on board, plus slow wi-fi.

ℹ Getting Around

Public transport within and between the islands of Shetland is managed by ZetTrans (www.zettrans.org.uk). Timetable information for all air, bus and ferry services can be obtained at www.travel.shetland.org, from the ZetTrans website and from Lerwick's **Viking bus station** (☏ 01595-694100; Commercial Rd).

AIR

Interisland flights are operated by **DirectFlight** (☏ 01595-840246; www.directflight.co.uk) from Tingwall airport, 6.5 miles northwest of Lerwick. There are big discounts for under-25s.

BOAT

Ferry services run by Shetland Islands Council (www.shetland.gov.uk/ferries) link Mainland to other islands from various points.

BICYCLE

If it's fine, cycling on the islands' excellent roads can be an exhilarating way to experience the stark beauty of Shetland. It can, however, be very windy and there are few spots to shelter. You can hire bikes from several places, including **Grantfield Garage** in Lerwick.

BUS

An extensive bus network, coordinated by ZetTrans (www.zettrans.org.uk), radiates from Lerwick to all corners of Mainland, and on (via ferry) to the islands of Yell and Unst. Schedules aren't great for day tripping from Lerwick.

CAR & MOTORCYCLE

Shetland has broad, well-made roads (think 'oil money'). Car hire is fuss-free, and vehicles can be delivered to transport terminals. Prices are usually around £40/200 for a day/week.

Bolts Car Hire (☏ 01595-693636; www.boltscarhire.co.uk; 26 North Rd, Lerwick) Office in Lerwick and does airport and ferry terminal rentals.

Grantfield Garage (☏ 01595-692709; www.grantfieldgarage.co.uk; North Rd, Lerwick; ☉9am-5.30pm Mon-Sat) The cheapest. A short walk towards town from the Northlink ferry terminal.

Star Rent-a-Car (☏ 01595-692075; www.starrentacar.co.uk; 22 Commercial Rd, Lerwick) Opposite the bus station. Has an office at Sumburgh airport.

Lerwick

POP 6800

Built on the herring trade and modernised by the oil trade, Lerwick is Shetland's only real town, home to a third of the islands' population. It has a solidly maritime feel, with aquiline oilboats competing for space in the superb natural harbour with the dwindling fishing fleet. Wandering along atmospheric Commercial St is a delight, and the excellent museum provides cultural background.

⊙ Sights & Activities

★ **Shetland Museum**   MUSEUM

(☎01595-695057; www.shetlandmuseumandarchives.org.uk; Hay's Dock; ⊙10am-5pm Mon-Sat, noon-5pm Sun May-Aug, 10am-4pm Mon-Sat, noon-5pm Sun Sep-Apr) FREE This is an impressive recollection of 5000 years' worth of culture, people and their interaction with this ancient landscape. Comprehensive but never dull, the display covers everything from the archipelago's geology to its fishing industry, via local mythology – find out about scary *nyuggles* (ghostly horses), or detect *trows* (fairies). Pictish carvings and replica jewellery are among the finest pieces; the museum also includes a working lighthouse mechanism, a small gallery, a boat-building workshop and an archive for tracing Shetland ancestry.

Clickimin Broch   RUINS

(⊙24hr) FREE This fortified site, just under a mile southwest of the town centre, was occupied from the 7th century BC to the 6th century AD. It's impressively large, and its setting on a tongue of land in a small loch gives it a feeling of being removed from the present day.

Shetland Textile Museum   MUSEUM

(Böd of Gremista; ☎01595-694386; www.shetlandtextilemuseum.com; Gremista Rd; adult/child £3/free; ⊙noon-5pm Tue-Sat, to 7pm Thu early May-early Oct) A mile north of the centre, this foursquare stone house, birthplace of P&O founder Arthur Anderson, was also once a fish-curing station. It now holds a good display on the knitted and woven textiles and patterns that Shetland is famous for.

Fort Charlotte   FORTRESS

(Charlotte St; ⊙9.30am-sunset) FREE Built in 1781, this occupies the site of an earlier fortification built in 1665 to protect the harbour from the Dutch navy. The five-sided fortress never saw action, but today houses local volunteer units and provides excellent views over the harbour.

Above and Underwater Shetland   BOATING

(☎07788-665565; www.auw-shetland.com) A cosy cabin cruiser runs a variety of trips out of Lerwick. Wildlife-focused trips are fun and take you to Bressay (adult/child £40/25, 3 hrs) or Noss (£45/25, 3½ hrs). Shorter two-hour cruises cost £30. An underwater mobile camera lets you see the submarine world.

✦ Festivals & Events

Shetland Folk Festival   MUSIC

(www.shetlandfolkfestival.com; ⊙late Apr or early May) This gets the islands buzzing.

⌂ Sleeping

Lerwick has very average hotels but excellent B&Bs. It fills year-round; book ahead. There's no campsite within 15 miles.

Islesburgh House Hostel   HOSTEL £

(☎01595-745100; www.islesburgh.org.uk; King Harald St; dm/tw/q £21/42/60; P@🛜) This typically grand Lerwick mansion houses an excellent hostel, with comfortable dorms, a shop, a laundry, a cafe and an industrial kitchen. Electronic keys offer reliable security and no curfew. It's wise to book ahead in summer.

Woosung   B&B £

(☎01595-693687; conroywoosung@hotmail.com; 43 St Olaf St; d £65, s/d without bathroom £35/60; 🛜🐾) A budget gem in the heart of Lerwick B&B-land, this has a wise and welcoming host, and comfortable, clean, good-value rooms with fridge and microwave. Two of them share a compact but spotless bathroom.

ORKNEY & SHETLAND LERWICK

UP HELLY AA!

Shetland's long Viking history has rubbed off in more ways than just street names and square-shouldered locals. Most villages have a fire festival, a continuation of Viking midwinter celebrations of the rebirth of the sun. The most spectacular happens in Lerwick.

Up Helly Aa (www.uphellyaa.org) takes place on the last Tuesday in January. Squads of *guizers* dress in Viking costume and march through the streets with blazing torches, dragging a replica longship, which they then surround and burn, bellowing out Viking songs from behind bushy beards.

Lerwick

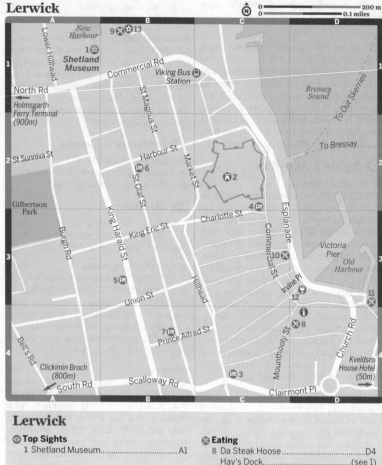

ORKNEY & SHETLAND LERWICK

Lerwick

The solid stone house dates from the 19th century, built by a clipper captain who traded tea out of the Chinese port it's named after.

★ Fort Charlotte Guesthouse   B&B **££**
(☏ 01595-692140; www.fortcharlotte.co.uk; 1 Charlotte St; s/d £40/80; 🛜🕿) Sheltering under the fortress walls, this friendly place offers summery en suite rooms, including great

singles. Views down the pedestrian street are on offer in some; sloping ceilings and oriental touches add charm to others. It has local salmon for breakfast and a bike shed. Very popular; book ahead.

Breiview Guest House   B&B **££**
(☏ 01595-695956; www.breiviewguesthouse.co.uk; 43 Kantersted Rd; s/d £55/80; 🅿🛜) On a hill a

little removed from the centre, this is a fine option with some water views. Rooms are spacious, light and furnished with blonde wood and have good bathrooms. Dieter is a lifeboat volunteer but guarantees to get your morning eggs perfect before dashing off to rescue a stricken ship.

Coming from the centre, turn left after passing the big Tesco supermarket and follow the signs.

Rockvilla Guest House
B&B **££**

(☏ 01595-695804; www.rockvillaguesthouse.com; 88 St Olaf St; s/d £65/90; ☎❄) Some of Shetland's B&Bs are aimed more at oilworkers than visitors, but this is quite the reverse: a relaxing, welcoming spot in a fine house behind a pretty garden. The three rooms are colour themed: Blue is bright, with a front-and-back outlook, Red is sultry with a sofa in the window, and smaller Green is shyer under the eaves.

Your hosts are friendly, and Jeff runs day tours to Sumburgh, Eshaness or Unst, among other places.

Eddlewood Guest House
B&B **££**

(☏ 01595-696734; http://eddlewood.wordpress.com; 8 Clairmont Pl; s/d £60/80; ☎ Jan-Nov; ☎) Cheerfully run, this sound selection has spacious, very well-kept en suite rooms with good showers. The top-floor rooms have plenty of character, with a cosy attic feel and good sea views. The friendly owner runs a welcoming, relaxed ship.

Kveldsro House Hotel
HOTEL **£££**

(☏ 01595-692195; www.shetlandhotels.com; Greenfield Pl; s/d £115/145; P ☎) Lerwick's best hotel overlooks the harbour and has a quiet but central setting. It's a dignified small set-up that will appeal to older visitors or couples. All doubles cost the same, but some are markedly better than others, with four-poster beds or water views. All boast new stylish bathrooms and iPod docks. The bar area is elegant and has fine perspectives.

✗ Eating

Mareel Cafe
CAFE **£**

(☏ 01595-745500; www.mareel.org; Hay's Dock; light meals £3-5; ☺10am-11pm Sun-Thu, 10am-1am Fri & Sat, food to 9pm; ☎) Buzzy, arty and colourful, this cheery venue in Mareel overlooks the water and does sandwiches and baked potatoes by day, and some cute Shetland tapas in the evenings. The coffee is decent, too, and it's a nice place for a cocktail.

Peerie Shop Cafe
CAFE **£**

(☏ 01595-692816; www.peerieshop.co.uk; Esplanade; light meals £3-8; ☺9am-6pm Mon-Sat; ☎) If you've been craving proper espresso since leaving the mainland, head to this gem, with art exhibitions, wire-mounted halogens and industrial-gantry chic. Newspapers, scrumptious cakes and sandwiches, hot chocolate that you deserve after that blasting wind outside, and – more rarely – outdoor seating give everyone a reason to be here.

★ Hay's Dock
CAFE **££**

(☏ 01595-741569; www.haysdock.co.uk; Hay's Dock, Shetland Museum; mains lunch £8-12, dinner £16-23; ☺10am-5pm Mon-Sat, noon-5pm Sun, plus 5.30-9pm Fri & Sat year-round & Tue-Thu Jun-Aug; ☎⬛) ✐ Upstairs in the Shetland Museum, this sports a wall of picture windows and a fairweather balcony that overlooks the harbour. Clean lines and pale wood recall Scandinavia, but the menu relies on carefully selected local and Scottish produce, with a substantial dash of international influence. Lunch ranges from delicious fish and chips to chowder, while evening menus concentrate on seafood and steak.

Fjarå
CAFE **££**

(☏ 01595-697388; www.fjaracoffee.com; Sea Rd; mains £8-18; ☺8am-10pm, food to 8pm; ☎) A cute wooden building in a super location, Fjarå is perched above a rocky shore and takes full advantage of its vistas, with big picture windows looking out over the water and perhaps some basking seals. It does a bit of everything, with breakfasts, sandwiches, salads and bagels at lunch, beers, cocktails and some decent seafood dinner plates.

It's across the road from the Tesco supermarket at the southern entrance to town.

Queen's Hotel
SCOTTISH **££**

(☏ 01595-692826; www.kgqhotels.co.uk; Commercial St; mains £11-22; ☺noon-2pm & 5.30-9.30pm; ☎) The dining room in this slightly run-down hotel wins marks for its harbour views – book one of the window tables. It's best visited for beautifully presented, classy local seafood dishes.

Da Steak Hoose
STEAKHOUSE **££**

(☏ 01595-696555; 5 Mounthooly St; mains £12-32; ☺noon-2pm & 5-9pm Tue-Sat, plus Mon Jun-Aug; ☎) Shetlanders have fine seafood but love their meat, so this friendly steakhouse was always going to be popular. Hidden away behind the tourist office, it offers uncomplicated steaks, ribs and burgers, served in sizeable portions with lots of garnishes. The dining area is atmospheric, with venerable, saggy floorboards and exposed walls; the downstairs bar is good for an apéritif at weekends.

You'll probably need to book. The kitchen might overcook your steak, so consider ordering it a grade less done. Few wines by the glass.

Drinking & Entertainment

Captain Flint's PUB

(☑ 01595-692249; 2 Commercial St; ⊙ 11am-1am; ☎) This port-side bar – Lerwick's liveliest – throbs with happy conversation and loud music, and has a distinctly nautical, creaky-wooden feel. There's a cross-section of young 'uns, tourists, boat folk and older locals. It has live music some nights and a pool table upstairs. Try a G&T with the seaweed-infused version of the local Reel gin.

Mareel ARTS VENUE

(☑ 01595-745500; www.mareel.org; Hay's Dock) Modern Mareel is a thriving arts centre, with a cinema, concert hall and cafe in a great waterside location.

Shopping

Best buys are the woollen cardigans and sweaters for which Shetland is world-famous. Check www.shetlandsartsandcrafts.co.uk for outlets around the islands, or grab the **Shetland Craft Trail** (www.shetlandartsandcrafts.co.uk) ✏ brochure from the tourist office.

OFFBEAT ACCOMMODATION

Shetland offers intriguing options for getting off the beaten accommodation track. There's a great network of *böds* – simple rustic cottages or huts with peat fires. They cost £10 per person, or £8 for the ones without electricity, and are available March to October. Contact and book via **Shetland Amenity Trust** (☑ 01595-694688; www.camping-bods.com; ⊙ 9am-5pm Mon-Thu, 9am-4pm Fri).

The same organisation runs three **Lighthouse Cottages** (☑ 01595-694688; www.shetlandlighthouse.com; per 3 days £279-321, per week £651-749) commanding dramatic views of rugged coastline: one, recently renovated and classy, at Sumburgh; one on the island of Bressay near Lerwick; and one at Eshaness. They sleep six to seven, and prices drop substantially off-season.

ⓘ Information

There are several free wi-fi networks around the centre, and the **Shetland Library** (☑ 01595-743868; www.shetland-library.gov.uk; Lower Hillhead; ⊙ 10am-8pm Mon & Thu, 10am-5pm Tue-Wed & Fri-Sat; ☎) offers both terminals and wireless access.

Gilbert Bain Hospital (☑ 01595-743000; www.shb.scot.nhs.uk) is on South Rd.

Lerwick Information Centre (p416) is helpful, with a good range of books and maps.

ⓘ Getting There & Away

Northlink Ferries (p416) from Aberdeen and Kirkwall dock at Holmsgarth terminal (Holmsgarth Rd), a 15-minute walk northwest from the town centre.

From **Viking bus station** (p416), buses service various corners of the archipelago, including regular services to/from Sumburgh Airport.

Bressay & Noss

POP 400

These islands lie across Bressay Sound just east of Lerwick. Bressay (*bress*-ah) has interesting walks, especially along the cliffs and up **Ward Hill** (226m), which has good views of the islands. Much smaller Noss is a nature reserve. As well as the crossing to Noss from Bressay, there are boat trips around the island from Lerwick.

Little **Isle of Noss** (☑ 0800-107 7818; www.nnr-scotland.org.uk/noss; boat adult/child £3/1.50; ⊙ 10am-5pm Tue-Wed & Fri-Sun mid-Apr–Aug), 1.5 miles wide, lies just east of Bressay. High seacliffs harbour over 100,000 pairs of breeding seabirds, while inland heath supports hundreds of pairs of great skua. Access is by dinghy from Bressay; phone in advance to check that it's running. Walking anticlockwise around Noss is easier, with better cliff-viewing. There's a small visitor centre by the dock.

With two daily departures, **Shetland Seabird Tours** (☑ 07767-872260; www.shetlandseabirdtours.com; adult/child £45/25; ⊙ May-Oct) runs three-hour cruises to watch gannets feeding, observe the raucous seabird colonies of Bressay and Noss, and do a bit of seal-spotting. You can book at the Lerwick Information Centre (p416).

Offering huge, colourful rooms and marvellous views back over the sound towards Lerwick, unusual **Northern Lights Holistic Spa** (☑ 01595-820257; www.shetlandspa.com; Uphouse; s/d £75/125; Ⓟ ☎) is appealingly decorated with Asian art. Room rates include sauna, steam room and Jacuzzi; massages and elaborate dinners (£37.50, BYOB) are available. Head for Uphouse; it's the big yellow building near the crest of the hill. Massages and spa treatments are also available for non-guests.

Ferries (passenger/car and driver return £5.30/13, seven minutes, frequent) link Lerwick and Bressay. The Noss crossing is 2.5 miles across the island.

Scalloway

POP 1200

Surrounded by bare, rolling hills, Scalloway (*scall*-o-wah) – Shetland's former capital – is a busy fishing and yachting harbour with a thriving seafood-processing industry. It's 6 miles from Lerwick.

There are pretty beaches and pleasant walks on the nearby islands (linked by bridges) of Trondra and East and West Burra.

Scalloway Museum (☑01595-880734; www.scallowaymuseum.org; Castle St; adult/child £3/1; ◷11am-4pm Mon-Sat, 2-4pm Sun May-Sep; ☞) has an excellent display on Scalloway life and history, with prehistoric finds, witch-burnings and local lore all featuring. It has a detailed section on the Shetland Bus and a fun area for kids, as well as a cafe.

During WWII, the Norwegian resistance movement operated the 'Shetland Bus' from here. The trips were very successful, carrying agents, wireless operators and military supplies to Norway for the resistance movement and returning with refugees, recruits for the Free Norwegian Forces and, in December, Christmas trees for the treeless Shetlands. **Shetland Bus Memorial** (Main St) is a moving tribute on the waterfront, built of stones from both countries. The Norwegian stones are from the home areas of 44 Norwegians who died running the gauntlet between Norway and here.

The town's most prominent landmark is **Scalloway Castle** (HES; www.historicenvironment.scot; ◷24hr) FREE, built around 1600 by Earl Patrick Stewart. The turreted and corbelled tower house is fairly well preserved. If you happen to find it locked, get keys from Scalloway Museum or Scalloway Hotel.

One of Shetland's best, **Scalloway Hotel** (☑01595-880444; www.scallowayhotel.com; Main St; s/d £95/135; ☑☞) is an energetically run waterfront place with very stylish rooms featuring sheepskins, local tweeds and other fabrics, and views over the harbour. Some rooms are larger than others; the best is the

fabulous superior, with handmade furniture, artworks and a top-of-the-line mattress on its four-poster bed. The **restaurant** (mains £18-25; ◷noon-3pm & 5-9.30pm Mon-Sat, noon-9pm Sun; ☞) is also excellent.

Buses run from Lerwick (£1.60, 25 minutes, roughly hourly Monday to Saturday, four Sunday) to Scalloway.

South Mainland

From Lerwick, it's 25 miles down this narrow, hilly tail of land to Sumburgh Head. Important prehistoric sights, fabulous birdwatching and glorious white-sand beaches make it one of Shetland's most interesting areas. The lapping waters are an inviting turquoise – if it weren't for the raging Arctic gales, you'd be tempted to have a dip.

Sandwick & Around

Opposite the scattered village of Sandwick, where you pass the 60-degree latitude line, is the small isle of Mousa, an RSPB reserve protecting some 7000 breeding pairs of nocturnal storm petrels. Mousa is also home to rock-basking seals as well as impressive Mousa Broch, the best preserved of these northern Iron Age fortifications.

On the island of Mousa, off Sandwick, **Mousa Broch** (◷24hr) FREE is a prehistoric fortified house, dating from some 2000 years ago, is an impressive sight. Rising to 13m, it's an imposing double-walled structure with a spiral staircase to access a 2nd floor. It features in Viking sagas as a hideout for eloping couples. In its walls nest hundreds of storm petrels, whose return to the nest at dusk is a stirring sight.

Mousa Boat (☑07901-872339; www.mousa.co.uk; adult/child return £16/7, daily except Saturday ◷Apr–mid-Sep) runs boat trips to Mousa from Sandwick, allowing three hours ashore on the island. It also offers night petrel-viewing trips (£20/10, dates on website).

Bigton, Boddam & Around

From **Bigton** it's another couple of miles to the largest shell-and-sand tombolo (sand or gravel isthmus) in Britain, **St Ninian's Isle**.

South of here, Shetland's best beach is gloriously white **Scousburgh Sands** (Spiggie Beach; Scousburgh). Back on the main road, from small Boddam a side road leads to the **Shetland Crofthouse Museum** (📞 01950-460557; www.shetlandheritageassociation.com; Boddam; ⏰ 10am-1pm & 2-4pm May-Sep) **FREE**.

South of Boddam, a minor road runs southwest to Quendale. Here you'll find the small but excellent, restored and fully operational 19th-century **Quendale Water Mill** (📞 01950-460550; www.quendalemill.co.uk; Quendale; adult/child £3/50p; ⏰ 10am-5pm mid-Apr–mid-Oct). The village overlooks a long, sandy beach to the south in the Bay of Quendale. West of the bay there's dramatic cliff scenery and **diving** in the waters between Garth's Ness and Fitful Head and to the wreck of the oil tanker *Braer* off Garth's Ness.

Near Scousburgh the **Spiggie Hotel** (📞 01950-460409; www.thespiggiehotel.co.uk; s/d/superior d £80/130/145; 🅿🛜) has compact rooms, self-catering annexes and tasty seafood and bar meals (noon to 2pm and 5.30pm to 8.30pm; mains £9 to £19). The rooms and dining room boast great views down over the local loch.

Sumburgh

With sea cliffs, and grassy headlands jutting out into sparkling blue waters, Sumburgh is one of the most scenic places on the island, with a far greener landscape than the peaty north. It has a handful of excellent attractions clustered near Shetland's major airport.

◉ Sights & Activities

★**Sumburgh Head**
Visitor Centre   LIGHTHOUSE, MUSEUM
(📞 01595-694688; www.sumburghhead.com; adult/child £6/2; ⏰ 11am-5.30pm Apr-Sep) High on the cliffs at Sumburgh Head, this excellent attraction is set across several buildings. Displays explain about the lighthouse, foghorn and radar station that operated here, and there's a good exhibition on the local marine creatures and birds. You can visit the lighthouse itself on a guided tour for an extra charge.

Jarlshof   ARCHAEOLOGICAL SITE
(HES; 📞 01950-460112; www.historicenvironment.scot; adult/child £5.50/3.30; ⏰ 9.30am-5.30pm Apr-Sep, 9.30am-dusk Oct-Mar) Old and new collide here, with Sumburgh airport right by this picturesque, instructive archaeological site. Various periods of occupation from 2500 BC to AD1500 can be seen; the complete change upon the Vikings' arrival is obvious: their rectangular longhouses present a marked contrast to the preceding brochs, roundhouses and wheelhouses.

WESTERN ISLANDS

Off West Mainland is **Papa Stour**, home to huge colonies of auks, terns and skuas but very few people. Buckled volcanic strata have been wonderfully eroded to dramatic caves, arches and stacks. There's a self-catering cottage, and a small campsite.

The island is served by Tuesday-only **DirectFlight** (p416) from Tingwall (return £69, 10 minutes, day return possible) and **ferries** (📞 01595-745804; www.shetland.gov.uk/ferries/) from West Burrafirth (passenger/car single £5.30/1.50, one hour).

Fifteen miles out in the Atlantic stands windswept **Foula**, perhaps Britain's most isolated community. Thirty-eight people are joined by 500,000 seabirds, including the rare Leach's petrel and Manx shearwater, and the world's largest colony of great skuas.

Accommodation is very limited and must be booked in advance. There is self-catering available, as well as centrally located **Leraback** (📞 01595-753226; www.originart.eu/leraback/leraback.html; Foula; B&B incl dinner per person £40; 🅿🛜), a simple B&B that offers evening meals.

DirectFlight flies to Foula from Tingwall (£79 return), with day trips possible from March to mid-October.

There are **ferries** (📞 01595-840208; www.bkmarine.org) from Walls (person/car single £5.30/20); bookings are essential. You can day trip to Foula on Wednesdays from Scalloway with **Cycharters** (📞 01595-810887; www.cycharters.co.uk).

Atop the site is 16th-century Old House, named 'Jarlshof' in a novel by Sir Walter Scott. There's an informative audio tour included with admission.

Old Scatness   ARCHAEOLOGICAL SITE
(☑ 01595-694688; www.shetland-heritage.co.uk/old-scatness; adult/child £5/4; ⊙ 10.15am-4.30pm Fri mid-May–Aug; 🖬) This dig brings Shetland's prehistory vividly to life; it's a must-see for archaeology buffs, but fun for kids, too. Clued-up guides in Iron Age clothes show you the site, which has provided important clues on the Viking takeover and dating of Shetland material. It has an impressive broch from around 300 BC, roundhouses and later wheelhouses. Best of all is the reconstruction with peat fire and working loom. At time of research, lack of funding had badly restricted the opening hours.

★ Sumburgh Head   BIRDWATCHING
(www.rspb.org.uk) At Mainland's southern tip, these spectacular cliffs offer a good chance to get up close to puffins, and huge nesting colonies of fulmars, guillemots and razorbills. If you're lucky, you might spot dolphins, minke whales or orcas. Also here is an excellent visitor centre (p422), in the lighthouse buildings.

❶ Getting There & Away

Bus 6 runs to Sumburgh and Sumburgh Airport from Lerwick (£2.70 to Sumburgh, £3.10 to the airport; one hour, eight Monday to Saturday, five Sunday).

North Mainland

The north of Mainland is very photogenic – jumbles of cracked, peaty, brown hills blend with grassy pastureland and extend like bony fingers into numerous lochs and out into the wider, icy, grey waters of the North Sea.

Brae & Around

The crossroads settlement of Brae is no beauty, despite its bayside location, but has several accommodation options and is an important service centre for the whole of northern Shetland.

Busta House Hotel (☑ 01806-522506; www.bustahouse.com; Busta; s/d £99/125; P@🛜🐾) 🐾 is a genteel, characterful hotel near Brae. It has a long, sad history and inevitable rumours of a (friendly) ghost. Built in the late 18th century (though the oldest part dates

from 1588), its refurbished rooms – all individually decorated – are compact and retain a classy but homey charm. Sea views and/or four-poster bed cost a bit more. There's a fine restaurant.

Frankie's Fish & Chips (☑ 01806-522700; www.frankiesfishandchips.com; Brae; mains £6-12; ⊙ 9.30am-8pm Mon-Sat, noon-8pm Sun; 🛜) 🐾 is a famous Shetland chippie, which uses only locally sourced and sustainable seafood. As well as chip-shop standards, the menu runs to plump Shetland mussels in garlicky sauces and, when available, plump juicy scallops. It also does breakfast rolls, baked potatoes and fry-ups. Eat in, out on the deck with views over the bay, or take away.

Buses from Lerwick to Brae (£2.70, 45 minutes, eight daily Monday to Saturday) run via Tingwall and Voe. Some continue to Hillswick.

Eshaness & Hillswick

Eleven miles northwest of Brae the road ends at the red basalt cliffs of Eshaness, some of Shetland's most impressive coastal scenery. When the wind subsides there is superb walking and panoramic views from the headland lighthouse.

A mile east of Eshaness, a side road leads south to the **Tangwick Haa Museum** (☑ 01806-503389; ⊙ 11am-5pm mid-Apr–Sep) **FREE**, housed in a restored 17th-century house. The wonderful collection of ancient black-and-white photos captures the sense of community in this area.

Follow the puffin signpost a mile short of Hillswick to find, Shetland's finest welcome at **Almara** (☑ 01806-503261; www.almara.shetland.co.uk; s/d £40/80; P🛜) 🐾. With sweeping views over the bay, this house has a great lounge, unusual features in the excellent rooms and bathrooms (including thoughtful extras such as USB chargers) and a good eye on the environment. You'll feel completely at home and appreciated; this is B&B at its best.

St Magnus Bay Hotel (☑ 01806-503372; www.stmagnusbayhotel.co.uk; Hillswick; s/d £85/95; P🛜🐾) is a wonderful wooden mansion, built in 1896. The owners are involved in an ongoing renovation process – a major project – to return it to former glories, and are doing a great job. Try for a renovated room, but all are winningly wood-clad, and half boast big windows taking full advantage of the fine water views. It serves food all day until 9pm.

Three buses from Lerwick run (Monday to Saturday) to Hillswick (£3.30, 1¼ hours). Two buses run the return route. There are other connections at Brae, including a service to Eshaness and North Roe.

The North Isles

Yell, Unst and Fetlar make up the North Isles, which are connected to each other by ferry, as is Yell to Mainland. All are great for nature-watching; Unst has the most to offer overall. If you're going to spend a night on both Yell and Fetlar or Unst, visit Yell on the way back, as the ferry to Unst is free if you are coming from Mainland that same day.

Yell

POP 1000

Yell if you like but nobody will hear; the desolate peat moors here are typical Shetland scenery. Still, the bleak landscape has an undeniable appeal.

◉ Sights & Activities

Shetland Gallery   GALLERY
(☏ 01957-744259; www.shetlandgallery.com; Sellafirth, Yell; ☺ 11am-5pm Tue-Sat & 2-5pm Sun Easter-Sep) Not far from the ferry to Unst and Fetlar, this has rotating exhibitions of Shetland artists.

Windhouse   RUINS
Northwest of the small settlement of Mid Yell, on the hillside above the main road, stand the reputedly haunted ruins of Windhouse, dating from 1707. It's been uninhabited since the 1920s, although there are plans to refurbish it. Look out for the Lady in Silk, the most famous of the ruins' several ghostly presences.

Old Haa Museum   MUSEUM
(☏ 01957-722339; www.shetlandheritageassociation.com; Burravoe; ☺ 10am-4pm Mon-Thu & Sat & 2-5pm Sun May-Sep) **FREE** This has a medley of curious objects (pipes, piano, doll-in-cradle, tiny bibles, ships in bottles and a sperm-whale jaw) as well as an archive of local history and a tearoom. It's in Burravoe, 4 miles east of the southern ferry terminal in Ulsta. Monday opening varies.

Lumbister RSPB Reserve   BIRDWATCHING
(www.rspb.org.uk) At this nature reserve red-throated divers, merlins, skuas and other bird species breed. The area is home to a large otter population, too, best viewed around Whale Firth, where you may also spot common and grey seals.

🛏 Sleeping & Eating

Lots of excellent self-catering cottages are dotted around the island; check www.welcometoyell.com for options.

Windhouse Lodge   BÖD £
(☏ office 01595-694688, warden 01957-702350; www.camping-bods.com; Mid-Yell; dm £10; ☺ Mar-Oct) Below the haunted ruins of Windhouse, and on the A968, you'll find this well-kept, clean, snug camping *böd* (hut) with power and a pot-belly stove to warm your toes. It's one of the cosiest, with a modern interior. Mattresses are thin. Book via phone or the website.

Quam B&B   B&B ££
(☏ 01957-766256; www.quambandbyellshetland.co.uk; Westsandwick; d £70; 🅿 🛜) Just off the main road through the island, this farm B&B has friendly owners and three good rooms. Breakfast features eggs from the farm, which also has cute ponies that you can meet. Dinners (£15 per person) can be arranged.

Gutcher Goose   CAFE £
(☏ 01957-744382; www.facebook.com/gutchercafe; Gutcher; light meals £3-6; ☺ 8.30am-4.30pm Mon-Fri, 9.30am-4.30pm Sat; 🛜) Recently opened when we passed by, this place was hoping to expand into evening meals and a fuller lunchtime offering. Mostly a shop, just by the Unst ferry slip, it has decent coffee and makes a fine spot to wait for a ferry.

ⓘ Getting There & Away

Yell is connected with Mainland by **ferries** (☏ 01595-745804; www.shetland.gov.uk/ferries) between Toft and Ulsta (passenger/car return £5.30/7.70, 20 minutes, frequent). It's wise to book car space in summer.

One **bus** runs Monday to Saturday from Lerwick to Yell (£4.20), connecting with ferries to Fetlar and Unst; connecting services cover other parts of the island.

Unst

POP 600

You're fast running out of Scotland once you cross to rugged Unst (www.unst.org). Scotland's most northerly inhabited island is prettier than Yell, with bare, velvety-smooth hills and settlements clinging to waterside locations, fiercely resisting the buffeting winds.

FAIR ISLE

It's a stomach-churning ferry ride to Fair Isle but worth it for the stunning cliff scenery, isolation and squadrons of winged creatures. About halfway to Orkney, Fair Isle is one of Scotland's most remote inhabited islands. It's only 3 miles by 1.5 miles in size and is probably best known for its patterned knitwear, still produced in the island's cooperative, Fair Isle Crafts.

It's also a paradise for birdwatchers, who form the bulk of the island's visitors. Fair Isle is in the flight path of migrating birds, and thousands breed here. They're monitored by the Bird Observatory, which collects and analyses information year-round; visitors are more than welcome to participate.

The smart **bird observatory** (☑ 01595-760258; www.fairislebirdobs.co.uk; s/d incl full board £75/140; ⊙ May-Oct; ℗ @ ☎) offers good accommodation in en suite rooms. Rates include full board, and there are free guided walks and other bird-related displays and activities. Under-25s get a big discount, paying £35 per person.

From Tingwall, DirectFlight (p416) operates flights to Fair Isle (£84 return, 25 minutes). There's also a weekly service from Sumburgh.

Ferries sail from Grutness (near Sumburgh) and some from Lerwick (one way person/car £5.30/20, three hours) two to three times weekly.

◉ Sights

★ Hermaness Nature Reserve
NATURE RESERVE

(www.nnr-scotland.org.uk) At marvellous Hermaness headland, a 4.5-mile round walk takes you to cliffs where gannets, fulmars and guillemots nest, and numerous puffins frolic. You can see Scotland's most northerly point, the rocks of **Out Stack**, and **Muckle Flugga**, with its lighthouse built by Robert Louis Stevenson's uncle. Duck into the **visitor centre** (☑ 01595-711278; ⊙ 9am-5pm May-early Sep) FREE, with its poignant story about long-time resident Albert Ross.

The path to the cliffs is guarded by a squadron of great skuas who nest in the nearby heather, and dive-bomb at will if they feel threatened. They're damn solid birds too, but don't usually make contact.

★ Unst Bus Shelter
LANDMARK

(www.unstbusshelter.shetland.co.uk; Baltasound) At the turnoff to Littlehamar, just past Baltasound, is Britain's most impressive bus stop. Enterprising locals, tired of waiting in discomfort, decided to do a job on it, and it now boasts posh seating, novels, numerous decorative features and a visitors' book to sign. The theme and colour scheme changes yearly.

Unst Heritage Centre
MUSEUM

(☑ 01957-711528; www.unstheritage.com; Haroldswick; adult/child £3/free, combined ticket with Unst Boat Haven £5; ⊙ 11am-4pm Mon-Sat, 2-4pm Sun May-Sep) This heritage centre houses a modern museum with a history of the Shetland pony and a re-creation of a croft house.

Unst Boat Haven
MUSEUM

(☑ 01957-711809; Haroldswick; adult/child £3/free, combined ticket with Unst Heritage Centre £5; ⊙ 11am-4pm Mon-Sat, 2-4pm Sun May-Sep) This large shed is a boatie's delight, packed with a beautifully cared for collection of Shetland rowing and sailing boats, all with a backstory. Old photos and maritime artefacts speak of the glory days of Unst fishing.

Skidbladner Longship
MUSEUM

(☑ 01595-694688; www.vikingshetland.com; Haroldswick; ⊙ 24hr) FREE Unst has the highest concentration of Viking longhouse sites in the country. The Viking Unst project manages three excavation sites, and has as its centrepiece this replica Viking longship. A re-created longhouse is alongside.

Shetland Distillery Company
DISTILLERY

(☑ 01957-711711; www.shetlandreel.com; Saxa Vord, Haroldswick) This small producer distils the Shetland Reel gin that you see around the place. Its version infused with local seaweed is well worth a try. The plan is to produce a single malt here too. Call to arrange a tour and/or tasting.

Muness Castle
CASTLE

(Muness; ⊙ 24hr) FREE This picturesque, sturdy 16th-century tower house in the island's southeastern corner was built by Laurence Bruce, *foud* (bailiff) of Shetland, who was, by all accounts, a nasty piece of work,

WILDLIFE WATCHING IN SHETLAND

For birdwatchers, Shetland is paradise – a stopover for migrating Arctic species and host to vast seabird breeding colonies; June is the height of the season.

Every bird has its own name here: rain geese are red-throated divers, bonxies are great skuas, and alamooties are storm petrels. Clownish puffin antics are a highlight. The **RSPB** (RSPB; www.rspb.org.uk; walks adult/child £5/2) maintains several reserves, plus there are National Nature Reserves at **Hermaness**, **Keen of Hamar** and **Noss**. **Foula** and **Fair Isle** also support large seabird populations.

Keep an eye on the sea: sea otters, orcas and other cetaceans are regularly sighted. Latest sightings are logged at useful www.nature-shetland.co.uk.

Shetland Nature Festival (www.shetlandnaturefestival.co.uk) in early July has guided walks, talks, boat trips, open days and workshops.

overtaxing locals and replacing their elected officials with his cronies. It's an atmospheric visit; grab a torch from under the information panel to explore.

🛏 Sleeping & Eating

★ Gardiesfauld Hostel   HOSTEL, CAMPSITE £

(☑ 01957-755279; www.gardiesfauld.shetland.co.uk; 2 East Rd, Uyeasound; tent sites per adult/child £6/2, dm adult/child £15/8; ☺ Apr-Sep; P 🐾 🛜) This spotless hostel has very spacious dorms with lockers, family rooms, a garden, an elegant lounge and a wee conservatory dining area with great bay views. You can camp here too, with separate areas for tents and vans. The bus stops right outside. Bring 20p pieces for the showers.

Saxa Vord   HOSTEL £

(☑ 01957-711711; www.saxavord.com; Haroldswick; s/d £22.50/45; ☺ mid-May–mid-Sep; P 🐾 🛜) This former RAF base is not the most atmospheric lodging, but the tired barracks-style rooms offer great value for singles, and there's something nice about watching the weather through the skylight-style windows. The restaurant dishes out surprisingly decent food, and there's a bar – Britain's northernmost, by our reckoning – and a friendly, helpful atmosphere. Wi-fi only in public areas.

Part of the same complex, self-catering houses (£750 per week) are good for families and available year-round.

Baltasound Hotel   HOTEL ££

(☑ 01957-711334; www.baltasoundhotel.co.uk; Baltasound; d £98-110; ☺ May–mid-Oct; P 🛜) Brightly decorated, commodious rooms – some bigger than others – are complemented by wooden chalets arrayed around the lawn.

It's worth the upgrade to the 'large doubles', which sport good modern bathrooms. There's a lovely country outlook, and evening bar meals (mains £8 to £13; food served 6pm to 8pm) in a dining room dappled by the setting sun. 'Unserviced' rooms offer a cheaper deal.

North Base   CAFE £

(☑ 01957-711393; www.thenorthbase.co.uk; Saxa Vord, Haroldswick; light meals £4-10; ☺ 11.30am-5pm Mon-Sat, 1-4pm Sun Apr-Oct; 🛜) Tucked away in the former RAF base, this spot produces artisanal chocolates and also has a pleasant cafe that doles out lunchtime comfort food to frozen walkers and birders.

ℹ Getting There & Around

Hire **bikes** (☑ 01957-711393; www.unstcycle hire.co.uk; Haroldswick; per day/week £10/50; ☺ 11.30am-5pm Mon-Sat, 1-4pm Sun, can hire out of hours) in the chocolate shop at the Saxa Vord complex in Haroldswick.

Unst is connected with Yell and Fetlar by a ferry (p424) between Gutcher and Belmont (free if coming from Mainland that day, otherwise passenger/car £5.30/7.70 return, 10 minutes, frequent).

One **bus** runs Monday to Saturday from Lerwick to the Unst ferry (£4.20, two hours). There are connecting services around Unst itself.

Fetlar

Fetlar, a notable birdwatching destination, is the smallest but most fertile of the North Isles. Its name is derived from the Viking term for 'fat land'.

Four to nine daily ferries (p424) (free if coming from Mainland that day, otherwise adult/car £5.30/7.70 return, 25 minutes) connect Fetlar with Gutcher on Yell and Belmont on Unst.

Understand Scotland

Scotland Today

Although an integral part of Great Britain since 1707, Scotland has maintained a separate and distinct identity throughout the last 300 years, which strengthened with the return of a devolved Scottish parliament to Edinburgh in 1999. Since then Scottish politics has diverged significantly from Westminster, culminating in 2016 when 62% of Scots voters chose to remain in the EU, while the UK as a whole voted to leave.

Best on Film

Whisky Galore! (1949) Classic Ealing comedy about wily Scottish islanders outfoxing the government when a cargo of whisky gets shipwrecked.
Local Hero (1983) Gentle Bill Forsyth comedy-drama sees American oil executive beguiled by the Highland landscape and eccentric locals.
Trainspotting (1996) 'Who needs reasons when you've got heroin?' Danny Boyle's second film (based on the novel by Irvine Welsh) dives into the gritty underbelly of life among Edinburgh drug addicts.

Best in Print

Raw Spirit (Iain Banks; 2003) An enjoyable jaunt around Scotland in search of the perfect whisky.
Mountaineering in Scotland (WH Murray; 1947) Classic account of climbing in Scotland in the 1930s, when just getting to Glen Coe was an adventure in itself.
Adrift in Caledonia (Nick Thorpe; 2006) An insightful tale of hitchhiking around Scotland on a variety of vessels.
The Poor Had No Lawyers (Andy Wightman; 2010) A penetrating (and fascinating) analysis of who owns land in Scotland, and how they got it.

An Independent Scotland?

Since the return of the Scottish parliament to Edinburgh in 1999, politics north of the border has headed in a different direction from England. A perceived disconnect between Scotland's social-democratic aspirations and what many voters felt was an increasingly authoritarian and right-wing Westminster government led to a landslide victory for the Scottish National Party in the 2011 Scottish parliamentary election, and a commitment to put the question of Scottish independence to the vote.

A referendum took place on 18 September 2014, posing the question: 'Should Scotland be an independent country?' The result was that a majority (55%) voted 'No' (from a record turnout of 85%). Despite maintaining the status quo, the referendum campaign re-energised Scottish politics and led to a huge increase in membership of political parties and a flourishing of debate, not only in the mainstream media but also online and among local interest groups.

The subsequent Scottish parliamentary election of May 2016 saw the SNP fall short of a majority by two seats, and the Conservative Party overtake Labour to come second – a huge shock for Labour, which had dominated Scottish politics for decades prior to 2011. The Scottish Green Party came fourth, another big turnaround, pushing the Liberal Democrats into fifth place. (In a notable achievement for equality, the leaders of the three biggest parties in Scotland, including the First Minister, were all women, and four out of the five main party leaders were openly gay.)

But the June 2016 referendum on whether the UK should remain part of the EU heralded a new era of uncertainty. While the UK as a whole voted to leave the EU by a margin of 52% to 48%, Scotland voted to remain by 62% to 38%.

Within days of the result, Scotland's First Minister Nicola Sturgeon declared that Scotland should not be pulled out of the EU against its will, and that a second referendum on the subject of Scottish independence was almost inevitable. The hows and whens of the UK's exit from the EU will take months or years of deliberation, but interesting times lie ahead...

Renewable Energy

One of the central planks of the SNP's vision for an independent Scotland in 2014 was its energy policy. The then party leader, Alex Salmond, said that he wanted the country to be the 'Saudi Arabia of renewable energy' – becoming self-sufficient in energy by 2020, and a net exporter of 'clean' electricity.

In the first half of the 20th century the Scottish Highlands were one the first regions in the world to develop hydroelectric power on a large scale, and since 2000 wind turbines have sprung up all over the place. By 2009, renewables provided 27% of Scotland's energy consumption, a figure that rose to 50% in 2015; the government's target is to reach 100% by 2020.

However, the future of Scotland's energy industry arguably lies not on land, but in the sea: Scotland has access to 25% of Europe's available tidal energy, and 10% of its wave power. The country is at the leading edge of developing wave, tidal and offshore wind power, and in 2012 the waters around Orkney and the Pentland Firth were designated as a Marine Energy Park.

Development Versus Conservation

In 2010 the Scottish government gave the go-ahead to a 137-mile, high-voltage overhead power line from Beauly (near Inverness) to Denny in Stirlingshire, to connect wind- and marine-generated electricity from the north to the heart of the national grid. Construction of the 615 giant pylons, marching through some of the Highlands' most scenic areas, was completed in 2015.

Supporters pointed out that the scheme also involved the removal of almost 60 miles of low-voltage pylons from the Cairngorms National Park; opponents claimed that a seabed cable, while more expensive, would have been a better alternative, and that the scars on the scenery were like taking a razor blade to a Rembrandt. The pylons and their access tracks are cleary visible along much of the A9 road between Perth and Aviemore.

The debate reflected a larger tension that exists across the Highlands and islands – between those keen to develop the region's resources and conservationists who want to keep the area unspoiled.

POPULATION: 5.3 MILLION

AREA: 78,722 SQ KM

UNEMPLOYMENT: 5.9% (2015)

ANNUAL WHISKY EXPORTS: 1.19 BILLION BOTTLES (2015)

if Scotland were 100 people

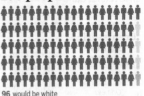

96 would be white
3 would be Asian
1 would be African, Afro-Caribbean or other

belief systems
(% of population)

44	32	16
Non Religious	Church of Scotland	Roman Catholic

6	1	1
Other Christian	Muslim	Other

population per sq km

EDINBURGH SCOTLAND UK

🧍 ≈ 65 people

History

Despite geographical isolation, Scotland was forged from the melting pot of several cultures and grew to wield great cultural, scientific and manufacturing influence globally. From the Vikings' decline onwards, Scottish history has been intertwined, often violently, to that of its southern neighbour, England. Battles and border raids were commonplace until shared kingship, then political union, drew the two together. Even then, Jacobite risings reflected divisions in Scottish and British society. More recently a trend towards self-determination led to devolved parliament in 1999, and 2014's independence referendum.

Top Prehistoric Sights

....

Jarlshof (Shetland)

....

Skara Brae
(Orkney)

....

Maeshowe
(Orkney)

....

Kilmartin Glen
(Argyll)

....

Callanish (Lewis)

....

Tomb of the Eagles
(Orkney)

....

Scottish Crannog
Centre (Kenmore)

Early Days

Hunters and gatherers have left fragments of evidence of Scotland's earliest human habitation. These people came in waves from northern Europe and Ireland as glaciers retreated in the wake of the last Ice Age around 10,000 BC.

The Neolithic was similarly launched by arrivals from mainland Europe. Scotland's Stone Age has left behind an astonishing diary of human development, unforgettable memories in stone of a distant past. Caithness, Orkney and Shetland have some of the world's best-preserved prehistoric villages, burial cairns and standing stones. Further south, crannogs (round structures built on stilts over a loch) were a favoured form of defensible dwelling through the Bronze Age.

The Iron Age saw the construction of a remarkable series of defence-minded structures of a different sort. Brochs (again a northeastern island development) were complex, muscular stone fortresses, some of which still stand well over 10m high.

Romans & Picts

The Roman occupation of Britain began in AD 43, almost a century after Julius Caesar first invaded. However, the Roman onslaught ground to a halt in the north, not far beyond the present-day Scottish border. Between AD 78 and 84, governor Agricola marched northwards and spent several years trying to subdue tribes the Romans called the Picts

TIMELINE	4000 BC	2200 BC	AD 43
	Neolithic farmers move to Scotland from mainland Europe; sites from these ancient days dot Scotland, with the best concentrated in Orkney.	Beaker culture arrives in Scotland. The Bronze Age produces swords and shields. Construction of hill forts, crannogs and mystifying stone circles.	Claudius begins the Roman conquest of Britain, almost a century after Julius Caesar first invaded. By AD 80 a string of forts is built from the Clyde to the Forth.

(from the Latin *pictus,* meaning 'painted'). By the 2nd century Emperor Hadrian, tired of fighting in the north, decided to cut his losses and built the wall (AD 122–28) that bears his name across northern England. Two decades later Hadrian's successor, Antoninus Pius, invaded Scotland again and built a turf rampart, the Antonine Wall, between the Firth of Forth and the River Clyde. In northern Britain, the Romans had met their match.

Little is known about the Picts, who inhabited northern and eastern Scotland. The Roman presence probably helped forge disparate Celtic tribes into a unified group; we can assume they were fierce fighters given the trouble the hardy Roman army had with them. The main material evidence of their culture is their fabulous carved symbol stones, found across eastern Scotland.

Eventually the Romans left Britain and at this time there were at least two indigenous peoples in the northern region of the British Isles: the Picts in the north and east, and the Britons in the southwest. A new group, the Celtic Scots, probably arrived around AD 500, crossing from Ireland and establishing a kingdom called Dál Riata in Argyll. St Ninian was the earliest recorded bringer of Christianity to the region, establishing a mission in Whithorn in Scotland's southwest. In the 6th century, St Columba, Scotland's most famous missionary, resumed St Ninian's work. Columba was a scholar and monk who was exiled, tradition has it, after involvement in a bloody battle. After fleeing Ireland in 563, he established a monastery on Iona – an island that retains an ancient, mystical aura – and also travelled northeast to take his message to the Picts. By the late 8th century most of Scotland had converted.

The First Kings of Scotland

The Picts and Scots were drawn together by the threat of a Norse invasion and by political and spiritual power from their common Christianity. Kenneth MacAlpin, first king of a united Scotland, achieved power using a mixture of blood ties and diplomacy. He set his capital in Pictland at Scone and brought to it the sacred Stone of Destiny, used in the coronation of Scottish kings.

Nearly two centuries later, MacAlpin's descendant Malcolm II (r 1005–18) defeated the Northumbrian Angles, a Germanic tribe who had settled in eastern England, at the Battle of Carham (1018) bringing Edinburgh and Lothian under Scottish control and extending Scottish territory as far south as the Tweed.

But the Highland clans, inaccessible in their glens, remained a law unto themselves for another 700 years. A cultural and linguistic divide grew up between the Gaelic-speaking Highlanders and the Lowlanders who spoke the Scots tongue.

Top Pictish Stones

St Vigeans Museum (Arbroath)

Aberlemno Stones (Angus)

Dupplin Cross (Dunning)

Groam House Museum (Rosemarkie)

Meigle Museum (Meigle)

Inverness Museum (Inverness)

Tarbat Discovery Centre (Portmahomack)

AD 142	AD 397	5th century	Early 500s
Building of Antonine Wall marks the northern limit of the Roman Empire. It is patrolled for about 40 years, but after this the Romans decide northern Britain is too difficult to conquer.	The first Christian mission beyond Hadrian's Wall, in Whithorn, is initiated by St Ninian. The earliest recorded church in Scotland is built to house his remains.	Roman soldiers are recalled to Rome as the Empire faces attack from barbarian tribes. The last Romans depart and Emperor Honorius tells Britons to fend for themselves.	A Celtic tribe, the Scots, cross the sea from northern Ireland and establish a kingdom in Argyll called Dál Riata.

Robert the Bruce & William Wallace

When Alexander III fell to his death in Fife in 1286, the succession was disputed by no fewer than 13 claimants, but in the end it came down to two: Robert de Brus, lord of Annandale, and John Balliol, lord of Galloway. King Edward I of England was asked to arbitrate. He chose Balliol, whom he thought he could manipulate more easily.

Seeking to tighten his feudal grip on Scotland, Edward – known as the 'Hammer of the Scots' – treated the Scots king as vassal rather than equal. The humiliated Balliol finally turned against him and allied Scotland with France in 1295, thus beginning the enduring 'Auld Alliance' and ushering in the Wars of Independence.

Edward's response was bloody. In 1296 he invaded Scotland and Balliol was incarcerated in the Tower of London; in another blow to Scots pride, Edward took the Stone of Destiny from Scone to London.

Enter William Wallace. Bands of rebels were attacking the English occupiers and Wallace led one such band to defeat the English at Stirling Bridge in 1297. After Wallace's execution, Robert the Bruce, grandson of Robert de Brus, saw his chance, defied Edward (whom he had previously aligned himself with), murdered his rival John Comyn and had himself crowned King of Scotland at Scone in 1306. Bruce mounted a campaign to drive the English out of Scotland but suffered repeated defeats. Persistence paid off and he went on to secure an illustrious victory over the English at Bannockburn, enshrined in Scottish legend as one of the finest moments in the country's history.

Scottish independence was eventually won in 1328, though 'the Bruce' died the next year. Wars with England and civil strife continued, however. In 1371 Robert the Bruce's grandson, Robert II, acceded to the throne, founding the Stewart (Stuart) dynasty, which was to rule Scotland and, in time, the rest of Britain, until 1714.

Robert the Bruce Trail

Melrose Abbey
(Melrose)

Scone Palace
(Perth)

Bannockburn
(Stirling)

Arbroath Abbey
(Arbroath)

Dunfermline Abbey
(Dunfermline)

The Renaissance

James IV (r 1488–1513) married the daughter of Henry VII of England, the first of the Tudor monarchs, thereby linking the two royal families through 'the Marriage of the Thistle and the Rose'. This didn't prevent the French from persuading James to go to war against his in-laws, and he was killed at the Battle of Flodden in 1513, along with some 10,000 of his subjects. Renaissance ideas, in particular Scottish poetry and architecture, flourished during this time; some of the finest Scottish Renaissance buildings can be seen within the fortress of Stirling Castle.

Mary, Queen of Scots & the Reformation

In 1542 King James V, childless, lay on his deathbed: broken-hearted, it is said, after his defeat by the English at Solway Moss. Then news came

685	780	848	1040
The Pictish king Bridei defeats the Northumbrians at Nechtansmere in Angus, an against-the-odds victory that sets the foundations for Scotland as a separate entity.	From the 780s onwards, Norsemen in longboats from Scandinavia begin to pillage the Scottish coast and islands, eventually taking control of Orkney, Shetland and the Western Isles.	Kenneth MacAlpin unites the Scottish and Pictish thrones, uniting Scotland north of the Firth of Forth into a single kingdom.	Macbeth takes the Scottish throne after defeating Duncan. This, and the fact that he was later killed by Duncan's son Malcolm, are the only parallels with the Shakespeare version.

that his wife had given birth to a baby girl. Fearing the end of the Stewart dynasty, and recalling its origin through Robert the Bruce's daughter, James sighed, 'It cam' wi' a lass, and it will gang wi' a lass.' He died shortly thereafter, leaving his week-old daughter, Mary, to inherit the throne as Queen of Scots.

She was sent to France and Scotland was ruled by regents, who rejected overtures from Henry VIII of England urging them to wed the infant queen to his son. Furious, Henry sent his armies to take vengeance on the Scots. The 'Rough Wooing', as it was called, failed to win hearts and minds and in 1558 Mary was married to the French dauphin. When he became king the next year, Mary was briefly queen of France as well as Scotland.

While Mary was in France, being raised Catholic, the Reformation tore through Scotland, to where, following the death of her sickly husband, the 18-year-old returned in 1561. She was formally welcomed to her capital city and held an audience with John Knox. The great reformer harangued the young queen and she later agreed to protect the budding Protestant Church in Scotland while continuing to practise Catholicism in private.

She married Lord Darnley in the Chapel Royal at Holyrood and gave birth to a son (later James VI) in 1565. Any domestic bliss was short-lived and, in a scarcely believable train of events, Darnley was involved in the murder of Mary's Italian secretary Rizzio (rumoured to be her lover), before he himself was murdered, probably by Mary's new lover and third-husband-to-be, the earl of Bothwell.

The Scots had had enough; Mary's enemies – an alliance of powerful nobles – finally confronted her at Carberry Hill, east of Edinburgh, and Mary was forced to abdicate in 1567 and thrown into prison at Castle Leven. She escaped and met her enemies in battle at Langside, but was defeated and fled to England, where she was imprisoned for 19 years by Elizabeth I and finally executed in 1587.

History, however, has a habit of providing a twist in the tale. Mary's son James VI (r 1567–1625) had meanwhile been crowned at Stirling, and a series of regents ruled in his place. In England, Elizabeth died childless,

Mary Queen of Scots by Antonia Fraser is the classic biography of Scotland's ill-starred queen, digging deep behind the myths to discover the real woman caught up in the labyrinthine politics of the period.

THE DECLARATION OF ARBROATH

During the Wars of Independence, a group of Scottish nobles sent a letter to Pope John XXII requesting support for the cause of Scottish independence. Having railed against Edward I's tyranny and sung the praises of Robert the Bruce, the declaration famously stated: 'For so long as a hundred of us remain alive, we will yield in no least way to English dominion. For we fight, not for glory nor for riches nor for honours, but only and alone for freedom, which no good man surrenders but with his life.' The Pope initially supported the Scottish cause, but English lobbying changed his mind.

1263	1296	1298–1305	1314
Norse power is finally broken at the Battle of Largs, which marks the retreat of Viking influence and eventually the handing back of the Western Isles to Scotland.	King Edward I marches on Scotland with an army of 30,000 men, razing ports, butchering citizens and capturing the castles of Berwick, Edinburgh, Roxburgh and Stirling.	William Wallace is proclaimed Guardian of Scotland in March 1298. After Edward's force defeats the Scots at the Battle of Falkirk, Wallace resigns as guardian and goes into hiding, but he is fatally betrayed after his return in 1305.	Robert the Bruce wins a famous victory over the English at the Battle of Bannockburn – a victory that would turn the tide in favour of the Scots for the next 400 years.

The Royal Stuarts: A History of the Family that Shaped Britain (2010) is a gripping portrait of the dynasty by Scottish journalist Allan Massie.

and the English, desperate for a male monarch, soon turned their attention north. James VI of Scotland became James I of England and moved his court to London. His plan to politically unite the two countries, however, failed. For the most part, the Stewarts (Stuarts) ignored Scotland from then on.

Union with England

Civil war and 17th-century religious conflict left the country and its economy ruined. Scotland couldn't compete in this new era of European colonialism and, to add to its woes, during the 1690s famine killed up to a third of the population in some areas. Anti-English feeling ran high: the Protestant king William, who had replaced the exiled Catholic James VII/II to the chagrin of many in Scotland, was at war with France and employing Scottish soldiers and taxes – many Scots, sympathetic to the French, disapproved. This feeling was exacerbated by the failure of the Darien Scheme, an investment plan designed to establish a Scottish colony in Panama, which resulted in widespread bankruptcy in Scotland.

The failure made it clear to wealthy Scottish merchants and stockholders that the only way they could gain access to the lucrative markets

THE LORDS OF THE ISLES

In medieval times, when overland Highland travel was slow, difficult and dangerous, the sea lochs, firths (estuaries), kyles (narrow sea channels) and sounds of the west coast were the motorways of their time. Cut off from the rest of Scotland, but united by these sea roads, the west coast and islands were a world unto themselves.

Descended from the legendary Somerled (a half-Gaelic, half-Norse warrior of the 12th century), the chiefs of Clan Donald claimed sovereignty over this watery kingdom. It was John MacDonald of Islay who first styled himself Dominus Insularum (Lord of the Isles) in 1353. He and his descendants ruled their vast territory from their headquarters at Finlaggan in Islay, backed up by fleets of swift *birlinns* and *nyvaigs* (Hebridean galleys), an intimate knowledge of the sea routes of the west and a network of coastal castles.

Clan Donald held sway over the isles, often in defiance of the Scottish kings, from 1350 to 1493. At its greatest extent, in the second half of the 15th century, the Lordship of the Isles included all the islands on the west coast of Scotland, the west-coast mainland from Kintyre to Ross-shire, and the Antrim coast of northern Ireland. But in a greedy grab for territory, Clan Donald finally pushed its luck too far. John MacDonald made a secret pact with the English king Edward IV to divide Scotland between them. When this treason was discovered 30 years later, the Lordship was forfeited to King James IV of Scotland, and the title has remained in possession of the Scottish, and later British, royal family ever since. Lord of the Isles is one of the many titles held today by Prince Charles, heir to the British throne.

1328	1410	1468–69	1513
Continuing raids on northern England force Edward III to sue for peace and the Treaty of Northampton gives Scotland its independence, with Robert I, the Bruce, as king.	One of Europe's most venerable educational institutions, the University of St Andrews, is founded.	Orkney and then Shetland are mortgaged to Scotland as part of a dowry from Danish King Christian I, whose daughter is to marry the future King James III of Scotland.	James IV invades northern England and is soundly defeated in Northumberland at the Battle of Flodden. It marks a watershed in war history, with artillery on the upswing and archery on the way out.

of developing colonies was through union with England. The English parliament favoured union through fear of Jacobite sympathies in Scotland being exploited by its enemies, the French.

On receiving the Act of Union in Edinburgh, the Chancellor of Scotland, Lord Seafield – leader of the parliament that the Act of Union abolished – is said to have murmured under his breath, 'Now there's an end to an auld sang'. Robert Burns later castigated the wealthy politicians who engineered the union in characteristically stronger language: 'We're bought and sold for English gold – such a parcel of rogues in a nation!'

The Jacobites

The Jacobite rebellions of the 18th century sought to displace the Hanoverian monarchy (chosen by the English parliament in 1701 to ensure a Protestant succession to the childless Stuart queens Mary II and Anne) and restore a Catholic Stuart king to the British throne.

James Edward Stuart, known as the Old Pretender, was the son of James VII/II. With French support he arrived in the Firth of Forth with a fleet of ships in 1708, but was seen off by English men-of-war.

The earl of Mar led another Jacobite rebellion in 1715 but proved an ineffectual leader; his campaign fizzled out soon after the inconclusive Battle of Sheriffmuir.

The Old Pretender's son, Charles Edward Stuart, better known as Bonnie Prince Charlie or the Young Pretender, landed in Scotland for the final uprising. He had little military experience, didn't speak Gaelic and had a shaky grasp of English. Nevertheless, supported by an army of Highlanders, he marched southwards and captured Edinburgh, except for the castle, in September 1745. He got as far south as Derby in England, but success was short-lived; an Hanoverian army led by the duke of Cumberland harried him all the way back to the Highlands, where Jacobite dreams were finally extinguished at the Battle of Culloden in 1746.

Although a heavily romanticised figure, Bonnie Prince Charlie was partly responsible for the annihilation of Highland culture, given the crackdown following his attempt to recapture the crown. After returning to France he gained a reputation for drunkenness and mistreatment of mistresses. France had serious plans to invade Britain during the mid-18th century, but eventually ceased to regard the prince as a serious character. When French ambitions were thwarted by British naval victories in 1759, the Bonnie Prince's last chance had gone. He died in Rome in 1788.

The Highland Clearances

In the aftermath of the Jacobite rebellions, Highland dress, the bearing of arms and the bagpipes were outlawed. The Highlands were put under military control and private armies were banned.

> Jacobite, a term derived from the Latin for 'James', is used to describe the political movement committed to the return of the Catholic Stuart kings to the thrones of England and Scotland.

> Bonnie Prince Charlie's flight after the Battle of Culloden is legendary. He lived in hiding in the remote Highlands and islands for months before being rescued by a French frigate. His narrow escape from Uist to Skye, dressed as Flora MacDonald's maid, is the subject of the 'Skye Boat Song'.

1567	1603	1692	1707
Mary, Queen of Scots is deposed and thrown in prison. Though her last stand is still to come, the days of wilful royal action in Scotland seem to be over.	James VI of Scotland inherits the English throne in the so-called Union of the Crowns, becoming James I of Great Britain.	The Massacre of Glencoe causes further rifts between those clans loyal to the Crown and those loyal to the old ways.	Despite popular opposition, the Act of Union – which brings England and Scotland under one parliament, one sovereign and one flag – takes effect on 1 May.

The clansmen, no longer of any use as soldiers and uneconomical as tenants, were evicted from their homes and farms by the Highland chieftains to make way for flocks of sheep. A few stayed to work the sheep farms; many more were forced to seek work in the cities, or to eke a living from crofts (smallholdings) on poor coastal land. Men who had never seen the sea were forced to take to boats to try their luck at herring fishing, and many thousands emigrated – some willingly, some under duress – to the developing colonies of North America, Australia and New Zealand.

If you do much walking in the Highlands and islands, you are almost certain to come across a pile of stones among the bracken, all that remains of a house or cottage. Look around and you'll find another, and another, and soon you'll realise that this was once a crofting settlement.

John Prebble's wonderfully written book *The Highland Clearances* tells the terrible story of how the Highlanders were driven out of their homes and forced into emigration.

The Scottish Enlightenment

During the period known as the Scottish Enlightenment (roughly 1740–1830) Edinburgh became known as 'a hotbed of genius'. Philosophers David Hume and Adam Smith and sociologist Adam Ferguson emerged as influential thinkers, nourished on generations of theological debate. Medic William Cullen produced the first modern pharmacopoeia, chemist Joseph Black advanced the science of thermodynamics, and geologist James Hutton challenged long-held beliefs about the age of the Earth.

After centuries of bloodshed and religious fanaticism, people applied themselves with the same energy and piety to the making of money and the enjoyment of leisure. There was a revival in Scottish history and literature. The writings of Sir Walter Scott and the poetry of Robert Burns achieved lasting popularity. The cliched images that spring to mind when you say 'Scotland' – bagpipes, haggis, tartans, misty glens – owe much to their romantic depictions of the country.

Most clan tartans are in fact a 19th-century invention (long after the demise of the clan system), partly inspired by the writings of Sir Walter Scott.

The Industrial Revolution

The development of the steam engine ushered in the Industrial Revolution. Glasgow, deprived of its lucrative tobacco trade following the American War of Independence (1776–83), developed into an industrial powerhouse, the 'second city' of the British Empire. Cotton mills, iron and steelworks, chemical plants, shipbuilding yards and heavy-engineering works proliferated along the River Clyde in the 19th century, powered by southern Scotland's abundant coal mines.

The Clearances and the Industrial Revolution had shattered the traditional rural way of life, and though manufacturing cities and ports thrived in these decades of Empire, wealth was generated for a select few by an impoverished many. Deep poverty forced many into emigration and others to their graves. The depopulation was exacerbated by WWI,

1745–46	1740s–1830s	1914–32	1941–45
The culmination of the Jacobite rebellions: Bonnie Prince Charlie lands in Scotland, gathers an army and marches south. Though he gains English territory, he is eventually defeated at the Battle of Culloden.	Cultural and intellectual life flourishes during the Scottish Enlightenment. Meanwhile the Industrial Revolution brings preeminence in production of textiles, iron, steel and coal – and above all in shipbuilding.	Scottish industry slumps during WWI and collapses in its aftermath in the face of overseas competition and the Great Depression. About 400,000 Scots emigrate between 1921 and 1931.	Clydebank is blitzed by German bombers in 1941 with 1200 deaths; by 1945 one out of four males in the workforce is employed in heavy industries to support the war effort.

which took a heavy toll on Scottish youth. The ensuing years were bleak and marked by labour disputes.

War & Peace

Scotland largely escaped the trauma and devastation wrought by WWII on the industrial cities of England (although Clydebank was bombed). Indeed, the war brought a measure of renewed prosperity to Scotland as the shipyards and engineering works geared up to supply material. But the postwar period saw the collapse of shipbuilding and heavy industry, on which Scotland had become over-reliant.

After the discovery of North Sea oil off the Scottish coast, excitement turned to bitterness for many Scots, who felt that revenues were being siphoned off to England. This issue, along with takeovers of Scots companies by English ones (which then closed the Scots operation, asset-stripped and transferred jobs to England), fuelled increasing nationalist sentiment. The Scottish National Party (SNP) developed into a third force (later, a second as they eclipsed the Conservatives, and then first as they won power from the Labour Party) in Scottish politics.

Devolution

In 1979 a referendum was held on whether to set up a directly elected Scottish Assembly. Fifty-two per cent of those who voted said yes to devolution, but Labour Prime Minister James Callaghan decided that everyone who didn't vote should be counted as a no, so the Scottish Assembly was rejected.

From 1979 to 1997 Scotland was ruled by a Conservative government in London, for which the majority of Scots hadn't voted. Separatist feelings, always present, grew stronger. Following the landslide victory of the Labour Party in 1997, another referendum was held on the creation of a Scottish parliament. This time the result was overwhelmingly and unambiguously in favour.

Elections were held and the Scottish parliament convened for the first time in 1999 in Edinburgh, with Labour's Donald Dewar, who died in office the very next year, becoming First Minister. Labour held power until 2007, when the pro-independence Scottish National Party formed government. They were overwhelmingly re-elected in 2011 and pushed for a referendum on independence. In a campaign that engaged the nation and resulted in a huge turnout, in September 2014, the Scots voted against becoming an independent nation by 55% to 45%.

One of the major factors for many Scots was the guarantee of continued EU membership by remaining part of the UK, so when, in June 2016, the UK population narrowly voted to leave the EU, this again brought the issue of independence into the spotlight.

Charlie, Meg & Me by Gregor Ewing (2013) is an entertaining account of one man and his dog retracing Bonnie Prince Charlie's epic 500-mile trek through the Scottish Highlands in 1746.

Between 1904 and 1931 around one million people emigrated from Scotland to begin a new life in North America and Australasia.

1970s	1999–2004	2014	2016
The discovery of oil and gas in the North Sea brings new prosperity to Aberdeen and the surrounding area, and also to the Shetland Islands.	Scottish parliament is convened in May 1999 after a three-century hiatus. The new parliament building is opened in Edinburgh by Queen Elizabeth II in 2004.	Scotland votes on and rejects becoming a fully independent nation by 55% to 45%, and so remains part of the UK.	Scots vote 62% to remain in the EU, but the UK as a whole votes to leave, raising further questions about Scotland's future path.

The Scottish Larder

Traditional Scottish cookery is all about basic comfort food: solid, nourishing fare, often high in fat, that will keep you warm on a winter's day spent in the fields or at sea. But Scotland has been a frontrunner in the recent British culinary revolution and an inspiring array of local and sustainable produce is on offer. Scotland's traditional drinks – whisky and beer – have also found a new lease of life, with single malts being marketed like fine wines, and numerous new microbreweries.

A Caledonian Feast by Annette Hope is a fascinating and readable history of Scottish cuisine, providing a wealth of historical and sociological background.

Breakfast, Lunch & Dinner

The Full Scottish

Though it's making a comeback, surprisingly few Scots eat porridge for breakfast – these days a cappuccino and a croissant is just as likely – and even fewer eat it in the traditional way; that is, with salt to taste, but no sugar.

The typical 'full Scottish' breakfast offered in a B&B or hotel usually consists of fruit juice and cereal, toast and jam, a pot of coffee or tea and a fry-up combination of any or all of bacon, sausage, black pudding (a type of sausage made from dried blood), grilled tomato, mushrooms, potato scones and a fried egg or two. Most B&Bs offer a vegetarian version these days. An increasing number are eliminating the fried plate in favour of a healthier option like fruit salad.

Fish for breakfast may sound strange but was not unusual in crofting (smallholding) and fishing communities where seafood was a staple; many hotels still offer grilled kippers (smoked herrings) or smoked haddock (poached in milk and served with a poached egg) for breakfast – delicious with lots of buttered toast.

Broth, Skink & Bree

Scotch broth, made with mutton stock, barley, lentils and peas, is nutritious and tasty, while cock-a-leekie is a hearty soup made with chicken and leeks. Warming vegetable soups include leek and potato soup, and lentil soup (traditionally made using ham stock – vegetarians beware!).

Seafood soups include the delicious Cullen skink, made with smoked haddock, potato, onion and milk, and *partan bree* (crab soup).

Seafood Pleasures

Scottish seafood is among the world's best, and is a major highlight of a visit to the country, particularly along the west coast. There's an increasing awareness of sustainability issues and most serious seafood

SSSSSMOKIN'!

Scotland is famous for its smoked salmon, but there are many other varieties of smoked fish – plus smoked meats and cheeses – to enjoy. Smoking food to preserve it is an ancient art that has recently undergone a revival, but this time it's more about flavour than preservation.

There are two parts to the process – first the cure, which involves covering the fish in a mixture of salt and molasses, or soaking it in brine; and then the smoke, which can be either cold smoking (at less than 34°C), which results in a raw product, or hot smoking (at more than 60°C), which cooks it. Cold-smoked products include traditional smoked salmon, kippers and Finnan haddies. Hot-smoked products include *bradan rost* ('flaky' smoked salmon) and Arbroath smokies.

Arbroath smokies are haddock that have been gutted, de-headed and cleaned, then salted and dried overnight, tied together at the tail in pairs, and hot-smoked over oak or beech chippings for 45 to 90 minutes. Finnan haddies (named after the fishing village of Findon in Aberdeenshire) are also haddock, but these are split down the middle like kippers, and cold smoked.

Kippers (smoked herring) were invented in Northumberland, in northern England, in the mid-19th century, but Scotland soon picked up the technique, and both Loch Fyne and Mallaig were famous for their kippers.

There are dozens of modern smokehouses scattered all over Scotland, many of which offer a mail-order service as well as an on-site shop. A few recommended ones include **Hebridean Smokehouse** (☏01876-580209; www.hebrideansmokehouse.com; Clachan, North Uist; ☉8am-5.30pm Mon-Fri, plus 9am-5pm Sat Easter-Oct) for peat-smoked salmon and sea trout; **Inverawe Smokehouse & Fishery** (☏Easter-Dec 01866-822808, Jan-Easter 01866-822777; www.inverawe-fisheries.co.uk; Inverawe, near Taynuilt; ☉9am-5pm mid-Mar–Oct, 9am-noon Dec; ☎🚻) for delicate smoked salmon and plump juicy kippers; and **Loch Duart Artisan Smokehouse** (☏01870-610324; www.lochduartsmokedsalmon. com; Lochcarnan; ☉8.30am-4.30pm Mon-Fri), famous for its flaky, hot-smoked salmon. **Marrbury Smokehouse** (☏01671-820476; www.marrbury.co.uk; Carsluith Castle, A75; ☉10am-6pm), supplier to Gleneagles Hotel and other top restaurants, is another one to try.

places will give information on provenance. Tucking into some local hand-dived scallops and creel-caught langoustines as the sun sets over some west-coast or island bay is one of Europe's great gastronomic pleasures.

And it's not all about crisp linen, claw-crackers and fingerbowls. A number of simple seafood shacks serve up delicious fresh fare in very no-frills ways – a great way to eat straight from the boats without busting the budget.

Juicy langoustines (also known as Dublin Bay prawns, Norway lobsters or, in some places, simply 'prawns') are a highlight; crabs, squat lobsters, lobsters, oysters, mussels and scallops are also widely available.

Scottish salmon is famous worldwide, but there's a big difference between the now-ubiquitous farmed salmon and the leaner, more expensive, wild fish. Also, there are concerns over the environmental impact of salmon farms on the marine environment.

Smoked salmon is traditionally dressed with a squeeze of lemon juice and eaten with fresh brown bread and butter. Trout, salmon's smaller cousin – whether wild, rod-caught brown trout or farmed rainbow trout – is delicious fried in oatmeal.

As an alternative to kippers, you may be offered Arbroath smokies (lightly smoked fresh haddock), traditionally eaten cold. Herring fillets fried in oatmeal are good, if you don't mind picking out a few bones.

Mackerel pâté and smoked or peppered mackerel (both served cold) are also popular.

Puddings

Traditional Scottish puddings are irresistibly creamy, high-calorie concoctions. Cranachan is whipped cream flavoured with whisky, and mixed with toasted oatmeal and raspberries. Atholl brose is a mixture of cream, whisky and honey, flavoured with oatmeal. Clootie dumpling is a rich steamed pudding filled with currants and raisins (so called for being wrapped in a 'cloot', or linen cloth, for steaming).

From the Turf

Steak eaters will enjoy a thick fillet of world-famous Aberdeen Angus beef, and beef from Highland cattle is much sought after. Venison, from the red deer, is leaner and appears on many menus, particularly in the Highlands. Scotland, particularly Ayrshire, has some quality pork that appears in various forms.

A variety of meat-based deli products are beginning to appear from smaller, often organic, producers, with pork, mutton and venison being used in a very tasty array of smoked and charcuterie products.

Vegetarian & Vegan

Scotland has the same proportion of vegetarians as the rest of the UK – around 8% to 10% of the population – and vegetarianism is now firmly in the mainstream. Even the most remote Highland pub usually has at least one vegetarian dish on the menu, and there are many dedicated vegetarian restaurants in the cities. If you get stuck, there's almost always an Italian or Indian restaurant where you can get meat-free pizza, pasta or curry. Vegans, though, may find the options a bit limited outside of Edinburgh and Glasgow.

One thing to keep in mind is that lentil soup, a seemingly vegetarian staple of Scottish pub and restaurant menus, is traditionally made with ham stock.

Most B&Bs offer a vegetarian fry-up option these days, though vegans are advised to explain beforehand to their host exactly what the term means – just in case.

Eating with Kids

Following the introduction of the ban on smoking in public places in 2006, many Scottish pubs and restaurants have had to broaden their appeal by becoming more family friendly. As a result, especially in the cities and more popular tourist towns, many restaurants and pubs now have family rooms and/or play areas. Children's menus are common, though not usually very imaginative.

You should be aware, though, that children under the age of 14 are not allowed into the majority of Scottish pubs, even those that serve bar meals; and in family-friendly pubs (those in possession of a Children's Certificate), under-14s are only allowed in between 11am and 8pm, and must be accompanied by an adult aged 18 or older.

Farmers Markets & Food Festivals

Many towns, city districts and villages, particularly in the south of Scotland, have a regular farmers market that showcases local produce. There's an inspiring variety of new, sustainably grown fare, with everything from chorizo to tea being brought from farm to table by small-scale producers. Local food festivals are another increasingly popular way to publicise regional delicacies.

What Are Ye Drinkin'?

A Pint...

Scottish breweries produce a wide range of beers, with generic multinational lagers alongside traditional-style real ales and a huge and growing selection of craft-brewed beers from small regional brewing operations.

Traditional Scottish ales use old-fashioned 'shilling' categories to indicate strength (the number of shillings was originally the price per barrel; the stronger the beer, the higher the price). The usual range is from 60 to 80 shillings (written 80/-). You'll also see IPA, which stands for India Pale Ale, a strong, hoppy beer first brewed in the early 19th century for export to India (the extra alcohol meant that it kept better on the long sea voyage).

Draught beer is served in pints (568ml, usually costing from £2.60 to £3.80) or half pints; alcoholic content generally ranges from 3% to 6%. What the English call bitter, Scots call heavy, or export.

The craft beer revolution of recent years has hit Scotland with full force, and a large number of small breweries are producing beers

Scotland's most famous soft drink is Barr's Irn Bru: a sweet fizzy drink, radioactive orange in colour, that smells like bubble gum and almost strips the enamel from your teeth. Many Scots swear by its restorative effects as a cure for a hangover.

HAGGIS – SCOTLAND'S NATIONAL DISH

Scotland's national dish is often ridiculed by foreigners because of its ingredients, which admittedly don't sound promising – the finely chopped lungs, heart and liver of a sheep, mixed with oatmeal and onion and stuffed into a sheep's stomach bag. It actually tastes surprisingly good.

Haggis should be served with *champit tatties* and *bashed neeps* (mashed potatoes and turnips), with a generous dollop of butter and a good sprinkling of black pepper.

Although it's eaten year-round, haggis is central to the Burns Night celebrations of 25 January, in honour of Scotland's national poet, Robert Burns, when Scots worldwide unite to revel in their Scottishness. A piper announces the arrival of the haggis and Burns' poem *Address to a Haggis* is recited to this 'Great chieftan o' the puddin-race'. The bulging haggis is then lanced with a *dirk* (dagger) to reveal the steaming offal within, 'warm-reekin, rich'.

Vegetarians (and quite a few carnivores, no doubt) will be relieved to know that veggie haggis is available in some restaurants.

Takeaways serve deep-fried haggis with chips – tasty but don't tell your cardiologist.

ranging from organic lagers to traditional Scottish ales, American-influenced pale ales and various styles of dark beer. An increasing number of pubs have given over one or more taps to local craft beers or real ales, immeasurably improving the Scottish beer scene.

Visit www.scottishbrewing.com for a comprehensive list of Scottish breweries, both large and small.

Traditional Scottish Pubs

The traditional Scottish pub ranges from the grandiose, purpose-built, Victorian pubs typical of Edinburgh and Glasgow, through former coaching inns dotted along ancient highways, to cottage drinking dens hidden away in Highland glens and island villages.

What they have in common today is that they have preserved much of their original 18th- or 19th-century decor – timber-beamed ceilings, glowing mahogany bartops, polished brass rails and stained-glass windows – and generally serve cask-conditioned real ales and a range of malt whiskies.

Pubs like these are often the social hub of rural communities, a meeting place and venue for live music, quiz nights and ceilidhs (p446).

...or a Wee Dram?

Scotch whisky (always spelt without an 'e' – whiskey with an 'e' is Irish or American) is Scotland's best-known product and biggest export. The spirit has been distilled in Scotland at least since the 15th century and probably much longer.

TOP 10 SINGLE MALTS – OUR CHOICE

After a great deal of diligent research (and not a few sore heads), Lonely Planet's *Scotland* writers have selected their 10 favourite single malts from across the country.

Ardbeg (p265; Islay) The 10-year-old from this noble distillery is a byword for excellence. Peaty but well balanced. Hits the spot after a hill walk.

Bowmore (p265; Islay) Smoke, peat and salty sea air – a classic Islay malt. One of the few distilleries that still malts its own barley.

Bruichladdich (p265; Islay) A visitor-friendly distillery with a quirky, innovative approach – famous for very peaty special releases.

Glendronach (Highland) Only sherry casks are used here, so the creamy, spicy result tastes like grandma's Christmas trifle.

Highland Park (p402; Orkney) Full and rounded, with heather, honey, malt and peat. Award-winning distillery tour.

Isle of Arran (p273; Arran) One of Scotland's newer distilleries, offering a lightish, flavoursome malt with flowery, fruity notes.

Macallan (p237; Speyside) The king of Speyside malts, with sherry and bourbon finishes. The distillery is set amid waving fields of Golden Promise barley.

Springbank (p261; Campbeltown) Complex flavours – sherry, citrus, pear drops, peat – with a salty tang. The entire production process from malting to bottling takes place on site.

Talisker (p382; Skye) Brooding, heavily peated nose balanced by a satisfying sweetness from this lord of the isles. Great postdinner dram.

The Balvenie (Speyside) Rich and honeyed, this Speysider is liquid gold for those with a sweet tooth.

For more distilleries, see pages 237 and 265.

At a bar, older Scots may order a 'half' or 'nip' of whisky as a chaser to a pint or half pint of beer (a 'hauf and a hauf'). Only tourists ask for 'Scotch' – what else would you be served in Scotland? The standard measure in pubs is either 25ml or 35ml.

As well as whiskies, there are whisky-based liqueurs such as Drambuie. If you must mix your whisky with anything other than water, try a whisky-mac (whisky with ginger wine). After a long walk in the rain there's nothing better to put a warm glow in your belly.

Whisky Bars

Some pubs, especially in the whisky-distilling region of Speyside, have become known as whisky bars, because of their staggering range of single malt whiskies – the famous Quaich bar in the Craigellachie Hotel (p238), established in 1894, offers more than 800 different varieties.

The revival of interest in single malts since the late 1990s has seen a new wave of whisky bars open across the country, mainly in the cities. Places like Glasgow's Òran Mòr (p129) have more than 300 malts stacked behind the bar.

Scottish Culture

For a guide to Scottish film locations, check out www.scotlandthemovie.com.

Arts

The notion of 'the Scottish arts' often conjures up cliched images of bagpipe music, incomprehensible poetry and romanticised paintings of Highland landscapes. But Scottish artists have given the world a wealth of unforgettable treasures, from the songs and poems of Robert Burns and the novels of Walter Scott to the architecture of Charles Rennie Mackintosh.

Literature

Scotland has a long and distinguished literary history, from the era of the medieval makars ('makers' of verses; ie poets) to the present-day crime novels of Val McDermid, Christopher Brookmyre, Louise Welsh and Ian Rankin.

Burns & Scott

Scotland's most famous literary figure is, of course, Robert Burns (1759–96). His works have been translated into dozens of languages and are known the world over. Burns wrote in Lowland Scots (Lallans); in fact, his poetry was instrumental in keeping Lallans alive to the present day. He was also very much a man of the people, satirising the upper classes and the church for their hypocrisy. Although he is best known for the comical tale of *Tam O'Shanter* and for penning the words to *Auld Lang Syne,* his more political poems – including *Such A Parcel Of Rogues In A Nation* (about the 1707 Act of Union) and *A Man's a Man for a' That* (about class and solidarity) – reveal his socialist leanings.

The son of an Edinburgh lawyer, Sir Walter Scott (1771–1832) was Scotland's greatest and most prolific novelist. Scott was born in Edinburgh and lived at various New Town addresses before moving to his country house at Abbotsford. His early works were rhyming ballads, such as *The Lady of the Lake,* and his first historical novels – Scott effectively invented the genre – were published anonymously. Plagued by debt in later life, he wrote obsessively in order to make money, but will always be best remembered for classic tales such as *Waverley, The Heart of Midlothian, Ivanhoe, Redgauntlet* and *Castle Dangerous.*

RLS & Sherlock Holmes

Along with Sir Walter Scott, Robert Louis Stevenson (RLS; 1850–94) ranks as Scotland's best-known novelist. Born at 8 Howard Pl in Edinburgh into a family of famous lighthouse engineers, Stevenson studied law at Edinburgh University but was always intent on pursuing the life of a writer. An inveterate traveller, but dogged by ill health, he finally settled in Samoa in 1889, where he was revered by the local people and known as 'Tusitala' – the teller of tales. Stevenson is known and loved around the world for those tales: *Kidnapped, Catriona, Treasure Island, The Master of Ballantrae* and *Strange Case of Dr Jekyll and Mr Hyde*.

Sir Arthur Conan Doyle (1859–1930), the creator of Sherlock Holmes, was born in Edinburgh and studied medicine at Edinburgh University. He based the character of Holmes on one of his lecturers, the surgeon Dr Joseph Bell, who had employed his forensic skills and powers of deduction on several murder cases in Edinburgh.

McDiarmid to Muriel Spark

Scotland's finest modern poet was Hugh MacDiarmid (born Christopher Murray Grieve; 1892–1978). Originally from Dumfriesshire, he moved to Edinburgh in 1908, where he trained as a teacher and a journalist, but spent most of his life in Montrose, Shetland, Glasgow and Biggar. His masterpiece is 'A Drunk Man Looks at the Thistle', a 2685-line Joycean monologue.

The poet and storyteller George Mackay Brown (1921–96) was born in Stromness in the Orkney Islands, and lived there almost all his life. Although his poems and novels are rooted in Orkney, his work, like that of Burns, transcends local and national boundaries. His best-known novel *Greenvoe* (1972) is a poetic evocation of an Orkney community threatened by the coming of modernity.

Dame Muriel Spark (1918–2006) was born in Edinburgh and educated at James Gillespie's High School for Girls, an experience that provided material for perhaps her best-known novel, *The Prime of Miss Jean Brodie*, a shrewd portrait of 1930s Edinburgh.

The Contemporary Scene

The most widely known Scots writers today include Iain Banks (1954–2013; *The Crow Road*), Irvine Welsh (b 1961; *Trainspotting*), Janice Galloway (b 1955; *The Trick Is To Keep Breathing*) and Liz Lochhead (b 1947;

Six Essential Scottish Novels

Waverley (Sir Walter Scott, 1814)

The Silver Darlings (Neil M Gunn, 1941)

A Scots Quair (Lewis Grassic Gibbon, trilogy 1932–34)

The Prime of Miss Jean Brodie (Muriel Spark, 1961)

Greenvoe (George Mackay Brown, 1972)

Trainspotting (Irvine Welsh, 1993)

SCOTTISH CULTURE ARTS

THE SCOTTISH LANGUAGE

From the 8th to the 19th centuries the common language of central and southern Scotland was Lowland Scots (sometimes called Lallans), which evolved from Old English and has Dutch, French, Gaelic, German and Scandinavian influences. As distinct from English as Norwegian is from Danish, it was the official language of state in Scotland until the Act of Union in 1707.

Following the Union, English rose to predominance as the language of government, church and polite society. The spread of education and literacy in the 19th century eventually led to Lowland Scots being perceived as backward and unsophisticated – children were often beaten for speaking Scots in school instead of English.

The Scots tongue persisted, however, and has undergone a revival – there are now Scots language dictionaries, university degree courses in Scots language and literature, and Scots is studied as part of the school curriculum.

Scottish Gaelic (*Gàidhlig* – pronounced 'gaa-lik') is spoken by about 60,000 people in Scotland, mainly in the Highlands and islands. It is a member of the Celtic family of languages, which includes Irish Gaelic, Manx, Welsh, Cornish and Breton.

Gaelic culture flourished in the Highlands until the Jacobite rebellions of the 18th century. After the Battle of Culloden in 1746 many Gaelic speakers were forced from their ancestral lands, and Gaelic was regarded as little more than a 'peasant' language of no modern significance.

It was only in the 1970s that Gaelic began to make a comeback. After two centuries of decline, the language has been encouraged through financial help from government agencies and the EU, and Gaelic education is flourishing at every level from playgroups to tertiary institutions.

Mary Queen of Scots Got Her Head Chopped Off). The grim realities of modern Glasgow are vividly conjured in the short story collection *Not Not While the Giro* by James Kelman (b 1946), whose controversial novel *How Late it Was, How Late* won the 1994 Booker Prize.

The Scottish crime-writing charts are topped by Val McDermid (b 1955) and Ian Rankin (b 1960). McDermid's novels feature private investigator Kate Brannigan and psychologist Tony Hill; *Wire in the Blood* became a successful TV series. Rankin's Edinburgh-based crime novels, featuring the hard-drinking, introspective Detective Inspector John Rebus, are sinister, engrossing mysteries that explore the darker side of Scotland's capital city. He has a growing international following (his books have been translated into 22 languages).

Music

Traditional Music

Scotland has always had a strong folk tradition. In the 1960s and 1970s Robin Hall and Jimmy MacGregor, the Corries and the hugely talented Ewan McColl worked the pubs and clubs up and down the country. The Boys of the Lough, headed by Shetland fiddler Aly Bain, was one of the first professional bands to promote the traditional Celtic music of Scotland and Ireland. It was followed by the Battlefield Band, Alba, Capercaillie and others.

The Scots folk songs that you will often hear sung in pubs and at *ceilidhs* (evenings of traditional Scottish entertainment, including music, song and dance) draw on Scotland's rich history. A huge number of them relate to the Jacobite rebellions in the 18th century and, in particular, to Bonnie Prince Charlie – 'Hey Johnnie Cope', the 'Skye Boat Song' and 'Will Ye No Come Back Again', for example – while others relate to the Covenanters and the Highland Clearances.

In recent years there has been a revival in traditional music, often adapted and updated for the modern age. Bands such as Runrig pioneered with their own brand of Gaelic rock, while Shooglenifty blend Scottish folk music with anything from indie rock to electronica, producing a hybrid that has been called 'acid croft'.

But perhaps the finest modern renderings of traditional Scottish songs come from singer-songwriter Eddi Reader, who rose to fame with the band Fairground Attraction and their 1988 hit 'Perfect'. Her album *Eddi Reader Sings the Songs of Robert Burns* (2003, re-released with extra tracks in 2009) is widely regarded as one of the best interpretations of Burns' works.

Bagpipes

The bagpipe is one of the oldest musical instruments still in use today. Although no piece of film footage on Scotland is complete without the drone of the pipes, their origin probably lies in the Middle East; when they first arrived in Scotland is unknown, but was certainly pre-medieval.

The traditional Highland bagpipe consists of a leather bag held under the arm, kept inflated by blowing through the blowstick; the piper forces air through the pipes by squeezing the bag with the forearm. Three of the pipes, known as drones, play a constant note (one bass, two tenor) in the background; the fourth pipe, the chanter, plays the melody.

Highland soldiers were traditionally accompanied into battle by the skirl of the pipes, and the Scottish Highland bagpipe is unique in being the only musical instrument ever to be classed as a weapon. The playing of the pipes was banned – under pain of death – by the British government in 1747 as part of a scheme to suppress Highland culture in the wake of the Jacobite uprising of 1745. The pipes were revived when the Highland regiments were drafted into the British Army towards the end of the 18th century.

The Traditional Music & Song Association (www.tmsa. org.uk) website has listings of music, dance and cultural festivals around Scotland.

The Living Tradition (www.living-tradition.co.uk) is a bimonthly magazine covering the folk and traditional music of Scotland and the British Isles, as well as Celtic music, with features and reviews of albums and live gigs.

Bagpipe music may not be to everyone's taste, but Scotland's most famous instrument has been reinvented by bands like the Red Hot Chilli Pipers, who use pipes, drums, guitars and keyboards to create rock versions of trad tunes. They feature regularly at festivals throughout the country.

Ceilidhs

The Gaelic word *ceilidh* (*kay*-lay) means 'visit'. A *ceilidh* was originally a social gathering in the house after the day's work was over, enlivened with storytelling, music and song. These days, a *ceilidh* means an evening of traditional Scottish entertainment including music, song and dance. To find one, check the village noticeboard, or just ask at the local pub; visitors are always welcome to join in.

Rock & Pop

It would take an entire book to list all the Scottish artists and bands that have made it big in the world of rock and pop. From Glasgow-born King of Skiffle, Lonnie Donegan, in the 1950s, to the chart-topping Dumfries DJ Calvin Harris today, the roll call is long and impressive, and only a few can be mentioned here.

The '90s saw the emergence of three bands that took the top three places in a 2005 vote for the best Scottish band of all time – melodic indie-pop songsters Belle and Sebastian, Brit-rock band Travis, and indie rockers Idlewild, who opened for the Rolling Stones in 2003. Scottish artists who have made an international impression in more recent times include Ayrshire rockers Biffy Clyro; indie rock group Frightened Rabbit; Glasgow synthpop band Chvrches; and Edinburgh hip-hop trio Young Fathers.

The airwaves are awash with female singer-songwriters, but few are as gutsy and versatile as Edinburgh-born, St Andrews–raised KT Tunstall. Although she's been writing and singing since the late 1990s, it was her 2005 debut album *Eye to the Telescope* that introduced her to a wider audience. Others include Glasgow-born Amy Macdonald, who was only 20 years old when her first album *This is the Life* (2007) sold three million copies; and Karine Polwart, whose songs combine folk influences with modern themes and subjects.

As far as male singer-songwriters are concerned, few are more popular than bespectacled twin brothers Craig and Charlie Reid, better known as The Proclaimers. Nine studio albums from 1987 to 2012 provided ample material for the hugely successful movie based on their music, *Sunshine On Leith* (2013); their 10th album *Let's Hear It For The Dogs* (2015) reached number 27 in the UK album charts.

Painting

Perhaps the most famous Scottish painting is the portrait of *Reverend Robert Walker Skating on Duddingston Loch* by Sir Henry Raeburn (1756–1823), held in the National Gallery of Scotland. This image of a Presbyterian minister at play beneath Arthur's Seat, with all the poise of a ballerina and the hint of a smile on his lips, is a symbol of Enlightenment Edinburgh, the triumph of reason over wild nature. However, recent research has suggested it may not be the work of Raeburn after all, but may have been painted by French artist Henri-Pierre Danloux.

Scottish portraiture reached its peak during the Scottish Enlightenment in the second half of the 18th century with the paintings of Raeburn and his contemporary Allan Ramsay (1713–84), while Sir David Wilkie (1785–1841), whose genre paintings depicted scenes of rural Highland life, was one of the greatest artists of the 19th century.

In the early 20th century the Scottish painters most widely acclaimed outside of the country were the group known as the Scottish Colourists –

Scottish Pop Playlist

Take Me Out by Franz Ferdinand

Suddenly I See by KT Tunstall

Letter from America by The Proclaimers

Same Jeans by The View

Bubbles by Biffy Clyro

This is the Life by Amy Macdonald

Loch Lomond by Runrig

Top of the Pops by The Rezillos

Don't You (Forget About Me) by Simple Minds

Say What You Want by Texas

SJ Peploe (1871–1935), Francis Cadell (1883–1937), Leslie Hunter (1877–1931) and JD Fergusson (1874–1961) – whose striking paintings drew on French post-Impressionist and Fauvist influences. Peploe and Cadell, active in the 1920s and 1930s, often spent the summer painting together on the Isle of Iona, and reproductions of their beautiful landscapes and seascapes appear on many a print and postcard.

Cinema

Perthshire-born John Grierson (1898–1972) is acknowledged around the world as the father of the documentary film. His legacy includes the classic *Drifters* (1929; about the Scottish herring fishery) and the Oscar-winning *Seawards the Great Ships* (1961; about Clyde shipbuilding). Writer-director Bill Forsyth (1946–) is best known for *Local Hero* (1983), a gentle comedy about an oil magnate seduced by the beauty of the Highlands, and *Gregory's Girl* (1980), about an awkward teenage schoolboy's romantic exploits.

In the 1990s the rise of the director-producer-writer team of Danny Boyle (English), Andrew Macdonald and John Hodge (both Scottish) – who wrote the scripts for *Shallow Grave* (1994), *Trainspotting* (1996) and *A Life Less Ordinary* (1997) – marked the beginnings of what might be described as a home-grown Scottish film industry; followed up more than 20 years later with a sequel, *T2: Trainspotting*.

Other Scottish directorial talent includes Kevin Macdonald, who made *Touching the Void* (2003), *State of Play* (2009) and the TV series of Stephen King's *11.22.63* (2016); and Andrea Arnold, who directed *Red Road* (2006), the BAFTA-winning *Fish Tank* (2009), and *American Honey* (2016), which won the Jury Prize at Cannes.

> *Rob Roy* (1995) is a witty and moving cinematic version of Sir Walter Scott's tale of the outlaw MacGregor – despite dodgy Scottish accents from Liam Neeson and Jessica Lange.

Architecture

The leading Scottish architects of the 18th century were William Adam (1684–1748) and his son Robert Adam (1728–92), whose revival of classical Greek and Roman forms influenced architects throughout Europe. Among the many neoclassical buildings they designed are Hopetoun House, Culzean Castle and Edinburgh's Charlotte Sq, possibly the finest example of Georgian architecture anywhere.

Alexander 'Greek' Thomson (1817–75) changed the face of 19th-century Glasgow with his neoclassical designs, while in Edinburgh, William Henry Playfair (1790–1857) continued Adam's tradition in the Greek temples of the National Monument on Calton Hill, the Royal Scottish Academy and the National Gallery of Scotland.

The 19th-century resurgence of interest in Scottish history and identity, led by writers such as Sir Walter Scott, saw architects turn to the towers, pointed turrets and crow-stepped gables of ancient castles for inspiration. The Victorian revival of the Scottish Baronial style, which first made an appearance in 16th-century buildings such as Craigievar Castle, produced many fanciful abodes such as Balmoral Castle, Scone Palace and Abbotsford.

> *Scotland's Castles* by Chris Tabraham is an excellent companion for anyone touring Scottish castles – a readable, illustrated history detailing how and why they were built.

Scotland's best known 20th-century architect and designer was Charles Rennie Mackintosh (1868–1928), one of the most influential exponents of the art-nouveau style. His finest building is the Glasgow School of Art (1896), which still looks modern more than a century after it was built.

Sport

Many Scots are sports-mad and follow football or rugby with a fierce dedication, identifying closely with local teams and individuals. The most popular games are football (soccer), rugby union, shinty, curling and golf, the last two of which the Scots claim to have invented.

Football

Football (soccer) in Scotland is not so much a sport as a religion, with thousands turning out to worship their local teams on Wednesday and weekends throughout the season (August to May). Sacred rites include standing in the freezing cold of a February day, drinking hot Bovril and eating a Scotch pie as you watch your team getting gubbed.

Scotland's top 12 clubs play in the Scottish Premiership (www.sspfl. co.uk), but two teams – Glasgow Rangers and Glasgow Celtic – have dominated the competition. On only 18 occasions since 1890 has a team other than Rangers or Celtic won the league; the last time was when Aberdeen won in 1985.

However, Rangers made headlines in 2012 when they were forced into liquidation over a tax dispute and kicked out of the premier league. Celtic had an easy run while their traditional rivals clawed their way back to the top from the fourth division, eventually gaining readmittance to the premiership in 2016.

Rugby Union

Traditionally, football was the sport of Scotland's urban working classes, while rugby union (www.scottishrugby.org) was the preserve of middle-class university graduates and farmers from the Borders. Although this distinction is breaking down – rugby's popularity soared after the 1999 World Cup was staged in the UK, and the middle classes have invaded the football terraces – it persists to some extent.

Each year, from January to March, Scotland takes part in the Six Nations Rugby Championship. The most important fixture is the clash against England for the Calcutta Cup – it's always an emotive event; Scotland has won twice and drawn once since 2006.

At club level, the season runs from September to May, and among the better teams are those from the Borders such as Hawick, Kelso and Melrose. At the end of the season, teams play a rugby sevens (seven-a-side) variation of the 15-player competition.

Golf

Scotland is the home of golf. The game was probably invented here in the 12th century, and the world's oldest documentary evidence of a game being played (dating from 1456) was on Bruntsfield Links in Edinburgh.

Today there are more than 550 golf courses in Scotland – that's more per capita than in any other country (see www.scottishgolfcourses.com). The sport is hugely popular and much more egalitarian than in other countries, with lots of affordable, publicly owned courses. There are many world-famous championship courses too, including Muirfield in East Lothian, Turnberry and Troon in Ayrshire, Carnoustie in Angus and St Andrews' Old Course in Fife.

Highland Games

Highland games are held in Scotland throughout the summer, and not just in the Highlands. You can find dates and details of Highland games held all over the country on the Scottish Highland Games Association website (www.shga.co.uk).

The traditional sporting events are accompanied by piping and dancing competitions and attract locals and tourists alike. Some events are peculiarly Scottish, particularly those that involve trials of strength: tossing the caber (heaving a tree trunk into the air), throwing the hammer and putting the stone. The biggest Highland games are staged at Dunoon, Oban and Braemar.

Curling, a winter sport that involves propelling a 19kg granite stone along the ice towards a target, was probably invented in Scotland in medieval times. For more information, see www.royal caledoniancurling club.org.

Shinty (*camanachd* in Gaelic) is a fast and physical ball-and-stick sport similar to Ireland's hurling, with more than a little resemblance to clan warfare. It's an indigenous Scottish game played mainly in the Highlands, and the most prized trophy is the Camanachd Cup. For more information, see www.shinty.com.

Natural Scotland

Visitors revel in rural Scotland's solitude and dramatic scenery. Soaring peaks, steely blue lochs, deep inlets, forgotten beaches and surging peninsulas evince astonishing geographic diversity. Scotland's wild places harbour Britain's most majestic wildlife, from the emblematic osprey to the red deer, its bellow reverberating among large stands of native forest. Seals, dolphins and whales patrol the seas, islands moored in the rough Atlantic are havens for species long hunted to extinction further south, while the northeastern archipelagos clamour with seabird colonies of extraordinary magnitude.

Scottish Natural Heritage (www.snh.gov.uk) is the government agency responsible for the conservation of Scotland's wildlife, habitats and landscapes. A key initiative is to reverse biodiversity loss.

The Land

Scotland's mainland divides neatly into thirds. The Southern Uplands, ranges of grassy rounded hills bounded by fertile coastal plains, occupy the south, divided from the Lowlands by the Southern Uplands Fault.

The central Lowlands lie in a broad band stretching from Glasgow and Ayr in the west to Edinburgh and Dundee in the east. This area is underlain by sedimentary rocks, including beds of coal that fuelled Scotland's Industrial Revolution. It's only a fifth of the nation by land area, but has most of the country's industry, its two largest cities and 80% of the population.

Another geological divide – the Highland Boundary Fault – marks the southern edge of the Scottish Highlands. These hills – with most of their summits around 900m to 1000m – were scoured by Ice Age glaciers, creating a series of deep, U-shaped valleys, some now flooded by the long, narrow sea lochs that today are such a feature of west Highland scenery. The Highlands form 60% of the Scottish mainland, and are cut in two by the Great Glen, a long, glacier-gouged valley running southwest to northeast.

Despite their pristine beauty, the wild, empty landscapes of the western and northern Highlands are artificial wildernesses. Before the Highland Clearances many of these empty corners of Scotland supported sizeable rural populations.

Offshore, some 800 islands are concentrated in four main groups: the Shetland Islands, the Orkney Islands, the Outer Hebrides and the Inner Hebrides.

Some 90% of Britain's surface fresh water is found in Scotland, and Loch Lomond is Britain's largest body of fresh water.

The Water

It rains a lot in Scotland – some parts of the western Highlands get over 4m of it a year, compared to 2.3m in the Amazon Basin – so it's not surprising there's plenty of water about. Around 3% of Scotland's land surface is fresh water; the numerous lochs, rivers and burns (streams) form the majority of this, but about a third is in the form of wetlands: the peat bogs and marshes that form a characteristic Highland and island landscape.

But it's salt water that really shapes the country. Including the islands, there's over 10,000 miles of tortuous, complex Scottish shoreline.

Wildlife

Scotland's wildlife is one of its biggest attractions, and the best way to see it is simply to spend time in the great outdoors. Pull on your boots, grab your binoculars, go quietly and see what you can spot. Many species that have disappeared from, or are rare in, the rest of Britain survive here in Scotland.

Animals

While the Loch Ness monster still hogs headlines, Scotland's wild places harbour a wide variety of animals, including red deer, otters and 75% of Britain's red squirrels.

Other small mammals include the Orkney vole and various bats, as well as stoats and weasels. The mountain hare swaps a grey-brown summer coat for a pure-white winter one.

Rarer beasts slaughtered to the point of near-extinction in the 19th century include pine martens, polecats and Scottish wildcats. Populations of these are small and remote, but are slowly recovering.

Of course, most animals you'll see will be in fields or obstructing you on single-track roads. Several indigenous sheep varieties are still around, smaller and stragglier than the purpose-bred supermodels to which we're accustomed. Other emblematic domestic animals include the Shetland pony and gentle Highland cow with its broad horns, shaggy reddish-brown coat and fringe.

The waters are rich in marine mammals. Dolphins and porpoises are fairly common, and in summer minke whales are regular visitors. Orcas are regularly sighted around Shetland and Orkney. Seals are widespread. Both the Atlantic grey and common seal are easily seen on coasts and islands.

Birds

Scotland has an immense variety of birds. For birdwatchers, the Shetland Islands are paradise. Twenty-one of the British Isles' 24 seabird species are found here, breeding in huge colonies. Being entertained by the puffins' clownish antics is a highlight for visitors.

Large numbers of red grouse – a popular game bird – graze the heather on the moors. The ptarmigan plays the Arctic trick of changing its plumage from mottled brown in summer to dazzling white in winter. In heavily forested areas you may see capercaillie, a black, turkey-like bird and the largest member of the grouse family. Millions of greylag geese winter on Lowland stubble fields.

The Royal Society for the Protection of Birds (RSPB; www.rspb.org. uk) is very active in Scotland. As well as the successful reintroduction of species, the population of several precariously placed bird species has stabilised, including ospreys (absent for most of the 20th century), golden eagles, white-tailed eagles, peregrine falcons and hen harriers.

National Parks

Scotland has two national parks – Loch Lomond & the Trossachs and the Cairngorms. There's a huge range of other protected areas: 47 National Nature Reserves (www.nnr-scotland.org.uk) span the country, and there are also marine areas under various levels of protection.

Environmental Issues

Scotland's abundance of wind and water means the government hasn't had to look far for sources of renewable energy. The ambitious grand plan is to generate 100% of the country's energy needs from renewable sources by 2020. And things are going to plan, with a level of

NATURAL SCOTLAND WILDLIFE

A beautifully written book about Scotland's wildlife, penned by a man who lived and breathed alongside the country's critters in a remote part of the Highlands, is *A Last Wild Place* by Mike Tomkies.

One of the best-loved pieces of Scottish wildlife writing is *Ring of Bright Water* by Gavin Maxwell, in which the author describes life on the remote Glenelg peninsula with his two pet otters in the 1950s.

FIVE ICONIC SCOTTISH SPECIES

Red Deer

The red deer, Britain's largest land animal, is present in large numbers in Scotland. You're bound to see them if you spend any time in the Highlands; in winter especially, harsh weather will force them down into the glens to crop the roadside verges. But the most spectacular time to spot them is during the rutting season (late September and October) when stags roar and clash antlers in competition for females.

Best places to spot Jura, Rum, Torridon, Galloway

Golden Eagle

Perhaps the most majestic wildlife sight on moor and mountain is the golden eagle, which uses its 2m wingspan to soar on rising thermals as it hunts for its favourite prey, the mountain hare. Almost all of the 400 or so pairs known to nest in the UK are to be found in the Scottish Highlands and islands, as they prefer remote glens and open moorland well away from human habitation.

Best places to spot Harris, Skye, Rum, Mull

Red Squirrel

Scotland's woods are home to 75% of Britain's red squirrel population; in most of the rest of the UK they've been pushed out by the dominant grey squirrel, introduced from North America. The greys often carry a virus that's lethal to the reds, so measures are in place to try to prevent their further encroachment.

Best places to spot Galloway Forest Park, Glen Affric, Landmark Forest Adventure Park, Rothiemurchus

Otter

From a low point in the late 20th century, when the population was decimated by hunting, pollution and habitat loss, otters have made a comeback and are now widespread in Scotland. They frequent both fresh and salt water, but are easiest to spot along the coast, where they time their foraging to coincide with an ebbing tide (river otters tend to be nocturnal).

Best places to spot Orkney, Shetland, Skye, Outer Hebrides; the piers at Kyle of Lochalsh and Portree are otter 'hot spots', as they have learned to scavenge from fishing boats.

Scottish Wildcat

Trapping, hunting, habitat loss and interbreeding with feral domestic cats have made the Scottish wildcat Britain's most endangered mammal; it is thought that fewer than 400 purebred individuals survive. It hunts around the edges of woodland at dawn and dusk and is very wary of humans; seeing one in the wild is extremely rare.

Best places to spot Angus Glens, Strathpeffer area, Highland Wildlife Park (in captivity)

50% achieved by 2015, and a solid commitment against fracking and nuclear power.

Though a major goal is to halt a worrying decline in biodiversity, climate change is a huge threat to existing species. Temperature rises would leave plenty of mountain plants and creatures with no place to go; a steady decline in Scotland's seabird population is also surmised to have been partly caused by a temperature-induced decrease of plankton.

The main cause, however, of the worrying level of fish stocks is clear: we've eaten them all. In 2010 the Marine (Scotland) Act was passed. It's a compromise solution that tries to both protect vulnerable marine stocks and sustain the flagging fishing industry. It may well be too little, too late.

Survival Guide

Directory A–Z

Accommodation

For budget travel, the options are campsites, hostels and cheap B&Bs. Above this price level is a plethora of comfortable B&Bs, pubs and guesthouses (£35 to £55 per person per night). Midrange hotels are present in most places, while in the higher price bracket (£65-plus per person per night) there are some superb hotels, the most interesting being converted castles and country houses, or chic designer options in cities.

If you're travelling solo, expect to pay a supplement in hotels and B&Bs, meaning you'll often be forking out over 75% of the price of a double for your single room.

Almost all B&Bs, guesthouses and hotels (and even some hostels) include breakfast – either full Scottish or a continental style – in the room price. If you don't want it, you may be able to negotiate a lower price, but this is rare.

Prices increase over the peak tourist season (June to September) and are at their highest in July and August. Outside of these months, and particularly in winter, special deals are often available at guesthouses and hotels.

Booking Services

VisitScotland tourist offices offer an accommodation booking service, which can be handy, but note that they can only book places that are registered with VisitScotland. There are many other fine accommodation options that, mostly due to the hefty registration fee, choose not to register with the tourist board.

VisitScotland (www.visitscot land.com/accommodation) Book accommodation approved by the official tourist board.

Scottish Cottages (www. scottish-cottages.co.uk) Booking service for self-catering cottages.

Lonely Planet (www.lonely planet.com/scotland/hotels) Recommendations and bookings.

B&Bs & Guesthouses

B&Bs – bed and breakfasts – are an institution in Scotland. At the bottom end you get a bedroom in a private house, a shared bathroom and the 'full Scottish' (fruit juice, coffee or tea, cereal and cooked breakfast – bacon, eggs, sausage, baked beans and toast). Midrange B&Bs have en suite bathrooms, TVs in each room and more variety (and healthier options) for breakfast. Almost all B&Bs provide hospitality trays (tea- and coffee-making facilities) in bedrooms. Common B&B options range from urban houses to pubs and farmhouses.

Guesthouses, often large converted private houses, are an extension of the B&B concept. They are normally bigger and less personal than B&Bs.

Bothies, Böds, Barns & Bunkhouses

Bothies are simple shelters, often in remote places; many are maintained by the Mountain Bothies Association (www. mountainbothies.org.uk). They're not locked, there's no charge, usually no toilets – and you can't book. Take your own cooking equipment, sleeping bag and mat. Users should stay one night only, and leave the place as they find it.

Camping barns – usually converted farm buildings – offer shared sleeping space for around £5 to £10 per night. Take your own cooking equipment, sleeping bag and mat.

Bunkhouses, a grade or two up from camping barns, have stoves for heating and cooking and may supply utensils. They may have mattresses but you'll still need a sleeping bag. There will be toilets but probably no showers. Most charge from £10 to £15 per person.

In Shetland, the Shetland Amenity Trust (www.camping-bods.com) has created a number of **böds** – converted croft houses or fishing huts with bunks and washing and cooking facilities, but often no electricity or heating – many in remote and dramatic locations. Beds cost £8 to £10 but you will need to prebook through the trust in Lerwick, who will give you the keys.

Camping & Caravan Parks

Free wild camping (p33) became a legal right under the Land Reform Bill of 2003. However, campers are obliged to camp on unenclosed land, in small numbers and away from buildings and roads.

Most commercial campsites offer a variety of pitches for touring campers – hardstanding and grass, with or without electricity – and accept tents, campervans and caravans; some are caravan-only.

VisitScotland (www.visitscotland.com/accommodation) Bookings for registered campsites; listings also available on a free map available at tourist offices.

Cool Camping (www.coolcamping.co.uk) Booking service for offbeat, remote and interesting campsites, including 'glamping' options.

Camping & Caravanning Club (www.campingand caravanningclub.co.uk) Listings of sites across the country.

Hostels

Backpacker hostels offer cheap, sociable accommodation, and in Scotland the standard of facilities is generally very good. The more upmarket hostels have en suite bathrooms in their dorms, and all manner of

luxuries that give them the feel of hotels, if it weren't for the bunk beds.

Hostels nearly always have facilities for self-catering, and, apart from very remote ones, internet access of some kind. Many can arrange activities and tours.

INDEPENDENT HOSTELS

There are a large number of independent hostels, most with prices around £13 to £25 per person. Facilities vary considerably. Scottish Independent Hostels (www.hostel-scotland.co.uk) is an affiliation of over 100 hostels in Scotland, mostly in the north. You can browse them online or pick up their free *Scottish Independent Hostels* map-guide from tourist offices.

SCOTTISH YOUTH HOSTEL ASSOCIATION

The **Scottish Youth Hostels Association** (SYHA; ☑01786-891400; www.syha.org.uk; annual membership 26yr & over/25yr & under £15/6, life membership £150) has a network of decent, reasonably priced hostels and produces a free booklet, which is available from SYHA hostels and tourist offices. There are dozens to choose from around the country, ranging from basic walkers digs to mansions and castles. You've got to be a HI member to stay, but nonmembers can pay a £3 supplement per night that goes towards the annual membership fee. Prices vary according to the month, but average around £18 to £25 per adult in high season.

Most SYHA hostels close from around mid-October to early March, but can be rented out by groups.

Hotels

There are some wonderfully luxurious places, including elegant country-house hotels in fabulous settings, and castles complete with crenellated battlements, grand staircases and the obligatory rows of stag heads. Expect all the perks at these places, often including a gym, a sauna, a pool and first-class service. Even if you're on a budget, it's worth splashing out for a night at one of the classic Highland hotels.

In the cities, dullish chain options dominate the midrange category, though there are some quirkier options to be had in Glasgow and Edinburgh.

Increasingly hotels use an airline-style pricing system, so it's worth booking well ahead to take advantage of the cheapest rates.

Rental Accommodation

Self-catering accommodation is very popular in Scotland and staying in an apartment in a city or a cottage in the country gives you an opportunity to get a feel for a place and its community. The minimum stay is usually one week in the summer peak season, and three days or less at other times.

Accommodation of this type varies very widely, from rustic one-bedroom cottages with basic facilities and sheep cropping the grass outside, to castles, historic houses and purpose-built

PRACTICALITIES

Newspapers Leaf through Edinburgh's *Scotsman* (www. scotsman.com) newspaper or Glasgow's *Herald* (www. heraldscotland.com); the latter is well into its third century. Have a giggle at rival tabloids the *Daily Record* and the *Scottish Sun*, or try the old-fashioned *Sunday Post* for a nostalgia trip.

TV Watch BBC1 Scotland, BBC2 Scotland and ITV stations STV or Border. Channel Four and Five are UK-wide channels with unchanged content for Scotland. BBC Alba is a widely available digital channel broadcasting in Scottish Gaelic.

Radio Find out what's hitting the headlines on BBC Radio Scotland (www.bbc.co.uk/radioscotland) by listening to *Good Morning Scotland* from 6am weekdays.

Smoking In Scotland you can't smoke in any public place that has a roof and is at least half enclosed. That means pubs, bus shelters, restaurants and hotels – basically, anywhere you might want to.

Weights and Measures Scotland uses the metric system for weights and measures, with the exception of road distances (in miles) and beer (in pints). The pint is 568mL, more than the US version.

designer retreats with every mod con.

The best place to start looking for this kind of accommodation is VisitScotland (www.visitscotland. com/accommodation) website, which lists numerous options all over Scotland. These also appear in the regional accommodation guides available from tourist offices. A quick internet search will reveal many websites listing thousands of self-catering places all across the country.

Expect a week's rent for a two-bedroom cottage to cost from £250 in winter, and up to £500 or more July to September.

University Accommodation

Many Scottish universities offer their student accommodation to visitors during the summer holidays (late June to August). Most rooms are comfy, functional single bedrooms, some with shared bathroom, but there are also twin and family units, self-contained flats and shared houses. Full-board, half-board, B&B and self-catering options are often available. Rooms are usually let out from late June to mid-September.

Activities
Birdwatching

Scotland is the best place in the British Isles (and in some cases, the only place) to spot bird species such as the golden eagle, white-tailed eagle, osprey, corncrake, capercaillie, crested tit, Scottish crossbill and ptarmigan. The country's coast and islands also provide some of Europe's most important seabird nesting grounds.

There are more than 80 ornithologically important nature reserves managed by Scottish Natural Heritage (www.snh.gov.uk), the Royal Society for the Protection of Birds (www.rspb.org.uk) and the Scottish Wildlife Trust (www.swt.org.uk).

Further information can be obtained from the Scottish Ornithologists Club (www. the-soc.org.uk).

Cycling

Cycling is an excellent way to explore Scotland. There are hundreds of miles of forest trails and quiet minor roads, and dedicated cycle routes along canal towpaths and disused railway tracks. Depending on your energy and enthusiasm, you can take a leisurely trip through idyllic glens, stopping at pubs along the way, or head off on a long and arduous road tour.

The network of signposted cycle routes maintained by Sustrans (www.sustrans. org.uk) makes a good introduction. Much of the network is on minor roads or cycle lanes, but there are long stretches of surfaced, traffic-free trails between Callander and Killin, between Oban and Ballachulish, on Royal Deeside, and along the Union and Forth & Clyde canals between Glasgow and Edinburgh.

But it's the minor roads of the Northwest Highlands, the Outer Hebrides, Orkney and Shetland that are the real attraction for cycle tourers, offering hundreds of miles of peaceful pedalling through breathtaking landscapes. The classic Scottish cycle tour is a trip around the islands of the west coast, from Islay and Jura north via Mull, Coll and Tiree to Skye and the Outer Hebrides (bikes travel for free on Calmac car ferries).

Many regional tourist offices have information on local cycling routes and places to hire bikes. They also stock cycling guides and books. Other resources include:

VisitScotland (www.visitscotland.com/see-do/active) Publishes a useful free brochure, *Active Scotland*, and has a website with more information.

Sustrans (www.sustrans.org.uk) For up-to-date, detailed information on Scotland's cycle-route network.

Cyclists' Touring Club (www.ctc.org.uk) A membership organisation offering comprehensive information about cycling in Britain.

Fishing

Fishing – coarse, sea and game – is enormously popular in Scotland; its lochs and rivers are filled with salmon, sea trout, brown trout and Arctic char. Fly-fishing in particular is a joy – it's a tricky but rewarding form of angling, closer to an art form than a sport.

Fishing rights to most inland waters are privately owned and you must obtain a permit to fish in them – these are usually readily available from the local fishing tackle shop or hotel, which are also great sources of advice and local knowledge. Permits cost from around £5 to £20 per day, but salmon fishing on some rivers – notably the Tweed, Dee, Tay and Spey – can be much more expensive (up to £150 a day).

For wild brown trout the close season is early October to mid-March. The close season for salmon and sea trout varies between districts; it's generally from mid-October to mid-January.

FishPal (www.fishpal.com/scotland) provides a good introduction, with links for booking fishing on various rivers and lochs.

Mountain Biking

A combination of challenging, rugged terrain, a network of old drove roads, military roads and stalkers' paths, and legislation that enshrines free access to the countryside has earned Scotland a reputation as one of the world's top mountain-biking destinations. Fort William has hosted the UCI Mountain Bike World Cup every year since 2007.

Scotland offers everything from custom-built forest trails with berms, jumps and skinnies to world-class downhill courses such as those at Laggan Wolftrax and Nevis Range. But perhaps the country's greatest appeal is its almost unlimited potential for adventurous, off-road riding. Areas such as the Galloway hills, Angus Glens, Cairngorms, Lochaber, Skye and most of the Northwest Highlands have large roadless regions where you can explore to your heart's content.

Top trails include Glen Feshie, Glenlivet and Rothiemurchus Forest in the Cairngorms, Spean Bridge to Kinlochleven via the Lairig Leacach and Loch Eilde Mor, and the stretch of the West Highland Way between Bridge of Orchy and Kinlochleven. The 37-mile loop from Sligachan on Skye (south through Glen Sligachan to Camasunary, over to Kilmarie, and back north via Strath Mor) was voted by *Mountain Bike Rider* magazine as the best off-road trail in Britain. Check out the Where to Ride link on www.dmbins.com.

Children

Scotland offers a range of child-friendly accommodation and activities suitable for families.

It's worth asking in tourist offices for local family-focused publications. *The List* magazine (available at newsagents and bookshops) has a section on children's activities and events in and around Glasgow and Edinburgh.

The **National Trust for Scotland** (☏0131-458 0200; www.nts.org.uk) and **Historic Environment Scotland** (Historic Scotland, HES, HS; ☏0131-668 8999; www.historicenvironment.scot) organise family-friendly activities at their properties throughout the summer.

Children are generally well received around Scotland, and every area has some child-friendly attractions and B&Bs. Even dryish local museums usually make an effort with an activity sheet or child-focused information panels.

A lot of pubs are family-friendly and some have great beer gardens where kids can run around and exhaust themselves while you have a quiet pint. However, be aware that many Scottish pubs, even those that serve bar meals, are forbidden by law to admit children under 14. In family-friendly pubs (ie those in possession of a Children's Certificate), accompanied under-14s are admitted between 11am and 8pm. There's no clear indication on which is which: just ask the bartender.

Children under a certain age can often stay free with their parents in hotels, but be prepared for hotels and B&Bs (normally upmarket ones) that won't accept children; call ahead to get the low-down. More hotels and guesthouses these days provide child-friendly facilities, including cots. Many restaurants (especially the larger ones) have highchairs and decent children's menus available.

Breastfeeding in public is accepted and is actively encouraged by government campaigns.

The larger car-hire companies can provide safety seats for children, but they're worth booking well ahead.

See also Lonely Planet's *Travel with Children*.

Customs Regulations

Travellers arriving in the UK from EU countries don't have to pay tax or duty on goods for personal use, and can bring in as much EU duty-paid alcohol and tobacco as they like. However, if you bring in more than the following, you'll probably be asked some questions:

➔ 800 cigarettes
➔ 1kg of tobacco
➔ 10L of spirits
➔ 90L of wine
➔ 110L of beer

Travellers from outside the EU can bring in, duty-free:

➔ 200 cigarettes *or* 100 cigarillos *or* 50 cigars *or* 250g of tobacco
➔ 16L of beer
➔ 4L of non-sparkling wine
➔ 1L of spirits *or* 2L of fortified wine or sparkling wine
➔ £390 worth of all other goods, including perfume, gifts and souvenirs

Anything over this limit must be declared to customs officers on arrival. Check www. hmrc.gov.uk/customs for further details, and for information on reclaiming VAT on items purchased in the UK by non-EU residents.

Electricity

230V/50Hz

Discount Cards

Historic Sites

Membership of Historic Environment Scotland (HES) and/or the National Trust for Scotland (NTS) is worth considering, especially if you're going to be in Scotland for a while. Both are organisations dedicated to the preservation of the environment, and both care for hundreds of spectacular sites. You can join up at any of their properties.

Historic Environment Scotland (Historic Scotland, HES, HS; ☎0131-668 8999; www. historicenvironment.scot) This organisation cares for hundreds of sites of historical importance. An annual membership costs £49.50/91.50 per adult/family, and gives free entry to HS sites (half-price entry to sites in England and Wales). Also offers a short-term Explorer Pass – three days out of five for £30, or seven days out of 14 for £40. It can be great value, particularly if you visit both Edinburgh and Stirling castles.

National Trust for Scotland (☎0131-458 0200; www. nts.org.uk) NTS looks after hundreds of sites of historical, architectural or environmental importance. An annual membership, costing £54/95 for an adult/family, offers free access to all NTS and National Trust properties (in the rest of the UK). If you're 25 or under, it's a great deal at only £24.

Hostel Cards

If travelling on a budget, membership of the **Scottish Youth Hostels Association** (SYHA; ☎01786-891400; www. syha.org.uk; annual membership 26yr & over/25yr & under £15/6, life membership £150) is a must.

Senior Cards

Discount cards for those over 60 years are available for train travel (p467).

Student & Youth Cards

The most useful card is the International Student Identity Card (www.isic.org), which displays your photo. It gives you discounted entry to many attractions and on many forms of transport.

Health

➔ If you're an EU citizen, a European Health Insurance Card (EHIC) – available from health centres or, in the UK, post offices – covers you for most medical care. An EHIC will not cover you for non-urgent cases or emergency repatriation.

➔ Citizens from non-EU countries should find out if there is a reciprocal arrangement for free medical care between their country and the UK. Australian travellers are eligible for free essential health care, for example.

➔ If you do need health insurance, make sure you get a policy that covers you for the worst possible scenarios, including emergency flights home.

➔ No vaccinations are required to travel to Scotland.

➔ The most painful problems facing visitors to the Highlands and islands are midges (p459).

Insurance

Insurance not only covers you for medical expenses, theft or loss, but also for cancellation of, or delays in, any of your travel arrangements.

Lots of bank accounts give their holders automatic travel insurance – check if this is the case for you.

Always read the small print carefully. Some policies specifically exclude 'dangerous activities', such as scuba diving, motorcycling, skiing, mountaineering and even trekking.

There's a variety of polcies and your travel agent can give recommendations. Make sure the policy includes health care and medication in the countries you may visit on your way to/from Scotland.

You may prefer a policy that pays doctors or hospitals directly rather than forcing you to pay on the spot and claim the money back later. If you have to claim later, make sure you keep all documentation. Some policies ask you to call back (reverse charges) to a centre in your home country where an immediate assessment of your problem is made.

Not all policies cover ambulances, helicopter rescue or emergency flights home. Most policies exclude cover for pre-existing illnesses.

Worldwide travel insurance is available at www.lonelyplanet.com/travel-insurance. You can buy, extend and claim online anytime – even if you're already on the road.

Internet Access

➡ If you're travelling with a laptop or smartphone, you'll find a wide range of places offering a wi-fi connection. These range from cafes to B&Bs and public spaces. Nearly all accommodation offers it.

➡ Wi-fi is often free, but some places (typically, upmarket hotels and SYHA hostels) charge.

➡ There are good deals on pay-as-you-go mobile data from mobile network providers.

➡ If you don't have a laptop or smartphone, the best places to check email and surf the internet are public libraries – nearly all of which have at least a couple of computer terminals, and they are free to use, though there's often a time limit.

> ## MIDGES
>
> If you've never been to the Scottish Highlands and islands before, be prepared for an encounter with the dreaded midge. These tiny, 2mm-long blood-sucking flies appear in huge swarms in summer, and can completely ruin a holiday if you're not prepared to deal with them.
>
> They proliferate from late May to mid-September, but especially mid-June to mid-August – which unfortunately coincides with the main tourist season – and are most common in the western and northern Highlands. Midges are at their worst during the twilight hours, and on still, overcast days – strong winds and bright sunshine tend to discourage them.
>
> The only way to combat them is to cover up, particularly in the evening. Wear long-sleeved, light-coloured clothing (midges are attracted to dark colours) and, most importantly, use a reliable insect repellent.

➡ Internet cafes also still exist in the cities and larger towns and are generally good value, charging approximately £2 to £3 per hour.

Language Courses

Scotland is a popular place to learn English, and there are numerous places to do it. Dedicated language academies offer intensive tuition at a price and can also arrange accommodation in residences or with local families. Much cheaper are colleges, some of which even offer free English classes for foreigners.

A good resource to start you off is the English UK Scotland (www.englishukscotland.com) website, which has details of many colleges and language schools, mostly in Edinburgh and Glasgow.

Legal Matters

➡ The 1707 Act of Union preserved the Scottish legal system as separate from the law in England and Wales.

➡ Police have the power to detain, for up to 24 hours, anyone suspected of having committed an offence punishable by imprisonment (including drugs offences).

➡ If you need legal assistance, contact the **Scottish Legal Aid Board** (☏0131-226 7061; www.slab.org.uk; 91 Haymarket Tce, Edinburgh).

➡ Possession of cannabis is illegal, with a spoken warning for first offenders with small amounts. Fines and prison sentences apply for repeat offences and larger quantities. Possession of harder drugs is much more serious. Police have the right to search anyone they suspect of possessing drugs.

LGBTIQ Travellers

Although most Scots are tolerant of homosexuality, couples overtly displaying affection away from acknowledged 'gay' venues or districts may encounter disapproval.

Edinburgh and Glasgow have small but flourishing gay scenes. The website and monthly magazine *Scotsgay* (www.scotsgay.co.uk) keeps folk informed about LGBTIQ-scene issues.

Maps

If you're going to do some hill walking, you'll require maps with far greater detail than the free maps supplied by tourist offices. The Ordnance Survey (OS) caters to walkers, with a wide variety of maps at 1:50,000 and 1:25,000 scales. Alternatively, look out for the excellent walkers maps published by Harveys; they're at scales of 1:40,000 and 1:25,000.

Money

ATMs

ATMs (called cashpoints in Scotland) are widespread and you'll usually find at least one in small towns and villages. You can use Visa, MasterCard, Amex, Cirrus, Plus and Maestro to withdraw cash from ATMs belonging to most banks and building societies in Scotland.

Cash withdrawals from some ATMs may be subject to a small charge, but most are free. If you're not from the UK, your home bank will likely charge you for withdrawing money overseas; it pays to be aware of how much, as it may be much better to withdraw larger amounts less often.

If there's no ATM, it's often possible to get 'cash back' at a hotel or shop in remote areas – ie make a payment by debit card and get some cash back (the cash amount is added to the transaction).

Credit & Debit Cards

Credit and debit cards can be used almost everywhere except for some B&Bs that only accept cash. Make sure bars or restaurants will accept cards before you order, as some don't. The most popular cards are Visa and MasterCard; American Express is only accepted by the major chains, and virtually no one will accept Diners or JCB. Chip-and-PIN is the norm for card transactions;

only a few places will accept a signature. Contactless card payments (up to £30) are increasingly accepted.

Money Changers

Be careful using bureaux de change; they may offer good exchange rates but frequently levy outrageous commissions and fees. The best-value place to change money in the UK tend to be travel agents. A handy tool for finding the best rates is the website http://travel money.moneysavingexpert. com/buy-back.

You'll normally find better rates in London than in Scotland, so do your changing there if you're visiting that city first.

Banks, post offices and some of the larger hotels will change cash and travellers cheques.

Opening Hours

Opening hours may vary throughout the year, especially in rural areas where many places have shorter hours, and a few close completely, from October or November to March or April. In the Highlands and Islands Sunday opening is restricted and it's common for there to be little or no public transport.

Banks 9.30am to 4pm or 5pm Monday to Friday; some open 9.30am to 1pm Saturday.

Post offices 9am to 6pm Monday to Friday, 9am to 12.30pm Saturday (main branches to 5pm Saturday).

Nightclubs 9pm or 10pm to 1am or later. Often only open Thursday to Saturday.

Pubs & Bars 11am to 11pm Monday to Thursday, 11am to 1am Friday and Saturday, 12.30pm to 11pm Sunday; lunch is served noon to 2.30pm, dinner 6pm to 9pm daily.

Shops 9am to 5.30pm (or 6pm in cities) Monday to Saturday, and often 11am to 5pm Sunday.

Restaurants Lunch noon to 2.30pm, dinner 6pm to 9pm

or 10pm; in small towns and villages the chippy (fish-and-chip shop) is often the only place to buy cooked food after 8pm.

Public Holidays

Although bank holidays are general public holidays in the rest of the UK, in Scotland they only apply to banks and some other commercial offices.

Scottish towns normally have four days of public holiday, which they allocate themselves; dates vary from year to year and from town to town. Most places celebrate St Andrew's Day (30 November) as a public holiday.

General public holidays:

New Year 1 and 2 January

Good Friday March or April

Christmas Day 25 December

Boxing Day 26 December

Telephone

You'll mainly see two types of phone booths in Scotland: one takes money (and doesn't give change), while the other uses prepaid phonecards and credit cards. Some phones accept both coins and cards. Payphone cards are widely available.

The cheapest way of calling internationally is via the internet, or by buying a discount call card; you'll see these in newsagents, along with tables of countries and the number of minutes you'll get for your money.

Mobile Phones

The UK uses the GSM 900/1800 network, which covers the rest of Europe, Australia and New Zealand but isn't compatible with the North American GSM 1900. Most modern mobiles can function on both networks but check before you leave home just in case.

Roaming charges within the EU have been eliminated (though charges may reappear when the UK leaves the EU). Other international roaming charges can be prohibitively high, and you'll probably find it cheaper to get a UK number. This is easily done by buying a SIM card (around £1) and sticking it in your phone. Your phone may be locked to your home network, however, so you'll have to either get it unlocked, or buy a cheap phone to use.

Operators offer a variety of packages that include UK calls, messages and data; a month's worth will typically cost around £20.

Though things are improving, coverage in Highland and island areas can be sketchy; don't rely on mobile data.

Pay-as-you-go phones can be recharged online or by buying vouchers from shops.

Phone Codes & Useful Numbers

Dialling the UK Dial your country's international access code then ☏44 (the UK country code), then the area code (dropping the first 0) followed by the telephone number.

Dialling out of the UK The international access code is ☏00; dial this, then add the code of the country you wish to dial.

Making a reverse-charge (collect) international call Dial ☏155 for the operator. It's an expensive option, but not for the caller.

Area codes in Scotland Begin with ☏01; eg Edinburgh 0131, Wick 01955.

Directory Assistance There are several numbers; ☏118500 is one.

Mobile phones Codes usually begin with ☏07.

Free calls Numbers starting with ☏0800 are free; calls to ☏0845 numbers are charged at local rates.

Time

Scotland is on UTC/GMT +1 hour during summer daylight saving time (late March to late October), and UTC/GMT +0 the rest of the year.

Los Angeles	8hr behind
Mumbai	5½hr ahead, 4½hr Mar-Oct
New York	5hr behind
Paris, Berlin, Rome	1hr ahead of Scotland
Sydney	9hr ahead Apr-Sep, 10hr Oct, 11hr Nov-Mar
Tokyo	9hr ahead, 8hr Mar-Oct

Tourist Information

The Scottish Tourist Board is known as **VisitScotland** (www.visitscotland.com). You can request regional brochures to be posted out to you, or download them from the website.

Most larger towns have tourist offices ('information centres') that open 9am or 10am to 5pm Monday to Friday, and on weekends in summer. In small places, particularly in the Highlands, tourist offices only open from Easter to September.

If you want to email a tourist office, it's [inserttown-name]@visitscotland.com.

Travellers with Disabilities

Travellers with disabilities will find a strange mix of accessibility and inaccessibility in Scotland. Most new buildings are accessible to wheelchair users, so modern hotels and tourist attractions are fine. However, most B&Bs and guesthouses are in hard-to-adapt older buildings, which means that travellers with mobility problems may pay more for accommodation. Things are constantly improving, though.

It's a similar story with public transport. Newer buses have steps that lower for easier access, as do trains, but it's wise to check before setting out. Tourist attractions usually reserve parking spaces near the entrance for drivers with disabilities.

Many places such as ticket offices and banks are fitted with hearing loops to assist the hearing-impaired; look for a posted symbol of a large ear.

An increasing number of tourist attractions have audioguides. Some have Braille guides or scented gardens for the visually impaired.

Download Lonely Planet's free Accessible Travel guide from http://lptravel.to/AccessibleTravel.

VisitScotland (www.visitscotland.com/accommodation) Details accessible accommodation and many tourist offices have leaflets with accessibility details for their area. Also produces the guide *Accessible Scotland* for travellers using wheelchairs. Many regions have organisations that hire wheelchairs; contact the local tourist office for details. Many nature trails have been adapted for wheelchair use.

Disability Rights UK (☏020-7250 8191; www.disabilityrightsuk.org) This is an umbrella organisation for voluntary groups for people with disabilities. Many wheelchair-accessible toilets can be opened only with a special Royal Association of Disability & Rehabilitation (Radar) key, which can be obtained via the website or from tourist offices for £5.40.

Disabled Persons Railcard (www.disabledpersons-railcard.co.uk) Discounted train travel. Costs £20.

Tourism for All (☏0845-124 9971; www.tourismforall.org.uk) Publishes regional information guides for travellers with disabilities and can offer general advice.

Visas

➤ If you're a citizen of the EEA (European Economic Area) nations or Switzerland, you don't need a visa to enter or work in Britain – you can enter using your national identity card.

➜ Visa regulations are always subject to change, which is especially likely after Britain's 2016 EU referendum result, so it's essential to check before leaving home.

➜ Currently, if you're a citizen of Australia, Canada, New Zealand, Japan, Israel, the US and several other countries, you can stay for up to six months (no visa required), but are not allowed to work.

➜ Nationals of many countries, including South Africa, will need to obtain a visa; for more info, see www.ukvisas.gov.uk.

➜ The Youth Mobility Scheme, for Australian, Canadian, Japanese, Hong Kong, Monegasque, New Zealand, South Korean and Taiwanese citizens aged 18 to 31, allows working visits of up to two years, but must be applied for in advance.

➜ Commonwealth citizens with a UK-born parent may be eligible for a Certificate of Entitlement to the Right of Abode, which entitles them to live and work in the UK.

➜ Commonwealth citizens with a UK-born grandparent could qualify for a UK Ancestry Employment Certificate, allowing them to work full time for up to five years in the UK.

➜ British immigration authorities have always been tough; dress neatly and carry proof that you have sufficient funds with which to support yourself. A credit card and/or an onward ticket will help.

Volunteering

Various organisations offer volunteering opportunities in Scotland, with conservation, organic farming and animal welfare projects to the fore.

Women Travellers

Solo women travellers are likely to feel safe in Scotland.

The contraceptive pill is available only on prescription; however, the 'morning-after' pill (effective against conception for up to 72 hours after unprotected sexual intercourse) is available over the counter at chemists.

Work

Whatever your skills, it's worth registering with a number of temporary employment agencies; there are plenty in the cities.

Low-paid seasonal work is available in the tourist industry, usually in restaurants and pubs.

At the time of research, EU citizens didn't need a work permit, but this may change as a result of Britain's referendum vote in June 2016 to leave the EU.

The Youth Mobility scheme allows working visits for some foreign nationals.

Transport

GETTING THERE & AWAY

Flights, cars and tours can be booked online at lonelyplanet.com/bookings.

Air

There are direct flights to Scottish airports from Britain, lots of European countries, the Middle East, the US and Canada. From elsewhere, you'll probably have to fly into a European or Middle Eastern hub and get a connecting flight to a Scottish airport – London has the most connections. This will often be a cheaper option anyway if flying in from North America.

Airports

Scotland has four main international airports: Aberdeen, Edinburgh, Glasgow and Glasgow Prestwick, with a few short-haul international flights landing at Inverness.

London is the main UK gateway for long-haul flights. Sumburgh on Shetland has summer service from Norway.

Aberdeen Airport (ABZ; ☎0844-481 6666; www.aberdeenairport.com) Located at Dyce, 6 miles northwest of the city centre. There are regular flights to numerous Scottish and UK destinations, including Orkney and Shetland, and international flights to several European countries.

Edinburgh Airport (EDI; ☎0844 448 8833; www.edinburghairport.com) Eight miles west of the city, this airport has numerous flights to other parts of Scotland and the UK, Ireland and mainland Europe, as well as long-haul flights to the US, Canada, the UAE and Qatar.

Glasgow Airport (GLA; ☎0844 481 5555; www.glasgowairport.com) Glasgow's principal airport offers connections all over Scotland, Britain and Europe. Long-haul destinations include the US, Canada and Dubai.

Glasgow Prestwick (PIK; ☎0871 223 0700; www.glasgowprestwick.com) Southwest of Glasgow near Ayr, this airport is a Ryanair hub serving mainly holiday destinations in southern Europe.

Inverness Airport (INV; ☎01667-464000; www.hial.co.uk) At Dalcross, east of the city, this airport has direct flights to several British and western European destinations.

London Gatwick (www.gatwickairport.com) London's second airport, with numerous flights to Scotland.

London Heathrow (www.heathrow.com) Britain's principal international airport.

Departure Tax

An Air Passenger Duty, essentially a departure tax, is payable for air travel originating in the UK. It's included in the ticket price. If you have to cancel a flight, you can reclaim it even if the rest of the ticket is non-refundable.

CLIMATE CHANGE & TRAVEL

Every form of transport that relies on carbon-based fuel generates CO_2, the main cause of human-induced climate change. Modern travel is dependent on aeroplanes, which might use less fuel per kilometre per person than most cars but travel much greater distances. The altitude at which aircraft emit gases (including CO_2) and particles also contributes to their climate change impact. Many websites offer 'carbon calculators' that allow people to estimate the carbon emissions generated by their journey and, for those who wish to do so, to offset the impact of the greenhouse gases emitted with contributions to portfolios of climate-friendly initiatives throughout the world. Lonely Planet offsets the carbon footprint of all staff and author travel.

Land

Bus

Buses are usually the cheapest way to get to Scotland from other parts of the UK.

Megabus (☏0141-352 4444; www.megabus.com) One-way fares from London to Glasgow from as little as £1 if you book well in advance. Has some fully reclinable sleeper services.

National Express (☏0871 781 8181; www.nationalexpress. com) Regular services from London and other cities in England and Wales to Glasgow and Edinburgh.

Scottish Citylink (☏0871 266 3333; www.citylink.co.uk) Daily service between Belfast and Glasgow and Edinburgh via Cairnryan ferry.

Car & Motorcycle

Drivers of EU-registered vehicles will find bringing a car or motorcycle into Scotland fairly easy.

The vehicle must have registration papers and a nationality plate, and you must have insurance. The International Insurance Certificate (Green Card) isn't compulsory, but it is excellent proof that you're covered.

If driving from mainland Europe via the Channel Tunnel or ferry ports, head for London and follow the M25 orbital road to the M1 motorway, then follow the M1 and M6 north.

Train

Travelling to Scotland by train is faster and usually more comfortable than the bus, but more expensive. Taking into account check-in and travel time between city centre and airport, the train is a competitive alternative to air travel from London. The **National Rail Enquiry Service** (☏03457 48 49 50; www.nationalrail.co.uk) has timetable and fare info for all trains in Britain.

Virgin Trains East Coast (www.virgintrainseastcoast.com) Trains between London Kings Cross and Edinburgh (4½ hours, every half hour).

Eurostar (www.eurostar.com) You can travel from Paris or Brussels to London in around two hours on the Eurostar service. From St Pancras, it's a quick and easy change to Kings Cross or Euston for trains to Edinburgh or Glasgow.

Caledonian Sleeper (www.sleeper.scot) This is an overnight service connecting London Euston with Edinburgh, Glasgow, Stirling, Perth, Dundee, Aberdeen, Fort William and Inverness. There are two departures nightly from Sunday to Friday.

Virgin Trains (www.virgintrains.co.uk) Trains between London Euston and Glasgow (4½ hours, hourly).

Crosscountry (☏0844 811 0124; www.crosscountrytrains.co.uk) Trains between Wales and southwest England to Glasgow, Edinburgh and Aberdeen.

TransPennine Express (www.tpexpress.co.uk) Trains from Manchester to Glasgow and Edinburgh.

Sea

Car-ferry links between Northern Ireland and Scotland are operated by **Stena Line** (☏08447 70 70 70; www.stenaline.co.uk) and **P&O** (☏0800 130 0030; www.poferries.com). Stena Line travels the Belfast–Cairnryan route and P&O Irish Sea the Larne–Cairnryan routes. At time of research, ferries from Troon had been discontinued.

GETTING AROUND

Air

Most domestic air services are geared to business needs, or are lifelines for remote island communities. Flying is a pricey way to cover relatively short distances, but certainly worth considering if you're short of time and want to visit the Hebrides, Orkney or Shetland.

Airlines in Scotland

Eastern Airways (☏0870 366 9100; www.easternairways.com) Flies from Aberdeen to Stornoway and Wick.

Flybe/Loganair (☏0371 700 2000; www.loganair.co.uk) The main domestic airline in Scotland, with flights from Glasgow to Barra, Benbecula, Campbeltown, Islay, Kirkwall, Sumburgh, Stornoway and Tiree; from Edinburgh to Kirkwall, Sumburgh, Stornoway and Wick; from Aberdeen to Kirkwall and Sumburgh; from Inverness to Kirkwall, Benbecula, Stornoway and Sumburgh; and from Stornoway to Benbecula. It (as Loganair only) also operates inter-island flights in Orkney.

Hebridean Air (☏0845 805 7465; www.hebrideanair.co.uk) Flies from Connel airfield near Oban to the islands of Coll, Tiree, Colonsay and Islay.

TRAIN FARES

The complex British train ticketing system rewards advance planning, particularly on long routes. A one-way fare from London to Edinburgh, for example, can cost over £150, but a fare purchased well in advance, at off-peak times, can be as low as £30. Regional fares in Scotland have a lot less variation.

Bicycle

Scotland is a compact country, and travelling around by bicycle is a perfectly feasible proposition if you have the time. Indeed, for touring the islands a bicycle is both cheaper (for ferry fares) and more suited to their small sizes and leisurely pace of life. For more information see http://active.visitscotland.com and the Sustrans (www.sustrans.org.uk/scotland/national-cycle-network) pages about the National Cycle Network.

Boat

The Scottish government has introduced a scheme called the Road Equivalent Tariff (RET) on most ferry crossings. This reduces the price of ferry transport to what it would cost to drive the same distance by road, in the hope of attracting more tourists and reducing business costs on the islands. Fares on many crossings have been cut by as much as 60%, and initial signs are that the scheme has been successful, with visitor numbers well up.

Caledonian MacBrayne (CalMac; ☎0800 066 5000; www.calmac.co.uk) Serves the west coast and islands. A comprehensive timetable booklet is available from tourist offices and on the website. There's a summer timetable and one for winter, when services are somewhat reduced. CalMac Island Hopscotch offers more than 20 tickets, giving reduced fares for various combinations of crossings; these are listed on the website and in the CalMac timetable booklet. Bicycles travel free with foot passenger tickets.

Northlink Ferries (☎0845 600 0449; www.northlinkferries.co.uk) Ferries from Aberdeen and Scrabster (near Thurso) to Orkney; from Orkney to Shetland; and from Aberdeen to Shetland.

Bus

Scotland is served by an extensive bus network that covers most of the country. In remote rural areas, however, services are geared to the needs of locals (getting to school or the shops in the nearest large town) and may not be conveniently timed for visitors.

First (www.firstgroup.com) Operates local bus routes in several parts of Scotland.

Postbuses (www.royalmail.com) Minibuses, or sometimes four-seater cars, driven by postal workers delivering and collecting the mail. There are no official stops, and you can hail a postbus anywhere on its route. Although services have been cut severely in recent years, it's still the only public transport in some remote parts of Scotland.

Scottish Citylink (www.citylink.co.uk) National network of comfy, reliable buses serving main towns. Away from main roads, you'll need to switch to local services.

Stagecoach (www.stagecoachbus.com) Operates local bus routes in many parts of Scotland.

Bus Passes

Holders of a **National Entitlement Card** (www.entitlementcard.org.uk), available to seniors and people with disabilities who are Scottish citizens, get free bus travel throughout the country. The youth version, for 11- to 26-year-olds, gives discounted travel, and SYHA members receive a 20% discount on Scottish Citylink services. Students do, too, by registering online.

The **Scottish Citylink Explorer Pass** offers unlimited travel on Scottish Citylink (and selected other bus routes) services within Scotland for any three days out of five (£41), any five days out of 10 (£62) or any eight days out of 16 (£93). Also gives discounts on various regional bus services, on Northlink

and CalMac ferries, and in SYHA hostels. Can be bought in the UK by both UK and overseas citizens.

Car & Motorcycle

Scotland's roads are generally good and far less busy than in England, so driving is more enjoyable.

Motorways (designated 'M') are toll-free dual carriageways, limited mainly to central Scotland. Main roads ('A') are dual or single carriageways and are sometimes clogged with slow-moving trucks or caravans; the A9 from Perth to Inverness is notoriously busy.

Life on the road is more relaxed and interesting on the secondary roads (designated 'B') and minor roads (undesignated), although in the Highlands and islands there's the added hazard of suicidal sheep wandering onto the road (be particularly wary of lambs in spring).

Petrol is more expensive than in countries like America or Australia, but roughly in line with the rest of western Europe. Prices tend to rise as you get further from the main centres and are more than 10% higher in the Outer Hebrides. In remote areas petrol stations are widely spaced and sometimes closed on Sunday.

Driving Licences

A non-EU licence is valid in Britain for up to 12 months from time of entry into the country. If bringing a car from Europe, make sure you're adequately insured.

Hire

Car hire in the UK is competitively priced by European standards, and shopping around online can unearth some great deals, which can drop to as low as £12 per day for an extended hire period. Hit comparison sites like Kayak to find some of the best prices.

The minimum legal age for driving is 17, but to rent a car, drivers must usually be aged 23 to 65 – outside these limits special conditions or insurance requirements may apply.

If planning to visit the Outer Hebrides or Shetland, it'll often prove cheaper to hire a car on the islands, rather than pay to take a hire car across on the ferry.

Avis (www.avis.co.uk)

Budget (www.budget.co.uk)

Europcar (www.europcar.co.uk)

Hertz (www.hertz.co.uk)

Sixt (www.sixt.co.uk)

Road Rules

➜ The *Highway Code*, widely available in bookshops, and also online and downloadable at www.gov.uk/highway-code, details all UK road regulations.

➜ Vehicles drive on the left. Seatbelts are compulsory if fitted; this technically applies to buses too.

➜ The speed limit is 30mph (48km/h) in built-up areas, 60mph (96km/h) on single carriageways and 70mph (112km/h) on dual carriageways.

➜ Give way to your right at roundabouts (traffic already on the roundabout has right of way).

➜ Motorcyclists must wear helmets. They are not compulsory for cyclists.

➜ It is illegal to use a hand-held mobile phone or similar device while driving.

➜ The maximum permitted blood-alcohol level when driving is 50mg/100mL (22mg per 100mL of breath); this is lower than in the rest of the UK but equivalent to the limit in many other countries.

➜ Traffic offences (illegal parking, speeding etc) usually incur a fine for which you're given 30 to 60 days to pay. In Glasgow and Edinburgh the parking inspectors are numerous and without mercy – never leave your car around the city centres without a valid parking ticket, as you risk a hefty fine.

Hitching

Hitching is fairly easy in Scotland, except around big cities and built-up areas, where you'll need to use public transport. Although the northwest is more difficult because there's less traffic, long waits are unusual (except on Sunday in 'Sabbath' areas). On some islands, where public transport is infrequent, hitching is so much a part of getting around that local drivers may stop and offer you lifts without even asking.

It's against the law to hitch on motorways or their immediate slip roads; make a sign and use approach roads, nearby roundabouts or service stations.

Hitching is never entirely safe, however, and LP doesn't recommend it. Travellers who hitch should understand that they are taking a small but potentially serious risk.

Tours

There are numerous companies in Scotland offering all kinds of tours, including historical, activity-based and backpacker tours. It's a question of picking the tour that suits your requirements and budget.

Discreet Scotland (☏07989-416990; www.discreetscotland.com) Luxurious private tours in an upmarket 4WD that range from day trips from Edinburgh to full weeks staying in some of Scotland's finest hotels.

Timberbush Tours (☏0131-226 6066; www.timberbush-tours.co.uk) Comfortable small-group minibus tours around Scotland, with Glasgow and Edinburgh departures.

Train

Scotland's train network extends to all major cities and towns, but the railway map has a lot of large, blank areas in the Highlands and the Southern Uplands where you'll need to switch to road transport. The West Highland line from Glasgow to Fort William and Mallaig, and the Inverness to Kyle of Lochalsh line, offer two of the world's most scenic rail journeys.

National Rail Enquiry Service (www.nationalrail.co.uk) Lists timetables and fares for all trains in Britain.

ScotRail (www.scotrail.co.uk) Operates most train services in Scotland; its website has downloadable timetables.

Costs & Reservations

Train travel is more expensive than bus, but usually more comfortable.

Reservations are recommended for intercity trips, especially on Fridays and public holidays. For shorter journeys, just buy a ticket at the station before you go. On certain routes, including the Glasgow–Edinburgh express,

---

SINGLE-TRACK ROADS

In many country areas, especially in the Highlands and islands, you will find single-track roads that are only wide enough for one vehicle. Passing places (usually marked with a white diamond sign, or a black-and-white striped pole) are used to allow oncoming traffic to get by. Remember that passing places are also for overtaking – you must pull over to let faster vehicles pass. It's illegal to park in passing places.

and in places where there's no ticket office at the station, you can buy tickets on the train.

Children under five travel free; those five to 15 years usually pay half-fare.

Bikes are carried free on all ScotRail trains but space is sometimes limited. Bike reservations are compulsory on certain train routes, including the Glasgow–Oban–Fort William–Mallaig line and the Inverness–Kyle of Lochalsh line; they are recommended on many others. You can make reservations for your bicycle from eight weeks to two hours in advance at main train stations, or when booking tickets by phone or online.

There's a bewilderingly complex labyrinth of ticket types. In general, the further ahead you can book, the cheaper your ticket will be.

Advance Purchase Book by 6pm on the day before travel; cheaper than Anytime tickets.

Anytime Buy any time and travel any time, with no restrictions.

Off Peak There are time restrictions (you're not usually allowed to travel on a train that leaves before 9.15am); relatively cheap.

It's always worth checking the ScotRail website for current family or senior offers.

Discount Cards

Discount railcards are available for people aged 60 and over, for people aged 16 to 25 (or mature full-time students), for two over-16s travelling together, and for those with a disability.

The **Senior Railcard** (www.senior-railcard.co.uk; per year £30), **16-25 Railcard** (Young Persons Railcard; www.16-25railcard.co.uk; per year £30), **Two Together Railcard** (www.twotogether-railcard.co.uk; per year £30) and **Disabled Persons Railcard** (www.disabledpersons-railcard.co.uk; per year £20) are each valid for one year and give one-third off most train fares in Scotland, England and Wales.

You'll find they pay for themselves pretty quickly if you plan to take a couple of long-distance journeys or a handful of short-distance ones. Fill in an application at any major train station. You'll need proof of age (birth certificate, passport or driving licence) for the Young Persons and Senior Railcards (proof of enrolment for mature-age students) and proof of entitlement for the Disabled Persons Railcard. You'll need a passport photo for all of them. You can also buy railcards online, but you'll need a UK address to have them sent to.

Train Passes

ScotRail (☑0344-811 0141; www.scotrail.co.uk) has a range of good-value passes for train travel. You can buy them online, by phone or at train stations throughout Britain. Note that Travelpass and Rover tickets are not valid for travel on certain (eg commuter) services before 9.15am weekdays.

Central Scotland Rover covers train travel between Glasgow, Edinburgh, North Berwick, Stirling and Fife; costs £36.30 for three days travel out of seven.

Spirit of Scotland Travelpass gives unlimited travel on all Scottish train services (with some restrictions), all CalMac ferry services and on certain Scottish Citylink coach services (on routes not covered by rail). It's available for four days travel out of eight (£134) or eight days out of 15 (£180).

Highland Rover allows unlimited train travel from Glasgow to Oban, Fort William and Mallaig, and from Inverness to Kyle of Lochalsh, Aviemore, Aberdeen and Thurso. It also gives free travel on the Oban/Fort William–Inverness bus, on the Oban–Mull and Mallaig–Skye ferries, and on buses on Mull and Skye. It's valid for four days travel out of eight (£81.50).

Glossary

bag – reach the top of (as in to 'bag a couple of peaks' or 'Munro bagging')

bailey – the space enclosed by castle walls

birlinn – Hebridean galley

blackhouse – low-walled stone cottage with thatch or turf roof and earth floors; shared by both humans and cattle and typical of the Outer Hebrides until the early 20th century

böd – once a simple trading booth used by fishing communities, today it refers to basic accommodation for walkers etc

bothy – hut or mountain shelter

brae – hill

broch – defensive tower

burgh – town

burn – stream

cairn – pile of stones to mark path or junction; also peak

camanachd – Gaelic for *shinty*

ceilidh (*kay*-li) – evening of traditional Scottish entertainment including music, song and dance

Celtic high cross – a large, elaborately carved stone cross decorated with biblical scenes and Celtic interlace designs dating from the 8th to 10th centuries

chippy – fish-and-chip shop

Clearances – eviction of Highland farmers from their land by *lairds* wanting to use it for grazing sheep

Clootie dumpling – rich steamed pudding filled with currants and raisins

close – entrance to an alley

corrie – circular hollow on a hillside

craic – lively conversation

craig – exposed rock

crannog – an artificial island in a *loch* built for defensive purposes

crofting – smallholding in marginal agricultural areas following the Clearances

Cullen skink – soup made with smoked haddock, potato, onion and milk

dene – valley

dirk – dagger

dram – a measure of whisky

firth – estuary

gloup – natural arch

Hogmanay – Scottish celebration of New Year's Eve

howff – pub or shelter

HS – Historic Scotland

laird – estate owner

linn – waterfall

loch – lake

lochan – small *loch*

machair – grass- and wildflower-covered dunes

makar – maker of verses

Mercat Cross – a symbol of the trading rights of a market town or village, usually found in the centre of town and usually a focal point for the community

motte – early Norman fortification consisting of a raised, flattened mound with a keep on top; when attached to a *bailey* it is known as a motte-and-bailey

Munro – mountain of 3000ft (914m) or higher

Munro bagger – a hill walker who tries to climb all the *Munros* in Scotland

NNR – National Nature Reserve, managed by the *SNH*

NTS – National Trust for Scotland

nyvaig – Hebridean galley

OS – Ordnance Survey

Picts – early inhabitants of north and east Scotland (from Latin *pictus*, or 'painted', after their body paint decorations)

provost – mayor

RIB – rigid inflatable boat

rood – an old Scots word for a cross

RSPB – Royal Society for the Protection of Birds

Sassenach – from Gaelic 'Sasannach': anyone who is not a Highlander (including Lowland Scots)

shinty – fast and physical ball-and-stick sport similar to Ireland's hurling

SMC – Scottish Mountaineering Club

SNH – Scottish Natural Heritage, a government organisation directly responsible for safeguarding and improving Scotland's natural heritage

sporran – purse worn around waist with the kilt

SYHA – Scottish Youth Hostel Association

wynd – lane

GAELIC & NORSE PLACE NAMES

The Gaelic language has left a rich legacy of place names, often intermixed with Old Norse names brought by the Vikings who occupied the western and northern islands. The spellings may be Anglicised, but the meaning is usually still clear.

Gaelic Place Names

ach, auch	from *achadh* (field)
ard	from *ard* or *aird* (height, hill)
avon	from *abhainn* (river or stream)
bal	from *baile* (village or homestead)
ban	from *ban* (white, fair)
beg	from *beag* (small)
ben	from *beinn* (mountain)
buie	from *buidhe* (yellow)
dal	from *dail* (field or dale)
dow, dhu	from *dubh* (black)
drum	from *druim* (ridge or back)
dun	from *dun* or *duin* (fort or castle)
glen	from *gleann* (narrow valley)
gorm	from *gorm* (blue)
gower, gour	from *gabhar* (goat), eg Ardgour (height of the goats)
inch, insh	from *inis* (island, water-meadow or resting place for cattle)
inver	from *inbhir* (rivermouth or meeting of two rivers)
kil	from *cille* (church), eg Kilmartin (Church of St Martin)
kin, ken	from *ceann* (head), eg Kinlochleven (head of Loch Leven)
kyle, kyles	from *caol* or *caolas* (narrow sea channel)
more, vore	from *mor* or *mhor* (big), eg Ardmore (big height), Skerryvore (big reef)
strath	from *srath* (broad valley)
tarbert, tarbet	from *tairbeart* (portage), meaning a narrow neck of land between two bodies of water, across which a boat can be dragged
tay, ty	from *tigh* (house), eg Tyndrum (house on the ridge)
tober	from *tobar* (well), eg Tobermory (Mary's well)
tom	small hill

Norse Place Names

a, ay, ey	from *ey* (island)
bister, buster, bster	from *bolstaor* (dwelling place, homestead)
geo	from *gja* (chasm)
holm	from *holmr* (small island)
kirk	from *kirkja* (church)
pol, poll, bol	from *bol* (farm)
quoy	from *kvi* (sheep fold, cattle enclosure)
sker, skier, skerry	from *sker* (rocky reef)
ster, sett	from *setr* (house)
vig, vaig, wick	from *vik* (bay, creek)
voe, way	from *vagr* (bay, creek)

Behind the Scenes

SEND US YOUR FEEDBACK

We love to hear from travellers – your comments keep us on our toes and help make our books better. Our well-travelled team reads every word on what you loved or loathed about this book. Although we cannot reply individually to your submissions, we always guarantee that your feedback goes straight to the appropriate authors, in time for the next edition. Each person who sends us information is thanked in the next edition – the most useful submissions are rewarded with a selection of digital PDF chapters.

Visit **lonelyplanet.com/contact** to submit your updates and suggestions or to ask for help. Our award-winning website also features inspirational travel stories, news and discussions.

Note: We may edit, reproduce and incorporate your comments in Lonely Planet products such as guidebooks, websites and digital products, so let us know if you don't want your comments reproduced or your name acknowledged. For a copy of our privacy policy visit lonelyplanet.com/privacy.

OUR READERS

Many thanks to the travellers who used the last edition and wrote to us with helpful hints, useful advice and interesting anecdotes:
Beck Robey, Charlotte Walber, Dirk Gudde, Erin Fredericks, Fran Boersma, John Charles, Judy Pengelly, Kim MacDonald, Kristine Quint, Lucy Graham, Mario Pennacchio, Sebastian Braden, Stephanie Lacasse, Vanessa Mattingly

WRITER'S THANKS

Andy Symington
I owe thanks to many, but firstly to Jenny Neil and Brendan Bolland for being great friends and superb hosts, to Juliette and David Paton for their perpetual generosity and warm welcome and to my father for the whisky and much more. Gratitude goes also to Morwynne Carlow, Riika Åkerlind and numerous helpful folk met along the way. Big thanks also go to co-author Neil Wilson, editor James Smart and the LP team.

ACKNOWLEDGEMENTS

Climate map data adapted from Peel MC, Finlayson BL & McMahon TA (2007) 'Updated World Map of the Köppen-Geiger Climate Classification', *Hydrology and Earth System Sciences*, 11, pp1633–44.

Illustrations p56-7, p100-101 and p180-1 by Javier Zarracina.

Cover photograph: Steam train crossing the Glenfinnan Railway Viaduct, Nick Fox/Shutterstock ©

THIS BOOK

This 9th edition of Lonely Planet's *Scotland* guidebook was researched and written by Neil Wilson and Andy Symington, who also wrote the previous two editions. This guidebook was produced by the following:
Destination Editor James Smart

Product Editors Kate Chapman, Ross Taylor, Amanda Williamson
Senior Cartographer Mark Griffiths
Book Designer Cam Ashley
Assisting Editors Peter Cruttenden, Bruce Evans, Gabrielle Innes, Bella Li, Anne Mason, Kate Mathews, Lauren O'Connell, Gabrielle Stefanos, Fionnuala Twomey, Simon Williamson
Assisting Cartographer Gabe Lindquist
Cover Researcher Naomi Parker
Thanks to Cheree Broughton, Daniel Corbett, Sasha Drew, Claire Naylor, Karyn Noble, Martine Power, Lauren Wellicome, Tony Wheeler

Index